# The Battle of the Atlantic

# The Battle of the Atlantic

*How the Allies Won the War*

## JONATHAN DIMBLEBY

VIKING

*an imprint of*

PENGUIN BOOKS

VIKING

UK | USA | Canada | Ireland | Australia
India | New Zealand | South Africa

Viking is part of the Penguin Random House group of companies
whose addresses can be found at global.penguinrandomhouse.com.

First published 2015

001

Copyright © Jonathan Dimbleby, 2015

The moral right of the author has been asserted

Extracts from the writings of Winston Churchill are reproduced with permission
of Curtis Brown, London, on behalf of the Estate of
Winston S. Churchill. © The Estate of Winston S. Churchill.
Extracts from Mass Observation are reproduced with permission of Curtis Brown Group Ltd,
London, on behalf of The Trustees of the Mass Observation Archive.
While every effort has been made to contact copyright holders, the publishers will be happy
to correct an errors of omission or commission brought to their attention

Set in 12/14.75 pt Bembo Book MT Std
Typeset by Jouve (UK), Milton Keynes
Printed in Great Britain by Clays Ltd, St Ives plc

A CIP catalogue record for this book is available from the British Library

HARDBACK ISBN: 978–0–241–18660–2
TRADE PAPERBACK ISBN: 978–0–241–18661–9

For Daisy and Gwendolen
in the hope that one day they will want to know
how Britain was saved from the Nazis

# Contents

Contents

# Maps and Illustrations

## Maps

## Illustrations

### SECTION I

11. German Admiral Erich Raeder, commander-in-chief of the Kriegsmarine (*Everett Collection/Mary Evans*)
12. Admiral Karl Dönitz, commander-in-chief of the U-boat fleet (*Sueddeutsche Zeitung Photo/Mary Evans*)
13. Hitler presents the Knight's Cross to Günther Prien (© *akg-images/ Ullstein Bild*)
14. Otto Kretschmer, German submarine commander (© *Ullstein Bild/ Getty Images*)
15. New recruits to the Merchant Navy (© *IWM [A 4469]*)

### SECTION 2

16. Survivors from the SS *Athenia*, sunk on the first day of the war (© *IWM [HU 51008]*)
17. The German pocket battleship *Admiral Graf Spee* sinks in the River Plate, Montevideo, Uruguay (*Everett Collection/Mary Evans*)
18. The destroyer HMS *Eskimo*, damaged during the Battle of Narvik, May 1940 (© *IWM [N 233]*)
19. The German battleship *Bismarck*, sunk on 27 May 1941 (© *akg-images*)
20. Survivors from the *Bismarck* are pulled aboard HMS *Dorsetshire*
21. Teams drawn principally from the ranks of the WRAF and the WRNS charting the shifting positions of the Atlantic adversaries (© *IWM [A 9891]*)
22. A U-boat entering one of the bomb-proof pens in the port of Lorient
23. Survivors of the SS *City of Benares* (© *AP/Press Association Images*)
24. British housewives queue to buy eggs in 1940 (*Grenville Collins Postcard Collection/Mary Evans*)
25. Officers on the bridge of a British Warship escorting an Atlantic convoy in 1941 (© *IWM [A 5667]*)
26. The torpedo room of a German U-boat (© *akg-images*)
27. A German U-boat crew at rest (© *akg-images/Ullstein Bild*)
28. A Hedgehog anti-submarine mortar mounted on the destroyer HMS *Westcott* (© *IWM [A 31000]*)
29. PQ17 in Hvalfjord, Iceland, June 1942 (© *IWM [A 8953]*)

## SECTION 3

30. Arctic conditions on an Allied merchant ship (© *AP/Press Association Images*)
31. At least 400 US merchant ships were sunk by U-boats in the first half of 1942 (© *Hulton Archive/Getty Images*)
32. By 1943, Atlantic convoys frequently exceeded sixty vessels in size (© *akg-images*)
33. U-boat POWs were few in number (*Everett Collection/Mary Evans*)
34. Patriotic poster distributed in British ports (© *IWM [Art.IWM PST 14440]*)
35. Officers in the Plot Room at the Admiralty in December 1942 (© *IWM [A 13205]*)
36. Bletchley Park, the secret headquarters of the Government Code & Cypher School (GC&CS) (© *Bletchley Park Trust/Getty Images*)
37. The Enigma machine, which the German high command used to encrypt secret military traffic (*Interfoto/Mary Evans*)
38. An emergency feeding centre in Liverpool (© *IWM [V 50]*)
39. A rating inscribing another U-boat kill on board HMS *Hesperus* (© *IWM [A 20897]*)
40. D-Day, 6 June 1944: British commandos land on Gold Beach (© *IWM [B 5246]*)

N

Orkneys — *Scapa Flow*

*N o r t h*

*S e a*

Glasgow ○ ○Edinburgh

○Newcastle

Belfast ○

Dublin○ ○Liverpool

Wilhemshaven○

**HOLLAND**

**ENGLAND**

**Amsterdam** ☐

**G E R M A N Y**

○ **London** ☐
Bristol

Southampton ○Dover

Plymouth

Dunkirk○ ○Antwerp

Calais○ **Brussels** ☐

**BELGIUM**

*E n g l i s h    C h a n n e l*

Cherbourg○

Dieppe○

○Le Havre

**Paris** ☐

*A T L A N T I C   O C E A N*

Brest○

Lorient○

Saint-Nazaire○ ○Nantes ○Tours

**F R A N C E**

*B a y*

*o f*

*B i s c a y*

○La Pallice (La Rochelle)

Lyon○

Bordeaux○

| 0 | 100 | 200 | 300 miles |

| 0 | 100 200 300 400 | 500 km |

The Home Waters

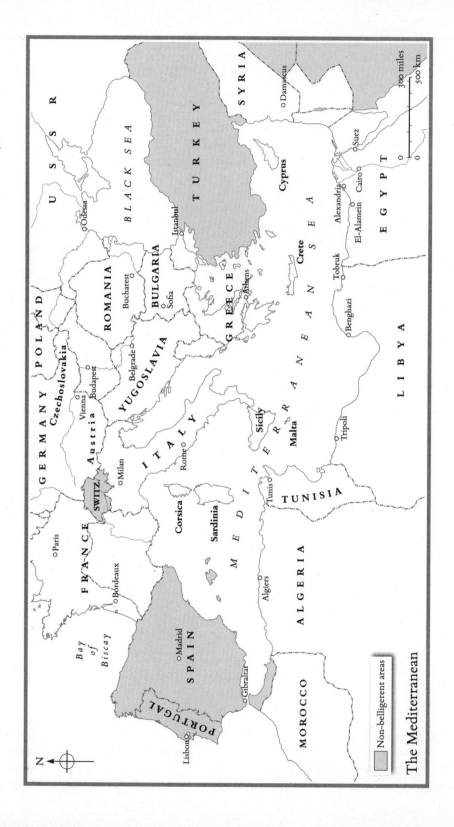

The Mediterranean

Non-belligerent areas

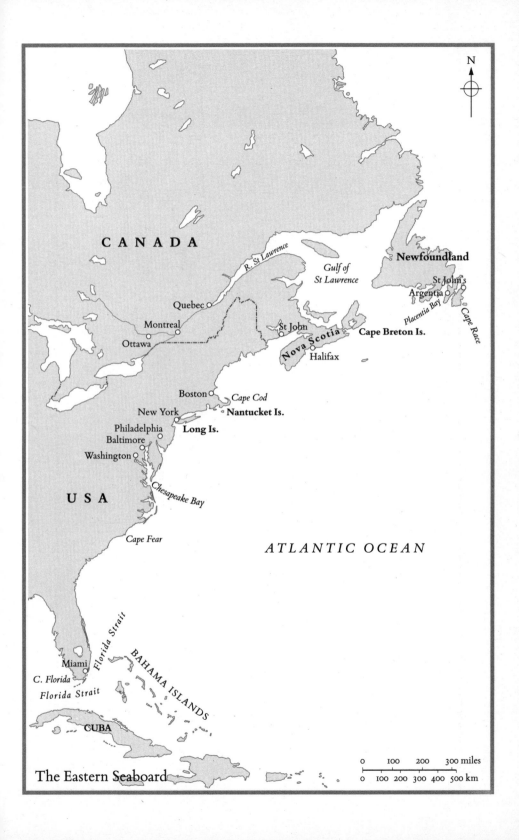

N

CANADA

R. St Lawrence

Gulf of
St Lawrence

Newfoundland

St John's

Quebec

Argentia

Montreal

Placentia Bay

Cape Race

St John

Ottawa

Nova Scotia

Cape Breton Is.

Halifax

Boston

Cape Cod

New York

Nantucket Is.

Philadelphia

Long Is.

Baltimore

Washington

Chesapeake Bay

USA

Cape Fear

ATLANTIC OCEAN

Florida Strait

Miami

BAHAMA ISLANDS

C. Florida

Florida Strait

CUBA

The Eastern Seaboard

| 0 | 100 | 200 | 300 miles |
|---|-----|-----|-----------|

| 0 | 100 | 200 | 300 | 400 | 500 km |
|---|-----|-----|-----|-----|--------|

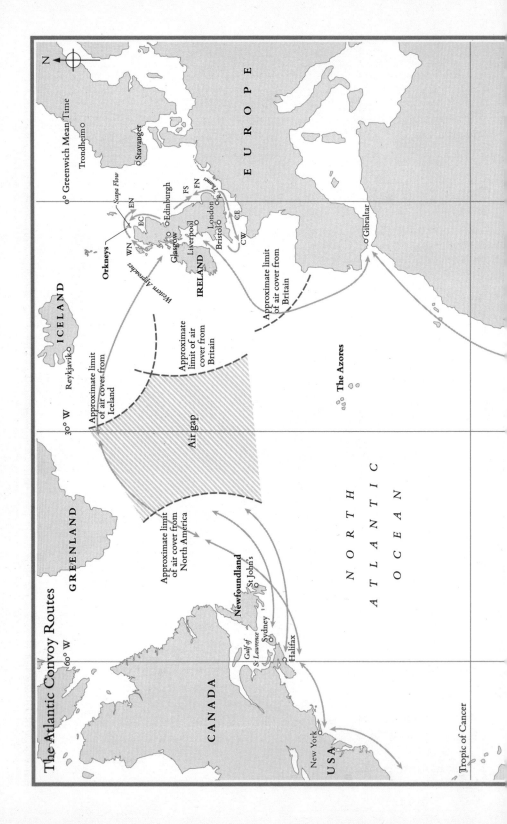

The Atlantic Convoy Routes

N

EUROPE

0° Greenwich Mean Time

Trondheim
Stavanger
Scapa Flow
Orkneys
EN
EC
WN
Edinburgh
FS
FN
Thames
Glasgow
Liverpool
London
Bristol
CE
CW
IRELAND
Western Approaches

ICELAND
Reykjavik
30° W
Approximate limit of air cover from Iceland
Approximate limit of air cover from Britain

GREENLAND
60° W
Approximate limit of air cover from North America
Air gap

Gibraltar
Approximate limit of air cover from Britain

The Azores

NORTH
ATLANTIC
OCEAN

CANADA
Newfoundland
St John's
Gulf of St Lawrence
Sydney
Halifax
New York
USA

Tropic of Cancer

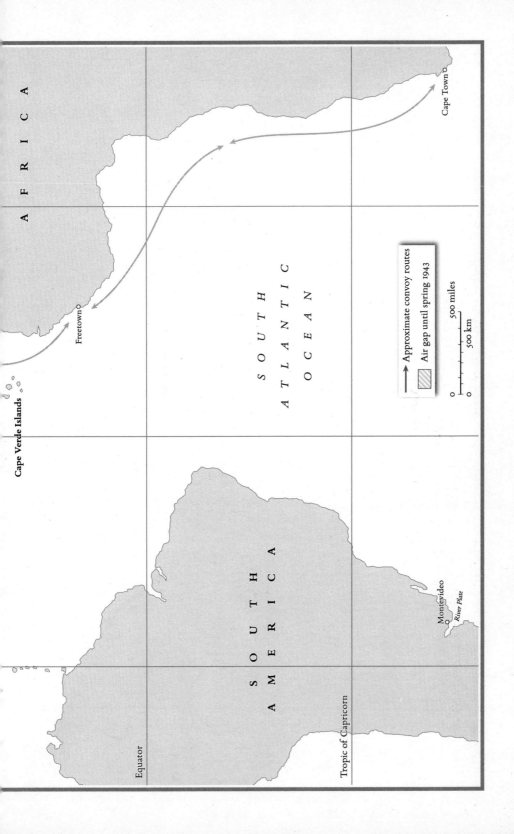

AFRICA

Cape Town

Freetown

Cape Verde Islands

SOUTH
ATLANTIC
OCEAN

SOUTH
AMERICA

Montevideo
River Plate

Equator

Tropic of Capricorn

Approximate convoy routes
Air gap until spring 1943

500 miles

500 km

0
0

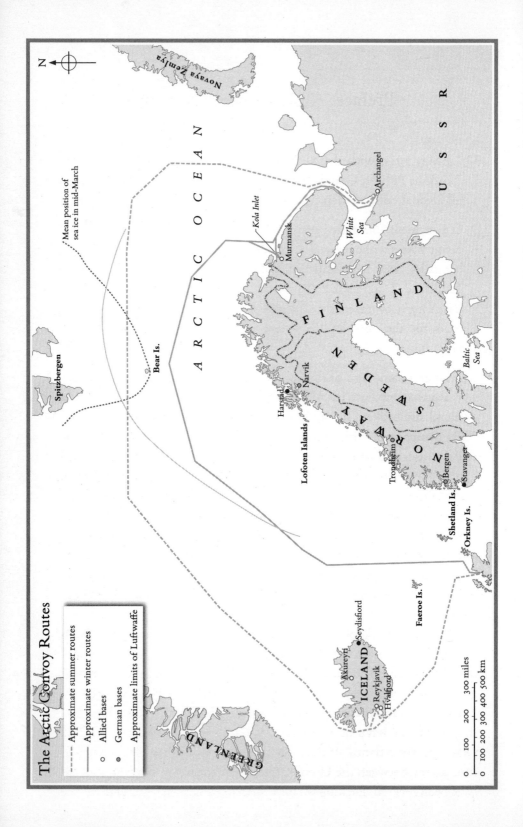

The Arctic Convoy Routes

- – – – – Approximate summer routes
- ———— Approximate winter routes
- ○ Allied bases
- ● German bases
- ———— Approximate limits of Luftwaffe

| 0 | 100 | 200 | 300 miles |
| 0 | 100 200 | 300 400 | 500 km |

N

Novaya Zemlya

ARCTIC OCEAN

Mean position of
sea ice in mid-March

Spitzbergen

Bear Is.

Archangel

Kola Inlet

Murmansk

White
Sea

U S S R

FINLAND

SWEDEN

NORWAY

Baltic
Sea

Narvik

Harstad

Lofoten Islands

Trondheim

Bergen

Stavanger

Shetland Is.

Orkney Is.

Faeroe Is.

Akureyri

Seydisfjord

ICELAND

Reykjavik

Hvalfjord

GREENLAND

# Preface: A Momentous Victory

On 4 May 1945, with the Third Reich crumbling about him, Hitler's successor as Führer, Grand Admiral Karl Dönitz, despatched a message to all U-boat commanders across the globe:

> U-boat men! Undefeated and spotless you lay down your arms after a heroic battle without equal. We remember in deep respect our fallen comrades, who have sealed with death their loyalty to Führer and Fatherland. Comrades! Preserve your U-boat spirit, with which you have fought courageously, stubbornly and imperturbably through the years for the good of the Fatherland. Long live Germany! Your Gr. Admiral.[1]

The longest campaign of the Second World War and the most destructive naval campaign in all history was finally over: Germany was defeated and broken. It could so easily have been otherwise.

By comparison with a global death toll of more than 60 million, the raw statistics of death and destruction in the Atlantic during the Second World War may appear modest – if any death in war can be so described. Though there are no precise figures, it is widely accepted that more than 3,000 merchant ships were sunk in the Atlantic, causing the deaths of more than 30,000 seamen. On the Axis side, in a macabre equivalence, some 27,000 officers and crew – or 75 per cent of those who went to war in the Kriegsmarine's U-boats – lost their lives; a higher death rate than that of any branch of the armed forces on any side of the conflict between 1939 and 1945.[2]

When we think of the great struggles of those years, our minds generally turn to the Blitz, El Alamein, Anzio, Arnhem, Moscow, Leningrad, Stalingrad, Berlin, or a host of others by which our parents or grandparents may have been affected. Although territorial struggles in Europe delivered the coup de grâce against the Third Reich, those battles could not have been fought, let alone won, without the Allied victory in the Atlantic. If the German U-boats had prevailed, the maritime artery between the United States and the United Kingdom would have been severed. Lacking oil for transport or heating, and without the

raw materials required to manufacture weapons of war, it would have
been impossible to prosecute the war against Germany. 'Blood, toil,
tears, and sweat' would have been to no avail. Even more fundamentally, in the absence of basic foodstuffs – most of which were imported
from Africa, Asia, South America and the United States – the British
people would have faced the prospect, in the words of the military historian John Keegan, of 'a truly Malthusian decline'.[3] Mass hunger would
have consumed the nation. Not only would it have been physically
and spiritually impossible to 'fight on the beaches . . . on the landing
grounds . . . in the fields and in the streets', but Churchill – or, more
probably, his successor – would have had little choice but to sue for
peace with Hitler. It is for these reasons that Churchill wrote 'The Battle
of the Atlantic was the dominating factor all through the war. Never for
one moment could we forget that everything happening elsewhere, on
land, at sea, or in the air, depended ultimately on its outcome, and amid
all other cares we viewed its changing fortunes day by day with hope or
apprehension.'[4]

Even if the U-boats had failed to starve out Britain, mere survival
would not have been enough to stave off disaster. Had the German
*Wolfsrudel* (wolf packs) – remained free to prowl the ocean at will, they
would have prevented the Allied armies from crossing the Atlantic in
sufficient numbers to join the British in the invasion of Europe: there
would have been no D-Day. It is very possible that, as a result, Stalin
would have elected to make a cynical accommodation with Hitler of
the kind that had produced the Ribbentrop–Molotov Pact in August
1939. In this case, the outcome of the Second World War in Europe
would have been – from the perspective of those who believe in freedom and democracy – catastrophically different.

Anyone with a modicum of imagination knows the fear of the deep that
is in all of us. Good mariners exercise constant vigilance. Distances are
distorted and dangers are magnified. In the gloom of twilight, cans,
tyres, beer bottles – the unsinkable detritus of the sea – strain the
detecting eye and become imagined hazards. Conversely, a faraway
light turns out to be a tanker that threatens imminent collision. A
cormorant's neck or the head of a curious seal are mistaken for a
barely submerged rock or – fatally – vice versa. All but the most foolhardy know that the delights of the sea are invariably tinged with

anxiety even when the waters are benign and the air is balmy. When nature delivers a hurricane that builds a gentle swell into mountainous walls of water which no human force can resist, any mariner of substance acknowledges the spasm of terror that shivers through body and spirit.

And that is in peacetime. In the Battle of the Atlantic every seaman on either side was on edge for hours and weeks at a time. The enemy was always at hand, lurking just over the horizon or prowling beneath the waves. In the air, warplanes laden with bombs emerged suddenly from the clouds to wreak havoc below. Ships and submarines may have been forbidding in appearance but their hulls were a skin of metal so thin that, as Winston Churchill once remarked of battleships in action, they were like 'eggshells pounding each other with hammers'.[5] Sinkings were rarely prolonged, and neither was survival in the icy waters – something every sailor knew only too well.

Most of those who perished at sea lost their lives in the grimmest circumstances. The fortunate ones died swiftly, blown up by torpedoes or, in the case of the U-boat crews, by depth charges or machine-gun fire. Others were trapped in sinking hulls or asphyxiated by toxic fumes. Some died from their wounds in vessels which lacked anaesthetics or surgeons or, very often, both; some drowned because lifeboats had been smashed into flotsam or because, after days or weeks adrift without food and water, they succumbed to insanity and threw themselves overboard.

On the Allied side, survivors of the Battle of the Atlantic have left first-hand accounts of their travails which are as vivid as those from any other military front. However, with the possible exception of British naval commanders such as Peter Gretton, Donald Macintyre, and 'Johnny' Walker, none of them achieved popular renown in their lifetimes. Their war was played out far from the correspondent's notebook or the photographer's lens. Their experiences were thus largely overlooked except in so far as official announcements of the time would permit. It was not until Nicholas Monsarrat, who had served in a wartime corvette, published his novel *The Cruel Sea* in 1951 that a wider public was able to appreciate the purgatory of the war at sea. In this volume, I have drawn extensively from the oral and written testimonies of those who fought in the ships that saved Britain and survived to tell their tales.

By contrast, the U-boat crews were hailed at the time as heroes of the Third Reich. Their most successful commanders – so-called 'aces' such as Otto Kretschmer, Erich Topp, Joachim Schepke, Günther Prien and Reinhard Hardegen – were household names throughout Germany, their acts of derring-do spread across the popular press and on cinema screens. Feted like film stars, they were garlanded with the highest honours, very often by the Führer himself. As those U-boats which were destroyed generally sank with the loss of every member of the crew, there are very few accounts of what it was like to go down in a fatally stricken vessel, but the exhausting combination of boredom, elation and terror has been vividly described by several U-boat commanders and a few of those who served under them. *The Battle of the Atlantic* draws no less from these first-hand testimonies.

As a phrase, memorable though it is, the 'Battle of the Atlantic' is misleading in a number of pertinent ways. It suggests a single conclusive encounter like the defeat of the Spanish Armada in 1588 or Nelson's destruction of the French fleet in 1805. But the former was accomplished within ten days and the latter lasted no more than a few hours. The Battle of the Atlantic not only lasted from the very first to the very last day of the war but, so far from being a single battle, it involved hundreds of hostile encounters on a wide variety of fronts, some of which lasted a few hours, some many days. It was not a battle but a campaign.

Moreover, it was a campaign fought not only in the strategic bubble of a single ocean but also in the seaways which both conjoined and separated the combatant nations via a network of arteries. Though navigators may chart the cross-hairs of latitude and longitude by which cartographers have distinguished the Atlantic from the Indian, Pacific and Arctic oceans, they were as strategically and militarily entwined as the commingling waters which flow from one to the other. To treat the Battle of the Atlantic in isolation from the naval battles fought in these waters (as well as in the Caribbean, the Mediterranean and the North Sea) is like presuming the carotid artery is the only means of pumping blood through the body. Yes, it was vital, but the 'capillary' routes along which a multitude of vital supplies flowed until they reached their final destination were of no less significance. For that reason, although the principal focus of *The Battle of the Atlantic* is on the campaign in that ocean, its narrative is not to the exclusion of other maritime fronts.

Nor should the war at sea be viewed only through a military prism. Of course, in such a long contest, the strategies and tactics adopted by both sides were not only critically important but also changed constantly through the experience of triumph and disaster which were themselves the product of new types of weaponry, novel technologies and breakthroughs in the gathering of crucial intelligence. With each innovation the advantage would switch suddenly and fatally from one side to the other. These are important ingredients in any account of this prolonged maritime struggle, but the full story of the Battle of the Atlantic is as much about the competing objectives, judgements and imperatives within and between the high commands of the principal protagonists as it is about a maritime clash of arms. For that reason, this book focuses as much on the individuals who wielded power and influence in the war capitals of Europe and America – London, Berlin, Moscow, and Washington – as on the men who fought and died on the high seas at their behest.

Those responsible for the direction of the war on the Allied side were swift to appreciate the critical importance of the Battle of the Atlantic but rather slower to give their navies the tools to finish the job. In the early years of the war Winston Churchill juggled with many competing priorities as he sought to safeguard Britain from invasion and to defend a global empire. As a result, the nation's resources were stretched to the limit and sometimes beyond it; to the profound frustration of the prime minister, who found it exceptionally difficult to reconcile his boundless ambition with the fact that the men, the armour, and especially the ships were not available in sufficient force to achieve everything at once. Nonetheless it remains one of the great conundrums of his leadership that, although he was to reflect that 'the only thing that ever really frightened me during the war was the U-boat peril',[6] he failed to follow through the logic of this foreboding until it was almost too late and certainly well beyond the point at which that 'peril' could have been eliminated. For every month from the start of hostilities until the early summer of 1943, Britain was losing merchant ships at a faster rate than they could be replaced, largely because they were inadequately protected against the Third Reich's rapidly expanding U-boat fleet.

From the British perspective, the story of the Battle of the Atlantic is in significant measure about a prolonged struggle between the Admiralty and the Air Ministry which became so fierce that a senior admiral was driven to comment that it was 'a much more savage one than our war with the Huns'.[7] Their hostilities were suspended only when, after three and a half years of war, Allied losses in the Atlantic reached such an alarming level that for a while it looked as though the U-boats were on the verge of severing Britain's lifeline, a prospective catastrophe which forced a resolution in favour of the Admiralty.

This damaging clash between two branches of the wartime government owed much to Churchill. In the summer of 1940, as the Battle of Britain raged overhead, the new prime minister was naturally obsessed not only with the need to stiffen national morale but also to orchestrate action against Germany which would reverse Britain's fortunes and, in time, lead on to victory. As he cast around for a means to this end, he swiftly concluded that 'an absolutely devastating, exterminating attack by very heavy bombers from this country upon the Nazi homeland' was the 'only one sure path' to the defeat of Hitler.[8] The ethical controversies provoked by this misapprehension have persisted to this day. By contrast, the consequences for the course of the Second World War have received less scrutiny. Yet Churchill's failure to insist that an adequate number of aircraft be released from the bombing of Germany to do battle against the U-boats in the Atlantic until it was almost too late was a strategic error of judgement that made a fateful contribution to Britain's failure to nullify the U-boat threat until many months later than would otherwise have been possible. The price of this delay may be measured in the thousands of lives and hundreds of ships which were lost unnecessarily in consequence. It may also be measured in terms of its strategic implications.

There is a tempting, indeed mind-boggling, scenario for those students who are lured by the 'what if' or 'if only' school of historiography: if the U-boat threat had been aborted several months earlier than it was, could the mass transportation of American troops and armaments from the United States to Britain have started in time to countenance a cross-Channel invasion of France in the autumn of 1943? Might the Allied armies have advanced deeper into Germany before the Red Army's own push towards the German capital in the summer of 1944? If so, would the Allies have been in a position at Yalta to ensure that the Cold War map of Europe was drawn more nearly to reflect their own strength on the ground, greatly to the strategic advantage, therefore, of not only the post-war West but also those millions of Europeans who later found themselves entrapped behind the 'Iron Curtain'?

It is a tempting vision that is explored later in these pages. What is surely beyond doubt, though, is that the prospect of an earlier victory in the Atlantic – by, say, the early autumn of 1942 rather than the early summer of 1943 – would have had a powerful impact on the fractious debate between London and Washington over Allied strategy in the prolonged build-up to D-Day (which this book also describes in some detail). In a cable to Roosevelt, which he despatched in July 1941, Churchill made it clear that he foresaw the liberation of Europe by a seaborne invasion 'when the opportunity is ripe'.[9] The single greatest obstacle in the way of this undertaking was the threat posed by the U-boats to the Atlantic convoys. Had this threat been eliminated earlier than it was, the strategic disputes between the Western Allies would have been even fiercer than they became by 1943; in particular the British would have found it far more difficult to persuade the Americans that victory in the Mediterranean (via North Africa and then Sicily) should precede the cross-Channel invasion of France. As it happened, of course, all such speculation, however intriguing, is rendered profitless because the prime minister was unwilling to prioritize the destruction of German U-boats over the destruction of German cities.

Churchill was a titanic leader whose strategic vision has often been unjustly disparaged but, in relation to the war at sea, his impetuous nature led him to embrace a false dichotomy. Contrasting the indubitably 'offensive' character of strategic bombing with the ostensibly 'defensive' task of forcing a lifeline passage for the convoys through U-boat infested oceans, he invariably favoured the 'offensive' initiatives hatched in the Air Ministry over the 'defensive' role assigned to the Admiralty. However, the prime minister was not alone in making this misleading distinction. Not only was it shared by his colleagues in the War Cabinet but also by the British chiefs of staff, including the First Sea Lord, Admiral Pound, who had most to lose. Although Pound became increasingly dismayed by Churchill's refusal to withdraw from Bomber Command the aircraft needed to nullify the U-boat onslaught, he fatally weakened his case by failing to question the prime minister's underlying premise. This collective mindset was evidently unable to recognize that the Atlantic convoys were no less 'offensive' in character than the wagon trains which opened up the American Midwest in the nineteenth century or (to borrow a twenty-first-century parallel) the military escorts which forced a way through the Taliban-infested deserts in Afghanistan to succour front-line towns and settlements. As it was, the Battle of the Atlantic soon materialized into a conflict that essentially was an asymmetric conflict between the convoys and the U-boats, a struggle in which, for month after month, the pendulum of triumph and disaster swung wildly from one side to the other.

The White House was no less aware of the strategic importance of the Atlantic lifeline. In May 1941 President Roosevelt made this unambiguously clear in a cable to Churchill. 'I believe the outcome of this struggle is going to be decided in the Atlantic and unless Hitler can win there he cannot win anywhere in the world in the end.'[10] But Roosevelt viewed the Battle of the Atlantic from a specifically American perspective and he was also under very different and strongly competing pressures. Until the Japanese attack on Pearl Harbor in December 1941, a sizeable majority of the American people – whose views were reflected vehemently in the media and in Congress – remained stubbornly averse to any military entanglement that might bring the United States into a faraway struggle in Europe from which they could detect no significant threat to the homeland.

Following Pearl Harbor, their visceral response was that retribution should be exacted against the Japanese at the expense of any other objective. That view was shared by some of the president's most powerful military advisors, most notably Admiral King, the commander-in-chief of the US Navy, whose ill-concealed prejudice in favour of prioritizing Japan over Germany was to aggravate the mood of negotiations with his British counterpart. However, in what was to prove the most important strategic presumption of the Second World War, Roosevelt had long been persuaded that the destruction of German Nazism should precede the elimination of Japanese imperialism: his mantra, to which all his subordinates were obliged to subscribe, was 'Germany First'.

However, since the White House had not only to prepare for a 'two-ocean war' but also to heed public opinion, he had to move in a crablike fashion towards his overriding strategic objective – which he accomplished with a legerdemain that Houdini would have envied.

Thus, by the autumn of 1941, not only was the US Navy preparing for action in the Pacific but openly confronting the Third Reich in the Atlantic. By the ruse of extending America's security zone to encompass virtually half the Atlantic Ocean, Roosevelt engineered a de facto – though not a de jure – declaration of war against Hitler three months before the attack on Pearl Harbor.

But there was a twist to this quasi-subversive commitment to the British cause. Although he was an Anglophile, his support for Churchill was strategically contingent. Partly as a result of the prime minister's seductive diplomacy, FDR was convinced that a Nazi victory in Europe would ultimately threaten the regional if not the global interests of the United States. However, following the German invasion of Russia in June 1941, he rapidly appreciated that the Soviet Union had the key to the destruction of the Third Reich. Though Britain mattered, Russia mattered even more – and this would lead to almost as much tension between London and Washington as it did between those two capitals and Moscow.

From the moment Hitler launched Operation Barbarossa in June 1941 it became an American priority to despatch military supplies by every means possible to the beleaguered Soviet regime. And since the Atlantic flowed into the Arctic, the former was an essential conduit via which the United States could turn warm words about Stalin into effective support for the Red Army. The prime minister did not fail to acknowledge that the Soviet Union was indispensable to the defeat of the Third Reich but – for reasons explored in these pages – he repeatedly found cause to delay or suspend the Arctic convoys. This often irritated the White House and invariably infuriated the Soviet leader. The extensive correspondence between Roosevelt, Churchill and Stalin reveals in the starkest way the scale of the diplomatic and personal challenges posed by their overlapping but often competing priorities.

The military significance of the supplies despatched to Russia was to be a matter of much debate. Higher estimates suggest that 10 per cent or even more of the Soviet Union's military and material needs were despatched through Washington's Lend-Lease programme which was initiated by Roosevelt following the German invasion. Whether it was as high as that figure or as low as 4 per cent (as some Soviet analysts were to assert), Allied assistance indubitably played a crucial part in providing vital raw materials and military equipment that Moscow could not otherwise source.[11] Certainly, Stalin behaved as though the West's military support was vital to the Red Army's prospects of arresting and reversing the Wehrmacht's advance. Of the three supply routes to Russia – via the Far East, Persia and the Arctic Ocean – the last, though lowest in terms of total tonnage, was the most important in the critical period up to 1943. When Arctic convoys were suspended, either because the conditions were judged too perilous or because the ships were required for other major Allied operations, Stalin railed openly against Churchill, and less aggressively against Roosevelt, whose correspondence with the Soviet Union was invariably warmer in tone than that adopted by the British prime minister. In language that would in other circumstances have led to a breakdown in diplomatic relations, his Western partners were variously and not infrequently accused of bad faith or breaching solemn commitments. Stalin did not let diplomatic niceties stand in his way; on one occasion, Churchill even refused to accept delivery of a particularly abusive cable, returning it in person to the Soviet ambassador in London ostensibly unread.

If the Soviet leader conducted his diplomatic relations with his Western counterparts like a bear with a sore head, he did not lack cause. Both Churchill and Roosevelt habitually gave him the impression that they regarded their military assistance to the Soviet Union as though it were a charitable donation rather than an essential contribution to a common cause. This clearly aggravated Stalin's suspicion that he and his people were being taken for granted by London and Washington, and that their unique contribution to the arrest of Nazism was being undervalued or even ignored. Between the lines of his correspondence, it is possible to detect a twin-edged resentment that, despite their warm words, the two Western leaders regarded Red Army lives as more expendable than those of their own combatants and that they were content to allow the Soviet armies to absorb crushing losses until they were ready to come in to reap the benefit. Whether or not this was so, Roosevelt's and Churchill's attitude towards Stalin bordered on the cavalier. This was particularly so when it came to an even graver source of discord between East and West: the opening of a Second Front via a cross-Channel invasion of Nazi-occupied Europe, which thereby became a source not only of disputatious debate within the Western Alliance, but also of bitter recrimination between the Western Allies and Moscow. Once London and Washington had agreed their own priorities, they were only too inclined to allow Stalin to believe that a tentative proposition was a cast-iron commitment. Thus they indicated a resolve to launch a Second Front in 1942 and, when that failed to materialize, they reiterated their determination to make it happen in 1943, only to postpone it once again until 1944. In the light of their own strategic priorities, these decisions were inevitable; but, sometimes by concealment and on occasion with downright duplicity, they stretched diplomatic propriety to its limits by allowing the Soviet leader to believe on each occasion that their contingent commitments to him were unequivocal. It was not surprising that Stalin's manner frequently betrayed his grievance at being gulled by allies who purported to be in awe of the gallantry displayed on the battlefield by a Red Army yet behaved as though the Soviet Union's main contribution to the defeat of Nazism was merely to drain the resources of the Third Reich in time for the eventual victory of the West.

The Allies were fortunate that Adolf Hitler was the final arbiter of German strategy for the Battle of the Atlantic and not Admiral Dönitz, the commander-in-chief of the U-boat fleet. Like Admiral Erich Raeder, the commander-in-chief of the Kriegsmarine, Dönitz believed that Britain was Germany's 'mortal enemy'.[12] Mercifully from the Allied perspective, the two admirals fell out over the best means of defeating their foe. Dönitz was adamant that the Third Reich's overriding military priority should be a U-boat campaign to throttle Britain's supply lines by sinking merchant ships at a faster rate than they could be replaced – the tonnage war, as he called it. Raeder acknowledged that U-boats had an important task but also saw a greater role for the battle fleet and especially the mighty surface raiders like the *Bismarck*, *Scharnhorst* and *Tirpitz*. In the absence of the single-minded conviction required to persuade Hitler that his overriding priority should be to build a U-boat fleet of sufficient size and power to achieve victory in the Atlantic before the Allies had put in place enough countermeasures to blunt the impact of Dönitz's plan of attack, the U-boat commander was deprived of the means required to secure an unequivocal victory in the Atlantic.

As it was, Raeder soon found himself sidelined by Hitler, who took greater heed of those members of his high command who were more effective at wheedling or blustering their way into his misplaced confidence. Crucially, the Führer's designated successor, Hermann Göring, the devious and preposterous commander-in-chief of the Luftwaffe, not only drowned out Raeder but, in his role as Reichsmarschall, was instrumental in denying the Kriegsmarine the resources needed to build the U-boat fleet rapidly enough to inflict terminal damage on the British convoys. This internal battle within the German high command – which closely mirrored that between the Air Ministry and the Admiralty in London – was critical to the outcome of the Battle of the Atlantic.

In January 1943, after enduring what he described as 'a vicious and impertinent harangue' from the Führer,[13] Raeder was peremptorily dismissed. His replacement was Karl Dönitz, whose influence grew so rapidly that in the final stages of the war he became Hitler's chosen successor. But, by the time he found himself at the helm of the Kriegsmarine, the Ship of State was already heading for the rocks. Had Dönitz been given a free hand to shape the war at sea, the Second World War might have taken an alarmingly different course. Like Churchill and Roosevelt, he understood that Germany's fate would be settled in the Atlantic Ocean. Happily, Hitler had no such strategic clarity.

In the chapters that follow I have sought to weave the themes outlined above into a narrative about a sustained drama in which the motives and actions of every combatant – from the most senior members of the competing high commands in London, Washington, Berlin and Moscow to those individuals who fought and died in the Battle of the Atlantic – are crucial to a full appreciation of the epic scale of the campaign. To place the stories of those who fought and died at sea for either side against the background of the momentous dilemmas and decisions of those who sent them there is not to diminish but to illuminate the epic scale of their endeavour. In so doing, I hope I have been able to establish that the Allied victory in the Battle of the Atlantic was a precondition for the defeat of Nazism and therefore as important as any other struggle on any other front between 1939 and 1945.

# 1. The Phoney War that Wasn't

On Sunday 3 September 1939, at 11.15 a.m., Nella Last, a housewife who lived in Barrow-in-Furness, turned on her wireless to hear the prime minister, Neville Chamberlain – honouring his commitment to Poland – announce that Britain had declared war against Germany. Listening with her was her husband, a joiner by trade, and her two sons, one of whom had just been called up for National Service. Later, she watched her 'boys' with others on the local beach at Walney as they filled sandbags against the threat of air raids. 'I could tell by the dazed look on many faces that I had not been alone in my belief that "something" would turn up to prevent war . . .' she wrote in the diary that she was to keep throughout the war and beyond.[1] That evening, with her family about her, she tried to relax but found it impossible: 'I've tried deep breathing, relaxing knitting and more aspirins than I can remember, but all I can see are those boys with their look of "beyond".'[2]

On the same day, immediately after Neville Chamberlain's broadcast, Winston Churchill left his apartment with his wife, Clemmie, and walked a hundred yards down the street to the open basement which had been reserved as a bomb shelter for local residents and where the tenants of some half a dozen flats had already gathered. He stood at the door of the property and in his imagination 'drew pictures of ruin and carnage and vast explosions shaking the ground; of buildings clattering down in dust and rubble, of fire-brigades and ambulances scurrying through the smoke, beneath the drone of hostile aeroplanes'.[3] After the all-clear he went down to the House of Commons, where he took his customary place on the backbenches, at which point, he wrote later, 'a very strong sense of calm came over me . . . I felt a serenity of mind and was conscious of a kind of uplifted detachment from human and personal affairs.'[4] This reverie was interrupted by a meeting with Chamberlain in his room at which the prime minister invited his scourge of many years to serve in the War Cabinet as First Lord of the Admiralty. By 6 p.m. that evening he was at his desk. Churchill's 'wilderness years' were over. The word was soon out as, to his great satisfaction, the Board of the Admiralty sent a signal to every man in the fleet: 'Winston is back'. Within hours, the first crisis of the Second World War was upon him.

On that day, too, Barbara Bailey, the thirty-four-year-old daughter of a London solicitor, was a passenger aboard the SS *Athenia* when she heard the news that Britain was at war. As soon as the ship's captain posted Chamberlain's declaration on the ship's notice board, a shiver of apprehension rippled swiftly through the vessel. Barbara Bailey broke down in tears, not so much from fear as the sense that she was alone and friendless. Two days earlier, just before the liner's departure from Liverpool bound for Montreal, she had written a letter to her mother from the Adelphi Hotel. Distraught at the collapse of a love affair, she had decided to make a fresh start in Canada. 'Darling, darling, mother,' she wrote,

> Perhaps I am wrong to leave, but I am just letting fate guide me . . . It's all so strange but I'll be all right – please don't worry about me – it's you all I am so worried over – please take care of each other. I'm terribly sorry for my lack of patience – especially with Daddy. I am determined to come back well and helpful to you all . . . And now, goodbye to you all and take care of yourselves, my darling family. All my love.[5]

As dusk began to haze the evening sky, the *Athenia* was steaming at fifteen knots into a heavy swell some 200 miles from the Irish coast. The press of people wanting to escape Europe as the storm clouds threatened ever more ominously meant that the liner was more heavily laden than usual. Among the 1,102 passengers on board were 311 Americans, 469 Canadians and some 150 refugees from the Continent, 34 of whom were German Jews. The remainder were British and Irish nationals, including a party of children on their way to a place of safety in Canada. Sharp-eyed passengers noticed great activity on deck as the ship's crew removed the covers from the vessel's twenty-six lifeboats (more than enough to accommodate the ship's complement), readied fire hoses and placed shields over deck lights. By the evening, many passengers had succumbed to seasickness and retreated to their cabins. Barbara Bailey elected to take supper in the dining room.

At 7.43 p.m., a little over eight hours after Chamberlain's announcement, there was an explosion on board, the sound of which reverberated along the hull and through every deck. The vessel tilted to port. Chairs and tables slid in the same direction, passengers flailed about one another, falling to their hands and knees as they sought a door handle or a rail to give them a purchase. Barbara Bailey managed to remain seated as dishes crashed about her and fellow diners fled for the stairs in alarm. When her two dining companions leapt up to follow the rush, she sought to restrain them, raising her voice above the wailing hubbub to exclaim, 'For God's sake, sit still. We're probably doomed, but don't let's get crushed to death.'

As the torpedo struck, the lights in the lounge went out. Passengers stampeded towards the staircase leading up to the upper decks. Still in the dining room, which was now otherwise deserted, Barbara Bailey sat as if paralysed by shock but in fact stricken by waves of misery at the memories of the lover she had lost and the endless rows with her father; she kept repeating to herself, 'Nobody loves me, nobody loves me.'[6] She was startled from this reverie when the chief steward peered into the gloom shouting, 'Is everybody out?' She left her seat and joined the throng on deck.

As the *Athenia* settled more heavily into the Atlantic, the crew acted with speed and proficiency as they sought to muster the passengers into orderly queues for the lifeboats and to quell the panic by which some of them had been seized. It was not easy. In the melee, husbands were separated from wives and parents from children. A woman shouted 'For God's sake help me find my baby.' A little boy screamed 'I'll never see my Daddy again.' The confusion on the crowded decks was aggravated by mutual incomprehension. Few, if any, of the English-speakers understood Polish, Czech, Romanian or German. The converse was also true. Refugees from Nazi-occupied Europe, determined to clamber into crowded lifeboats clinging to the suitcases, baskets and blanketed bundles which contained the remains of their worldly goods, were uncomprehending as other passengers yelled at them in the frenzy of fear. For the most part, however, a semblance of order and restraint soon prevailed. On the basis of many interviews with survivors, Max Caulfield was to write, 'While some were still a little hysterical and emotional, others stood like graven statues, too stunned to move, trying to reconcile the sight of the sprawling bodies around No. 5 hatch with the normality of ship life as it had been only an hour before . . .'[7] At one point, a young Protestant minister clambered onto an elevated portion of the deck, where he was seen to raise his arms to the heavens.

Below him a knot of passengers knelt as he offered them all prayers for salvation.

With great dexterity, the crew managed to manoeuvre every lifeboat into the water with little mishap. It was a tricky evacuation. Isabelle Coullie, who had managed to find her way through the throng of confused and terrified passengers to find the lifeboat station, lost her grip as she clambered down the rope into the boat allocated to her and her husband, John, and, like several others, fell into the ocean. Her husband at once leapt in to save her. With difficulty they were both hauled into the lifeboat, where John helped four others to row their heavy cargo of women and children clear of the stricken liner. In the process, he recalled 'we shipped a lot of water, and also got soaked . . . Bell [Isabelle] got sick and then sometime later I was sick – we had swallowed so much oil and the taste was awful. Then it got cold and we were utterly miserable.'[8]

By contrast, Barbara Bailey had recovered herself. The motion of the boat disturbed her not at all and she was suddenly exhilarated by the spray that whipped across her face. When two women became distressed as the lifeboat started to ship water, she told them, 'I love the sea. The sea is kind. The sea hasn't done this to you. And if death were to come, it would come quickly.'[9] As night fell, the sea around the *Athenia* was speckled by lifeboats filled with survivors in varying degrees of relief, exhaustion and distress waiting to be rescued from the Atlantic chill. Still on board the *Athenia*, the wireless operator had managed to send out an SOS distress signal to all ships in the vicinity. A clutch of destroyers and other vessels was soon steaming at full speed to the scene, most of them arriving in the early hours of the following morning. After nine hours adrift, the Coullies were among those picked up by a Swedish ship, where they were wrapped in blankets and dosed with hot soup. One by one, and with difficulty in a rising sea, most of those who had escaped from the *Athenia* were similarly plucked to safety.

Fourteen hours after the torpedo struck her on the port bow, the SS *Athenia* reared up and, with barely a sound, slipped under the waves. Altogether, 118 people lost their lives, 93 of whom were passengers, including 16 children. If the *Athenia* had not remained afloat for so long, and if there had been no rescue ships in the area, the loss of life would have been very much higher.

The sinking of the *Athenia* was not only a disaster for those directly affected but it came as a profound shock to the Admiralty, which had lulled itself into the assumption that the German U-boats would avoid attacking passenger liners, which were supposedly exempt from enemy action under the elaborate rules of engagement negotiated between the world's major naval powers in the years leading up to the outbreak of war. Moreover, the sinking revealed in a single blow how unready Britain was for a conflict in which the U-boat would become Germany's principal weapon against Allied merchant shipping.

The rejoicing in the Royal Navy at Churchill's return to the Admiralty was more equivocal than the new First Lord had allowed himself to presume. For some, who had long memories of the First World War, the signal 'Winston is back' was greeted with mixed feelings. Though his eloquent belligerence towards the enemy boded well, he had acquired a well-earned reputation in those years for interfering in matters which were either beneath or beyond his competence as a cabinet minister. As a result he fell out with a succession of senior officers who were obliged to defer to him as their political master. His habit of sending signals to the fleet without the authority of his peers on the Board and, in the view of one of their number, of issuing 'peremptory orders' to the Sea Lords, rankled greatly.[10] He was bombastic, impetuous, intemperate and tactless – traits which led the loyal biographer of another First Sea Lord, Prince Louis of Battenberg, to liken the new incumbent to a 'thwarted spoilt school boy'.[11]

With contumely heaped upon him by his political adversaries and by a press which bayed for his removal from high office after the debacle at Gallipoli in 1915 – for which he was held primarily responsible – Churchill was a much diminished force until the emergence of Hitler on the European stage. His outspoken denunciation of Chamberlain's policy of appeasement won him few political friends at Westminster but his lonely defiance against the weight of the political establishment made him, once again, a force to reckon with. Now, with the outbreak of a war which, almost alone, he had both foreseen and advocated, his exile was at an end. His political gifts were suddenly indispensable to the damaged credibility of the prime minister; his place in the Cabinet assured.

'So it was', he wrote later, 'that I came again to the room I had quitted in pain and sorrow almost exactly a quarter of a century earlier.'[12] Wholly unrepentant about his role in the Gallipoli fiasco, which he attributed to misfortune and the tactical errors of others, he lost no time in letting those about him know that he was indeed back, not only in charge but as interventionist as ever. Within hours he summoned Admiral Dudley Pound, the First Sea Lord, to his presence. Churchill had been sharply critical of the way in which the British fleet in the Mediterranean, under Pound's command, had been deployed earlier in the year. Now, by Churchill's account, 'We eyed each other amicably if doubtfully.'[13] Pound had been in the role for three months and only because his predecessor Admiral Roger Backhouse (who had himself been in the post for only seven months) had developed a brain tumour and been forced to retire prematurely. As a front-line admiral, Pound had been relieved to have been overlooked in favour of Backhouse, telling a friend, 'I can hardly believe my luck . . . Just think I am not to be First Sea Lord but instead I am to stay with the fleet for another extra year . . . and then they tell me they will make me an Admiral of the Fleet and I can retire straight from the sea.'[14] Now, unexpectedly, he found himself in the top job at a critical moment.

Pound was the son of an Eton scholar who favoured life in the Devon countryside. His mother was a domineering American of eccentric habits, which included an apparently uncontrollable urge to shoplift. When she and her husband separated, Dudley, who was still a child, was brought up by his father in a bucolic backwater where his life was in every way unexceptional: his tastes were conventional and his talents indeterminate. In 1891, at the age of thirteen, he joined HMS *Britannia*, a floating hulk moored in the River Dart which served as the training centre for the navy's officer class. Though the course required proficiency in mathematics, it was otherwise notable for its absence of intellectual rigour. As Pound's biographer has noted, 'The cadets were strained physically, but not mentally, and it may be said that education, as opposed to professional training, ended for many at 13.'[15] Pound emerged from his exertions at *Britannia* with enough qualifications to promote an upwardly mobile career: 'Very zealous and of very good judgement' was the characteristic assessment of one of his commanding officers. By 1915, a captain at the comparatively young age of thirty-seven, he was posted to work as a staff officer under Admiral Fisher, the brilliant and mercurial First Sea Lord brought out of retirement at the start of the war.

Pound was less impressed by Fisher than Churchill had been, confiding to a colleague later that the septuagenarian was 'a very old man, and really only able to put in about 2 hours work a day at the Admiralty, and spent the rest of the day at his own leisure'.[16] This was not only uncharitable but untrue; the young captain seemed to have forgotten or not known that Fisher was usually at his desk by 5 a.m., well before others, including Pound, were accustomed to arrive for work. But like many ambitious young men, Pound was not generously endowed with benevolence. His training had been stern and narrow and this was reflected in his demeanour and attitude. However, within the confines of the prevailing orthodoxies, he was distinguished by a calm intelligence, a gift for clear if cautious thought, and a propensity for tireless work. His talent for painstaking organization may not have excited envious comment but it helped assure his seamless rise to the top. One close observer noted, 'He wore a lugubrious air and his mere entry into the room made the occupants feel grave.'[17] If his physical presence was not immediately commanding, his manner was forceful and, though he was generally equable, a well-developed sense of his own status went hand in hand with a quick temper.

On one occasion he castigated two young officers for damage caused to their destroyers in a gale which put both ships temporarily out of commission. Allegedly frothing at the mouth in fury, he paraded them on his quarterdeck and ordered their courts martial. However, once he had simmered down, he was persuaded to establish a court of inquiry instead; and when this exonerated the two men of any blame, he was swift to atone for his impetuosity by signalling the news to the whole fleet. This was not the only such incident. More startling was his decision to court-martial a trusted colleague, Commander Norris, for allegedly allowing his 'despatch vessel' to drag aground during a storm. Norris was to recall that, on appointing him, Pound had warned that 'if I ever put a foot wrong in this job I could expect nothing else than "three times the stick" . . . [just as] he would serve out to others'.[18] Even though Norris had already been cleared by a court of inquiry, Pound persisted in establishing a court martial in his cabin. This similarly exonerated Norris. To celebrate this verdict, Pound immediately presented his friend with a bottle of champagne.

By the time of his appointment as First Sea Lord, Pound had acquired a reputation for diligence and decency. But he had yet to face any test comparable to the multiplicity of challenges that now faced him. The sinking of the *Athenia* on the very first day of the war exploded like a howitzer shell in the Admiralty, a reminder of a terrible period in the Great War when the Germans waged 'unrestricted' submarine warfare against Allied shipping that would have been calamitous if the United States had not come to Britain's rescue in 1917.

For the first two years of the First World War, the threat from what was then a new form of maritime technology – the submarine – was recognized but not given due weight. With the singular exception of a sage warning by Admiral Fisher, the Admiralty had convinced itself that the main danger to Britain's trade came not from the German navy's small posse of U-boats but from Kaiser Wilhelm II's fleet of capital ships, the so-called 'commerce raiders' which, it was believed, had made convoys redundant in the age of steam. Departing from a tradition which had originated in the Napoleonic wars, the admirals allowed themselves to believe that coal-fired ships travelling together in large numbers and pumping smoke into the atmosphere would form plumper targets for marauding enemy ships than if they travelled alone. Moreover, they also regarded the convoy system as outmoded because merchant ships, travelling independently, could now be adequately protected by a radio communications network through which the Admiralty in London could identify enemy surface raiders and send Royal Navy cruisers to trap them at those focal points where the international shipping routes converged. Underlying these twin presumptions was an aversion to using warships defensively as convoy escorts when they could be better deployed offensively, operating aggressively – and exhilaratingly – as 'hunting patrols' to confront the enemy in open battle. No less significantly, the wartime government was also under pressure from a phalanx of British shipowners and speculative investors, who argued vehemently against any suggestion that their ships should be shepherded through the war zone under the protection of the Royal Navy. By sailing independently, they insisted, their vessels would sail more rapidly and more frequently to their destinations without the logjams which were bound to occur when upwards of thirty merchant ships arrived en masse at the same destination. That this powerful group profited as handsomely when disaster struck as when their vital cargoes reached port safely may have played a part in their reckoning; it is not an exaggeration to note that the more ships the enemy sank, the richer these individuals became.

They not only benefited from huge insurance payouts every time one of their ships went to the bottom but simultaneously from the growing demand for vessels to replace these losses. Despite the introduction of an excess profit tax, the rewards remained phenomenal.

For all these reasons, the British were slow to recognize the worsening threat from German submarines. By the late autumn of 1916, not only was the U-Boat fleet much larger than it had been at the start of the conflict, but the 'on-off' campaign it had waged against merchant shipping since the start of the war had been resumed with a vengeance. To the British government's consternation, it soon became apparent that vital food stocks – especially of imported grain for bread – were falling faster than they could be replenished. In February 1917 the impending crisis was deepened when the Kaiser formally lifted all restrictions on submarine warfare, warning that any vessel on the high seas was now a target for his U-Boats – which duly started to run amok. By the following month, 25 per cent of the ships setting out on voyages were being sunk before they returned. In turn this led neutral states to curtail their trade with the Allies, which thus fell by a catastrophic 75 per cent. It was now clear that Britain was perilously close to losing the campaign at sea, and thereby its means of prosecuting the war against the Kaiser.

In this critical atmosphere Lloyd George (who had unseated Asquith as prime minister in December) began to press the Admiralty to reinstate the convoy system. The admirals were not only short of suitable escorts but deeply reluctant to change tack, although on those routes where convoys were initiated, the impact was immediate. Between March and May on three cross-Channel routes, the naval staff historian records that 'only nine vessels were lost – all at night – out of a total of 4,000 convoyed. Air escorts were provided by day.'[19] Still, though, the Admiralty was slow to heed the lesson.

In July the Kaiser decided to raise the ante. Allegedly in retaliation for the increasingly successful 'hunger blockade' imposed by the Allies on the Central Powers,[20] he announced that the Kaiserliche Marine (Imperial Navy) would no longer abide by the so-called Prize Rules which ordained that no merchant vessel could be sunk by a submarine until it had been searched and its crew provided with a place of safety. The Kaiser's decision shattered what was left of the international consensus about the conduct of a just war at sea; henceforth, he declared, U-boats would not only be permitted to engage in unrestricted warfare against all merchant ships entering the war zone but also to sink them on sight and without warning.

Following this unilateral repudiation of the Prize Rules, the overall number of sinkings rose sharply. This led the Admiralty to jump to the conclusion that the two were causally linked: that the surge in sinkings was a direct consequence of Germany's no-holds barred onslaught. In fact, as the available statistics showed, the cause was due to a simultaneous surge in the number of U-boats on patrol, from fewer than thirty at the start of the war to almost seventy by the spring of 1917. As a result, for several months the U-boats continued to wreak havoc in those parts of the ocean where merchant ships lacked close protection by Allied warships and, where possible, by air patrols (including airships) as well.

By this time, however, the United States had entered the war. The sinking of the *Lusitania* on 7 May 1915 with the loss of more than 1,000 lives, including 128 Americans, had outraged opinion in America and round the world but was not of itself regarded as a casus belli by the White House. There were other factors, but the incident which finally goaded President Woodrow Wilson into declaring 'a war to end all wars' against Germany on 6 April 1917 was the sinking of seven unarmed US merchant ships a few weeks earlier. America's intervention was the Kaiser's undoing. It not only helped to deliver the coup de grâce on the battlefield but, with the deployment of some forty US warships on escort duty, transformed the course of the war at sea as well. According to the naval staff historian, drawing on detailed figures which were available to the Admiralty at the time, when merchant ships were under escort, the U-boats were virtually unable to launch an effective attack: 'Submarine after submarine was sighted and attacked before it dived, or was else forced to dive to escape detection . . . Down to the end of December 1917 there was only one instance of a ship in a convoy with air escort being sunk by a U-boat.'[21] In this way, the United States not only saved Britain from being starved into surrender but demonstrated unambiguously the unique contribution of the convoy system, which the Admiralty had resisted for so long, to the catastrophe which now engulfed Germany.

It was against this backdrop that, in 1921, following the Treaty of Versailles, the US government convened a meeting of the major sea powers in Washington. Its purpose was to prevent a naval arms race and, especially, to impose a new set of rules on maritime warfare to control the threat posed by submarines in any future conflict. Instead the participants were seduced into an elatorate diplomatic quadrille that was to last for the next eighteen years as Britain, the United States, France and Italy sought ways to enhance their naval might vis-à-vis one another, while corralling the latent threat posed by Germany – the recusant at the centre of this masquerade – at the same time.

In the flush of victory, Britain sought to call the tune by pressing for submarines to be outlawed altogether as weapons of war. This was presented as though it were a moral campaign against an inhuman form of warfare but it carried little conviction for those able to detect the self-serving motive behind the British case. Compared with a battleship with which a great maritime nation could rule the waves, the submarine was cheap to build and, with one torpedo, could inflict a mortal blow on any surface warship; greatly to the disadvantage of the British Empire, the submarine thus threatened to alter the balance of maritime power. The Admiralty's proposal was rejected.

Instead, the Americans proposed a new international law defining rules of engagement under which submarines would be subjected to the same protocols as other warships, specifically to an even tougher set of Prize Rules than those the Kaiser had repudiated. Not only would U-boat commanders be required to search a merchant ship before seizing it and to sink it only after its crew had been disembarked but, if this were to prove impracticable, they would also be required by the first article of the US resolution 'to desist from attack and from seizure and to permit the merchant vessel to proceed unmolested'.[22] Despite vigorous objections from the French and Italians, Washington prevailed. On 4 February 1922 a new Submarine Code, framed in virtually the same terms that the United States had originally proposed, was signed into law by all four nations as a key component of what became known as the Washington Naval Treaty.

The French soon backtracked, refusing to ratify the agreement. This led to further debate at the London Naval Conference in 1930. Once again Britain (whose maritime supremacy lay in the Royal Navy's surface fleet) proposed that U-boats should – like chemical weapons – be abolished altogether. This time the United States, alarmed by the rapid production of submarines by Japan, concurred. France still vacillated, insisting that submarines were not offensive but 'defensive' instruments of war. It took several months of negotiation before the British team cobbled together a final draft to which, by the autumn of 1930, the United States, France, Germany and Japan felt able to put their signatures.

The London Naval Treaty, as it was called, was so ambiguously phrased as to leave almost every important issue unresolved. Six years later, in March 1936, despite – or perhaps because of – these embedded ambiguities, more than thirty nations, including Germany and the Soviet Union (but excluding Japan and Italy, which both now reneged), added their signatures to what had morphed into the Second London Naval Treaty. This document modified the first in minor ways but left its essential elements intact, notably with a series of protocols which outlawed 'unrestricted warfare' on the high seas. As Churchill observed, it was 'the acme of gullibility' to suppose any belligerent nation would uphold the Submarine Code that it embraced.[23]

The Admiralty was convinced that the Kaiser's campaign of unrestricted submarine warfare had proved so disastrous that no German leader would make the same mistake ever again. Preoccupied by the threat to the British Empire from the Japanese in the Far East, naval staff officers neglected to analyse data (available since 1920) which showed conclusively that it was the introduction of escorted convoys, supported wherever possible by aircraft, that had saved the nation from collapse in 1917. Instead, they derived comfort from the fact that the leader of the German mission, Joachim von Ribbentrop, had put his signature to an Anglo-German agreement which imposed a permanent restriction on the size of the Kriegsmarine in relation to the Royal Navy (in the ratio of a little over 1 to 3). So long as Hitler adhered to this treaty, the Royal Navy would still be free to confront the Japanese in the Pacific. With the benefit of hindsight, the Admiralty's eagerness to take Ribbentrop at his word is as breathtaking as the spirit of appeasement which clearly infused the British negotiators. While the talks were still in progress, an internal Admiralty memorandum noted: 'In the present mood of Germany it seems probable that the surest way to persuade them to be moderate in their actual performance is to grant them every consideration in theory. In fact they are more likely to build up to submarine parity if we object to their theoretical right to do so, than if we agree that they have a moral justification.'[24]

The Admiralty's readiness to overlook the resurgent U-boat threat in favour of maintaining a battle fleet in the Far East was reinforced by the Royal Navy's traditional romance with battleships and cruisers. After all, it was those great warships that throughout history had taken the fight to the enemy in set-piece battles of the kind made glorious by Admiral Nelson and which, despite the best efforts of the Germans at the Battle of Jutland, had ensured that the British continued to rule the waves. By comparison with the dash and excitement of raiding and plundering their way across the oceans, the task of escorting merchant ships in convoy seemed singularly mundane. In later correspondence with the naval historian Arthur Marder, the Admiral of the Fleet, Sir Caspar John, was to sum up the attitudes of his fellow officers in those years: 'Convoy protection was regarded with martial antipathy by the Navy . . . it was far too defensive in outlook.'[25]

Nor were the shipowners to be ignored. In 1935, the Admiralty's financial secretary, Lord Stanley, told the Commons that, even in the event of hostilities, a convoy system would not be introduced until 'conditions had become so intolerable that they [the shipowners] were prepared to make the necessary sacrifices'. Citing the inevitable delays caused by the need to marshal a convoy at either end of its voyage and pointing to the fact that the fastest vessels in convoy could only travel at the speed of the slowest, Stanley was insouciance personified. Convoys, he reiterated, would be required only 'when sinkings are so great that the country no longer feels justified in allowing ships to sail by themselves but feels that for the protection of their crews the convoy system is necessary'.[26] It was not until 1938, when the risk of war with Germany could no longer be ignored, that the Admiralty felt obliged to modify Stanley's formula. Preparations were now made for the convoy system to be available on the outbreak of war but still with the proviso that this extreme measure would be introduced only if the German U-boats were to breach the 1936 Treaty by once again engaging in 'unrestricted' warfare.

The sinking of the *Athenia*, within hours of Britain's declaration of war, shattered the Admiralty's wishful thinking. The notion that any pretensions to chivalry as defined by the Prize Rules would be at a pre-mium in a clash of maritime arms with the Third Reich seemed to have been mercilessly dispelled. As it turned out, this conclusion proved to be premature but it was enough to set the alarm bells ringing in the

Admiralty. As the news of what had happened spread swiftly around the world, Churchill's first action as First Sea Lord on the morning of 4 September was to ask for an estimate of the existing and potential size of the U-boat fleet. He was informed that the Germans had sixty U-boats and that a further hundred would be ready by early 1940. Two days later, on 6 September, the Admiralty made the formal decision to introduce the convoy system forthwith. But this speed of response masked the fact that the Royal Navy was alarmingly short of escort vessels while those that were available were frequently unsuitable in size and type and their crews were often untrained and ill-prepared. The air support, which in 1917 had played such a large part in deterring the enemy's submarines, was also notable by its absence. To make matters worse, the RAF, an offspring of the naval and army air services which had sprung into independent life in the closing stages of the First World War, was reluctant to release its limited supply of fighters and bombers for what was so widely regarded as the mundane task of safeguarding Britain's maritime supply lines. The Royal Navy – though prepared to do battle against the German and the Japanese surface fleets – was thus woefully ill-equipped for the onslaught that could now be expected from the German U-boats while the Admiralty's enduring disdain for defensive as opposed to offensive warfare was soon to bring the nation perilously close to defeat once again.

The Führer was aghast when he heard that the *Athenia* had been torpedoed by a U-boat. While he was still hopeful that it might be possible to come to terms with Chamberlain's government, Hitler was simultaneously anxious to avoid any provocation which might tilt the United States from neutrality towards belligerency. The Third Reich was far from ready to contemplate conflict with America; in Hitler's mind the subjugation of Europe and the conquest of the Soviet Union were to come first. For this overriding political imperative, Admiral Raeder, the commander-in-chief of the German Navy, had been instructed to ensure that the U-boat fleet should adhere to the rules enshrined in the 1936 Treaty. Raeder disagreed strongly with Hitler's cautious diktat, believing that the U-boat arm of the Kriegsmarine could secure victory by waging 'unrestricted' warfare against all merchant shipping even if America were thereby sucked into the conflict. Nonetheless he duly ordered the commander of the U-boat forces to remind his men of this directive. Accordingly, at 2 p.m. on 3 September Dönitz issued what he evidently regarded as an unambiguous instruction to the men under his command: 'U-boats to make war on merchant shipping in accordance with operations order . . .', a form of words, he noted in his War Diary for that day, that 'should exclude any misunderstanding as the operations are under the express orders for war on merchant shipping in accordance with Prize Law'.[27]

The sinking of the *Athenia* was a flagrant breach of the Prize Rules as defined in the 1936 Treaty and Berlin was forced swiftly to counter an acute diplomatic embarrassment. Masterminded by the Führer's information minister, Joseph Goebbels, the Third Reich's first wartime effort at 'damage limitation' was both crass and incredible. 'The *Athenia* must have been sunk in error by a British warship or else struck a floating mine of British origin,' the propaganda minister announced on the day of the disaster.[28] In the following days, as Dönitz's biographer, Peter Padfield, has noted, such 'inventions took wing, and the affair was soon shrouded in a fog of absurd distortion'.[29] On 5 September Berlin Radio solemnly announced that, if indeed the *Athenia* had been torpedoed, 'it could only have been done by an English submarine. We believe the present chief of the British Navy, Churchill, capable of even that crime.'[30] Raeder did not shrink from adding to this nonsense by declaring that the British allegation implicating one of the Kriegsmarine's U-boats was an 'abominable lie'.[31] It must have been something of a relief to Berlin (as well as a vindication of Goebbels's methodology) that many Americans appear to have been gulled by this chicanery to the point of concluding that who did what to whom was an open question (which was not finally settled until the Nuremberg trials six years later).

The offending attacker was U-30. After rising to the surface to confirm that he had crippled the *Athenia*, Kapitänleutnant Fritz-Julius Lemp continued to hunt for prey in the seaways around Britain, eventually returning to the submarine base at Wilhelmshaven on 27 September. Under interrogation by Dönitz, he immediately confirmed that he had fired the offending torpedo. Claiming that the *Athenia* had been steering a zigzag course and that her lights had been doused, he protested it was reasonable for him to have concluded that the *Athenia* was an armed merchant cruiser and therefore fair game under the 1936 Treaty Prize Rules. Whether he was sincere or whether the prospective exhilaration of his first kill had warped his judgement cannot be known.

According to his War Diary for 4 September, Dönitz initially thought it 'inconceivable' that a U-boat should have been responsible for the tragedy, but after cross-examining Lemp he ordered the hapless commander to Berlin to repeat his story to Raeder, who passed on the gist of it to Hitler.[32] Returning to Wilhelmshaven, Lemp was placed under 'cabin arrest' by Dönitz but spared the humiliation of a court martial which would have drawn public attention to what he had done. Nor did Dönitz have any qualms about concealing the truth from the outside world. Lemp and his crew were sworn to secrecy while the U-boat's log was doctored to suggest that U-30 had been nowhere near the scene of the sinking. At no point in the internal correspondence between the principals involved in this cover-up is there a word of regret at the loss of innocent human life caused by Lemp's violation of international law.

Lemp had – no doubt inadvertently – defied Hitler's will. The Führer's overriding concern was still to avoid a premature expansion of the war and, within hours of the sinking, he made his displeasure unambiguously clear. Further tightening the restrictions already imposed on submarine warfare by the 1936 Treaty, he announced: 'By order of the Führer and until further orders no hostile action will be taken against passenger liners even when sailing under escort.'[33] This instruction was swiftly followed by others, all designed to reduce the risk that America or France (even after the latter's declaration of war against Germany) might be provoked into retaliation. In his memoirs, Dönitz complained that these orders 'had a very restricting effect on the operations of our U-boats, made very high demands on the powers of observation and identification of their commanders and burdened them with a heavy responsibility. In addition they not infrequently enhanced the danger to which the U-boats were exposed.'[34] This, had they known about it, might have offered a crumb of comfort to those in the Admiralty who had chosen to take German protestation of goodwill at face value.

Dönitz's dismay was shared by Raeder. Both men believed in a no-holds-barred confrontation with the enemy. However, this was the extent of their common ground. Dönitz was a man of clear views but narrow horizons. His presence immediately impressed itself on those about him: he was upright and lean, his demeanour calm and measured. When he spoke, he was terse to a degree that brings to mind the style of General Bernard Montgomery. He cared greatly for the psychological and material well-being of those who served under him but he inspired more awe than affection. Though he rarely lost his temper, he was as quick to rebuke as he was to praise. He never betrayed anxiety and his certainties rarely, if ever, appeared to be afflicted by self-doubt.

His memoirs, written after his release from Spandau (where he was imprisoned until 1956 after his conviction as a war criminal at Nuremberg), are to be distrusted for their omissions, distortions and self-exculpations but they reveal more about their author than perhaps he intended: that his ambition was vaunting, that he was ruthless, and that he generally held others responsible for his own shortcomings. With an infamous disregard for the evidence, he failed to express any remorse for the deaths of millions of innocent people. It is clear that he either averted his gaze from the crimes of Nazism or was indirectly complicit in them. But his record also reveals that he was an outstanding leader of men who was to pose a greater threat to Allies in the Second World War than any other military commander in the Third Reich.

Dönitz was born in Berlin, in 1891, the son of a modestly prosperous engineer. The heroic stamp of Germany's Prussian heritage was impressed upon him from childhood. Kaiser Wilhelm II's *Weltpolitik* (the policy designed to show the world that Germany was a great power), which had replaced Bismarck's *Realpolitik* (a practical approach to the exercise of power), required the creation of a strong navy to establish the Empire's global hegemony and, in Paul Kennedy's phrase, 'the coming mastery of the German race in the world'.[35] When he was seventeen the Dönitz family moved to Weimar, where Karl came under the spell of Goethe and Schiller, to the extent that he formed a literary society at his college. However, his artistic leanings were overridden by an urge to join the Imperial German Navy, which, under the tutelage of its commander-in-chief, Admiral Tirpitz, was emerging as a force to rival British sea power.

The training of the officer corps was modelled on the Prussian army. In the words of Dönitz's biographer, 'this meant adopting a harsh, high, rather nasal barking, a deliberately crude, often ungrammatical mode of speech, a prickly concern for personal and caste honour . . . and on board ship insistence on exaggerated marks of deference from specialist officers, petty officers and ratings to the person of the elite executive officer'.[36] This extreme environment helped foster the resentment which led to a naval mutiny in 1918 that in turn spawned the revolutionary uprising that accelerated the downfall of the German Empire and the establishment of the Weimar Republic in the following year. It is a mark of Dönitz's intelligence and ambition that, despite the limitations of his upbringing, he was not contaminated by the sterile authoritarianism of the navy but readily adapted to the changing order.

In January 1917 the twenty-six-year-old Oberleutnant zur See was posted to his first U-boat, which was based in the Adriatic. There is no reason to doubt his enthusiasm for his new world. 'I was fascinated by that unique spirit of comradeship engendered by destiny and hardship shared in the community of a U-boat's crew, where every man's well-being was in the hands of all and where every single man was an indispensable part of the whole,' he was to write. 'Every submariner, I am sure, has experienced in his heart the glow of the open sea and the task entrusted to him, has felt himself to be as rich as a king and would change places with no man.'[37]

His superior officers were quick to discern his qualities. As he rose smoothly up through the long chain of command, via submarines and torpedo boats, report after report portrayed him in ever more glowing terms: 'Excellently gifted for the post, above average, tough and brisk officer . . . Quick in thought and action, prompt in resolution, absolutely reliable . . . All in all – a splendid officer of worthy personality, equally esteemed as officer and man, an always tactful subordinate and excellent comrade,'[38] wrote one of his superior officers when describing the thirty-eight-year-old Korvettenkapitän in 1929. Soon after that, when he was promoted to become a senior staff officer at Wilhelmshaven, his chief of staff noted that he was 'very ambitious and consequently asserts himself to obtain prestige, finding it difficult to subordinate himself and confine himself to his own work sphere'.[39] This intensity of purpose did him no harm. Following the death of President Hindenburg and Hitler's assumption of untrammelled power in 1933, Dönitz, by now in command of a cruiser, the *Emden*, joined every other individual serving in the Reich's armed services to declare his 'unconditional obedience' to Adolf Hitler. Three months later, on the eve of an extended world tour of duty, his commander-in-chief, Raeder, introduced him to the Führer; there is no record of what if anything he contributed to the conversation but, as an old man, he made it clear he had been greatly impressed by his 'brave and worthy' leader.[40]

★

Erich Raeder was fifteen years older than Dönitz. His love for the Fatherland had similarly been instilled in him as a child. Born in Hamburg, the son of a language teacher, his intellectual horizons were narrowly circumscribed by an authoritarian father, who – despite the fervour of the age – banned all political discussion at home. The values that he thus inherited reflected the spirit of the time: contempt for an ailing parliamentary system combined with devotion to the Catholic Church and a visceral faith in the Kaiserliche Marine as 'both the expression of and the instrument for Germanism throughout the world'.[41] Much later, he spoke of his decision to join the navy at the age of eighteen as though it had been preordained, a matter of fate. Physically unprepossessing, his cleverness and diligence nonetheless distinguished him as an outstanding cadet with a gift for coherent strategic analysis. By the outbreak of the First World War, he had risen to the rank of lieutenant commander and was selected to play a key part in planning Germany's naval operations against Britain. He worked closely with Admiral Franz Ritter von Hipper, who commanded the German battle-cruiser force at the Battle of Jutland in June 1916, during which Raeder's tactical judgement earned the Admiral's lasting gratitude. 'Whatever was granted to me in this war, whatever I have received in the way of honors or distinction,' he wrote later, 'I owe to your clear, energetic and sympathetic support . . . You were my good star and it turned pale when you left me.'[42]

His experience of being Hipper's right-hand man in a battle which had carved a swathe through both navies but ended in a marginal victory for the German fleet marked Raeder indelibly. Following his promotion to commander-in-chief of the Reichsmarine (as the Kaiserliche Marine had been renamed) in 1928, he made it his overriding purpose to rebuild a Hochseeflotte (high seas fleet) that would be worthy of a resurgent Fatherland and as powerful as any in the world. Only the decadence of the Weimar Republic seemed to stand in the way of this vision. Its 'distortion of social life . . . in certain customs and manners alien to our German way of life' was repugnant to him; jazz and modern dance, for example, were not symptoms of a nation resolved to shake off the chains of a national humiliation but of moral decay, manifestations of a society which had lost its bearings. The 1918 naval mutiny – which had begun as a protest but turned into a violent and anarchic uprising by enlisted sailors against the authority of their commanding officers – was an abhorrent memory. Politically, Raeder was frozen in aspic. Unable or unwilling to distinguish between bolshevism and social democracy, his patriotism was purblind.

As behoved his patrician outlook, he resolved to reinvigorate the Kriegsmarine with 'a distinctive *esprit de corps*' among the officers and men under his command that would stand in exemplary contrast to the virus of degeneracy by which Germany had been afflicted.[43] The emergence of the Nazis seemed to offer precisely that framework for the renaissance he craved both for the nation and for the navy. Facing his accusers at Nuremberg, he portrayed himself as 'only a sailor and soldier, not a politician',[44] whose commitment during the Third Reich had been less to National Socialism than to his country's national interest; and that he had sought to serve the State rather than the Party. Under the Nazis, however, State and Party became so entwined as to be almost inseparable and Raeder – who had no qualms about taking a personal oath of loyalty to the Führer in 1934 – showed little inclination to distinguish between the two.

As he consolidated his hold on the nation, Hitler warmed to Raeder's vision of a dominant Hochseeflotte. In 1935 the Reichsmarine was renamed the Kriegsmarine, while its commander-in-chief had already proved himself equally mutable, adept at sidestepping or subverting the limitations on Germany's rearmament imposed by the Versailles Treaty. Following the Austrian Anschluss in 1938, when it became clear that Czechoslovakia was next in line for occupation, Raeder at once began to prepare the Kriegsmarine for a maritime confrontation with Britain, which he was certain was now inevitable. His only fear was that Hitler would provoke that conflict before the new Hochseeflotte was in a fit state to challenge the might of the Royal Navy.

Raeder's Z-Plan, as it was codenamed, envisaged the construction of an Atlantic naval force capable of severing the British Empire's supply lines and intimidating any other potential adversary. The fleet would comprise a new generation of ten battleships – bigger, faster and with greater firepower than any nation had yet constructed – supported by fifteen pocket battleships (*Deutschland* class heavy cruisers), sixty-five cruisers of varying sizes, eight aircraft carriers and – in a subordinate role, if not as an afterthought – a fleet of 249 U-boats. The vessels would be organized into battle groups powerful enough to cripple Britain's trade, by killing merchant ships in the Atlantic without fear of effective reprisal. However, as he made clear to Hitler, this was a long-term strategy: his armada would not be ready to challenge Britain's naval hegemony until 1948, a decade hence.

The Führer, who had no experience of naval warfare, could not resist interfering at every level of operational detail, 'from the size and armaments of individual ships to the composition of the fleet'. This habit grew ever more irksome to the precise and organized mind of a naval strategist who had enough self-esteem to regard himself as 'the architect of Germany's naval renaissance'.[45] Since neither man was intimidated by the other, the auguries for an enduring relationship between the pair were not auspicious.

Raeder had to contend not only with Hitler but also with Dönitz, whose own perspective was unencumbered by an appetite to re-establish either a global land empire or its maritime equivalent. As a relatively junior officer – although commanding the nascent U-boat fleet, he was still only a captain in 1938 – Dönitz was not in a position to confront Raeder openly. However, his experience of the First World War had led him ineluctably to the conclusion that a submarine fleet was the most effective weapon with which to destroy Britain's maritime lifeline. Raeder's failure to prioritize the construction of a U-boat fleet over battleships and cruisers infuriated the younger man.[46] So intractable was their dispute that Raeder postponed making any decision about the number of U-boats to be built or at what rate they should come off the production line. As a result only one U-boat was launched in 1937 and only six more in the following year. In exasperation, Dönitz 'pressed with increasing vehemence for an acceleration' in the programme but to no avail.[47]

Raeder's preoccupation with creating a surface fleet that would eventually allow the Third Reich to rule the waves in Britannia's stead was all consuming. In January 1939, apparently convincing himself that the Munich Agreement had given him a licence to treat the entire continent of Europe as Germany's backyard, Hitler reiterated his commitment to the Z-Plan but – conscious that Britain might in due course be roused to object – demanded that the deadline for its completion should be advanced by three years to 1945. When Raeder remonstrated, arguing it would be impossible to complete the construction of so many warships before 1948, Hitler retorted that at least six battleships (including the *Bismarck* and the *Tirpitz*, which were already nearing completion) must be operational by 1944 at the latest: 'If I can build the Third Reich in six years,' he fulminated, 'then the Navy can surely build these ships in six years.'[48]

It was a ludicrous parallel that in any event became redundant the following month when, without warning, Hitler formally abrogated the 1935 agreement between Britain and Germany which had limited the overall size of the Kriegsmarine to 35 per cent of the Royal Navy's total tonnage. Raeder was appalled. Though the Führer's defiance had liberated Raeder from the restraints hitherto imposed by the pretence that the Third Reich would honour its international treaty obligations, Germany still lacked the wherewithal to deliver his master plan for a high seas fleet to challenge the world by 1945. Nor was it much comfort that Hitler chose this moment to promote him to the rank of Grossadmiral (grand admiral). This display of gratitude could not mask the fundamental fact that the German navy was not fit for purpose in anything like the way that either man had intended two years earlier.

Raeder, who had clung to the hope that the Führer would prove wily enough to avoid a premature war against the world's greatest maritime power, was aghast when the Heer (army) invaded Poland on 1 September 1939. Bemoaning the fact that it would no longer be possible to accomplish 'the final solution to the English question',[49] he drafted a memorandum in which he wrote resentfully, 'Today the war against England-France broke out, which the Führer had previously assured us we would not have to confront until 1944 and which he believed he could avoid up to the last minute.' There would be little that the Kriegsmarine's gallant servicemen could now hope to achieve except to demonstrate 'that they know how to die gallantly and thereby to create the foundation of a future rebirth'.[50]

Initially, Dönitz's reaction to Chamberlain's declaration of war was similarly bleak. Newly promoted to the rank of commodore, the U-boat commander was in his operations room at Wilhelmshaven when the news reached him. Evidently unmindful of the staff officers around him he expostulated, 'My God! So it's war against England again,' and walked out of the room. But, collecting himself, he returned soon afterwards, and, with his customary bravura, announced, 'We know our enemy. We have today the weapon and a leadership that can face up to this enemy. The war will last a long time; but if each does his duty we will win. Now to your tasks.'[51] In contrast to Raeder, he exuded an optimism which was unfeigned. While Raeder continued to regard the U-boat as no more than a useful adjunct to his now chimerical Hochseeflotte,

Dönitz genuinely believed that the U-boat was the weapon that would win the war.

There was, though, one proviso. Less than a month earlier he had presented Hitler and Raeder with a shopping list for a grand total of 300 U-boats. Until he had that number at his disposal, he warned, '[we] shall have to content ourselves with a series of pin-pricks against [Britain's] merchant navy'.[52] Three weeks after the sinking of the *Athenia* he seized the opportunity to make the case once more, but this time in a face-to-face meeting with the Führer at Wilhelmshaven. In front of both Raeder and the commander-in-chief of the armed forces, General Keitel, Dönitz delivered Hitler a seven-point plan for victory at sea. The blueprint envisaged a coordinated and concentrated deployment of the U-boat fleet 'to attack merchantmen massed in convoy'; the U-boat, he argued, was 'a weapon capable of dealing Britain a mortal blow at her most vulnerable spot'. Once again, though, he insisted, 'The minimum requisite total is 300 U-boats . . . Given this number of boats, I am convinced that the U-boat arm could achieve decisive success.'[53] Hitler said nothing in response.

Dönitz was not naive. For some five years he had been agitating for an expansion of the U-boat arm, but from his relatively lowly position in the hierarchy of the Third Reich he had achieved little. On the outbreak of war, he had no more than forty-six U-boats under his command (rather fewer than the sixty which the British Admiralty had estimated). Of these, only twenty-two – the Type VIIs – were suitable for prolonged operations in the Atlantic although repairs and maintenance meant that no more than seven would be available to take on the enemy at any one time. To have anything like the number required to inflict the mortal blow he envisaged, the high command would have to approve a major U-boat construction programme as a matter of urgency. This put him at loggerheads with Raeder, who had yet to surrender his ambition to establish a world-class battle fleet in the hope of weakening the Royal Navy by forcing the Admiralty to concentrate its own resources against this threat, thus exposing the British merchant fleet to the depredations of the U-boats and individual surface raiders.

Regardless of their competing views, both men knew that a tug-of-war between the navy, the army and the air force for an inadequate supply of scarce resources – machinery, manpower, and raw materials – was now inevitable. As the Luftwaffe's commander-in-chief and the Führer's designated deputy, Reichsmarschall Hermann Göring had also been entrusted with responsibility for Germany's 'four-year plan'. As the first among equals in the high command, he had snaked his way into Hitler's confidence with a combination of cunning and flattery. This gave him unique authority to dispose of the resources required to realize the Führer's vision. Fully aware of his leader's implacable resolve to secure Lebensraum for the Third Reich by force of arms, he not only offered unquestioning support for the project but also did all in his considerable power to thwart any competing strategy. A continental war to subjugate Europe and then to invade Russia would require a close partnership between the Heer and the Luftwaffe, which meant that the Kriegsmarine would have to take third place in the queue for resources.

Thus on the outbreak of hostilities, both Britain and Germany were ill-prepared and ill-equipped for what was to prove a decisive struggle for mastery in the Atlantic. The mutual self-delusion of the inter-war years – Hitler's belief that he could cheat and lie his way to the conquest of Europe without riling Britain to the point of war mirroring Chamberlain's belief that the Führer would respond favourably to his diplomatic overtures – provided a framework within which both the Royal Navy and the Kriegsmarine were far from ready to face the exigencies of the unfolding conflict. Both Admiral Pound and Grossadmiral Raeder were still convinced, as were their respective political masters, that the war at sea would be won and lost by great battle fleets. As a great maritime power with imperial pretensions that were threatened by the Italians and Japanese as well as the Germans, the British had the most powerful navy in the world. However, the price of this was a shortage of suitable escorts to protect the merchant convoys on which the survival of the nation depended. Conversely, hobbled by global aspirations but strapped for the resources to build a battle fleet to match, the Kriegsmarine lacked the U-boats it needed to sever the enemy's Atlantic lifeline. Thus, fortuitously, the two sides were more evenly matched than the crude balance of naval firepower might suggest. As a result the Battle of the Atlantic acquired a switchback momentum on which neither high command was able to capitalize as each side reacted to sudden and unexpected shifts in fortune with urgent measures to seize the advantage or nullify the threat from the other. At sea, there would be no 'phoney' war. As the sinking of the *Athenia* had inadvertently demonstrated, it was mortal combat from the outset.

## 2. Caught Hopping

By the end of 1939 the British people faced the prospect of grave food shortages. The nation had long been dependent on the free flow of trade not merely for prosperity, but also for survival. At any one time some 3,000 merchant ships were plying to and fro across the great oceans that linked Britain to her trading partners and her colonies. Without copper, zinc, manganese, tin, bauxite, tungsten, lead, rubber, iron ore, aluminium, nickel, timber, cotton and jute, not to mention a huge array of other precious minerals and metals, let alone fuel oil – 95 per cent of which was imported – British industry would be brought to a standstill. Without sustenance – 70 per cent of the nation's food supply was imported – the population would starve. Once the stresses of war were added to the combined effects of mass hunger and mass unemployment, any British government would rapidly be driven to the point of unconditional surrender.

To meet this threat, the government established a Ministry of Food within five days of the outbreak of war. Its primary role was to control the supply and distribution of food across the nation. At first it stuttered. Its attempt to control the distribution of fresh fish was so clumsily organized that the market fell into chaos: supplies fell and prices soared. In her diary for 19 December Nella Last wrote, 'There was very little bacon in town today and women were anxiously asking each other if they knew of a ship which had any in. We eat so little bacon and cheese, but I'll get my ration and start using it in place of other things – meat and fish – in my cooking. Fish is very dear, and, in my budget, not worth the price for the nourishment.'[1]

Politically, the ministry's initial attempt to manipulate the market was toxic. Those who were viscerally averse to the very idea of controls even in wartime had been handed a propaganda tool with which to berate the government. Thus the ministry's plan to introduce ration books to control the sale of sugar, meat, bacon and fats, which had been expected to be a formality, became 'a matter of violent controversy' which led the War Cabinet to postpone their introduction until 8 January 1940.[2]

Butter, bacon, and sugar became the first basic foodstuffs which could be bought only with coupons. In due course tea, chocolate, biscuits, cereals, eggs, lard, canned fruits and meat would be added to the list. By the standards of a later age, the rations were meagre (initially half a pound of butter, bacon, and sugar per head per week), but they were regarded as sufficient to provide a balanced diet and to satisfy the prevailing dictum that the British nation should be 'fed like an army'.[3] Bread and potatoes were excluded from these controls. Similarly, fresh vegetables and fruit could be bought freely, though they were often hard to obtain. Lemons and bananas virtually disappeared from the shelves.

Nor did other 'essentials' escape: later in the year, it became impossible to buy petrol without coupons (for an allowance of between four and ten gallons a month). Soon afterwards, other basic commodities – from clothing to coal, from soap to gas and electricity – would similarly be brought under state control.

'Make do and mend' was Nella Last's patriotic mantra. Like millions of other housewives she managed to make the most of her newly straitened circumstances with 'a nip and tuck'. In addition to cooking three meals a day for her husband, she played her part in the war effort by working at a WVS centre where she made 'wax blossoms and dollies to raffle' as well as knitting scarves, gloves, socks and balaclavas for serving sailors. But food was an enduring preoccupation.

Nella was rarely at ease. BBC news bulletins reporting the losses of ships at sea plagued her imagination. 'When I went to bed', she wrote on one occasion, 'I slept so lightly and seemed to "make pictures" of things I'd read or heard on the wireless. If the wind swished rain on the window, I woke trembling with the thought of men struggling in water – seeing hands trying to clutch at support that was not there.'[4] On another occasion, she almost gagged on a glass of water which she tried to swallow too quickly.

> The feeling of slight chokiness gripped me and sent my mind over green cold water, where men might be drowning as I sat so warm and safe – and so useless to help . . . Arthur [her elder son] always laughs at me for what he calls my 'fixation' about my shipwrecked sailors, at my shameless begging for used woollen vests and socks, and the hours of patient mending to make them whole; but if he knew the dreadful wakenings

from even more dreadful dreams sometimes – dreams of men in open boats or on rafts, where I can hear the splash of cold waves and feel the numbing coldness that is of death – he would understand.[5]

Her nightmares might well have been provoked by any number of reports which, though redacted and bowdlerized for the sake of national security and to protect the public from gruesome reality, were vivid enough to agitate all but the dullest imagination. By the New Year of 1940 there were already more than enough maritime disasters to arouse such an intensity of feeling. Between September and December 1939, 221 merchant ships went to the bottom, 110 of which were sunk by German U-boats. Of the remainder, seventy-eight were destroyed by mines and ten by the Luftwaffe; the rest were unaccounted for. The first merchant casualty was the *Bosnia*, a 2,407-ton vessel belonging to the Cunard White Star Line. On the third day of the war she was steaming alone some 120 miles off the coast of Portugal en route for Glasgow, laden with a cargo of sulphur. In the half-light of morning her presence was detected by the commander of U-47, Günther Prien, who saw a 'plume of smoke' on the horizon which emerged 'like a dragonfly flitting over a stream'. U-47 dived and Prien watched his prey through the periscope until the freighter passed above the submerged submarine unaware of the threat. Once the *Bosnia* was clear, he surfaced astern of her and fired a warning shot from its deck-mounted cannon which landed in front of his quarry. The *Bosnia* ignored this and Prien fired a second round. This time, instead of stopping engines, the merchantman altered course and began to flee. In the same moment, U-47's signaller intercepted a message from his prey – 'Under attack and fire from a German U-boat. Urgently require assistance.' Prien ordered his gunnery crew to open fire once more, whereupon the *Bosnia* 'hove to and lay there like a wounded animal'. A column of yellow smoke began to rise from the stricken vessel as her crew lowered lifeboats to escape. In the rush to safety, one boat half-capsized and started to fill with water. 'It was pathetic to see the men drift helplessly away,' Prien noted. 'Some of them shouted for help while others beckoned to us. We steered towards the sinking boat.'[6] Some of the sailors were thrashing wildly in the water, unable to swim. Two members of Prien's crew hauled one of these aboard the submarine. He was a teenager, trembling with cold and fear but defiant. According to Prien's account, the boy, who spoke with a cockney accent, said, 'Of course, we got a fright, Sir. You can't imagine what it's like; you looks over the water and sees nothing, on'y sky and water and then suddenly a bloomin' big thing pops up beside yer, blowing like a walrus. I thought I was seein' the Loch Ness monster.'

Meanwhile another merchant ship, the *Eidanger*, flying the Norwegian ensign, had responded to the *Bosnia*'s message. Norway was a neutral state and, under the Prize Rules, her ships were therefore immune to attack. With the help of U-47's crew, the Norwegian vessel picked up the rest of the *Bosnia*'s company and, after an exchange of courtesies with Prien, sailed away. It was a laborious process and, for Prien, tinged with anxiety by the possibility that a Royal Navy destroyer might also respond to the *Bosnia*'s appeal. The U-boat commander had not only obeyed international law but the unwritten law of the sea by demonstrating a common humanity – rather than speeding away and leaving the crew of the *Bosnia* to fend for themselves.

The *Bosnia* was soon engulfed by flames but still remained afloat. Prien decided that the only way to sink her was with a torpedo. It was the first he had fired in earnest. He invited his crew on deck to watch the spectacle. They had seen photos from the First World War and expected the steamer to rear dramatically before plunging to the bottom. In fact, Prien wrote, the sinking was 'much less showy and all the more impressive for that. There was a dull explosion and huge columns of water rose up [as] high [as] the mast. And then the stricken ship simply broke in two pieces which in a space of seconds disappeared into the sea. A few bits of driftwood and the empty [life]boats were all that was left.'[7] Thirty-three of the *Bosnia*'s crew survived, one died.

Prien was not given to false sentiment. Two days later, 260 miles to the north-west of Cape Finisterre, he attacked another British merchant ship, the *Gartavon*. On this occasion the vessel hove to after one warning and the ship's crew took swiftly and efficiently to the lifeboats. Prien watched the men row rapidly away and then turned back towards the *Gartavon* to see that the crewless vessel had turned in an arc and was steaming at speed directly towards U-47. It was obvious to him that her crew had set the engines to 'full ahead' and fixed the rudder, hoping to cut the submarine in half. The ruse nearly succeeded. As he shouted for his own crew to take avoiding action, he watched as the vessel passed so close that her rigging cast a shadow over the U-boat's hull while her wash knocked the submarine off course. By his own account, he was gripped by 'a cold fury'. He gave orders for U-47 to chase after the escaping lifeboats. Tempted to destroy them, he kept saying to himself, 'Don't forget that these people are shipwrecked.' Once he had caught up with the fleeing crew, he used a megaphone to demand that their captain identify himself. When 'a slim and fair man stood up' in the stern of one of the lifeboats, Prien collected himself enough to observe the proprieties but made known his displeasure. 'Since you have committed a hostile act I shall not radio for you but I will send you the next neutral ship I meet.' The English captain, George Hunter, replied simply, 'OK, sir', and then asked, 'May I proceed?' Prien assented, the two men saluted, and the lifeboats made off. They were picked up later by a Swedish tanker, the *Castor*.

Prien noted of this encounter with the *Gartavon*'s captain: 'We were polite to each other, like knightly opponents in a novel. But behind this formality lay an icy hatred, the hatred of two peoples who are facing each other in the last decisive round.' Prien returned to where the abandoned *Gartavon* was still moving in dizzy circles and finished her off with shell fire. 'From then on', Prien wrote with evident relish, 'the war hardened with every day . . . Every vessel in an enemy convoy was liable to be torpedoed without warning and we worked according to the formula: *Any ship in convoy to the bottom*.'[8]

As the First Lord of the Admiralty, Churchill was reaching the peak of his remarkable powers. Restless, demanding, tireless, his appetite for responsibility knew no bounds. As the political visionary who had been a lone voice against Hitler in the wilderness years of the 1930s, he was quite incapable of confining his role in the War Cabinet to the immediate task of confronting the threat posed by the Kriegsmarine; or, rather, as he put it, 'I felt that as a member of the War cabinet I was bound to take a general view, and I did not fail to subordinate my own departmental requirements for the Admiralty to the main design.'[9] The situation facing the government was about as grim as it could be. Austria, Czechoslovakia and now Poland were under Nazi occupation; Italy had yet to declare war against Britain but Mussolini had signed the 'Pact of Steel' with Hitler; the Soviet Union – an ally against Germany in the First World War – had put its signature to Ribbentrop's Non-Aggression Pact; and the United States – which had belatedly come to Britain's rescue in 1917 – was demonstrably averse to repeating the experience. Though the British Empire was as yet intact, Britain was at bay.

Churchill had been swift to grasp the scale of the strategic threat to the nation's global interests and made it his business to ensure that fellow ministers in the War Cabinet were left in no doubt that his towering presence among them was not mere adornment but evidence of his unwavering conviction that the fainthearts were wrong: Britain could eventually emerge triumphant from the battle for national survival, in which he was determined to play a leading part. To this end he bombarded his colleagues with missives giving them the benefit of his experience and wisdom. Even Chamberlain did not escape the barrage. In a characteristic display of intellectual energy and self-confidence, Churchill initiated a correspondence with Neville Chamberlain (which appears to have been written as much for posterity as for immediate digestion) offering the prime minister detailed advice on every aspect of the war.

In one of these letters, written on 15 September, he pressed his leader to take urgent measures to reinforce the Maginot Line on which the first wave of more than 150,000 British troops were already stationed alongside their French allies to resist any German attack through Belgium. He ended with an admonishment: 'I hope you will consider carefully what I write to you. I do so only in my desire to aid you in your responsibilities, and discharge my own.' Chamberlain replied wearily, 'All your letters are carefully read and considered by me, and if I have not replied to them, it is only because I am seeing you every day . . .'[10] If Churchill detected a touch of irony in that response, it did not deter him from his overpowering need to impress upon the War Cabinet and the British people that he was not only in command of his own brief at the Admiralty but more than ready for the highest office as well.

A few days later he asked the prime minister's permission to address the House of Commons in his role as First Lord. Chamberlain assented and, on 26 September, Churchill seized the moment. Noting that, in the first three weeks of the conflict, British shipping losses had fallen from 65,000 tons in the first week to 9,000 tons in the third, he declared that 'the whole vast business of our world-wide trade continues without interruption or appreciable diminution. Great convoys of troops are escorted to their various destinations. The enemy's ships and commerce have been swept from the seas . . . But the British attack on the U-boats is only just beginning. Our hunting force is getting stronger every day.'[11] Admirably serving its immediate political purpose, to dispel despondency or alarm, his statement nonetheless fell little short of brag-gadocio; it was certainly misleading.

On the same day, 26 September, Admiral Dönitz was in his office at Wilhelmshaven, examining a set of photographs taken by a Luftwaffe pilot which showed a number of warships at anchor in Scapa Flow in the Orkney Islands. Although he had considered an assault on the most important of the Royal Navy's anchorages, he had been deterred ini-tially both by the fierce currents that swirl around Scapa – which at some stages of the tide flowed faster than the maximum speed of a sub-merged U-boat – and by the minefields, booms, nets and naval patrols he presumed were in place to protect the Home Fleet's sanctuary. But, encouraged by one of his most respected staff officers and by an intelli-gence report from a U-boat operating in the area, he came to the view that, although the enterprise would be hazardous in the extreme, it was not beyond the bounds of possibility. The photographs showed that the main entrances to Scapa Flow were indeed blocked, but, as he noted in the U-boat Command War Diary, they were of good enough quality to show at the eastern edge of the anchorage, 'a narrow channel about fifty feet wide . . . the shore on both sides is practically uninhabited. Here, I think, it would certainly be possible to penetrate – by night, on the sur-face at slack water.'[12]

He summoned one of his best commanders, Günther Prien, fresh from sinking the *Bosnia*. After talking him through the charts and photographs, Dönitz told him to decide within forty-eight hours whether he was willing to accept the task. According to Prien's (ghosted) recollection, Dönitz continued, 'You are perfectly free to make your own decision. If you come to the conclusion that the undertaking is impossible you will report that fact to me. No blame whatsoever will be attached to you, Prien, because we know that your decision will be based on your own honest conviction.'[13] Prien did not make up his mind at once – the thirty-one-year-old captain had a wife and two children living with him at the base – but after perusing the options told his commanding officer that he was willing to undertake the enterprise.

A little over two weeks later, on the evening of 13 October, U-47 was in Holm Sound, on the eastern approach to the British anchorage, gliding as quietly as possible across a calm sea. No one spoke or lit a cigarette. Prien had selected the night of the new moon when, even in a cloudless sky, they would still be protected by darkness. But they had failed to foresee the effect of the Northern Lights, whose brilliance could easily silhouette the submarine's hull for any watchful British lookout. They nosed through Holm Sound and into the narrows of Kirk Sound until they were well inside Scapa Flow. They passed a group of tankers, silent at their moorings and apparently unguarded. They continued until, close to the northern shoreline, they saw the outlines of what appeared to be a battleship; which was 'hard and clear, as if painted into the sky with black ink . . .' Prien wrote. 'Slowly we edged closer . . . Now we could clearly see the bulge of the gun turrets, out of which the guns jutted threateningly into the sky. The ship lay there like a sleeping giant.'[14]

A month earlier, on 14 September 1939, Churchill had himself taken leave from his other duties because he wanted to 'visit Scapa at the earliest possible moment'. He was met at Wick by the commander-in-chief of the Home Fleet, admiral Charles Forbes. When they left the harbour in the admiral's flagship, the *Nelson*, Churchill expressed his surprise that a 34,000-ton battleship was not accompanied by a protective phalanx of destroyers. Forbes told him there were none to spare. Over the course of the next three days they explored the range of predicaments posed to the fleet by the Kriegsmarine's surface 'raiders' and U-boats. Scapa Flow was top of their agenda. In 1938 this large stretch of sheltered water had been selected as the main base for the Home Fleet, but its defences had been allowed to decay. A single strand of looped wire had been laid across the three main entrances to serve as an anti-submarine net but the blockships, which had been filled with ballast and sunk to provide additional protection during the First World War, had largely disintegrated.

Nonetheless, Churchill evidently came away from his visit with 'a strong feeling of confidence' in Forbes and apparently reassured that the repairs required to restore the defences at Scapa Flow were in progress.[15] However, mindful of his ignominious removal from the Admiralty in 1915, he could not throw off a vague foreboding. 'I felt oddly oppressed,' he wrote. 'No one had ever been over the same terrible course twice with such an interval between. No one had felt its dangers and responsibilities from the summit as I had or, to descend to a small point, understood how First Lords of the Admiralty are treated when great ships are sunk and things go wrong. If we were in fact going over the same cycle a second time, should I have once again to endure the pangs of dismissal?'[16]

Back in London, he left the train at Euston to be met by Admiral Pound, who informed him that a U-boat had sunk the aircraft carrier *Courageous* in the Bristol Channel. Although the ship had been protected by four destroyers, U-29 had managed to penetrate closely enough at dusk on 17 September to launch its torpedoes with fatal precision. More than 500 men out of a total complement of 1,260 were drowned as the *Courageous* went to the bottom. This disaster had been preceded, three days earlier, by a similar attack on another aircraft carrier, the *Ark Royal*. But, on this occasion, U-39's three torpedoes had exploded prematurely. Not only was the *Ark Royal* spared but the three destroyers accompanying her managed to locate and sink the offending U-boat.

With the convoy system not yet in place, the Admiralty's response to the loss of one aircraft carrier and the near-loss of another was to avoid any similar disaster in future. This left the many hundreds of merchant ships to lumber towards the British coastline without aerial cover, a decision that was to have damaging repercussions that would haunt the Battle of the Atlantic for many months to come. As Admiral Dönitz was to note, the Admiralty's decision 'made things very much easier for the U-boats.'[17] But, by this point, the admirals had a very different role in mind for these precious vessels.

Despite the compelling evidence from the First World War, the Admiralty judged that the greater danger facing Britain's global trade came not from submarines but from the Kriegsmarine's warships – surface raiders – marauding through the shipping lanes of the oceans picking off any merchant ship at will. Churchill appreciated this danger, but he also recognized that the threat posed by the U-boats could not be ignored. On 10 September he had sent a private note to Chamberlain in which he wrote: 'I must make a great effort to bring forward the smaller anti-U-boat fleet. Numbers in this sphere are vital'. Yet he shared the same priorities as the naval staff and expressed them with characteristic force.[18] Within a fortnight of his appointment, he dictated a note to Pound urging a substantial redeployment of British warships to create powerful hunting groups with the task of scouring the ocean 'to catch and to kill' any German warship bold enough to venture out of its safe haven in the Baltic.[19] These 'task forces', as they later came to be called, were each to consist of a heavy cruiser, an aircraft carrier, four destroyers and two or three oil tankers (to allow the warships to range far from their bases without the need to return to port to refuel). The vision of the British Navy ruling the waves in this way appealed to both his offensive spirit and his romantic nature.

But it missed the essential point – which had been clearly demonstrated in the First World War – that the surest way to combat the threat to Britain's supply lines was to deploy suitable warships to escort merchant ships travelling in convoy.

Now, in October, Churchill's forebodings were about to be realized. As U-47 got closer to its prey, Prien saw the silhouette of what he thought was a second battleship half-concealed behind the first. Prien chose this vessel – which was in fact an elderly seaplane carrier, the *Pegasus* – as his first target, knowing that the nearer vessel, the *Royal Oak*, was already doomed. There was a hiss and then a click as a torpedo was snapped into its tube and, within moments, sent on its way. Within the next twenty minutes, Prien had crept around to another position which was no more than 1,500 metres from the *Royal Oak*. The first torpedo struck the bows, sending a column of water into the air, with no apparent effect. A few minutes later, a little before 1.30 a.m. on 14 October, three more torpedoes were on their way. The last of these struck the battleship's hull amidships: 'A wall of water shot up towards the sky. It was as if the sea suddenly stood up on end. Loud explosions came one after the other like drumfire in a battle and coalesced into one mighty ear-splitting crash . . . Behind this firework display the sky disappeared entirely.' Prien was transfixed by the inferno; it was 'as if the gates of hell had suddenly been torn open and I was looking into the flaming furnace'.[20] He called down to his crew to let them know that the battleship was sinking. 'For a moment there was silence,' he wrote. 'Then a mighty roar went through the ship, an almost bestial roar in which the pent-up tension of the past twenty-four hours found release.'[21] Prien immediately silenced them lest the cacophony revealed their whereabouts.

On board the *Royal Oak*, most of the 1,200 officers and men had been asleep in their hammocks below decks. The first torpedo to strike the ship caused little concern. The dull thud as it hit the bows was presumed to have been caused by an internal explosion – a refrigerator blowing up perhaps – which would have caused little damage. Surgeon-Lieutenant Dick Caldwell jumped down from his bunk wondering what had caused the noise. A few minutes later 'a tremendous shuddering explosion occurred and the ship took a list to starboard. I heard the tinkling of glass falling from ledges and pictures in what seemed to be the awe-struck silence which followed: a silence which was suddenly shattered by a third explosion. All the lights went out, the list increased, and it was obvious to everyone that we were for it.'[22] A fourth torpedo smashed through the battleship's hull into the ship's magazine which was filled with high explosive. The vessel lurched violently. All those who could scrambled for the upper decks. 'We were just going out and this hot orange blast came up through the decks . . . all I could do was to hide in a corner, cover my face and try to save my eyes and hope for the best.'

The *Royal Oak* was now listing heavily to starboard. Dick Caldwell stood on the sloping deck preternaturally calm:

> I can recall most vividly every thought and impression that passed through my brain; my new and rather expensive tennis racket, a book I had borrowed and promised to return, three pounds in the bottom of my drawer . . . [and the feeling] This can't be happening to me; you read about it in books and see it on the flicks, but it doesn't happen, it can't be happening to me.

Within moments, he was on the side of the ship clinging to the hull, then he was in the water. 'I seemed to go down and down and started fighting for breath.' When he came to the surface, he was covered in oil:

> I gulped it and retched at the filthy taste in my throat; oil, thick black oil smarting in my eyes. I swam and floundered about . . . I heard cries round me, saw black heads bobbing, and I swam frenziedly again . . . I repeatedly went under until quite suddenly I gave it up and thought 'I'm going to drown.' Perfectly dispassionately . . . and I thought of all the people I wanted to see again and things I wanted to do . . .

A few moments later he saw a group of heads and thrashed his way towards them. There were about a dozen of them clinging to the keel: 'Time dragged on, with no sign of us being picked up. We strained our eyes in the darkness for some glimmer of light but none came.' Eventually they saw the masthead light of a search vessel approaching them. 'We shouted again and again. When she was within twenty yards of us we left our upturned boat and struck out in her direction.' Twice Caldwell tried to climb aboard but his hands were numb with cold and each time he fell back in the water. 'I thought "Mustn't lose now. Come on, mustn't lose now" – but have no recollection whatsoever of finally succeeding.'[23] As soon as he had been plucked to safety, Caldwell and his fellow survivors were taken across to the *Pegasus* where they drank copious amounts of tea and wallowed in hot baths. '[W]e began to talk and recognise people and shake hands and try not to notice friends that were missing.'[24]

Surgeon-Lieutenant Caldwell was among the few to survive.* In all, 833 of his fellow officers and men had drowned. The *Royal Oak* settled on the bottom of the anchorage in almost 100 feet of water. When divers eventually reached the hull some days later, they were appalled by what they saw. 'God there were bodies everywhere . . .' one of them recalled. 'They told me to bang on the bottom of the ship and see if anyone tapped back. What was the point?'[25] U-47's attack had devastatingly fulfilled Churchill's worst imaginings.

Now Prien had to make his escape from Scapa Flow against the incoming tide. Even at full speed, U-47 could barely make headway. As the flames engulfing the *Royal Oak* began to die down, their place was taken by myriad pinpricks of light, beaming across the water from small naval craft sweeping the bay seeking to identify the whereabouts of the unknown assailant. At one point what appeared to be a destroyer approached close enough to signal the U-boat. But in the absence of any response from Prien, the vessel's commander seemed to have concluded that the unidentified object lying almost motionless in the water ahead was anything but the *Royal Oak*'s executioner and the warship disappeared into the night. Perhaps because it seemed almost inconceivable that an enemy submarine could have penetrated so deeply into Scapa Flow, the Royal Navy's desultory efforts to locate the U-boat soon petered out. In any case, at that moment the fate of those who had gone down with the *Royal Oak* mattered far more to their comrades than the prospect of wreaking vengeance on their persecutor.

Prien was thus left alone to slip away to the safety of open water without any further distractions. 'Laboriously, painfully, the boat

---

* On 10 December 1941 Surgeon-Commander Caldwell was aboard HMS *The Prince of Wales* when the battleship was sunk by Japanese bombers in the Pacific. He was shipwrecked but survived for a second time.

wriggled through the narrows,' the U-boat ace recalled. 'Before us lay the sea, broad and free, vast under the limitless sky. Taking a deep breath I turned to give the final command of this action. "All stations. Attention. One battleship destroyed . . . and we are through!" This time I allowed them to roar.'[26]

Prien's triumph was Germany's coup. On the approaches to Wilhelmshaven U-47 was greeted by the *Scharnhorst*, whose crew lined up on the battleship's decks in salutation. As the submarine reached the jetty, a band played, a crowd waved and cheered. Prien stepped ashore to be met by Dönitz, who congratulated him in the name of the Führer. Soon the entire crew was in Hitler's plane bound for Berlin, where their commander was to be awarded the Iron Cross by the Führer in person. At Tempelhof airport they were greeted by swarms of people who cheered them all the way to the Chancellery. As Hitler walked in to greet them, Prien was overwhelmed to be in the presence of his Führer. 'I had often seen him before but never had I felt his greatness as intensely as in this moment. Certainly I stood here, too, thus realizing a dream of my youth . . . But what was I in comparison with this man who had felt the degradation of this land on his own, who had dreamed of a freer and happier Fatherland!'[27]

The loss of the *Royal Oak* was a psychological blow that the British Admiralty could ill afford. According to his assistant private secretary, John Higham, Churchill's eyes filled with tears when he was given the news as he muttered, 'Poor fellows, poor fellows, trapped in those black depths.' But the First Lord was nonetheless quick to reassure the War Cabinet that although the loss of the battleship had been 'an extremely regrettable disaster', it 'did not materially affect the general naval position'.[28] But, he was too astute a politician to ignore the possibility that the loss of so many lives would be regarded as evidence of complacency and incompetence. Well aware that the 'shock to public opinion' could easily have forced a lesser politician to fall on his sword to assuage popular feeling, he reflected, 'It might well have been politically fatal to any Minister who had been responsible for the pre-war precautions' – thus neatly exonerating himself from responsibility for the state of the Scapa defences and, by implication, transferring the blame on his immediate predecessor, Lord Stanhope.[29] If he felt any personal responsibility for the disaster, he was careful not to admit it. Although he did not discount what he called the 'U-boat menace', Churchill persisted in the belief that the best way of countering it was to establish 'an independent flotilla which will work like a cavalry division . . . [and] could search large areas over a wide front. In this way these areas would become untenable to U-boats.'[30] The First Sea Lord and his fellow admirals did not hesitate, but the young commanders required to lead these cavalry charges were not persuaded. Captain Donald Macintyre, who was later to become renowned for his exploits as an escort commander, complained, 'We were sent on one wild goose-chase after another to the positions of the latest sinkings only to find – as expected – that the guilty U-boat had fled the scene . . .'[31]

Sub Lieutenant (later Admiral) John Adams was similarly unimpressed. 'Where I drew the line,' he recalled, 'was one particular report from the lighthouse on the south corner of the Isle of Man that a periscope had been sighted 6 miles away. Well, you're jolly lucky to see a periscope at 1,000 yards, let alone 6 miles, and yet we were sent out from Liverpool to go and chase that particular contact which was obviously hopeless before we started.'[32] The high seas were too vast and the prey too elusive to justify the use of such a precious and scarce resource as maritime cavalry when – as events would prove – it would have been better deployed shepherding merchant convoys safely, if prosaically, to their destinations.

More generally, the crucial lessons of the Great War had been overlooked. The fact that in 1918 the U-boats had been vanquished so comprehensively had lulled the Admiralty into a false sense of security. This illusion was reinforced by the invention of ASDIC, a sonar device (named after the Allied Submarine Detection Investigation Committee, under whose auspices it had been devised) that could be fitted to the hulls of surface ships and was capable of locating a submerged U-boat by 'pinging' an echo from its hull back to the surface. The naval staff presumed that ASDIC would render submarines so vulnerable to being depth charged to oblivion as to become virtually obsolete. However, they failed to take into account either that the device was far from fail-safe (it was far less accurate in rough seas) or to foresee that the U-boats would generally attack by night and on the surface, in which conditions ASDIC was of little use. Their misplaced faith in ASDIC was exacerbated by their credulous presumption that the Germans would adhere strictly to the Prize Rules which had been so painstakingly negotiated with the representatives of the Third Reich. For these reasons, they determined that the principal threat to Allied merchant shipping in the Second World War would come from surface raiders – battleships and cruisers – and not from the submarine, which, they concluded as late as 1937, 'would never again be able to present us with the problem we were faced with in 1917'.[33] They could hardly have been more wrong.

On 13 November Churchill invited Chamberlain and his wife to dinner at the Admiralty. It was their first such encounter and, by his own account, Churchill relished 'the only intimate social conversation' that ever flowed between them. At one point, according to his own, possibly embroidered account, they were interrupted by an officer who came up from the war room in the basement to report that a U-boat had been sunk. A while later, he came again to report that a second had been destroyed. Before they had finished their meal, he appeared once again to announce a third sinking. The First Lord's guests were suitably impressed. Churchill noted later, 'As the ladies left us, Mrs Chamberlain with a naive and charming glance, said to me, "Did you arrange all this on purpose?" I assured her that if she would come again we would produce a similar result.'[34] It was not until after the war that he discovered that all three reports were false: there had been no such sinkings that night. Such over-optimism was not infrequent. On both sides of the war at sea, the temptation to misinterpret wishful thinking as firm evidence was hard to resist; but it proved far harder to confirm a claim than to make it.

In Berlin, meanwhile, Hitler was facing pressure from the Kriegsmarine to rewrite the rules of U-boat warfare by approving an 'unrestricted' offensive against any merchant ship anywhere on the high seas. The ostensible justification for jettisoning the Prize Rules, so carefully elaborated between the wars, was the alleged perfidy of British merchant skippers. According to Dönitz's commanders, they invariably radioed for help as soon as they were ordered to 'heave to', while on more than one occasion an enemy warplane had arrived overhead before the U-boats had been able to complete their authorized stop-and-search procedures. This, they argued correctly, was a violation of international maritime law that put their own boats in grave danger. At a meeting with Raeder on 23 September 1939 Hitler conceded that U-boat commanders should henceforth be permitted to 'fire upon vessels which used their wireless'.[35] Dönitz's restatement of the Führer's decision was unequivocal: 'They are subject to seizure or sinking without exception.'[36]

Still believing that the British government would, in due course, seek to negotiate an accommodation with the Third Reich, Hitler nonetheless remained anxious to avoid any unnecessary provocation at sea. To the frustration of Raeder and Dönitz, he therefore refused to authorize an overt breach of the Prize Rules by sanctioning unrestricted submarine warfare against merchant ships that might be trading with the enemy. But Dönitz was not to be thwarted. Exploiting the ambiguities embedded in the Prize Rules, he issued his commanders with a secret instruction authorizing them to sink any merchant ship sailing without lights in 'sea areas where only English vessels are to be expected'. To avoid any doubt that he was violating the spirit, if not the letter, of the law, he continued, 'Permission to take this step is not to be given in writing, however, but need merely be based on the unspoken approval of the naval operations staff . . . the sinking of a merchant ship must be justified in the War Diary as due to possible confusion with a warship or auxiliary cruiser.'[37]

On 24 November, Berlin approved a further violation of the Prize Rules. Henceforth, it was announced publicly, 'in waters around the British Isles and in the vicinity of the French coast, the safety of neutral ships can no longer be taken for granted'.[38] In other words, it was open season on all merchant shipping of any nationality in these latitudes. Unrestricted U-boat warfare was now the official, though still unstated, policy of the Third Reich. For Dönitz, the implications were merciless: 'Rescue no one and take no one with you. Have no care for the ships' [life]boats. Weather conditions and the proximity of land are of no account. Care only for your own boat and strive to achieve the next success as soon as possible! We must be hard in this war. The enemy started this war in order to destroy us, therefore nothing else matters.'[39]

But victory could not be achieved by the violation of the rules of maritime warfare alone. Dönitz still lacked enough U-boats to deliver more than the 'series of pinpricks' about which he had warned in his memorandum to Hitler in August. Although he was now liberated to pick off individual merchant ships sailing alone, the targets that really mattered in the tonnage war were the convoys. His tactics were clear: 'Our object must be to locate the convoys and destroy them by means of a concentrated attack by the few U-boats available,' he instructed his commanders. 'The greater the concentration and the greater the measure of surprise achieved, the more certain and complete will be the success.'[40] But, as he constantly complained, 'the few' were not yet available, and in any case, without a commitment by the high command to build a fleet of 300 U-boats, he insisted, the great opportunity to strangle Britain's Atlantic lifeline would come to naught.

Raeder appreciated Dönitz's argument but was fettered by two factors: on the one hand, his own strategic priorities which favoured the surface fleet and, on the other, the unrelenting hostility of Hitler's closest ally, Reichsmarschall Göring, who enjoyed the additional advantage that planes could be built much faster than ships and could thus more swiftly satisfy the Führer's hunger for action. Raeder's ambitious proposal to create a world-class fleet of warships to rival the Royal Navy – the Z-Plan – was in tatters but, like the British First Lord and the First Sea Lord (whose roles he combined as commander-in-chief of the Kriegsmarine), he still believed that naval warfare was essentially a test of firepower between rival 'surface fleets'. Thus, in competing for scarce resources with the other two branches of the Wehrmacht, he was hampered by the fact that, to realize the classic naval objective of offering a twin-pronged threat to the enemy, he had to argue simultaneously and with equal vehemence for an expansion both of the battle fleet and of the U-boat arm. Unwisely, Raeder also sought to acquire emergency powers to deliver these overly ambitious goals. Even on a war footing, Germany's industrial machine was incapable of turning out twenty-nine U-boats a month, as Raeder demanded, without proportionately depriving Göring's Luftwaffe of warplanes. In a Wehrmacht driven by internecine animosities and strategic self-contradictions, Raeder had overreached himself and Göring, the most cunning schemer in Hitler's entourage, was swift to pounce on his rival's political ineptitude. Heeding his deputy's advice, Hitler decided on 10 October to approve Raeder's construction programme in principle but to hobble it in practice. Bluntly refusing to grant Raeder his emergency powers, Hitler's rebuff was formally delivered to him in the form of a curt communiqué: 'As Reichsmarschall Göring already possesses the widest possible powers, the Führer and Supreme Commander of the Armed Forces has refrained from granting any subsidiary emergency powers to cover the period of the U-boat building programme.'[41]

This was a pivotal moment at a critical time. Deprived of any right of compulsion, Raeder was forced to scale back the U-boat construction programme to twenty-five boats a month. Even this target proved impossible to achieve: in the first six months of 1940 the production lines proved incapable of delivering more than two boats a month, which was barely enough to make good the fleet's losses over the same period. Given the devastation that the U-boats were to inflict despite this shortfall, it is hard to contemplate what might have been if Hitler had granted Raeder's demand. It was Britain's great good fortune that Hitler's acolyte had outsmarted the commander-in-chief of the Kriegsmarine.

Like Raeder, Churchill seized every opportunity to range far beyond his own brief as First Lord. In a speech at the Mansion House on 20 January 1940 he invited his listeners (who included those tuned in to the BBC as well as those who had gathered to hear him in person) to accompany him on a tour d'horizon, sharing with them a glimpse of the promised land that would in due course be theirs. 'The day will come,' he averred, 'when the joybells will ring again throughout Europe, and when victorious nations, masters not only of their foes but of themselves, will plan and build in justice, in tradition, and in freedom a house of many mansions where there will be room for all.' The eloquence of his vision may have stirred his audience, but the foundations on which it was constructed were far more fragile than he cared to allow. When he went on to claim that it seemed 'pretty certain that half the U-boats with which Germany began the war have been sunk', and that the U-boat campaign against British shipping had already been 'utterly broken', he indulged in a wild and unwarranted surmise: in reality, only ten U-boats – not half but rather less than a fifth of the fleet – had been eliminated. The others remained a potent threat.

In a somewhat desultory fashion, the Admiralty had started to shore up the defences which were supposed to protect Britain's naval anchorages but, as an enterprising U-boat commander was about to demonstrate, they remained far from impenetrable. On 12 January 1940 the twenty-seven-year-old commander of U-23, Kapitänleutnant Otto Kretschmer, took his vessel into a bay on the east side of the Orkneys only four miles from where Prien had sunk the *Royal Oak* three months earlier. In contrast to Prien, Kretschmer was not a convivial character.

One of his crew, Volkmar König, would later recall: 'Kretschmer would never sit at a bar and drink a beer with one of his crew. He was in authority.'[42] Nor was he given to rhetoric. Horst Elfe, second watch officer on Kretschmer's next command, U-99, remembered that 'Silent Otto' 'wasn't someone who gave big encouraging speeches. He was always very matter-of-fact, very unemotional, but he was not without a heart.'[43] More importantly, he was trusted and respected by his men. Already singled out by his superiors as 'worth watching for the future', he had been twice decorated since the opening of hostilities. Judging him to be 'unusually quiet but inwardly strong . . . a lone wolf, Dönitz sent an appreciation to naval headquarters in Berlin at the end of 1939, citing 'his unconcern, calm, decisiveness' as 'outstanding characteristics in action' which made him 'specially suited for the carrying out of difficult tasks'.[44]

Inganess Bay, near Kirkwall in Orkney, was ostensibly protected by shore batteries and two ASW (anti-submarine warfare) trawlers, armed with ASDIC sonar equipment and depth charges. Nonetheless, Kretschmer was able to slip into the anchorage undetected. A 10,500-ton Danish oil tanker, the *Danmark*, was moored in a corner of the bay. 'We could see the people on the bridge with their cigarettes,' U-23's watch officer, Hans-Jochen von Knebel, recalled.

> We shot at it, and yes, it worked – the torpedo did explode at the right time. We were very proud and happy. The English didn't believe we could be so close by in the anchorage, and when the torpedo exploded they searched the sky with lights because they thought we were the Luftwaffe. They were even firing into the air . . . Then we turned back and again we sailed very close to the lookouts but got out of there in one piece.[45]

In the wake of Prien, Kretschmer had demonstrated for a second time that individual U-boats, operating with stealth and dash, could penetrate Britain's defences more or less with impunity.

The embarrassment set nerves jangling in the Admiralty. The naval officer in charge at Kirkwall, Vice-Admiral Raikes, was ordered to produce an official report on the incident. This unhappy document recorded lamely that 'there were no indications or suspicions of the presence of the enemy'. This did not satisfy Vice-Admiral Binney, commanding Orkneys and Shetlands, 'I consider that the negligence and inefficiency of [the two ASW trawlers] allowed this submarine to escape,' he thundered two weeks later. When Raikes protested that his superior officer had been unfair, Binney fired back that 'it should not have been possible for a submarine to have got into position to fire into Inganess Bay at all'. For good measure, the director of submarine warfare added, 'It is a thoroughly bad show when a ship which is protected by two A/S vessels is torpedoed and the U-boat is allowed to escape.'[46]

In his Mansion House speech, Churchill had been careful to warn there would be 'many losses and misfortunes' in the months ahead, but could not resist claiming that 'things are not going so badly after all. Indeed they have never gone so well in any naval war.'[47] On the basis of this blithe presentation, no one would have known that, at that very moment, the Admiralty was seeking to establish how one of Dönitz's U-boats had once again been able to humiliate the Royal Navy in its own backyard. The audacity was magnificent, but the First Lord's optimism was, to put it mildly, premature.

## 3.   Rash Moves


'Britons Acclaim Men of Altmark'. The headline in *The New York Times* for 18 February 1940 did not exaggerate. As its London reporter wrote, 'Huge crowds cheered themselves hoarse when the destroyer, HMS *Cossack*, with a Royal Air Force escort, slid into Leith with some 300 British seamen who had suddenly and almost at the last moment been snatched by the British Navy from their long imprisonment aboard what has come to be known among the British public as the German "hell ship" the *Altmark*.'[1] This triumphant arrival marked the end of a sustained maritime drama which had begun in the South Atlantic, garnered headlines all over the world, and then, in obedience to the laws of unintended consequences, led to a skirmish in the neutral waters of Norway, which itself produced a diplomatic crisis that foreshadowed a military disaster for which the First Lord of the Admiralty, Winston Churchill, bore great responsibility – and which had great bearing on what did and did not happen thereafter in the Battle of the Atlantic.

The drama began in December 1939. Four months earlier, the only ships available for deployment from the Kriegsmarine's entire surface fleet were two pocket battleships – *Deutschland* and *Admiral Graf Spee*. Accordingly, these two warships were sent, respectively, to the North and South Atlantic, with their specific task defined as 'the disruption and destruction of all enemy shipping by all possible means'.[2] Both were accompanied by supply vessels which allowed them to remain away from their home ports for many months. Their task was simple: to sink as many Allied merchant ships as they could find without putting themselves at risk. For this reason, they were also under instruction to avoid contact with any enemy warships even if they were of inferior size and power.

The Admiralty plans to counter this elusive threat in the South Atlantic was constrained by a shortage of warships. As Britain lacked enough naval escorts to protect every merchant convoy along the myriad of trans-continental shipping routes that criss-crossed these vast waters, 'evasive routing', as it was called, was virtually the only way of avoiding the German marauders roving the ocean like hungry sharks after easy meat. Evasive routing worked only if a stricken merchant ship had time to give its location before one or other of the pocket battleships had sent it to the bottom of the sea. Thus alerted, all other ships in the area were ordered to alter course in the hope of avoiding a similar fate.

Evasive routing was not of itself enough to mitigate the threat. Every merchant ship plying those seas that linked the ports of the Far East, India, Africa and South America to Britain carried precious supplies on which Britain was heavily dependent. As soon as news reached London on 30 September that a British merchant ship, the SS *Clement*, had been sunk by a battleship off the coast of Brazil, the Admiralty redeployed no fewer than eight hunting groups from other locations around the globe to track down and sink the assailants. Sent variously to the West Indies, the north-east of Brazil, Argentina, the Cape of Good Hope and Senegal, these task forces comprised in total five aircraft carriers, four battleships, and fourteen cruisers (three of which were French) as well as their accompanying destroyers; individually, however, it was by no means certain that any one of these groups was powerful enough to prevail against the firepower of a pocket battleship. They would not find out until they had traced the enemy in an apparently deserted ocean of limitless horizons.

Although one or two sightings were reported to London, the *Graf Spee* ranged freely for almost ten weeks, criss-crossing some 35,000 miles of the South Atlantic to accost nine merchant ships, all but two of which were sunk after their crews had been transferred to the pocket battleship's accompanying supply ship, the *Altmark*. Finally, though, on 13 December, the *Graf Spee* was sighted by HMS *Exeter*, the most powerful cruiser in Force G, one of the three British hunting groups in this part of the ocean, some 150 miles off the coast of Uruguay. At just after 6 a.m., while Lieutenant Commander Richard Jennings was still in his pyjamas, he was summoned to action stations in the *Exeter*'s control tower. As he crossed the compass platform, he was hailed by his captain, F. S. 'Hooky' Bell, with the words, 'There's the fucking *Scheer*!'[3] Within minutes, as senior gunnery officer, Jennings ordered the first broadside to be fired at what he only later discovered to be the *Graf Spee*, which, at distance of 20,000 yards, was 'as large as life on the horizon'.

Able Seaman Len Foghill had come off middle watch and was asleep in his hammock when he was woken by the summons to action: 'I was out of bed and at my action stations before the bugler had finished sounding general quarters. I dashed off with my socks on and my shoes under my arm . . . There were flashes all around us and the sound of guns.' As Foghill kept watch on the enemy warship through his binoculars, the *Exeter* came under a barrage of accurate fire. 'Shells were passing right through the superstructure. There was shrapnel flying everywhere. In the first ten minutes we lost five officers and fifty-six ratings . . . The bridge from where the captain was controlling the ship was out of action, most of the personnel being killed or injured.'[4]

The *Exeter* was supported in the attack by two light cruisers, HMS *Achilles* and HMS *Ajax*, in which the force commander, Commodore Henry Harwood, flew his pennant. Harwood's decision to attack the German battleship was audacious: a broadside from the *Graf Spee* outweighed the combined firepower of the three British cruisers by a factor of more than two to one. Although the *Exeter* inflicted more damage on the enemy warship than her crew imagined at the time, it was an unequal contest. Under the relentless precision of the *Graf*'s 11-inch guns, the turrets housing the British cruiser's 8-inchers were soon knocked out. Soon afterwards the 'nerve centre' of the ship was also shattered; all communications were destroyed and all orders had to be transmitted by a chain of runners.

One of these was Foghill:

It seemed as if I bore a charmed life because all the time I was going about, my shipmates were being killed. I was losing friends but oblivious to it at the time. I was just doing the things I was trained to do. When I went through the waist, the deck where the torpedo tubes are, I saw injured men lying around dying. Even the padre was down there handing out tots of whisky to the injured . . . There were bodies everywhere. A piece of shrapnel took the back of our sub-lieutenant's head off. I'd never seen anyone die before.[5]

Surgeon-Commander Roger Lancashire did what he could to tend the wounded:

The casualties were pretty devastating. There were two or three who literally died in my arms. These were people I had been living with, as it were, for three years. There were cases where, if I'd had the facilities and an endless supply of blood transfusions, things might have been different, but it wasn't like that. I did a quick assessment of who was most likely to benefit and then went to work on them.[6]

The only time that he left the sick-bay was to tend his captain, who had been one of only three people to survive the blast which destroyed the bridge. 'Hooky' Bell was wounded by shrapnel and half-blinded by splinters of metal in both eyes but, evidently undaunted, he accompanied the surgeon-commander along the deck to watch Jennings direct fire from the lid of gun turret Y, which housed the last of the *Exeter*'s big guns still in working order. Lancashire was to recall that the gunnery officer

> gave me a running commentary on what was going on. It was fantastic. I was spellbound. There in the distance you could see the *Graf Spee*, firing every now and then. The exciting thing was that *Ajax* and *Achilles* had made a smokescreen and they were taking it in turns to dodge in and out of it and give a rapid and accurate six-inch broadside, which the *Graf Spee* didn't much like.

Clearly aware that his own ship was in worsening trouble, Bell told Lancashire, 'If he gives me half a chance and heads this way I intend to ram the bugger.'[7]

He did not get his chance. With *Exeter* severely damaged and almost out of action, Harwood ordered all three cruisers to withdraw. Between them they had lost seventy-one lives, almost all of them from *Exeter*. But the *Graf Spee* did not emerge unscathed. One of the *Exeter*'s big guns had almost destroyed the battleship's main steering gear, which meant that offensive action of any kind was impossible. Captain Hans Langsdorff decided to make for Montevideo, the Uruguayan capital on the northern bank of the River Plate, where he knew he could anchor safely in neutral waters. Like almost every other South American state, Uruguay had still not been pressed to choose sides in what still seemed to be a faraway European conflict of little global moment. As the *Graf Spee* dropped anchor in the harbour at Montevideo, the *Ajax* and *Achilles* and Force G's fourth cruiser, HMS *Cumberland* – in place of *Exeter*, which was already heading for the British base at Port Stanley in the Falklands for emergency repairs – took up station just outside Uruguay's territorial waters. By this time Harwood, who had just been promoted to rear admiral, had radioed the Admiralty asking for reinforcements from the two other British hunting groups in the region.

Captain Langsdorff had reached sanctuary but the reprieve was only temporary and he knew it. Under the rules of maritime warfare, the *Graf Spee* was entitled to remain at Montevideo for twenty-four hours, though, following representations from the German embassy, the Uruguayan authorities extended this grace period by a further seventy-two hours. This happened to suit Harwood very well. It would take three days before the reinforcements he had summoned would reach the River Plate. Conversely, Langsdorff believed – wrongly but perhaps deceived by British Intelligence – that two powerful British warships – the aircraft carrier HMS *Ark Royal* and the battlecruiser HMS *Renown* – were already on the point of joining the British blockade. When it became clear that the repairs to the *Graf Spee* would not be completed before his seventy-two hours were up, he faced two drastic options. Either he could hand over his ship to be interned for the duration by the Uruguayan authorities or he could scuttle her. He cabled Berlin accordingly, advising that 'escape into open sea and breakthrough to home waters [is] hopeless'.[8] This did not find favour with the Kriegsmarine's commander-in-chief, who thought that Langsdorff had a third choice. A month earlier Admiral Raeder had made clear what he expected of those who served under him: 'The German warship and her crew are to fight with all their strength to the last shell, until they win or go down with their flag flying'[9] – an instruction that chimed with one of Hitler's more than usually fatuous admonitions – 'Rather death with honour than strike the flag.'[10] In this case, Raeder secured the Führer's ready assent before cabling Langsdorff, urging him to fight it out and go down with all guns blazing. Rather than impose a moment of suicidal glory on his men, the *Graf Spee*'s captain declined to accept Raeder's instruction.

Instead, as night began to fall on 17 December, the citizens of Montevideo watched the pocket battleship steam slowly out of the harbour towards the open sea. The *Graf Spee* was followed closely by a German merchant vessel, the *Tacoma*. As she reached the mouth of the Plate, thousands of onlookers on the banks of the estuary watched as the two vessels drifted to a halt while the skeleton crew who had remained on board was transferred to the *Tacoma*. Minutes later the *Graf Spee* burst into flames as a series of explosions tore a gaping hole in her hull just below the waterline. Soon afterwards the much-feared battleship settled ingloriously on the mud of the river bed, her superstructure still looming fatuously above the surface of the still water.

Almost unobserved, the *Tacoma* meanwhile slipped out of Montevideo and steamed across the estuary to the Argentinean capital, Buenos Aires, where Langsdorff and his crew were duly interned by the authorities. From there, Langsdorff sent a letter to the German ambassador in Montevideo. 'I am fully content to pay with my life for any possible discredit on the honour of the flag,' he wrote. 'I shall face my fate with firm faith in the cause and the future of the nation and of my Führer.'[11] Accordingly, on 20 December, he put a pistol to his head and – at the second attempt – killed himself.

The news that a major German warship had been scuttled in the River Plate made headlines around the world. In an absurd attempt to limit the damage to the Third Reich's prestige, Goebbels concocted a story almost as preposterous as his efforts to lay the blame for the sinking of the *Athenia* on the First Lord of the Admiralty. According to the account broadcast by German radio, the *Graf Spee* had inflicted severe damage on a powerful British fleet, scoring a heroic victory before succumbing to overwhelming odds. Only muttonheads were fooled. Others, though, found pathos in the demise of the German battleship. Indulging a common romance with great warships, *The New York Times* correspondent in Montevideo allowed himself to mourn the sight of 'the broken and twisted mass of black and burning wreckage', commenting that such ships 'represent so much in tradition and honor that no one can visit the tragic ruins of the *Graf Spee*, as this correspondent did this afternoon, without being deeply impressed that anything so noble should have been sentenced wilfully to so ignoble an end'.[12]

In London, the mood could scarcely have been more different. By his own account, Churchill had found it 'most exciting to follow the drama of this brilliant action' from inside the Admiralty War Room;[13] so exciting, evidently, that he had to be restrained from cabling Harwood with an avalanche of tactical advice, which he based on a series of unconfirmed reports gleaned spasmodically from a commercial radio station based in the United States. He was prevented from doing so only when Admiral Pound, with unusual firmness, intervened to insist that not even the First Lord should pester a British commander as 'The Battle of the River Plate' – as it was soon to be known – was still in progress. However, when the government released the news, Churchill was no longer to be tethered. On 18 December he took to the airwaves to inform the nation that 'News which has come from Montevideo has been received with thankfulness in our island, and with unconcealed satisfaction throughout the greater part of the world . . . and through-out a vast expanse of water peaceful shipping of all nations may, for a spell at least, enjoy the freedom of the seas.'[14]

In the course of the broadcast, he made a point of referring to the 'constant menace of U-boats' and warned of the 'rough and violent times' which lay ahead. However, for good reason, he refrained from drawing attention to the disturbing fact that while virtually half the British navy had been despatched to hunt for the *Graf Spee*, Dönitz's submarines had sunk no fewer than 114 merchantmen, of which more than 100 were sailing independently; by contrast, only two merchant ships were lost from the fourteen 'fast' convoys that had been escorted across the Atlantic to Britain by the end of the year.[15] The truth was that the First Lord and his admirals were still locked in a First World War mindset which led them to deploy a disproportionate number of ships in the hunt for an elusive 'surface raider' in a vast ocean when they might better have been used for the mundane task of shepherding otherwise unprotected merchant convoys through the shoals where the threat came from vessels lurking under the surface. Though Dönitz had lost nine U-boats – one sixth of his fleet – in the four months from September to December 1939, the loss of more than 400,000 tons of British shipping was but a portent of what was to be unleashed upon Britain's merchant fleet in the months ahead.

A month after Churchill's broadcast, on 19 January, under the headline '300 British Seamen Suffer on Nazi Tanker That Supplied Graf Spee', the London correspondent of *The New York Times* reported that the British seamen captured by the *Graf Spee* from the merchant ships she had sunk before her own demise were being held prisoner in a German auxiliary tanker, the *Altmark*, which was now on her way back to European waters. According to the American reporter's colourful account, the British captives were

> cooped up in the holds without room to move between mattresses covered by vermin. Exercise and fresh air are limited to an hour and fifteen minutes daily. Food is scarce and bad . . . The total water ration is

one quart daily . . . the prisoners' sanitary arrangements are primitive . . . Machine guns are mounted on the tanker's deck with guards standing by ready to fire at the slightest sign of unrest . . .[16]

Unsurprisingly, this predicament seized global headlines but it foreshadowed a far greater drama, the choreography of which was already preoccupying the high commands in London and Berlin.

With the demise of the *Graf Spee*, the *Altmark* had no further purpose in the South Atlantic. As soon as he felt confident that the British warships had left the region, her master, Captain Heinrich Dau, set course for his home port of Hamburg. Dau had been taken prisoner in the First World War and the experience had apparently soured his feelings for the British; twenty years on, he clearly felt under no obligation to provide his captives with more than the bare necessities of life. Unaware that his ship was about to garner as much international attention as the pocket battleship now resting on the bed of the River Plate, Dau set a course which took the *Altmark* north towards Greenland and thence, avoiding the busy shipping lanes of the North Atlantic, towards the safety of Norway's territorial waters, taking care to steer well clear of Scotland.

Despite intense diplomatic overtures from London and Berlin, the Norwegian government, like its neighbours Sweden and Denmark, clung tenaciously to a perilous neutrality. For almost four months Churchill had been agitating in the War Cabinet in favour of military action in the neutral waters of Scandinavia to prevent the free passage of merchant ships carrying Swedish iron ore from the Norwegian port of Narvik to Germany. Less than a month after the outbreak of war, he presented the Cabinet with a detailed memorandum arguing that 'drastic action' might be needed to intercept these convoys and thus 'greatly reduce [Germany's] power of resistance'.[17] He proposed laying mines inside Norway's territorial waters, hoping thereby to force the enemy's merchant ships into international waters where they could be intercepted and if necessary sunk by the Royal Navy and the RAF. As the First Lord's proposal would constitute a clear breach of international law, it was hardly surprising that the Foreign Secretary, Lord Halifax, stamped on the idea – or as Churchill noted ruefully, he was 'unable to obtain assent to action'. This did not stop him pressing repeatedly and passionately for what he persisted in calling 'the simple and bloodless operation' of mining these neutral waters.[18] Nor was he detained in this by the niceties of maritime law, telling his own officials how obvious it was that 'we should be prepared to violate Norwegian neutrality'.[19]

In December he went a step further. Insisting that it 'cannot be too strongly emphasized that British control of the Norwegian coast-line is a strategic objective of first-class importance', he urged the invasion and occupation of the strategically important port of Narvik. As for Britain's treaty obligations, there were overriding *raisons d'état* which rendered them irrelevant. 'No technical infringement of International Law, so long as it is unaccompanied by inhumanity of any kind, can deprive us of the good wishes of neutral countries,' he insisted. 'Small nations must not tie our hands when we are fighting for their rights and freedom ... Humanity, rather than legality, must be our guide.'[20] Though he pleaded the case at length and with characteristic forcefulness, his colleagues in the War Cabinet were as yet unwilling to countenance such a cavalier breach of a set of international laws which had originally been established at the behest of a British government.

Simultaneously, and mirroring Churchill's ambition, plans were already well advanced in Germany for the occupation of both Norway and Denmark. On 10 October, aware that in due course the Führer intended to occupy the Low Countries and northern France, Raeder urged Hitler to authorize the seizure of key ports along the Norwegian coast from which the Kriegsmarine could more conveniently take the offensive in the Atlantic. More critically, these bases were essential to ensure the safe transit of the 'absolutely vital' shipments of Swedish iron ore needed to sustain Germany's armaments programme. Raeder's advocacy of this course was, as his biographer has noted, 'a calculated risk, with implications both for the immediate and long-term future of his fleet'.[21] Although such a move, as he would later concede, 'breaks all rules of naval warfare', he believed that the argument for taking this risk was compelling, not least because it would give the Kriegsmarine its first opportunity to make a 'decisive' impact on the course of the war.[22]

Raeder's overriding objective was to secure the resources required to expand his fleet to the size needed to triumph eventually in a global maritime war. In both supreme commander of the armed forces (OKW) Field Marshal Wilhelm Keitel and commander of the Luftwaffe Reichsmarschall Hermann Göring (who had already been designated by the Führer to be his successor), Raeder faced formidable opponents. Like

Hitler, their priority was the continental battle for Lebensraum in Europe rather than global war. By advocating the invasion of Norway, Raeder hoped not only to play the principal role in an important operation but also thereby to protect the Kriegsmarine from the financial depredations of his rivals in the army and air force.

London and Berlin were by now engaged in a form of military blind-man's buff as each groped around in uncertainty but determined to prevent the other from seizing the strategic advantage in Norway. Their planning was further complicated by the Soviet invasion of Finland in November 1939. The Molotov–Ribbentrop Pact – signed a little over three months earlier, on 23 August, with a high degree of cynicism on both sides – incorporated a secret protocol which carved the nations sandwiched between them into Nazi and Soviet 'spheres of influence' wherein each dictatorship would be licensed to behave with impunity.

Both the German and British high commands presumed that the Finns would swiftly collapse before the overwhelming might of their Soviet neighbour. When it became clear that, on the contrary, the small but highly motivated Finnish army would fight for every inch of its sovereignty against the Red Army's ill-equipped and poorly led conscripts, the British chiefs of staff began to lay tentative plans to send men and weapons to support Helsinki's resistance. The obvious way for these reinforcements to reach the far north would be overland through Norway and Sweden via the port of Narvik. For Churchill this held out the promise of a double whammy. As he later explained with engaging candour,

> I sympathized ardently with the Finns and supported all proposals for their aid; and I welcomed this new and favourable breeze as a means of achieving the major strategic advantage of cutting off the vital iron-ore supplies of Germany. If Narvik was to become a kind of Allied base to support the Finns, it would certainly be easy to prevent the German ships loading ore at the port.[23]

Berlin suspected that such a move was afoot. On the day that the Red Army marched into Finland, Raeder warned Hitler that it was now vital 'to occupy Norway';[24] to lose Norway, he argued, would turn the Baltic into a battleground and make it very much more difficult for the Kriegsmarine to operate in the Atlantic. Hitler agreed. By December, partly as a result of a meeting with the Norwegian national leader,

Vidkun Quisling, and partly on the basis of reports from the German intelligence service, the Abwehr, Raeder became even more convinced that a British move on Narvik was imminent.

He was not far off the mark. Churchill continued to press the point and was rewarded at a meeting of the Supreme War Council in Paris in early February, when the governments of Britain and France agreed in principle that they should send up to 40,000 troops to the Finnish front line via Norway and Sweden. This undertaking would require an intense diplomatic effort to persuade the governments in Oslo and Stockholm to permit their territories to be crossed for the purpose. Whether or not this arm-twisting would have worked was never to be known. Within days of the agreement in Paris, the 'Aid to Finland' project had foundered in the storm which now broke over Norway.

On 14 February, three weeks after leaving the South Atlantic, the *Altmark* sailed into Norwegian waters, where she was detected by an RAF reconnaissance plane on patrol over the North Sea. For the First Lord of the Admiralty this was fortuitous manna, the pretext he needed to incite a major incident, an excuse – however threadbare – to take the battle to the enemy by an assault on Germany in Norwegian waters. In a questionable, if not disingenuous, interpretation of international law, he told Pound that the *Graf Spee*'s former supply ship was 'violating neutrality in carrying British prisoners of war to Germany . . . The *Altmark* must be regarded as an invaluable trophy.'[25] A small flotilla of destroyers, under the command of Captain Philip Vian aboard HMS *Cossack*, was despatched to 'intercept' the German ship. But the *Altmark* ignored the British signals and, escorted by two Norwegian torpedo boats, took shelter in Josing Fjord, one of many narrow, steep-sided and snowy inlets along that coast. As darkness fell, *Cossack* entered the fjord and Vian invited the captain of one of the torpedo boats, the *Kjell*, to come aboard. The Norwegian skipper insisted that the *Altmark* had been inspected three times and that no British sailors or weapons had been found on board. In an effort to end the stand-off, he then informed Vian that he had been instructed to use force if necessary to prevent the British boarding the German vessel. The British captain at once contacted the Admiralty for further instructions. These soon arrived.

Without feeling any need to consult the First Sea Lord, Churchill sent a personal order to Vian, instructing him to 'board *Altmark*, liberate the prisoners, and take possession of the ship pending further instructions',[26] adding, for good measure, that he should avoid engaging the Norwegian torpedo boat except in self-defence. 'Suggest to Norwegian destroyer [sic]', the First Lord concluded artlessly, 'that honour is served by submitting to superior force.' The argument from force majeure duly prevailed and the Norwegian captain wisely withdrew. The captain of the *Altmark* proved less amenable. According to Vian's account, which was contradicted in almost every significant respect by Dau, the latter put his engines full astern as the *Cossack* approached as though to ram the British warship. They nearly collided before the German vessel went aground on the ice-covered shoreline. At this point, thirty-three British crewmen, led by Lieutenant Commander Turner, managed to leap aboard the *Altmark*, whereupon Captain Dau and his crew surrendered. But one of the German armed guards evidently took aim and shot at the boarding party, one of whom was wounded. Vian reported later that, after a brief exchange of fire, 'the armed guard decamped; they fled across the ice, and began to snipe at the boarding party from an eminence on the shore. Silhouetted against the snow they made easy targets, and their fire was quickly silenced.'[27] Six Germans were killed and six more were seriously wounded. According to Dau's account, however, the British boarding party had fired 'wildly and blindly' and had then shot 'with the utmost intensity at innocent German sailors not only fleeing for their lives but without firing a single shot in retaliation'.[28] In any event, the prisoners were swiftly released from their prison quarters in the tanker. According to the legend which swiftly built up around this episode, one of Vian's men broke open the hatches covering the hold and hailed below, 'Any British down there?'

As the news seeped out, the British press, led by the *Daily Mail* and the *Daily Express*, reached for the heights of hyperbole: according to the former – in the course of a derring-do account in which mere facts came a poor second – 'the crew of the destroyer *Cossack* wrote a chapter in British naval history as daring and inspiring as any exploit of Raleigh or Drake'.[29] An *Express* reporter attending the funeral of the German sailors killed in the skirmish relished 'the "fine collection" of black eyes among the surviving German crew, clearly administered by British fists'. As for Captain Dau, he was 'a bullying shrimp . . . scowling, beard a-quiver, forever bleating "Heil Hitler!"' who had subjected his captives to boundless torment in his German 'hell ship'.[30]

It was not until the men arrived back in Scotland that the ghoulish

accounts of their incarceration, which had become encrusted by colourful embellishments over the weeks since the initial reports, were shown
to be somewhat exaggerated. Though their privations had been severe
and distressing, 299 merchant seamen emerged into the light of day
remarkably unscathed. To welcome them on their arrival at the port of
Leith, the government had laid on ambulances, doctors, reporters and
cameramen. However, it was soon clear that Captain Dau's victims were
not in need of medical attention and therefore that the journalists had no
story. As Churchill noted ruefully, 'it appeared they were in good
health . . . and came ashore in a hearty condition, [so] no publicity was
given to this aspect'.[31] Nonetheless, the myth was to prevail. A narrative
which began with a great sea battle in the course of which a German
battleship was sunk, which featured a wicked German captain and his
'hell ship' and its noble British victims and which led to a further victory
in a Norwegian fjord that culminated in a safe homecoming: the saga
was far too compelling to be subverted by a cold dose of reality.

However, the *Altmark* incident was genuinely of more than passing
moment. The skirmish in the Norwegian fjord – the first direct confrontation between Britain and Germany in mainland Europe – had
thrown a harsh light on the disdain of both belligerents for the niceties
of neutrality. For this reason, the propaganda battle that now ensued
was, in its own terms, far more intense than the clash which inspired it.
To counter the British coup, Berlin responded with an impressive display of simulated outrage. Casting around for parallel examples of
British 'brutality', the German Foreign Ministry alighted on an episode
in the Napoleonic Wars, more than a century earlier, when Admiral
Nelson (ignoring orders by putting his telescope to his blind eye) sank
or seized the bulk of the Danish fleet at the Battle of Copenhagen in
1801. In a surge of self-righteous bombast, Berlin declared that Britain's
'unheard-of violation of international law' was liable to provoke 'the
most severe consequences'.[32] More ominously, the Germans simultaneously conveyed the same threat in identical terms to Oslo, warning that
Norway's failure to protect her territorial waters could not be ignored.

For their part, the Norwegians, squeezed between the belligerent
purposes of two great powers, remonstrated impotently with each of
them. In almost the same breath, the country's hapless foreign minister,
Halvan Koht, declared that the British action was 'the grossest violation
of neutrality' but that 'even such a case does not give Germany the right

to send its war forces to Norway'. However, if Berlin was now looking for a casus belli – however specious – the *Altmark* incident was clearly going to serve as well as any. Having what a later generation of diplomats might call a 'colourable case', Berlin made the most of it for days on end. Heeding Goebbels's instruction that 'all propaganda must be focused on this single incident',[33] the Propaganda Ministry ensured that the number of column inches of print and minutes of airtime devoted to Britain's perfidy in Norway rivalled the attention German radio had given to the 'liberation' of Poland.

The *Altmark* incident did not cause the events which now unfolded but it was the trigger that unleashed them. Raeder had been preparing outline plans for the invasion of Norway since December. Now, galvanized by the unambiguous evidence of the threat posed by Britain to Germany's vital interests so cruelly exposed by Oslo's inability to defend its neutrality, he issued a directive on 1 March authorizing the invasion of Norway (at a date yet to be confirmed) to pre-empt any 'major operation' by the British to occupy Narvik. By 1 April, it was clear that his intentions had hardened and his horizons had broadened. In a meeting with his senior commanders, he warned that, although Operation Weserübung – as the invasion of Norway was codenamed – would be one of the 'rashest undertakings in the history of modern warfare', it would finally give Germany open access to the Atlantic Ocean and the high seas beyond. It was 'intolerable', he fulminated, 'that every successive German generation should be confronted with the problems of British pressure. The conflict with England was inevitable, sooner or later; it must be fought to a finish.'[34]

In London, three days later, after what Churchill was to describe as seven months of 'vain boggling, hesitation, changes of policy, arguments between good and worthy people, unending',[35] the British War Cabinet finally yielded to the First Lord's pressure and authorized the Admiralty to mine Norwegian waters to obstruct the flow of Swedish iron ore to Germany. But, as he was still to seethe many years later, it was now too late. 'Hitler was ready, and ready with a far more powerful and well-prepared plan. One can hardly find a more perfect example of the impotence and fatuity of waging war by committee . . . now all was to be disaster.'[36] With this self-serving – if perceptive – reflection, Churchill side-stepped his own responsibility for what now took place.

In the early hours of 8 April, four British destroyers duly laid a minefield in the channel leading to the port of Narvik. But a large German fleet – virtually every surface vessel in the Kriegsmarine – was already at sea heading for Norway. Organized into six battle groups and laden with troops, their mission was the seizure of the country's principal ports, including Narvik. As a part of an unrelated plan conceived by Churchill a fortnight earlier, British troops were already at Rosyth waiting to embark on another quartet of British cruisers which were to land them at the southern ports of Stavanger, Bergen and Trondheim, ostensibly to forestall any German move against Norway. But it was now impossible for them to reach Norway in time to arrest the German occupation.

The Home Fleet, under Admiral Forbes, was already at sea but heading in the opposite direction to intercept *Scharnhorst* and *Gneisenau*, assuming – wrongly – that the two battleships were about to break out into the Atlantic to harass Britain's trade routes; in fact, they had been sent to the north merely as a diversionary tactic. On 9 April the prime minister's private secretary, Jock Colville (who was given to gallows humour) noted that while 'Norway and Denmark had been invaded by the Germans . . . most of our fleet is busy chasing German ships towards the North Pole'.[37] After attending the War Cabinet and the Supreme War Council, he added, 'The Germans have scored a considerable success . . . and we, who started the whole business, seem to have lost the initiative . . . The First Lord (who at last sees a chance of action) is jubilant.'[38]

Outsmarted by the speed and scale of the German invasion, the War Cabinet flailed around in confusion and dismay. A series of false starts, misunderstandings, personal animosities, and contradictory orders combined rapidly to crumble into what Churchill was to call, with self-exculpatory understatement, an 'improvised campaign'[39] which, in the words of an eminent but waggish naval historian of that era, consisted largely of 'order, counter order, disorder'.[40]

Churchill bore a greater responsibility for this shambles than he would ever acknowledge. Although Chamberlain bore him no animosity and had no cause to doubt the sincerity of his protestations of loyalty, he was irked by the First Lord's methods and manner. In a letter to his sister Ida he complained that Churchill

> goes to bed after lunch for a couple of hours or so and holds conferences
> up to 1 in the morning at which he goes into every detail, so I am

informed, that could quite well be settled by subordinates . . . Officers and officials in his own and other departments are sent for and kept up until they are dropping with fatigue and Service Ministers are worn out in arguing with him.[41]

If Chamberlain was tempted to echo the well-briefed diplomatic correspondent of *The Times* who noted in his diary (presumably on the basis of the malicious gossip of resentful officials and envious ministers) that Churchill was 'overdoing himself and taking the strain by stoking himself unduly with champagne, liqueurs etc.',[42] he refrained from doing so.

More serious, from the prime minister's perspective, was the way in which Churchill conducted the business of the Military Co-ordinating Committee, which had been set up to streamline the affairs of the War Cabinet. When the First Lord took the chair he could not help but leave the impression that he regarded the presence of his colleagues as redundant. The prime minister told another of his sisters,

> I am bound to say that I don't think Winston did mean to supersede this body, but he does enjoy planning a campaign or an operation so much, and he believes so earnestly in all his own ideas (for the moment) that he puts more intense pressure on his staff than he realizes. The result is apt to be that they are bullied into a sulky silence – a most dangerous position in a war.[43]

Nonetheless, though Churchill frequently changed his mind, flitted from one idea to another, and contradicted himself as well as his subordinates, he demonstrated precisely those characteristics that marked him out as a great wartime leader: an implacable will, an indomitable spirit, an inexhaustible supply of energy and a matchless gift for public rhetoric.

With the War Cabinet still bemused by the speed and turn of events, ten German destroyers swept into Narvik without meeting any significant resistance. In a bid to wrest back the initiative, the Admiralty gave the go-ahead to a small flotilla of Royal Navy destroyers, under the command of Captain Bernard Warburton-Lee, to fight their way into Narvik and challenge the German occupiers. In the early hours of the following morning, 10 April, battered by high seas and a heavy snowstorm, Warburton-Lee in HMS *Hardy* led two other destroyers into the inner harbour. 'All we knew was that there was a big German force up there,' one of Warburton-Lee's crewmen would recall, 'but we did not know how big. We soon found out.'[44] The harbour was choked with an armada of twenty-three merchant ships of various nationalities as well as the German warships. Taken by surprise, the German destroyers were at first slow to react and two of them were put out of action almost at once by a volley of torpedoes from the advancing British destroyers. But then came return fire from a shore battery, soon followed by the arrival of several more German destroyers which circled round and hit *Hardy* at almost point blank range. The British destroyer was badly damaged and ran aground. Warburton-Lee was mortally wounded but retained his composure, ordering, 'Abandon Ship. Every Man for Himself. And good luck.'

*Hardy*'s crew jumped overboard and swam to the shore. 'It was so cold that a moment after we got into the water there was no feeling in our hands or feet . . .' an anonymous survivor recalled. 'And all the time we were still under fire. German shells were dropping round us. They had seen we were in trouble and they let us have it.'[45] Despite this, 170 men reached the shore and, with the help of a sympathetic Norwegian family, set off on the fifteen-mile hike to the village of Ballangen. Seventeen of their shipmates had been killed and two were reported missing. *Hardy*'s last signal was 'Keep on engaging the enemy', but when another British destroyer was sunk and two more severely damaged, the British had little choice but to flee. Warburton-Lee was carried to the shore, where he died on the beach; his leadership under fire was judged so heroic as to merit the first Victoria Cross of the Second World War to be awarded posthumously.

Churchill was furious at the ease with which the Kriegsmarine had outsmarted the Royal Navy and gave vent to his feelings in a letter to the First Sea Lord. Urging Pound to 'concentrate on Narvik, for which long and severe fighting will be required', he issued an unequivocal order: 'Narvik must be fought for. Although we have been completely outwitted, there is no reason to suppose that prolonged and serious fighting in this area will not impose a greater drain on the enemy than on ourselves.' Blithely ignoring the fact that Germany had a prima facie case for charging Britain with an earlier violation of Norwegian neutrality, he also had the audacity to add that 'Norwegian neutrality and our respect for it have made it impossible to prevent this ruthless *coup*'.[46] That the cause for which Britain was fighting had a moral justification that Germany entirely lacked does not alter the fact that, inspired by the First Lord, the British government had espoused a course of action which was no less a violation of international law, extenuating circumstances notwithstanding.

At 10 Downing Street that morning the War Cabinet discussed 'the line that should be taken in answer to criticisms of our failure to forestall or prevent the German occupation of Norway'. Among other points, Churchill said that he proposed to emphasize the 'bad weather' which had favoured the Germans and – preposterously – that 'the blame attached not to us but to the neutrals, and we should take every opportunity of bringing this point home'.[47] Facing a wrathful House of Commons the following day, Churchill did just that. In the process, he allowed himself to be distinctly more economical with the truth than the facts justified. Accusing Berlin of abusing the 'Norwegian corridor', he complained brutally: 'The strict observance of neutrality by Norway has been a contributory cause to the sufferings to which she is now exposed.'[48] In an attempt to account for the embarrassing fact that the Home Fleet had been on a wild-goose chase in pursuit of the *Scharnhorst* and the *Gneisenau* while the bulk of the Kriegsmarine was about to occupy Norway, he went on to explain: 'When we speak of the command of the seas it does not mean command of every part of the sea at the same moment, or at every moment. It only means that we can make our will prevail ultimately in any part of the seas which may be selected for operations, and thus indirectly make our will prevail in every part of the sea.'[49] In the circumstances, this conventional proposition was less than compelling but it contained the kernel of an important truth that the Admiralty had not yet fully recognized but which was to be driven home within weeks, and with fearful authority, in the Atlantic Ocean.

Chastened by the humiliating turn of events, Pound ordered that every German warship still in Narvik should be destroyed forthwith. On 13 April, the battleship HMS *Warspite*, with a screen of nine destroyers and escorted in the air by dive-bombers from the aircraft carrier HMS *Furious*, entered the harbour to wreak the Royal Navy's revenge. Peter Gretton was first lieutenant aboard the destroyer *Cossack*. The inner harbour was littered with the wrecks of British and German warships crippled in the earlier battle. 'By some chance', Gretton wrote later, 'the ship dodged the wrecks although there were some close shaves.'[50] Within moments, the British destroyer came under fire both from the shore and from the German warships still in the harbour. Shells began to burst all around, some on the water and some on the super-structure. Torpedoes snaked haphazardly towards the ship across the bay. Smoke and the smell of cordite filled the air. The battleship brought her big guns to bear. A gunner's mate, Petty Officer Daniel Reardon, rejoiced to hear the turret officer above his station call out: 'Tell the crew we have hit a destroyer and she is burning nicely.' One by one, almost at leisure, the *Warspite*'s heavy weapons despatched the German warships. 'After a while,' Reardon reported, ' "Check fire" is ordered and the ship seems to be stopping. "Crew may go on top of turrets," and up there it is a sight – burning and sinking enemy ships all around us, and our own destroyers searching into every little corner that might hide something.'[51]

Sweeping close to the edge of the harbour at a speed of twelve knots, *Cossack* suddenly went aground. Gretton was jolted by the unexpected impact:

> A semi-armour-piercing shell had exploded in the foremost boiler room, instantly killing the crew, cutting all leads from the bridge to the steer-ing engine and to the telegraphs, and fracturing the main steam pipe, so that the engines were temporarily useless and the ship could not be steered. We had eight hits in all . . . There were about twelve killed and rather more wounded – a surprisingly small number considering the punishment we had taken.[52]

After a semblance of order had been restored, *Cossack*'s gunnery crew started to lob shells into the merchant ships floating alongside the jetty that was used to load the Swedish iron ore bound for Germany, in what Gretton described as

> a rather cold-blooded manner . . . We were getting a little excited by then and the gun's crews were taking too much advantage of this glori-ous opportunity of plastering a town at no expense. There was hardly a prominent building in sight in which some keen-eyed enthusiast did not spot a sniper, usually imaginary, and it was necessary to damp their ardour.[53]

Much to Gretton's frustration, Admiral Whitworth, who was in overall command aboard his flagship, *Warspite*, refused *Cossack*'s request to send a platoon ashore to take the town with the hope of making contact with

*Hardy*'s surviving crew members, who were presumed by now to have reached shelter in the village of Ballangen. Nonetheless, Whitworth had secured a modest triumph. For the loss of three destroyers and at a cost of fifty-five lives, the British force had put eight German destroyers out of action and sunk one U-boat. However, this triumph presaged a greater tragedy.

Following hard on *Warspite*'s initial success at Narvik, Admiral of the Fleet Lord Cork, who at Churchill's behest had been charged by Pound to take command of the naval forces now gathering in Norwegian waters, sailed hurriedly for the German-held port. His task as he had interpreted it, after a verbal briefing from both Churchill and Pound, was 'to turn the enemy out of Narvik at the earliest possible moment'.[54] At the same time, but without any coordination between the War Office and the Admiralty, Major-General Pierse Mackesy, who was in command of a brigade of British soldiers, was on his way to the same destination with a similar purpose. However, his instructions were couched in far more cautious language. 'It is not intended that you should land in the face of opposition . . .' he was told, 'the decision whether to land or not will be taken by the Senior Naval Officer in consultation with you.'[55] Thus Mackesy and Cork, who had never met, found themselves sailing independently, each unaware of what the other had been told. Their paths crossed on 15 April at the port of Harstad, some seventy miles to the north of Narvik, and they fell out at once.

Urged on by Churchill, who was widely thought to have 'a private line' to Cork from which the First Sea Lord was excluded, the Admiral of the Fleet was resolved to make a swift assault on Narvik, regardless of what he recognized to be the significant risks involved. Mackesy demurred, bluntly insisting that the operation was too hazardous and that his troops were armed and equipped for only an unopposed landing. As one of the Admiralty's most senior officers noted at the time, 'I gather the General and the Admiral up in the northern area are fighting cat and dog. But if you will send two men from Whitehall with a completely and utterly different conception of what they are to do, and not meet until a battle is imminent, what are you to expect?'[56] Churchill was scathing about Mackesy's attitude, noting that 'nothing I or my colleagues or Cork could do or say produced the slightest effect on the General. He was resolved to wait until the snow melted.'[57] Meanwhile the weather closed in, snow fell heavily, and the Germans consolidated their hold on Narvik. Thus the Norwegian campaign – ill-judged, poorly planned, and lamentably executed – stumbled towards its bathetic nadir with a vainglorious squabble between two British commanders as Churchill fumed impotently from the sidelines.

As the principal advocate of Operation Weserübung, Admiral Raeder could derive quiet satisfaction from its success so far. Despite losing a large proportion of the German surface fleet (thus making the invasion of Britain an even greater challenge), the invasion of Norway had appeared to demonstrate that the Kriegsmarine was crucial to Germany's overall war aims. Admiral Dönitz, however, was in a state of the highest dudgeon. Although he had been required to deploy thirty-five U-boats at various points along Norway's long and ragged coastline, they had been unable to make any significant impact on the campaign. In the early days, they had found themselves everywhere that the enemy wasn't. Far more worryingly, though, even after they had located suitable targets, they had failed to destroy them. What was intended as a killing spree had turned into a fiasco. One after another, his top commanders radioed back to Wilhelmshaven with the same bad news. On 11 April U-25 reported firing torpedoes at two destroyers but failing to hit either. The following day U-51 reported a similar failure. On 15 April U-48 got close enough to the *Warspite* to unleash two torpedoes at the British battleship but, again, both failed to make contact; had they done so, it is hard to imagine that Churchill would have survived the political storm which would have followed the demise of another great battleship on his watch. As it was, the next day U-47 – commanded by Günther Prien, the hero of Scapa Flow – located six transport ships at anchor in Bygdenfjord, where they were unloading troops under the protective eye of two British battlecruisers. That night he fired eight torpedoes at this wall of vessels, all of which missed. Three days later he reported: 'Sighted *Warspite* and two destroyers and attacked the battleship with two torpedoes at a range of 900 yards. No success. As a result of the explosion of one of them at the end of its run I was placed in a most awkward predicament and was pursued by destroyers coming from all directions.'

Initially, Dönitz was incredulous. It seemed incomprehensible that in the space of a week, not one of his U-boats had registered a significant kill. After 'four attacks on a battleship, fourteen attacks on a cruiser, ten on a destroyer and ten on transports . . .' he recorded, 'the net result had merely been the sinking of one transport'. The fact that six deep-draught transport ships in Bygdenfjord had escaped unscathed from U-47's bombardment was compelling evidence that the torpedoes rather than the U-boats were to blame. 'To have missed these ships, lying motionless and overlapping each other, would have been quite impossible . . . And so we found ourselves equipped with a torpedo which refused to function in northern waters either with contact or with magnetic pistols . . . To all intents and purposes, then, the U-boats were without a weapon.' As Dönitz rapidly discovered, this threatened to have a devastating effect on the morale of even the most hardened U-boat commanders. On his return to Wilhelmshaven, after cutting short his mission, Prien evidently told him that he 'could hardly be expected to fight with a dummy rifle'.[58]

Noting in the U-boat War Diary the 'absurdity' that, as the U-boat supreme commander, he 'should have to be burdened with lengthy discussions and investigations into the causes of torpedo failures and their remedies',[59] Dönitz angrily contacted Raeder to demand an urgent inquiry, which was convened at once. Its preliminary findings did nothing to assuage Dönitz. 'The facts are worse than could have been expected,' he wrote.

> I have been informed . . . that the correct functioning of the AZ [pistol] in peacetime was considered to have been proved by only *two* shots and these not even perfect. Such methods of working can only be described as criminal . . . The result is staggering . . . I do not believe that ever in the history of war have men been sent against the enemy with such useless weapons.[60]

The intensity of Dönitz's frustration at what he described as a lost opportunity for 'certain success'[61] could not be contained within the confines of official memoranda but seeped out to rekindle the conflict between the Kriegsmarine U-boat arm and its commander-in-chief over the latter's pre-war decision to prioritize the construction of capital ships over submarines. Raeder responded to this upsurge of frustration by castigating his senior staff for failing to 'counter objectively the all too temperamental assertions of younger officers'.[62] Attempting to silence the critics by claiming – disingenuously – that the decision to construct battleships at the expense of U-boats had been made by the

Führer (and, by implication, was beyond rebuke), he argued that this choice had been vindicated by the success of the Norwegian campaign. Demanding an end to 'cheap, destructive criticism calculated to undermine what until now has been our finest asset: the navy's unity', he urged them to seek out 'daring actions' which would demonstrate the vital role of the surface fleet in the war against Britain.[63]

None of this was of any comfort to Dönitz, who was ever more convinced that Raeder's fixation with the surface fleet was hobbling the U-boat arm at precisely the moment when it should have been wreaking havoc on what both men regarded as Germany's mortal enemy. In the meantime, he had little choice but to recall the bulk of his fleet to base until the torpedo problem had been remedied. To his even greater chagrin they therefore played no part in the final act of the maritime drama which now reached its climax in the North Sea as Britain's first significant attempt to arrest Hitler's progress ended in tragedy and recrimination.

With the stand-off between Cork and Mackesy over the seizure of Narvik still unresolved, the British and French leaders came up with a parallel scheme to drive the Germans out of Norway. Supported by their principal advisors, they alighted on Operation Hammer, a plan to capture Trondheim, a major port 500 miles to the south of Narvik. Trondheim was large enough to act as a base for some 50,000 troops, it had excellent communications by rail and air and, no less pertinently, its seizure would serve notice on Hitler that the Allies still meant business. The problem was not the end but the means. Churchill, whose mind was still set on the seizure of Narvik, was sceptical, but, in the absence of any planning or preparation, the War Cabinet found itself borne along on the crest of a wave of misplaced optimism which – despite the setbacks at Narvik – reached well beyond the confines of government.

The principal agent of the hubris by which Whitehall's armchair strategists were now gripped was Sir Roger Keyes, a retired Admiral of the Fleet who had been heavily involved in the Dardanelles fiasco. Keyes had latterly become a Member of Parliament, a status he exploited to bombard Pound and Churchill with detailed plans for the seizure of Trondheim. Not content with that, he demanded that he should be recalled to take command of a naval task force to storm the Norwegian citadel. At a meeting with Churchill, he expressed himself so vehemently and at such length that Churchill was driven to curtail their discussion before the retired admiral had finished. Keyes continued to lobby with an excess of zeal which was not, however, without effect. Before long a consensus had formed among the military cognoscenti in favour of the 'smashing' blow at Trondheim which he had advocated with such formidable resolve. Even Churchill, who later wrote that 'left to myself I would have stuck to my first love, Narvik', succumbed to what he now came to regard as 'this exciting enterprise to which so many staid and cautious Ministers had given their strong adherence, and which seemed to find so much favour with the Naval Staff and indeed among all our experts'.[64] On 17 April, the die was apparently cast.

It was not to be. The next day what the First Lord described as a 'decisive stopper' was put in the works by the very same chiefs of staff whose endorsement for the amphibious assault on Trondheim had so recently convinced even the most timid cabinet ministers. To Churchill's indignation, they abruptly executed a 180 degree turn, advising the bewildered politicians that, as it stood, the plan they had drawn up only a few days before was, on reflection, too fraught with hazard to contemplate with any degree of confidence. Infuriated by this volte-face, Churchill was tempted to overrule their objections and give his 'old friend' Admiral Keyes, in whom he detected 'a passionate ardour for action and glory',[65] the chance he craved to lead a task force into Trondheim and take the port by storm. The First Lord was restrained from this folly only by the realization that to give Keyes so important a role over the heads of the chiefs of staff would have precipitated Pound's resignation. Operation Hammer, for a few days very much alive, was now dead and buried.

In its stead, the chiefs of staff opted for an alternative to the frontal assault demanded by Keyes: a two-pronged attack on the coast to the north and south of Trondheim with a view to achieving the same objective but at far less risk. It was a disastrous decision. At Churchill's behest, two of the five troopships heading for Narvik were diverted to the remote island ports of Namsos and Åndalsnes, where, within two days, more than 13,000 soldiers from Britain, France and Poland landed unopposed. They began to move on Trondheim. At first they met little resistance, but they had allowed neither for the Luftwaffe, which had control of the skies, nor for the better trained and better equipped Wehrmacht troops whom they started to encounter in growing numbers.

After ten days on Norwegian soil, the operation had to be aborted to avoid the humiliation of a mass surrender. By 2 May the entire expeditionary force had been evacuated from the city. At a cost of several hundred British lives, Trondheim was safe in German hands. As Churchill put it, 'Both claws of the feeble pincers were broken.'[66]

As the principal architect of the Norwegian venture, the First Lord did not seek to exculpate himself entirely from the opprobrium which was heaped now on the government's head in Westminster, but he was careful to scatter the blame liberally over the heads of his colleagues as well. 'Considering the prominent part I played in these events and the impossibility of explaining the difficulties by which we had been overcome or the defects of our staff and governmental organization and our methods of conducting war,' he was to reflect, 'it was a marvel that I survived and maintained my position in public esteem and Parliamentary confidence.'[67]

Ironically, the flow of events which were about to propel him into the post for which his genius was uniquely fitted sprang directly from the debacle in Norway. On 7 May Sir Roger Keyes, still smarting from his rebuff, took his seat in Parliament for a day-long debate on the crisis. In full dress uniform, the Admiral of the Fleet was the first backbencher to speak. Delivering himself of a withering indictment of the government's conduct of the campaign, he set the tone for a debate from which the government was unable to extract any jot of comfort. Chamberlain, who made a narrow and self-serving speech, won the vote but with a severely dented majority, losing the Commons and the nation in the process. It was clear he would have to go.

On the evening of 10 May, as the first panzers crossed into Belgium, Churchill seized the moment for which he had been waiting so long and which he regarded as properly his. Although Chamberlain had wanted Halifax to succeed him, his Foreign Secretary declined to take up the challenge, leaving the way clear for the First Lord of the Admiralty. Three days later the new prime minister gave a timely illustration of why he was the only politician in the land remotely capable of rallying the nation for what lay ahead. In a speech to his colleagues in the House of Commons he promised simply, 'I have nothing to offer but blood, toil, tears and sweat.'[68] It was a phrase that would not only reverberate down the years but that also marked the moment in the Second World

War when fear yielded to defiance, the threat of defeat to the hope of victory.

The Norwegian fiasco was not yet at an end. At Narvik, the stand-off between Lord Cork and General Mackesy had given the 6,000 German defenders time to dig in around the town. Although *Warspite* had given the British control of the port, allowing more than 13,000 allied troops to disembark, it was not until the end of the month, by which time their numbers had been reinforced by another 11,000 men, that the Allied forces (supported by those units of the Norwegian army which had refused to crumble prematurely) finally dislodged the enemy from their hillside stronghold. The removal of Mackesy (engineered by Churchill) and his replacement by General Claude Auchinleck (who was later to emerge as one of the great generals of the Second World War) gave new impetus to the battle: Narvik was taken and its defenders forced to retreat deeper into the mountains. However, to the dismay of those defiant Norwegians who had not surrendered their souls to the Nazis, no sooner had this victory been achieved than it was snatched away from them. Unbeknown to them, the War Cabinet had decided some days earlier that the British troops were needed elsewhere, their modest triumph overtaken by the cataclysmic events now unfolding further south. So far from being the start of an offensive, the only purpose of the struggle for the high ground around Narvik had been to secure safe passage to the troop-carriers waiting in the port below – although in the process they managed to damage the port's handling facilities which took some time to repair.

A few days later, in the late afternoon of 8 June, the aircraft carrier HMS *Glorious*, shielded by two destroyers, was steaming at full speed towards Rosyth when she was detected by the two battleships, *Scharnhorst* and *Gneisenau*, which were roaming the North Sea in search of easy prey. *Glorious* failed to detect the attackers until at least twenty minutes after they had identified her. Inexplicably, not one of her aircraft was either on reconnaissance or standing by on the flight deck. By the time her crew was summoned to action stations, the ship's fate was sealed. Within twenty minutes of the first shell landing, the old aircraft carrier was listing heavily. Within two hours she had sunk. There were just thirty-nine survivors of a ship's crew which had numbered more than twelve hundred, among whom were at least forty of the RAF's most highly trained pilots and aircrew who, against great odds, had already shown themselves to be dauntless in battle.

In an attempt to shield the carrier, her two escorts, HMS *Ardent* and HMS *Acasta*, had laid a protective smokescreen between the *Glorious* and the two battleships. Under cover of this shroud, they turned to attack the enemy with torpedoes. It was a suicidally audacious move. Within moments the German big guns were firing at the diminutive British warships at point-blank range. *Ardent* was overwhelmed and sank almost at once with the loss of 164 crew. *Acasta* turned as if to flee, but it was a ruse. 'You may think we are running away from the enemy, we are not,' her captain told his crew. '[O]ur chummy ship (*Ardent*) has sunk, the *Glorious* is sinking, the least we can do is make a show, good luck to you all.'[69] Altering course to starboard, the destroyer fired a barrage of torpedoes at the two German battleships. One of them hit the *Scharnhorst*, forcing her captain to disengage and head to Trondheim for repairs. For the crew of the *Acasta* it was a moment of intense exhilaration. Leading Seaman Carter, who was one of the torpedo handlers, recalled, 'I'll never forget the cheer that went up . . .'

A few moments later, a retaliatory shell crashed into the destroyer's engine room. Carter was hurled to the deck but got to his feet again only to see that every other member of his team had been killed by the blast. He was consumed by a sudden rage. 'I climbed back into the control seat, I see those two ships, I fired the remaining torpedoes, no one told me to, I guess I was raving mad.'[70] Moments later, the destroyer was engulfed in flames. Her captain gave the order to abandon ship and Carter jumped overboard. Once in the water, he looked up. 'I saw the Captain, leaning over the bridge, take a cigarette from a case and light it. We shouted to him to come to our raft, he waved "Goodbye and good luck" – the end of a gallant man.' He and 152 of his crew were lost. These deaths contributed to an overall Allied casualty figure for the Norwegian campaign of 6,602, of whom 4,369 were British. The equivalent German figure was 5,296. Norway had been overrun, occupied and annexed. The Wehrmacht's victory was absolute.

With the benefit of hindsight, the decision to confront the Third Reich in Norway may be seen as a ghastly error of strategic judgement compounded by an embarrassingly long list of tactical and operational confusions and contradictions. Even at the time it should surely have been clear that Hitler would discern even the whisper of British action as a mortal threat to which he would respond with the speed and ferocity which he had already demonstrated elsewhere. Although Dönitz was often at odds with the Kriegsmarine's commander-in-chief, he was in no doubt that Raeder had been right to insist on Operation Weserübung: 'What was certain was that, had the British occupied Norway, our supplies of iron ore from the Scandinavian countries would have ceased.' This, he did not need to add, would have been catastrophic. If the British had been allowed to occupy Norway, they could have advanced on the Baltic to point a dagger at the very heart of the Fatherland. More immediately, Dönitz feared that by controlling Norway's ports and airfields, the British would be in a position to block the Kriegsmarine's 'emergence into the Atlantic via the North Sea' which, in turn, would have made it 'very much more difficult' to sever the transatlantic lifeline.[71]

As it happened, the perceived need to occupy Norway very soon became redundant. By the time the last Allied troops had arrived back from Trondheim, Dunkirk was in German hands, Paris was about to fall and Marshal Pétain was preparing the armistice that would surrender French sovereignty to the Third Reich. This humiliation not only gave Hitler mastery of Europe, it also provided Dönitz with a fistful of French ports in the Bay of Biscay from which to launch his U-boats directly and swiftly at the merchant convoys on which Britain depended for survival. The Battle of the Atlantic was about to start in earnest.

# 4.  The End of the Beginning

In Washington the news of France's collapse was greeted with incredulity and dismay. President Roosevelt was trapped between the Scylla of the threat posed by Hitler and the Charybdis of America's aversion to any involvement in the European imbroglio. He had never been in much doubt about the Führer. Soon after he entered the White House as president for the first time in March 1933, less than two months after the Führer's appointment as German Chancellor, Roosevelt told the French ambassador, 'Hitler is a madman and his counsellors, some of whom I personally know, are even madder than he is.'[1] But with vivid memories of the horrors of the First World War still embedded in the collective memory of the American electorate, and his campaign theme song 'Happy Days Are Here Again' reverberating expectantly across the nation, his initial response to the rise of Hitler was to lead the international call for global disarmament.

By the autumn of 1937 he was still in thrall to the pendulum of congressional opinion, which swung only narrowly from isolationism to appeasement and back again, sometimes hovering over both at once. In his Quarantine Speech of 5 October that year he felt compelled to warn that 'the epidemic of world lawlessness is spreading' and that war was 'a contagion' that could 'engulf states and peoples remote from the original scene of hostilities',[2] but he was careful to say nothing that might be interpreted as an intention on his part to steer his fellow Americans into the vortex of the worsening European crisis. In a carefully calibrated speech that did not mention either Germany or Japan, he tried to navigate a course past both Scylla and Charybdis by promising to shield America from involvement in foreign conflicts without committing himself to eternal appeasement. It was an adroit performance that defined the challenge facing the nation. But despite the dexterity with which he wove together the threads of a subtle argument, the impact of his words served merely to illuminate his political dilemma. The openly isolationist press, led by the Hearst empire and the *Chicago Tribune*, was predictably venomous and, though loyal commentators did not desert him, the speech failed to dispel the corrosion of public scepticism. Two years later, with Britain at war with Germany and Japan at the gates of the Chinese capital, Nanking, the president was still hogtied. He summed up his predicament in a letter to a sympathetic newspaper editor: 'My problem is to get the American people to think of conceivable consequences without scaring [them] into thinking they are going to be dragged into this war.'[3]

It was not just a matter of public relations. Since the summer of 1935 a succession of Neutrality Acts had imposed a wide-ranging embargo on the provision of war materials to any nation at war, regardless of its character or predicament. On 4 January 1939 Roosevelt – who had already lobbied Congress in vain for their repeal – used his annual message to America's legislators to warn that 'our neutrality laws may operate unfairly and unevenly – may actually give aid to the aggressor and deny it to the victim'.[4] Yet again his appeal for the laws to be amended was to no avail. In September he made the pilgrimage to Capitol Hill to make the same pitch. This time Congress relented to the extent of amending the legislation to allow private companies – not the government – to sell arms to belligerents, which in practice meant Britain and France. But this was only authorized on a 'cash-and-carry' basis; no grants, loans or post-dated cheques would be permitted. Roosevelt had to work overtime to secure even this concession, insisting repeatedly that there were no circumstances in which he would lead the United States into a war against Germany.

It was progress of a kind, but Roosevelt still had to take great care to avoid any risk that he might be identified by isolationists either in Congress or in the media as a 'warmonger'. In a deepening international crisis, he had to move with stealth and cunning, making a virtue of ambiguity and masking his intentions without openly practising deception. It was a perilous course which opened him to the charge of vacillation and inconstancy. But so far from being a ditherer, he was a master of timing. Given the prevailing mood of the American electorate, this was the only way in which he could build and sustain a strategy which, though he could not have known it at the time, would eventually ensure the Allied victory in the Second World War.

Roosevelt's predicament was becoming a nightmare for Churchill. In his eight months as First Lord of the Admiralty he had been careful to nurture an informal correspondence with the president, who had written to congratulate him a week after his return to the Cabinet in September. 'It is because you and I occupied similar positions in the World War [Roosevelt had served as Assistant Secretary of the Navy from 1913 to 1920] that I want you to know how glad I am that you are back again in the Admiralty', the president had written. Inviting Churchill to 'keep me in touch personally with anything you want me to know about', he suggested that the First Lord send letters 'through your or my pouch'.[5] Churchill did not let this offer slip by. Now as prime minister, with a touch of self-conscious whimsy, he signed himself 'Former Naval Person' as he initiated a correspondence and, through it, a relationship which would determine Britain's fate. In contrast to Roosevelt, his authority as both Prime Minister and Minister of War – subject only to the will of a generally acquiescent War Cabinet and Parliament – was as absolute as any democratic dictator might have wished; the conduct of all British policy was in his hands to shape and direct as he saw fit. Yet even if, by comparison, Roosevelt was trammelled by domestic constraints, his relationship with Britain was nonetheless one of benefactor to supplicant: America could survive without Britain, but Britain could not survive without America. Churchill was well aware of this and too astute to resent it. Instead he deployed his masterly way with words to lubricate an understanding with the White House which was in due course to give him far more influence with Roosevelt and over American policy than the relative balance of power between them might otherwise have bestowed on him.

However, with the first of the 950 messages which he was to send the president in the next four years, Churchill fared less well than he had hoped. His primary objective was to secure arms and munitions and, above all, several dozen American destroyers, both to combat the U-boat threat and to guard the English Channel against the prospect of a Nazi invasion. To this end, on 15 May 1940, with Germany in occupation of the Netherlands and Belgium, the French army already crumbling before the German blitzkrieg, and the British expeditionary force starting to fall back towards Dunkirk, the Former Naval Person opted for a frontal assault on the White House:

> I trust you realize, Mr President, that the voice and force of the United States may count for nothing if they are withheld too long. You may have a completely subjugated, Nazified Europe established with astonishing

swiftness, and the weight may be more than we can bear. All I ask now is that you should proclaim non-belligerency, which would mean that you would help us with everything short of actually engaging armed forces. Immediate needs are, first of all, the loan of forty or fifty of your older destroyers to bridge the gap between what we have now and the larger construction we put in hand at the beginning of the war.[6]

Shorn of the diplomatic language, Roosevelt's reply the following day gave Churchill short shrift. Without even bothering to dismiss Churchill's request that America declare a state of 'non-belligerency' (and thereby take an inevitable step closer to war by openly siding with Britain and France), he made it clear that 'except with the specific authorization of Congress' it would not be possible to provide the destroyers. And he added drily, 'I am not certain that it would be wise for that suggestion to be made to the Congress at this moment.' As if to seal this rejection, he added 'it seems to be doubtful from the standpoint of our own defense requirements . . . whether we could dispose even temporarily of these destroyers'.[7] In this respect, the president was not dissembling. Although he had authorized a modest expansion of the US Navy during the inter-year wars, it was – in crude terms – still markedly weaker than the Royal Navy: 15 battleships, 5 aircraft carriers, 36 cruisers and 127 destroyers in the former's fleets, compared with 15 battleships, 7 aircraft carriers, 66 cruisers, and 184 destroyers in the latter's.[8]

But this was not all. In the spring of 1940, the main part of the US Navy was already stretched paper-thin by the deployment of its warships not only in the Atlantic but, more heavily, on the West Coast to counter the growing menace posed by the Japanese navy – the world's third largest, but most modern – in the Pacific. Moreover, Washington feared that, with the collapse of France now imminent, Berlin would soon acquire France's naval bases in her West African colonies and from these launch attacks on vulnerable South American states. To counter this nascent threat to its backyard, the Americans would be obliged to patrol that seaboard as well. Hardly surprisingly, the Navy Department – supported by Congress – made it abundantly clear in Washington it would not be possible to surrender even one mothballed First World War destroyer, let alone four dozen as the prime minister had sought.

If Roosevelt hoped his reply to Churchill would be the end of the matter, Churchill was swift to disabuse him. Four days later, on 20 May, with the German panzers breaking through the French lines on all fronts, he appealed again: 'I understand your difficulties, but I am very sorry about the destroyers . . .' To reinforce his chagrin, he postulated an apocalyptic vision in which he and his government were 'finished' by the turn of events: in such circumstances, he warned, others might come 'to parlay amid the ruins', in which case,

> you must not be blind to the fact that the sole remaining bargaining counter with Germany would be the fleet, and if this country was left by the United States to its fate no one would have the right to blame those responsible if they made the best terms they could for the surviving inhabitants. Excuse me, Mr President, putting this nightmare bluntly. Evidently I could not answer for my successors who in utter despair and helplessness might well have to accommodate themselves to the German will.[9]

This was an astute thrust which went to the heart of Washington's growing fear that the Axis powers, reinforced by the acquisition of the British and French navies, might, before long, not only rule the high seas but, in ever closer alliance with Japan, all the oceans. The president did not reply.

In the critical days between the middle of May and the middle of June, American public opinion veered wildly. On the one hand, the polls showed a clear majority in favour of supporting the beleaguered peoples of France and Britain; on the other, when asked specifically about the supply of armaments, there was a similar majority against. Roosevelt railed against isolationists and Nazi fellow-travellers. When Charles Lindbergh, exploiting his celebrity status as the first man to fly solo across the Atlantic, used a national radio broadcast on 19 May to declare that America was not under any threat that could not easily be seen off and that no aid should be sent to Britain or France, the president raged privately that the argument 'could not have been better put if it had been written by Goebbels himself'.[10]

It was not merely a matter of public opinion, however. The United States was in no position to wage war even if the president had been so minded. The nation's armed forces had been run down so steeply following the end of the First World War that, as late as 1939, Roosevelt's newly appointed chief of staff, General George Marshall, had taken himself up to Capitol Hill to lobby Congress in person, arguing that it was dangerous and irresponsible for the world's largest economy to rely on armed forces which were weaker than those of sixteen other countries, including Spain and Portugal. He made little headway. In exasperation, he warned Roosevelt that if the necessary resources were not appropriated, 'I don't know what is going to happen to this country.'[11]

But it took another year for Congress to get the message. Only as the German offensive on the far shores of the Atlantic intensified did the nation's legislators eventually realize that it would be impossible for the United States to immunize itself from the virus of Nazism merely by averting its gaze. In the last days of May 1940 they finally agreed to pour resources into the defence of the nation, appropriating even more than the billions of dollars the president had requested for that purpose. The standing army was to be expanded fourfold, from 280,000 to 1,200,000 men, the National Guard was to be put fully at Roosevelt's disposal, and 16 million civilians were soon to be conscripted; America's industrial complex would be cranked up to deliver a throughput of 50,000 aeroplanes; and the shipyards would begin a crash programme to provide the navy with 9 new battleships, 31 cruisers and 181 destroyers. 'The problem', as historian Waldo Heinrichs noted, 'was no longer money but time and capacity.'[12] From the French and British perspective, he might have added, it was also that, in the collective mind of the American people, these programmes were intended only for the defence of the United States, not to prop up a disintegrating Europe.

In growing desperation, Paul Reynaud, the French premier, supported with passion by Churchill, besought the president for direct military assistance. Roosevelt responded with warm words. In reply to the French leader, he cabled

> Your message of June 10 has moved me very deeply. As I have already stated to you and to Mr. Churchill, this Government is doing everything in its power to make available to the Allied Governments the material you so urgently require . . . This is because of our faith in and support of the ideals for which the Allies are fighting.[13]

Encouraged by this declaration, the prime minister urged Roosevelt to reiterate this promissory note in public, believing (as he confided to the French premier) that if he did so, the United States would inevitably be driven 'to take the only remaining step, namely, becoming a belligerent in form as she already has constituted herself in fact'.[14] To his disappointment, however, the president refused to fall into this elephant trap. To release his cable into the public realm, Roosevelt explained, would be widely misinterpreted as a promise of 'military participation in support of the Allied Governments' – for which, he reminded the prime minister, 'there is of course no authority under our constitution except in the Congress to make any commitment of this nature'.[15] It was 'imperative', he added, to avoid 'any possible misunderstanding' about this. Exasperated by this rebuff, Churchill reacted sharply: 'I understand all your difficulties with American public opinion and Congress,' he wrote tartly, 'but events are moving downward at a pace where they will pass beyond the control of American public opinion when at last it is ripened.'[16]

By this time it was too late for France. But Churchill detected a chink in the presidential armour that he could widen to Britain's advantage. More than once, Roosevelt had laid bare his deepest strategic anxiety. Before the collapse of France, he had written, 'It is most important to remember that the French and British Fleets continue [in] mastery of the Atlantic and other oceans . . . Naval power in world affairs still carries the lesson of history.'[17] In a note to Churchill alone, he reiterated, 'As naval people, you and I fully understand the vital strength of the fleet in being, and command of the seas means in the long run the saving of democracy and the recovery of those suffering temporary reverses.'[18] With France on the verge of signing an armistice with the German occupiers, Churchill moved at once to exploit the opportunity that this disaster had inadvertently given him.

Commenting later that it was 'a matter of life and death', he wrote again to the president on 15 June, to reiterate his warning about what might happen 'if resistance were beaten down here': a new government would come to power in Britain that 'might present to a shattered or starving nation an almost irresistible case for submission to the Nazi will'. In this case, the country would become 'a vassal state of the Hitler Empire', the Royal Navy would be at the Third Reich's disposal and, 'if it were joined by the Fleets of Japan, France, and Italy,* overwhelming sea-power would be in Hitler's hands . . .' To drive this message home, he added,

---

* Mussolini, sensing an Axis victory in the offing, had declared war on Britain five days earlier.

If we go down you may have a United States of Europe under the Nazi command far more numerous, far stronger, far better armed than the New World. I know well, Mr President, that your eye will have already searched these depths, but I feel I have the right to place on record the vital manner in which American interests are at stake in our battle.[19]

Once more, he followed this apocalyptic prospect by pleading with Roosevelt to release the US warships for which he had asked a month earlier. Explaining that 'the bulk of our destroyers' would have to be deployed against the threat of a German invasion, he asked rhetorically, 'how shall we be able to cope with a German-Italian attack on the food and trade by which we live?' To offer these destroyers, he concluded, would be a 'practical and possibly decisive step which can be taken at once, and I urge most earnestly that you will weigh my words'.[20] If Roosevelt did so, he must have found them wanting when balanced against competing priorities. The triple lock of American public opinion, the threat from Japan, and the paucity of warships available to the US Navy, still counted far more with him than even the most eloquent exposition of the apocalypse foretold by the British prime minister. Once again, he failed to respond; the destroyers remained on the American side of the Atlantic.

Opinion in Washington was hardening against supplying any war materials to London. In a phrase that eighteen months later Churchill was gleefully to hurl back at defeatists in Congress, the simile doing the rounds of the Capitol Building was that Britain, following the rest of Europe, was soon to have 'its neck wrung like a chicken' and it was too late to stop it. Roosevelt's military planners expressed the same sentiment but less crudely, advising him that the supply of weaponry should be made 'only if Great Britain displayed an ability to withstand German assault . . .'[21] A few days later, as though publicly to pinion the president to its will, Congress went even further 'by forbidding the sale of Army and Navy supplies [to any nation, including Britain] unless service chiefs declared it unessential to the national defence'.[22] Roosevelt was not only boxed in by isolationism per se but by his own political ambition. He was only weeks away from accepting his party's nomination for an unprecedented third term as president. With the race for the White House promising to be an exceptionally close contest against Wendell Wilkie, a challenger who had already unfurled an isolationist banner, it was hardly a moment to ignore the mood of the nation – especially as he rated Britain's chances of survival as 'about one in three'.[23]

Towards the end of June 1940 Otto Kretschmer, who had already made a name for himself by sinking the *Danmark* six months earlier and soon afterwards by adding a British destroyer to his list of kills, was about to enjoy the fruits of Britain's predicament even more thoroughly. Singled out for promotion by Dönitz, he had been plucked from the small coastal Type IIC boat, U-23, to take command of a much larger and more powerful U-boat, the new Type VIIB, which had a displacement of 750 tons and a top speed on the surface of over seventeen knots. Armed with fourteen torpedoes, U-99 had a range that offered the young ace the prospect of many more kills than he could possibly have achieved in U-23. Kretschmer did not waste his chance. In the course of the next nine months he was to pioneer a devastating means of attack and to sink a greater tonnage of merchant shipping than any other U-boat commander. In the process, he would become the most decorated hero in the Kriegsmarine.

U-99's campaign began inauspiciously on 17 June, when Kretschmer's course took him along the Norwegian coast, where the *Scharnhorst*, newly repaired from the damage inflicted by *Acasta*, was on patrol. Mistaking U-99 for a British submarine, one of the battleship's aircraft dive-bombed the semi-submerged vessel and very nearly sent Kretschmer and his forty-four-man crew to the bottom. U-99 was forced to return to Wilhelmshaven for repairs. By early July, though, he was on patrol in the Atlantic, fully laden with torpedoes and with enough fuel for at least a month at sea. Soon after midday on the 5th, he saw a steamship zigzagging (the standard procedure for avoiding a torpedo attack) in his direction. The vessel, a 2,000-ton freighter, failed to see the German submarine until too late. Peering through U-99's periscope, Kretschmer lined up the merchantman in his sights and ordered his first torpedo to be released. Within a few seconds there was flash followed by a dull roar and U-99's first victim was claimed. As her crew scrambled into the lifeboats, her stern tipped up and the ship broke in two. Adopting a practice for which he was to become renowned, Kretschmer eased towards the lifeboats and spoke to the ship's captain. Establishing the name of the sunken vessel – the *Magog* – and that none of the crew had been hurt, he pointed the shipwrecked mariners towards the Irish coast, about fifty-eight nautical miles distant, and ordered his wireless officer, Jupp Kassel, to hand over a bottle of brandy to help them on their way. As U-99 made off, he heard *Magog*'s skipper shout out his appreciation for the gesture.

Two days later, Kretschmer sighted another merchant ship, the *Bissen*. The Swedish cargo vessel was sailing alone and he sank her with his second torpedo. Her crew of twenty survived to be picked up by a British destroyer. Later the same day, he found a third victim, the *Sea Glory*, also sailing independently. This time every member of her twenty-nine-man crew went down with their ship. Late that night U-99's lookout sighted the outlines of several ships sailing as a group. It was Convoy HX53, forty-four ships on their way from Halifax, Nova Scotia, to Liverpool. This was the first convoy to be sighted by Kretschmer and his first attempt at a manoeuvre which had yet to be tried by any other U-boat commander. Instead of treading water until the convoy drew parallel with the U-boat, he accelerated until he was well in front of the foremost ships. He then submerged and allowed U-99 to drift back below the surface until the convoy was passing directly overhead. He watched through his periscope as the merchant ships rumbled past to port and starboard. His intention was to pick them off one by one as they came into his sights. Selecting a suitable target, he gave the order 'Fire!' but the torpedo settings had been wrongly adjusted and the weapon veered harmlessly away into the night. However, U-99 had not been detected and Kretschmer fired again. The same thing happened. Finally, more by chance than design, one of his stern torpedoes hit the *Humber Arm*, a 5,000-ton freighter. The flash as the torpedo made contact illuminated the sky. U-99 dived to weave a way out of the convoy and to give Kretschmer a chance to investigate why the torpedoes had malfunctioned.

U-99 was silent and motionless beneath the surface but not forgotten. After a short while, Kassel's hydrophones detected the sound of an approaching warship. In his War Diary, Kretschmer noted, 'I think my crew are going to get their baptism of depth charging this time. Escort approaching fast as though to attack.' Four minutes later he added, 'This is the attack.'[24] Travelling at the U-boat's maximum underwater speed of seven knots, he dived to 350 feet and reduced speed to save the life of the batteries that supplied the electric motors which drove the propellers. The British escort had picked up an ASDIC signal which pinpointed U-99's position. Again and again it ran in to release a battery of depth charges, the blasts from which shook the U-boat from stem to stern. The battering lasted for two hours, by which time the oxygen supply to the U-boat had begun to fail. Kretschmer ordered his crew to put on their breathing masks which were connected to cases of alkali that partially purified the stale air. To conserve air and energy, the men lay down at their stations. The destroyer did not give up. Its bombardment lasted another four hours.

By this time, according to Kretschmer's biographer (on the basis of extensive interviews with U-99's commander), 'Most of the crew were now breathing in large gasps behind their masks, and it was obvious that they could not stay alive much longer.'[25] As the depth charges exploded, U-99's hull juddered so violently that it seemed the hull must soon split under the pressure. But, according to Kassel, who was on his hydrophones in the control room, Kretschmer not only appeared unperturbed but sat nearby apparently engrossed in a novel. After a while, the wireless operator noticed that Kretschmer had not turned a single page. He looked more closely and saw that the book was upside down. The nearest the U-99's captain came to revealing any emotion was in his War Diary, where he wrote, 'Each noise was strange, and every roll and crack inside the U-boat seemed to herald the end.'[26]

By this point, U-99's batteries were almost drained. The propellers no longer had the power to maintain the vessel horizontally on an even keel. Gradually U-99 sank towards the bottom until it was 700 feet under the surface, 150 feet below the depth at which the Type VII was certified to dive safely. Kretschmer estimated that very soon they would have to surface to avoid being crushed by the pressure of water. Yet, after searching for the U-boat for no less than fourteen hours and releasing 127 depth charges, the attacker eventually gave up the chase. In the early hours of the following morning U-99 finally rose to the surface. Kretschmer had just enough strength to open the hatch and climb on to the conning tower. A foul yellow air belched up from below. As the diesel engines came back to life, the crew crawled up behind their commander to lie under the dark canopy of an Atlantic sky and gulp in the fresh night air. Kretschmer noted: 'We all felt like school-children at Christmas time. Everything about the depth-charging had been new to us, and we didn't know what to expect next . . . Now we have received all the presents the enemy can give us. We all have a fresh confidence in our ship.'[27]

He was not alone. His fellow ace Günther Prien and his crew in U-47 were similarly elated. In the last half of June they were hunting for prey in the Western Approaches. At first they had little success. They torpedoed a lone freighter, piled high with crates containing aeroplane parts, but, for a week thereafter, they scoured the seas in vain. On the seventh day, however, they came across a convoy of some thirty ships only lightly escorted. 'They made a lovely silhouette against the evening sky,' Prien wrote later. 'I chose the three biggest ones, a tanker of twelve thousand tons, another of seven thousand tons and a third, a freighter of seven thousand tons.' Prien peered into his periscope and gave the orders to fire. The first two torpedoes hit their targets. The third, which was released a moment too early, missed its intended victim but smashed into another. Three torpedoes: three ships and U-47's killing spree was not over.

Two days later Prien came across a cargo ship carrying grain; on this occasion he ordered the ship's crew to take to their lifeboats before sinking their vessel with a volley of shells. The following day he scored again, sinking two more cargo ships, one laden with timber, the other with diesel. On 29 June he sunk the 4,000-ton *Empire Toucan*, noting admiringly that her radio operator stayed on board until the last moment, continuing to signal her position until, carrying a red light above his head, he finally leapt into the sea. 'As he struck the water,' Prien recalled, 'the red light went out. We stopped at the place where he had disappeared but we could not find him. Then shadows appeared in the north, dark shapes in the dusk, probably destroyers. As we had only one usable torpedo left, we decided to push off.' His own radio officer picked up the *Empire Toucan*'s last message: 'Torpedoed by U-boat sinking fast SOS.'

The following day Prien decided to use what he thought was his last functioning torpedo to sink a Greek freighter. He was about to turn for home when he was told that the torpedo crew had managed to repair a fault in another of U-47's torpedoes which had failed to fire earlier:

> It was a clear and calm summer morning. We were steaming along in the vicinity of the [Irish] coast. The lookout reported 'A steamer on the starboard bow.' A huge vessel with two funnels approached us out of the sun in wild zigzags . . . 'Fellows,' I said and I felt their excitement. 'Cross your fingers and let's try and get it.' Then the command, 'Fire'.

Then we waited counting, counting. Painfully, slowly, the seconds slipped by. The ship was a great distance away, too great a distance I feared. Then suddenly right amidship[s] a column of water rose up far beyond the mast and immediately after we heard the crash of the detonation.

Prien's victim was a cruise liner, the *Arandora Star*. Originally painted white, except for her two red, white and blue funnels, she had been nicknamed 'The Wedding Cake'. On the outbreak of war, she was requisitioned by the government and repainted battleship grey, soon after being used to evacuate troops from Norway and, very recently, from Dunkirk. On this occasion, she was sailing from Liverpool to St John's in Newfoundland, with some 1,200 German and Italian citizens and eighty-six prisoners of war who were on their way to be incarcerated in a Canadian internment camp, when the torpedo struck on 1 July 1940. The survivors spoke of the chaos below decks as the lights went out, glass shattered and 'ruptured pipes spewed out noxious fumes. Those rushing up the companionways towards the open air found their escape barred by the barbed wire the guards had secured in place to keep the internees below decks.'[28] British soldiers, shocked into immobility, were reported to have remained on guard, bayonets fixed, to prevent their prisoners escaping. Though many nonetheless found a way to the upper decks, hundreds of passengers, notably a number of elderly Italians, were trapped below. Those who did escape had not been given any emergency drill. Some were too terrified to jump into the sea; others leapt and broke their necks in the process.

From the conning tower of U-47, Prien watched the *Arandora Star*'s crew hurriedly lower the lifeboats: 'hundreds of heads . . . bobbing in the water . . . It was not possible to help them because the coast was too close and the ship was still afloat. On her fo'c's'le a number of guns were clearly visible. We retreated underwater. When a few minutes later we surfaced only the lifeboats were visible on calm sea.'[29] Within half an hour of being struck, the *Arandora Star* had reared up and disappeared beneath the ocean's surface. More than 800 prisoners, internees, guards and crew lost their lives – among them 243 of his fellow countrymen, though Prien would never learn that. He and his crew left the scene celebrating a tour of duty which they judged – over-optimistically – had netted them a record 66,587 tons of enemy shipping. For weeks afterwards the decomposing bodies of those who had perished were washed up along the coastline of the British Isles.

The ease with which both Prien and Kretschmer had been able to harvest their catch was, for the British, a harbinger of far worse to come. In June alone, Dönitz's U-boats had sunk fifty-eight merchant ships, with a total displacement of 284,113 tons. This was only a little under half the number lost from all causes – bombings, mines, and collisions – in the entire three-month period from March to May but less than half the 600,000 tons a month at which Dönitz was aiming. Nonetheless, though the number of operational U-boats was to remain very small, these statistics were about to soar. It was the moment for which Dönitz had been waiting and planning. During the battle for Norway, he had been in a state of perpetual frustration and frequent rage because the malfunctioning torpedoes had made his small fleet virtually useless. Despite this, in the eight months of so-called 'phoney war', a handful of U-boats had sunk no fewer than 240 merchant ships on their way to and from Britain. Although these kills had come at a price – twenty-two U-boats had been sunk – the Kriegsmarine had not only been able to replace these vessels but the defective torpedoes had been re-engineered and – as Kretschmer, Prien and other aces like Joachim Schepke and Erich Topp had demonstrated – these weapons were now far more reliable than they had been six weeks earlier. With only eight or nine U-boats operating at any one time, they and their fellow U-boat commanders were making a mockery of the complacent belief of the pre-war Admiralty that the U-boat would not constitute a significant threat to Britain's trade routes and that, in any case, the Royal Navy's surface ships were ineffably superior to any challenge from the Kriegsmarine.

The fall of France in June 1940 transformed the strategic map of the maritime war greatly to Dönitz's advantage: 'it would mean that we should now have an exit from our "backyard" . . . on the very shores of the Atlantic, the ocean in which the war at sea against Britain must be finally decided'.[30] Rather than sailing from their German bases through the North Sea and around the coast of Scotland to reach the killing grounds of the Atlantic, the U-boat fleet could now access the major sea lanes from the French ports in the Bay of Biscay which were now occupied by their own forces. The potential impact was game-changing.

Even before the ink was dry on the Franco-German armistice agreement, Dönitz had ordered a train to be on standby at Wilhelmshaven, laden with torpedoes and other equipment, ready to head for the Bay of Biscay, where he had elected to base his headquarters just down the road from the port of Lorient at a château in the small village of Kerneval. On 23 June he went in person to survey his new demesne, where 'from the windows of the grand salon which let in the tangy smells of the foreshore and fish jetty immediately beyond',[31] he could see the open sea in one direction and, in the other, the quays where the U-boats would soon be moored. By the end of the month, the first U-boats began to arrive in Lorient and within days the port was a functioning base on the new front line. Some newly recruited U-boat commanders were so certain that Britain would soon crumble that they feared the war would be over before they had seen any action for themselves. 'There's no need to get excited,' Dönitz told them. 'In the many months that lie ahead you'll get so much fighting that you'll be fed up to the back teeth with the whole business. Don't forget that we're fighting the strongest sea power in the world.'[32]

This may have been so, but the Royal Navy was stretched to breaking point by the summer of 1940. On 4 August Churchill conveyed his deepening concern in a note to both his successor as First Lord, A. V. Alexander, and to the First Sea Lord, Admiral Pound. 'The repeated losses in the North-western Approaches are most grievous . . . No doubt this is largely due to the shortage of destroyers through invasion precautions. Let me know at once the whole outfit of destroyers, corvettes, and Asdic trawlers, together with aircraft, available and deployed in this area . . . we cannot go on like this.'[33] It was not only U-boats. Two pocket battleships, the *Admiral Scheer* and the *Admiral Hipper*, along with half a dozen merchant raiders – fast cargo vessels armed with powerful guns and torpedoes but usually disguised as innocent traders – were also marauding through the ocean, disrupting the flow of supplies across the Atlantic. Although these surface raiders sank relatively few ships (*Scheer*, the most successful of the Kriegsmarine's commerce raiders, sank no more than seventeen vessels in a five-month voyage during which she covered 46,000 miles), their very presence posed a threat that the Admiralty could not ignore.

In his Mansion House speech as First Lord, seven months earlier, Churchill had stressed that the safest way for merchant ships to travel was in convoy, a view which more shipowners came to share. As a result the convoys grew in number and size. However, except for those ferrying troops to various fronts, they were still poorly protected (often by no more than a couple of small warships) against the risk of being selected as prey by the *Scheer* or the *Hipper*. For this reason, Atlantic convoys were subjected to frequent delays or postponement. In turn, this disrupted the flow of supplies from which, among others, the shipowners derived their income. To avoid these delays and the congestion they caused at the ports, some of these owners continued to require their skippers to choose the Russian roulette option of sailing independently.

The shortage of escort warships to protect every major shipping route across the great oceans of the world – on which the nation depended for its very means of survival – was reaching critical proportions that were relished by Admiral Dönitz. By June, in a measured assessment of the opportunity his U-boats now savoured, he was able to pinpoint three fundamental reasons why they were soon to enjoy their 'First Happy Time': 'The U-boats encountered a large number of vessels sailing independently while convoys were weakly escorted, and not all of them accompanied by aircraft.'[34]

By August 1940 the Admiralty faced an intractable dilemma. The only available way of protecting the Atlantic convoys as they lumbered to and fro across the ocean was to transfer Royal Navy vessels from the flotillas then patrolling along England's southern and eastern coastlines against the prospect of a German invasion. It was an unpalatable choice which led to a dispute between the admirals and particularly between the commander-in-chief of the Home Fleet, Admiral Forbes, based in Rosyth, and his fellow commander-in-chief charged to protect Britain's southern flank. The stark character of the division between them could hardly have been more fundamental; in the words of the navy's official historian, it 'lay only in the question whether the means employed to defeat invasion were the best, having regard to the country's other vital need – to avoid starvation'. The preponderant view in the Admiralty was against Forbes, who insisted that the Royal Navy should not be 'tied down to provide passive defence to our country' when it could be better used 'to carry out its proper function – offensively against the enemy and in defence of our trade'.[35] To this end, he urged that destroyers and armed trawlers be diverted from the English Channel to escort duties in the Atlantic. Throughout August and into September 1940, as the Luftwaffe intensified its attempt to soften up the nation's defences in preparation for the presumed launch of Operation Sealion (the code-name for the invasion of Britain), the admirals were unable to reconcile their competing perspectives.

Without the fifty US destroyers which he had so far failed to secure from Roosevelt, the prime minister was no less at a loss than the Admiralty. There was nothing for it: he would attempt to breach the White House barricades once again. Advising the president at the end of July that four British destroyers had been sunk in the previous ten days and a further seven had been damaged, he warned that this rate of attrition was impossible to sustain: 'If we cannot get a substantial reinforcement the whole fate of the war may be decided by this minor and easily remediable factor.' This was to raise the stakes yet again, but he pressed further:

> I am confident, now that you know exactly how we stand, that you will leave nothing undone to ensure that fifty or sixty of your oldest destroyers are sent to me at once. I can fit them very quickly with Asdics and use them against U-boats on the Western Approaches, and so keep the more modern and better-gunned craft for the Narrow Seas against invasion. Mr. President, with great respect I must tell you that in the long history of the world this is a thing to do *now* . . . I feel entitled and bound to put the gravity and urgency of the position before you.[36]

Serendipitously, Roosevelt came under pressure at this point from the Century Group, an assortment of politicians and business leaders who were both Anglophile and interventionist,[37] who suggested that the destroyers might be exchanged for 'immediate naval and air concessions in British possessions in the Western Hemisphere'.[38] Finally convinced by Churchill's latest plea that Britain's very survival – and therefore America's strategic interests – was indeed at stake, the president seized on this idea and proposed it to the prime minister. As both men knew, it would be a cruelly lopsided deal from which Britain would obtain temporary relief in return for handing the United States a ninety-nine-year lease on a chain of seven island strongholds (Newfoundland, Bermuda, the Bahamas, Jamaica, St Lucia, Trinidad and British Guiana) in strategic waters stretching from Newfoundland to the Caribbean. But Churchill had little choice but to accept.

Inevitably the president was anxious to sell the trade-off to his fellow Americans as a great bargain secured at no risk. In a letter to Senator Walsh, the chairman of the Naval Affairs Committee, who threatened to torpedo any such deal, Roosevelt pointed to the great strategic bene-fit to the United States of acquiring the seven military bases in return for 'fifty ships, which are on their last legs anyway . . . By the way, the fifty destroyers are the same type of ship which we have been from time to time striking from the naval list and selling for scrap for, I think, $4,000 or $5,000 per destroyer . . .'[39]

With the outlines of a deal swiftly agreed, Churchill and Roosevelt found themselves at loggerheads over its presentation to their respective electorates. While the president wanted to publicize it as a financial and strategic coup d'état for the White House, Churchill was equally deter-mined to conceal the true nature of what he had agreed. Acutely sensitive to the mood in Parliament, he reflected that 'if the issue were presented to the British as a naked trading away of British possessions for the sake of the fifty destroyers it would certainly encounter vehe-ment opposition'.[40] After a prolonged correspondence between London and Washington, the two leaders and their aides engineered a com-promise that dissembled by omission but duly satisfied both Congress and Parliament. Roosevelt was persuaded to use a form of words ambiguous enough to save the prime minister's face but not so complicit as to leave Congress in any doubt about the real nature of the contract while Churchill was spared the humiliation of announcing the terms of the trade-off; on 31 August, he described it as 'simply measures of mutual assistance rendered to one another by two friendly nations, in a spirit of confidence, sympathy and goodwill . . .'[41]

In his letter to Senator Walsh, Roosevelt had volunteered, 'I am abso-lutely certain that this particular deal will not get us into war anyway unless Germany wishes to attack us.'[42] Conversely, although Churchill told the Commons that 'only very ignorant persons would suggest that the transfer of American destroyers to the British flag . . . affects in the smallest degree the non-belligerency of the United States', he derived private comfort precisely because he felt sure that in fact it 'brought the United States definitely nearer to us and to the war . . . [and] marked the passage of the United States from being neutral to non-belligerent'.[43] This was no less important to him than the fact that the scrap-value destroyers were finally on their way across the Atlantic – a material, as well as a symbolic, demonstration of America's growing commitment to the British cause.

One day in early June 1940 John Julius Cooper (later Viscount Norwich), the ten-year-old son of the Minister of Information, Duff Cooper, had a 'disgusting' lunch with his mother, Lady Diana Cooper, at his 'rather seedy' boarding school in Northamptonshire. Lady Diana was a noted beauty, actress, and writer, and socialite whose grace, wit and intelligence was in great demand. On this occasion, though, he recalled, 'She wasn't her normal ebullient self. And at the end of lunch she said "I've got some news for you. We are going to send you off to America next week." She thought I was going to burst into tears.'[44] So far from feeling any distress, the small boy was intoxicated by the vision of skyscrapers, Hollywood and the Wild West. Some days later, accompanied by his nanny, he was aboard the SS *Washington* bound for New York. A little under two years earlier his father, Duff Cooper, had achieved great prominence when he'd resigned from Chamberlain's government in protest at the Munich Agreement, declaring that he might have been able to accept 'War with honour or peace with dishonour', but that 'war with dishonour' was too much. Echoing Churchill, he thereafter became a very public opponent of appeasement.

On a lecture tour of America, in the late autumn of 1939, Cooper had provoked the wrath of isolationists. Arriving at one venue in Brooklyn with Diana, he found it surrounded by a phalanx of police, nightsticks at the ready. Outside the hall, a group of bedraggled young men stood with placards bearing slogans like 'Send Duff Home', 'We Won't be Dragged into War' and 'Don't Listen to English Lies'. But inside, where even more police were in place, the audience did listen and even cheered when he left by the stage door.[45] As a result of his stance, Cooper was presumed to be high on the Nazi 'hit list' in the event of invasion. Convinced that their offspring would be seized by the Germans and held hostage for her husband, Diana decided that her only child, on whom she doted, should be evacuated to a place of safety on the other side of the Atlantic. The young Cooper was one of an estimated 14,000 children whose parents had decided to use their relative wealth to evacuate their children abroad in this period. But when Churchill heard that the child of a government minister was 'fleeing the country' he was furious. Duff Cooper temporized but, according to his son, 'when my mother had made up her mind, there was nothing to be done'.[46]

Most of the passengers on John Julius's voyage to the New World in SS *Washington* were American families, some with very young children, similarly fleeing from the storm clouds. The children played shuffle-board, visited the 'Novelty' shop and put on a cabaret, at the end of which five of the children sang 'God Save the King' out of tune and the ten-year-old John Julius wrote home to his mother, 'I do hope the air raids on London are not too bad . . . I do wish you both were here.'[47]

In fact the Luftwaffe's onslaught was intensifying. From her privil-eged vantage point, Lady Diana Cooper chronicled the impact of the bombardment on the British capital for the benefit of her beloved son (who, by September, was settled in Upper Canada College, a Toronto boarding school regarded as that nation's 'Eton'):

> September 8th – and a bad news Sunday. The raid last night . . . was on a far bigger scale that we have had before – damage and death and fire and I fear much agony . . . Chapel Street [the family home in Westmin-ster which they had closed up for the duration] may be a heap of ruins for all I know.
>
> Sept. 9th. Another appalling raid on London last night . . . I had a dinner party tonight for the American Ambassador* . . . There's a bad A.A. gun just outside that bangs away and bombs drop *all* the time but our talk drowned out some of the noise and a glass of wine gave me a bit of Dutch courage. It's really not the place to sleep, the eighth floor [they had taken residence in the Dorchester Hotel where the rooms were cheaper near the roof]. I never closed an eye but Papa sleeps like a baby in a pram.
>
> Sept. 10th. Here there are five or six raids a day . . . One could bear it better if one could see any end to it . . . Is it the beginning of an invasion scheme or is it just to break our spirit? It won't do that.
>
> Sept. 17th. A terrific night of bombardment. A bomb fell in Park Lane not fifty yards away, another blew all the glass out of Berkeley Square. Papa has just gone to the meeting of the House of Commons. There's a

---

*Joseph Kennedy, whose visceral Anglophobia was barely constrained by his diplo-matic duties. He was relieved of his role in October 1940 to be replaced by John Winant.

raid on as usual and I'm terribly afraid of the Huns bombing it and getting a rich bag. Winston should have just begun to make his statement.
I do hope he cuts it short.[48]

He did not. In his secret session on that day, Churchill referred
briefly to the destruction wrought by the German bombers in the vicinity of Whitehall before providing the House with the evidence on which
he had based his public warning that 'at any moment a major assault
may be launched upon this Island'. More than 1,700 self-propelled barges
and more than 200 ships, some of them very large, were already gathered in the Channel ports now occupied by Germany. 'If this is all
pretence and stratagem to pin us down here, it has been executed with
surprising thoroughness and on a gigantic scale.' Some of these vessels
were 'fully loaded with all the munitions needed for the invading armies
and to beat us utterly. The shipping available and now assembled is sufficient to carry in one voyage nearly *half* a million men.'[49]

While Churchill was delivering this bleak assessment of Britain's
prospects, an 11,000-ton liner, the SS *City of Benares*, four days out of
Liverpool, was ploughing into an Atlantic storm some 200 miles
south-west of Rockall bound for Quebec. Among the 407 passengers
were ninety children aged between five and fifteen whose parents had
decided it was better for them to be sent across a hazardous ocean to a
place of safety in Canada than to face the prospective perils of the Blitz
and Nazi invasion. Their circumstances were markedly different from
those which had been enjoyed by Diana Cooper's son a few months earlier. These evacuees were travelling courtesy of the Children's Overseas
Reception Board (CORB), a body hastily set up by the government –
with Churchill's reluctant approval – after the fall of France.

CORB was a means-tested scheme designed largely to counter widespread coverage in the press of 'the children of the well-to-do posing
happily on the country estates of Long Island and Quebec'. Editorial writ-
ers asked an obvious but provocative question: 'Why should the son of the
rich man sleep in security in New York's gay lighted towers while the son
of the poor man dozed in crowded shelters below our dangerous cities,
menaced by the bomber's drone?' CORB was bombarded with applications from families hoping to billet their children with one of the many
hundreds of American and Canadian citizens who had responded to Britain's plight by offering their homes as refuge. So great was the demand

that by 4 July CORB's in-tray had been swamped by 211,000 applications and the scheme was abruptly suspended, although all those who had already been enrolled remained free to take up their berths.[50]

Around a dozen CORB ships had left the embarkation port of Liverpool with some 2,000 child evacuees before the Dutch liner, the *Volendam*, was torpedoed off Ireland on 31 August 1940 with 230 children on board. The vessel sank but, perhaps because all the children were rescued, this near-tragedy was not enough to deter the parents of a further ninety children, who were entrusted to a party of 'escorts' who had volunteered to chaperone their offspring to Canada on the *City of Benares*, which had left Liverpool on 13 September at the head of OB213, a convoy of twenty vessels which was escorted by one destroyer and two sloops.*

The *Benares* had run into heavy weather soon after leaving the Mersey, but, driving in to head seas at eight and a half knots, the convoy was making steady if uncomfortable progress across the Atlantic. As Churchill rose to address the Commons on 17 September the vessel passed longitude 20°W, the point beyond which, the Admiralty had decreed, U-boats would pose little or no danger. Their allotted task duly accomplished, the escort vessels turned back, unaware that U-48, commanded by Heinrich Bleichrodt, was lurking some sixty miles further to the west, and had already detected the slow-moving convoy.

A little after ten o'clock that night, the *Benares* shuddered violently and the ship was plunged into darkness. Mary Cornish, one of the volunteers escorting the children, heard 'a muffled thud, followed by a noise of crashing glass and splintering woodwork'. U-48's third torpedo – the first two had missed – struck the hull amidships, passing just below the cabins where the children had been put to bed some hours earlier. Cornish, who had at once set off in the dark to find her fifteen charges, found herself 'gazing down into a black abyss . . . a vast hole in the centre of the ship, a hole that was quickly filling with the sea'.[51]

---

* Sloops were designed before the war as escort vessels. At a length of 266 feet and with a speed of up to nineteen knots, they were longer and faster but more expensive to build than the far more numerous corvettes which succeeded them. Similar in size to a destroyer but very much slower, the sloop cruised at half its speed but required one-tenth the horsepower, which meant it consumed much less fuel and had far greater range.

Helped by members of the crew, she and her fellow escorts managed to extricate the children from the debris and took them to the promenade deck, where they waited for the order to abandon ship, which came at 10.20 p.m. 'Don't worry,' Cornish recalled telling them repeatedly, 'it's only a torpedo.' After she was sure that her children were safe in one of the lifeboats, she waited until she was ordered to climb into Lifeboat No. 12, which was swinging from its davits nearby. By this time the emergency lighting had come on to illuminate the commotion about her. People were sliding down ropes from the upper deck. There were shouts and cries as the boats were lowered into a heaving sea. One capsized as it hit the water, the children screaming as they fell into the sea. The crew lowered rafts and threw down lifebelts for them but no one on deck could see how many of them thus saved themselves or were drowned.

Lifeboat No. 12 was not lowered until Fourth Officer Cooper had convinced himself that there were no more children trapped alive below decks. The water had risen swiftly and was now waist-high in their cabins; all who could escape to the upper decks must have done so. Cooper boarded No. 12 and the lifeboat swung wildly but securely down to the water below. As they drew slowly away from the sinking liner, Mary Cornish looked in wonderment at the towering, foam-crested waves that now bore down on them. At 11 p.m., still ablaze with lights, she watched as – in the bald words of the official report later submitted by Cooper – 'the vessel commenced to go down stern first[;] raising her bow out of the water she appeared to list heavily to port, then disappeared'.[52] Although the lifeboat was already crowded, Cooper picked up more survivors from the water until it was filled with six small boys, two chaperones (a Roman Catholic priest and Cornish), a Polish shipping executive, four British crew members (one of whom was a ship's steward) and thirty-two Lascars (the name given to those Asian – usually Indian – sailors recruited by shipowners to serve in the merchant navy as deckhands and orderlies), who shivered in a huddle on the bottom of the boat.

Later that morning, Cooper ordered the steward to hand out the first rations – a sardine, a biscuit and a dipper (a small cylinder which held a quarter of a pint) for each person – while Cornish, an accomplished musician, tried to maintain the children's morale by organizing a sing-song – 'Roll Out the Barrel', 'There'll Always Be an England' and

'Run Rabbit Run' – telling stories and reminding them that this was 'the greatest adventure of their lives'. When she asked them 'Which would you rather: be bombed at home, or torpedoed in the Atlantic?' the boys were unanimous in their view that torpedoes were more exciting.[53] But spirits soon sagged. The sea raged, the boat bucked and reared, the wind shrieked, the mast groaned, and the cold bit through their clothing. They were short of blankets, there was no room to move or even stretch.

After four days at sea, the elements began to take their toll. The children became drowsy, their bodies weakened by the lack of food and water, their legs and feet benumbed by the cold. On Day 5, a Sunday, they saw a steamer and it saw them. It came close and hove to. Their spirits soared until, after a quick inspection, the vessel turned away and disappeared over the horizon. Day and night had started to drift timelessly into one another as one gale followed the next and the rain soaked them to the skin. Some of the Lascars began to fail. They lay listlessly on the bottom boards, giving Cornish the impression that they were slowly sinking into a coma; after five days at sea, several of them were no more than semi-conscious. The following night one of the boys became delirious. Cornish removed her jacket and wrapped it around his feet. With very little food or water to sustain them, the children's strength was ebbing fast. A second boy became delirious.

The following morning the gales abated, the sea became calm and No. 12 drifted across the ocean under a slack sail. Then, in the early afternoon, one of the boys saw a plane heading towards them. It was a Sunderland flying boat whose pilot swooped down, flew round in a circle and waved at them from his cockpit window before heading back in the direction from which he had come. Soon a second Sunderland arrived. It dropped a package of supplies – beans, salmon, and peaches – with a note informing them that a destroyer was on its way. It was HMS *Anthony*, which in compliance with the order to escort the *Athenia* only to the dispersal point at 20°W, had been one of the escorts ordered to 'abandon' them over a week before. Remarkably, with the exception of one of the Lascars, who died almost as he was rescued, all the shipwrecked occupants arrived safely back in the port of Greenock after eight days adrift in the ocean. In his official report, Fourth Officer Cooper noted that the children 'behaved splendidly and were looked after very efficiently by Miss Cornish whom I believe massaged them continuously . . . Everyone behaved very well, and a spirit of loyalty to orders and comparative cheerfulness prevailed throughout the entire seven days and nineteen hours which we were in the boat.'[54]

As soon as she disembarked with 'her' six boys, Cornish asked how all the other children had fared. To her anguish, she was told that almost all of them had drowned, including fourteen of the fifteen girls she had originally been allocated. Of the 407 passengers and crew who had left Liverpool in the *City of Benares* on 13 September, 147 perished. Of the ninety children, only thirteen – six of them in Lifeboat No. 12 – returned alive.

As in the case of the *Athenia*, Berlin sought to exculpate U-48's commander, Heinrich Bleichrodt, claiming that the *Benares* had been requisitioned by the Admiralty and converted into an auxiliary cruiser and was therefore a valid target under the rules of maritime warfare. This was not true. Nonetheless, it is quite possible – as he was to insist after the war – that Bleichrodt genuinely believed that he had torpedoed one of the Royal Navy's armed merchantmen. This was not good enough for Goebbels. A week after the tragedy, his news agency announced: 'If the ship was really torpedoed with the loss of 83 [sic] children, then the murderer's name is Churchill. Nothing is sacred to this monster. The world is beginning to recognize him more and more for what he is – a fiend in human form.'[55]

Amid an outpouring of horror in the British press at the callousness of this response, the government decided to end the resettlement programme, claiming – disingenuously – that the sinking of the *City of Benares* had illustrated how greatly foul weather had contributed to the dangers to which even passenger ships travelling in convoy were exposed. This was not quite the end of the matter. The parents of the CORB evacuees had evidently been assured that the *City of Benares* was to be protected for the entire voyage across the Atlantic. On 23 November, an editorial in *The Times* reported that 'the minds of some of the bereaved parents are still grievously troubled over the discrepancy between their expectations of a continuous escort and the facts established in the reports of the sinking and subsequent statements'. Whether the guarantee was 'implicit or explicit', the leader writer concluded, 'every imaginative mind has shared and continues to share deeply the unspeakable loss which a large number of parents have suffered, and will enter into the harrowing doubts and questions which are still their portion'.[56]

Propaganda and public relations aside, the sinking of the *Benares* exposed two harsh truths: firstly, that no part of the Atlantic ocean was safe from U-boats; and secondly, that the shortage of escort vessels was so acute as virtually to guarantee a future massacre of merchant ships, whether they were sailing independently or in convoy. Within days of the tragedy, both these facts were to be seared into the collective consciousness of the Admiralty and the War Cabinet.

# 5.  U-Boats on the Rampage

If 17 September 1940 was a day of tragedy at sea, it was also a day of bitter coincidence on land. For, as Churchill warned the Commons that a Nazi invasion seemed imminent, Hitler made the decision to abort Operation Sealion, the threat of which had caused so many children to be sent on that ill-fated voyage aboard the *Benares* into U-48's line of fire. As commander-in-chief of the Kriegsmarine, Admiral Raeder had played a crucial role in the Führer's decision to postpone the invasion of Britain. Although his staff had been charged to study the operational challenges of a cross-Channel invasion from the opening volleys of the war, Raeder had long been convinced that Sealion would present the German navy with what he described as 'impossible tasks' and should not be contemplated except as a last resort.[1] However, he had reckoned without a late-flowering enthusiasm for the project within the German high command – the OKW – and especially within the army, whose generals were elated beyond reason by the astonishing ease with which their panzers had colonized France.

In the summer, relations within the OKW had been soured by a violent clash between gung-ho generals and wary admirals over the timing, the scale and the speed with which Sealion could be accomplished. After a series of acrimonious exchanges on paper and in person, Raeder and General Franz Halder, the army chief of staff, were ordered by Hitler to find a way out of their impasse, an injunction which they were unable to obey. The Führer was himself ambivalent about Sealion. He recognized that any attempt to land on English soil would be a hazardous enterprise or 'an exceptionally bold and daring' undertaking, as he described it.[2] Yet, still harbouring the illusion that the British could be persuaded or intimidated to the conference table, he appeared to believe that compelling evidence of an imminent invasion would be enough to drive the British government to see sense and therefore, in Churchill's favoured term, to parlay with the Third Reich.

Knowing Hitler's mercurial mind, Raeder was too canny openly to oppose an invasion; initially he proposed to delay the landings until the spring of 1941. Hitler objected, insisting that, to maintain the psycho-logical pressure, the Wehrmacht should prepare for an invasion in mid-September at the very latest. But the operation was contingent on the success of the Luftwaffe's bombing campaign and the vagaries of weather in the English Channel. Moreover, Raeder had been careful to secure an undertaking from Hitler that the starting gun would be in his hand and his alone. This gave the Kriegsmarine decisive influence which Raeder exploited to the full. As Hitler's 'S-day', 20 September, approached, the admiral secured one postponement after another on the basis of this or that operational snag. But his clinching argument against Sealion was impossible to gainsay.

In a memorandum for Hitler which Raeder submitted on 14 Septem-ber and which contained no trace of the schadenfreude he surely felt, he pointed out that a crucial prerequisite for the success of Sealion had yet to be delivered. He noted: 'The present air situation does not provide conditions for carrying out the operation, as the risk is still too great.'[3] The following day, Göring's grossly exaggerated claim for the Luft-waffe's bombing campaign against England was exposed by the 'never was so much owed by so many to so few' pilots, who decimated a raid by 100 bombers, which had been chaperoned to their target zone by 400 Luftwaffe fighters. With fifty-four of his aircraft destroyed by the RAF in a single raid, Göring was forced to concede that the Battle of Britain was proving impossible to sustain at such a level. Since the RAF had not yet been broken, it was impossible to give Sealion the protec-tion required to secure a successful landing on British soil. Hitler's reaction was to postpone the operation 'until further notice';[4] in reality, the invasion – which Raeder judged would have been 'disastrous'[5] – was dead in the water.

Dönitz was as relieved as Raeder when he heard Sealion had been abandoned, noting later, 'we possessed control neither of the air nor of the sea; nor were we in any position to gain it'.[6] But his relief was short lived. Once again the problem lay with his commander-in-chief. Raeder had a vision for victory which knew virtually no limits and which he laid before Hitler even before the abandonment of Sealion. Nor was it quite so quixotic as it was to be depicted by his enemies within the high command. At its heart was an unyielding belief that Britain was Ger-many's bitterest foe whose defeat was a prerequisite for the global hegemony that was Germany's proper destiny. But rather than a head-on assault, he argued that victory could better be achieved by launching a peripheral attack on Britain's pivotal interests in the Middle East, and, specifically, the Nile Valley and the Suez Canal, the artery which linked Britain to its most productive imperial possessions in Africa and Asia.

On 11 July he outlined this vision for the benefit of the Führer. Offering him global horizons to conquer, he explained that Germany would need to become 'an oceanic naval power of the first rank'[7] with a battle fleet to match. Though he did not spell out the implications of this in detail, he had already assessed that to establish this brave new world and to police its boundless perimeter, the Kriegsmarine would eventually require 'up to 80 battleships, 20 aircraft carriers, 225 cruisers and 500 U-boats'.[8] Raeder's timing was unfortunate. Hitler was already agitated by another destiny which was far more pressing: the invasion of Russia, the destruction of bolshevism and thereby – the sine qua non of a thousand-year Reich – the establishment of Lebensraum for Nazi Germany. Nonetheless, he did not openly dismiss Raeder's strategic proposal. Instead the admiral would remain at liberty to persist in the delusion that he might persuade the Führer to choose his Mediterranean strategy over what was to become Operation Barbarossa. As it turned out, Hitler was to find himself fatally trapped between his overriding urge to conquer the Soviet Union and the strategic necessity to confront Britain in the Middle East, a disagreeable distraction that would be forced on him by the military incompetence of his Axis partner, the Italian dictator Benito Mussolini, who had declared war on Britain a month earlier.

Dönitz believed that Raeder was in grave danger of losing the plot. Conceding that to confront Britain in the Mediterranean and the Middle East would 'strike a grievous blow' against the enemy, he argued that, since the Raeder plan would entail diverting the Kriegsmarine's limited resources from 'fighting against the greatest sea power in the world in the decisive theatre of operations, the Atlantic', it would be a dangerously high price to pay. Furthermore, he believed that Raeder's fixation with battleships both betrayed a fundamental misunderstanding about the essential character of the conflict with Britain and endangered its prosecution. What mattered above all else, Dönitz insisted, was to strangle Britain's lines of communication. The Kriegsmarine's overriding priority 'should be to sink as much enemy shipping as quickly as we could'. The only way to achieve this was with a large fleet of U-boats. So obvious did this seem to him that, as he wrote later, 'I lost no opportunity to state it forcibly and unequivocally.'[9] His persistence did not endear him to Raeder, nor — to his deepening frustration — did it deliver what he wanted at a point when he rightly believed it might have made a decisive impact on the course of the war.

In October 1940 the force of Dönitz's argument was demonstrated with an authority that sent a chill through the British Admiralty which reached into the heart of the War Cabinet. Churchill, who scrutinized the relevant statistics with intense concern, had already begun to detect an 'ominous fall in imports'.[10] The significance of this weighed the more heavily on him because it seemed so intractable. Dönitz's U-boats may not have been of 'the requisite number' to assure success, but they had started to run amok in the shipping lanes of the Atlantic Ocean and to demonstrate the gravity of the threat they posed to the convoys.

For this reason, the codenames for two of these convoys – HX79 and SC7 – were to be woven into the folkloric history of the Battle of the Atlantic. Out of a total of eighty-three merchant ships which set off from Nova Scotia for Liverpool in early October, more than one in three were to be sunk before they reached their destination. This was an unsustainable rate of destruction that was made even more alarming by the fact that it was achieved by no more than eight U-boats, not one of which was lost in the process.

The first of these ill-fated convoys, SC7, set off from Sydney, Nova Scotia, bound for Liverpool on 5 October. It was the first of a series of 'slow convoys' containing vessels hitherto regarded as too ponderous for inclusion in the 'fast' HX convoys bound for Britain, the rate at which they were being picked off when sailing independently having forced a change of policy. SC7 comprised thirty-five ageing merchant ships, the oldest of which, the *Thoroy*, was a tanker that had been at sea for almost half a century.[11] The vessels were incapable of maintaining an average speed of more than seven knots even in good weather without some of them falling behind to become easy prey for the wolf packs. They sailed in eight columns half a mile apart from one another, the entire convoy stretching over an area of some five square miles. For the first eleven days of the crossing the convoy was escorted by only one lightly armed warship, a sloop called HMS *Scarborough*, whose captain, Commander N. V. Dickinson, had already been alerted to the havoc being caused on the Western Approaches by individual U-boats on the prowl. On his way across to Nova Scotia from Britain, he had picked up a message from a solitary merchant ship which had broken away from an earlier convoy (HX72), reporting that six ships had been torpedoed in one night attack. As one of the war's most distinguished commanders, Captain Donald Macintyre, was later to note, 'A deep sense of futility in the face of their skilful and elusive tormentors could not but weigh on the minds of Dickinson and his men.'[12]

On the fourth day out from Nova Scotia, a gale sprang up from the south. Four small steamers, which were designed for the relatively benign conditions of the Great Lakes, soon dropped out of the convoy, unable to cope with the size of the Atlantic waves. (Only one made it to port; the other three were sent to the bottom by an opportunistic U-boat.) The remaining thirty-one ships lumbered on at a reduced speed for another seven days, by which time the convoy had reached the outer edges of the Western Approaches, where they were joined by two more British warships, the sloop HMS *Fowey* and one of the first Flower class corvettes to come off the production line, HMS *Bluebell*. The latter's crew was not enamoured of the new vessel. Don Kirton, a twenty-two-year-old who had already served in the Royal Navy for three years, recalled the moment he first set eyes on her: 'She seemed more like a rowing boat than [a] fighting ship. The funnel was the biggest part of her. She had a very old 4-inch gun. It was a 1914 weapon and I thought, "Well, we won't get far with this." '[13]

At just over 200 feet in length and with a maximum speed of sixteen knots, the Flower class corvettes, 267 of which were to be built in the course of the war, came to play an indispensable role in the Battle of the Atlantic. Named – somewhat whimsically – after common British plants, they were bog-standard vessels which could be built at speed in small yards around the country. They were cramped and were so uncomfortable in rough weather that the word soon went round that 'a corvette would roll on wet grass'; even hardened mariners suffered severely from seasickness. Nonetheless, because they pitched and tossed and rolled their way over and around the waves like corks rather than diving into them, they proved to be virtually immune even to the heaviest seas and decidedly less likely to founder than much bigger and ostensibly stronger vessels. For this reason above others, corvette crews gradually if reluctantly came to regard their spartan little vessels with an emotion somewhat akin to affection.

None of this was any comfort to those on board *Bluebell* or any of the other ships in SC7 as the convoy wallowed towards the Western Approaches, where Dickinson knew that an unknown number of U-boats were surely lying in wait. An atmosphere of growing menace was heightened by the inexperience of the three escort commanders. The low priority which had hitherto been given by the Admiralty to what was regarded as the mundane task of escorting convoys across the Atlantic meant that the three senior officers, who had not trained or worked together before, were bereft of tactical doctrine or any coherent plan of action with which to confront the dangers they were about to encounter.

On the night of 16 October, the dark hulls of the slow-moving convoy were etched against the skyline, clear enough to be easily detected by U-48 (which, with Heinrich Bleichrodt in command, had sunk the *City of Benares* only four weeks earlier). SC7's position, speed and direction were radioed back to Dönitz's headquarters in Lorient, which in turn made contact with a flotilla of six more U-boats patrolling to the north-east of Rockall, a seagull-stained Atlantic outcrop 286 miles to the west of the British coastline. Their commanders were ordered to link up with U-48, which was deputed to shadow the convoy until the flotilla was ready to attack. Bleichrodt could not wait to pounce on such easy pickings. Impatient for a kill, U-48 closed on the convoy and, unnoticed by any of the escorts, torpedoed two merchant ships and quietly withdrew without being detected. It was the start of a catastrophic forty-eight hours which served notice on the British government that Dönitz's U-boats – working as teams in wolf packs – had the potential gravely to imperil the nation's Atlantic lifeline.

As the two sloops, *Scarborough* and *Fowey*, began a fruitless search for the offending U-boat, HMS *Bluebell* stood by the stricken merchantmen to rescue their crews. As a result, the convoy, ploughing towards even greater danger, was without any naval protection at all. *Scarborough* took up her station again as SC7's escort, but a passing Sunderland flying boat, which reported sighting another U-boat over the horizon, prompted her captain to set off in pursuit, once again leaving the convoy without protection. It was a cardinal error: by the time Dickinson decided to rejoin the convoy, *Scarborough* had fallen so far astern that, at a maximum speed of fourteen knots, it proved impossible to regain contact. Realizing what had happened, the other wild-goose-chasing sloop,

HMS *Fowey*, under the command of Lieutenant Commander Robert Aubrey, hastened back to rejoin the convoy, where he was soon joined by *Bluebell*. With alarm bells now ringing in the Admiralty, two further escorts were already on their way to reinforce the threatened merchant ships. They arrived in the early hours of 17 October. But they were to make precious little difference. Directed by radio instructions from Lorient, U-28, U-46, U-93, U-99, U-100, U-101 and U-123 were in position, waiting to attack. Dönitz had sprung his trap.

On board the *Beatus*, a freighter carrying steel, timber and aeroplane parts, an assistant steward, Frank Holding, watched a streak of white light reaching from the ship to the horizon, the reflection of the moon dancing on the water. He was not lulled by the beauty of the moment: 'You're thinking "Someone's out there."' In this case, he was right. Within minutes, the *Beatus* had sailed into the waiting jaws of the wolf pack.

When a seaman reported seeing a torpedo cross close to the ship's bows, Holding knew they were in trouble:

> The next thing I heard was this explosion and a sound like breaking glass from down near the engine room. The ship stood still . . . We knew we were sinking. While we were standing on the deck by the funnel, all this wet ash came up over us – the sea must have got into the engine room where the fires were.

With one lifeboat uselessly waterlogged in the sea, the crew scrambled into the other one and pulled away from the sinking vessel. Holding produced a mouth organ.

> I started playing. I was enjoying this. It's a funny thing isn't it? . . . But then the second engineer said, 'Knock that off, will you? There's a U-boat on the surface.' I was short-sighted, but I could hear the engines racing and I could hear them shouting out in German. They were excited. They were in the chase, these U-boat men.[14]

The wolf pack was headed by the Kriegsmarine's most celebrated ace, Otto Kretschmer, who had already secured his reputation by his fearless and pioneering attacks on British shipping earlier in the year. Before leaving Lorient, he had written a twelve-point list of standing orders for his crew. It contained a firm injunction: 'It should not be necessary to fire in the first instance more than one torpedo for one ship.' The corollary of this diktat was revolutionary: it entailed firing at close range on the surface, which, Kretschmer explained, 'can be done only by penetrating the escort's anti-submarine screen and at times getting inside the convoy lanes. This should be the objective of all our attacks.'[15] Although the newly established Anti-Submarine Division of the naval staff in London was just beginning to work out the variety of tactics for which the U-boat commanders had been carefully trained and drilled, Kretschmer's unique plan of action had never even been guessed at. At 10 p.m. on 18 October, he went for it.

As the other U-boats in the wolf pack took up flanking positions from which to unleash their torpedoes from outside the escort screen, U-99 headed at full speed directly at the convoy. Passing between two British warships, Kretschmer surged towards the outer column of merchantmen. Despite the fact that the moon shone over a warscape that was by now eerily illuminated by a confusion of gun flashes, star shells* and distress flares, U-99 was still undetected. Kretschmer's first victim was an elderly tramp steamer, the *Creekirk*, laden with iron ore. Despite the laconic style favoured by U-99's commander, his meticulous log fails to conceal the intensity of the moment: '10.06 p.m. Vessel of some 6,500 tons sinks within 20 seconds. I now proceed head-on into the convoy.' By that time, not only was the *Creekirk* on the ocean bed but thirty-seven members of the crew, including her captain, had gone down with her.

Thereafter, the disaster facing SC7 unfolded at such speed and in so great a confusion that those who were trapped in the inferno of destruction could barely comprehend what was happening to them. After sinking the *Creekirk*, Kretschmer saw a large gap between two ships travelling line astern. Seizing the moment, he veered sharply to penetrate into the very heart of the convoy until he was surrounded by merchant ships, all aware of their possible fate but none knowing how to escape. One victim tried a 'valley of death' tactic. A sharp-eyed lookout on a large freighter caught a glimpse of U-99, the ship fired a star shell into the air and, in Kretschmer's words, 'turns towards us at full speed continuing even after we alter course'. The chase lasted for some minutes until Kretschmer noted, 'the ship turns off, fires one of her

---

* Much like a firework, the star shell contained a fuse which ignited a magnesium flare at a given height, illuminating a wide arc of the sea below.

guns and again takes her place in the convoy'. Undeterred, Kretschmer lined up another large freighter but, as he gave the order to fire, the ship turned towards U-99. As a result 'the torpedo passes ahead of her and hits an even bigger ship after a run of 1,740 metres. This ship of 7,000 tons is hit abreast the foremast . . .' It was the *Empire Miniver*, which was laden with iron and steel.

Seeing what had happened to the *Creekirk*, the *Empire Miniver*'s captain, Robert Smith, tried to find a way of escape. It was to no avail: 'There was a dull thud, a big flash and a cloud of bluish smoke. Then everything went black; all the lights went out, the engines stopped, the ship shuddered, lay still and lost her way.' The explosion 'blew all the hatches off her and the pig-iron was blown into the air just like shrapnel'. Smith and his crew had time to lower the lifeboats and row well clear of the stricken vessel. 'About 25 minutes after the attack there was a terrific explosion amidships. She broke her back and sank immediately,' he recalled.[16]

According to one of his crew, Kretschmer now stood at the front of U-99's conning tower and declared, 'Well, here goes. We are going in to tear down this convoy.'[17] U-99's next target was a Greek cargo ship carrying 5,426 tons of sulphur. Kretschmer's log – dictated as the drama unfolded – provided a staccato running commentary: 'Immediately after the torpedo explosion there is another explosion, with a high column of flame from bow to bridge. Smoke rises 300 metres. Bow apparently shattered. Ship continues to burn with a green flame.' By midnight, manoeuvring with impunity, he had accounted for three merchant ships in the very heart of a convoy that was supposedly chaperoned by four British warships. Belatedly, however, three of the four closed in. But Kretschmer was too smart and too quick for them: 'I make off at full speed to the south-west and again make contact with the convoy.'

With other members of the wolf pack firing at will from outside the screen which the escorts had failed to provide, the convoy was at the mercy of the U-boats. From his vantage point in HMS *Bluebell*, Sub Lieutenant Keachie witnessed a chaotic spectacle: 'I remember feeling so helpless when we saw these ships being sunk. What do we do? Ships were sunk from different places in the convoy and we would scurry around to try and find the submarine. The ASDIC was useless.' Kretschmer relished the Royal Navy's humiliation. 'The destroyers [sic] do not know how to help and occupy themselves by constantly firing star-shells which are of little effect in the bright moonlight.'[18] Attacking from astern of the convoy, the U-boat ace was now in a position to pick off his victims like a marksman aiming at ducks in a shooting gallery. Nor did he relent until he had despatched another five merchant ships. The *Fiscus* went down with her captain and entire crew of thirty-eight; the *Thalia* lost twenty-two of her twenty-four-man crew; the *Empire Brigade* apparently sank within one minute of being hit, though in this case, thirty-six members of her forty-one-man crew managed to launch the lifeboats in time to escape before she went under; the *Snefield*'s crew managed to escape in similar fashion while the *Clintonia*, on which Kretschmer had expended his last torpedo, was kept afloat by her cargo of timber which gave her crew time to abandon ship with only one casualty, a crewman who was killed when another submarine, U-123, arrived to finish her off with a round of shellfire.

Their task accomplished, Kretschmer's wolf pack slipped away in the early hours of 19 October, leaving the British escorts to trawl the deserted battleground for survivors – among them French, Swedish, Jamaican, and Indian, as well as British, sailors. One by one, the *Bluebell* scooped them to safety. 'You could see the red bulbs on their lifejackets,' Kirton recalled. 'We put scrambling nets over the side. Two of the lads would go over the gunwales, and there found eager hands to take them forward to where there was shelter. Many of them were violently sick from the fuel oil that they had swallowed. Some were completely naked.'[19] Among the last to be picked up by the *Bluebell* were the survivors from the *Beatus* including Frank Holding. In worsening weather, the corvette steamed for the Clyde, heavily laden with exhausted and seasick sailors.

U-99's contribution to the destruction of SC7 was greater than that of the other U-boats in the wolf pack, but between them they had accounted for the sinkings of seventeen ships in a little over forty-eight hours. Of the thirty-five vessels which had set off from Nova Scotia two weeks earlier, only fifteen arrived in Liverpool, the other twenty had all been sunk with the loss of more than 140 lives. In Lorient, the fate of SC7 became known – in a self-congratulatory reference to the Nazi Party's internecine purge that began on 30 June 1934 – as 'the Night of the Long Knives'. Another such night was imminent.

In this second, almost simultaneous, grisly encounter, the lessons for the Admiralty were even starker. Although the proportion of merchant ships lost from convoy HX79 was lower – 25 per cent to SC7's 57 per cent – the damage inflicted by the U-boats was more alarming. Largely because of the value of their cargoes, the forty-nine vessels in convoy HX79 were heavily protected: Britain could ill-afford the loss of eighteen freighters laden with iron and steel and seven tankers carrying oil and gas. So, although the convoy had left Halifax, Nova Scotia on 8 October 1940 shielded initially by only two armed merchant cruisers, eleven days later these were replaced by two destroyers, a minesweeper, three corvettes and three anti-submarine trawlers. Yet their presence made no discernible difference to the shambles that ensued. Detected by the U-boat ace, Günther Prien, now a hero in Germany after sinking the *Royal Oak* a year earlier, the convoy came under attack from six U-boats at the very moment that Kretschmer was completing the slaughter of SC7. In one night, Prien's wolf pack added a further twelve ships to Dönitz's tally for those two days. The ease with which this slaughter was accomplished made it clear beyond reasonable doubt that naval escorts could not prevail by numbers alone: they needed to be well led, highly trained, closely coordinated, and equipped with a coherent plan of action. All these ingredients were notable by their absence.

The exhausted survivors of HX79's ill-fated crossing reached Liverpool on 23 October to discover the full value that was placed on their contribution to Britain's war effort by the state and by their employers. The prime responsibility for their care fell on charities such as the Anglican Missions to Seamen and the Salvation Army, whose resources were already stretched to the limit by the destruction wrought by the Luftwaffe's bombers which blasted the city at a rate of three or four raids a week. As the employees of private shipping companies, they were regarded as casual labourers. In recompense for their tribulations, they were entitled to fourteen days' leave and a one-off payment of £30. This was barely enough to replace the clothes and other personal possessions which had gone down with their ships. One radio officer reflected with wry bitterness, 'There was no compensation for lost money, cameras, radios, [eye]glasses . . . Any complaints received the answer, "You shouldn't take any more than is essential to sea with you." '[20] This response not only reflected a bureaucratic indifference to the mortal challenge these sailors had just endured but ignored the fact that impecunious seafarers had little choice but to take their meagre possessions wherever they went as they had no alternative home for them.

The individual suffering of merchant seamen – many of whom were not British citizens but 'volunteers' from the Empire, Asia (especially China) and South America – mattered less to a necessarily hard-headed War Cabinet than the loss of the ships which they had manned. Altogether, the twelve vessels that went down in HX79 took with them some 37,480 tons of oil and petroleum products, 11,700 tons of steel, 3,000 tons of iron, 1,700 tons of lead and zinc, 8,000 tons of grain, 19,400 tons of timber, and 8,333 tons of sugar. Such losses would be unsustainable; if replicated on a regular basis they would soon have brought Britain to the brink of despair. Total imports of food and raw materials, excluding oil, which had been around 60 million tons a year before the outbreak of war, were falling at such a rate that by the end of December 1940 they had dropped by 10 per cent to 54 million tons. Nor was there any early prospect of reversing the trend. 'There was the risk that we would suffer such a dramatic fall in our imports, we would have to cut our food consumption to impossibly low levels,' a member of the prime minister's Statistical Branch, Donald MacDougall, recalled. 'Further reductions would also threaten the country's ability to prosecute the war . . . It was frightening all the time.'[21]

The scale of the challenge facing the convoys was demonstrated by a single episode which afflicted HMS *Folkestone*, a sloop escorting a convoy of forty-seven ships which set off from Liverpool to cross the Atlantic on 15 October. In the early hours of the 17th, three freighters were torpedoed. One of these was a Norwegian tramp steamer, the *Dokka*, whose captain and crew managed to save themselves by scrambling on to a couple of rafts. After a while, a submarine, U-93, loomed up beside them. Its commander, Kapitänleutnant Korth, who was on his first mission, demanded to know the identity of the ship he had just sunk. The *Dokka*'s master, Captain Pedersen, had just given him a false name when *Folkestone* approached at speed. U-93 turned and started to flee. Pedersen gesticulated and shouted at *Folkestone*'s captain, Lieutenant Commander C. F. H. Churchill, 'There is the submarine – go and get her.' Churchill reacted rapidly enough to fire five rounds at the U-boat, the last of which hit the conning tower. The U-boat dived, which should have been Churchill's moment. The U-boat had a maximum speed of eight knots under water, half the speed of which *Folkestone* was capable: it should have been at his mercy.

Knowing that he was almost over his quarry, Churchill ordered depth charges to be dropped at the point where U-93 had disappeared beneath the waves. But the submarine managed to dodge away. A few minutes later, *Folkestone*'s ASDIC detected the vessel once more and Churchill came in for a second run. But he now found himself in a quandary for which he was ill-prepared and for which he had no answer. To remain in sonic contact with U-93, he had to attack slowly enough to avoid so churning the water as to distort or suppress the echo which was his sole means of locating the submarine accurately. This created a catch-22 for him. To maximize the chances of hitting a target that was twisting and turning like an eel to escape, the depth charges needed to be released as nearly as possible from immediately above the U-boat; but by going slowly enough to manoeuvre into this position, he ran the risk of disabling his own ship in the process. Only by travelling fast enough over the target to ensure that the *Folkestone* was away from the explosive impact of her own depth charges could he avoid disabling the electronic systems and thereby crippling the destroyer even as he sent the submarine to the bottom. In frustration and near-despair, Churchill called off the chase, writing subsequently, 'I was at a loss to know how I could have done better.'[22] In truth, he was not to blame: here was disconcerting evidence that, in a struggle of competing technologies, ASDIC was not the wonder-weapon it was once presumed to be.

From the Admiralty's perspective, the trend was disturbing. In August 1940 U-boats sank fifty-six merchant ships; in September, the number rose to fifty-nine; and the haul for October was sixty-three, the great majority of these sinkings being accomplished at night with torpedoes fired from the surface and not, as the Admiralty had originally presumed, from beneath the waves. The grand loss for the three months was 178 ships with a total displacement of more than 700,000 tons, which was below Dönitz's target of 600,000 in a single month but serious enough to demonstrate that the need for more effective countermeasures was pressing. As yet, though, none were forthcoming. For some time senior officials in the Admiralty had urged a range of possible solutions which included accelerating the development of radar (radio detection and ranging) systems that were both powerful and compact enough to be fitted to aircraft as well as warships; and more sophisticated radio communication systems which were also still at a relatively primitive stage of evolution. So far, however, the failure to foresee the

U-boat threat in the years leading up to the outbreak of war meant that neither of these potential game-changers had been developed to the point where they posed a serious threat to the enemy.

The War Cabinet had been slow to appreciate the degree to which the Atlantic lifeline was endangered. At a regular meeting of the Defence Committee, a few days before the mutilation of SC7 and HX79, the prime minister and his colleagues, including his successor as First Lord of the Admiralty, A. V. Alexander, did not even discuss the U-boat threat. On 15 October their focus had been on whether to send reinforcements to the Middle East and Malta (to counter an Italian invasion of Egypt from Libya in the previous month) and the need to disable the *Bismarck* and the *Tirpitz* with 'a large scale bombing attack'.[23] However, a few days after Kretschmer and his colleagues had demonstrated the existential threat posed to Britain's imports from the wolf packs, the committee hurriedly approved the Admiralty's recommendations. In addition it was agreed that, as Admiral Forbes, the Home Fleet's commander-in-chief, had urged two maths earlier, more vessels should be diverted from both the east and south coasts – even at the expense of weakening the navy's anti-invasion precautions on those fronts – to protect the Atlantic convoys. This was the first clear evidence that the government intended to take decisive action to meet the crisis.

However, the Admiralty still found it difficult to discard Churchill's earlier obsession with hunting groups. Even though the number of shepherding escorts gradually rose to an average of two per convoy, they were still frequently ordered to leave their flocks to search for U-boats reportedly seen in far distant waters. Captain Donald Macintyre, who had been despatched on so many pointless hunting expeditions earlier in the war, continued to face 'exasperating futile days when the ships so badly needed to escort convoys were being battered by fruitless hunts in storm-swept seas, without any hope of reaching the enemy before he had slipped away into the vast blank spaces of the ocean'.[24]

Far more disturbing in its baleful impact on the Battle of the Atlantic was another prime ministerial obsession. At its 15 October meeting, the Defence Committee also agreed that the RAF should 'deliver on Germany the maximum load of bombs that it was possible to carry'.[25] This simple determination by the War Cabinet reflected an unquestioned assumption that, in the words of Stanley Baldwin eight years earlier, 'the bomber will always get through' – though as yet it was not an open endorsement of the former prime minister's stated belief that 'The only defence is offence, which means that you have to kill more women and children more quickly than the enemy if you want to save yourselves.'[26] This – in the form of the area bombing of German cities – was to come later.

However, Churchill was already some way down that route. Almost three months earlier, in July, casting around for some way of arresting Germany's apparently irresistible progress, he had written to Lord Beaverbrook (in whom he placed unwarranted trust),* asserting, 'when I look round to see how we can win the war I see there is only one sure path . . . and that is an absolutely devastating, exterminating attack by very heavy bombers from this country on the Nazi homeland. We must be able to overwhelm them by this means, without which I do not see a way through'.[27] A week later, the Chief of the Air Staff and commander-in-chief of Bomber Command, Air Marshal Sir Charles Portal, seized on Churchill's fixation, writing in the course of an internal Air Ministry debate:

> we have the one directly offensive weapon in the whole of our armoury, the one means by which we can undermine the morale of a large part of the enemy people, shake their faith in the Nazi regime, and at the same time and with the very same bombs, dislocate the major part of their heavy industry and a good part of their oil production.[28]

The implications of the use of the word 'morale' in this context may be open to dispute but, shorn of any contextual ambiguity, it is hard to resist the conclusion of the historian John Terraine that the word implies 'either the threat or the reality of blowing men, women and children to bits'.[29]

On 3 September Churchill elaborated this theme in a fateful memorandum which was placed before his colleagues in the War Cabinet. Entitled 'The Munitions Situation', it was a sweeping assessment of the

---

* As Minister for Aircraft Production, Beaverbrook showed such energy and initiative that Churchill was enthralled. The newspaper magnate was an unscrupulous flatterer, so self-regarding and ambitious that Churchill's wife, Clemmie, would later write to her husband – in vain – urging 'Try ridding yourself of this microbe.' Instead, Churchill entrusted him with ever more responsibilities.

challenges facing the three armed services that opened with a categorical assertion:

> The Navy can lose us this war, but only the Air Force can win it. Therefore our supreme effort must be to gain overwhelming mastery in the air. The Fighters are our salvation, but the Bombers alone provide the means of victory. We must therefore develop the power to carry out an ever-increasing volume of explosives to Germany, so as to pulverize the entire industry and scientific structure on which the war effort and economic life of the enemy depend.[30]

This intuition, for which there was no objective evidence, was widely shared within the British high command. There were, though, doubters. Among them was the air minister, Sir Archibald Sinclair, who argued that 'our small bomber force could, by accurate bombing, do very great damage to the enemy's war effort, but could not gain a decision against Germany by bombing the civilian population'. However, Sinclair was a man of weak convictions, weakly held. According to the historian Sir Max Hastings, his relationship with the prime minister was sometimes described as 'Head of school's fag'. More significantly, he carried very little political weight. Concealing his misgivings, he readily became 'the RAF's political representative rather than its master' and a malleable mouthpiece for Portal and Bomber Command.[31]

Though it had yet to be enshrined formally in doctrine or strategy, Churchill's forceful guidance was to have a devastating impact on the Royal Navy's faltering efforts to combat the U-boats in the Atlantic. Subject to a few minor provisos – which did not apply to the Admiralty – Churchill's counsel was unequivocal: 'The Air Force and its action on the largest scale must therefore . . . claim the first place over the Navy or the Army.'[32] At the time this injunction went unchallenged, but its implications were soon to precipitate a prolonged conflict between the RAF and the Admiralty of such intensity that, more than two years later, the Second Sea Lord, Admiral William Whitworth, would be moved to write 'our fight with the Air Ministry becomes more and more fierce as the war proceeds. It is much more savage than our war with the Huns, which is very unsatisfactory and such a waste of effort.'[33] This was far more than a turf war between two competing departments. It went to the very heart of the struggle against the Nazis and it is virtually impossible to exaggerate its malign impact not only on the conduct of the struggle against the U-boats but on the course of the Second World War itself.

The immediate impact of Churchill's decree was to give the Kriegsmarine's U-boat arm a renewed lease of life. In October 1940 Hitler asked Dönitz whether the submarine bases at Lorient and elsewhere in the Bay of Biscay would require protection from British bombing raids. Dönitz did not waste this chance. Within weeks the 'truly gigantic task', as he described the project of building impenetrable submarine pens, was well under way. In the following months this construction programme was monitored by reconnaissance aircraft from Coastal Command (the RAF's maritime arm), which took photographs of the rapid expansion of the facilities at Lorient. The evidence for a major building programme was not to rely exclusively on aerial photography. Six months after Dönitz initiated the project the survivors from U-100, which had been depth charged in mid-Atlantic on 17 March, would be interrogated about their home base at Lorient. In addition to describing their living conditions and the rules governing fraternization with the French – a law 'forbids intercourse with any French woman except those installed at the approved brothel which closes at 10 p.m.' – they would tell their inquisitors that the port was being developed 'into an important harbour'. To deliver this project, they said,

> a great number of workmen from the Todt building organization and the NSKK [the National Socialist Motor Corps] . . . are working day and night . . . one informant, more willing and reliable than the others, said that the Germans were intending to build such concrete shelters as was being done in Heligoland and in other German harbours. In the dock a partition is being built so that two U-boats can use it simultaneously.[34]

This should have been enough to alert not only the Admiralty but, in turn, the War Cabinet to a dangerous development that required an urgent response. However, aside from a few desultory raids in early 1941 – which were all but suspended in May on the grounds that they 'had achieved sufficient success and that they were claiming too much of the available bombing effort'[35] – Bomber Command was not instructed to divert a substantial number of its long-range aircraft from the strategic bombing of Germany in order to blast the Biscay bases. As with the refusal to allocate sufficient resources to the protection of the

Atlantic convoys, so this decision betrayed a failure of foresight which would be of great consequence for the course of the Battle of the Atlantic.

By the autumn of 1941 the rapidly growing U-boat fleet based at Lorient, Saint-Nazaire, Brest and La Pallice (La Rochelle) would be sheltered under an impenetrable shield of concrete sixteen feet deep. To the bemused relief of Admiral Dönitz, whose tonnage war would otherwise have been imperilled if not thwarted, this had been accomplished without any significant interruption. As he would observe, 'It was a great mistake on the part of the British not to have attacked these pens from the air while they were under construction . . . but Bomber Command preferred to raid towns in Germany. Once the U-boats were in their concrete pens it would be too late.'[36]

However, long before this work had been completed, Dönitz's single-minded focus on the tonnage war was already bearing fruit. After the triumph of the tactics spearheaded by Kretschmer and Prien in wreaking havoc against HX79 and SC7, their commander-in-chief was exhilarated but far from complacent; he was still far away from reaching his target of 600,000 tons a month. In a report written immediately after those successes, he outlined his key conclusions. Emphasizing that a 'concentration of ships in a convoy' required 'a concentration of U-boats' to confront them, he reiterated the need to have many more submarines at his disposal, both to attack particular convoys with even greater effect and to attack more of them; at the moment, he argued, too many convoys escaped while the U-boats were on their way back to their bases to reload with torpedoes. Doubtless mindful of Kretschmer and Prien, he added, almost as an aside, 'The main thing will always be the ability of the commander.'[37]

Writing later of the 'heavy loss' inflicted on the British when, in October 1940, eight U-boats 'operating simultaneously' sank sixty-three merchant ships, he noted in reflective frustration, 'I had asked not for eight but for 100 U-boats operating simultaneously as the number required to achieve decisive results in the war on British shipping . . . it was essential that we should throw into it [the Battle of the Atlantic] as quickly as we possibly could a really large number of U-boats.'[38] As it was, by the end of the year he had at most thirty operational U-boats at his disposal, of which – because of the need to service, maintain, and repair sophisticated submarines which were tested to the limit in the Atlantic battle – only a small proportion could be at sea at any one time.

It was one of the pregnant ironies of this point in the conflict that, just as Churchill was already fixated on the air war, Hitler was no less obsessed by the land war. Though he recognized that the maritime struggle mattered, his obsession with Barbarossa meant that he was unable to focus, except spasmodically, on the operational implications of this. Had he done so, the Battle of the Atlantic would assuredly have taken a very different course: were Germany to succeed in throttling the life-giving artery across the Atlantic, not only would D-Day have been impossible but long before that Britain would have been forced to sue for peace; conversely, by allowing the convoys to escape the noose, Hitler ensured that the massive preponderance of Allied power that was thus able to descend on Europe was bound eventually to force the Third Reich to its knees. In short: victory in the Atlantic for one side all but guaranteed the eventual defeat of the other.

As it was, Dönitz would be left to observe bitterly that Hitler and the German high command were 'both, unfortunately, quite incapable of grasping' the fact that 'out there in the Atlantic a handful of U-boats was being called upon to fight a battle that would decide the issue of the war'.[39] The same could not be said of Churchill. Nonetheless, despite his post-war protestations that 'The only thing that ever really frightened me during the war was the U-boat peril,'[40] the prime minister did not at this point react to the threat of 'slow strangulation' facing the nation with either the alacrity or the means required to avert this prospective catastrophe. Despite his confessional spasm, Churchill, at the time, was juggling competing priorities; the Battle of the Atlantic was but one of these and most certainly not *primus inter pares*.

On 10 November 1940 Nella Last prepared Sunday lunch: 'I made cabbage soup today, and added a shredded carrot and a leek. My husband said, when I put the second course on, "After that soup we don't need much – don't forget there is a war on" – what I call his battle-cry. I ruffled his hair and said, "Oh, eat your lunch and don't worry." ' The main course was half a rabbit's leg diced and mixed with scrambled egg on toast. This left the other half leg for the following day's lunch – 'not bad for 1s. 8d. these days'.[41] By now, the sugar and tea ration had been cut respectively to eight ounces and two ounces a week while the supply of 'inessentials' like cups, cutlery, kettles, clocks and prams had been sharply curtailed to make way for the production of wartime munitions. Four weeks later, Nella Last wrote out her grocery order for the week. Toilet rolls had risen in price from 6d to 11d and, she noted, they were 'a lot smaller at that'. Envelopes and reels of cotton had likewise gone up in price and down in size and quality. 'I foresee', she wrote 'a very great simplicity after Christmas.'[42]

Nella Last's tribulations were a microcosm of the toll exacted by the U-boats combined with the rapidly spiralling cost to the nation of an ever-expanding war. With only $2 billion left in its coffers, the Treasury was running out of reserves so rapidly that, Churchill noted later, 'Even if we divested ourselves of all our gold and foreign assets, we could not pay for half we had ordered, and the extension of the war made it necessary for us to have ten times as much.'[43] But, with the US Treasury expressing deep scepticism about Britain's prospective bankruptcy, he felt constrained to write again to Roosevelt on 8 December 1940. His letter, which, he later reflected, was 'one of the most important I ever wrote', was an eloquent scattergun of a plea for assistance on a wide variety of fronts, not least to combat 'a mortal danger' arising from 'the steady and increasing diminution of sea tonnage', which, he wrote, threatened to cripple 'our ability to feed this Island and import the munitions of all kinds we need'. Noting that Britain's shipping losses in the autumn had been 'on a scale almost comparable to those of the worst year of the last war', he stressed that it was 'in the shipping and in the power to transport across the oceans, particularly the Atlantic ocean, that in 1941 the crunch of the whole war will be found'. Then came the prime minister's own crunch. Pressing Roosevelt to make available to Britain 'every ton of merchant shipping, surplus to its own requirements', he simultaneously demanded 'heavy bombers, on which, above all others, we depend to shatter the foundations of German military power', not to mention 'the small arms, artillery and tanks' with which to provision the Empire's growing armies. Nor did he beat about the financial bush: 'The more rapid and abundant the flow of munitions and ships which you are able to send us, the sooner will our dollar credits be exhausted,' he confessed, elaborating that the orders placed or in negotiation already 'many times exceed the total exchange resources remaining at the disposal of Great Britain'.

If Churchill regarded this declaration of imminent insolvency as a national humiliation, he concealed it with characteristic panache:

I believe you will agree that it would be wrong in principle and mutually disadvantageous in effect if at the height of this struggle Great Britain were to be divested of all saleable assets, so that after the victory was won with our blood, civilization saved, and the time gained for the United States to be fully armed against all eventualities, we should stand stripped to the bone . . . If, as I believe, you are convinced, Mr President, that the defeat of the Nazi or Fascist tyranny is a matter of high consequence to the people of the United States and to the Western Hemisphere, you will regard this letter not as an appeal for aid, but as a statement of the minimum action necessary to achieve our common purpose.[44]

This was Churchill at his magnificent best, identifying an approaching abyss while cloaking his audacity in language calculated to appeal to America's national interest and to her president's own commitment to freedom and democracy. And it worked.

The president was on a yachting holiday in the Caribbean when Churchill's missive was delivered to him the following day. After a long pause for private thought but very little, if any, debate with his advisors, he evidently decided that Churchill had made a compelling case that could be ignored no longer. His authority as president buttressed by the fact that he had been re-elected for an unprecedented third term, he invited the Secretary of the Treasury, Henry Morgenthau, to lunch at the White House on 17 December. 'You should say to England [sic],' he instructed, 'we will give you the guns and ships that you need, provided that when the war is over you will return to us in kind the guns and ships we have loaned you.'[45] In that single utterance, Roosevelt gave birth to a simple but crucial programme that both saved Britain from bankruptcy and made possible the eventual destruction of Nazism. At a press conference the following day the president alighted upon a folksy analogy to fly the Lend-Lease kite before the American public:

Suppose my neighbor's house catches fire and I have a length of garden hose four or five hundred yards away and connect it up to his hydrant, I may help him put out the fire. Now what do I do. I don't say to him before that operation, 'Neighbor, my garden hose cost me fifteen

dollars; you have to pay me fifteen dollars for it.' No! What is the trans-
action that goes on? I don't want fifteen dollars – I want my garden hose
back after the fire is over.[46]

A fortnight later, on 29 December, in one of his regular Fireside
Chats he warmed to this theme. Warning adroitly that there was 'danger ahead', he advised the nation that 'we cannot escape danger by
crawling into bed and pulling the covers over our heads . . . If Britain
should go down, all of us in all the Americas would be living at the
point of a gun . . . We must produce arms and ships with every energy
and resource we can command . . .' And he ended with the memorable
assertion. 'We must be the great arsenal of democracy.'[47] Not all were
convinced; the polls showed that a stubborn 40 per cent of the American
population were still more concerned to stay out of the war than to aid
Britain, which in turn meant that Congress could by no means be taken
for granted. For this reason Roosevelt went out of his way to reassure
the isolationists that 'You can . . . nail any talk about sending armies to
Europe as deliberate untruth. Our national policy is not directed toward
war. Its sole purpose is to keep war away from our country and our
people.'[48] Despite, or perhaps because of, his wily promise to avoid direct involvement in the European war, the Fireside Chat was a persuasive
triumph. From those who read or heard his words, the president won an
approval rating of 80 per cent, which was enough to give him the confidence to instruct the Treasury to draft a Bill enshrining the principles
and the details of Lend-Lease. In the following weeks, deploying his
great flair for tough-minded ambiguity – hedging here and dodging
there, accepting this or that amendment – he nudged the Bill through
Congress until, on 11 March 1941, the Lend-Lease Act (formally An Act
to Promote the Defense of the United States) was signed into law with
the overwhelming approval of both the House and the Senate. The vote
was no less a triumph for Churchill – it is no wonder he came to relish
his 'most important' letter of 8 December – than it was for Roosevelt.
Both men knew that the die was cast: the fates of the United States and
Great Britain were now so closely entwined as to ensure that the inex-
orable logic of war – de facto if not yet de jure – would make them
inseparable.

## 6.  Churchill Declares 'The Battle of the Atlantic'

The Atlantic storms of the winter of 1940 were as cruel as any seafarer could recall. Those thousands of men in warships and freighters who endured the battering of giant waves and the ferocity of bitter winds for day after day lived a purgatorial existence. In such conditions the weather was an even greater threat than the enemy. On what he described as 'one black morning', First Lieutenant Peter Gretton, still serving aboard the destroyer HMS *Cossack* after its heroics at the Battle of Narvik, was washed into the sea by a wave which swept over the upper deck but – by an astonishing trick of fate – was hurled back on board again by the next wave. Badly bruised but with no bones broken, he went immediately to the bridge to report his mishap to the captain who – with the strained jocularity that so often prevailed in such circumstances – merely 'issued a monumental reprimand for leaving the ship without permission'. Gretton was helped below, where he collapsed from shock.

Two crew members who were swept overboard by the same wave were less fortunate; their bodies were not recovered. As Gretton commented, 'Once over the side there was little chance. The water was icy cold and it took time to turn the ship in the dangerous seas. These large destroyers did not ride over the waves, but seemed to dip the lee gunwale right under when they rolled. The force of the sea was unbelievable.'[1]

Despite such tribulations, there was a certain cachet to serving in destroyers. They cut a dash, they were sleek, fast, manoeuvrable and aggressive and, by virtue of their role as the bodyguards of great battle fleets, they were frequently exposed to the fatal firepower of more powerful enemy warships, a vulnerability which bestowed on their crews an unmatched reputation for derring-do. The same was not true of a corvette. The ugly ducklings of the Atlantic were slow and ungainly. Corkscrewing over the waves rather than slicing through them, they induced seasickness in even the most hardened mariners. Below decks there was little space and no comfort. Sodden with seawater that infiltrated hatches and sluiced down the pipes that housed the anchor chains, the accommodation was humid and ill-ventilated, leaving cabins, clothes and bedding perpetually dewy with condensation. In lesser spirits, such conditions might have stirred mutinous thoughts. And yet these privations appeared to have the opposite effect, inspiring a camaraderie that touched almost every sailor who served in one of the more than 200 Flower class corvettes that for five years of war chivvied the merchant convoys back and forth across the Atlantic.

The testimonies to this are legion: 'Well, I think we were all going through the same sort of thing. We were in the same sort of danger . . . you were in it together. There was no running away from it, was there? You were there and you had to get on with it'; 'on bigger ships you have a great deal more bullshit. But that was the way corvettes were: very special. It was a family and it ran itself'; 'I think the magic of the "Flower Class" corvette is that it's small, a very close knit company of a crew and everyone of you have shared the same experiences, the same feelings . . . It was a family affair.'[2]

Seaman Dennis Jolley, who had been drafted from a frigate to serve in a corvette, noted a sharp contrast as soon as he joined HMS *Crocus*.

> One bloke was speaking to me, and I didn't know who he was, and I said to someone, 'Who was that?' and he said, 'Oh, he's a Jimmy, the first lieutenant; he comes next one down from the skipper.' And he came and spoke to me and asked me who I was and where I came from, and where I'd been and all that, in a nice manner. He didn't have a hat on; he had shorts on, his shirt was hanging out. Now on the *Wye* you weren't allowed on deck without your hat on, you weren't allowed on deck without your lifebelt . . . On the *Crocus* they never worried, it was a different navy, different navy altogether.[3]

Such familiarity evidently failed to breed contempt; nor did the enforced proximity between officers and men erode significantly the distinctions of class and rank by which they were formally separated. 'There was a great division between the wardroom and lower deck which was not breached very much,' Commission Warrant John Arthur recalled, 'Socially ashore there was no contact [which] the Americans didn't understand and the Australians certainly didn't, the fact that you were on the same ship but one was wardroom and one was messdeck.'[4]

The lack of space below decks was especially acute in the galley area. With only enough refrigeration to provide a crew of seventy-five with fresh meat and vegetables for three days, by which time the bread was mouldy, the crew otherwise lived exclusively on dried and tinned food, of which bully beef and hardtack biscuits were the staple. Aside from the occasional tot of rum, the staple drink was Kye, which was made by grating blocks of pure but gritty cocoa into a jar or a pan and boiling it up with water. 'They always used to say, if you could make it so's the spoon would stand up in it, that was okay for drinking,' Leading Seaman Geoffrey Drummond recalled. 'It was bitter to eat, but it made super stuff that stuck to the lining of your stomach . . . I think you really needed something like that on cold nights.'[5]

In rough weather, even Kye failed to alleviate the wretchedness the crew had to endure. The winds were sometimes so fierce and the seas so mountainous that the convoys were unable to make any headway against a storm; even with engines at full power, the pitch-and-toss was so extreme that the screws of a merchant ship would thrash vainly in the air as frequently as under the foaming water. Waves crashed onto foredecks with such power that inch-thick iron stanchions carrying guard wires were bent horizontal as though they had been struck by a giant hammer. Lifeboats were stove in as though they were matchwood. Chests and lockers welded or bolted to the deck were ripped from their fastenings and hurled into the sea. Ordinary Seaman Cyril Stephens reflected a common view: 'It's very, very frightening because a ship rolls and it rolls over and you think it's never going to get back up again. That's frightening, that is frightening.'[6] It was even worse when there was ice. In sub-zero weather seawater would freeze to virtually every part of the superstructure exposed to the elements including the deck, railings and gun emplacements. When this happened even the sturdy corvette became suddenly and alarmingly top heavy. To avert a capsize, the crew was deployed for hour after hour, day and night, to chip away at the weight of ice; to touch bare metal inadvertently without wearing gloves was to have the skin ripped from the palm of your hand.

In one of the many vivid descriptions that would later make him famous as a novelist, Nicholas Monsarrat, who served as an officer in corvettes for much of the war, was moved to a stream of consciousness as he recorded the 'long nightmare' of one Atlantic storm:

> five hundred miles, and six days, of screaming wind and massed, tumbling water, of sleet and snow storms, of a sort of frozen malice in the weather which refused us all progress. Nothing could keep it out:

helmets, mittens, duffle-coats, sea-boot stockings – all were like so much tissue paper. 'Cold?' said the signalman, as he pulled his hand away from the Morse-lamp and left a patch of skin on the handle: 'Cold? I reckon this would freeze the ears off a brass monkey' . . . icy water finds its way everywhere – neck, wrists, trouser-legs, boots: one stands out there like a sodden automaton, ducking behind every rail as every other wave sends spray flying over the compass house, and then standing up to face, with eyes that feel raw and salt-caked and streaming, the wind and rain and the treachery of the sea.

Poor weather was a perpetual torment inflicted with an arbitrary ferocity that seemed to provoke in Monsarrat a parallel anger and resentment that mingled with wonder to produce a resilience that those of his fellow seamen less gifted with the power of language shared in equal measure. Tested to the extreme by the severity of the conditions, their display of stoicism was every bit as heroic, if less dramatic, than that form of courage displayed by soldiers in the heat of battle in the deserts of North Africa, the jungles of Borneo or the barren Russian steppe. In Monsarrat's case, an armoury of words was at his disposal to fling back at the elements:

> Apart from the noise it produces, rolling has a maddening rhythm that is one of the minor tortures of rough weather. It never stops or misses a beat, it cannot be escaped anywhere. If you go through a doorway, it hits you hard: if you sit down, you fall over; you get hurt, knocked about continuously, and it makes for extreme and childish anger. When you drink, the liquid rises towards you and slops over: at meals, the food spills off your plate, the cutlery will not stay in place. Things roll about, and bang, and slide away crazily: and then come back and *hurt* you again. The wind doesn't howl, it *screams* at you, and tears at your clothes, and throws you against things and drives your breath down your throat again . . . Sometimes, at the worst height of a gale, you may be hove-to in this sort of fury for days on end, and all the time you can't forget that you are no nearer shelter than you were twenty-four hours before.[7]

The only comfort to be derived from a gale was the knowledge that the conditions made it virtually impossible for a U-boat to launch its torpedoes with any prospect of success. The Kriegsmarine's submariners suffered no less than their adversaries on the surface: similarly cramped conditions with little room to stand and none to sit in comfort; the sourness of stale air, dirty clothes and unwashed bodies laced with the stench of trapped diesel fumes; and the absence of fresh food, the dependence on tins of vegetables and fruit to vary a diet of smoked sausage (as opposed to bully beef) and biscuits. In bad weather, a U-boat motoring on the surface was every bit as uncomfortable as a corvette. Peter Cremer, one of the few U-boat commanders to survive the war, was to describe his own experience of a January storm, when he was in U-333. He evidently endured a very similar experience to Monsarrat's:

> As far as the eye could see there were only rolling hills with strips of foam coursing down their sides like veins in marble. On the surface the U-boat literally climbed the mountainous seas, plunging through the wave crests, hung for a moment with its stern in the empty air and plunged down the other side into the trough of waves. When it buried its nose, the screws in the stern seemed to be revolving in air . . . Striking high up in front against the conning tower and from behind into the open bridge screen, the seas smothered us and we had to shut the conning tower hatch for a while to prevent foundering.[8]

With the seas crashing down on U-333's deck 'like an avalanche', he felt as though he and his crew were 'whirling about' in 'a dice cup'; it was impossible to perform any useful function, impossible to prepare food and impossible to sleep in hammocks which 'swayed to and fro like washing hung to dry'. On one occasion, despite the distracting tempest, Cremer managed to detect a tanker a mere 3,000 metres away. In quieter conditions, this would have been easy prey. But with the wind at Force 10, the tanker was at one moment on top of 'a mountainous wave' and at the next, 'had disappeared into the valley'. An attack was out of the question. Though he attempted to keep station with his quarry in the hope that the weather might abate, Cremer soon lost sight of the vessel, which escaped into the night. The same thing happened the next day and the day after that. When the conditions became 'unendurable' Cremer ordered all hands to diving-stations. U-333's wild gyrations eased but the turmoil of the ocean ran so deep that the only way absolutely to escape the misery of the 'dice cup' was to go down until they were at least fifty metres beneath the surface. At this level, U-333 lay quite still. 'The cook brought a delicious-smelling stew to table and everyone fell to. Eat and sleep, hear nothing, see nothing."[9] When the storm eased, the hunting and the killing began again.

The weather did not entirely disrupt the tonnage war. In the last three months of 1940, 267 British, Allied and neutral ships – a total of just over 1.1 million tons – was sent to the bottom; in the first three months of 1941, the figure was 314 ships or just over 1.2 million tons. The great majority of these vessels were sunk by U-boats. This rate of attrition was starting to be felt in towns and cities throughout Britain. With food imports running at two-thirds of the pre-war level, a freelance journalist, Maggie Joy Blunt, noted:

> We are not starving, we are not even underfed, but our usually well-stocked food shops have an empty and anxious air. Cheese, eggs, onions, oranges, luxury fruits and vegetables are practically unobtainable . . . Housewives are having to queue for essential foods . . . Prices are rising . . . The outlook really seems very grim indeed.[10]

A fortnight later Nella Last noted:

> With everybody killing and fighting each other, and sinking each other's ships, and crops not getting planted, and the labour shortage everywhere due to men being soldiers instead of growing food – how soon will there be famine over the world? . . . Nowadays when my husband and I hear bad news on the radio, we just look at each other and don't talk much about it.[11]

The following month she went to her local market, where she found 'closed stalls everywhere . . . I wandered about with a sadness in my heart. I loved the market and the joyous spirit there . . . Now grim-faced women queue and push – and hurry off to another queue when served.'[12]

During a fortnight that straddled the end of April and the beginning of May, the Luftwaffe targeted Barrow-in-Furness, killing eighty-three citizens and damaging or destroying 10,000 houses. Nella Last did not escape. 'A night of terror,' she wrote on 4 May,

> Land mines, incendiaries and explosives were dropped, and we cowered thankfully under our indoor shelter . . . I've got a sick shadow over me as I look at my lovely little house that will never be the same again. The windows are nearly all out, the metal frames all strained, the ceilings

down, the walls cracked . . . The house rocked, and then the kitchenette door careered down the hall.[13]

The next day, in the hope of restoring her spirits, she went shopping to discover that there was no meat for sale in town. For a nation where a meal without beef, mutton, chicken or pork was no meal at all, the introduction of meat rationing in March 1940 had been particularly demoralizing. With imports providing well over half the nation's needs, reserve stocks fell steadily; by January the following year, the reserves were almost exhausted. The Ministry of Food responded by cutting the weekly allowance repeatedly until, by the spring of 1941, butchers frequently ran out of supplies. For Nella Last it was a cause for modest rejoicing when, three days after her house collapsed around her, she was able to buy 'a veal jelly-bone, with enough meat on it to make a little bowl of potted meat, and a shank-end mutton bone for a stock-pot – all for 2s. 1d.'[14]

Churchill was acutely sensitive to these shortages and the effect they might have on public morale but he did not allow himself the luxury of despair. On the contrary. In the spirit of wishful thinking which frequently carried him through hard times, he coined a new phrase to match the moment, and used it for the first time to issue a 'Most Secret' Battle of the Atlantic Directive for the benefit of his colleagues and senior officials in Whitehall: 'The next four months should enable us to defeat the attempt to strangle our food supplies and our connection with the United States', he wrote on 6 March 1941. Ordering an onslaught against the German submarine fleet, he instructed that the U-boats were to be 'hunted' at sea and bombed in the building yards and in the docks and that the Admiralty was to have first call on all short-range anti-aircraft guns, of which 'a constant flow' was to be made available.

But the battle also had to be fought at home. With Britain losing merchant ships at a faster rate than the shipyards could replace them, the directive emphasized the urgent need to simplify and accelerate the repair of damaged shipping. An additional 40,000 workers were to be taken on to reduce the 'terrible slowness of the turn-round of ships in British ports', while the Ministry of Transport was to 'ensure' that there was 'no congestion at the quays'.[15] This was much easier said than done.

In significant measure, the prime minister had himself to blame for what now promised to become a critical shortage of merchant ships. As First Lord of the Admiralty, he had been instrumental in the appointment of a Scottish shipping magnate, Sir James Lithgow, as Controller of Merchant Shipbuilding and Repair, with the task of shaping wartime policy for the industry. Lithgow had form. Over the previous decade, as chairman of the National Shipbuilders Securities (NSS), he had earned the lasting enmity of the shipbuilding unions by overseeing the contraction of Britain's shipbuilding capacity by a third with the loss of tens of thousands of jobs. In this process, he came to regard the unions with loathing, a feeling that was reciprocated in full measure by those who found themselves on the dole as a result of decisions for which he bore overarching responsibility. In an unforgiving reflection on those times, the Confederation of Shipbuilding and Engineering Unions (CSEU), the country's largest shipbuilding union, was to use an official inquiry in 1942 to lambast Lithgow's NSS, claiming, in the words of a senior official, that the employers had destroyed the livelihoods of workers 'who had given a lifetime of service . . . In the carrying out of their policy they deliberately lowered the building capacity of the Industry without regards to the nation's need, either in peace or war.'[16]

In his new wartime role, Lithgow did little to repair this damage. Instead he contrived to establish a policy which reflected the narrow interests of his peers. Backed by the Admiralty's bureaucrats, he opposed an all-out expansion of production, he opposed standardization of design and parts and he opposed centralization of control, endorsing instead a light regulatory regime which made it easy for individual shipbuilders to maximize their profits while minimizing the power of the unions to bring effective pressure on their employers. In this way, an official in the Ministry of Labour noted, 'the hidden hand' of the owners contributed to the lamentable failure of the industry to increase output on anything like the scale required to meet the worsening shortfall.[17]

The damage wrought by Lithgow's boneheaded approach to the crisis was compounded by an acute shortage of skilled labour. Churchill could call for 40,000 additional workers but they could not be conjured out of the rhetorical ether. The collapse of the shipping industry in the thirties as a result of the Depression had steered younger labourers into other industries. However, apprentice schemes had been curtailed while many of those who had lost their jobs were either reluctant to return to the yards or were no longer equipped to do so. Despite the efforts of Ernest Bevin – whom Churchill had appointed Minister of Labour in May 1940 – to broker a rapprochement between the owners and the unions (where he had latterly been a formidable figure as leader of the Transport and General Workers Union), the mutual acrimony persisted.

Attitudes hardened on both sides so that in early 1942, a junior government minister, Philip Noel-Baker, would be informed by a correspondent that:

> Lithgow is acting as a deterrent to production in the West of Scotland Shipyards. Rightly or wrongly, he is referred to locally as the King of Scotland . . . he is considered to be the cause of all the unemployment and evil times which the Clydeside Shipping Industry has suffered during the last fifteen years. Mistrust is so deep that enthusiasm for the war effort is not possible so long as the choice seems to lie between Lithgow and Hitler.[18]

Although, as the historian Kevin Smith has noted, only a small minority in the shipyards 'idled their time away, overmanned their jobs, wasted materials, and knocked off work thirty minutes before dinner and again at day's end', the malaise was deep seated. An Admiralty employee, in correspondence with Noel-Baker, observed:

> The workers feel that this is their harvest after years of want; the longer the war lasts the better for them, that when the war ends they will return to their poverty and the dole. The end of the war is a major catastrophe, since it will bring with it the end of their prosperity . . . to ask them to increase their efforts is at the same time to bring about their ruin.[19]

Observing this stand-off from his perspective as a naval officer on escort duty in the Atlantic, Nicholas Monsarrat was aghast but did not blame the workers so much as the owners:

> Many of these men who strike now were treated like dirt for years before the war: almost literally like dirt – they were tipped and shovelled out of the way and on to a sort of slag-heap of unemployed and unemployables. They didn't learn love of country from that . . . Now they have power, almost paramount power, and they use it to square up the account. It isn't patriotism (the system that pauperized them wasn't

patriotism either): it is not in the end even common sense; but it is assuredly human nature.[20]

To combat alienation and apathy in the shipyards and docks, Bevin resorted to patriotic propaganda, hoping to persuade the workers that they were helping to feed the nation, not merely serving their bosses. A poster depicting a soldier wearing a tin helmet and carrying a rifle urged a Liverpool dockworker, manhandling a wooden crate, 'GO TO IT CHUM! That's war work – we get munitions in return for that lot!' In a strapline across the bottom of the poster, the message was rammed home with a quotation from Bevin, 'WE MUST HAVE EXPORTS'.[21] Despite such efforts and the willingness of the great majority of those working for firms like Cammell Laird, Harland and Wolff, and Grayson Rollo to honour their contracts of employment, it nonetheless proved impossible to staunch the shipping haemorrhage either by accelerating turnaround times to any significant degree or by replacing merchant ships at a faster rate than they were being damaged or destroyed. Although the problem was aggravated by the Luftwaffe's bombing raids on Merseyside in which some 4,000 people were killed and 10,000 homes destroyed, the seeds of a worsening crisis had been sown before the war by the crude rationalization of the shipping industry and the deep and persistent antagonism thus engendered between crass owners and resentful workers.

The losses in the Atlantic continued to grow inexorably. In February 1941 400,000 tons of shipping was sunk; in March the figure was well over 500,000 tons; by April it was to approach 700,000 tons. These figures were so disturbing that Churchill ordered the Minister of Information, Duff Cooper, to discontinue the publication of weekly sinkings:

> When the Press asks why have the week's figures not come out, the answer will be that they are to be published monthly instead of weekly. When the comment is made that we are afraid to publish weekly, because, as you say, we 'desire to cover up the size of our most recent shipping losses', the answer should be, 'Well, that is what we are going to do anyway.'

Aware that this degree of censorship would provoke adverse speculation, he added drily, 'We shall have a lot worse to put up with in the near future.'[22]

The relentless pressures of the mortal danger posed by the U-boats in the Atlantic imposed a severe strain on the prime minister's relations with the Admiralty and, in particular, with his successor as First Lord, A. V. Alexander. One of the most telling illustrations of this was prompted by Churchill's assiduous efforts to solicit the White House for support. Noting in March, 'It is to the United States [ship]building that we must look for relief in 1942,'[23] he was relieved when, in the weeks following Roosevelt's Lend-Lease victory in Congress, the president undertook to provide the Royal Navy with ten coastguard vessels requisitioned for the purpose from a reluctant US Navy. However, the Admiralty's response to this offer was less than ecstatic. With a prudence and caution that were inimical to Churchill, Alexander opted to look Roosevelt's gift horse in the mouth and cabled the British naval attaché in Washington accordingly: 'Is it the intention that these ships will be manned by USA or by ourselves? . . . Also please confirm whether vessels are of newer type speed 20 knots or of older type speed 16½ knots. Newer type would be of considerably greater value.'[24] Insensitivity of this order could not have been better calculated to get under Churchill's skin; similarly the pettifogging response to the news that the ten coastguard cutters – each of which required a crew of around a hundred – would have to be brought across the Atlantic by British sailors. Instead of welcoming America's largesse and finding ways to acknowledge it, the navy's bureaucrats merely complained that they did not have the men for the task.

By contrast, Churchill was purring with rare delight because the president had sent him a personal note to confirm the arrangement. On 5 April the PM wrote at once to the First Lord and the First Sea Lord: 'let me be assured that all is in train for manning and bringing into action these vessels at the earliest moment'.[25] This was precisely the assurance that neither of them could provide. Pound drafted a reply to the prime minister, which the First Lord duly forwarded under his own name, explaining among other things that the ratings who had been earmarked to crew the US cutters had been serving overseas on battleships for four years without a break and would very soon be required to serve on the new *Duke of York*. 'The welfare side must be considered,' he wrote. 'They require leave in England, and to send them at once on escort duties without seeing their homes should be avoided if possible.'[26]

Churchill's response verged on the vindictive:

This is a great pity, and I am very sorry to hear of these delays. Considering the vital character of the Battle of the Atlantic, I am surprised that the Admiralty take such an easy-going view of their responsibilities . . . Remember that our merchant seamen are to be drowned and their ships sunk in the interval. I am entirely out of sympathy with these kind of proposals.[27]

Pound resented the prime ministerial slur and, for once, his response, via Alexander, was robust:

The prime minister refers to the question of leave. I consider that it should be pointed out to him that since the first day of the war, the Navy have been working under a degree of stress which no Navy has ever worked under before and which is on a different level to anything that either of the other Services have done. When men are being worked under such extreme pressure it is essential that they should receive certain consideration, and the consideration which is necessary is a matter which only the Admiralty can judge.[28]

Alexander decided against forwarding Pound's message to the prime minister; indeed, noting that Churchill's minute 'was rather ill-tempered, and it did not specifically call for any answer', he didn't give one.[29] In the circumstances, it was a judicious decision.

President Roosevelt was well aware that the Atlantic lifeline not only mattered greatly to Britain but was also essential to the security of the United States. In a cable to Churchill on 3 May he wrote: 'I believe that the outcome of this struggle is going to be decided in the Atlantic and unless Hitler can win there he cannot win anywhere in the world in the end.'[30] This unequivocal statement not only reflected his own intuition but was the fruit of extensive debate with his most senior advisors. By January 1941 the Secretary of the Navy Frank Knox, the Army Chief of Staff General George Marshall, Secretary of War Henry Stimson and Chief of Naval Operations Admiral Harold ('Betty') Stark had reached a strategic consensus of the greatest importance. Notwithstanding the growing threat posed to American interests in the Pacific by the expansionist drive of the Japanese government, they resolved that the defence of Britain should be an overriding priority for the United States. At a meeting on 17 January, Roosevelt endorsed their judgement but, ever mindful of public opinion, refused to contemplate direct military action against Germany as they had urged. Nonetheless, he not only agreed that the maintenance of the supply lines to Britain was in America's vital interest but ordered the US Navy to make plans to provide an armed escort for merchant convoys heading towards Britain across the Atlantic. To that end, he initially authorized Stark to transfer three battleships, an aircraft carrier, four cruisers and a number of other smaller vessels from the US Pacific Fleet. However, he later drew back from this step for fear that, as he told reporters, such a move would bring America 'awfully close to war . . . [which was] about the last thing we have in our minds'.[31] The polls remained his overriding constraint: a majority of voters opposed the very principle of escorting merchant ships, to the point where – by 50 per cent to 40 per cent – they were against being drawn into war against the Third Reich even if German submarines were to sink American warships which were guarding unarmed merchantmen. To avoid reawakening this leviathan and provoking a legislative backlash in Congress, Roosevelt moved adroitly but decisively to achieve very much the same purpose but by different and – ostensibly – more cautious means.

On 10 April he told his military advisors that he intended unilaterally to extend the US Security Zone far out into the Atlantic to longitude 25°W, an invisible north–south line some 2,600 miles from the coast of America that runs from Greenland in the north to the Azores in the south. Within this vast expanse of ocean, US air and naval patrols would be charged to monitor the movement of hostile craft and report their whereabouts to the Royal Navy so that the convoys might take avoiding action. In outlining his plan to the prime minister the next day, Roosevelt wrote: 'We will want in great secrecy notification of movement of convoys so our patrol units can seek out any ships or planes of aggressor nations operating west of the new line . . . We will immediately make public to you [the] position [of] aggressor ships or planes when located in our patrol area.'[32] From Churchill's point of view this was a dramatic breakthrough, a convincing demonstration that the president was finally ready to nudge the United States a little closer to open conflict with Germany. Thus it was with 'the greatest relief' that he thanked the president for his 'momentous message'.[33] Although Hitler had instructed the Kriegsmarine to avoid any confrontation with

American warships, the possibility of an inadvertent maritime clash was self-evident to everyone.

In parallel to these critical moves on the Atlantic chessboard, the early months of 1941 were hectic with transatlantic diplomacy which placed Churchill's Battle of the Atlantic in its wider context. In the eight weeks between the end of January and the end of March, British and American officials met in Washington in an attempt to hammer out a framework of priorities were the United States to form an alliance with Britain to confront Germany in what was still essentially a European war. These talks – codenamed ABC-1 – were tortuous and complex but by the end of March had yielded a plan that was to shape the contours of Allied policy in the years ahead. In the early stages of these negotiations, Admiral 'Betty' Stark had sent Knox a note defining as a major national objective for the United States the 'prevention of the disruption of the British Empire, with all that such a consummation implies'. To this end, he forecast presciently, it would ultimately be necessary 'to send large air and land forces to Europe or Africa, or both'.[34]

Although this presentiment did not figure in the ABC-1 agreement, the document contained at its core an overt understanding that Europe and the Atlantic should be defined as the decisive theatre of the war even if the United States and Japan were to go to war with each other. By implication, the document also endorsed Churchill's own commitment to the British Empire and therefore to the Middle East, North Africa, and the Mediterranean as well as the Far East. Although this strategic vision would be subjected to extreme stress within the US administration once that moment arrived in December 1941, Roosevelt himself never deviated from his commitment to the belief he shared with Churchill that the defeat of Hirohito's Japan should follow the defeat of Hitler's Germany and Mussolini's Italy.

In addition to these diplomatic initiatives over which he presided from a distance, Churchill was preoccupied in the first half of 1941 with a host of overlapping setbacks: the 'disastrous' rout of Wavell's army in North Africa by the Afrikakorps, which had arrived in February under the command of General Erwin Rommel;[35] the Wehrmacht's rapid thrust southwards through Europe to occupy Romania, overrun Yugoslavia and, in April, to raise the Swastika over Athens – a development which led to a British expeditionary force fleeing the country; the loss of Crete (to where the British survivors of the ill-judged Greek campaign had been evacuated); and an urgent diplomatic drive to shore up the neutrality of Turkey, the survival of which bore directly on British interests in Iran, the Persian Gulf, and the Middle East, not to mention the Middle East itself. The only good news from the imperial front in those testing weeks had been the defeat of the Italian Empire in East Africa, Ethiopia and Eritrea (where Indian troops under the Middle East Command had fought with notable valour) in February. This rare victory had allowed Roosevelt to remove the Red Sea from the list of combat zones forbidden to US vessels, which, in turn, allowed the Americans to transport Lend-Lease military supplies across the Atlantic, round the Cape and into the Indian Ocean, thence to Suez to provision the armies under Wavell's Middle East Command. However, set against manifold losses, that victory was but a small mercy.

It is hard to exaggerate the sense of foreboding that prevailed in both London and Washington during this period. From London, Averell Harriman, Roosevelt's special envoy and coordinator of the Lend-Lease programme, wrote to Harry Hopkins, the president's closest confidant, in near despair: 'It has been as if living in a nightmare, with some calamity hanging constantly over one's head. I have not expected any war news that would make us happy.' After a visit with Churchill to the bomb-devastated city of Portsmouth, he added, 'the destruction was fantastic (I think the details had best be omitted) but the people are amazing . . . But how long can they last out unless there continues real confidence in victory?'[36] On 2 May Churchill's private secretary described a conversation between Churchill and Harriman at the end of a day of particularly bleak news from all fronts, noting that the prime minister, 'in worse gloom than I have ever seen him . . . sketched out a world in which Hitler dominated all Europe, Asia and Africa and left the US and ourselves no option but an unwilling peace'.[37] When he reflected on 'the unceasing tumult of war', Churchill himself found it impossible to recall 'any period when its stresses and the onset of so many problems all at once or in rapid succession bore more directly on me and my colleagues than the first half of 1941'.[38]

With Britain's Atlantic lifeline under growing strain, the embattled Admiralty was no less anxious than Churchill, albeit with a narrower focus. The gloom was pervasive, pierced only occasionally by good news. In March 1941 the confirmation that Germany's three most famous U-boat aces had been removed from the fray caused a frisson of elation and a degree of relief. Four months earlier Günther Prien, Joachim Schepke, and Otto Kretschmer had met for dinner in a restaurant a few miles outside Lorient to celebrate the fact that, with the addition of five oak leaves to his Iron Cross, Kretschmer had just been honoured by Hitler in person with the highest award for gallantry in the German armed services. Following his devastating role in the attack on convoy HX72 in September (when eleven out of forty-three ships were sunk), he had gone on to sink three British armed merchant cruisers in November as well as yet more merchant ships. On his return to Lorient he had been summoned to the Chancellery in Berlin, where Hitler showered him with praise, handed him his glittering prize and then, *summa cum laude*, invited him to sit with him to discuss the progress of the U-boat campaign. Seizing the moment and reflecting Dönitz's frustration, Kretschmer pressed the need not only for more U-boats – only twenty-four were currently operational – but for air reconnaissance as well. Apparently impressed, Hitler nodded, rose from his seat and said, 'Thank you, commander. You have been admirably frank, and I shall do what I can for you and your colleagues.'[39]

While Kretschmer was making the most of his encounter with the Führer, Dönitz was putting similar pressure on the naval high command, urging that aircraft deployed on reconnaissance should be placed under the direct control of the U-boat Command. Some days later, he pressed the point again at a meeting with Admiral Raeder and, immediately afterwards, with General Alfred Jodl, the Wehrmacht's head of operations. He clearly made a compelling case because, on 7 January, Hitler – perhaps with Kretschmer's words still in his mind – authorized the transfer of a group of reconnaissance aircraft from the Luftwaffe to the U-boat Command. Dönitz was delighted, noting in his War Diary: 'This order is a great step forward.'[40] As head of the Luftwaffe, Göring was furious that Hitler had taken this decision without consulting him. The Reichsmarschall invited Dönitz to join him on the train which was retained in perpetual readiness for his personal use. According to the U-boat commander-in-chief, who had not met him before, Göring 'did his utmost to persuade me to agree to a cancellation of the Fuehrer's order, but this I refused to do. He then invited me to stay to dinner, but I declined the invitation, and we parted bad friends.'[41] Hitler's decision was to prove less propitious than Dönitz had hoped but it marked a signal personal victory for the commander of the U-boat arm and one that Göring would not easily forgive.

At their celebration dinner outside Lorient, Schepke, the most boisterous member of the trio, suggested a wager. All three aces believed they had each sunk more than 200,000 tons of shipping – though in fact only Kretschmer had surpassed that total – and there was an unstated rivalry between the three very different individuals. According to Dönitz, Prien, who had made his reputation by sinking the *Royal Oak* in Scapa Flow, was 'a great personality, full of zest and energy and the joy of life' whom he held in 'great affection and esteem', Schepke was 'a real thruster', but Kretschmer's 'exploits stood alone'.[42] Like the other two, the most successful U-boat commander of the Second World War evinced no fear but, if he lacked Schepke's charm and exuberance or Prien's swagger (not to mention his sharp tongue and quick temper), Kretschmer inspired unquestioning loyalty. According to his biographer, he ran his ship like a 'martinet, who nonetheless was a captain in whom any of his crew could safely confide their troubles'.[43] After dinner, as they followed the wine with coffee and brandy, Schepke allegedly said, 'Let us wager on which of us reaches 250,000 tons first. I offer to provide the champagne for the three of us if either of you beats me to it. If I win, then you will see to it that I am wined and dined with suitable trimmings. Is it a bet?'[44] The other two assented.

On 19 February Prien left Lorient in U-47, followed soon after by Kretschmer and Schepke. On 25 February, in the North Atlantic, he located a convoy of thirty-nine ships guarded by seven escorts. He signalled U-boat headquarters at Lorient: 'Enemy convoy in sight on westerly course at estimated speed seven knots. Am being driven off by air patrols.'[45] It was an 'outbound' convoy, OB290, en route to Halifax. Soon after midnight Prien attacked, sinking three ships and damaging one more. Still tracking the convoy while reloading his torpedoes, his signals alerted three Condor bombers from Gruppe 40 (transferred from the Luftwaffe to the U-boat arm) and later that day they sank another seven enemy freighters.

Two days later Prien and Kretschmer in U-99 stumbled across one another close to the position from where Prien had signalled. Exchanging messages by semaphore, Kretschmer told Prien that Schepke in U-100 was close behind. The two aces then set off in pursuit of the convoy, which was still invisible in the mist. Suddenly this veil lifted to reveal not only the convoy but two destroyers, one of which immediately turned to head towards them. U-47 and U-99 dived at once and managed to escape unharmed. By now, with the wind rising to gale force, making it far too rough to make it worth expending a torpedo with very little chance of scoring a hit, the three U-boats merely tried to keep station with the convoy, alternately making contact before finally losing it for good.

On 6 March Prien sighted another convoy heading westwards. The thirty-seven ships in OB293 were escorted by two corvettes and two destroyers, HMS *Wolverine* and HMS *Verity*. In the early hours of the following morning four U-boats went on the attack, led by Prien in U-47 and Kretschmer in U-99. Adopting the technique which had brought him so many kills already, Kretschmer engineered his way into the middle of the convoy and swiftly added two more to his tally. Another merchantman was sunk by U-70. But, on this occasion, the escorts responded with alacrity as the two corvettes, HMS *Camellia* and HMS *Arbutus*, charged towards the submarine, forcing her captain, Joachim Matz, to crash-dive to avoid being rammed.

For the next four hours the pair hunted U-70 without a moment's pause. Eventually, after dropping more than fifty depth charges, they scored a direct hit which inflicted terminal damage. Despite frenzied efforts by Matz and his crew, the submarine fell uncontrollably to a depth of more than 650 feet. At this point, Matz blew all his ballast tanks with high-pressure air, which proved just enough to force the stricken vessel to the surface. When the captain opened the conning tower hatch, the pressure inside the vessel was so great as to blow him and a number of his crew up on to the bridge deck. Twenty-six of them, including Matz, jumped into the sea, where they were rescued by life rafts dropped by *Arbutus*. The remaining twenty-five men, who did not have time to escape, were trapped inside the hull and perished as U-70 sank beneath the waves.

More by chance than skill, Kretschmer managed to escape this bombardment despite a barrage of depth charges dropped by the two British destroyers which exploded close enough to cause U-99 to rock, pitch and groan under the impact. Prien, meanwhile, had apparently continued to shadow the convoy, sending out reports through the night of its position and speed. Then the signals from Prien ceased. Dönitz became concerned and signalled: 'U-47 report position, conditions and successes.'[46] There was no reply. The much-garlanded thirty-three-year-old ace, who had sunk the *Royal Oak* in Scapa Flow and twenty-nine other ships in the space of his short career, was not heard from again. Soon afterwards the Admiralty announced that 'the circumstantial evidence' was strong enough to validate the claim by HMS *Wolverine*'s captain for his ship to be credited with the demise of one of Germany's most feared U-boat commanders. Much later, the Admiralty was to revise its verdict, judging the evidence to be too flimsy to stand. Although it made good wartime propaganda for a hard-pressed British government to announce that a British destroyer had wreaked vengeance on the U-boat captain who had humiliated the Royal Navy at Scapa Flow, the precise cause of Prien's disappearance would remain a mystery.

Some days later Kretschmer and Schepke were both patrolling in the Western Approaches when they received a signal from Lorient ordering them to close on a convoy some 150 miles south of Iceland. HX112, which comprised forty-one merchant ships bound for Liverpool from Nova Scotia under protection from six Royal Navy escorts, had been detected on the evening of 15 March by Fritz-Julius Lemp. Another of Dönitz's young aces, Lemp had recently graduated from U-30, in which he had sunk the *Athenia* on the first day of the war, to take command of U-110, a new type IXB vessel which had greater range and speed than the type VIIs in which he and his fellow U-boat commanders had already inflicted so much damage. After reporting his find to Dönitz, Lemp went on the offensive, torpedoing a 6,200-ton tanker, the *Erodona*, in the early hours of 16 March.

On board the destroyer HMS *Walker*, the escort commander, Captain Donald Macintyre (who had played a prominent role in the Narvik battle as the commander of HMS *Hesperus*) watched aghast as the *Erodona* exploded: 'I had never before seen this most appalling of all night disasters . . . we were shocked into silence by the horror of it and the immediate thought that none could survive.'[47] Galvanized by what he had just witnessed, Macintyre summoned a posse of warships to join him in the search for the offending U-boat. However, their ASDICs failed to detect any answering echo from beneath the waves. Lemp had got away.*

---

* Despite Macintyre's initial fears, fifteen members of her fifty-one crew survived the inferno and had time to take to the lifeboats. That night there were no further attacks and the following day also passed without incident, while the crippled *Erodona* was towed back to Iceland. The ship was later repaired and returned to service in 1943.

By this time, Macintyre had ordered a 'drastic alteration of course' by which – he dared to hope – any pursuing wolf pack might have been thrown off the scent. For a while the tactic seemed to have worked: U-99 and U-100, accompanied by U-37 (under the command of Asmus Clausen), had indeed temporarily lost contact with the convoy. Soon after 10 p.m., however, HX112 was once again in their sights and, within minutes, Kretschmer, in his customary fashion, penetrated into the very middle of the convoy. Within the hour, five more ships had been sent to the bottom.

Macintyre was at a loss: 'I was near to despair and I racked my brains to find some way to stop the holocaust.'[48] As the escorts under his command churned back and forth through the water 'searching in vain for the almost invisible enemy', Macintyre steered *Walker* into a gentle curve while he stared into the night for the tell-tale white wake of a retreating U-boat. A few moments later he saw what he wanted. As he ordered full speed ahead, the U-boat crash-dived, a swirl of phosphorescent water marking the spot precisely for the destroyer to drop ten depth charges. A crescendo of explosions and the fountains of water that rose to mast height convinced Macintyre that he must have killed his quarry: 'We could hardly have missed; it had been so quick we must have dropped them smack on top of him.'

It was not so. In the absence of any wreckage rising to the surface, Macintyre had little choice but to extend the search. Half an hour later, *Walker*'s ASDIC made contact again. Macintyre summoned a sister destroyer, HMS *Vanoc*, to join the hunt, and together the two ships dropped a pattern of depth charges where their target was presumed to be. But the submarine – U-100 with Schepke in command – proved to be an elusive prey, twisting and turning with such panache that the two destroyers were flummoxed. The sea was so agitated by the multiple explosions that the British ASDIC operators were unable to distinguish between the ping from one or another depth charge and the same sound from the U-boat. Macintyre was forced to suspend the chase.

However, at least one of the twenty-nine depth charges released by the two British warships had hit its mark. U-100 had been badly damaged. The explosions had 'smashed instruments, knocked out the pumps, and caused heavy flooding'.[49] With its control systems knocked out of action, the U-boat sank, involuntarily, to a depth of 750 feet, deeper than any U-boat had ever been before. Fearing that the hull might implode under the extreme pressures to which it was now being subjected and apparently still believing that he had a chance to torpedo one of his persecutors, Schepke ordered his crew to blow the tanks. When the submarine rose to the surface at around 3 a.m. on 17 March, he opened the conning tower only to see a destroyer heading in his direction at high speed. The British warship had detected the U-boat from a distance of about 1,000 yards, but with neither the naked eye nor binoculars. *Vanoc* had been equipped with one of the first seaborne radar devices, a quantum leap in technology that was eventually to prove decisive in the Battle of the Atlantic and 'the first verifiable British surface-ship radar contact on a U-boat'.[50]

Schepke, of course, knew none of this but only that his crippled vessel was in imminent danger of being run down. In the hope of arresting *Vanoc*'s headlong advance, he tried to manoeuvre into a position which would allow him to fire the last of his torpedoes. At first neither the diesel nor the electric engines would start, and when they did, the disoriented commander ordered 'Full Ahead' rather than 'Full Astern', as he had surely intended. By now it was too late. At 03.18, according to *Vanoc*'s log, the destroyer sliced through U-100's conning tower. Schepke ordered his crew to abandon ship. There were six survivors from a crew of fifty. Schepke was not among them. As he gave his last order he was crushed to death between U-100's bridge and *Vanoc*'s bow. His body fell into the sea and disappeared from view.

So far Kretschmer, the ace of aces, had eluded detection and had hopes of slipping away and heading home to Lorient. But he reckoned without a careless lookout who failed to see that U-99 was gliding along the surface perilously close to *Walker*. When the officer on watch saw that the British warship was not much over a mile away, Kretschmer ordered a crash-dive. No one aboard *Walker* had noticed the U-boat, but once it was underwater the destroyer's sonar operator detected the tell-tale ping, and shouted 'Contact! Contact!' Macintyre was at first incredulous; it seemed impossible that another U-boat should be found so swiftly after the sinking of U-100. But as the sonar echo got louder and louder there could be no doubt. *Walker* ran in to attack, dropping a pattern of six depth charges. The blast waves rocked the enemy boat, shattering dials, chronometers and gauges, including the main depth gauge, which meant Kretschmer had no idea how deep they were. With all lights fused and oily water rising above their ankles in the crew's quarters, Kretschmer decided that he had no choice but to blow the ballast tanks and rise to the surface. But the petty officer in charge of the control room was unable to release the relevant air valve. As the boat began to sink further, Kretschmer's trusted navigator, Warrant Officer Peterson, reading from a second depth gauge in the forward compartment, calmly recorded their free fall towards the bottom. When they had reached a depth of 720 feet, there was a sound of cracking from the stern; they were well below the depth at which U-99's hull might have been expected to implode. At that moment two seamen, summoning the strength of otherwise doomed men, managed to shift the air valve. Kretschmer shouted, 'Open it wide and fast!'[51] Nose first, U-99 rushed to the surface, to settle there like a sitting-duck, unable to move in any direction.

*Walker* was about to make a second run at U-99, which Macintyre presumed to be still somewhere below the surface, when *Vanoc* signalled 'U-boat surfaced astern of me'. Gun crews from both warships fired tracer bullets and heavier shells from their 4-inch guns. According to Macintyre the blinding flashes and tracer 'made a great display, though I fear their accuracy was not remarkable'.[52]

By the time Kretschmer opened the conning tower hatch, U-99 was on her side, lolling helplessly in the swell. Still hoping that he could use a torpedo to hit one of the destroyers which was lying astern only a little way off, he urged his engineers to get the U-boat moving again. But, although they managed to fire up the engines, the propellers had either been blown off or badly buckled, which made it impossible to maintain steerage way. Kretschmer watched impotently as some of *Walker*'s crossfire hit its mark, pinging into the U-boat's delicate hull. With his command slowly sinking beneath him, he ordered U-99's crew to come up on deck in preparation for the order to abandon ship.

Apparently Kretschmer then sat himself down under the shelter of the conning tower and 'to his men's amazement, proceeded to light a cigar'.[53] He had intended to scuttle the submarine but it proved impossible to open the door to the locker where the necessary charges were stored. With the U-boat settling deeper into the water, Kretschmer made a short speech to his men before ordering them to collect warm clothes and lifebelts from below. Suddenly the submarine reared up at a sharp angle. As some of the crew fell into the sea and water poured in through the open hatches, Kretschmer ordered Peterson to signal the nearest destroyer: 'From Captain to Captain . . . Please pick up my men drifting towards you in the water stop I am sunking [sic].'[54] At night, with the destroyer heaving uneasily in a heavy swell, *Walker*'s signaller had some excuse for only picking up the last three words, which Macintyre immediately presumed to be an act of surrender.[55]

Whatever his message was intended to convey, Kretschmer had no intention of allowing U-99 to be seized by the enemy. The only way to do this was sink his vessel by flooding the ballast tanks. An engineer volunteered to descend into the hull again for this purpose. It is likely that he succeeded. Within a few minutes, the U-boat disappeared beneath the waves, taking the indomitable engineer with her. Kretschmer and the rest of the crew were washed off into the sea, where they formed up in a line, linking arms to make sure they did not become separated from one another. Macintyre manoeuvred *Walker* to pick up these survivors, some of whom, he recorded, were already 'in the last stages of exhaustion from the cold of those icy northern waters'.[56]

Kretschmer, still wearing his captain's hat, was the last man to be picked up. According to his biographer, he was 'pulled on the destroyer's deck, weak after hours of action and tension' whereupon 'a large Colt .45 pistol was poked in his face' by a 'cheerful, grinning Petty Officer'.[57] Macintyre did not mention this but only recalled 'an amusing little incident [when] Kretschmer found to his surprise that he still had slung around his neck his Zeiss binoculars, a very special pair made at Dönitz's orders for presentation to a selected few aces'. According to Macintyre, Kretschmer had always sworn that no enemy would ever obtain these prize binoculars and, for this reason, the U-boat commander now tried to throw them into the sea. But he was too late. They were snatched from him by one of *Walker*'s crew and handed over to Macintyre, who duly recorded, 'I claimed them as my prize of war. For the rest of the war they were my inseparable companions and played their part in bringing several of Kretschmer's successors to a similar fate.'[58]

It was only at this point that *Walker*'s crew realized that their prisoner was the most renowned and successful U-boat commander of the war. By Kretschmer's own account, he and his crew were treated with consideration and courtesy by Macintyre, who made his own cabin available for the German ace. Before the war, Kretschmer had been a student at Exeter University, an experience which had evidently tempered any animosity he may have harboured for the British. Macintyre was surprised to discover that his adversary was 'far from the fanatical Hitlerite we had half-expected. Indeed as a professional naval officer and a most skilful one, he had much the same attitude to politics as we had ourselves and preferred to restrict himself to his duties and lament the mess the politicians had made of things.'[59] This assessment was later confirmed inadvertently by Kretschmer himself when secret recordings were made of a conversation between him and a fellow POW from U-99 in which he said: 'I only hope that the war will soon be over, as it is no fun to sit here caged up, and one gets nothing out of war either. For a long time I have felt no more enthusiasm for the war.'[60] In the same conversation Kretschmer also confided that he had spent much of his time in the British destroyer playing bridge and drinking whisky with his captors, from whom he derived the impression that, like him, they too thought 'the war is absurd and hope it will soon be over'. The regard in which officers in the Kriegsmarine and the Royal Navy still held each other, despite a mutual urge to destruction, undoubtedly stemmed from their shared appreciation of the perilous nature of war at sea and a common respect for the skill, enterprise and character required by those individuals who fought to the death in the isolation of the ocean.

When the 'battered and salt-stained' *Walker* docked back in Liverpool at Prince's Landing Stage, which was usually reserved for what her captain described as 'more lordly vessels', Macintyre and his crew were gratified to be welcomed in person by the newly appointed head of Western Approaches Command, Admiral Sir Percy Noble, who was renowned for his affability as well as a clear mind and a talent for organization. Noble was accompanied by a gaggle of senior officers, 'all anxious to give us their congratulations'.[61] Kretschmer was impressed by the untoward respect he too was accorded by the Royal Navy: 'When I came off the destroyer I was treated like a young god. A small car was standing by and there was a great number of officers. It was a really imposing ceremony. There was a silence and I came down with slow and measured tread. I must say it was all done very well.'[62]

Next day, however, when Kretschmer and his crew were taken from their prison cells to be led through the streets of Liverpool to Lime Street station for their journey to London, where they were to be interrogated, the mood was very different. 'The people were furious, I can tell you. You just can't imagine it,' Kretschmer told his cellmate later, 'The women were the worst. If I'd fallen into their hands, they'd have torn me to bits. There was a whole crowd of little children at the railway station with stones in their hands and they wanted to throw them at us.' Then – apparently forgetting that the Luftwaffe had been subjecting their city to an unmerciful bombardment – he added with indignation, 'There was a lot of hooting and they all pointed their fingers at me, and when you think that these people are supposed to be the lords of the world, then it is high time that was changed.'[63]

The realization that Prien and Schepke had been lost and Kretschmer was *hors de combat* was cause for cautious satisfaction in London and profound distress in Lorient. For Dönitz, the news – in personal as well as professional terms – that his three aces had fallen one after the other came as 'particularly heavy blows', though he consoled himself that this 'sudden increase in losses in March had not been due to any particular cause' but was 'purely fortuitous'.[64] This supposition was soon confirmed to his own satisfaction by figures for March and April suggesting that his U-boats had sunk eighty-four ships totalling just under 500,000 tons. That figure excluded a further seventy-four ships sunk in the South Atlantic, where a large number of Allied and neutral merchant ships still plied the ocean independently. In the absence of all but a handful of patrolling Royal Navy vessels, there were easy pickings to be had on the Cape route via Freetown, the capital of Sierra Leone, an important Allied convoy station.

In London, the demise of the three aces – who between them had accounted for an extraordinarily high percentage of the sinkings – was a source of rejoicing in the press and some respite for the Admiralty. But Churchill, though gratified by this unexpected bonus, was far from euphoric about progress in the Battle of the Atlantic. Indeed, the news was so discouraging that he did not wish it to be shared with the nation. On 9 April 1941, as he prepared to deliver an eloquent tour d'horizon to the House of Commons, he was irked to discover that the Admiralty had released a batch of discouraging statistics. Upbraiding the First Lord, he asked scathingly, 'Was it very wise to have published the fact that you have captured no more than 50 officers and 400 men from the German U-boats during the whole war? This would actually amount to the crews of 5 or 6 U-boats. Most people reading the figures would take this as a confession of marked failure.'[65] His 'War Situation' speech itself, which he delivered the same day, put the Royal Navy's gallant but modest successes at sea into troubling perspective, reminding a crowded House not only that 'everything turns upon the Battle of the Atlantic', but adding, 'Our losses in ships and tonnage are very heavy . . . these losses could not continue indefinitely without seriously affecting our war effort and our means of subsistence . . . what is to happen in the future if these losses continue at the present rate?'[66] It was a rhetorical question but one to which no one yet had an answer.

## 7.   Moving the Goalposts Again

Twelve days after Churchill's cautionary address, on 21 May 1941, a 5,000-ton American freighter, the SS *Robin Moor*, was ploughing steadily through an Atlantic swell when she was stopped by a U-boat in the South Atlantic some 700 miles off Freetown. With a complement of nine officers, twenty-nine crew, and eight passengers (including three women and a child), she was bound for Mozambique with a general cargo of commercial goods for the Portuguese colony. Claiming – illegitimately – he was acting in accordance with the Prize Rules, the U-boat's captain, Jost Metzler, gave the *Robin Moor*'s passengers and crew time to scramble into four lifeboats before he fired a single torpedo into the hull and several shells at the superstructure. Within thirty minutes the ship had disappeared beneath the waves. After Metzler had handed out a modest supply of rations to every lifeboat and promised to radio their position to all ships in the vicinity, U-69 turned away and soon disappeared over the horizon. Whether or not the U-boat commander was as good as his word is not known, but by good fortune three of the lifeboats were found after thirteen days adrift in the ocean, and the fourth, whose occupants included the *Robin Moor*'s captain, five days after that. In the United States, images of the survivors and reports of their struggle against the elements filled many pages of newsprint and hours of broadcasting, generating much public outrage. On the face of it, this was the 'inciting' incident for which many of those around the president had fervently wished: a legitimate casus belli.

Three days after the sinking of the *Robin Moor*, Roosevelt delivered one of the defining speeches of his wartime presidency. In a radio address to the nation, which he delivered from the White House, he put the United States on a war footing by proclaiming an 'unlimited national emergency'. Declaring that 'what started as a European war has developed, as the Nazis always intended it should develop, into a war for world domination', he laid out in some detail his plans to counter the threat that this now posed directly to the United States. Lend-Lease, he explained, was based 'on hard-headed concern for our own security' and, he emphasized, every dollar of aid sent to Britain and other threat-ened democracies 'helps to keep the dictators away from our own hemisphere'. Declaring that 'the Battle of the Atlantic now extends from the icy waters of the North Pole to the frozen continent of the Antarctic', he warned that the 'supreme purpose' of the Axis powers now was to 'obtain control of the seas' as the essential precondition of world domina-tion. Praising Britain's 'epic resistance', he made a commitment that gave great comfort to Churchill. The United States, he promised:

> would give every possible assistance to Britain. Our patrols are helping now to ensure delivery of the needed supplies to Britain. All additional measures necessary to deliver the goods will be taken. Any further methods or combination of methods, which can or should be utilized, are being devised by our military and naval technicians, who with me, will work out and put into effect such new and additional safeguards as may be needed.
>
> I say that the delivery of needed supplies to Britain is imperative. I say this can be done; it must be done; it will be done.[1]

That evening, the president retired to the Monroe Room, where, to his delight, the composer Irving Berlin was persuaded to play 'Alexan-der's Ragtime Band' for him and a small group of family and friends. Roosevelt was no less pleased to discover that of the 1,000 or more tel-egrams by which the White House had been bombarded following his declaration of a national emergency, the overwhelming majority approved. 'And I figured,' he said, as he riffled through them, 'I'd be lucky to get an even break on this speech.'[2]

For the most part the American media interpreted Roosevelt's words as 'a solemn commitment: the entry of the United States into the war against Germany was now considered inevitable and even imminent'.[3] As it turned out, however, the president had no such purpose. The very next day he used a press conference to dismiss any suggestion that such a step was in his mind: the US Navy would not be used to escort the transatlantic convoys; nor did he seek to change the neutrality laws which prevented the United States openly coming to the assistance of any other belligerent nation. To the disappointment of those who were eager for America to declare war on the Third Reich, his clarion call had heralded not so much the start of a military crusade against Nazism as a false dawn.

The most plausible explanation for Roosevelt's apparent volte-face lay with the president's acute political antennae and the opinion polls, both of which told him that the American people were still not ready for war. A slew of Gallup polls concluded that there were 'about an equal number of convinced Interventionists to Isolationists, with a Central block of slightly over half the nation who agree with the president's present policy' – which the pollster interpreted to mean that Roosevelt was 'hoping to avoid war, but would be prepared for war rather than see us defeated'.[4]

Roosevelt's closest confidant, Harry Hopkins, was among those of his most loyal supporters to be perplexed and frustrated by his apparent vacillation. A fortnight later, however, Hopkins alighted – so he believed – on the touchpaper by which the entire nation might be ignited in favour of war. At the time of his 'unlimited emergency' speech on 27 May, Roosevelt was almost certainly unaware of the fate which had befallen the *Robin Moor* in the South Atlantic: as he spoke, the survivors were still adrift and therefore the truth of how they had come to be shipwrecked was as yet unknown. On 13 June, however, *The New York Times* opened America's eyes. One of its correspondents reported that the American consul in the Brazilian port of Recife, to which some of the *Robin Moor*'s crew had been taken, confirmed that their vessel 'undoubtedly was sunk by a German submarine'. Berlin did not pretend it was otherwise but responded to the newspaper's report by stating baldly and provocatively: 'Germany will continue to sink every ship with contraband for England.'[5] This was just what Hopkins needed.

The following day, he sent the president a note which stated 'The sinking of the ROBIN MOOR violated international law; it violates your policy of freedom of the seas.' Implying that the incident could be used to ratchet up US policy towards Germany, he urged Roosevelt to charge the Navy Department 'with the duty of providing security for all the American flag ships traveling on the seas outside of the danger zones' rather than operating merely in an 'observational' role; the US Navy, he proposed, should be given the freedom to decide 'what measures of security are required to achieve this objective'.[6]

Hopkins had been in Roosevelt's inner circle for almost a decade. A principal architect of the New Deal programme, he had also proved himself to be a skilled and tireless administrator. By the spring of 1940 he had forged so strong a bond of friendship with both the president and

Eleanor Roosevelt that they provided him with his own room on the second floor of the White House, where he stayed as their guest and as the president's confidant for the next three years. Instrumental in planning and administering the Lend-Lease programme, he soon became an influential advocate of Britain's case in the heart of the US administration. Though he was already gaunt and grey with stomach cancer, he was an energetic emissary and a skilled diplomat on whose judgement the president placed great reliance. Reviled by some of his colleagues who resented his unique role and who, in the words of his biographer, generally regarded him 'as a sinister figure, a backstairs intriguer, and an Iowan combination of Machiavelli, Svengali and Rasputin',[7] he nonetheless wore his authority lightly and with a charm that belied a steely clarity of perspective and purpose.

Early in 1941 Roosevelt had sent Hopkins to London to establish at first hand the extent of Britain's predicament. Travelling the country at the prime minister's side, he met ministers, civil servants and senior figures from the three armed services as well as well-wishers among the public, who clearly warmed to the frail and dishevelled American unobtrusively accompanying Churchill on his prime-ministerial walkabouts through the bombed quarters of London and other cities. Though he was as reserved and taciturn in public as Churchill was expansive and voluble, people seemed to detect that his heart was with them: a quotation from the Book of Ruth which he deployed in an impromptu speech at a dinner in Glasgow given by the Lord Provost – 'Whither thou goest, I will go . . . even to the end'[8] – evaded the censorship imposed on the occasion and whistled along the grapevine, where it was widely interpreted as a statement of presidential intent.

The sentiment certainly reflected Hopkins's own attitude. In a letter from London, hand-written on Claridges notepaper, he was unequivocal:

> The People here are amazing from Churchill down, and if courage alone can win – the result will be inevitable. But they need our help desperately, and I am sure you will permit nothing to stand in the way . . . Churchill is the govn't in every sense of the word – he controls the grand strategy and . . . I cannot emphasize too strongly that he is the one person over here with whom you need to have a full meeting of minds . . . This island needs our help now, Mr President, with everything we can give them.[9]

To Churchill he said simply, 'The President is determined that we shall win the war together. Make no mistake about it.'[10] Not unnaturally, the prime minister was bowled over by what he described as 'that extraordinary man . . . a crumbling lighthouse from which there shone the beams that led great fleets to harbour'. Such hyperbole, constructed in hindsight, was a mark of genuine affection but it also reflected the key role Hopkins played in Churchill's diplomatic overtures towards the White House on which the success of the Battle of the Atlantic was to hang.

By the early summer of 1941 Hopkins was more than ever convinced that the sooner the United States took up arms against the Nazis, the better it would be for the nation and the world. Nor was he alone in attempting to persuade Roosevelt to respond more aggressively to the threat from Germany and in support of a beleaguered Britain. To varying degrees, Henry Stimson, Frank Knox and Harold Ickes (respectively the US naval, war and interior secretaries) were all frustrated by what they regarded as the president's overly cautious stance. They were further frustrated when Roosevelt opted to deliver another message to Congress rather than demonstrating the retaliatory belligerence for which they had pressed him after the sinking of the *Robin Moor*. On 20 June, in a speech which otherwise echoed the sentiments of his unlimited national emergency of 27 May, his tone was stern as he told the nation's legislators, 'The Government of the United States holds Germany responsible for the outrageous and indefensible sinking of the *Robin Moor*.' Yet, though he demanded 'full reparation for the losses and damages suffered by American nationals', he failed to issue any warning about the consequences that Germany would face if such recompense were to be denied (which, of course, it was). Instead of belligerence, he had offered defiance, declaring, 'We are not yielding and we do not propose to yield.'[11] To which a latter-day sceptic might have retorted, 'Yes, but where's the beef?'

It would be a mistake, though, to conclude that Roosevelt was irresolute. Nor was his caution solely inspired either by the opinion polls or by a well-founded concern that Congress was not yet ready to endorse military action against Germany. Of greater immediate moment for the president in the summer of 1941 was America's worsening relationship with Japan and his anxiety to avoid waging war on two oceanic fronts simultaneously. Although he had authorized the construction of more than 200 warships – including seven battleships and twelve aircraft carriers – the US Navy as yet lacked the firepower, the structure or the training to prevail in both theatres at once. And there was a further and even greater dilemma posed by the drama that was now unfolding on a new battlefront, 5,000 miles away on the edge of the Russian steppe.

On 15 June 1941 Roosevelt was alerted by Churchill to the imminent invasion of Russia by the German panzers. This prospect not only dwarfed every other crisis but presented the United States with a new set of strategic challenges. Of one thing only was he certain: that nothing should be done to restrain Hitler from embarking on a military adventure that would only be recognized as a madcap gambit much later. London and Washington were convinced not only that the communist state would fall into Nazi hands within a matter of months, if not weeks, but that it was far better for the Nazis to expend their energies on the conquest of the Soviet Union than on opening a new front against the United States. Yet, once Hitler had unleashed Operation Barbarossa on 22 June, both Churchill and Roosevelt had no doubt that in the interim they had no choice but to support the Third Reich's new adversary. The question for both America and Britain was not 'whether' but 'how much and in what way' they should succour a communist regime which, until so very recently, had been an apparently enthusiastic signatory to the Nazi–Soviet Pact of August 1939. The answers to those questions would bring a new and divisive dimension to the Battle of the Atlantic in which not only Roosevelt and Churchill but now Stalin as well had a direct and pressing interest.

In Berlin, Admiral Raeder had done his best to divert Hitler from Operation Barbarossa. As the most outspoken member of the German high command, he persisted in pressing both for his Mediterranean strategy against Britain and for an immediate challenge to the US Navy in the Atlantic before the most powerful nation in the world had time to build up a fleet of sufficient size and power to vitiate the U-boat campaign to throttle Britain's maritime lifeline. In part this dual strategy reflected his unshakeable belief that *Seekrieg* – the war at sea – was the initial means of achieving victory in the *Gesamtkrieg* – total war – on which the Third Reich had embarked. But this strategic vision also happened to dovetail with a narrower aspiration to build the Kriegsmarine into a world-beater. Disentangling the twin motives or assessing which of them was cause and which was effect is a futile endeavour; in either case he was not easily deterred from the equally Herculean task of trying to change Hitler's mind.

In his obduracy, Raeder did not shrink from risking Hitler's wrath to a degree that few of his peers would have dared. The Führer had a degree of sympathy with some of the admiral's proposals. A month before launching Barbarossa, he instructed the Kriegsmarine to prepare for 'the occupation of the Azores in order to deploy long-range bombers against the United States', which he intimated would be on the Third Reich's agenda in the autumn.[12] Consumed by hubris, he had convinced himself that, at this point, the United States was so 'politically unstable'[13] as to pose little challenge to the Third Reich. Even if America were to be forced into war with the Axis powers, he believed that Roosevelt would focus on the threat from Japan in the Pacific rather than confront Germany – the obverse of what had in fact been agreed in the 'Europe First' strategy to which the United States had made a hypothetical but tentative commitment at the ABC-1 talks in Washington during the spring of 1941.

Soon after the invasion of Russia, Hitler's self-delusion had reached such proportions that he informed the Japanese ambassador not only that 'The Russian War has been won' but also that the moment to attack the United States would very soon be at hand. 'We must jointly annihilate' the United States, he declared.[14] But timing was all. He was determined to avoid war with the United States until the Soviet Union had been broken. On the very day before the invasion of Russia, he instructed the obstinate Admiral Raeder that 'he should avoid *every* incident with the United States until Barbarossa unfolded itself. After a few weeks the situation would be cleared up.'[15]

Raeder's repeated attempts to turn the Russian tide were not only fruitless but counterproductive. In the process of proselytizing for a doomed strategy, he signally failed to make the much simpler case for extending the U-boat campaign in the Atlantic. Admiral Dönitz, whose unyielding focus was on the tonnage war in the Atlantic, was exasperated by Raeder's ill-focused perspective and his lack of clout with the Führer. As a result the U-boat campaign was failing to achieve its full potential. On frequent occasions, with two of his submarines permanently at sea to provide weather reports for his Lorient headquarters, he had only four operational U-boats in the Atlantic at any one time. Even so, merchant ships were being sunk (by surface raiders and bombers as well as U-boats) at three times the rate at which they could be replaced. If this trend were accelerated, Britain would soon face unsustainable shortages of food and raw materials: people would go hungry and industry would be paralysed. Under such circumstances, whoever emerged from the British elite to replace Churchill would be obliged to negotiate terms with Hitler. Dönitz's frustration was all the greater because he was convinced that this was both the raison d'être of the tonnage war and a realizable objective.

Mindful of the fact that the balance could already have been even more heavily in favour of the Third Reich if he had been allocated the number of U-boats he deemed necessary to throttle Britain's supply lines, Dönitz lamented his lack of direct access to the Führer. Rueing the fact that 'my only way of convincing him of the true state of affairs was by means of reports and proposals submitted to him through Naval high command', he blamed Raeder for succumbing to the pressure for 'more and more' U-boats to be withdrawn for what he dismissed as 'subsidiary operations' rather than convincing Hitler that 'every available U-boat should be concentrated on the Battle of the Atlantic'.[16]

The first of these subsidiary operations followed immediately in the wake of Barbarossa when Dönitz was ordered to despatch eight U-boats to seek out Soviet vessels in the Baltic, where, he wrote, 'they found practically no targets and accomplished nothing worth mentioning'. Similarly, in the following month a further six U-boats were summoned to the Arctic, where they too roamed empty seas. In this case the U-boat commander-in-chief protested vehemently, informing his superiors: 'The decisive factor in the war against Britain is the attack on her imports. The delivery of these attacks is the U-boats' principal task which no other branch of the Armed Forces can take over from them. The war with Russia will be decided on land, and in it the U-boats can play only a very minor role.'[17] This reproach was both stinging and valid but he – or rather Raeder on his behalf – did not prevail. Nor was that all. To his bemused dismay, Dönitz was also frequently ordered to detach U-boats from their proper role as a strike force to escort the Kriegsmarine's auxiliary cruisers, supply ships and prize vessels on their long voyages in the Atlantic and Pacific, 'regardless of the fact the U-boat would stand very little chance of being able to protect its charge if it were attacked and would be quite powerless to help, if it were sunk by the enemy'.[18] Thus, at a period when Britain would have been hard pressed to withstand an all-out U-boat campaign in the Atlantic, Dönitz was thwarted. The Battle of the Atlantic, which could have taken a decisive turn in his favour, was no closer to resolution: from the perspective of the U-boat commander-in-chief, with no more than a total of sixty-five operational submarines at his disposal, a golden opportunity had been missed.[19]

Although Roosevelt was as anxious as Hitler to avoid a shooting war in the Atlantic Ocean, neither was able to resist the torrent of events that had already begun to drive them at an accelerating pace towards that inevitability. The extension of the US Security Zone in the Atlantic to 25°W not only failed to deter the wolf packs but coincided with a westwards shift in their operations to the most exposed part of the lifeline between Britain and America: the so-called Atlantic Gap was a black hole some 300 miles from east to west and 600 miles from north to south, 180,000 square miles of ocean which, at this point in the war, was beyond the range of any RAF Coastal Command aircraft. In the absence of any aircraft carriers – which were all deployed elsewhere – the Atlantic convoys were thus without aerial protection in this vast region, making them even more vulnerable to the wolf packs which now began to hunt in these waters in surging numbers, knowing themselves safe from any threat from the sky.

The Admiralty's reaction to this westwards shift by the U-boat fleet was to escort merchant convoys for the entire Atlantic crossing rather than, as hitherto, within the rectangular boundaries of the Western Approaches, which stretched from the northernmost tip of Scotland to the southernmost tip of England and extended westwards into the Atlantic to a point some 300 miles to the south of Iceland where, at 30°W, it overlapped the US Security Zone. However, an acute shortage of suitable vessels meant that most of these convoys – despite being reinforced by the Royal Canadian Navy – were accompanied only by a skeletal force of warships. In the vastness of the ocean to the south of Iceland, therefore, not only were the convoys vulnerable but those merchant ships which fell out of line with engine trouble or in poor weather provided easy pickings for the marauding submarines.

No less threatening from the Admiralty's perspective was the Kriegsmarine's fleet of surface raiders. By April, *Scheer* and *Hipper* had between them accounted for more than twenty merchant ships while the two battleships *Scharnhorst* and *Gneisenau*, which similarly roamed the Atlantic between January and March, had sunk or captured a further twenty-two vessels. According to the navy's official historian, 'this completely dislocated our Atlantic convoy cycles, with serious consequences for our vital imports. Their depredations forced the widespread dispersal of our already strained naval resources.'[20] It might have been even worse. Although by April all four of these capital ships had returned to their bases in either Norway or France for maintenance, repairs and refits, the Admiralty knew no relief.

Intelligence reports suggested that an even mightier German warship would soon be on the rampage in the Atlantic. In the collective imagination of all navies, the *Bismarck* was no ordinary battleship but a supreme example of marine engineering: faster, more powerful, and more dangerous than any rival. Mounted with 15-inch guns (compared with the 11-inch guns on *Gneisenau* and *Scharnhorst*) the *Bismarck* was the first real battleship to be built in Germany since the First World War. Although she was not invulnerable – she was inadequately protected against aerial bombardment – her very name inspired admiration, envy and fear. For the Kriegsmarine, the *Bismarck* foreshadowed a future in which Germany would eventually rule the waves in Britannia's stead. For the admirals on both sides – with the notable exception of Dönitz – the *Bismarck* represented a twentieth-century symbol conjured from a quasi-romantic vision of a past in which the fate of nations had been decided by bloody encounters between rival battle fleets as famous warships bore down upon one another, all guns blazing, until the vanquished either raised the flag of surrender or sank beneath the waves. Down the ages, a host of famous, if half-forgotten, maritime victories or defeats – Lepanto, Cadiz, Chesapeake, Trafalgar and Jutland – were etched in every naval imagination by innumerable paintings and, latterly, photographs which captured symbolic moments of triumph and disaster. By the Second World War, these set-piece slugfests – encounters that corresponded in some measure to the cavalry charge or the tank battle on land – were still vivid in the minds of naval warriors and their political leaders but they no longer defined the terms on which nations fought one another on the high seas. This was particularly true of the Battle of the Atlantic which was not about instant triumph but slow strangulation. Yet, here too, the big ships remained a potent threat.

It was this that made Churchill so anxious. The thought of the apparently invincible *Bismarck* and the other four capital ships prowling the Atlantic where, in Churchill's words, they 'would subject our naval strength to a trial of the first magnitude',[21] was chilling to contemplate. This was precisely Raeder's intention. The 'one and only' object of his surface raiders, he had declared, was 'the battle against enemy commerce. The main target is, as always, only the convoys.'[22]

To counter this threat, the Admiralty had decided that not only the North Atlantic convoys but those on the route to Freetown – especially those carrying troops via the Cape to the Middle East – should be escorted, whenever possible, by battleships or cruisers. The Royal Navy's resources were thereby stretched to the limit. If the *Bismarck* were to break out into the Atlantic, she would not only wreak further havoc but – so Raeder hoped – validate his belief that the Kriegsmarine's capital ships were critical to German hegemony in the North Atlantic and its controlled extension to other parts of the ocean.

On 22 May reports reached London that the *Bismarck* and a heavy cruiser, *Prinz Eugen*, accompanied by a small flotilla of destroyers, had slipped their moorings in Norway heading north for the Denmark Strait, a wide but treacherous channel between Iceland and Greenland, the safest route by which to break out into the Atlantic. The strait was covered by British cruisers, HMS *Norfolk* and HMS *Suffolk*, with the battleship HMS *Prince of Wales* and the battlecruiser HMS *Hood* standing by, all with their accompanying destroyers, to intercept the two German raiders once they had been alerted by the cruisers. It was a tall order. The intention was to launch a surprise attack but the British squadron found it extremely difficult even to locate let alone to maintain contact with the German warships despite the new – albeit primitive – radar sets that had just been installed in some of the pursuing vessels. The endeavour was further hampered both by poor weather and snowstorms, which frequently obliterated visibility, and by the need to maintain radio silence to avoid detection by the German vessels. Despite this, the British managed to close on the Germans until by 6 a.m. on 24 May the two fleets were no more than fourteen miles apart. The *Hood* and the *Prince of Wales* started to manoeuvre into positions from which they could open fire on their quarry.

The outcome of the battle would depend partly on chance but heavily on the speed, efficiency and teamwork with which the gun crews could unleash the massive firepower of their big guns. In this, the Germans proved themselves superior; after spending 'many months testing and perfecting their equipment in the Baltic' their crews were quicker on the draw and their range finders more precise in their targeting.[23] That was not all: Vice-Admiral Lancelot Holland, the squadron commander, who 'flew his flag' aboard *Hood*, had made a succession of tactical miscalculations that had culminated in an angle of approach towards the German ships which was so oblique that some of his 15-inch guns (which had a maximum range of up to twenty-two miles) could not be brought to bear effectively; as a result, in the stern words of the First Sea Lord (who enjoyed the luxury of hindsight), the squadron found itself 'fighting with one hand only when it had got two'.[24] In what was to become a very confused battle, the superior tactics of the German ships prevailed.

It was the first time that Lieutenant Esmond Knight, on the bridge of the *Prince of Wales*, had experienced action. As the first salvo from the battleship soared towards its target, he enjoyed a moment of 'unendurable ecstasy, then the pulverizing crashing roar, which for a second seems to knock one senseless'. As the *Bismarck* opened fire almost simultaneously, adrenalin coursed through Knight's body:

> Now followed the most exciting moments that I am likely to experience – those desperate and precious seconds racing past while guns were reloaded and the enemy's first salvo was roaring to meet us . . . Then again that horrible rushing noise, and suddenly an enormous geyser of sea-water rising on our starboard side . . . there was an ear-splitting crack as HE [High Explosive] shells from *Prinz Eugen*, exploding practically overhead, rained showers of shrapnel on to the decks . . . I ran to the other side of the ship, where to my horror, I saw a great fire burning on the boat-deck of the *Hood* . . . enormous reaching tongues of pale-red flame shot into the air . . . *Hood* had literally been blown to pieces.

Soon afterwards, Knight heard the 'horrible rushing noise' once again and then all went 'hazy'. At first he had a sensation as though he was dying but he came round to hear voices shouting 'Stretcher bearer!' and 'Clear the way there!' A moment later 'Strong hands lifted the dead men off me; there was a horrible smell of blood, and the uncanny noise that men make when they are dying.' Once in the sick bay, a medical officer told him 'Open your eyes, old boy,' but when he tried to do so,

Knight could see nothing.[25] He was fortunate to survive; nine others were wounded but thirteen of his shipmates were killed.*

Meanwhile, the destroyers hurried to pick up the survivors from *Hood*. But when HMS *Electra* arrived, her crew saw only devastation. The *Bismarck*'s heavy guns had been mortally effective. The battle-cruiser had been travelling at her maximum speed of thirty knots, which meant that when those sailors not killed in the explosions that ripped the ship apart or trapped fatally below decks jumped or fell into the sea (from a height of more than a hundred feet), they invariably landed with such force that a broken neck was almost inevitable. Only three men survived. One of these, an unnamed able seaman, told one interviewer what had happened when he leapt into the freezing water to escape the 'furnace' which threatened to incinerate him:

> The sailor leapt into the sea but hadn't a clue what happened after he hit the water. All he did know — and he couldn't get over the horror of it — was that when he came to the surface and looked round for the ship he found she had gone. Then he'd had to duck again as *Prince of Wales*, her guns blazing, came charging up from astern.[26]

In the space of a few minutes, 1,415 of the *Hood*'s complement of 1,418 had perished. The *Bismarck* had fully lived up to her reputation. In an earlier age this might have settled the contest between two great powers. In the Second World War, it meant only that the fearsome battleship was free to continue about her business of destroying the merchant ships that sustained the transatlantic lifeline — or so it seemed.

Admiral Dönitz had little faith in the strategic or tactical utility of battleships, which he regarded as 'dinosaurs'[27] in the new age of submarine warfare, and he had long resented Raeder's preoccupation with capital ships, which he derided as 'bloated surface vessels'.[28] Nonetheless when Raeder ordered the *Bismarck* into the Atlantic, he did not hesitate to put his U-boats at the service of Admiral Günther Lütjens, commanding the German battle group. Immediately after the *Bismarck*'s triumph in the Denmark Strait, Dönitz went further, ordering 'a complete

---

* Knight had been permanently blinded in one eye and almost blinded in the other. An actor by profession, he was to earn renown after the war with his portrayal of the *Prince of Wales*'s captain in the 1960 film *Sink the Bismarck*.

cessation of operations against merchant shipping' in favour of giving whatever support Lütjens might now require. This was an emergency instruction. Although the British did not yet know it, the *Bismarck* had been hit in the bows by a shell from the *Prince of Wales* in the course of their brief encounter in the Denmark Strait. The damage was so serious that, so far from being a menace, the great battleship was a crippled giant trailing a long slick of oil in her wake. The leak from a forward oil tank meant the planned Atlantic foray had to be aborted. Lütjens signalled the naval high command that he had decided to divert towards the sanctuary of Saint-Nazaire in the Bay of Biscay, more than 1,000 miles to the south-east. The *Bismarck*'s hunting days were over before they had begun.

When Vice-Admiral Holland went down with *Hood*, his place as the British squadron's commanding officer was taken by Rear Admiral William Wake-Walker, who flew his flag in *Norfolk*. As yet unaware that the German titan was in trouble, he had opted to track the German warship on her southerly course. But mid-morning, however, a Sunderland flying boat reported seeing the giveaway trail of oil which was now flowing freely from the stricken battleship, which suggested that, far from being on the offensive, the *Bismarck* and *Prinz Eugen* might be in flight.

At this point, the commander of the Home Fleet, Admiral John Tovey, flying his flag in the new battleship *King George V* and accompanied by the veteran battlecruiser HMS *Repulse*, the aircraft carrier HMS *Victorious*, four cruisers and nine destroyers, was some 330 miles away to the south-east of the unfolding drama.[29] He now hastened to intercept the *Bismarck* while the Admiralty ordered all other vessels in the vicinity to close on the *Bismarck* as well. Before long an armada of nineteen warships, including two aircraft carriers, was converging on the stricken vessel, which by this time had been forced to reduce speed from thirty to twenty-four knots to conserve her dwindling supply of fuel. Even so, it would still be possible to reach the safety of Saint-Nazaire before her pursuers could make contact.

In London, the prime minister followed this drama with intense focus. Still unaware of the extent of the damage to the *Bismarck*, or that the crippled vessel was heading towards the Bay of Biscay, he could barely concentrate on anything else. Even as he scanned the stream of messages and despatches which flowed onto his desk from all corners of the Empire, he recalled that 'only one scene riveted my background thoughts: this tremendous *Bismarck*, 45,000 tons, perhaps almost invulnerable to gunfire, rushing southwards towards our convoys'.[30]

Lütjens, meanwhile, was desperate to shake off his pursuers. And, in the early hours of 25 May, it looked as though he had done so. The *Suffolk*, which was equipped with the latest radar technology, had been zigzagging behind the fleeing battleship but, straying to the outer limits of her radar range, lost contact with the quarry. Although Admiral Tovey's squadron was little more than a hundred miles away, Lütjens had altered course to head directly for Saint-Nazaire and thereby evaded this threat. It was a narrow margin but it was enough: the British commanders had no idea where the *Bismarck* now was or in which direction she was heading.

In London, the anxiety and strain in the Admiralty was all but palpable as the best brains in the building struggled to solve this conundrum, hoping to second-guess Lütjens. As the day wore on, they finally resolved that his destination was almost certainly the port of Brest. Accordingly, as evening fell, Tovey's squadron and all the other ships now engaged in the hunt were instructed to alter course. On 26 May, soon after 10 a.m., the Admiralty's hunch seemed to be confirmed when a Catalina flying boat from Coastal Command caught a glimpse of the *Bismarck* through a gap in the clouds and reported that her position was 690 miles north-west of the French port. At the speed she was travelling, the battleship would reach safety by the late evening of 27 May. This gave her pursuers a maximum of twenty-four hours to reach her before she reached the protective umbrella of the Luftwaffe's bombers. It was, at best, a slender chance.

By this time, late on 26 May, Dönitz had ordered 'All U-boats with torpedoes to proceed at once and at full speed toward *Bismarck* grid square BE29.'[31] Were any of these to sight the approaching British warships – at least two of which, *Renown* and *Ark Royal*, were without escorts – the hunters could very easily become the hunted. But in a freshening storm only U-556, commanded by Herbert Wohlfahrt, was able to reach the appointed location. As he was in any case returning to port after a long mission during which he had expended all his torpedoes, he could do no more than report the position of any British ships in the vicinity. Later that evening, he noted, 'Alarm. A battleship of the *King George* class and an aircraft carrier, probably the *Ark Royal*, came in right through the mist from astern, travelling at high speed . . . If only I had had a few torpedoes! I could have stayed where I was and got them both.'[32]

By this time, when it looked as though the *Bismarck* might escape, the prime minister – who was in a state of barely suppressed agitation – was with the First Sea Lord in the Admiralty. So great was his anxiety that he now intervened directly by instructing Pound to send Tovey a message: '*Bismarck* must be sunk at all costs.' In so doing, both breached a cherished protocol – the prime minister by interfering in what was an operational matter, and Pound by agreeing to instruct the commander-in-chief of the Home Fleet accordingly. The prime minister did not hold the strong-minded but prickly Tovey in high regard, once describing him as 'negative, unenterprising and narrow-minded';[33] it was perhaps with this in mind, that his tone was unusually unequivocal and even brutal. Although he was aware that the admiral's flagship was running low on fuel and that, in such circumstances, discretion would advise a tactical withdrawal from the enemy-infested waters, Churchill went on to instruct that 'if . . . it is necessary for *King George V* to remain on the scene' to ensure the *Bismarck*'s destruction 'she must do so even if it means subsequently towing'.[34] As Churchill would have known, any ship under tow was at grave risk of being sunk either from the air or by a U-boat. For the prime minister, however, the stakes were too high for any other course to be considered.

In the event, with the battleships unable to close with the *Bismarck*, it was the squadron of Swordfish biplanes which took off from the *Ark Royal* just before 9 p.m. on 26 May that moved the drama decisively towards its denouement. The flying conditions were atrocious. As the navy's official historian put it, in 'low rain cloud, strong wind, stormy seas, fading daylight and intense and accurate enemy gunfire . . . individual aircrews pressed in most gallantly and two of the thirteen torpedoes released found their mark'.[35] One of these wrecked the *Bismarck*'s steering gear and jammed the rudders. As a result the 'masterpiece of naval construction', as Churchill was to describe her, began to turn in slow circles, out of control and therefore doomed.[36] At midnight the commander of U-556 noted, 'What could I now do to help the *Bismarck*? It's a horrible feeling to be so near and yet not able to do anything.'[37] Almost simultaneously, Admiral Lütjens signalled 'Ship unmanoeuvrable. We shall fight to the last shell. Long live the Führer.'[38]

1. Winston Churchill and Franklin D. Roosevelt at their first formal meeting, at Placentia Bay, in August 1941. The president eluded his own press corps by pretending to depart for a holiday in the presidential yacht; in a similar shroud of secrecy, the prime minister was accompanied by 'a retinue which Cardinal Wolsey might have envied'.

2. Sir Charles Forbes, commander-in-chief of the Home Fleet, 1938–40. Churchill visited the fleet's base in Scapa Flow with him on 14 September 1939. He returned with a 'strong feeling of confidence' that repairs to the defences there were progressing well.

3. Churchill and Admiral Sir John Tovey arriving on board his flagship, HMS *King George V*, in October 1942. Tovey was commander-in-chief of the Home Fleet, 1940–43, and responsible for the protection of the Arctic convoys.

4. Admiral Sir Percy Noble addressing the ship's company of Captain 'Johnny' Walker's HMS *Stork* at Liverpool on 19 December 1941. Commander-in-chief, Western Approaches Command, 1941–2, Noble was renowned for his affability, clear mind and talent for organization.

5. (*above left*) Admiral Sir Dudley Pound, the First Sea Lord, 1939–43. On Churchill's appointment as First Lord of the Admiralty, the future prime minister recalled, 'We eyed each other amicably if doubtfully.' In early 1942 Pound warned that the loss of merchant ships and oil tankers threatened to paralyse Allied operations on the battlefield, stating: 'If we lose the war at sea we lose the war.'

6. (*above right*) Admiral Sir Max Horton, commander-in-chief, Western Approaches Command, 1942–5, in his office overlooking the Operations Room at Derby House, his Liverpool HQ, in 1943. Horton's domineering and sometimes brutal manner concealed a fine analytical mind; in the judgement of one of his peers, he also 'had an intuition of what the Hun would do, which was quite uncanny'.

7. (*above left*) Sir Arthur Harris, commander-in-chief, Bomber Command. He considered any attempt to use his aircraft to combat U-boats as a wasteful diversion from what he regarded as their only valid task, obliterating German cities. In a secret memo to the prime minister, he spelt out the advantages, in his view, of the RAF over the navy: 'Why nibble at the fringes of the enemy's submarine and sea power when we can obliterate with comparative ease the very sources of that power?'

8. (*above right*) Admiral Ernest King was promoted from commander-in-chief of the US North Atlantic Fleet to Chief of Naval Operations in 1942. He inspired admiration, fear and hostility. General Dwight D. Eisenhower once wrote: 'One thing that might help us win this war is to get someone to shoot King.'

9. (*right*) Admiral Harry 'Betty' Stark, the US Navy's Chief of Naval Operations, 1939–42. In early 1941 he defined as a major national objective for the United States the 'prevention of the disruption of the British Empire'.

10. Harry Hopkins, Roosevelt's closest aide, posing with Soviet leader Josef Stalin during his August 1941 visit to Moscow to discuss the delivery of Lend-Lease supplies to the Soviet Union. Hopkins noted that 'his hands are as huge as his mind. His voice is harsh ... he seems to have no doubts.'

11. (*top*) German Admiral Erich Raeder inspecting the crew of the battle cruiser *Scharnhorst* in April 1942, after their escape from Brest through the English Channel. Commander-in-chief of the Kriegsmarine, Raeder believed that Britain was Germany's 'mortal enemy'. He was sacked by Hitler after what he called a 'vicious and impertinent harangue' from the Führer.

12. (*bottom*) Admiral Karl Dönitz, commander-in-chief of the U-boat fleet. In constant conflict with Raeder, Dönitz replaced him as commander-in-chief in January 1943. In 1945 he succeeded Hitler as Führer.

13. (*above*) Hitler presents the Knight's Cross to Günther Prien for sinking the British battleship *Royal Oak* at Scapa Flow in October 1939. Prien was among the U-boat aces who were hailed as heroes of the Third Reich.

14. (*left*) Otto Kretschmer, German submarine commander, who was regarded by Dönitz as the best of his aces. He was captured by Captain Donald Macintyre's HMS *Walker* and became a prisoner of war in Britain in 1941.

15. New recruits to the Merchant Navy, in which 185,000 men
volunteered for service. More than 30,000 of them lost their lives.

By this time five British destroyers had reached the scene. Their commander, Captain Philip Vian, ordered them to complete the destruction of the *Bismarck* with a fusillade of torpedo fire. But though the battleship was otherwise disabled, her massive guns were still intact and the destroyers were unable to get close enough to inflict significant damage. By dawn on 27 May, however, two battleships, HMS *King George V* and HMS *Rodney*, arrived to finish the task. They opened fire just before 9 a.m. and a little over an hour later the *Bismarck* was 'a flaming shambles, and all her guns were silent'.[39] It had taken hundreds of heavy shells and at least eight torpedoes to sink her, but at 10.40 a.m., her ensign still aloft, she disappeared beneath the waves. Although, between them, two British warships picked up 110 survivors and a German U-boat, with the help of another vessel, picked up a further five, almost 2,000 of her crew, including Lütjens himself, went down with their ship. Within one week of leaving Scandinavian waters, the pride of the German navy was on the bottom of the ocean.

The news was passed to Churchill as he resumed his seat in Church House (whence Parliament had been forced to adjourn following the destruction of the Commons Chamber) after apprising his fellow MPs of the loss of the *Hood*. He rose again immediately to announce: 'I have just received news that the *Bismarck* is sunk.' Afterwards, he reflected, 'They seemed content.'[40] Churchill had invested the sinking of the *Bismarck* with almost supernatural significance:

> Had she escaped, the moral effects of her continuing existence as much as the material damage she might have inflicted on our shipping would have been calamitous. Many misgivings would have arisen regarding our capacity to control the oceans, and these would have been trumpeted round the world to our great detriment and discomfort.[41]

He was probably right in this surmise but that was principally because it reflected an attitude towards naval warfare which was shared in Tokyo and Washington and Berlin no less than in London. While it was, of course, true that the Royal Navy's big ships were needed to secure control of the high seas against the Italians and Japanese, the British underestimated the potential of the U-boat to challenge Britain's maritime supremacy by inflicting terminal damage on merchant shipping in the Atlantic. Only Dönitz appeared to realize this with any degree of clarity.

Churchill's glow of satisfaction did not last for long. Though the *Bismarck* had been sunk, the *Prinz Eugen* was still at large somewhere in the Atlantic and, he thought, might offer yet another chance for him to achieve his overriding diplomatic objective – to suck the United States into Britain's war. To impress upon them the significance of this, he sent Alexander and Pound one of his 'Action This Day' notes stressing that the search for the German cruiser raised 'questions of the highest importance'. These, he indicated, did not so much concern the need per se to eliminate a hostile warship as the role the US Navy might be persuaded to play in her detection:

> It would be far better, for instance, that she should be located by a United States ship, as this might tempt her to fire upon that ship, thus providing the incident for which the United States Government would be so thankful . . . If only we can create a situation where the *Prinz Eugen* is being shadowed by an American vessel, we shall have gone a long way to solve [sic] the largest problem.[42]

Though he did not know it, Churchill was jumping the presidential gun. While a number of Roosevelt's advisors were no less eager than the British prime minister to engineer a casus belli, Roosevelt himself had yet to go this far – as the response to the sinking of the *Robin Moor* had demonstrated. In any case, Churchill's scheme was thwarted at least for the moment, because the *Prinz Eugen* evaded detection by any warship to escape into the vastness of the Atlantic – though only to develop serious engine trouble which forced her return to Brest for major repairs.

By chance, Roosevelt's 'unlimited national emergency' broadcast on 27 May coincided to the day with the sinking of the *Bismarck*, about which he learned nothing until afterwards. By this time, however, he was in any case contemplating a decision of far wider strategic import. A little over a week later he initiated a move which Admiral 'Betty' Stark, the Chief of Naval Operations, described as 'practically an act of war':[43] the occupation of Iceland. Although he did not announce this decision publicly for another month, it became the catalyst for an incident which did indeed bring the United States into the Battle of the Atlantic.

Unaware as yet of the circumstance in which the *Robin Moor* had been sunk, the president's move in the first week of June was not

retaliatory but pre-emptive: a number of strategic and tactical imperatives had combined to create a compelling military logic. Most notable
among these was the fear that, if he did not act first, Hitler might beat
him to the draw, using Norway as a jumping-off point from which to
launch an aerial and naval invasion of Iceland. If Germany were to
establish bases on the island, the convoy routes between the United
States and Great Britain would be even further imperilled. By the same
token, from the Anglo-American perspective, the establishment of a
mid-Atlantic terminus on the island would provide an invaluable
refuelling base for the escorts; it would also provide aerial cover over
the Denmark Strait, through which – notwithstanding the fate of the
*Bismarck* – other German raiders might yet again break out into the
Atlantic to wreak havoc in every part of that ocean and beyond. For
Roosevelt, the occupation of Iceland promised to kill two birds with
one stone: it would signal his own commitment to Britain and could be
sold simultaneously to the American people as an act of self-defence
against Nazi aggression.

The president's decision was somewhat complicated by the fact that
Iceland was already under foreign occupation. A little over a year earlier, on 10 May 1940, the day on which Churchill became prime minister,
a Royal Naval task force (which had been despatched while he was still
First Lord of the Admiralty) had landed at Reykjavik and seized control
of the country. Later, citing with approval an unnamed strategist who
had commented: 'Whoever possesses Iceland holds a pistol firmly
pointed at England, America, and Canada', Churchill claimed that the
invasion enjoyed 'the concurrence of its people'.[44] This was disingenuous. The islanders had been given no advance warning of the British
operation and the Icelandic government protested furiously that the
nation's neutrality had been 'flagrantly violated'. But though the use of
force majeure blatantly violated international law – and to that extent
provided an uncomfortable parallel with some of the actions of the
Third Reich – the fear that the pistol might soon be in Hitler's hands
following the collapse of Denmark (with which Iceland was in close
and formal union) a month earlier meant that such niceties cut no ice in
the British War Cabinet.

The Icelanders were in no position to offer physical resistance and
within hours of the landing, the handful of Germans resident on
the island, including a very surprised German consul who expressed

his outrage at the indignity of it all, was swiftly rounded up by a party of Marines and despatched to Britain for internment. Within a couple of days, two 10,000-ton freighters were offloading trucks, Bren-carriers, ammunition and supplies for the British advance party. The officer in command of the operation was Rear Admiral Sir Kenelm Creighton. He did not warm to Reykjavik. 'Everywhere I went there were piles of cods' heads in various stages of de-composition,' he recalled, and 'no sooner had I breathed a sigh of relief and whipped the handkerchief away from my nose after passing one heap than I had to clap it back again quickly on being confronted by another.'[45] Beyond the capital the landscape was desolate and the population unwelcoming:

> Like other small neutrals they had hoped to evade the world conflagra-
> tion and to them it seemed that we were just as aggressive planting
> ourselves on their island as the Germans walking into Denmark . . .
> they were distant, reserved and inclined to turn their backs when any of
> our men [who soon numbered 25,000 British and Canadian troops]
> passed in the street.[46]

Among those British soldiers was a young army officer, Theodore Gadian, a former GP who had signed up in 1939 to serve in the Royal Army Medical Corps (RAMC). In the early summer of 1940 his Field Ambulance Group (146) – which had been fortunate to emerge unscathed from the Norwegian debacle in May – was despatched to what he described as 'one of the remotest outposts of empire . . . bleak and forbidding and yet with a beauty of its own'. Like many other servicemen on other fronts, he did not know how long his new posting would last or whether he would ever again see the new love in his life, Golda Alexander, whom he had left behind in England.* No less testingly for them both, for many weeks he was forbidden to tell her where his posting had taken him. Their letters to one another were an emotional lifeline:

> I have spent a long time this week-end reading and rereading your let-
> ters; and I feel happier and happier each time I do so. I feel, as you do,
> that they form an intimate contact between us, and that they might
> seem a bit maudlin to others, to ourselves, who know and appreciate the

---

* Theodore Gadian and Golda Alexander were married in February 1942.

depths of our love to one another, they are while we are apart, everything, and mean more than anything in the world.

Although he had been billeted in a small community far from the capital, Gadian was constrained by military censorship and an evident reluctance to burden her with his cares. He rarely complained about his lot, although, on one occasion, he did allow himself to bemoan the fact that, in the early days, the new garrison had 'no papers and no wireless that works . . . no cinema, or dance hall'. However, he was far readier to describe those occasions on which this tedium was lifted. When a transatlantic liner came into port, heavily escorted by British warships, he rejoiced in describing the 'magnificent' officers' party where 'the ladies wore evening dress' and they danced the night away in the ballroom of the requisitioned vessel to the accompaniment of the ship's orchestra.

A few days after this party, the reality of war intervened when Gadian was airlifted to attend the crew of a Grimsby fishing boat which had been attacked by a German dive-bomber some sixty miles off the coast of Iceland. The survivors' stories incensed the young medical officer:

> The crew of fifteen took to the [life]boat and were machine-gunned while helpless and unarmed . . . They rowed 45 miles in the worst of seas and were picked up by an Icelandic boat. They were taken to a little village . . . one was dead, one desperately wounded . . . It is against this barbarity and savagery that we have to fight.

The RAMC did not only tend British servicemen. One day in September, a fifteen-year-old Icelandic girl was brought to the hospital where Gadian was based. She was accompanied by her father, who showed him her arm in silent rebuke.

> A soldier had tattooed an enormous heart, with an arrow through it . . . I was expected to remove it! It had been done with Indian ink and apart from burning it off with acid, which would leave a big scratch, there is nothing one can do. So [the young girl] will bear this keepsake and memory of the Army occupation to her grave.[47]

It may be presumed that such incidents, though small in themselves, did little to break down the barrier of distrust from behind which the Icelanders faced the British occupying force. Yet relations gradually improved to the point where, by the summer of 1941, Gadian felt able to note that 'The Icelanders are beginning to like us a bit more.'

The US decision to occupy Iceland was precipitated by America's own strategic priorities, but the negotiations by which the transfer of power was confirmed were initiated on 28 May 1941 at a meeting between the president and the British ambassador, Lord Halifax (the former advocate of appeasement who had been appointed to his new post five months earlier following the death of Lord Lothian). Roosevelt's proposal could hardly have come at a better moment for Churchill, who was quick to grasp its significance. In a joint note to Halifax's successor as Foreign Secretary, Anthony Eden, and to the First Lord, Alexander, some weeks earlier, he had remonstrated with both men for what he had interpreted as a grudging and pedantic response by departmental officials to an unrelated proposal emanating from the American side. 'I would rather that telegrams of this kind should not be sent without my seeing them first,' he wrote. 'What does the convenience of our shipping mean compared to engaging the Americans in the war? A negative answer like this is chilling and ill-suited to our present purpose.'[48] The angry urgency in Churchill's tone was unfeigned.

Britain had endured setbacks and crises on all fronts. In February, the 'Army of the Nile' – as Churchill now dubbed the Western Desert Force under the command of General O'Connor – had driven a much larger Italian army out of Egypt and harried them more than halfway back to Tripoli. But, impelled by the political urge to demonstrate that, hard-pressed as it was, the British government would stand by its allies, the prime minister chose this moment to rush four divisions – some 60,000 men – from the Libyan front line to Greece in a doomed attempt to stave off a full-scale invasion by the Wehrmacht. This ill-judged venture ended in a military debacle a few weeks later when the expeditionary force was forced to flee the overwhelming might of the advancing panzers. Although the Royal Navy managed to rescue over 40,000 men from the beaches around Athens, 15,000 or more British Empire and Commonwealth troops were either taken prisoner or killed.

To compound this disaster, the decision to redeploy so many men to Greece had brought O'Connor's advance on Tripoli to an abrupt halt, not only dashing all hope of driving the Italians out of North Africa but precipitating a humiliating reverse in the Western Desert at the hands of

General Erwin Rommel. On 24 March the Desert Fox had launched a surprise attack on the British front line some 200 miles south-west of Benghazi at Beda Fomm and then, ignoring orders from his superiors, led a blitzkrieg across the desert, not only driving O'Connor's bewildered troops all the way back to within 100 miles of the Egyptian border but laying siege to the port of Tobruk in the process. The rout had taken six days.

The high command in London feared the worst: 'I suppose you realize we shall lose the Middle East,'[49] the Chief of the Imperial General Staff confided to his director of military operations, Major-General John Kennedy. The gloom was widespread. In June, after a counter-offensive by his 'Army of the Nile' foundered against Rommel on the Libyan border with heavy loss of life, even Churchill succumbed: 'I went down to Chartwell [his estate in Kent], which was all shut up, wishing to be alone. Here I got the reports of what had happened. I wandered about the valley disconsolately for some hours.'[50] As he had long been aware, Britain's only escape route from the prospect of further disasters lay through the White House, and the longer Roosevelt temporized, the graver became the predicament. Thus his untempered delight when Halifax told him that the Americans would be happy to replace the British troops in Iceland.

On 30 May he responded to Roosevelt's offer by suggesting that the American takeover should be 'at the earliest possible moment . . . If it could be done in the next three weeks or less, or even begun, it would have a moral significance even beyond its military importance. You only have to say the word and our staffs can get to work at once.'[51] His eagerness was partly inspired by the thought that the British force could be transferred to the hard-pressed fronts in the Middle East but principally by his appreciation of the fact that – as Stark had observed – Roosevelt's offer would inevitably suck America even closer towards an outright military alliance with Britain against Germany.

With this green light, Roosevelt demonstrated the careful decisiveness which was his hallmark. On 5 June he ordered the US Navy to make the necessary preparations for a landing on Iceland. Following up on this twelve days later, Admiral Stark pressed Hopkins for formal presidential confirmation of an initiative which contained 'so much potential dynamite'. Affirming that a US task force would be ready to depart on 22 June, he concluded, 'I will wait for the final "execute" until

I get word from the president, for as you know the invitation from the government of Iceland has not yet arrived.'[52] This 'invitation' was no more than a fig leaf to save Icelandic face. The authorities in Reykjavik had been left in no doubt that, while their consent was desirable, it was by no means a precondition for the US occupation; as the president's trusted envoy in Iceland, Lincoln MacVeagh, was to tell him some months later, '[T]rue military occupation is not relished. But the wiser heads know that it is preferable to invasion.'[53] After a conversation with Churchill on 24 June, the prime minister of Iceland duly sent a formal 'invitation' to the president, which appears to have been drafted in Washington and was, of course, accepted with alacrity.[54]

The diplomatic niceties accomplished, the president alerted Congress to his decision on 7 July, by which time the US task force had already arrived off Reykjavik, where the advance party of an eventual force of 40,000 US military personnel landed the following day. His decision had required more than a little political courage as well as diplomatic thuggery. In an analysis of public opinion written for the Foreign Office some days later, a British official in Washington cited an unnamed 'observer' who had likened the American people to 'an audience watching an exciting movie. Hitler is the cunning villain: England is the brave but not too bright hero. The sympathy of the entire audience is with the hero but that's about all. They do not see that they are called upon to do anything about it.'[55] Sooner or later, though, the military implications of the occupation of Iceland were all but certain to force the US Navy on to the offensive. Though Roosevelt was still not ready to take that plunge, the momentum of events, regardless of what the audience might hope or fear, was unstoppable.

Although they were initially reluctantly welcomed by the population, the American forces based in Iceland did not endear themselves to the local population. The conditions in Iceland were hardly conducive to high morale. There were few opportunities to escape the tedium of barrack life or to find recreational alternatives to the mess room. In summer it was possible for the new arrivals to explore the island beyond their military bases but the beauty of a lunar landscape surrounded by mountains soon palled; the midnight sun shone throughout high summer and in deep winter Iceland was shrouded in darkness for eighteen hours a day. Although the temperature was relatively mild in the lowlands, ranging from 14° F in the winter to 70° F in summer, when the hurricanes blew, the storm winds shrieked across a polar desert surrounded by lashing waves. Iceland was not for the faint-hearted.

In an effort to counter low morale among the troops, the US ambassador sought to remind them that theirs was a vital mission. As he explained to Roosevelt, he did this by asking them a rhetorical question: 'What would be our situation if Germany were in control there [Iceland] rather than we or our allies?'[56] At the time he wrote those words, in November 1941, the United States was still not formally at war with Germany but Roosevelt had declared a full state of 'belligerency' in the Atlantic. The incident that was finally to provoke the president to this de facto declaration of hostilities was sparked – not deliberately but inevitably – by his strategic decision to occupy this remote outcrop in the Atlantic Ocean. As he explained to the American people with a homely but arresting image: 'When you see a rattlesnake poised to strike, you do not wait . . . you crush him.'[57]

# 8.  America Goes for It

The loss of the *Bismarck* was the beginning of the end of Raeder's influence in the German high command. For the admiral, the loss of the iconic battleship was a tragic end to an heroic endeavour. For Hitler it was a humiliation for which he held the Kriegsmarine's commander-in-chief personally responsible. 'Hitler's attitude changed radically and unalterably,' Raeder recalled. Whereas once 'he had given me a relatively free hand as long as government policies or the other armed forces were not involved, he now became extremely critical and very apt to insist on agreement with his own views'.[1]

Hitler's immediate reaction was to forbid Raeder to despatch any further surface ships into the Atlantic – no battleships, no cruisers, no aircraft carriers, no destroyers. Instead they were to remain in port against future deployment once the Russian campaign was over. This was a devastating blow to a man who had invested his reputation in the creation of a fleet of great capital ships to rival any in the world. Not only was this vision in tatters but, in effect, his cherished surface fleet which had waged war at sea 'with daring and initiative' was now deemed irrelevant.[2] A proud and obstinate man, Raeder continued to plan for further breakouts into the Atlantic, only to have his proposals peremptorily vetoed by the Führer. For the time being at least, the fleet was effectively out of commission, if not quite in mothballs. Only the so-called 'auxiliary' cruisers – merchant raiders armed with heavy weapons but heavily camouflaged to conceal their identity – were still free to roam the oceans, but even their modest contribution to Germany's war at sea was to last only a few more months. From now on the Atlantic convoys had only the U-boats (and to a lesser extent the Luftwaffe) to contend with. For a while this lulled the British towards the conclusion that the Royal Navy was winning the U-boat war; and for a while it looked as though they might be right.

Raeder's exclusion from Hitler's inner counsel had also denied Dönitz a direct route to the Führer. Hitler's veto on the deployment of the surface fleet had inadvertently vindicated his unswerving belief that the

U-boat campaign was the only realistic way of defeating the British in the Atlantic. The sinking of the *Bismarck*, he was to reflect, had nevertheless shown that 'the enemy had improved his system of patrolling the Atlantic to such a degree that our own surface vessels could obviously not operate in these sea areas'.[3] But, to his frustration, the U-boat commander-in-chief was still far from securing the fleet of 300 U-boats he had said he needed to win the tonnage war.

In July and August, he complained, he had at most a dozen U-boats to patrol 'the whole vast sea area from Greenland to the Azores', potentially the most fruitful killing ground in the entire ocean. The 180,000 square miles of the Atlantic known to the British as the Atlantic Gap was beyond the range of British aircraft. Although the US-built Liberator Mark 1, with a range of up to 2,700 miles, was capable of covering the area, the first tranche of these long-range bombers to be delivered to the Air Ministry in the summer of 1941 was appropriated by the RAF for the bombing campaign against Germany; as a result these aircraft were unavailable to play what could have been a crucial part in the Battle of the Atlantic (and would remain so for a further – profoundly controversial – eighteen months; see Chapter 18). If Dönitz had been able fully to exploit their absence at this point, the wolf packs might well have been able to sever Britain's vital supply route across the Atlantic. However, twelve U-boats could not begin to stem the flow, let alone to cover the waterfront. As it was, it was impossible to deliver that killer blow. 'Time and time again', Dönitz wrote, '. . . the U-boats swept the seas fruitlessly in a vain attempt to find the enemy.' By his reckoning, the total sinkings in all oceans for July and August thus amounted to a 'meagre' 174,519 tons, a sharp drop from their haul during the previous three months.[4]

The figures for June would have been even more disappointing if Dönitz had not been required to shift a proportion of his fleet from the Freetown patrol to the busy sea lanes between Britain and Gibraltar. The British fortress held a commanding position at the entrance to the Mediterranean; so long as it was in Britain's hands it would be virtually impossible for the Axis forces to enter or leave what Mussolini regarded as Italy's maritime backyard. In Il Duce's mind, the Mediterranean was not so much a sea as an Italian lake on the far side of which lay Libya, the most important colony in what he dreamt would one day form part of a great Italian empire in Africa. Only Britain – by virtue of its commanding position in the Middle East – stood between his vision and reality. In the meantime, the Rock of Gibraltar not only inhibited Italy's access to the Atlantic but was a bulwark against any attempt by Hitler to use Spain as a stepping stone from which to occupy North Africa and the Azores, from where the Luftwaffe's long-range bombers might threaten the coast of South America, which Washington already regarded as its backyard.

From Britain's perspective, it was a strategic necessity to hold Gibraltar. Although most of the civilian population (some 15,000 people) had been evacuated in 1940, the garrison housed the 1st and 2nd Gibraltar Brigades; the Royal Navy Harbour was a base both for Force 'H' – a pioneering carrier task force, spearheaded by *Ark Royal*, *Renown* and the light cruiser HMS *Sheffield*, supported by other warships including twenty destroyers – and for RAF Coastal Command's 202 Squadron's Swordfish biplanes and flying boats (Catalinas and Sunderlands). Were Dönitz's U-boats to succeed in disrupting the supply of food, fuel, and armaments to the Rock, they would not only threaten the survival of the garrison but make it even more difficult to protect the convoys carrying emergency supplies to Malta. This beleaguered fortress island was pivotal to the conduct of the campaign against the Axis forces in the Western Desert as a base from which to interdict the Italian convoys carrying supplies from Libya for Rommel's assault on Egypt. As the German high command was equally aware of all these strategic complexities, the approaches to the Rock had become as perilous as any waters in any ocean. For this reason, the convoys which regularly plied from Liverpool to Gibraltar and back were invariably given heavy protection.

One of these convoys, OG71, left Liverpool on 13 August. It comprised twenty-three merchant ships, accompanied by thirteen Royal Navy escorts, one of which was the corvette HMS *Campanula*, whose first lieutenant was Nicholas Monsarrat. The future novelist had applied to join the RNVR (Royal Naval Volunteer Reserve) early in 1940 and had served in *Campanula* since then. After a year at sea, he was a seasoned officer who had endured the worst Atlantic weather and had already witnessed hideous human suffering. His father had been a surgeon, which was deemed sufficient reason for him to be appointed to that post in *Campanula*, although he had never studied medicine, let alone used a scalpel. Thus began what he later described as 'the worst horror-film of my life'. His patients were generally merchant sea-men plucked from the ocean after their vessels had been torpedoed in convoy:

> Survivors climbing on board with gasping lungs, or hauled over the side like oil-soaked fish from the scrambling nets, or hoisted up with a rope to torture anew a shattered body . . . They could have swallowed mouthfuls of corrosive fuel oil, and be coughing up their guts until they died; they could be shuddering in the last bitter extremity of cold and exhaustion; they might have sustained gross wounds and the shock that went with them; they could be screaming with the pain of deep, hope-less burns, and broken limbs.[5]

In the absence of an operating theatre (there was no space for such a luxury in the confines of a corvette) or the benefit of anaesthetics, he had to stitch up gashed throats, coax 'a dangling eyeball' back into its socket and stuff innards back into open stomach wounds, without knowing until that moment that they 'could actually *smell* so awful'.[6]

The young first lieutenant had to school himself into the clinician's necessary detachment. In the early hours of his thirty-first birthday he buried eight men:

> Eight men, eight sailors, eight comrades in this fearful enterprise – I should be in tears, I should be wearing a mourning band around my heart . . . But . . . I still found a ready appetite for the fried bread, the powdered-egg omelette, and the thin brew of coffee essence which was our reward one hour later.[7]

It was impossible, though, to be unmoved by the suffering he so often witnessed when men of all nationalities were plucked from the ocean, frightened and bewildered by the horror of being torpedoed. 'Survivors in the mess-decks, filling every available space . . . talking, shivering, wolfing food, staring at nothing.'[8]

Monsarrat's task was made no easier by the fact that he loathed his captain, Lieutenant Commander Richard Case.\* As 'a long-term pro-fessional sailor in the RNR [Royal Naval Reserve]', Case evidently

---

\* Perhaps to spare his embarrassment, Monsarrat did not identify Case by name in his war memoir, *Three Corvettes*, which was originally published in three separate vol-umes before the end of the war.

despised 'the pink-cheeked amateurs' of the RNVR – a disdain, the junior officer believed, that flowed from the 'traditional stupid and childish feud' between two branches of the naval reserve; a feud he saw mirrored in the rift between the full-time naval officers and those called up as reservists. But, in Monsarrat's account, Case was an unusually obnoxious and domineering individual. Using 'raucous prison slang', the captain appeared to relish humiliating his subordinate officer with questions barked as though they were orders: 'Monsarrat! Where's that bloody steward?' 'Monsarrat! That stem-wire's slack again! Hop to it!' 'Monsarrat! There's too much noise over my cabin!' And on one occasion, 'Monsarrat! I've been calling you for ten minutes!' 'Sorry, Sir, I was in the lavatory.' 'Don't go to the lavatory! Bake it!'[9] The first lieutenant and his colleagues had no choice but to endure in obedient but no less disdainful silence.

Now, in August 1941, came 'the most horrible voyage of all'. OG71 had been routed far out into the Atlantic to stay out of range of Luftwaffe bombers flying from the French coast. *Campanula* had been given a refit, she was fitted with a new radar set and the sea was calm and the breeze balmy. To Monsarrat, the conditions 'seemed to take the whole ship away from war and into the simple warming joys of being alive and afloat'. There were whales and basking sharks, and once they saw a turtle. The crew chatted and told hoary jokes culled from years at sea; they were over halfway towards their destination and it was blissful.

Dawn broke on 17 August as though to lull the mood once again. But as the sun rose over the horizon, the calm was broken by a lookout who saw an approaching enemy aircraft. It was a long-range Focke-Wulf reconnaissance plane which circled overhead, keeping well out of gunfire range. The mood in *Campanula* changed at once. They had been discovered, their speed and direction plotted and signalled back to Lorient, where Dönitz at once ordered a pack of eight U-boats to close on the slow-moving convoy still some 500 miles from its destination. The trap was soon set and in the early hours of 19 August it was sprung. At this point, as Monsarrat put it, 'the cutting edge of war sliced our brief paradise to bloody rags'.[10]

Unusually, Dönitz ordered his wolf pack to attack the escorts before sinking any of their charges. The first ship to go was an elderly 'four stack' destroyer, one of the vessels delivered to the Royal Navy by the United States under the 'destroyers for bases' deal but transferred to the

Norwegian navy earlier in the year. HNoMS *Bath* exploded and sank with heavy loss of life. Over the course of the next five days, despite frantic efforts by the escorts, supported by RAF Catalinas and Sunderlands despatched from Gibraltar, a further nine ships were sunk. Six of these were merchantmen carrying supplies and weapons for the defence of Gibraltar; the other two were a passenger ship, the SS *Aguila*, and another Flower class corvette, HMS *Zinnia*.

The passengers aboard *Aguila* included some ninety service personnel, including twenty-two members of the Women's Royal Naval Service who had volunteered for the Gibraltar posting to serve as cipher and wireless operators. Kapitänleutnant Schnee in U-201, whom Dönitz regarded as 'an exceptionally brilliant' individual,[11] tracked the convoy for a day and most of the night before taking his chance in the early hours of 19 August. Finding a gap in the escort screen, he fired four torpedoes in rapid succession. One of them hit the *Aguila*, which sank almost immediately, taking with her fifty-eight members of the crew, the convoy's commodore and eighty-nine passengers. None of the Wrens survived.*

Altogether four ships went down on 19 August. Two more were sunk on the 22nd and on the following night another four were lost. The last of these was the *Zinnia*, which was torpedoed by another U-boat ace, Reinhard 'Teddy' Suhren, in U-564. *Zinnia*'s loss was keenly felt by the crew of the surviving corvette. Monsarrat himself watched the explosion as the torpedo hit the *Campanula*'s sister ship and felt 'saddened and sickened' by the experience.

When dawn broke, *Campanula* joined the search for survivors. Monsarrat was put in charge of the scrambling nets as the crew 'yanked' six men to safety. The *Zinnia*'s captain, Lieutenant Commander Charles Cuthbertson, whom Monsarrat greatly respected, was not among them. It was a great relief to him, therefore, to be told that Cuthbertson had been among another group of nine men rescued by other vessels. Seventy-five of their shipmates had not been so fortunate.

A few days later, after the U-boats had disappeared as discreetly as they had arrived, *Campanula* was back in Gibraltar. Cuthbertson came aboard but said very little. 'I could only tell him,' Monsarrat wrote,

* At its peak in 1944 the WRNS numbered 75,000. Around 100 Wrens died while on duty in the Second World War.

'that I had looked after his stunned survivors, and buried his dead; those rows of sailors like ourselves, their badges proclaiming their faithful service, their wide-open eyes attesting their last surprise.'[12]

On 13 August – the day that OG71 embarked on its fateful passage to Gibraltar – HMS *Prince of Wales* was sailing at full speed away from the Canadian naval base of Argentia in Newfoundland. On board was a party of British diplomats, military advisors and Churchill, on his way back from his first summit with the president of the United States. The two men had met briefly more than twenty years earlier but this encounter was of an altogether different order. Although the cognoscenti on both sides of the Atlantic had suspected for some time that such a get-together was imminent, the preparations for the occasion were made in great haste and in the utmost secrecy. Once again Harry Hopkins was the go-between.

On 14 July he had arrived in Britain to see Churchill for the second time, but on this occasion he was accompanied by a phalanx of senior US military officers. The principal purpose of their visit was to discuss the need to open a new convoy route through the Arctic to provide aid to Russia without starving the supply lines to Britain across the Atlantic. But Hopkins had also been charged to raise his doubts about Churchill's determination to defend the British Empire without jeopardizing the defence of the Home Front against a German invasion. Hopkins did not mince his words, advising Churchill that the conviction was growing in Washington that the Middle East was indefensible, that the British should contemplate withdrawal from that distant front and that, instead, all their efforts should focus on the Battle of the Atlantic, which, in the view of the US administration, was where 'the final decisive battle of the war' would be fought.[13] Moreover, this shift of resources would in due course free up warships and freighters which, the US director of the War Plans Division, Admiral Robert L. Ghormley, warned, 'might be needed in the Pacific and the Indian Ocean'.[14]

Happily for Churchill, as Hopkins freely explained, the president 'had a somewhat different attitude' to his advisors as he recognized that 'the British have got to fight the enemy wherever they find him'.[15] Snatching eagerly at this crumb of comfort, the British chiefs of staff countered their American counterparts by claiming respectively that the navy, the army and the RAF were all getting stronger by the day.

Churchill himself asserted – prematurely – that prospects in the Battle of the Atlantic were improving. Rather more persuasively, he also warned that by 'smashing down through Spain and past Gibraltar into North and West Africa', the Axis powers could establish a launch pad for an assault on the American hemisphere. Were the United States to be drawn into the war against Hitler, he argued, it would be well to pre-empt this danger by establishing a forward base in North Africa from which to attack the Wehrmacht in Europe. In this case, he hardly needed to add, it would be crucial for Britain to protect its strategic interests in the Mediterranean and the Middle East. With the issue unresolved, the talks were adjourned for another, unspecified, date.

If Washington's scepticism about Britain's imperial pretensions was a bitter pill for Churchill, Hopkins knew how to sugar it. Sitting with the prime minister in the Rose Garden at Number 10 one afternoon during these talks, he issued an invitation from the president suggesting that the two men get together to discuss their mutual concerns. According to Churchill's private secretary, the waspishly observant Jock Colville, this prospect made the prime minister 'as excited as a schoolboy on the last day of term'.[16] More decorously, Churchill himself acknowledged that he had 'the keenest desire to meet Mr. Roosevelt', clearly undaunted by a scribbled note which Roosevelt had handed to Hopkins before the latter's departure from Washington, which stated baldly, 'No talk about war'.[17] Roosevelt was evidently not willing to be subjected to one of Churchill's eloquent disquisitions on the need for the United States to declare war against Germany forthwith.

While he was in London, Hopkins was simultaneously seized by a moment of inspiration on the president's behalf. He cabled Roosevelt to suggest that before his return to the States he should fly to Moscow as the president's emissary to Stalin. The long and arduous journey by air would have much the same purpose as his first visit to London – to establish at first hand the scale of the predicament facing the Soviet Union. Roosevelt immediately gave him the go-ahead for what turned out to be one of the most important journeys of the war. Hopkins took with him two messages for the Soviet leader. One was from Roosevelt expressing 'the great admiration all of us in the United States have for the superb bravery displayed by the Russian people in the defense of their liberty and in their fight for the independence of Russia',[18] and the other was from Churchill, who asked Hopkins to tell Stalin that 'Britain has but one ambition today, but one desire – to crush Hitler. Tell him that he can depend upon us.'[19] If ever there was a case of 'my enemy's enemy is my friend', this overture from the two leaders of the capitalist world to the leader of the world's only communist state was its acme.

The meetings between Stalin and Hopkins lasted for three days and produced a long shopping list of Soviet requirements as well as – from Hopkins's pen – a vivid portrait of America's new ally:

> No man could forget the picture of the dictator of Russia as he stood watching me leave – an austere, rugged, determined figure in boots that shone like mirrors, stout baggy trousers, and snug-fitting blouse. He wore no ornament, military or civilian. He's built close to the ground, like a football coach's dream of a tackle . . . His hands are huge, as hard as his mind. His voice is harsh but ever under control . . . He seems to have no doubts. He assures you that Russia will stand against the onslaughts of the German Army. He takes it for granted that you will have no doubts either.[20]

His meeting with Stalin had confirmed Hopkins's instinct that the Western military observers who had been sending back deeply pessimistic messages to Washington and London were mistaken about the Soviet Union's ability to resist the Wehrmacht. Roosevelt's confidant was evidently impressed by the Soviet leader's long and detailed assessment of the relative strengths of his own and Hitler's forces. Stalin, he concluded, was clear-minded, well informed, confident and resolute; with appropriate military support from the Western Allies there was no reason to expect the Red Army would crumble before the might of the advancing Wehrmacht. Though he had made it clear to the Soviet leader that he could not personally make a formal commitment on behalf of the United States or Britain, Hopkins was readily persuaded that the Western Allies should not only authorize the early despatch of anti-aircraft guns, machine guns and rifles to Russia but, in due course, should also consider sending heavy artillery, tanks and bombers as well.

The two men went on to explore the best means by which this aid might be delivered. The overland route via Persia (modern day Iran) was rudimentary and little suited as yet for the transport of heavy goods, while the threat posed by the Japanese navy in the Pacific effectively prohibited the use of the far eastern Russian port of Vladivostok by

American vessels. Although both these routes would later surpass it in importance, the only practical option for many months ahead would be to despatch maritime convoys through the Arctic Ocean to the northern ports of Murmansk and Archangel. Hopkins left Moscow convinced that this hazardous enterprise should be essayed at the earliest opportunity.

In Washington, suspicion and distrust of the Soviet Union still prevailed. Thus, when the Soviet ambassador, Konstantin Oumansky, asked Secretary of State Stimson for the 'delivery of military secrets' he was told 'quite bluntly' that until American observers were permitted to enter the war zone 'this extraordinary privilege' would not be granted.[21]

In similar vein, the outspoken but widely respected Assistant Secretary of State, Adolf Berle, warned Hopkins not to be carried away by enthusiasm for the Russian cause: the Soviet leadership was 'unpredictable' and the prospect of a rapprochement between the USSR and Germany could not be discounted: 'there might be a military coup in Germany with a General appearing as dictator and an immediate Russo-German alliance. Judging by their propaganda, the Russians are apparently playing for something like this now . . . So for God's sake, tell the sentimentalists to watch themselves.'[22]

Mindful of these concerns but impressed by Hopkins's analysis, Churchill and Roosevelt decided to honour their verbal commitments to Stalin by authorizing the first convoy to depart for Russia forthwith. On 21 August 1941 six merchant ships, escorted by three British destroyers, two minesweepers and two armed trawlers, left Reykjavik for Archangel, arriving in the Russian port ten days later without incident.

On the eve of its arrival, the US ambassador in Moscow, Laurence Steinhardt, was instructed to reassure the Kremlin that the flow of materials had begun. The initial shipments were to include fighter planes, fuel, tanks and ammunition, raw materials and food.[23] These supplies, the Kremlin was told, were to be delivered through the autumn and into the winter.

While Hopkins was with Stalin, Washington and London scrambled to organize the transatlantic rendezvous which had been arranged for 10 August in the remote waters of Placentia Bay in Newfoundland, which

sheltered the US naval base at Argentia. Hopkins was determined to get
back to Britain in time to join Churchill for the voyage across the Atlantic in the *Prince of Wales*. As soon as his talks in the Kremlin were over,
he flew to Scotland, ignoring advice to delay his departure on account
of the adverse weather conditions en route. After a rough flight, battling
strong headwinds, the frail American arrived at Scapa Flow feeling
'desperately ill',[24] not from the turbulence but because the bag of drugs
on which he depended to alleviate the pain of his stomach cancer had
gone astray somewhere in Moscow. As the prime minister's party prepared to board the battleship, even Churchill noted solicitously that his
new friend looked 'dead-beat'.[25]

The need for total secrecy had required cloak-and-dagger preparations for the meeting of the leaders to ensure that neither the American
nor the British public – let alone the German military intelligence service, the Abwehr – would discover what was in the offing. Roosevelt
eluded his own press corps by pretending to depart for a holiday in the
presidential yacht, the *Potomac*. Once he had eluded the pack, he
switched to the USS *Augusta* for the voyage to the secret rendezvous. In
a similar shroud of secrecy, Churchill – accompanied by 'a retinue
which Cardinal Wolsey might have envied'[26] – departed on schedule on
4 August. Initially the *Prince of Wales* was flanked by a flotilla of destroyers but, in worsening weather and high seas, the battleship was soon
forced to abandon its escorts, which were unable to maintain the high
speed required to reach their destination on schedule. Thereafter, the
warship zigzagged alone across the Atlantic to avoid any marauding
U-boats. Though the voyage was hardly risk free, the *Prince of Wales*'s
maximum speed of almost thirty knots made it far less hazardous than
it would have been in a slower vessel. Churchill's party duly arrived
undetected in Placentia Bay six days later.

On 10 August 1941, in Placentia Bay, the prime minister and the
president came face to face aboard the *Augusta* for three days of intense
discussion and debate. Colonel Ian Jacob, who was in the British party
as military assistant to the War Cabinet,* recalled that the encounter

---

* Soon to be promoted by Churchill to the rank of lieutenant-general, Jacob was
almost invariably at the prime minister's side on his multiple wartime trips abroad.
After the war he joined the BBC and, following a brief secondment to Number 10 in
1951, he returned to become the Corporation's director-general in 1952.

'had something of the nature of a first meeting between stags; the two great men wanted to have a good look at each other'.[27] There was little self-delusion in their burgeoning relationship. Though they established an easy rapport, neither of them was to forget for a moment 'what he was or represented or what the other was or represented'; Churchill 'quickly learned that he confronted in the president a man of infinite subtlety and obscurity – an artful dodger who could neither be pinned down on specific points, nor hustled or wheedled into definite commitments against his judgement or his will or instinct'.[28] For his part, Roosevelt swiftly observed how pertinacious the prime minister could be in pursuance of an objective.

Notwithstanding the president's 'No talk of war' injunction, Churchill's objective was to establish an alliance so close as to leave the impression that, strategically, the two leaders were joined at the hip. To that extent, the two men were at one with each other, though the degree to which this union would or should go beyond rhetorical expressions of mutual amity was far more difficult to establish. However, the Atlantic Conference, as it became known, did have symbolic significance. Not only did it affirm a close transatlantic bond but it enshrined a set of common values and aspirations which were codified in the Atlantic Charter which had been drafted by the British side before being negotiated, refined and approved by the two leaders on the day that their talks ended. The Charter's language was rich with benign promise. It confirmed that the two nations were in favour of self-determination, free trade, and an end to 'fear and want' in a world where – following the 'final destruction of Nazi tyranny' – sovereign nations would undertake to rid themselves of weapons of war for the sake of international peace and security.* But how this might be accomplished and, specifically, the part that might be played by the United States in the process was carefully sidestepped: for the moment, in public at least, 'No talk of war' remained Roosevelt's lodestar. Nonetheless, though it lacked any policy of substance, the sonorous declarations which emerged from the first summit did serve as a useful public platform on which to construct the framework within which to develop a crucial diplomatic and military

---

*The Atlantic Charter, www.un.org/en/aboutun/charter/history/atlantic.shtml. The Charter would later serve as a blueprint for the founding of the United Nations Charter which came into force one month after Hitler's overthrow in 1945.

relationship while sidestepping Churchill's obdurate commitment to the British Empire.

On his return to Washington, Roosevelt was given a notably cool reception by the White House press corps, who liked to believe their relationship was based on mutual trust and honesty. Now, smarting at the ease with which the president had given them the slip a week earlier, many were less ready than usual to give him the benefit of the doubt. As recompense, they expected at the very least some titbits of truth and insight from him. Instead, when he invited them aboard the *Potomac*, he gave them nothing, refusing point-blank to elaborate on the meaning behind the words of the Charter. Asked by one frustrated reporter if his meeting with the British prime minister had brought the United States closer to war, his answer was an unequivocal 'No'. However, anxious to avoid upsetting Churchill, he used the rules of the White House Lobby to insist that even this reply should not be quoted verbatim.

The president had good cause to be so unforthcoming. Behind the veil of the Atlantic Charter both he and Churchill had concealed the true and immediate import of their talks. The president's son, Elliott, an army air force officer who had joined his father for the talks aboard *Augusta*, was to claim that Churchill had used his very first meeting with the president to declare, 'It's your only chance. You've got to come in beside us! If you don't declare war, declare war I say, without waiting for them to strike the first blow, they'll strike it after we've gone under, and their first blow will be their last as well.'[29] Though this hyperbole assuredly reflected Churchill's private sentiments, the younger Roosevelt was a notoriously unreliable witness; it would have been an unlikely lapse of judgement on the prime minister's part to have defied the presidential request to avoid talking about the war quite so brazenly. But Churchill certainly did raise the banned topic with members of the president's entourage and later claimed to have told Roosevelt's circle that he 'would rather have an American declaration of war now and no supplies for six months than double the supplies and no declaration'.[30]

No detailed minutes were kept of the private talks between the two men but, in reporting back to the War Cabinet, the prime minister felt able to quote Roosevelt as telling him that 'he would wage war, but not declare it, and that he would become more and more provocative'. Moreover, he added, the president had also 'made it clear that he would look for "an incident" which would justify him in opening hostilities'.[31]

Whether or not Roosevelt had spoken in quite these terms, the prospect of such an incident became very much more likely as a result of a decision which Roosevelt made aboard the *Augusta* on the eve of his meeting with Churchill.

Summoning his military advisors, the president told them that, starting on 1 September, not only would US warships be required to escort American merchant ships to Iceland but – crucially – that merchant ships of any other nation would be free to join the American convoys and thereby fall under the protection of the US government. And he went further, instructing his chiefs of staff that any number of foreign merchant ships would be permitted to shelter under the US flag so long as every such convoy contained one American or Icelandic vessel. The precise role of the US escorts was deliberately ill defined, but the potential repercussions were self-evident. As Roosevelt pointedly instructed his advisors, 'it would be too late for escorts to start shooting after an attack began'.[32]

The president's decision combined the conviction and cunning that were his hallmarks, achieving by stealth what – given the prevailing mood in Congress – would have been exceptionally difficult if not impossible to achieve by an open and frontal approach to the prospect of war with Germany. However, by its implicit commitment to ensuring that Britain's Atlantic lifeline could not be severed, his instruction also made it clear that he was indeed willing to contemplate being drawn into a shooting war in the Atlantic Ocean. As with his decision to extend the US Security Zone to longitude 25°W, he had surreptitiously raised the stakes once again.

Roosevelt was well aware that the British navy was already overstretched in the Atlantic, the Mediterranean and the Far East, and that if he were to ask Britain to escort the convoys carrying US aid to the Soviet Union, something would have to give somewhere. So when Churchill used his first formal meeting at Placentia Bay to advise Roosevelt that Britain needed to withdraw at least four dozen warships from escort duty in the western Atlantic 'to bolster convoy protection along the Gibraltar and West African routes' (where Dönitz had recently redeployed most of his U-boats from the North Atlantic) he found himself pushing at an open door. Roosevelt readily assented.

Thus reassured, the prime minister made his farewells and sailed for Britain on 12 August. As soon as he was at sea, he despatched messages to King George VI, the Australian prime minister, Robert Menzies, and the Labour leader, Clement Attlee, who held the post of deputy prime minister in the wartime coalition. His tone was upbeat, reflecting the fact that he believed it was 'astonishing' that a 'technically neutral' power had joined 'with a belligerent power' in calling for the destruction of Nazism.[33] When he was told that Roosevelt had ordered two US destroyers to escort the *Prince of Wales* as far as Iceland, he was delighted by this token of presidential goodwill. His cup was already brimming when the great battleship caught up with a convoy of seventy-three ships lumbering towards Britain carrying oil, tanks, armoured cars, aircraft, wheat and other foodstuffs. The prime minister insisted on steaming through the middle of the convoy at twenty-two knots, flying a signal which read 'Good luck – Churchill'. Sir Alexander Cadogan, a senior Foreign Office official not noted for expressing exaggerated sentiment, observed that the 'forest of funnels looked almost like a town . . . it was a beautiful and inspiring sight', but added 'it is disturbing to see what a target they offer and how little protection they have'.[34]

Whether or not they shared this anxiety, the crews aboard the merchant ships were not disposed to let it detract from this moment. According to one of the *Prince of Wales*'s crew, they

> went mad. It was a great moment . . . for none more so than the prime minister. Quickly every ship was flying the 'V' flag; some tried a dot-dot-dot-dash salute on their sirens. In nearer ships men could be seen waving, laughing, and – we guessed though we could not hear – cheering. On the bridge the prime minister was waving back at them, as was every man on our own decks, cheering with them, two fingers on his right hand making the famous V-sign.[35]

Churchill was so elated by this experience that he demanded a rerun. The great battleship duly executed a U-turn, waited for the convoy to wallow by, and repeated the sail-past for the delectation of all. The anonymous crewman added, 'If dusk had not been approaching I believe we should have done it again.'[36]

In the ship's wardroom, according to the journalist A. V. Morton, who – to the annoyance of the American press corps – had been infiltrated by the British into Churchill's party for the Atlantic Conference, the mood among the *Prince of Wales*'s officers was more subdued: 'What we had all subconsciously hoped for was a declaration that America was coming into battle with us; the only thing that seemed to us to justify the dramatic encounter.' But, as they listened to the BBC broadcast in which Attlee read out the full text of the Atlantic Charter, they became increasingly bemused: 'We sat looking at one another . . . We knew that, sooner or later, somehow, and in some way, America would come in with us and fight; then we asked ourselves, why not now?'[37]

In London the mood was equally sombre. As politicians, diplomats, and journalists pored over the Charter, they were disappointed to discover that the warm words of mutual aspiration, valuable as they were, failed to contain any commitment by the United States to join Britain in belligerency.

A few days later, on 24 August, Churchill's broadcast to the British people offered little enlightenment, although his message was couched in such grandiloquent but imprecise language as to leave the impression that the United States was indeed on the brink of declaring war against Germany: 'I thought you would like me to tell you something about the voyage which I made across the ocean to meet our great friend, the president of the United States,' he began, before reporting that he had returned 'across the ocean waves, uplifted in spirit, fortified in resolve'. The president, he confided, had 'pledged' America to the 'final destruction of Nazi tyranny . . . a solemn and grave undertaking' which 'must be made good. It will be made good.'[38] In using the word 'pledge' to describe America's commitment, Churchill had not only gone some way beyond any interpretation that the words of the Atlantic Charter could reasonably have been thought to bear but also beyond any commitment that Roosevelt had made or even implied at Placentia Bay. Reality had fallen victim either to wish fulfilment or a misplaced attempt to bounce the president into a greater commitment than he was yet able or willing to give.

In either case, Churchill was cast into gloom when he heard that Roosevelt had insisted firmly and in public that the United States was not on the brink of declaring war against Germany on the back of their talks aboard *Augusta*. He gave vent to his disappointment in a bleak private note he sent to Hopkins on 28 August:

> The president's many declarations with regard to United States being no closer to war and having made no commitments have been the cause of concern in high circles here in London and in the Cabinet. This feeling

is also going to be felt in Parliament. I don't know what will happen if England [sic] is fighting alone when 1942 comes. I will be very pleased if you can give me any hope.[39]

In reporting Churchill's reproachful tone with Roosevelt, Hopkins concluded that 'the only thing we can make out is that Churchill is pretty depressed and takes it out on us in this fashion'. Intriguingly, though, the president gave Hopkins the impression that he was quite unaware that the British had allowed themselves to believe that 'ultimately we would get into the war'. If so, Roosevelt was also unaware of the degree to which his habitual opacity could mislead friends as well as foes. Hopkins was in no doubt how serious this ambiguity could become; in the same memorandum he noted that his own conversations in London had left him with the impression that, should the British ever conclude that the United States had no intention of becoming a belligerent, it 'would be a very critical moment in the war and that British appeasers might have more influence on Churchill'.[40]

Strategically, Roosevelt was torn. At Placentia Bay he and Churchill had discussed not only Nazism but also the growing challenge to their interests posed by Japanese imperialism. Churchill repeatedly urged Roosevelt to react more aggressively against an expansionist power that threatened both American and British spheres of influence in Asia. But the president faced a dilemma that his principal advisors – divided among themselves – were unable to resolve for him. He did not doubt that Japan was on the offensive, but he was reluctant to make any move that might provoke war while America's armed forces were insufficiently prepared to fight on two fronts at once. As he told his Secretary of the Interior, Harold Ickes, a little over a month before his meeting with Churchill in Placentia Bay, 'it is terribly important for the control of the Atlantic for us to help to keep peace in the Pacific. I simply have not got enough Navy to go round – and every little episode in the Pacific means fewer ships in the Atlantic.'[41]

Nonetheless, when it became clear later in July that Japanese forces were preparing to tighten their grip on Indochina (today's Vietnam, Cambodia, and Laos) by threatening Thailand, the Malay Peninsula and Singapore, as well as the Burma Road (which linked Japanese-occupied China with the British colony) and the Dutch East Indies (today's Indonesia), Roosevelt was goaded to respond. In collaboration with the other Western powers affected, the White House imposed a further range of trade and financial embargoes. Almost incidentally these included an oil embargo which, if effective, would soon lead to the collapse of the Japanese economy. This was as far as Roosevelt was willing to go. As the diplomatic historian Robert Dallek has written, 'Roosevelt remained eager to extend the discussions with Tokyo as a means of deferring a war in the Pacific for as long as he could' so that the scarce resources at his disposal could 'be marshalled to fight Hitler'.[42]

Churchill – who appeared to be either unaware of or indifferent to the president's dilemma – came away from Placentia Bay apparently believing that he had persuaded Roosevelt to ratchet up the pressure on Japan and that, on his return to Washington, he would formally warn that, if the Emperor's armed forces encroached further into the south-west Pacific, the United States 'would be compelled to take counter-measures, even though these might lead to war' between the two nations.[43] When Roosevelt failed to deliver this warning in such combative terms, Churchill was dismayed. Yet the president's caution was well judged. On 12 August, despite a personal appeal to Congress, the House passed a Bill extending military service by only one vote (203 to 202), and then only to eighteen months rather than for the duration of the emergency as the government had requested. Roosevelt was not yet strong enough either militarily or politically to take the United States into any war – let alone a war on two fronts at once – without the irresistible momentum that would be created by a deliberate act of aggression specifically directed against the people of the United States.

It is not unreasonable to suppose that this was precisely what the president intended to engineer. In his unhappy message to Hopkins on 28 August, Churchill had sought to bolster his case for American belligerency with a pair of crude statistics: 'The Germans have thirty submarines on a line from Northern Ireland to the eastern point of Iceland and we have lost 50,000 tons in the last two days,' he wrote plaintively, apparently overlooking the implications of the president's decision to deploy American warships to protect convoys en route from the United States to Iceland – namely that a confrontation with the German submarines lurking in those waters waiting to attack these convoys was highly likely, if not inevitable.[44] The US Naval Academy historian, Robert W. Love, was left in no doubt that the president's decision 'was intended to create an incident at sea with Germany's U-boats'.[45]

On Monday, 1 September – the day the US Navy began its escort duties in the Atlantic, the president – perhaps influenced by Hopkins – used his Labor Day address to give Churchill some encouragement. 'I know,' he declared, 'that I speak the conscience and determination of the American people when I say that we shall do everything in our power to crush Hitler and his Nazi forces.'[46] This was not only significantly more aggressive than the wording he had approved for the Atlantic Charter but also, on the face of it, a direct contradiction of his assertion that the United States was no closer to war as a result of his meeting with the British prime minister at Placentia Bay. However, it was not as yet a declaration of war and, significantly, he was also careful to avoid mentioning the orders he had given to the US Navy about its new role in the western Atlantic which came into force as he spoke.

Three days later, on the morning of 4 September, the US destroyer USS *Greer* was en route to Iceland about 125 miles south-west of Reykjavik, cruising at seventeen and a half knots, when her captain, Commander G. W. Frost, received a message from a passing RAF bomber. The signal read: 'Enemy U-boat observed submerging about 10 miles northwest'.[47] The *Greer* accelerated to twenty knots and zigzagged towards the submarine's reported position. There followed a deadly game of aquatic cat and mouse. U-652, under the command of Oberleutnant Georg-Werner Fraatz, was soon detected by the *Greer*'s sonar equipment. In compliance with existing orders to trail and report the presence of U-boats, Frost began to track U-652, always keeping the submarine on the American warship's bow.

The stalk lasted for three hours until the British aircraft, evidently frustrated by the lack of action, demanded to know whether the *Greer* intended to attack. In conformity with his rules of engagement, Frost answered in the negative. At this, the British plane dropped four depth charges 'more or less at random' on the presumed position of the U-boat before returning to its base to refuel.[48] Assuming that the depth charges had been released by the *Greer*, Fraatz – who was himself under direct orders from Hitler to all U-boats not to initiate an attack on US warships – fired a torpedo at the American destroyer in what he regarded as self-defence. This, assuredly, was the excuse for which Roosevelt had been waiting and hoping.

The *Greer* saw the torpedo carving through the water and had time to dodge out of the way, avoiding it by a hundred yards. Frost counter-attacked with depth charges. U-652 fired a second torpedo, which the *Greer* similarly sidestepped but lost contact in the process. Two and half hours later, after searching the ocean in a series of widening arcs, the *Greer*'s sonar picked up the tell-tale ping of a submarine. Frost ordered eleven more depth charges to be released above U-652. None hit its target and, after losing contact once again, the *Greer* was ordered to resume her course for Iceland. It was a minor incident but a major encounter.

A week later, Roosevelt made the most of the moment. In his Fireside Chat on 11 September (long-remembered for the 'rattlesnake' reference to Nazi Germany), he exploited the U-boat attack on the *Greer* to draw the United States closer to the brink. 'If the destroyer was visible to the submarine when the torpedo was fired, the attack was a deliberate attempt by the Nazis to sink a clearly identified American warship,' he confided; on the other hand, 'if the submarine was beneath the surface of the sea [as it indeed was] . . . then the attack was even more outrageous. For it indicates a policy of indiscriminate violence against any vessel sailing the seas – belligerent or non-belligerent.' With no mention of the depth charges dropped by the RAF bomber which had provoked the U-boat to retaliate, Roosevelt had delivered himself of a masterly distortion of the truth, confirming in the process that he had indeed been looking for such a confrontation in the full knowledge of what it meant.

In this, it served its purpose admirably. Insisting that U-652's action 'was piracy, legally and morally', Roosevelt reminded his listeners about the U-boat attack on the *Robin Moor* three months earlier and about a number of other American-owned freighters sunk elsewhere on the high seas, urging them 'to stop being deluded by the romantic notion that the Americas can go on living happily in a Nazi-dominated world'. In far more contemptuous language than he had yet essayed in public, he ridiculed the 'tender whisperings of appeasers that Hitler is not interested in the Western Hemisphere'. After the *Greer* incident, he insisted, such 'soporific lullabies' would not for much longer affect 'the hard-headed, far-sighted and realistic American people'. The attack on the US destroyer was 'one determined step towards creating a permanent world system based on force, on terror, and on murder'.

It was a brilliantly choreographed performance. While artfully insisting that the United States did not seek 'a shooting war with Hitler', he announced that henceforth 'if any German or Italian vessels of war enter the waters, the protection of which is necessary for American defense, they do so at their own peril'.[49] In short, the US Navy was now at liberty to 'shoot on sight' any Axis warship entering the western hemisphere. In effect, the United States was now at war with Germany in the Atlantic.

In reaching this point Roosevelt had displayed rare political leadership, strategic judgement and moral courage. Unwilling to be goaded into intemperate action, carefully balancing the competing pressures to which he was persistently subjected, happy to be advised but not steered by others, willing to conceal and deceive in the national interest, he spoke an unvarnished truth when, towards the end of his broadcast, he said, 'I have no illusions about the gravity of this step. I have not taken it hurriedly or lightly. It is the result of months and months of constant thought and anxiety and prayer.'[50]

The president had judged American opinion to a T. Even when a congressional inquiry uncovered the manifest distortions in his account of the *Greer* incident, no one demanded that he reverse or amend the policy. Nonetheless, following a meeting with the president at the White House, the British ambassador, Lord Halifax, informed Churchill that Roosevelt believed a large majority of the American people wanted to avoid war against Germany on the one hand, but on the other were willing to support whatever action might be needed to defeat Hitler. For this reason, Halifax reported Roosevelt as saying, 'if he asked for a declaration of war, he wouldn't get it, and opinion would swing against him. He therefore intended to go on doing whatever he best could to help us, and declarations of war were out of fashion.'[51]

This was Roosevelt at his most astute and most devious. In effect, his 'shoot on sight' policy had skilfully reconciled America's interests with Britain's needs. By bringing the United States closer to an open confrontation with the Third Reich, he had laid down a gauntlet that Hitler could only interpret as a declaration of aggressive intent by the most powerful nation in the world; simultaneously he had sent a powerful 'we are all in it together' message to the people of Britain. It was a commitment that was to have a crucial impact on the next stage in the Battle of the Atlantic.

# 9. Secret Weapons

In the summer of 1941 Admiral Dönitz was perplexed. Although his fleet had grown to more than sixty-five operational U-boats, their quarry seemed ever more elusive. In the months of June and July, a significant number of convoys appeared to have been diverted from the expected route across the Atlantic as if to avoid his waiting wolf packs. He needed an explanation for these missed kills. At his headquarters at Kerneval, he and his staff planned and directed the movement of his U-boat fleet with meticulous care. They worked in two situation rooms, where they 'thrashed out our daily appreciation of the situation and arrived at all our decisions . . . The walls were covered with maps and charts. On them were marked with pins and little flags the positions of all our boats and such enemy dispositions as were known to us; on them, too, were indicated anticipated convoys and the routes they would probably take.'[1] The atmosphere was remarkably informal. Though he was a disciplinarian who could sometimes lapse into an 'evil mood' and did not suffer fools, he encouraged his planners to challenge his ideas and to come up with their own;[2] his presence may have been intimidating but he did not seek to lead by fiat alone. One of his closest colleagues, Viktor Oehrn, recalled: 'Dönitz very seldom "ordered". He convinced, and because all that he wanted was very precisely considered, he really convinced. He sought discussion with everyone who had an opinion without regard to rank. Anyone who had no opinion, he soon left aside.'[3]

In relation to the question of the disappearing merchant ships, however, not even the best brains at Kerneval could come up with an explanation.

Mirroring this activity at Lorient was the Operations Room at Derby House in Liverpool, where Admiral Noble, the commander-in-chief of the Royal Navy's Western Approaches Command, presided over the 'Citadel', an underground, bomb-proof bunker in a nondescript building a few streets back from the edge of the Mersey. Noble's style was not unlike that of his adversary at Kerneval. He was man of greater charm than Dönitz but he had a similar depth of experience in the navy and he was renowned for listening to others. For these reasons, he was not only liked but also respected by his fellow officers. Among these, Admiral Creighton observed that 'he got his way' by reason of his personality rather than 'the power of his position'.[4]

Noble's power was considerable. From his office, he could look down through a glass window at a massive table on which was spread a situation map that showed the latest estimated positions of both the transatlantic convoys and the U-boat wolf packs. Each convoy was represented by a piece of wood about six inches long, shaped like a toy boat and painted in one of a range of hues (green, yellow, blue, black) to represent its point of origin. This provided a visual ready-reckoner, which was updated constantly. A chart on the wall above the table, which was in his direct line of sight, provided the same information but in much greater detail. A team of uniformed women, drawn from the ranks of the WRAF and the WRNS, worked in shifts around the clock, charting as precisely as possible the shifting positions of the Atlantic adversaries. The plotters were rarely entirely confident of their findings. A 'good fix' came to mean 'within 40–50 miles', which meant a possible range of up to 100 miles; even what they knew to be 'appallingly bad' fixes of 'up to 200 miles' were logged. Inaccurate as they were, they at least made it possible to assert 'with remarkable confidence that a set of bearings, poor as they were, certainly did <u>not</u> emanate from such and such an area. All was fish which came into the plotter's net and rarely was a set of bearings discarded as utterly useless.'[5]

It was on the basis of such sketchy evidence that Noble had to decide how best to deploy his fleet to counter the enemy's efforts to torpedo the convoys. Such decisions not only took a quick and cool brain but a readiness to gamble when the stakes could scarcely have been higher or – at this stage of the war – the odds more heavily loaded against him. In these circumstances, Noble recognized the importance of boosting the morale of the men serving under him so that they would believe – as he did – that Britain would eventually prevail in a maritime struggle which was a battle as much of wills as of weaponry. To this end, 'he constantly went to sea in the little ships and flew in the lonely aircraft of Coastal Command, sharing their dangers and their discomforts'.[6]

But morale alone was not enough. At both Derby House and Kerneval, the protagonists strove for pinpoint accuracy with an imprecise technology. An error of one decimal point in the navigator's fix from an aircraft or the inevitable drift from a radio signal, both magnified by human error in transferring these statistics to the chart, gave mortal meaning to the term hit-and-miss.

Dönitz had started to notice the effectiveness of Noble's operation in Derby House in the spring; how, in the war of the 'plotters', the enemy too often had the upper hand and that, as a result, in the convoy routes to the south of Greenland, the advantage seemed to be slipping away from him towards his adversary. 'Time and time again there occurred between one convoy battle and another a long hiatus during which the U-boats swept the seas fruitlessly in a vain attempt to find the enemy,' he wrote, attributing this setback to a continuing shortage of U-boats and the resultant 'lack of "eyes" with which to search the vast Atlantic expanses'. After a while, though, he began to wonder if 'there might be other reasons to account for our meagre success in locating shipping? Was there any chance, for example, that the enemy had some means of locating U-boat dispositions and of routing his shipping clear of them?'[7] His immediate suspicion was that the enemy might have planted spies in his own headquarters. To reduce this risk, 'the circle of those with access to operational details was cut to the minimum'[8] to the extent that Lorient even stopped informing any other command where U-boats were positioned. However, he was following a false trail. It was soon clear that there were no traitors in his camp and the restrictions he had imposed on the flow of information made no difference.

Dönitz had long been aware the British had use of land-based radio direction finders (D/F) to locate radio transmissions between U-boat commanders and his headquarters. In the early months of the war this caused him little anxiety because he supposed – correctly – that as the source of the D/F signal became more distant, the more prone it was to error. As a rule of thumb, he judged that 'at a distance of some 300 miles the average error is 60–80 miles'.[9] Nonetheless, by the summer of 1941 he presumed – also correctly – that the chain of D/F had extended – via Newfoundland, Greenland and Iceland – to cover the entire North Atlantic. As a result, the British would be able to pinpoint the location of a U-boat signal in most of those waters. This posed a dilemma for him. To avoid any risk of detection the radio traffic between Lorient and the U-boats would have to be terminated. But these signals were indispensable both for planning attacks on convoys and for directing the wolf packs to their quarry. As a compromise, U-boat commanders were ordered to transmit messages only when it was essential and then with extreme brevity (as a result of which it became more difficult to coordinate wolf pack operations). But this still failed to solve the riddle of the ocean: how was it possible for so many convoys to dodge the wolf packs? It was one of the most important questions of the war and one to which neither he, nor any of his colleagues, were ever to find an answer.

Three months earlier, on 1 March 1941, a party of 600 British commandos landed on the Norwegian Lofoten Islands, which lie inside the Arctic Circle, some 900 miles from the British mainland. Although the islands were ostensibly under German control, the soldiers met no resistance. The ostensible purpose of the raid was the destruction of the local fishing industry, including trawlers and the processing plants for the production of fish oil and one of its by-products, glycerine, which was essential to the manufacture of high explosive. To this extent Operation Claymore, as it was codenamed, was one of several hit-and-run missions of the kind much favoured by Churchill, designed to take the enemy by surprise, cause disruption and demonstrate the flair and resolve of the British armed forces. But there was an ulterior motive of far greater significance, a fishing expedition which would yield an invaluable catch.

The destroyer HMS *Somali* acted as the command post for Claymore, which involved simultaneous landings at four separate ports. As she steamed between these locations to coordinate the operation, one of her lookouts saw what appeared to be an innocent trawler, with the name *Krebs* inscribed on her hull. However, she aroused suspicion as soon as she began to speed away from the British vessel. When the *Krebs* was two miles distant, the *Somali* opened fire and the fishing boat responded in kind, so accurately that one of its shells ripped a hole in one of the destroyer's pennants. However, that was all but that. The next shot from the *Somali* destroyed the armed trawler's wheelhouse, boiler room and ammunition store, killing the *Krebs*'s captain and a number of his crew.

A little later, one of the *Somali*'s young officers with a buccaneering streak, Lieutenant Sir Marshall Warmington, commandeered a Norwegian fishing boat and, taking two men with him, boarded the trawler brandishing pistols. The surviving crew members, five in all, surrendered at once. Warmington went below, broke open a drawer (by dint of firing his pistol at the lock) and discovered two discs or wheels which 'he immediately realized were for some kind of cipher machine'.[10] More importantly, he rescued a collection of documents, one of which contained the settings for the use of a German cipher machine in the waters around Britain. It was called Enigma.

The original Enigma machine had been developed by a German engineer hoping to sell a secure communications system to commercial companies in the early 1920s. By a circuitous route one of its operating manuals found its way to the Polish government's Cipher Bureau a decade later, where a small team of engineers managed not only to reconstruct the machine but to decrypt secret German military traffic in the years leading up to the war. On the eve of the German invasion in September 1939 the Poles decided to share their knowledge with the British code-breakers based at Bletchley Park, the secret headquarters of the Government Code & Cypher School (GC&CS). By early 1940 a team of gifted mathematicians, scientists, engineers and analysts, working in Huts 4 and 8, were on their way to breaking the Enigma code, thereby making a crucial contribution to the outcome of the Second World War. Each hut was inspired by two young academics, Alan Turing, a twenty-eight-year-old mathematician and scientist, in Hut 8 and Harry Hinsley, a twenty-one-year-old historian, in Hut 4. Despite his years and the fact that he did not enjoy the formal status implied by the phrase, Turing was known by his team as 'The Prof'. So prodigious were his gifts that, in his case, the overused term 'genius' is but his due. Initially, his demeanour and his character marked him out in ways that conventional observers regarded as eccentric. He eschewed gossip, he rarely laughed, he evidently preferred his own company, he worked with obsessive energy and appeared indifferent to the judgement of others. Modern psychologists, as Hugh Sebag-Montefiore has pointed out, might have regarded his behaviour as symptomatic of a mild form of autism, perhaps Asperger's syndrome (a disorder which was not formally recognized until some forty years after the war).[11] Whatever the case, he not only dressed shambolically but he was, by the prevailing standards at Bletchley Park, disorganized and undisciplined. These traits did not find favour with his immediate superior. Alfred 'Dilly' Knox, who was twenty-eight years his senior and had been a leading cryptologist for more than twenty years, regarded the young genius as someone 'very clever, but quite irresponsible, and [who] throws out a mass of suggestions of all degrees of merit. I have just, but only just, enough authority and ability to keep him and his ideas in some sort of order and discipline.'[12] Mercifully, Knox was not so affronted as to terminate Turing's contract. Without Turing, it is doubtful that the Enigma code would have been broken.

The Enigma machine looked like an electric typewriter, but inside the body of the machine were three parallel wheels, like aerofoils but with letters stamped along them. Each time a letter key on the 'typewriter' was depressed, at least one of the wheels would rotate and an electrical current would illuminate a different letter on a lampboard. In the words of one of the code-breaking team, the machine 'could be set up in millions of different ways so that if you typed out an ordinary sentence on it you would get nothing but a jumble of nonsense groups'.[13] To turn this gobbledegook back into the original German, Turing had to find a way of breaking the code embedded in the Enigma settings, a feat which its creators believed to be impossible. But they had reckoned without genius.

With the help of his Polish collaborators, Turing soon understood how the machine worked and by early 1940 he had invented an electromechanical device, or 'bombe', which replicated the action of several Enigma machines wired together. Turin's bombe was well able to recover message settings for the army and air force Enigma but had far greater difficulty in recovering message settings from the German navy, where a greater cipher discipline prevailed. The bombe was capable of churning through the millions of possible settings required to decrypt the daily messages sent between Lorient and the U-boat fleet on operations anywhere in the Atlantic Ocean, but without access to the key that was presumed to be embedded somewhere in the coded message, Turin's invention had no utility. To discover the key was impossible without a crib sheet – a means of identifying the letter grid used for enciphering the code – Turing and his team were stymied: 'Without cribs, they could not break any Enigma messages. If they could not break some Enigma messages, they would not be able to identify any cribs.'[14] The only way to break this circle was to get hold of the Enigma settings by capturing the relevant documents.

The codes recovered from the *Krebs* on 1 March did not reach Bletchley Park for almost a fortnight. Within hours of their arrival, however,

Turing and his team had used them to decrypt a number of messages. These had been sent in early February but, although the cribs were by now out of date, they provided important clues to the way in which the settings were arranged. But there was more to it than that. Once decrypted, these messages were sent across for further analysis to the Naval Intelligence Section in Hut 4, where Hinsley presided with an authority which belied his youth.

As a twenty-year-old Cambridge undergraduate, Hinsley had been in Germany before the outbreak of war but managed to cross the border into France just before hostilities began. Two weeks after his return to Cambridge to complete his history degree, he was summoned to the Foreign Office. A few days later he was in Bletchley Park. He was so highly regarded by his colleagues there that, by the time he was poring over the decrypted documents seized from the *Krebs*, he had been nick-named 'The Cardinal'.[15] As Hinsley scoured the encrypted data supplied by Turing, he detected a pattern in the flow of messages and soon, by his own account, he was 'able to show conclusively that the Germans were keeping a number of weather ships on station in two areas, one north of Iceland and the other in the mid-Atlantic'. Even more significantly, he also deduced that 'though their routine weather reports were different in outward appearance from Enigma signals, the ships were carrying the naval Enigma'.[16] Armed with these insights, on 26 April 1941 Hinsley wrote to the Admiralty urging immediate military action: 'The seizure of one of these ships, if practicable, would . . . offer an opportunity for obtaining cyphers.'[17] The Admiralty needed no further prompting.

Just over a week later, on 5 May, a posse of three cruisers and four destroyers, with the redoubtable Warmington in HMS *Somali* to the fore, sped towards the position at which one of these weather ships, the *München*, was expected to have taken up station. When he saw the British warships steaming over the horizon towards him, the *München*'s captain fired a coded recognition signal in the hope that they belonged to the Kriegsmarine. The *Somali* replied by opening fire on the trawler in the hope this would cause the trawler's crew to panic. It did. Not waiting for more of the same, they lowered two lifeboats into the water and rowed rapidly away from the weather ship, though not before dumping the Enigma machine overboard in a weighted bag. As Warmington's boarding party leapt onto the *München*, they interrupted the radio officer who had stayed on board to tap out a message, presumably to alert his base to what had happened. He was swiftly removed from his chair and placed under arrest. Warmington conducted a cursory search of the trawler but was under orders to summon a prize crew from the cruiser HMS *Edinburgh*, which was standing off about 200 yards away, rather than remove any documents himself. The Admiralty wanted be certain that nothing of significance could be missed and, to that end, had sent a senior officer from the Operational Intelligence Centre (OIC), Captain Jasper Haines, to join the *Edinburgh*'s prize crew. Once aboard the trawler, Haines made his way to the captain's cabin where he soon found what he wanted. Within three days a sheaf of documents encased in maroon covers had been handed over to Bletchley Park, the *München* was under tow on its way to the Faeroes, where her crew, none of whom had been injured, was taken into captivity as prisoners of war. This was accomplished in conditions of the utmost secrecy. Some days later, to avoid the enemy linking the seizure of the *München* to the possibility that the British were after the Enigma code, the Admiralty issued a communiqué which stated: 'One of our patrols operating in northern waters encountered the *München*, a German armed trawler. Fire was opened, and the crew of the *München* then abandoned and scuttled their ship. They were subsequently rescued and made prisoner.'[18]

Quite fortuitously, two days after the capture of the German trawler, Bletchley Park received another bonanza. At the end of the first week in May, U-110, under the command of Fritz-Julius Lemp (who had sunk the *Athenia* on 3 September 1939), was on patrol some 300 miles to the west of Ireland. Lemp was not in the mould of a disciplinarian like Kretschmer or Prien but had a reputation for waywardness and eccentricity. He was known to encourage his men to go on drinking binges and to sing English songs which were forbidden by the Kriegsmarine. Once, near the end of a patrol, when he was instructed to stay put to file weather reports rather than to return home to Lorient, he responded by signalling 'Shit, Lemp'.[19] This streak of rebelliousness was about to prove his undoing.

Alerted by Lorient to an approaching convoy of forty vessels, OB318, en route from Liverpool to Canada with an escort of eight British warships, U-110, along with three other submarines, raced to intercept. Lemp was impatient for action. Rather than waiting for the cover of darkness as cooler heads would have counselled, he decided on the far riskier option of an underwater attack in the middle of the day. At noon on 9 May he fired torpedoes at four of the freighters in the convoy. Two struck their targets. Almost immediately, U-110's radio operator, sweeping his hydrophones from left to right, detected an unmistakable and ominous pinging sound. They were being hunted by a warship equipped with ASDIC sonar equipment. Lemp ordered an emergency dive.

Within moments his crew heard the vibration from the propellers of a British warship steaming at speed and passing directly overhead. The first depth charges exploded near enough to make the U-boat shudder under the pressure but not so close as to cause any damage. Lemp went deeper, zigzagging in growing desperation to avoid a cluster of warships which now closed in on U-110, crossing and recrossing the submarine's track to seek and destroy. There were more depth charges. Then, no less terrifyingly, there was the silence and the wondering as they waited for the next attack. With characteristic panache, Lemp told his men, 'It's OK. We are all going to be fine.' Then, in apparent reference to the *Athenia*, he added jokily, 'You don't think I am going to let them catch me and shoot me, do you?'[20]

Soon afterwards, one of the depth charges found its mark, putting U-110's rudders out of action, damaging the batteries and shattering the depth meters. With water and oil leaking into the hull, the submarine was now a wreck. To avoid death by drowning, Lemp decided to surface. He had not intended to surrender but when he saw three destroyers opening fire and two of them bearing down on U-110 at speed, he shouted, 'We're surrounded! All hands abandon ship.'[21]

A German newspaperman, Helmut Ecke, who had been assigned to Lemp's U-boat to write a series of propaganda articles, described the moment when the British warships 'opened fire on us with tracer shell. It was like a New Year's Eve party at two o'clock in the afternoon. A crewman in front of me took a dive, and during his flight from the tower into the water he lost half his head.'[22] Once it was clear that there would be no resistance and with most of U-110's crew thrashing around in the water, the British ceased fire. Heinz Wilde, one of U-110's radio operators, recalled thinking, 'Well, that's it. What am I going to do in the North Atlantic? The water is freezing. The chance of survival is tiny. I can't go on swimming for ever. I'll probably die of exposure, and because I have the *Tauchretter* [a breathing apparatus, similar to a gas mask, designed for submariners] I will float as a corpse in the Atlantic.'[23] He survived because a corvette, HMS *Aubretia* (which had fired the fatal depth charge), came to the rescue, dropping scramble nets and helping the rapidly weakening German sailors on to the deck. Wilde remembered that the British crew tried to help him stand up 'but I didn't have any feeling in my legs. They stripped me naked on a cold May day south of Greenland, wrapped me in a blanket and massaged me warm . . . Then I got a cup of tea. I can remember the taste of the tea to this day.'[24]

U-110 did not sink as swiftly as Lemp had expected. Realizing this, he appears to have swum back to the vessel in the hope of sinking her before the British could board her. He did not make it. Like fourteen of his crew, he was presumed to have drowned, leaving thirty-two of his men to be incarcerated as POWs. Ecke, who had swallowed mouthfuls of oily seawater, remembers vomiting on deck just outside a wash-room where an English lieutenant was shaving. 'He started to whistle "Deutschland Uber Alles" to me. He found it very, very funny.'

On board the destroyer, HMS *Bulldog* (which, in 1945, was to accept the surrender of the German garrison on the Channel Islands), the escort commander, Joe Baker-Cresswell, ordered a junior officer, Sub Lieuten-ant David Balme, to board U-110: 'Get on board as quickly as you can. I think she is completely abandoned, but there may be one or two left behind. Get hold of the signal books first, and then anything useful you can take away.'[25] Taking eight men with him, the twenty-year-old Balme rowed across to the stricken submarine and hauled himself aboard. The deck was wet and slippery. Carrying his revolver, he found his way below. 'I felt terribly vulnerable and very frightened,'[26] he recalled. Apart from his own breathing, all he could hear 'was a faint hissing, and the sound of the Atlantic waves lapping against the hull'.[27] He ordered the rest of the boarding party to join him.

As they struggled through the interior in the half light, they came across a chaos of charts, books and documents. Balme ordered them to form a human chain to pass all the papers up to the deck. They worked at speed for fear the U-boat would sink before they had recovered everything of possible significance. After a few minutes of this, Balme was called to the radio room, where his radiographer showed him a machine which looked like a typewriter but which, when he 'pressed one letter key on the keyboard, another letter was highlighted on a dis-play panel'.[28] The peculiar machine joined the documents to be taken back to the *Bulldog*, an operation which altogether took ninety minutes to complete. That evening the destroyer took U-110 in tow and set off slowly towards Iceland. When Baker-Cresswell alerted the Admiralty to his haul he was instructed, 'Your operation is to be referred to as Operation Primrose in all future signals. Reference to it is to be prefaced Top Secret and signals to be made only in cipher.'[29]

Next morning, the wind strengthened, the seas rose and U-110 was soon waterlogged. At around 11 a.m., the submarine reared up and slid beneath the surface until the only evidence of her existence was a severed tow rope drifting in the water. By comparison with the value of what had been retrieved from her interior, the loss of the submarine was of little moment. When the *Bulldog* reached Scapa Flow two days later, two Naval Intelligence officers came aboard. They could barely disguise their delight at seeing the first Enigma *machine* to be captured in the war. The same night, a briefcase containing the most valuable documents seized from U-110 was on Hinsley's table in Hut 4. As Baker-Cresswell steamed back to Iceland, he received a message from the First Sea Lord. 'Congratulations. The petals on your flower are of rare beauty.'[30]

The beauty was not quite so valuable as Pound had thought. Though Sub Lieutenant Balme was decorated with the Distinguished Service Cross by King George VI at Buckingham Palace, the stash of documents recovered from U-110 did not provide the breakthrough that Pound and the King – who, on hearing of the seizure, is said to have murmured 'Perhaps the most important single event in the whole war at sea'[31] – evidently hoped. But it mattered nonetheless. Once Hinsley and his team had assessed its significance, it became clear that Balme's exploit had provided another important piece in the Enigma jigsaw.

The task of interpreting the significance of the cryptic messages derived from breaking the Enigma code was a painstaking process that not everyone at the Admiralty adequately appreciated. In the early days, Hinsley's relationship with his naval counterparts in the OIC in London had been fraught. His precocious talent for prognosis had first surfaced a year earlier, when he had warned – presciently but to no avail – that the *Scharnhorst* and *Gneisenau* were closing in on the aircraft carrier HMS *Glorious* during the evacuation from Norway. Soon afterwards, the young master of Hut 4 was summoned to London to explain his methodology to the team in the division at OIC with which he had most dealings, the Submarine Tracking Unit. He stayed for a month and was not impressed by what he found. In a letter to Frank Birch (his immediate superior in Hut 4) of October 1940 he did not trouble to conceal his disdain, complaining, 'they not only duplicate our work and other people's work but duplicate it in so aimless and inefficient a manner, that all their time is taken up groping at the truth, and putting as much of it as is obvious to all on card indexes'. Frustrated by their inability 'to answer questions properly' and their 'personal opposition to Bletchley Park', he noted: 'They know facts . . . but they seem to have no general grasp of these facts in association. They lack imagination. They cannot utilize the knowledge they so busily compile.'[32]

Hinsley's youthful strictures were not entirely warranted. The OIC was by no means lacking talent or initiative. On the basis of the Enigma signals decoded by staff, Commander Roger Winn, the intelligence officer in overall charge of the Submarine Tracking Unit, was reputed to 'look into the very minds of Dönitz, and the commanders in his U-boats'.[33] Moreover, he was only too willing on this basis to predict the likely whereabouts and intentions of a wolf pack and therefore to advise on the evasive action that should be taken by a convoy. Very often the mind-reader was right; sometimes he was wrong. In a hit-and-miss discipline, he could hardly be faulted for undue caution or timidity.

With the arrogance of youth, Hinsley was intolerant of those he regarded as lesser mortals. The staff of the OIC, on the other hand, soon realized that the young man in their midst was gifted with a prodigious intellect whose rare analytical skills they could ill afford to overlook. Thus, on his return to Bletchley Park, after his four-week immersion in the OIC, Hinsley noticed the Centre began to do 'all in its power to ensure through regular exchange of visits, and with the assistance of new scrambler telephones, that there should be complete collaboration between the OIC and the Naval Section at Bletchley'.[34] And it was with evident satisfaction that he noted subsequently that, on one occasion, in response to an inquiry to the OIC from the Home Fleet asking 'What is your source?' the reply came back 'Hinsley'.[35]

It was again at Hinsley's instigation that, after the capture of the *München*, four British warships were despatched to seize another German weather ship – the *Lauenburg* – in the last week of June 1941. The haul this time included the Enigma settings for the following month. Though the complexity of their task was aggravated by the fact that these settings were changed on a monthly basis, the code-breakers now had almost every piece of the jigsaw in place. Thereafter, the time it took to decode the exchange of radio traffic between the situation rooms at Lorient and the U-boats in the North Atlantic fell to an average of no more than fifty hours, enough warning for the Admiralty to divert convoys away from the waiting U-boat patrols. It was essentially for this reason that – to Dönitz's perplexed frustration – his wolf packs so often found themselves prowling the convoy routes in vain. In July and August the German submarines sank less than 100,000 tons of shipping in each month, which was their worst performance for almost a year. In November, their tally fell to 62,000 tons.

In Lorient, Dönitz's team was at a loss. Their exasperated commander-in-chief became strident to the point of admonishing his U-boat crews as though they lacked the stomach for their appointed task. On 24 June, for example, he despatched a message to U-203 (which was intercepted by Bletchley Park) urging 'At them! Attack them! Sink them!'[36] A selection of the code-breakers' decrypts was sent to Churchill on a daily basis by the head of the Secret Intelligence Service (MI6), Sir Stewart Menzies, who by convention signed all his own messages with the letter 'C'. On this occasion Dönitz's abrupt injunction caught the prime minister's eye. Clearly irritated by the failure of Menzies to provide him with a thorough analysis of its import, he demanded an explanation. The head of MI6's response was withering: 'I understood your order to send Naval material of particular importance, and I did not judge the ordering of attacks on convoys to be within this category. I will, however, submit such Messages in future, if you so direct. I attach no significance whatsoever to the order at the end of the Message in question.'[37]

Before despatching this rebuff, Menzies sought clarification from Bletchley Park. Writing from Hut 4 on 28 June, the head of the German Naval Section, Frank Birch, described Dönitz's modus operandi with uncanny accuracy, a summary of which the head of MI6 passed on to the prime minister in a modified form the same day. Identifying Dönitz's total control of the U-boats, Birch wrote:

> He places them; he moves them; they only report as and when and what he bids them. A single ship they may sink on sight, but when they contact

a convoy, they must await his orders; they shadow while he directs others to the scene.

His interest in the game is, therefore, a very personal one. It engenders in him the enthusiasm of a crowd at a football match. Cries of encouragement are frequent though it is not often he gets as excited as this.

This particular mixture of sea-doggery and hysteria is due to the fact that for some time before he had been having a pretty lean time, which, as several fault-finding signals show, had made him rather tetchy. <u>At last</u> he has got hold of a convoy.[38]

Perhaps Birch exaggerated for effect but an entry in U-boat Command's War Diary reflected Dönitz's frustration at the ease with which the convoys escaped his clutches. On 28 September he noted, 'The most likely explanation is that our cipher has been compromised, or that there has been some other breach of security.'[39] With his own cipher experts insisting that the naval Enigma was 'one of the most secure systems for enciphering messages in the world', he asked the head of the Kriegsmarine's communications, Vice-Admiral Erhard Maertens, to investigate further. In October, Maertens reported back with his findings. In a letter to Dönitz on the 24th, he wrote reassuringly: 'The acute disquiet about the compromise of our Secret Operation cannot be justified. Our cipher does not appear to be broken.'[40] Dönitz accepted Maertens's conclusion but with deepening puzzlement.

As more and more convoys appeared to escape the clutches of the U-boats which he had sent to intercept them, he noted: 'Coincidence alone it cannot be ... A likely explanation would be that the British from some source or other gain knowledge of our concentrated dispositions and avoid them.'[41] With the benefit of hindsight, this verdict may seem so feeble as to beggar belief. But, since the cryptanalysts in the German high command would not even contemplate the notion that Enigma could be broken, Dönitz could only conclude that the explanation had to lie in 'a combination of U-boat radio traffic [derived from a D/F fix] and reports of [U-boat] sightings'.[42] As he himself conceded, this speculative analysis was of precious little use to him because he had no way of adapting U-boat tactics to vanquish this 'unknown unknown'. Unlike Enigma, the existence of Ultra – the code word used to describe the intelligence derived from breaking the German code – was, and would remain, an inviolable secret.

That, however, was not quite that. On 6 September Churchill visited Bletchley Park to see the code-breakers at work. Though he would never mention the existence of Enigma publicly, he was clearly impressed by what he saw and heard, if not by the rudimentary, cramped and chaotic environment in which the academics were obliged to work. The code-breakers clearly picked up on this because, some weeks after the prime minister's visit, Turing and three of his colleagues were emboldened to write a 'secret and confidential' letter of complaint to him. Their missive was not about their working conditions, however, but concerned an issue of far greater moment. Though their letter was couched in the most courteous language, it revealed an intense frustration with their unnamed superiors, among whom, assuredly, was Commander Alastair Denniston, the head of Bletchley Park.★

Dear Prime Minister,

Some weeks ago you paid us the honour of a visit and we believe you regard our work as important . . . We think, however, that you ought to know that this work is being held up, and in some cases not being done at all, principally because we cannot get sufficient staff to deal with it. Our reason for writing to you is that for months we have done everything we possibly can through the normal channels, and that we despair of any early improvement without your intervention . . . The trouble to our mind is that as we are a very small section with numerically trivial requirements it is very difficult to bring home to the authorities finally responsible either the importance of what is done here or the urgent necessity of dealing promptly with our requests . . . We have felt that we should be failing in our duty if we did not draw your attention to the facts and to the effects which they are having and must continue to have on our work, unless immediate action is taken.[43]

To write in such terms to the prime minister was to take an extreme step, but it worked. Churchill at once despatched an Action This Day note to General 'Pug' Ismay, who was effectively, but not formally, his chief of staff: 'Make sure that they have all they want on extreme

★ The Government Code and Cypher School officially became GCHQ in April 1946, when it left Bletchley Park for its former outstation at Eastcote, although it had adopted that acronym as a cover name before the outbreak of war.

priority and report to me that this has been done.' Some of these missives, written in moments of frustration and without due consideration, were not infrequently ignored. But in this case, Churchill had alighted on a critical problem in need of urgent solution; it was an example of how his quasi-dictatorial power as prime minister could prove invaluable. Ismay sent Churchill's orders to Menzies, who reported back on 19 November to inform the prime minister that, in Hinsley's words, 'every possible measure was being taken; though the arrangements were not then entirely completed, Bletchley's needs were being very rapidly met'.[44]

In Britain, Enigma was a carefully guarded secret to which only those with 'a need to know' – and they excluded most senior military commanders – were privy. Those who were in the know – the teams at Bletchley Park, senior staff in MI6, and the chiefs of staff – were careful to ensure that no one outside their charmed circle would hear even a whisper about the Third Reich's secret weapon or the fact that they had been privy to it; indeed, the very existence of Ultra and Enigma would not enter the public realm until almost three decades from the end of hostilities.

The code-breakers in Britain and Germany were like chess players exchanging moves in the dark; unable to see what the other side was up to, each chose to believe that their own secret messages were secure. Both were mistaken. The team at the Admiralty's Naval Intelligence Division (NID) were not quite so blindsided as their counterparts in the Kriegsmarine, but they were unaware that Dönitz had not been entirely thwarted. They knew about Bletchley Park's counterpart B-Dienst (Beobachtungsdienst – observation service), which they called the 'B service', though not how extensively the Germans had managed to penetrate the secret ciphers by which all movement of British convoys in the Atlantic and beyond was directed and controlled.

In August 1941 a hint of anxiety crept to the surface in the Admiralty. A report written by the NID and headlined 'Compromise of Convoy Movements Near the British Coast' detailed a number of cases which made them wonder if B-Dienst had discovered the sailing schedules and the positions of particular convoys around the British Isles. The authors began by stating, 'There is evidence that the Germans are now tapping a source of intelligence about convoys which they did not possess before 24/7.' Unable to provide an explanation for this, they offered a hypothesis instead: 'It is not clear whether the above reports are (a) forecasts based on incomplete information (e.g. d/f [direction finding], reconnaissance, non-current special intelligence) or (b) the result of non-current special intelligence, but the latter explanation would appear more probable owing to the (in some cases) very precise details given.'[45] It is tempting to draw a parallel between the German refusal to believe their communications could be penetrated and the British failure to detect that signals transmitted by the Admiralty were being intercepted by B-Dienst. Unlike their German counterparts, though, the British cryptanalysts did at least concede the possibility that the Germans were reading their codes. In the face of this suspicion, their problem was not so much denial as an astonishing failure to do anything of note about it. Their arrogance was to prove very expensive.

The consequences of this oversight were not fully appreciated until after the end of the war, when it was mercilessly exposed in a Top Secret report written for the Director of Naval Intelligence by Commander Tighe in November 1945. Tighe's analysis was regarded as so sensitive that only three copies of the document were distributed. However, many of its findings were reproduced in another Top Secret document which was based on the Tighe Report but written a year later. Even in his bowdlerized version of what Tighe had written, R. T. Barrett's analysis was excoriating. Throughout the war, he wrote, it had been 'generally assumed' by NID and other authorities that 'while the Germans could read low grade cyphers and codes, those used by the higher levels were beyond their reach'. It was only after the war that 'the evidence of captured documents and the questioning of German officers, WT [Wireless Telegraphy] staff and cryptanalysts gave a severe shock to this complacency.'[46]

From September 1939, according to Tighe (as reported by Barrett), 'the enemy was entirely at home with' Britain's naval codes; by the spring of 1940, B-Dienst was reading between 30 and 50 per cent of naval traffic, which, for instance, gave them 'a free run of everything of importance in connection with the Norway expedition'.[47] Extracts from German intelligence summaries, contained in a separate Admiralty document, show how the code-breakers in Berlin were able to track every move of HMS *Glorious* in the fateful hours before it was sunk during the evacuation from Norway by the *Scharnhorst* with the loss of almost everyone on board. On the basis of these decrypts, Barrett wrote, the Germans were able to conclude on 4 June 1940: 'The British naval force in the northern Norwegian area do [sic] not seem to feel itself endangered, except by air attack. They reported every German aircraft sighted, giving their own position, which was transmitted encoded merely according to the position reporting chart.' Four days later, as the two enemy battleships closed on the doomed aircraft carrier, the German code-breakers were able to report that her accompanying destroyers, *Acasta* and *Ardent*, had been 'proceeding on their usual routes' and that they 'were all hit and sunk'.[48]

Although the Admiralty regularly changed the Naval Codes as a precaution (much as the Germans changed the Enigma settings), these were invariably broken by B-Dienst within weeks. Before long, according to Tighe/Barrett, 'the enemy' was reading 'a great proportion of all signals in connection with convoys, not only in the North Atlantic, but in other areas where the cypher was used'. In perhaps their severest indictment of all, Tighe/Barrett wrote: 'The enemy achieved a high degree of success against codes used for communications with merchant ships. The money saved by failing to provide a proper code for our mercantile marine was a bad investment, costing us hundreds of times over in money, as well as grave loss of ships and life.'[49]

By breaking the Enigma code, Bletchley Park had rewritten the rules of the war at sea. But so had B-Dienst. And, since neither side knew what the other's rules might be or how to break them, the Battle of the Atlantic was very far from over.

## 10.  Fingers in the Dyke

In mid-September 1941 the hedgerows in the meadows around Barrow-in-Furness were heavy with blackberries. Nella Last picked more than enough for her own needs but was not sure what to do with the rest. 'I've too many to bake, and no fat or sugar to spare, and I am wondering whether to dip into my store and make a little jam. It would mean taking two pounds of sugar – and I'll have to see.' On her way back home she met a 'a little farm-boy' who turned out to be six years old. He was

> dirty, tousled and ragged. His poor little eyes were nearly closed with styes, and when I touched his cheeks as I turned his head to look at them, his flesh had the soft limp feeling of malnutrition. He went off to bring a herd of cows for milking, and as he passed he was chanting, 'Left, right, left, right,' in imitation of the soldiers. I called 'Hi, sergeant – like a toffee?' I gave him two sweets, and his dirty claw-like hand *grabbed* them unbelievably, as he said in a hushed tone 'Oooh – both for me.'[1]

By the late autumn, the list of foodstuffs that were rationed was growing. Milk had joined meat, tea, margarine, cooking fats, cheese (in 1940), jam, marmalade, treacle, syrup and eggs (one per head per week) on the list. The rations had been carefully calibrated by the Ministry of Food to ensure that every citizen could obtain at the least the minimum intake of calories and vitamins required for a modest but healthy diet. The most testing period was in the spring of 1941. Imports of dairy products and fruit had fallen to less than half the level of six months before and meat imports had fallen by two-thirds, which left a reserve of only two weeks.[2] Overall, imports had fallen to two-thirds the pre-war level, a trend that was a source of deepening concern to the War Cabinet.

The prime minister might have been excused for being otherwise preoccupied with an alarming increase in the rate of crises, setbacks and uncertainties on multiple fronts – Rommel's onslaught in North Africa, the Wehrmacht's occupation of Yugoslavia, the Greek debacle, the loss of Crete, the threat to Malta, let alone the Luftwaffe's raids on Plymouth, London, Coventry, Hull, Liverpool and Glasgow – but he still found time to worry about the nation's diet. Acutely aware that food shortages posed a greater threat to civilian morale than any number of German bombs and that, were citizens to go hungry, civil unrest and defeatism might soon follow, he did not allow even the gravest crisis on the battlefield to distract him for long from the overriding need to fill human stomachs, albeit on the plainest diet.

His sensitivity about this extended well beyond the statistics of supply and demand to embrace the way in which foodstuffs were controlled and rationed. In February 1941, to take one example among many, he had been agitated by the discovery that up to 500,000 tons of potatoes from Northern Ireland were to be destroyed as 'unsaleable' following a heavy decline in the pig population. 'It seems a great pity,' he reprimanded the Minister of Agriculture, Robert Hudson, 'that there should have been this great reduction in the number of pigs owing to the fear of shortage of feeding stuffs . . . We cannot afford in these days to throw away hundreds of thousands of tons of edible material.'[3]

In the first six months of 1941 more than 2.8 million tons of shipping was destroyed, mostly sunk by U-boats operating in the Atlantic. Although there was a lull in the late summer, the figure rose again towards the end of the year so that by December – despite more naval escorts, despite radar, and despite Ultra – over 1,000 merchantmen had been sent to the bottom of the seas, a total loss for the year of over 4 million tons. It was some comfort that the start of Lend-Lease in March not only promised a regular supply of weaponry and raw materials but also an urgently needed source of basic foodstuffs. These shipments – dried eggs, evaporated milk, bacon, beans, cheese, lard, orange juice and canned meat, which were 'crucial in the battle to maintain the quality of the nation's diet' – began to arrive in May,[4] and before long would contribute up to 10 per cent of the estimated dietary needs of the population.

To secure these supplies was not simply a matter of controlling demand; there was also the question of supply. The transatlantic wrangling that ensued as officials on both sides strove to establish some balance between these two components of what had become an artificial market tested the resolve of the British and the patience of the Americans to such a degree as 'to sour Anglo-American negotiations over food throughout the rest of the war'.[5] The disputes were by no means theoretical: every ship sent across the Atlantic with food was one less vessel available for other vital shipments at a time when the shortage of merchant ships was no less acute on the American than on the British side of the Atlantic. While the British negotiators wanted to ensure against any shortfall, the Americans wanted to cut the flow to the bare minimum required to sustain the war effort. In this diplomatic tug-of-war, the Ministry of Food tended to exaggerate the need while the US authorities did the opposite.

In the letter to Roosevelt on 8 December 1940, which he came to regard as 'one of the most important' he ever wrote (see p. 118), Churchill included a warning that was tantamount to blackmail:

> Unless we can establish our ability to feed this Island, to import the munitions of all kinds which we need, unless we can move our armies to the various theatres where Hitler and his confederate Mussolini must be met, and maintain them there, and do all this with the assurance of being able to carry it on till the spirit of the Continental Dictators is broken, we may fall by the way, and the time needed by the United States to complete her defensive preparations may not be forthcoming.[6]

Harry Hopkins told Churchill soon afterwards that his letter had deeply affected the president, describing how he sat alone in his deck-chair 'to read and reread' the prime minister's pitch and that for two days thereafter was 'plunged in intense thought, and brooded silently'.[7] Those hours of reflection had borne fruit in the form of Lend-Lease, the implementation of which had been placed in the hands of civil servants and military advisors.

When Hopkins was in London in January 1941 on his first fact-finding mission, he had been told by Whitehall officials that Britain needed 40 million tons of imports a year, of which 16 million tons was the food required to sustain the nation; in sub-Churchillian mode they had insisted, 'we cannot cut much further without reducing the stamina and morale of the people'.[8] In March, somewhat arbitrarily, the prime minister had reduced that global requirement to 'an import of not less than 31 million tons', of which food, he insisted, 'cannot be cut lower than 15 million tons'.[9] To their hard-pressed and competitive counterparts in Washington, these casually shifting calculations from Whitehall had all the authority of numbers totted up on the back of an envelope.

The individual charged by Churchill to deliver Britain's revised target was Sir Arthur Salter, a junior minister in the Department of Transport. Following Congress's approval of Lend-Lease, the prime minister despatched Salter to Washington in April to establish a British Merchant Shipping Mission. His task was to extract from Washington a commitment to provide Britain with as many merchant ships as he could persuade his opposite numbers were required to save Britain from collapse. He was an inspired choice. A former academic and civil servant, he moved effortlessly through the Washington bureaucracy on a diplomatic offensive to overcome the suspicion which confronted him on his arrival. He faced formidable obstacles. In an atmosphere spiky with distrust, he had to persuade the American negotiators to divert hundreds of ships and millions of tons of cargo space from what many of them regarded as higher commercial and military priorities elsewhere. His task was not made easier by the fact that, although the U-boats were continuing to sink freighters at a faster rate than they could be replaced, the number of US merchant ships that had been made available to Britain was still three times the size of the American fleet. Admiral Emory Land, the dyspeptic chairman of the US Maritime Commission, which was responsible for the allocation of the US vessels, was adamantly opposed to relinquishing even one merchant ship to the British, insisting, 'If we do not watch our step, we shall find the White House en route to England with the Washington Monument as a steering oar.'[10]

However, thanks to Churchill's close relationship with Hopkins, Salter was soon able to by-pass the 'usual channels' to make his case within the portals of the White House itself, where Hopkins listened carefully to what he had to say. In purely logistical terms, Salter's pitch was persuasive. Between August 1940 and April 1941, he told Roosevelt's confidant, 'dry-cargo' imports to Britain had fallen by more than half, from 44 million tons to just over 20 million. This was self-evidently an ominous trend and Hopkins was sympathetic. Salter was emboldened not only to seek the diversion of existing merchant ships to the British cause but to lobby for a massive boost to the American shipbuilding programme to 4 million tons a year, or some 500 new vessels. The president indicated that he shared Hopkins's attitude, but he was not disposed to tarry over the intricacies of Lend-Lease, preferring to confine himself to a general instruction to the relevant agencies, leaving others to 'fill in the necessary details, subject to his final approval'.[11] As a result, despite Salter's efforts, the chaotic and sometimes hostile American bureaucracy not only managed 'to bungle' the implementation of the presidential directive but was given leeway to display 'immense scepticism' about British estimates of what was required to save the nation.[12] Over the next two years, with the competition for available resources growing ever more intense, Salter's patience and resolve would be tested to the limit.

Had they been aware of how some British citizens responded to the advent of Lend-Lease, Washington's bureaucrats might have been even less minded to support the former colonial rulers in their hour of need. A surge in the cost of living in Britain had put the government under growing pressure. By the end of 1941 the average price of wholesale goods was to rise inexorably to 50 per cent above its pre-war level.[13] Shortages of food, clothing and other consumer 'necessities' had not only led to long queues outside shops but to profiteering, speculation and a burgeoning black market, all of which exacerbated divisions between the 'haves' and the 'have nots'. Envy and resentment threatened to undermine the fragile basis on which the unity of a nation at war had been constructed.

J. L. Hodson, a liberal-minded diarist who journeyed up and down the land, was moved to note:

> I grow weary of listening to stories of waste and bungling . . . Hotel life in Torquay is grotesque – evening clothes and dancing every night. The breakfast menu gives you fish and an egg or a brisket of beef, together with toast, porridge and jam. Dinner is seven shillings and sixpence – soup (or cocktail), entree of ham, poultry, sweet, coffee. Officers I know had a lunch the other day which included eggs, fish and meat.[14]

This subversive commentary illuminated a deeper malaise. Petty corruption had become endemic among those who had the means to exploit their positions of wealth or authority. In the spring of 1941 the chairman of the North Midland Region Price Investigation Committee reported 'cans of soup, sold by manufacturers at six shillings and sixpence a dozen, were reaching the public at fourteen shillings and sixpence a dozen, having passed through the hands of six middlemen, one of whom had bought the [same] goods twice'.[15] Such speculation was rampant and covered all manner of foodstuffs and other basic necessities.

Nor was it only those with power who exploited the system. Nella Last strongly approved of rationing as 'the only fair way' to distribute supplies. She was therefore moved to exasperation by the way in which it operated in her home town:

> The present rationing has been a farce. Those who have wanted to be greedy have got more than their share. I asked the Co-op coalman why he called so seldom . . . if I'd not carefully saved up all last summer and made fire-bricks out of any coal-dust or sawdust, I'd have been short. He answered, 'A lot of women have been going to different branch shops, ordering coal, and getting their three or four hundredweight as usual; but only enough for half-rations for everybody have been delivered at the coalyard, so that means muddle and shortage.'

When her sister 'spoke as if to get more than she is entitled to was a *grand game*', Nella was duly appalled.[16]

From his vantage point at sea in his corvette, Nicholas Monsarrat was roused to fury by these multiple malpractices. Assuredly reflecting the views of his fellow officers and men, the future author of *The Cruel Sea* not only castigated those who worked to rule or went on strike in the docks and the shipyards but reserved an even greater ire for

> food-wasters, black-market buyers and thieves, people wangling goods in excess of quota, people taking God knows what profit on the sale and re-sale of things they had hardly heard of in peace-time. Imagine what bloody fools we feel, knowing that a convoy of what we thought vital supplies has really gone to the comfort of such people; the comfort of stupid folk who cannot visualize the price in blood of what they are wasting, the profit of assorted vermin who see, in a shipload of necessaries, only the chance of a squeeze.

Reflecting on that 'price in blood' – his fellow sailors who had been blown to pieces, incinerated, or drowned – he had always held in his mind that 'offsetting the horror and pity' of this suffering was the 'idea that we were bringing in what was vital, that it goes straight to some threatening gap, that no part of it was wasted or diverted'.[17] In this respect, no corruption or criminality was more repellent to Monsarrat than that devised by 'petrol-wanglers', who in his judgement merited 'a special hell'. Petrol rationing had been in force since the outbreak of war and the restrictions became more severe the longer the war went on.

From a total of 823,000 tons a year in 1940, the amount that motorists could consume fell to 473,000 tons by 1942 and would fall lower still, to 301,000 tons, in 1943.[18] The restrictions imposed on the honest a degree of self-rationing that made even a short journey to visit a sick relative in hospital a decision to be weighed against necessary trips to work; recreational driving was virtually impossible and by February 1942, following the fall of Singapore, the Chancellor of the Exchequer, Sir Kingsley Wood, not only condemned 'personal extravagances' but ruled that no petrol would be allowed for 'pleasure motoring'.[19]

These restrictions were not hard for the rich or the ingenious to circumvent. You could acquire extra coupons for fuel by fraudulently licensing your car as a taxi; or by claiming dishonestly that you needed to attend church on a Sunday; or, if you had the means, by purchasing several cars, acquiring coupons for them all but only driving one. Were such men, Monsarrat asked rhetorically,

> Stupid? Incurably selfish? Traitorous? Do they feel clever when they've got their extra whack? Does it give them a sense of power to know that men, foolishly valorous, have fought and perished in hundreds, just to keep their cars ticking over sweetly? Once again, ten such are not worth the skin of the man who dies for them; and one sometimes wishes they could be individually flayed, just to prove it in simple terms.[20]

Like Nella Last, most people either could not or would not cheat the system. For this majority, the queues, shortages, coupons and rationing were quite testing enough in themselves without the crooks and spivs in their midst by whom – like Monsarrat – they were greatly aggrieved. Churchill frequently intervened in the complex tasks allotted to the Ministry of Food, which month after month was obliged to ratchet up controls and to extend the range of goods for which coupons were required. In July 1941, worrying about the irritation that would inevitably be provoked by rationing 'secondary foodstuffs' such as dried and canned fruit, rice and tapioca, syrup and treacle, he urged the minister responsible, Lord Woolton, to make the system as 'flexible' as possible by allowing coupons to be used in a variety of shops rather than in one authorized outlet only. 'Though rigid rationing might be easier to administer,' he argued, 'some system which left the consumer freedom of choice would seem much better. Individual tastes have a wonderful way of cancelling out.'[21]

Occasionally he even allowed himself a diversion into culinary advice. In one of his Action This Day memoranda sent to the Ministers of Food and Agriculture, he advocated an increase in the output of rabbit meat. Averring that 'rabbits are not by themselves nourishing [which suggests that the prime minister had never personally partaken of rabbit pie]', he claimed that they were 'a pretty good mitigation of vegetarianism. They eat mainly grass and greenstuffs, so what is the harm in encouraging their multiplication in captivity?'[22] At the end of the year, hearing that Woolton was about to impose rationing on sweets and chocolate, he urged him to postpone such a draconian step: 'I gather that it was admitted in the Lord President's Committee that a sweets ration would lend itself to irregularities more easily than our other rations . . . If we create artificial illegalities that are neither enforceable nor condemned by public opinion the habit of evasion may spread to cases where it would be injurious.'[23]

It may seem bizarre that the prime minister should have immersed himself in such details when he was confronted by an unprecedented global crisis but it reflected his sensitivity to the politics of food which only those who enjoyed absolute authority could dare to ignore. Although Churchill had quasi-dictatorial power over Britain's war strategy, he could not afford to lose sight of the fact that the War Cabinet he commanded was at the apex of a democracy whose mercurial mood swings could easily destabilize, if not derail, its best-laid plans. Ever aware of the precariousness of his power, he understood only too well the paramount need to sustain popular morale when news of setbacks on the battlefront seemed to postpone an end to the conflict into the mists of an uncertain future. It was this that made the Battle of the Atlantic – which was in significant measure a battle for food – such a consuming priority. But the competition between priorities was growing more intense by the week.

Towards the end of September 1941 Roosevelt wrote an uncharacteristically gushing letter to Stalin: 'I can't tell you how thrilled all of us are because of the gallant defense of the Soviet Armies . . . ways and means will be found to provide the material and supplies necessary on all fronts, including your own.'[24] Some weeks earlier he had issued a formal instruction to the US Secretary of State advising him that aid to the Soviet Union was of 'paramount importance for the safety and security of the United States'.[25] Stimson's task was to find a way of reconciling the competing demands of Britain and Russia with those of America's own armed forces.

The Russian Front was not only under severe pressure but in some places had broken down. Much of the Ukraine had fallen, Moscow was under siege and the panzers were, in Stalin's words, 'at the gates of Leningrad'. In a blunt letter to the prime minister, which Ivan Maisky, the Soviet ambassador in London, handed to Churchill on 4 September, the Soviet leader asserted that the Soviet Union was now faced by 'a mortal menace'. Commenting acidly that the Germans were 'transferring all their forces to the East with impunity, being convinced that no second front exists in the West and that none will exist', he warned threateningly that, in the absence of both a Second Front and the tanks and planes urgently required on the Eastern Front, the Soviet Union faced 'defeat' or, at the very least, would lose 'any capacity to render assistance to its Allies by its actual operations on the fronts of the struggle against Hitlerism'.[26]

After delivering Stalin's message, Maisky remained with Churchill for a further ninety minutes, during which, according to Churchill, he complained 'in bitter terms' that Russia had been left to face the German onslaught 'virtually alone'. Apparently detecting 'an underlying air of menace' in the ambassador's appeal, Churchill retorted angrily: 'Remember that only four months ago we in this Island did not know whether you were coming in against us on the German side . . . you of all people have no right to make reproaches to us.'[27]

On the same day that Maisky delivered the Soviet leader's letter to Churchill, Sir Stafford Cripps, the British ambassador in Moscow, wrote to Anthony Eden in language that was barely less accusatory than that of the Soviet ambassador in London. Castigating the British government's failure to 'to do anything to create a diversion' – namely a Second Front – as though 'the war here [was] no direct responsibility of ours', he advised that 'unless we can now at the very last moment make a super-human effort we shall lose the whole value of any Russian front, at any rate for a long period, and possibly for good'.[28]

Churchill was so irked by Cripps that he decided to reply himself. Dismissing his ambassador's complaints as 'unjust', he made it witheringly clear that, had Cripps not been ignorant of 'the practical and technical facts', he would have realized that to open a Second Front on mainland Europe would be to court a 'bloody repulse' at the hands of Hitler's forces. Nor was that all: the diversion of naval vessels required for such a venture, he continued, 'would entail paralysis of the support of the Middle Eastern armies and a breakdown of the whole Atlantic traffic. It might mean the loss of the Battle of the Atlantic and the starvation and ruin of the British Isles.' And in case his meddlesome ambassador had not yet got the message, he added tartly 'When you speak . . . of a "super-human" effort you mean, I presume, an effort rising superior to space, time and geography. Unfortunately these attributes are denied us.'[29]

Nonetheless, the combined effect of Stalin's letter, Maisky's complaints and Cripps's warning was enough to persuade Churchill to alert Roosevelt to the possibility that the Russians 'might be thinking of separate terms'.[30] From the president's perspective, the risk that Stalin might once again find a modus vivendi with Hitler was too grave to be ignored; it had to be averted at almost any price. Once again, however, he could not entirely ignore Congress.

The power brokers in Washington were far from united about the need to shore up the Soviet Union. There were many in whom isolationism and anti-communism were mutually reinforcing to a degree that exasperated Hopkins, the most insistent advocate of aid for Russia around the White House, who told Churchill that such 'thick heads' were apparently too stupid to appreciate 'the strategic importance of that front'.[31] However, Roosevelt did not need formal authorization from America's legislators before deciding that the nation's vital interests were at stake there: it was an urgent military, political and diplomatic priority to shore up the Soviet Union. This resolve was scheduled to be turned into a commitment at the First Moscow Conference (where the United States was represented by Averell Harriman and Britain by Lord Beaverbrook), which was due to open on 29 September.

Churchill acknowledged the force of the president's argument and could not but endorse it. However, he was unable to rid himself of the resentful thought that 'everything sent to Russia was subtracted from British vital needs'. Somewhat uncharacteristically, he even found himself sharing what he described as his 'stresses' about this unpalatable truth with his colleagues as together they 'endured the unpleasant process of exposing our own vital security and projects to failure for the sake of our new ally – surly, snarly, grasping, and so lately indifferent to our survival'.[32] In a frosty and sometimes barely courteous exchange of messages with the Soviet leader during September, he not only reiterated that a Second Front was out of the question but could also not resist pointing out that the monthly quotas proposed by Roosevelt for delivery to the Soviet Union were to be supplied 'almost entirely out of British production, or production which the United States would have given us under our own purchases or under the Lend-Lease Bill'.[33]

The Moscow Conference lasted for three days, by the end of which Harriman, supported by Beaverbrook, had negotiated the details of a long Soviet shopping list, which, under the terms of Lend-Lease, carried an interest-free price tag of $1 billion. Stalin was jubilant at the scale of this American largesse while Roosevelt cabled Churchill to declare that he was 'delighted with the outcome of the Moscow Conference . . . The important thing now is to get the goods to them.'[34] As he was bound to do, Churchill endorsed the American commitment, but not without qualms. He had conceded Britain's own contribution to the project only after what he described as 'prolonged and painful discussions' with the Americans that, for the British Service departments involved, had been 'like flaying pieces off their skin'.[35] Nonetheless, on 6 October he cabled Stalin with the news that the first of 'a continuous cycle of convoys, leaving every ten days' was already on its way to the Arctic port of Archangel.[36] It was a seminal moment.

The news from Russia was uniformly pessimistic. On 10 October the US military attaché in Moscow, Ivan Yeaton, citing reports that disgruntled Soviet troops had returned from the front, claiming that they had been 'in combat without ammunition and arms', warned that 'it is possible that the end of Russian resistance is not far away'.[37] Hopkins, whose own visit to Moscow had left him in no doubt about Russia's will to resist, was dismissive of such jeremiads. Doubtless mindful of the fact that such warnings might be used by critics to undermine America's present resolve, he wrote a personal note to Stimson advising that the military attaché's report 'should be accepted with the greatest reserve' and noting that, when he was in the Russian capital, 'Yeaton was outspoken in his criticism of the Russians and was insisting at that time – over ten to twelve weeks ago – that Moscow was going to fall at any time . . . he was so biased against the Russians that if his opinions were accepted here the Department may find itself very badly advised.'[38]

Russia's predicament had become acute. By mid-October a pincer movement by two German armies under General Fedor von Bock was advancing on Moscow at such a rate that the warnings of capitulation could hardly be ignored; officials prepared to evacuate the city as the Red Army under Marshal Semyon Timoshenko fell back to the out-skirts of the capital. On the 19th, with the panzers only forty miles from the Kremlin, Stalin was forced to proclaim that the city was under a state of siege and that 'Moscow will be defended to the last'.

As these seismic events moved towards their climax, an Allied con-voy of thirteen merchant ships, steaming variously under the flags of Britain, the Soviet Union, Panama, and Belgium, escorted by a heavy cruiser, two destroyers and five minesweepers, steamed into the Rus-sian port of Archangel. PQ1 – as the convoy was called – offloaded twenty heavy tanks and 193 fighter aircraft. This delivery was little more than symbolic – an earnest gesture of intent – but the convoys which now started to embark regularly on this hazardous route not only defined a new relationship with the Soviet Union but also marked the start of another critical stage in the Battle of the Atlantic.

In his headquarters at Lorient, Admiral Dönitz chafed under the yoke of Raeder's orders, which themselves emanated directly from Hitler. He had been intensely frustrated in July, when he had been instructed to detach a sixth of his operational U-boats from the Atlantic theatre to the Arctic, where, as he was to comment acidly, 'of course at that time there had not yet been any Allied convoys carrying supplies to Russia', and where, therefore, they had 'roamed the empty seas' in search of a non-existent prey. Protesting 'repeatedly' against this misuse of his pre-cious resources, he described the U-boat pickings in the Arctic as being 'meagre in the extreme',[39] but he railed in vain.

As if that were not enough, towards the end of September he was instructed to divert a further six U-boats on what he described as 'subsidiary' operations for which they were ill-suited. They were the first of some thirty U-boats which were soon either in or on their way to the Mediterranean, a deployment forced on the U-boat commander-in-chief to meet an emergency which the German liaison staff in Rome described as 'catastrophic'; which led Raeder to foresee 'the loss of the entire German-Italian position in North Africa' unless there was 'the utmost acceleration of relief measures'[40] for Rommel's forces in the

Western Desert, and Hitler to declare that an Axis defeat in the Mediterranean 'threatened the security of the [European] continent'.[41]

The battle for North Africa that raged back and forth between September 1940 and the autumn of 1942 was as much a struggle for supplies as it was for capturing enemy strongholds. Within this narrower context, the naval war in the Mediterranean was as vital to the protagonists in the desert as the Battle of the Atlantic was to the survival of Britain; whichever side ruled the Mediterranean waves had command of the land battles as well. Churchill left the War Cabinet in no doubt about the importance of the Mediterranean theatre. In a Most Secret directive on 28 April 1941 he insisted, 'The loss of Egypt and the Middle East would be a disaster of the first magnitude to Great Britain, second only to successful invasion and final conquest.'[42] Although the chiefs of staff by no means shared such an apocalyptic view, they were only too aware of the growing threat to Britain's hold on this theatre.

Ever since Italy's declaration of war in June 1940, no Allied merchant ships had been able to pass safely into the Mediterranean via the Straits of Gibraltar. This meant that supplies for Wavell's Middle East Command (which by 1941 totalled some 400,000 men) had to be sent round the Cape of Good Hope, along the east coast of Africa and up into the Red Sea to Suez – a mammoth logistical enterprise. Conversely, virtually all supplies for the Axis armies in North Africa – food, fuel and armaments – merely had to cross from ports in Italy and Sicily to Tripoli and, latterly, Benghazi, which Rommel had overrun the previous February.

Malta was a pivotal British outpost to be held at almost any price. Only 60 miles from Sicily and 220 miles from Tripoli, the island fortress was the only stronghold in the Mediterranean between the British bases at Gibraltar (1,000 miles to the west) and Alexandria (1,000 miles to the east), and the only base from which the Royal Navy and the RAF could interdict these supply lines. With triumph or disaster in the desert at stake, the naval struggle for the Mediterranean between the British and Italian navies was fought without quarter.

In March 1941, on the eve of the German advance against Greece, the British had enjoyed a rare triumph. Based on intelligence from Bletchley Park's cryptologists who – for the first time – had managed to penetrate the Italian navy's Enigma code, the Mediterranean Fleet, under the command of Admiral Andrew Cunningham, sailed in secrecy from its headquarters at Alexandria to intercept the pride of the Regia

Marina off the southernmost tip of Greece. The Battle of Cape Matapan had echoes of the pitched battles of a past age when wars were won and lost, empires seized and broken, by the action of great navies grappling with each other on the seven seas. In a battle that lasted a little over twelve hours on 28/29 March, Cunningham's fleet inflicted severe damage on an Italian battleship and sank three heavy cruisers and two destroyers, all at a cost of light damage to four cruisers and the loss of three British lives to 2,300 Italian.

The Matapan victory temporarily wrested control of the eastern Mediterranean from the Axis powers and gave a much-needed boost to the morale of the War Cabinet. But the satisfaction, as on so many past occasions, was short lived. When reports reached London that another panzer division had landed in Tripoli to join Rommel's Afrikakorps, which was dug in on high ground overlooking the Egyptian border at Sollum, Churchill was seized by fear that the Desert Fox would launch another blitzkrieg against Alexandria as a prelude to moving on Cairo, seizing the Suez Canal and occupying the entire Nile Delta. Were this to happen, his Middle East strategy would be in tatters. Moreover, if Hitler were to seize the moment, as the director of military operations, Major-General John Kennedy, advised the chiefs of staff, the Middle East Command would face a simultaneous threat 'from the north through Turkey and possibly from the north-east through the Caucasus and Persia'. 'Whether we can hold on in the Middle East,' he warned, 'depends on one thing and one thing alone – whether the Germans concentrate seriously against us there.' The prospect of this pincer movement led the prime minister to demand emergency action to prop up the Eighth Army. Judging that it would otherwise be impossible to defend the Middle East – by which, at this point in the conflict, his war strategy was defined – he demanded a move so bold that fainter spirits would not even have contemplated it. From his perspective, there was only one sure way to safeguard Britain's imperial presence in the region. Once again the burden would fall on the Admiralty.

So agitated was the prime minister by the fear that the Eighth Army might otherwise founder that he overrode the objections of the chiefs of staff to insist that a convoy of five vessels carrying more than 300 new tanks be sent via the Straits of Gibraltar through the enemy-infested western Mediterranean to Alexandria. Gambling that the risk of losing these tanks to Italian torpedo bombers was more than offset by the fact that, if they survived, they would reach the British front line at least two months sooner than if they had taken the Cape route, he brooked no opposition. In the event, a gamble which would have been judged unforgivably foolhardy if it had failed was vindicated: the dive-bombers were beaten off and, protected by *Renown* and *Ark Royal*, the convoy reached its destination on 12 May with the loss of only one merchant ship, the *Empire Song*, along with the fifty-seven tanks she was carrying for the North African front. Tiger, as Churchill's enterprise was codenamed, had been a triumph against the odds.

Yet again, though, the prime minister's relief was short lived. Less than three weeks later, following the Greek debacle in April, Crete fell to an airborne invasion by some 22,000 Axis assault troops. In ten days of fighting, more than 5,000 of these were killed or declared missing in action while the British suffered some 3,500 casualties and 12,000 Allied troops were taken prisoner. However, 15,000 of their colleagues – among them survivors of the ill-fated expeditionary force who had retreated there from the Greek mainland so very recently – were safely evacuated. This salvage operation was itself accomplished with skill and daring – albeit at great cost to the Royal Navy, which lost 2,000 service-men and twenty-two warships, nine of which were sunk and thirteen put out of action by the Luftwaffe's bombers.

With the loss of Crete, Malta was now Britain's only stronghold in the Mediterranean and it too was at Hitler's mercy. Had the Führer been as determined to wrest the Middle East from Britain as he sometimes declared himself to be and as Raeder continued to advocate, the occu-pation of Crete would have made his task of seizing the island base even simpler than it had been before the evacuation. As it happened – though the chiefs of staff could not have known it at the time – the Führer's dis-ordered mind was quite incapable of concentrating for long on any strategic objective apart from the Wehrmacht's now faltering efforts to conquer Russia. It was a fateful lack of focus on his part, for by autumn of 1941, when Hitler was eventually afflicted by a tremor of anxiety about the Mediterranean, the British had once again acquired the upper hand, reducing the flow of Axis supplies reaching Rommel's forces in Libya by some 40 per cent. This threat prompted Hitler to transfer an entire air corps from the Russian Front to Sicily and North Africa. However, the Luftwaffe arrived too late for Rommel, who was rapidly running out of fuel for his tanks and weaponry for his men.

In the meantime, Wavell, a great commander-in-chief who been given an insuperable set of simultaneous goals by Churchill and who was duly fired for failing to achieve them, had been succeeded in July 1941 by General Claude Auchinleck. The new commander-in-chief refused to be goaded by Churchill into a premature offensive, and it was not until 18 November 1941 that he launched a surprise attack on Rommel's front line, forcing a German withdrawal from the Egyptian border. After heavy fighting and despite some audacious counter-attacks, Rommel was also forced to lift the siege of Tobruk. With only eight operational tanks left, the Desert Fox began the long retreat to the starting line some two hundred miles to the south-west of Benghazi, whence he had unleashed his own whirlwind attack nine months earlier.

Operation Crusader was hailed as a triumph for Auchinleck's generalship, but it was not a moment to savour for long. The Luftwaffe's arrival led to a sustained and crippling bombardment of Malta. The ferocity of the onslaught forced the island's inhabitants to retreat underground, where many thousands lived a troglodyte existence in caves and tunnels dug out of the rock. By March 1942 the battering endured by Cunningham's ships had become so severe that the admiral (who was about to surrender his command for a posting to Washington for which he was ill-suited and was to dislike intensely) advised Pound that, although there were still 25,000 naval officers and men on station in Alexandria, 'there was now no fleet to go to sea in'.[43] By this time, the Axis armies in North Africa had been re-equipped, reorganized, and refreshed; Rommel had launched another desert offensive and Churchill was contemplating the removal of Crusader's architect, General Auchinleck, from his post as commander-in-chief, Middle East.

Aside from numerous examples of gallantry on the desert battlefield, the back-and-forth across that empty terrain had served to demonstrate with cruel clarity that, above all, the struggle for victory in North Africa hinged on logistics; that to control the seaways between the European mainland and North Africa was to prevail in the desert. To this extent, the conflict in the Mediterranean illuminated a broader truth about the wider war – that the struggle for victory over Hitler hinged on getting men, weapons, fuel and food from Britain and the United States to every front line. For Dönitz, whose U-boats were attempting to sever the British lifeline across the Atlantic, it was a truth that gnawed at his very being.

# 11.  Shifting Fortunes

Dönitz shared Hitler's belated realization that it was strategically important to sustain the Axis presence in North Africa. The U-boat
commander-in-chief also endorsed the high command's appreciation of
the fact that the only way to achieve this was to maintain Rommel's
campaign by protecting his supply lines across the Mediterranean. However, he believed this task was far better suited to aircraft and surface
vessels than to U-boats: his protests against their redeployment from the
Atlantic to escort Italian convoys bound for Tripoli were repeated and
vehement. 'I cannot accept responsibility for an increase in the number
of U-boats in the Mediterranean,' he told Raeder. 'It would weaken our
efforts in the main theatre of operations, without a proportionate increase
of our chances of success in the Mediterranean.'[1] He was overruled.

The only reason given him in late November 1941 was that 'the situation and the importance to our whole war effort of retaining our
position in the Mediterranean necessitate a complete reorientation of
the focal areas of U-boat activities until the situation has been restored'.[2]
But, as Dönitz had foreseen, his U-boats proved rather less effective in
combating British warships in the Mediterranean than they would have
been hunting merchant ships in the Atlantic. Although their presence
had a significant psychological and material impact on the disposition of
Cunningham's fleet, their achievement was modest – though far from
nugatory. On 13 November U-81 torpedoed the aircraft carrier HMS
*Ark Royal*; on 24 November U-331 sank the battleship HMS *Barham*;
and on 14 December U-557 sank the cruiser HMS *Galatea*. Nonetheless,
relative to their numbers, the contribution of the German submarines to
the intensifying struggle for supremacy in the Mediterranean was significantly greater than Dönitz chose to acknowledge.

Nonetheless, once they had passed through the Straits of Gibraltar,
the U-boats were doomed to a long and unproductive sojourn in Mussolini's 'Italian Lake'. The adverse currents flowing out of the
Mediterranean through the Straits were so fierce as to make it virtually
impossible for a submerged U-boat, travelling at a maximum speed of

seven knots, to re-enter the Atlantic and to attempt the passage on the surface was to court disaster at the hands of the RAF. Dönitz noted resentfully in his War Diary that his Mediterranean fleet was caught in 'a mousetrap' and was thus 'never again . . . available for operations in any other theatre'.[3]

To make matters worse, from his thwarted perspective, another group of U-boats that he had been instructed to deploy in the waters immediately around Gibraltar 'were compelled to remain almost continuously submerged and were exposed to constant and considerable danger' both from RAF Coastal Command and the Royal Navy's anti-submarine naval patrols. In this state of 'submerged immobility' his U-boat commanders saw 'no movement of shipping at all in an easterly direction' during the entire time they were required to remain on station. To compound Dönitz's exasperation at the tactical folly, no fewer than one in three Axis submarines in the Mediterranean were being destroyed or disabled by the British bombers. By the end of the war, even this daunting tally was to be far exceeded: as if to confirm Dönitz's grim presentiment, only one U-boat out of the forty deployed there ever managed to escape the 'mousetrap'; all the others were sunk.[4]

Seeking to arrest this slaughter, Dönitz confronted the Kriegsmarine's high command repeatedly. But his protests were to no avail. By the end of 1941 more than a third of his fleet of operational U-boats was stationed either in the Mediterranean or just off Gibraltar. As a result, Dönitz's operations in the Atlantic were severely curtailed, a strategic error which, in the words of the Royal Navy's official historian, 'brought us a most welcome easement in that vital theatre'.[5]

Dönitz was so driven by his urge to triumph in the 'tonnage' war against the Atlantic convoys, that he rarely saw the bigger picture. Perhaps for this reason, he seemed hardly to notice that in December the Axis forces in the Mediterranean had inflicted severe damage on the Royal Navy. Soon after the loss of the *Ark Royal* and the *Barham*, three Italian mini-submarines – or 'human torpedoes', as they became known – each piloted by two frogmen, penetrated the very heart of the naval base at Alexandria. Two of the trio managed to reach HMS *Queen Elizabeth* and HMS *Valiant* and attach limpet mines to their hulls. It was an extraordinarily daring enterprise which was also effective. Although the Italian commandos were captured for their pains, both battleships were severely disabled and put out of action for many months.

On the same day – 19 December – the Royal Navy endured yet another serious setback. 'K' Force sailed out of Valletta with the intention of intercepting an Italian convoy heading to Tripoli laden with supplies for North Africa. Instead it ran into a newly sown minefield. One cruiser was sunk, with the loss of almost 700 lives, while two more were damaged and a destroyer which had come to their rescue was put out of action. This accumulation of losses left only three cruisers and a clutch of destroyers in war-fighting condition in that vital sector of the Mediterranean – a blow to the Royal Navy which led Churchill to lament that 'in the course of a few weeks the whole of our Eastern battle fleet was eliminated as a fighting force'.[6] If Dönitz was aware of this, it did not in any way modify his obsessive belief that it was the Atlantic and only the Atlantic that mattered.

The absence of U-boats and a surfeit of gales following the autumnal equinox meant that the Battle of the Atlantic was virtually on hold in the last three months of 1941. But not entirely. Though the great majority of the transatlantic convoys arrived at their destinations without U-boat interference, the same was not true of the route between Britain and Gibraltar. Following the mauling of OG71 in August 1941 (see p. 174), a further five were lost from convoy OG74, which ran into a U-boat pack in the last week of September.

Four days before these sinkings, a convoy of twenty-five vessels left Gibraltar bound for Milford Haven, protected by no fewer than ten corvettes and destroyers. This protective phalanx was testimony to the rate at which new warships suitable for escort duties had started to come off the production line from small shipyards in Britain and Canada. Despite the addition of these new escorts, HG73 soon ran into even more serious trouble than its immediate predecessors. Rear Admiral Creighton, the convoy commodore, who had been almost constantly at sea since the outbreak of war and had helped oversee the British invasion of Iceland in May 1940, was aboard the 3,500 ton *Avoceta*. In addition to a cargo of oranges, the *Avoceta* carried 128 passengers, including sixty small children and babies. In the hope of avoiding marauding U-boats, the convoy steamed out of Gibraltar and headed due west, travelling at the speed of the slowest, a bare seven knots. On the fourth day out, when they were far out in the Atlantic and about to change course for Liverpool, the lumbering cavalcade was spotted by a

Focke-Wulf Condor, one of the Luftwaffe's fleet of long-range reconnaissance aircraft. In support of the convoy was HMS *Springbok*, one of the first Catapult Aircraft Merchant (CAM) ships – converted freighters from which aircraft were literally catapulted into flight. The CAM ships formed an effective launch pad but were too small for planes to land on, so their pilots had either to make for the nearest airport or – as happened on several occasions – ditch in the sea, not only putting their own lives in peril but also destroying a precious aircraft in the process. In this case, the *Springbok*'s RAF fighter managed to chase the Condor away before making a safe landing in Gibraltar.

This was not the end of the matter, though. The next day another Condor was circling overhead, spotting for the wolf pack that would soon be upon them. Creighton ordered the children to be brought up from their cabins to the smoking room immediately below the bridge in the hope that they would have a better chance of escape if the *Avoceta* were torpedoed. They were joined there by an elderly priest who sought to comfort the mothers who sat either clutching their children or, distracted by fear, muttering imprecations as they fingered their rosaries. A flurry of messages from the Admiralty confirmed the worst; the U-boats were just over the horizon waiting for nightfall and the chance to strike.

The first attack came at 11.30 p.m. on 25 September. Creighton was climbing to the upper bridge when a violent tremor shook the *Avoceta* and, as he recalled, 'she staggered like a stumbling horse and shuddered to a lurching stop'. The force of the blast flung the commodore against the side of the bridge ladder. From below came the scream of escaping steam 'which smothered some of the unearthly gargling sounds coming from [those] drowning and the tearing squeals of those trapped in the scalding agony of the engine room'. Before there was time to launch a single lifeboat the *Avoceta*'s bows reared towards the sky as the stern was sucked below the surface. Creighton was horrified: 'I clung to a stanchion feeling sick and helpless as I had to look on while the children were swept out into the darkness below by the torrent of water which roared through the smoking room.'[7]

Moments later Creighton was himself swept into the water. 'Everything became hazy. I suppose I was drowning. I felt curiously as if I was pleasantly drunk and enveloped in cotton wool.' But, as he was sucked down by the pressure of the *Avoceta*'s mast and rigging in which he had become entangled, he felt an agonizing pain in his chest. A moment later, he broke free and catapulted to the surface. Nearby, he saw a raft, no larger than a settee, to which a handful of people were clinging with a desperation born of the knowledge that to lose their grip would mean almost certain death. He swam up and asked, 'Any room for another?' He was hauled aboard, where he 'lay sodden, gasping, and . . . bitterly cold'. There were seven others on the raft, several of whom were coughing and choking, their throats clogged with fuel oil. 'Gradually, their strength ebbed, they became insensible, and slipped off unnoticed in the darkness.' All around, red battery-operated emergency lights attached to lifejackets twinkled in the water. Disconcertingly, these began to be extinguished one by one, along with their wearers' lives, Creighton presumed. But in fact a rescue vessel had arrived and was plucking survivors from the ocean. Three hours later the corvette HMS *Periwinkle* came alongside Creighton's raft to pull him and his fellow mariners aboard to warmth and comfort.[8] They were fortunate. Only twenty-eight of the *Avoceta*'s complement survived: those who did not – forty-three members of her crew and sixty-seven passengers – included thirty-two women and twenty of the sixty children who had boarded at Gibraltar a week earlier.

In the course of the following three days and nights, another nine of the twenty-five ships in the convoy were sunk by a pack of five U-boats. Not one of HG73's ten escorts managed to strike a blow in return. At the inquiry into these losses, which opened the day after the battered convoy trundled into Milford Haven, Admiral Sir Percy Noble, the commander-in-chief of Western Approaches Command, offered reassurance to the captains of the escort vessels that they had been summoned not to be reprimanded but to help the Admiralty establish what lessons might be learned from their tragic failure to drive off their assailants.

Creighton later offered a searing insight into the grief of others and into his own distress. Some days after returning home, he attended Sunday service at his local church, where thoughts of those lost from the *Avoceta* kept floating unbidden into his mind. In particular he remembered a nineteen-year-old wireless officer, a Canadian called Norman Larson, who had volunteered to serve although, as a farmer's son from the Canadian Midwest, he would have been exempt from any draft his government might introduce. 'I thought of him keeping his watch, all alone for hours each day and night . . . He saw the danger closing in on the convoy . . . he was all alone when it struck.' The commodore was so moved by this memory that he wrote to Larson's mother to commiserate. Larson's sister replied in a letter which, he noted, typified 'the grief, sadness and pride of so many families, whose husbands, fathers and sons gave their all in the cause of victory':

Dear Sir,

My mother, sister and I wish to thank you so very kindly for the information about Norman Larson, Telegraphist, RCNVR, a very dear son and brother . . . We find it very hard to believe that he is gone. We had a letter from him written on 7 September saying he had acquired a good coat of tan in Gibraltar.

My mother's heart is broken and we know it is so for all mothers who lose their sons in war. He always wrote faithfully to his mother and little souvenirs he sent us from England showed he thought of us at home . . .

In his last letter from England just before sailing for Gibraltar he mentioned one of the boys as having an accordion and they would have music on the way . . . I will close now. May God protect you and give you the strength to carry on in England's traditional way till victory is here.

I remain,

Yours very sincerely,
(Mrs.) Robert Livingstone.

Another of *Avoceta*'s crew, her chief engineer, had spent forty years at sea. Creighton had grown fond of him:

His cabin was an almost square box eight feet by seven just above the engine room. This little closet was his home . . . It was pathetic to see the lonely life he led – small photographs of his wife and family the only decoration in his cabin. We yarned often and I felt deeply for him . . . I picture him in the hour of disaster making his way to the engine room where the sea swept him up to his last home.[9]

Creighton, who had been temporarily deafened by being dragged so far below the surface, was not released swiftly from the grip of that trauma. Yet he retained a sense of humour. He needed it. One day when he was still on survivor's leave, a woman he knew quite well stopped him in the village street. 'I hear you were sunk in your last convoy,' she said. Creighton replied, 'Yes, I am afraid I was.' She said, 'But I thought a naval officer always went down with his ship.' Creighton retorted, 'I thought I had done so but I did not know that honour demanded that I should follow her 2,000 fathoms to the bottom.'[10] Their exchange ceased abruptly.

Quite why it was that ten escorts had been unable to protect HG73 more effectively was a disturbing conundrum for the Admiralty. A few weeks later a far more contentious inquiry brought the Admiralty's anxieties into even sharper focus. Overlapping with Creighton's departure from Gibraltar, another convoy of eleven merchant ships left Freetown on 14 September bound for Liverpool with an escort of five warships. SL87's cargo included palm oil, copper, and cocoa beans from West Africa, and, in the case of the 5,000-ton *Silverbelle*, phosphate, a crucial ingredient in the manufacture of incendiary bombs and mortar shells. A week after leaving the West African coast, when the convoy was south of the Azores, the *Silverbelle* became the first of seven freighters to be intercepted and torpedoed by a pack of three U-boats.

The court of inquiry into this disaster opened on 17 October under the presidency of a senior member of Admiral Noble's staff. In the coldly precise language adopted during such procedures, his report amounted to a scathing verdict which highlighted the combination of confusion, inexperience and incompetence which had apparently bedevilled the Royal Navy's futile efforts to protect its charges:

> The fact that 7 out of 11 ships were sunk with no retaliation against the enemy is to be deplored. The escort was a strong one for a convoy of this size . . . It is clear that the efforts of the escorts were poorly co-ordinated . . . The general inference to be drawn from this analysis is that the escort vessels were not sufficiently alive to the vital necessity of prosecuting the most vigorous possible search for the attacking U-boat immediately after the attack.

This was tantamount to an accusation of gross negligence if not cowardice to boot. Lieutenant Commander R. W. Keymer, captain of the sloop HMS *Gorleston* – an ex-US Coast Guard cutter – who had been the convoy's escort commander, responded with a furious rebuttal. 'This is not true and is a great slight on those who day after day twenty-four hours a day . . . were on their feet without sitting down let alone sleeping, in an effort to combat an enemy with ill-trained and ill-equipped ships most of whom were crocks.'[11] This was a resentful exaggeration on Keymer's part but it contained the kernel of a home truth.

Although SL 87's naval commanders had been given some training in the basic principles of convoy protection, they had not had a chance to plan or rehearse adequately for the exigencies of counter-submarine warfare and their crews – many of whom were conscripts pressed hurriedly into service – had been thrust into the front line of the Battle of the Atlantic with very little training. To make matters worse, only three of the five escort vessels attached to SL 87 were equipped with radio direction finders and two of these 'were out of action owing to breakdowns and lack of spare parts'.

Yet, it was the slight on the men serving under him that most irked Keymer. In a formal response to the Admiralty's Final Report, he wrote:

> The Ship's Company, a large proportion of whom, it is worth noting, are conscripts of the twenty-eight and thirty years of age class, and who joined this their first ship in July, although visibly shaken by the extraordinary series of attacks ... not only showed courage and good discipline at the most trying moments but also maintained an excellent morale.

Despite these protestations, Keymer could not be exculpated from the main charge laid against him; he did indeed 'fail to prosecute the most vigorous' counter-attack against the convoy's assailants. Rather, he had elected to peel away to go to the assistance of one vessel, the stricken *Silverbelle*, which was already being attended by another escort. The inquiry judged that it was 'particularly unfortunate that SO [Senior Officer] in command of the escorts [Keymer] spent so much time out of touch with his group'.[12] It was a charge to which Keymer was unable to offer a convincing defence. In committing himself to a well-meaning but redundant gesture, he had left his convoy mortally exposed.

Admiral Noble, who was admired and trusted by those serving under him at the Western Approaches Command, was appalled by the inquiry's findings. By nature mild-mannered and generally understanding of the tribulations endured by his colleagues at sea, he took the unusual step of circulating its key criticisms to every ship in his fleet. Although Keymer was spared a court martial, he was told that he would never again be allowed to serve as an escort group commander. It was a bitter blow, though somewhat ameliorated by the fact that the Royal Navy could not afford to dispense altogether with the services of such an experienced officer; Keymer continued to serve honourably on escort duties until the end of the war. In a sorry coda to the fate of HG73, as the *Northern Whig* (a Belfast newspaper) reported on 14 October, 'Eighty survivors from four ships forming part of a convoy recently sunk 100 miles from the Azores were landed at Lisbon yesterday. There were originally 100 in the lifeboats, but 20 died from hunger and thirst.'[13]

Though the fate of SL87 had its unique characteristics, similar complaints about lack of equipment and training abounded. This was partly explicable by the fact that the expansion of the escort fleet had been as belated as it was rapid. It was also demonstrably true that the Admiralty had failed to establish guidelines for the protection of the Atlantic convoys; decisions had to be made on the spur of the moment by individual commanders who had no general framework of reference on which to base them. This ad hoc approach was not only tactically incoherent but left inexperienced commanders floundering in the face of a coordinated U-boat attack. Nor was the rate of attrition sustainable. After a further two Gibraltar convoys lost another ten ships between them in October, it became a matter of urgency for the Admiralty to discover more effective means of combating a U-boat menace which showed no signs of evaporating.

With such a poverty of achievement – especially at a time when so large a proportion of Dönitz's modest fleet had been caught in the Mediterranean 'mousetrap' – the prime minister was edgy and sensitive about the implications for the Battle of the Atlantic. When the Admiralty released statistics which implicitly revealed how little the convoy escorts had accomplished, he remonstrated with both the First Lord and the First Sea Lord:

> I much regret that the number of U-boat prisoners taken by us should have been published. I commented unfavourably upon this publication six months ago. The figure is so small that it advertises to the world the failure of all our efforts against them. There was absolutely no need to make such a disclosure, gratuitously encouraging the enemy and discouraging our friends.[14]

In December, however, there was cautious reason to suppose that a solution to the U-boat menace off the Straits of Gibraltar might be in the offing. On the 15th, a convoy of thirty-two vessels left the British base bound for Liverpool to be escorted by a phalanx of seventeen warships. The overall command of this escort group had been given to an unusually dynamic and forceful character who was soon to become a legendary figure within the Royal Navy.

Commander F. J. 'Johnny' Walker had not been a high-flyer. Bombastic and outspoken, he lacked that degree of tact and decorum which found favour in the boardrooms of the pre-war Royal Navy. Although his intellectual gifts were beyond doubt, his impatience and arrogance were held against him and barred him from rapid promotion. By the time he left the battleship HMS *Valiant* in 1937, where he had served as second-in-command, the forty-six-year-old officer had managed to provoke his captain to such a degree that he was left in no doubt that little prospect of advancement awaited him; one adverse report went so far as to conclude that he was 'lacking powers of leadership'.[15] Nonetheless, he was posted to Portsmouth as commander of the Anti-Submarine Warfare School, HMS *Osprey*. Though this kept him away from the front-line duties he craved, his technical prowess was rewarded by a subsequent appointment as Staff Officer (Operations) at Dover. This gave him a chance to hone his expertise, though it still failed to satisfy his yearning to take command of his own ship. After the outbreak of war, he applied again and again for a chance to prove his worth at sea, but he was invariably informed, 'Request not approved.'[16]

It was not until September 1941 that he finally got his wish. At the behest of Admiral Noble, to whom he had been recommended by a mutual friend, he was plucked from Dover to assume command of HMS *Stork*, an escort sloop based at Liverpool. He was initially unimpressed by his fellow officers. Some, like himself, had been 'passed over' for promotion, but most had been drawn from the pool of the Royal Naval Volunteer Reserve, whom Walker regarded as 'weekend sailors churned out by the recruiting machine often with inadequate training'.[17] When, to his delight, he was given command of the 36th Escort Group, which comprised two sloops and seven corvettes, he was quickly disabused of such prejudice.

Walker now had 500 men under his command, to be welded into a cohesive fighting force with one overriding objective: to sink U-boats.

His work-up routine was remorseless and repetitive. Day after day and night after night he bludgeoned the 36th Escort Group into the semblance of a team. His operational instructions reflected his approach and his character: 'U-boats are the chief menace to our convoys. I cannot emphasize too strongly that a U-boat sighted or otherwise detected is immediately to be attacked continuously without further orders, with guns, depth charges and/or ram until she has been destroyed or until further orders are received.' Though he expected to take charge of most operations, he made it clear that it was 'essential' for officers 'to act instantly without waiting for instructions in situations of which I may be unaware or imperfectly informed . . . No officer will ever be blamed by me for getting on with the job in hand.'[18] This attitude was not unique, but it was still rare in a Royal Navy in which personal initiative and enterprise were not yet as highly prized as buccaneering officers would have liked. As convoy HG76 steamed out of the anchorage at Gibraltar led by the 36th Escort Group, Walker's operating principles were about to be put to the test in no uncertain fashion.

Walker's squadron was soon reinforced by two more sloops, three destroyers, three corvettes and the aircraft carrier HMS *Audacity*.* He was in no doubt that his convoy would very soon come under attack from one or another of the wolf packs that invariably lurked in these hunting grounds. He was right: Dönitz had been forewarned about HG76's departure, confirmed by German agents in Spain who passed the intelligence up to his headquarters. A *Gruppe Seerauber* (pirate pack) of six U-boats was waiting to pounce on the convoy almost as soon as it had left the security of the Rock. By chance, Walker evaded the waiting U-boats and his good fortune continued when, on the evening of the 15th, the Australian destroyer HMAS *Nestor* detected and depth charged a U-boat off Cape St Vincent, at the southernmost tip of Portugal. Notwithstanding this success, the escorts were on full alert; if one submarine was in the vicinity, others would be nearby.

At dusk on the 16th another of Walker's destroyers, HMS *Stanley*, reported sighting two aircraft in the distance. In his unconventional

---

* The *Audacity* was the first 'escort carrier' to be assigned specifically to this role. Originally a German merchant ship, the *Hannover*, built in 1939, she was captured in 1941 and adapted for her new purpose. She carried eight American-built Martlet fighter planes.

way, Walker noted in his War Diary, 'This report was pooh-poohed by *Audacity*, but *Stanley* stuck stoutly to his convictions. I have assumed that the enemy has now passed our full particulars to every U-boat not wearing a deaf-aid.'[19] By midnight – courtesy of Bletchley Park – his assessment had been confirmed by the Admiralty. From this moment on, the confrontation between the escorts and the U-boats took on an entirely new character. As a result of the losses incurred by earlier Gibraltar convoys, Walker had an unusually large number of escorts at his disposal as well as the *Audacity*. This gave him a freedom of man-oeuvre denied to his predecessors. Thus, on the 17th, when one of *Audacity*'s aircraft sighted a U-boat on a parallel course, some twenty miles away to port, he was able to go after it without leaving HG76 vulnerable to attack from other 'pirates'. Leaving twelve escorts to pro-tect the convoy, he set off at full speed in pursuit of the submarine accompanied by four warships, all of which he had rehearsed so assidu-ously for this, the real thing.

U-131 was under the command of Arend Baumann, an inexperienced officer on his first patrol. Surprised by the sudden appearance of *Auda-city*'s spotter aircraft, he put U-131 into an emergency dive. For half an hour all seemed well. But the illusory calm was shattered by a barrage of depth charges. Lights fused, batteries leaked chlorine gas into an already foetid atmosphere and – more seriously – the pressure of the explosions split the submarine's hull at the stern. Walker's posse had achieved what he expected of it.

Baumann was trapped. Tempted to court disaster by coming to the surface, he decided instead to seek escape by descending to 600 feet and crawling away at the U-boat's maximum submerged speed of five knots. After two hours, he thought it would be safe to surface. He rushed to the conning tower to scan the horizon. To his immediate relief, there was no sign of his assailants, but within minutes five enemy warships appeared, some seven miles distant, bearing down on the submarine at full speed. Walker's group had not given up after the initial attack but continued to sweep the area. On sighting the submarine, Walker sum-moned one of *Audacity*'s Martlet aircraft. The pilot, Sub Lieutenant George Fletcher, who had only recently qualified to fly in the Fleet Air Arm, dived at the U-boat and opened fire, but the submarine's gunnery team was ready. As the aircraft swooped into their sights, they opened fire and scored a direct hit. The Martlet plunged into the sea, killing

Fletcher. It was, though, a hollow triumph. At the same moment Walker's escorts found their range and raked the U-boat from stem to stern. Within twenty minutes U-131 was a scuttled wreck on its way to the ocean bed, her crew having had just enough time to leap into the water to be saved from drowning by their attackers.

The manner of U-131's sinking did not of itself change the course of the struggle but it had illuminated a yet-to-be widely recognized truism about the Battle of the Atlantic: that ships and planes operating in tandem could form a powerful shield and pose a formidable threat. A convoy thus protected, though by no means invulnerable, was very much more likely to arrive intact. Walker's feat had been possible on this occasion because he had been allocated enough ships to achieve what Keymer could not: retaliation without leaving the convoy unprotected.

Dönitz read the runes. Realizing that *Audacity*'s aircraft had made it impossible for the U-boats to close on the convoy without risking annihilation, he knew what was required: 'The sinking of the aircraft carrier is of particular importance not only in this case but also in every future convoy action,' he noted as soon as he was alerted to what had happened.[20] To this end, he decided to reinforce the *Seerauber* group – which, as a result of another sinking, had now lost three of its six boats – with three of his most experienced commanders, one of whom was the ace Engelbert Endrass, who had already sunk twenty-two merchant ships in the course of ten patrols.

Before their arrival, the surviving member of the *Seerauber* pack continued to stalk the convoy. After dark on the 19th, U-574 fired at the escort destroyer *Stanley* and scored a direct hit. Walker watched as 'she went up, literally in a sheet of flame hundreds of feet high'.[21] Out of a ship's complement of 161, only 25 survived. Walker at once ordered every vessel under his command to fire star shells into the air to illuminate the surface of the sea. *Stork* then closed to within half a mile of the burning wreck – no closer for fear of wounding or killing survivors – and dropped a pattern of depth charges which forced the U-boat to surface. In his report to the Admiralty, Walker described how the coup de grâce was delivered:

> I managed to ram her just before the conning tower and roll her over. She hung for a few seconds on the bow and then scraped aft where she was greeted by a pattern of ten depth charges. I was informed that a

Boche in the water, who was holding up his arms and crying '*Kamerad*', received the content of the depth charge thrower in his face instead.[22]

Such relish at the death of an adversary, rare among mariners even in war, was perhaps explicable in Walker's indignation at the demise of *Stanley* and did not prevent *Stork* from following the rules of maritime chivalry and circling round to pick up the surviving members of the U-boat crew.

The following day a Focke-Wulf appeared over the horizon. Two of *Audacity*'s fighters were scrambled and after a brief dog-fight the German plane was shot down. But the tension was starting to tell. No longer hopeful of evading further attack, Walker had set course directly for Liverpool, still six days away. Soon afterwards, a U-boat torpedoed the *Annavore*, the first merchant ship to be sunk since their departure from Gibraltar. HMS *Audacity*, whose captain, Commander D. W. MacKendrick, was of senior rank to Walker and therefore only nominally under the group commander's orders, opted – against Walker's advice – to take up station on the unprotected starboard side of the convoy. At 11 p.m. on the 21st, the aircraft carrier was torpedoed and, seventy minutes later, she sank with the loss of seventy-three lives. Dönitz's instructions had been fulfilled. Walker blamed himself for not insisting that MacKendrick follow his advice, commenting, 'I feel myself accordingly responsible for the loss.'[23]

Walker had little time for such reflection. Soon after 3 a.m. on the 22nd, the *Stork*'s crew heard a crash from the stern. Walker rushed aft to see that, in the confusion of battle, the sloop HMS *Deptford* had ploughed into *Stork*'s quarterdeck. As he surveyed the damage to his ship, Walker took a ghoulish satisfaction in noting that '*Deptford*'s stem had walked straight into the temporary prison and two of the five Boche captives there were pulped literally into a bloody mess. When I went aft in the dark later to inspect the damage I walked straight into the hole and found myself with my feet among the Boche corpses and my elbows on the quarterdeck.'[24]

Undeterred, Walker kept up the pressure on the U-boats, compelling Dönitz to call off the attack on 23 December. By the time HG76 reached Liverpool four days later, Walker had lost two warships; however, thirty of the thirty-two merchant vessels which had left Gibraltar two weeks earlier had arrived safely. As significantly, five U-boats had gone to the bottom, which, for Dönitz, was an unsustainable rate of attrition.

The reactions in Britain and Germany reflected this balance of victory and defeat. Walker arrived home to find that his triumph had been rewarded with a DSO. In the new year, as hero of the hour, he was summoned to the Admiralty in London, where, in a room stuffed with senior officers, Admiral Noble and Captain George Creasy, the director of anti-submarine warfare, asked him what his experience had taught him. His reply was unequivocal:

(1) Aircraft are absolutely invaluable for anti-submarine warfare ... *Audacity* [which had downed four enemy aircraft before her own demise], her staff and pilots, put up a matchless performance. (2) Convoys should be protected by both 'an outer and inner' screen of escorts, and (3) by day, ALL escorts should be used as striking forces for offensive lunges away from the convoy, attacking U-boats detected as far away as thirty miles.[25]

Giving impeccably sound advice was one thing, heeding it was quite another. Perhaps mindful of the futility of Churchill's amateurish enthusiasm for the creation of hunting groups to seek out enemy submarines, which Captain Macintyre, in very different circumstances, had likened to 'a search for a mouse in a ten-acre field' – the admirals were unwilling at this stage to accept Walker's last piece of advice. Nor were there yet enough ships available to provide the double screen of escorts that he had advocated. And, while they conceded that aircraft might indeed be 'absolutely invaluable', the admirals lacked the power or the influence to conjure them out of an ether which was barricaded from them by an Air Ministry that saw no cause whatsoever to divert RAF planes from their 'proper' task of defending Britain and bombing German cities. Walker was to die prematurely from a heart attack in 1944, but until that moment, frustrated as he and his colleagues were by the obdurate and purblind attitude of the Air Ministry, he continued to demonstrate the validity of his argument. In the process, he acquired a mythic status across the Royal Navy for innovation, resolution, quick-wittedness and aggression. More than fifty years later 'Johnny' Walker was permanently memorialized in the form of a statue that was erected on Pier Head in Liverpool in 1998.★

For a while, his success engendered a mild sense of euphoria but wiser

---

★ The statue was unveiled by the Duke of Edinburgh in 1998.

heads at the Admiralty were far from sanguine. The statistics told a far from encouraging story. In September 1941, by which time the U-boats were coming off the production line at an accelerating rate, it was estimated that Dönitz had a grand total of 184 boats at his disposal and that his losses were 44 (in fact, the figures were respectively 198 and 47). But it was only too clear that U-boats were being commissioned at a faster rate than they were being destroyed while the converse remained true for Allied merchant ships. To have any chance of reversing the trend, drastic measures would be required. One member of the Board of Admiralty reported: 'We require every single surface ship and every long-range aircraft we can possibly muster. Any suggestion that the corner has been turned is not supported by the facts.'[26]

Dönitz and his staff at Kerneval were dismayed by Walker's victory: the loss of five U-boats was unprecedented and seemed to foreshadow further slaughter. Fainter hearts even began to suggest that their commander-in-chief should give up what was becoming an unequal struggle or, as he put it, 'my staff was inclined to voice the opinion that we were no longer in a position to combat the convoy system because of recent experiences'. Dönitz rejected this muttering as unduly defeatist: 'our heavy defeat', he concluded, '. . . had been due to exceptional circumstances. This one isolated case was no reason for making any fundamental change in my views . . . and I was proved right by subsequent events.'[27] This was true – up to a point.

## 12.  Beating the Drum

In January 1942 the neon signs along the eastern seaboard from thousands of restaurants, bars and casinos from Miami to New York sent a spiral of multi-coloured lights into the darkness. On the 1,200 miles of freeway between these two hubs of American civilization the headlamps from scores of thousands of cars and trucks pierced the darkness to create an ever-flowing ribbon of movement which could be seen from several miles out at sea, a linear streak of peacetime reassurance which clearly illuminated the shoreline. To assist the mariner's task, lighthouses beamed ritual warnings and buoys flashed along safe channels. The tramp steamers, freighters and tankers which plied these busy sea lanes were similarly illuminated, their slow-moving bulk etched clearly against the night sky.

An innocent observer of this scene would have been unaware that less than a month earlier, on 7 December 1941, Japan had bombed Pearl Harbor and Germany and the United States were now at war. The attack on Pearl Harbor, which destroyed a large proportion of the US Navy, came as a shock to the American people. But many months of worsening tension between Washington and Tokyo had made military conflict between the two Pacific powers – whose competing vital interests were at stake – virtually inevitable. As the Japanese armies pressed forward to occupy and threaten ever greater swathes of the Far East and Indo-China, so the United States tightened the political and economic screws on Emperor Hirohito's regime. Japanese assets had been frozen, trade sanctions imposed and in the autumn of 1941 Washington imposed an oil embargo which, 'if fully implemented and joined in by the British and Dutch, would have [had] an immediate and growing impact and carry beyond deterrence to coercion'.[1] Diplomats in Washington were well aware of this, which is why they had wrangled between themselves over the use of such an overtly hostile initiative that would assuredly goad Japan towards a military confrontation.

As relations with Tokyo deteriorated towards the point of no return, Roosevelt had temporized, anxious to avoid all-out war in the Pacific when the position in Europe was looking ever more precarious. By late November the Wehrmacht had advanced to within thirty miles of Moscow and the Russian capital appeared to be on the verge of collapse. Although still reluctant to wage war simultaneously in the Pacific and the Atlantic when America's armed forces were ill-equipped for a large-scale confrontation on either front, Roosevelt knew by December that the question was not if but only when and where the Japanese would strike. Pearl Harbor was the answer.

Soon after daybreak on 7 December, more than 350 Japanese warplanes took off from six aircraft carriers to sink or seriously damage eighteen US warships, including eight of the Pacific Fleet's nine battleships, three cruisers, three destroyers, and 347 aircraft. More than 2,400 military personnel were killed and a further 1,178 were wounded. The 'surprise' attack cost Japan only twenty-nine planes (with a further seventy-four damaged), five midget submarines and sixty-four lives. The Japanese high command evidently believed that inflicting such losses on the United States would lead Washington to acquiesce in their imperial plans for the Far East. It was a fatal miscalculation.

As it transpired – if only as a result of force majeure – the Americans were to fight the Pacific War essentially with submarines backed up by aircraft launched from its carrier fleet. Battleships were swiftly proved to be almost redundant, useful principally to bombard the enemy's shorelines to 'soften up' Japanese defences prior to a landing by US Marines and ground troops.

This decisive change in the character of naval warfare, which was to make the difference between victory and defeat in the Pacific, was not apparent at once and certainly not to the Führer. Intoxicated by the apparent implications of Japan's démarche and, as ever, consumed by hubris, Hitler seized the moment of Pearl Harbor to declare war on the United States. In so doing, he abandoned a policy which had hitherto governed his entire war strategy. Until this point he had insisted that the Kriegsmarine should avoid any provocation in the Atlantic that might tempt the US Navy to retaliate; he had repeatedly insisted that, while war with the United States was inevitable, it should be avoided until the Soviet Union was securely under Nazi rule.

Dönitz had frequently chafed under these restrictions, warning Hitler that his U-boats in the Atlantic had been placed in an 'intolerable' position following Roosevelt's 'Shoot on Sight' order in September 1941.[2] However, Hitler been adamant – even after two Atlantic confrontations in October, when the USS *Kearny* (with the loss of seven crew) and then the USS *Reuben James* (with the loss of 114 crew) were both torpedoed in circumstances which Dönitz could, with some justice, claim to have been the inevitable consequence of America's undeclared war against the Kriegsmarine: nothing, the Führer insisted, should be done that might tempt the United States towards a declaration of war against the Third Reich.

Now, though, every such constraint was lifted – and all bets were off. In so far as he could indulge so powerful a feeling, Dönitz was exuberant. Hitler's Declaration of War was an opportunity to be seized at once. 'Here,' he wrote in his War Diary '. . . is an opportunity of getting at enemy merchant ships in conditions which elsewhere have ceased almost completely for a long time . . . Attempts must be made as quickly as possible to utilize these advantages which will disappear shortly, and to "beat the drum" along the American coast.'[3]

On 13 January, on the basis of a British intelligence decrypt, a message was flashed to all shipping along America's eastern seaboard from the most senior naval officer in the United States, the Chief of Naval Operations, Admiral 'Betty' Stark:

PRIORITY FROM OPNAV: ACCOUNT SUBMARINE MENACE ON NORTH ATLANTIC COAST INSTRUCT ALL COASTWISE MERCHANT SHIPPING PROCEEDING NORTH OF NEW YORK TO UTILIZE CAPE CODCAN [Cape Cod Canal] AND IF THIS IS NOT POSSIBLE TO KEEP AS CLOSE TO COAST IN THIS AREA AS NAVIGATIONAL SAFETY WILL PERMIT.[4]

Within hours, the first U-boat had arrived off the east coast of the United States and set about what would later be defined in an official US Navy document as a 'massacre'.[5] The lights along the seaboard were shining with a terrible brilliance.

Armed only with a large-scale nautical chart, a guidebook to New York and a street map of Manhattan Island, which marked the inlets and harbours around its perimeter and, for good measure, depicted the location of the Statue of Liberty, Captain Reinhard Hardegen was in command of U-123, the first long-range Type IX U-boat to arrive in the new killing ground.[6] Hardegen navigated his U-boat into the busiest shipping lanes in the United States without being detected. That evening, guided by shore lights and the rhythmic *dash-dot-dash-dash* light from the Montauk Point Lighthouse off Long Island, he picked his way cautiously towards the Ambrose Channel, the main approach to New York harbour.

At just after 1.30 a.m. on 14 January, his watch officer detected moving lights to port heading on a reciprocal course some 4,000 metres away. As it came closer, Hardegen saw that the vessel was fully lit from stem to stern. He manoeuvred U-123 into a firing position. Turning to the watch officer, he said, 'It's a tanker, Number One. A huge one. Two torpedoes. Aim for the bridge and aft mast.'[7] Less than a minute later, he watched as a spurt of flame shot into the sky to turn into a 'black, sinister mushroom cloud 150 meters high, and the fog-streaked sky took on an eerie orange cast'. The tanker lurched, sagged in the water and tilted to starboard but did not sink. One of the two torpedoes fired by the submarine had evidently missed. Three more were required before the vessel settled by the stern before coming to rest on the seabed, her bows still exposed clearly above the surface. By this time, Hardegen's radio operator had intercepted an SOS message from the stricken vessel: HIT BY TORPEDO OR MINE 40 MILES WEST OF NANTUCKET LIGHT SHIP X NORNESS.[8] By checking his Lloyds Register, Hardegen noted with satisfaction that the *Norness* was a modern 9,577-ton tanker almost 500 feet long and had evidently been fully laden.

On board the stricken tanker, Captain Harold Hansen had been asleep when the first torpedo struck. Pulling an overcoat over his pyjamas, he directed operations as the crew lowered the tanker's lifeboats and rafts into the sea. Two members of the forty-man crew – one seventeen-year-old, who was blown off the deck by the force of the second torpedo as it struck, and the other who fell into the icy water when a lifeboat capsized – were drowned. The only other victim was a puppy, called Pete. In his attempt to scramble into a lifeboat, Pete's owner, Paul Georgsen, missed his footing and fell into the sea. He managed to clamber back aboard the *Norness*, where he recovered his pet, picked him up and, this time, jumped aboard a life raft. But the waves poured across the low sides of the vessel, soaking everyone on board. The puppy whimpered and shivered so violently that Georgsen realized it could not survive. 'So, I said "goodbye" to him,' he recalled, 'then brained him on the deck.'[9] Later that day the survivors were spotted by a patrolling aircraft which directed a small armada to their rescue.

The sinking of the *Norness* signalled the start of an orgy of destruction by U-123 and a handful of other U-boats which, for almost four months, were to operate with impunity up and down the US coast. In Washington and London, Operation Drumbeat – Dönitz's codename for a maritime bombardment which would last for six months – was soon to provoke a degree of alarm which verged on hysteria. To an extent that, in retrospect, seems astonishing though not incomprehensible, the US Navy was quite unprepared for an onslaught which was severely to threaten the flow of oil and other crucial supplies both within the United States and across the Atlantic to Britain.

On the following day, 15 January, Hardegen torpedoed a British tanker, the *Coimbra*. On this occasion, only six survived when an oil leak caught fire, incinerating their thirty-five shipmates. On 18 January U-66, under the command of Richard Zapp, sank the *Allan Jackson*, a tanker belonging to Standard Oil en route from Cartagena to New York with 73,000 barrels of Colombian crude oil. In this case there were thirteen survivors but twenty-two men went down with their ship.

The two U-boats did not operate in tandem but as lone wolves picking off easy targets. In the early hours of 19 January Hardegen sank a freighter, the *City of Atlanta*, and immediately afterwards he attacked a tanker, the *Malay*, but failed to sink her. At 5 a.m. he torpedoed a freighter, the *Ciltvaira*, sailing southbound, lights blazing, from New York to Savannah. At much the same time, 200 miles to the east, Zapp fired a torpedo at a liner, the *Lady Hawkins*, sailing from Montreal for Bermuda carrying 212 passengers and 109 crew.

U-66's first torpedo struck the *Lady Hawkins* immediately below the bridge, catapulting most of those on deck into the sea. A second torpedo hit the engine room, destroying two lifeboats and extinguishing all the ship's lights. Disoriented by the dark and unable to find their way along steeply tilting passageways, many of those below were engulfed by water and drowned. Those who made it on deck either scrambled into lifeboats or leapt into the sea. Among the latter, Albert Johnson, his wife and their two-year-old daughter, Janet, were hauled aboard a lifeboat so heavily laden that most of the seventy-six men and women on board had to stand.

They were fortunate that one of their number was Chief Officer Percy Kelly, who at once set about creating order and discipline. With no power, the *Lady Hawkins* had been unable to radio for help, so Kelly had little idea when or whether they would be rescued. He rigged a sail, set a course for what he hoped would be the nearest landfall and, with very little food to go round, distributed 'a daily ration of one biscuit, a tablespoon of canned milk, and two ounces of water per person'.[10] Mrs Johnson recalled, 'We owe our lives to the chief officer, whose courage and tact kept our spirits up.'[11] Kelly himself later spoke fondly of the Johnsons' daughter.

> She set an example for all of us and took the whole experience as a picnic . . . She was soaked for five days but we heard hardly a whimper from her . . . She spent all her time in her mother's arms and got a thrill out of every waking minute. One night she had a little fever and we gave her a spoonful of brandy. It pulled her through, but for a time made her laugh so much that the whole boat laughed with her.[12]

Some were less fortunate. Five people in the lifeboat died of exposure. 'That was our worst time. It was awful to see them go . . . The spray and the water were bad. We never were entirely dry,' Kelly recalled.[13] A Canadian missionary, Marian Parkinson, who had been separated from her husband in the chaos of abandoning ship, performed the burial rights over the victims. Then, once they had been gently stripped of their clothes (which were handed to other passengers to help them avoid the same fate), their remains were slipped over the side into the sea. The death toll would have been far higher but for the fact that, after five days marooned at sea, they managed to attract the attention of a passenger ship and were rescued. No others from 321 passengers and crew who had originally embarked on the *Lady Hawkins* were found. Among the 250 to die was Marian Parkinson's husband. In his own terms, Zapp had scored a singular success.

As the shore lights continued to sparkle in the night sky despite the growing carnage, at sea the killing spree continued without pause or interruption. Yet, despite this massacre, the US authorities did nothing. Aghast at what he described as this 'reprehensible' failure to order a coastal blackout, the official US naval historian, who was himself a serving naval officer, explained, 'When this obvious defense measure was first proposed, squawks went up all the way from Atlantic City to southern Florida that "the tourist season would be ruined" . . . Ships were sunk and seamen drowned in order that the citizenry might enjoy business and pleasure as usual.'[14]

Dönitz was incredulous:

> The coast was not blacked-out, and the towns were a blaze of bright lights . . . Shipping followed the normal peace-time routes and carried the normal lights. There were, admittedly, anti-submarine patrols, but they were wholly lacking in experience. Single destroyers, for example, sailed up and down the traffic lanes with such regularity that the U-boats were quickly able to work out the time-table being followed. They knew exactly when the destroyers would return.[15]

To make matters even simpler for the U-boats, the merchant ships in their sights continued to use their radios as though this entailed no risk to their security. As a result, the German submarines were able to form a clear idea of the location, direction and destination of their slowly moving targets. 'It did not take the U-boats long to work out a very effective routine,' Dönitz wrote. 'By day they lay on the bottom at depths of anything from 150 to 450 feet and a few miles from the shipping routes. At dusk they approached the coast submerged and when darkness fell surfaced in the middle of the stream of shipping to deliver their attacks.'[16]

The pickings were so easy that Dönitz soon ordered all available U-boats to join Hardegen and Zapp. Yet again, though, he was frustrated by his own high command, which instructed him instead to divert eight U-boats to the north of Scotland and around the Faeroes to protect Norway, where Hitler had suddenly become agitated by the fear that Britain would launch another invasion. This was a false alarm. It is true that Churchill had briefly contemplated another such venture but this time he heeded the advice of his advisors that it would almost certainly end in yet another Norwegian fiasco. Although Dönitz argued strenuously against diverting the U-boats as the Führer had demanded, he failed to win the argument – a measure both of the Führer's inability to appreciate the critical nature of the Battle of the Atlantic and of Raeder's lack of clout within the German high command.

Thus, by the end of January, seven U-boats were on patrol off

Norway and three off the Straits of Gibraltar. To Dönitz's frustration, this left him with only six of the sixteen U-boats deployed in the Atlantic theatre available for what he regarded as 'the German Navy's most important task, the sinking of enemy shipping' off the coast of the United States; even so, he allowed that 'the successes achieved have been very gratifying'.[17] And so they must have been. Week by week the U-boats extended their area of operations until, by April 1942, they were sinking Allied shipping at random from the Panama Canal to Nova Scotia.

The forces ranged against this onslaught were pitiful. Initially, Admiral Adolphus Andrews, the US commander of the Eastern Sea Frontier (responsible therefore for the protection of almost 1,500 miles of coastline from Jacksonville, Florida, to the Canadian border), did not have a single warplane at his disposal, let alone any pilots who had been trained in anti-submarine warfare. The only aerial protection available to merchant shipping in these lanes was provided by nine short-range bombers, seconded from the US Army Air Forces (USAAF), which could only provide two daylight sweeps apiece every twenty hours. Although the total of naval and army planes available rose to 170 by April, they were notably unsuccessful, even embarrassingly so.

Experiencing their first taste of war, young pilots dropped depth charges in the ocean with enthusiastic abandon and claimed to have sunk U-boats with an intemperance to match. Before long, it would be noted later, 'the number of U-boats supposedly sunk in the ESF rivalled the amount in existence in Hitler's fleet worldwide'.[18] To sustain public morale against a stream of disaster stories in the press about the loss of merchant ships and their crews, the navy was prone to make much of these uncorroborated claims. Most notably, at the end of January, when a pilot named Donald Mason was reported to have signalled from the cockpit of his Lockheed Hudson bomber, 'Sighted sub; sank same', his laconic phrase made headlines across the nation. It emerged later, however, that the phrase was almost certainly concocted for him by the US Navy's public relations team.[19] More embarrassingly for Mason and the navy, it was also confirmed that, although he had indeed sighted a U-boat and released two bombs above it, he had missed his target: no U-boats were sunk that day. This did not prevent a memorable phrase seeping into the national psyche and, before the facts were known,

Mason was duly awarded a Distinguished Flying Cross for his 'achievement'. Such self-delusion was endemic. Despite repeated claims to the
contrary, not a single U-boat was sunk in the area until March, when
two were depth-charged off the coast of Newfoundland. One of the
pilots involved in this belated success was, as it happened, Donald
Mason, who was accorded the rare privilege of promotion from the
ranks to become a junior flying officer.

Even more disturbing than the absence of suitable aircraft and trained
pilots was the motley collection of warships available for the task of
defending America from the U-boat onslaught. Not only were these
similarly inadequate but they were also the beneficiaries of similarly
exaggerated claims made on their behalf. In this respect the navy secretary, Frank Knox – a former journalist and part-owner of the *Chicago
Tribune* – was a serial offender. Once, on a day when not a single U-boat
had been attacked with any degree of success, he allowed himself to
announce that 'three U-boats had been sunk and four heavily damaged'.
On 1 April he went so far as to report that no fewer than twenty-eight
U-boats had been sunk since the start of Operation Drumbeat. Whether
or not the nation was April fooled, the president knew better.

By late February Roosevelt had become so exasperated by the navy's
failure that, on the 26th, he despatched a memorandum to Knox castigating him for 'the inefficiency' of the department in failing to establish
the patrols required to confront the U-boat menace. 'When the submarine pack started to work on our own coast,' he wrote, 'I asked Betty
[Stark] for a report on a given hour on a given day on how many patrol
boats (as distinguished from destroyers) were at work between Eastport,
Maine and Key West.' Informed by Stark that a grand total of seven
ships were on patrol between the Canadian border and the southernmost tip of Florida, Roosevelt did not mince his words. 'This,' he
rebuked Knox, 'is a real disgrace.'[20]

If the statistics for February were bad, they were even worse for the
following month, when Roosevelt discovered that 'an all-time monthly
high record' of more than a million tons of shipping had been lost
and that, of the vessels sunk, '564,000 tons were cargo and 458,000 tons
were tankers'. The implications embedded in these figures were even
more alarming. According to the government official responsible for
collating this evidence for the president, the 'US, UK, and Canadian
construction of new ships aggregated 350,000 tons. Of this total, only

28,000 tons were tankers. This is equal to about 5% of the total tanker tonnage lost during the month.' He hardly had need to say more. At this rate of attrition, the Allies would soon lose the means to keep their economies alive, let alone to prosecute a world war. In his abrasive memorandum to Knox, Roosevelt had mentioned the fact that he had been relieved to learn that Rear Admiral Andrews had been put in over-all command of the patrols working on the eastern seaboard but did not refrain from fulminating, 'it has taken a hell of a long while to get it done. I first mentioned this just six weeks ago [mid-January]. Mean-while, the patrol of the Atlantic seaboard is totally insufficient. We cannot plead that we have not got the means, because we have got the means.'[21]

The president's rebuke sprang from a long-standing frustration at the navy's failure to convert private vessels for patrol work, despite his own prodding.

> For more than a year and a half, I have encouraged the buying of yachts . . .
> it has taken an unconscionable time to convert them . . . I have talked
> about the larger fishing boats but the Department did nothing about it.
> There are still several hundred fishing boats big enough to do patrol
> work except during very serious North Atlantic storms.[22]

In far more emollient terms he wrote to Andrews, a personal friend from the First World War, to proffer some presidential advice. Drawing on his own experience in the Navy Department as assistant secretary between 1913 and 1920, he wrote:

> I hope you will consider routing the coastwise shipping as close to shore
> as possible . . . Remember that from mid-April on you will get rela-
> tively good weather the whole length of the coast and in such weather
> smaller craft can operate on the average of 90% of the time . . . if I were
> in your place, I would buy (for junk prices) a lot of old ferry boats . . .
> Cut off their overhangs, build up a wooden bow, put a bulwark around
> the stern, take off the top hamper, and the silly looking things will be
> able to patrol . . . All it needs is one radio, one light gun and half a dozen
> depth charges.[23]

This DIY proposal did not find favour with the man who was responsible for the appointment of Andrews to his new command. Admiral Ernest King – who was himself about to be promoted from commander-in-chief, Atlantic Fleet, to the most senior rank in the navy as Chief of Naval Operations – was a formidable figure who inspired admiration, fear and hostility in equal measure. As a senior naval officer who had served with distinction in the First World War, he had garnered laurels and won respect. His natural authority and his sharp mind were widely envied but his arrogance had won him few friends and many foes. From those who had been on the receiving end of his foul temper (often induced by heavy drinking) he earned lasting enmity; his philandering, for which he was notorious, aroused similar emotions in those of his fellow officers who had thereby been cuckolded. Even that most tolerant of men, General Dwight Eisenhower, was among those of King's colleagues who found the admiral insufferable. On the day that he heard King was to be promoted by Roosevelt to succeed Stark as Chief of Naval Operations, he noted: 'One thing that might help win this war is to get someone to shoot King. He is the antithesis of cooperation, a deliberately rude person, which means he is a mental bully . . . but this fellow is going to blow up sooner or later, I'll bet a cookie.'[24]

Whatever his shortcomings of character, King was by no means immune to the scale of the crisis on the eastern seaboard, which he acknowledged to be 'desperate'.[25] Nonetheless, he was unwilling to acknowledge at any stage that he might have been in any way at fault for the unfolding debacle. Quick to disparage the president's belief that small vessels could be deployed in this manner as revealing an anachronistic 'predilection' that was 'something short of realistic in assessing the submarine menace',[26] he had no stopgap alternative to offer. The only realistic means of combating the U-boat menace that he could discern was 'to produce in quantity . . . a small destroyer of moderate speed, suitable for mass production'.[27] This was a succinct description of the role that had been played by the corvette, which had been in mass production in British and Canadian yards for over two years.

As no similar vessel was yet available in the US Navy, King had little option but to adopt Roosevelt's idiosyncratic prescription, despite his aversion to such a ramshackle notion; as he was later to concede, it was the only means at hand to combat 'the seriousness of the situation on the eastern seaboard'.[28] But it was not until a week or more after Roosevelt had pressed his old friend to seek out such craft that Andrews was formally instructed by King to scour the harbours for small craft under a hundred feet in length that were both 'capable of carrying depth charges and guns' and 'fit for sea patrol'.[29]

With the neon lights still blazing up and down the American coast-line and gas-guzzling automobiles still gliding blithely up and down its freeways, British officials did not trouble to disguise their anger at such official nonchalance. Writing from London to Hopkins in early March, Averell Harriman, the president's special envoy, sought to convey the scale of the growing frustration that he detected in the British capital. 'It was all very well when the British were suitors for our favor to expect them to make the biggest sacrifices while we were living off the fat of the land. Now they look on us as partners and when we ask them to make sacrifices they expect us to do the same.'[30]

When Roosevelt had told him three months earlier that the Japanese attack meant 'We are all in the same boat now', Churchill had gone to bed 'saturated and satiated with emotion', reflecting that he had slept the sleep 'of the saved and thankful'.[31] The whirl of events that followed left him elated. An initially reluctant Roosevelt had welcomed Churchill to the White House, where he embedded himself at the heart of the US admin-istration for the next three weeks. At the Arcadia Conference, as their Washington talks were codenamed, the prime minister set himself the central task of ensuring that Roosevelt still shared his view that 'the defeat of Japan would not spell the defeat of Hitler, but that the defeat of Hitler made the finishing off of Japan merely a matter of time and trouble'.[32]

In principle a commitment to this priority merely required the White House to reconfirm the Europe First strategy originally agreed in the ABC-1 talks two years earlier (see p. 134). But after Pearl Harbor, the world suddenly looked very different to the American people as, with anger and bewilderment, they watched the Japanese armies moving simultaneously against the Philippines, Guam and Midway. The polls were unequivocal: most of the electorate expected the president to reverse an order of priorities which had been established in secret when the United States was still a non-belligerent. By February, this attitude had hardened, one poll showing that, while only 25 per cent of the pub-lic thought the main focus should be on Germany, 62 per cent wanted their government to concentrate on the defeat of Japan.[33]

On this occasion, though, Roosevelt overrode popular opinion and held fast to the view that the destruction of Nazism should precede the defeat of Japan. To this end, even though it would prevent the United

States from launching an early offensive in the Pacific, it became even more essential, as a co-belligerent of Britain, to sustain the Atlantic lifeline. From the prime minister's perspective Arcadia (which lasted from 22 December 1941 to 14 January 1942) was an unalloyed triumph. Without Roosevelt's unshakeable belief that the destruction of the Third Reich should precede the defeat of Japanese imperialism and his courage in gainsaying public opinion, the decision would undoubtedly have gone the opposite way.

Yet, the will towards the means did not match the will towards the end, and by this time any euphoria the prime minister had experienced in the heady days after Japan's attack rapidly evaporated. Before his departure for London, Churchill was buttonholed by Sir Arthur Salter, whom he had sent to Washington a year earlier to compete on Britain's behalf for the shipping required to sustain a regular flow of transatlantic supplies. When Salter advised him that, following Pearl Harbor, he had started to face 'very great' difficulties in dealing with his American counterparts, Churchill asked him for a written report. Salter obliged at once. In reaction to the Japanese assault, he explained, the US forces had started to commandeer shipping that had been earmarked for Britain. As a result, he warned, the 'UK importing service is itself now in a very serious condition': at the present rate, the flow of goods to Britain (excluding oil) would fall from 'the 33 million [tons] which you instructed me to press for only a few weeks ago' to 23 million.[34] Churchill was aghast. Circling these two salient figures in Salter's report, he sent a note to Hopkins on 10 January. 'The statements marked by me in red would, if true, be catastrophic,' he wrote, urging – as Salter had advised – that the administration should set up a 'Joint Consultative Board so that your people can hear what we have to say before taking decisions on allocation'.[35]

This was far easier said than done. A hornets' nest of competing civilian and military agencies was already stirring over what was needed and by whom. The 'expanding demands, mistrust, confusion and rivalry'[36] were exacerbated by toxic levels of animosity within some parts of the US administration towards what they regarded as Salter's 'relentless' entreaties which 'polluted . . . the springs of cooperative effort . . . from the beginning'.[37] Despite the British envoy's ability to form tactical alliances with some key American officials, he had so far found it quite impossible to fulfil Churchill's directive to him.

The prime minister was also astonished to discover that the United States had failed to make any preparations to meet the threat of a direct attack on the American homeland; an insouciance which had allowed the U-boats to prowl US waters with what he was to describe as 'a freedom and insolence which were hard to bear'.[38] In early February he sent a private warning to Hopkins, in terms which did little to disguise the depth of his anxiety. 'It might be well to make sure the president's attention has been drawn to the very heavy sinkings,' he urged, following up soon afterwards with a formal offer to send twenty-four armed trawlers and ten corvettes to the rescue, noting, 'It was little enough, but the utmost we could spare.'[39] Although Churchill's offer was gratefully received and the vessels were despatched in time to arrive in early March, the U-boat slaughter did not abate.

By now thoroughly alarmed, Churchill wrote once again to Hopkins on 12 March in terms which guaranteed that his cable would land swiftly on Roosevelt's desk. 'I am most deeply concerned at the immense sinking of tankers . . . in a little over two months, in these [US] waters alone, about sixty tankers had been sunk or damaged.' Insisting that the situation was 'so serious that drastic action of some kind is necessary', he demanded that the crisis should be addressed 'at the highest level'.[40] Roosevelt summoned King to the White House for an explanation. The admiral, who was invariably dismissive of any criticism directed at him, was not to be browbeaten even by his commander-in-chief. Instead he chose to counter-attack, complaining that America's predicament had been brought about in large measure by the RAF's failure to bomb the U-boat pens in the Bay of Biscay. King's imprint was clearly stamped on the president's subsequent reply to Churchill. Using language so uncharacteristically stiff and formal that the prime minister detected 'a touch of strain' in it, Roosevelt wrote, 'Your interest in steps to be taken to combat the Atlantic submarine menace as indicated by your recent message to Mr Hopkins on this subject impels me to request your particular consideration of heavy attacks on submarine bases and building and repair yards, thus checking the submarine activities at their source and where submarines perforce congregate.'[41]

Had this implied rebuke been delivered a year earlier, the arrow would have been well aimed. Bomber Command's failure to bomb the U-boat pens when they were still in the early and vulnerable stage of construction had allowed the German engineers to complete their task without interruption. By the spring of 1942 they were impenetrable. Nonetheless, Churchill evidently felt obliged to reassure the president. 'In order to cope with future U-boat hatchings, we are emphasizing attacks on U-boat nests, and last night went to Lübeck with 250 bombers . . . Results are said to be the best ever. This is in accordance with your wishes.' The use of incendiary bombs in the raid on the old Hanseatic port destroyed or damaged more than 12,000 buildings and left 25,000 citizens homeless while many ancient buildings were engulfed by fire. Yet, the economic life of the city was rapidly restored and no U-boat facility was reported to have been damaged.

To mollify the president further, Churchill also informed him that the Admiralty and the RAF between them had 'evolved a plan' for day and night patrols in the Bay of Biscay and that the Admiralty was 'pressing to allocate four and later on six bomber squadrons to this new Biscay patrol'. He also reminded Roosevelt that 'the need to bomb Germany [was] very great . . . I find it very hard to take away these extra six squadrons from Bomber Command, in which Harris [Arthur Harris, the newly appointed commander-in-chief of Bomber Command] is doing so well.'[42] This aside was an oblique reference to the bitter rivalry that was about to erupt into all-out battle between the Admiralty and the Air Ministry over the allocation of bombers. Churchill's letter may have soothed the presidential brow; it did nothing to relieve his own deepening concern.

By April, nerves in London were fraying fast. On the 13th, the First Lord of the Admiralty, A. V. Alexander, wrote a note to Churchill, reminding him that the 'increasing losses on the USA coast and in the Caribbean' since the start of the month had been 'frightful'.[43] By mid-April the threat to Britain's oil supplies appeared to be so critical that the Minister of War Transport, the Conservative peer Fred Leathers, wrote to Hopkins expressing the 'grave anxiety [that] is felt in London' about the loss since the start of the year of 'over one million tons deadweight of Allied tanker tonnage . . . sunk or seriously damaged on the American Coast and in the Caribbean'.[44]

These figures served merely to rub salt in ever deepening White House wounds. At the present rate, as both Roosevelt and Hopkins had been advised, the United States would lose 'close to 10 million tons' of merchant shipping.[45] Already a handful of U-boats had destroyed 45 per cent of the shipping volume required to sustain the flow of oil to meet demand within the United States and Britain. On whichever side of the Atlantic they were read, these statistics were horrifying.

Masterminding this rampage from Kerneval, Dönitz found it quite as astonishing as Churchill that Drumbeat was proving so much more successful than he had dared even to imagine. On 15 April he noted:

> By attacking the supply traffic – particularly the oil – in the US zone, I am striking at the root of the evil, for here the sinking of each ship is not only a loss to the enemy but also deals a blow at the source of his ship-building and war production . . . I consider that we should continue to operate the U-boats where they can sink the greatest tonnage with the smallest losses, which is at present in American waters.[46]

Hitler was similarly taken aback by what a small number of U-boats was able to achieve. It must have been especially galling for the Admiralty to read a Bletchley Park decrypt of a conversation in which the Führer apparently told the Japanese ambassador in Berlin how he was 'surprised at the successes we have met with along the American coast lately. The United States kept up the tall talk and left her coast unguarded. Now I daresay she is quite surprised.'[47]

To the infuriated bemusement of the British, the American authorities remained extraordinarily reluctant to order a blackout along the American coastline. Although, in mid-February, the president had belatedly authorized the armed services to do whatsoever might be required 'to prevent the silhouetting of ships and their consequent destruction by enemy submarines',[48] it was not until 9 March that King finally instructed Adolphus Andrews to take the action required to achieve this modest objective by taking 'such steps as may within his province to control the brilliant illumination of Eastern Seaboard amusement parks and beaches'.[49] Five days later, King made it clear that even this 'request' did not require a total blackout; it would suffice merely to dim the offending lights.

The consequences of King's failure to go further than that were swiftly apparent. In the early hours of 14 March U-404 detected the silhouette of a freighter against the lights of Atlantic City and fired three torpedoes into the side of the SS *Lemuel Burrows*. Captain Grover Clark was in his cabin when the first torpedo struck. The force of the explosion threw him out of his chair. When he recovered his wits, he

16. (*top*) Survivors from the SS *Athenia*, sunk by U-30 on the first day of the war, 3 September 1939.

17. (*bottom*) The German pocket battleship *Admiral Graf Spee* sinks in the River Plate, Montevideo, Uruguay, after being scuttled by her crew in December 1939. The ship had been sent to the South Atlantic tasked to effect 'the disruption and destruction of all enemy shipping by all possible means'.

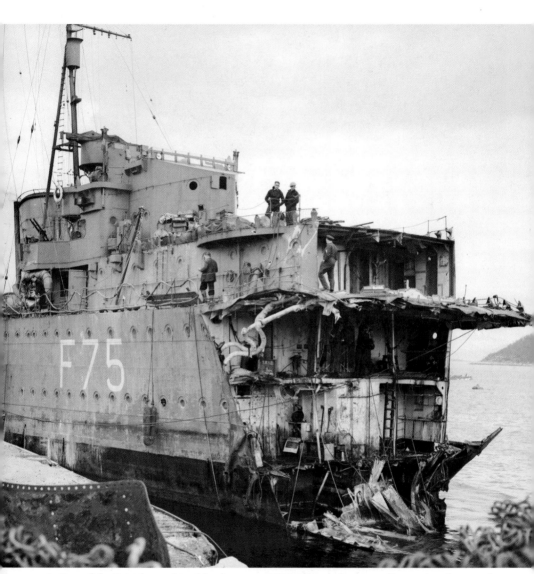

18. One of the British warships (the destroyer HMS *Eskimo*) that were damaged or destroyed during the Battle of Narvik, May 1940. The Norwegian campaign, initiated by Churchill as First Lord of the Admiralty, became a fiasco from which he emerged as prime minister.

19. (*above*) The German battleship *Bismarck*, sunk by the Royal Navy on 27 May 1941. Photograph taken from the deck of the *Prinz Eugen*.

20. (*left*) Survivors from the *Bismarck* are pulled aboard HMS *Dorsetshire*.

21. (*above*) Teams drawn principally from the ranks of the WRAF and the WRNS worked in shifts around the clock at Derby House, charting the shifting positions of the Atlantic adversaries.

22. (*right*) A U-boat entering one of the bomb-proof pens in the French port of Lorient, where Dönitz made his headquarters. The seizure of the Biscay ports in June 1940 transformed the Battle of the Atlantic to Hitler's immediate advantage.

23. (*top*) Survivors of the SS *City of Benares*, a passenger ship which was sunk by a German U-boat while en route to Canada in September 1940. The U-boat's third torpedo – the first two had missed – struck the hull amidships, passing just below the cabins where evacuee children were sleeping. Of the ninety children on board, only thirteen – six of them in Lifeboat No. 12 – returned alive.

24. (*bottom*) British housewives wait to buy eggs in 1940. Journalist Maggie Joy Blunt noted, 'Housewives are having to queue for essential foods ... Prices are rising ... The outlook really seems very grim indeed.'

25. (*right*) Officers on the bridge of a British warship escorting an Atlantic convoy in 1941. The U-boat menace was exacerbated by a shortage of suitable escorts, aircraft carriers and long-range bombers.

26. The torpedo room of a German U-boat. When Otto Kretschmer, commanding U-23, torpedoed the *Danmark* at Orkney, his watch officer recalled the reaction of its victims: 'The English didn't believe we could be so close by in the anchorage, and when the torpedo exploded they searched the sky with lights because they thought we were the Luftwaffe'.

27. A German U-boat crew at rest. They were tested to the limit. Of the 38,000 young men who served in the U-boat fleet, some 30,000 were killed in action.

28. (*top*) A Hedgehog anti-submarine mortar mounted on the bow of a destroyer (HMS *Westcott*). The Hedgehog could spray a volley of mortar rounds at a retreating U-boat that were primed to explode on contact (rather than being timed or fused like a depth charge).

29. (*bottom*) PQ17 in Hvalfjord, Iceland, June 1942, about to enter the annals of naval history as a maritime disaster that Churchill would describe as 'one of the most melancholy naval episodes in the whole of the war'. Only eleven of the thirty-three ships in this Arctic convoy reached their destination.

ran on deck and gave the order to abandon ship. The second torpedo hit amidships and, Clark recounted, the explosion 'blew my shoes off my feet and left me standing in my stocking feet'.[50] Although the starboard lifeboat had been smashed, twenty-six members of the crew had managed to get away in the port lifeboat, which was overturned almost at once by the size of the backwash from the explosion. As the men scrambled for a handhold on the upturned boat, Clark and seven other members of the crew released two life rafts and hurled them into the sea before jumping overboard themselves and swimming to clamber aboard them. At this point, U-404 drew alongside. Her captain, Otto von Bülow, demanded to know the name of the stricken vessel. When Clark refused to tell him, the U-boat withdrew and fired a third torpedo into *Lemuel Burrows*'s hull, which sent her to the bottom.

The men clinging to the upturned lifeboat soon succumbed to the hypothermic temperature of the surrounding air and, one by one, they began to slip silently into the water before, seven hours later, the survivors were rescued by a passing steamship. Clark's raft was also found and the men on board were rescued; the other was also found but with only one man aboard. Altogether fourteen members of *Lemuel Burrows*'s crew survived. Of the twenty who perished, three were later found floating in an oil slick, one was washed up on a beach, and a third corpse was found trapped under the upturned hull of the port lifeboat. None of the other bodies were recovered.

In the weeks that followed it was repeatedly pointed out by senior military officials that it was not enough merely to dim the shore lights; that the silhouettes of coast-hugging ships could still be detected from ten miles out to sea. Yet no blackout order was made until 18 April, and even then it applied only to waterfront lights and illuminations. Even in May, when army studies concluded that the night sky was still so clearly illuminated from the shore that 'like targets in a shooting gallery our ships are moving off in a backdrop of hazy light',[51] the authorities still shrank from imposing a general blackout. Finally on 18 May, the Eastern Defense Command of the US Army ordered 'a stringent dimout'.[52] And this was as far as the authorities or the American public, 'which wanted business and pleasure as usual',[53] were prepared to go. It was not enough.

On 4 May, almost five months after Hitler's declaration of war on America and four months on from the start of Drumbeat, U-333 arrived off the Florida coast. With withering clarity, the submarine's commander, Peter Cremer, described the contrast between the Europe he had left with what he now witnessed in the United States.

> Whether in Stettin, Berlin, Paris, Hamburg, Lorient or La Rochelle – everywhere had been pitch dark. At sea we tried not to show any light, even hiding the glowing cigarette in the hollow of the hand when smoking was allowed on the bridge. Not a ray of light came through the conning tower hatch. Yet here the buoys were blinking as normal, the famous lighthouse at Jupiter Inlet was sweeping its luminous cone far over the sea. We were cruising off a coastal road with darting headlights from innumerable cars. We were in so close that through the night glasses we could distinguish equally the big hotels and the cheap dives, and read the flickering neon signs . . . Before this sea of light, against this footlight glare of a carefree new world, we were passing the silhouettes of ships recognizable in every detail and sharp as the outlines in a sale catalogue. Here they were formally presented to us on a plate: please help yourselves![54]

Two days after his arrival off Florida, Cremer sank two tankers and a freighter. Within the next few days, three of his fellow U-boat commanders – 'Teddy' Suhren, Harro Schacht and Heinrich Bleichrodt – had sunk a further fourteen ships, including a Dutch freighter, off Cape Canaveral, in which seventeen crewmen perished. Such human tragedies were played out up and down the coast day after day. However, being minor in themselves when weighed in the scales of a global war, such losses were easily overlooked and rapidly forgotten except by those who grieved for the loved ones they had lost. By the end of May, though, the material impact of these killing sprees – the loss of approaching 400 merchant ships and their cargoes – was impossible to ignore any longer.

On 24 June Roosevelt returned to the fray with further sound counsel for his naval commanders. When Andrews wrote to him in dismay about some scurrilous gossip concerning the allegedly high life he was leading in such low times, the president was solicitous, but not to a fault:

> with the continued sinkings off the coast you are inevitably going to be criticized, as the whole Navy is being criticized . . . unfortunately the

Navy's publicity for the last four or five months has been none too good, for it has promised that the situation would get better within a few weeks and the promise has not been fulfilled . . .

Reminding Andrews that over a year earlier he, Roosevelt, had urged that ships large and small should be commandeered to cover the entire seaboard only to be thwarted by his own subordinates, he complained again about the purblind vision and lethargy of the Navy Department. Those responsible

> could not see anything less than 100 feet in length, and even after December Seventh [the date of Pearl Harbor] they moved as slowly as cold molasses in getting additional vessels. I am willing to bet that there are still 1000 vessels on this coast and on the Great Lakes which could have been picked up and put to work . . . It is the tendency of the Navy to seek perfection. The Navy is not good at improvising.

Reiterating that such small ships need only be armed with light weapons to be effective, Roosevelt added crucially that 'the whole purpose is to keep the submarine down day and night'.[55]

In alighting on this point, he had acutely identified an Achilles heel by which the high commands of both the British and US navies had long been crippled. Although commanders at sea had been swift to realize that even small ships could deter a torpedo strike when working in combination with aircraft patrols, their superiors were imprisoned by a traditional mindset which prioritized offence over defence. For these men, it was exceptionally hard either to reconcile their preconceptions with Roosevelt's insight or to appreciate that the mere presence of a small ship posed an existential threat to thin-skinned submarines.

King was never able to surrender his belief that 'small patrol craft' were 'inadequate for antisubmarine work'.[56] Nonetheless, a few days before Roosevelt's 'cold molasses' critique of the Navy Department, he was driven to order that

> there be acquired the maximum number of civilian craft that are in any way capable of going to sea in good weather for a period of at least forty-eight hours at cruising speeds . . . They will be fitted to carry at least four 300-pound depth charges and be armed with at least one machine gun, preferably 50 calibre; and will be equipped with a radio set, preferably voice.[57]

Those words could easily have been written by the president himself, so closely did they mirror his instructions to Andrews more than three months earlier – though King would never bring himself to admit any error of foresight or judgement on this or any other matter. Although the number of new vessels thus press-ganged to the cause would eventually number more than 1,700, the admiral's belated conversion – five months after the start of Operation Drumbeat – was a climbdown which came too late to save an untold number of ships and lives.

Far more important even than this or his refusal to impose a total blackout was King's parallel failure to insist that all merchant ships should travel in convoy. By June, General Marshall, in his role as army chief of staff, was so alarmed by the mounting losses that he challenged King openly in a formal letter. Writing on 19 June, his warning was apocalyptic: 'The losses by submarines off our Atlantic seaboard and in the Caribbean now threaten our entire war effort.' Acknowledging an acute shortage of suitable escort vessels, he questioned whether 'every conceivable improvised means' had been 'brought to bear on this situation'.[58] King's response, two days later, was icy:

> I have long been aware, of course, of the implications of the submarine situation as pointed out in your memorandum . . . I have employed – and will continue to employ – not only regular forces but also such improvised means as to give promise of usefulness. However, it is obvious that the German effort is expanding more rapidly than our defense.

Reiterating his criticism of the British for failing to bombard the U-boat bases and construction, he claimed to have been as committed to the convoy system, supported by escorts and aircraft, as anyone else.[59]

In an individual of less substance than King, this comment might have been dismissed as mere chutzpah, but in his case this was not so much audacity as arrogance. It is true that, at his direction, a rudimentary convoy system had been introduced along various parts of the American coastline in May, but the proportion of ships thus protected had been small and haphazardly organized. Nonetheless, King would brook no criticism – even when, a little over two weeks after Marshall's complaint, the president was even more specific. In a memorandum for the Chief of Naval Operations, he pointed out that on the Atlantic coast between 17 May and 27 June, when thirty-three merchant ships 'sailing independently' had been sunk by U-boats, 'only four were lost under convoy'; similarly, that in the Gulf of Mexico thirteen ships 'sailing independently were lost and only one under escort'; and that in the Caribbean sixty-nine ships 'sailing independently were lost and ten under escort'. Buttressed by these unassailable statistics, he gave vent to his profound dissatisfaction, insisting, 'We must speed things up and we must use the available tools even though they are not just what we would like to have.'[60]

In his reply, King sought to exculpate himself by insisting that by the middle of May he had already 'established convoy systems, beginning with the most dangerous, as acquisition of escort vessels permitted', adding, however, that while these 'were a step in the right direction', their escorts were 'unduly weak, consisting of a too large proportion of small craft with little fighting power'. Nonetheless, 'My goal – and I believe yours also – is to get every ship under escort. For this purpose we (the United States and Great Britain) need a very large number – roughly 1000 – sea-going escort vessels of DE [Destroyer Escort] or corvette type. I am doing my best to get them quickly.'[61]

It was true that King could claim that at no stage had he expressed any opposition to the principle of convoying merchant ships. As he was to make clear after the war, he had been among those senior staff officers who, in 1940, had been advocating the construction of suitable escort vessels. Not content to defend himself by referring back to this fact, he used his autobiography to turn the blame back on the president, accusing him of acquiescing in the need for such craft 'reluctantly and belatedly' and attributing this to the president's 'faith in the efficacy [of] small patrol craft [that were] unsuitable for antisubmarine work'.[62] This was unjust: no naval historian has since unearthed any files to suggest that Roosevelt ever opposed the construction of escort destroyers. The president had merely argued that smaller craft could, if necessary, be used to good effect along much of the coastline for much of the year, which was precisely the view to which King had been such a late convert. This was a grave error of judgement which led to the unnecessary loss of many lives and much cargo; it was not until almost five months from the beginning of the slaughter along the eastern seaboard, in June, that he finally succumbed and authorized the establishment of what almost immediately proved to be a remarkably effective network of convoys.

In his twin roles as commander-in-chief of the US Navy and Chief of Naval Operations, between the spring of 1942 and 1945, King made a major contribution to the eventual outcome of the Second World War. Even in those troubled Drumbeat months of 1942 he oversaw the resurrection of the US Pacific Fleet and victories over the Japanese Imperial Navy in two major battles (the Coral Sea in May and Midway in June). These successes not only altered the balance of power in the Pacific to the strategic advantage of the Allies but greatly boosted American morale after the humiliation of Pearl Harbor. However, this does not nullify his failure to respond swiftly or adequately to the challenge of Operation Drumbeat, a cardinal error of judgement and leadership from which only his most indulgent supporters have since sought to exonerate him.[63] Without mentioning King by name, the verdict of the US Navy's official historian, Samuel Eliot Morison, was measured but damning:

> This writer cannot avoid the conclusion that the United States Navy was woefully unprepared, materially and mentally, for the U-boat blitz on the Atlantic Coast that began in January 1942 . . . this unpreparedness was largely the Navy's own fault. Blame cannot justly be imputed to Congress . . . nor to the people at large . . . Nor can it be shifted to President Roosevelt . . . In the end the Navy met the challenge, came through magnificently and won; but this does not alter the fact that it had no plans for a reasonable protection to shipping when the submarines struck, and was unable to improvise them for several months.[64]

As Roosevelt had noted so presciently and acerbically, the evidence in favour of even weakly escorted convoys was compelling. By July, with more and more merchant ships travelling in convoy and the total number of sinkings on the eastern seaboard falling to three, it was conclusive. Realizing that the U-boat killing spree was over, Dönitz withdrew his fleet from the coast of America and despatched it once more to the North Atlantic. The 'Second Happy Time', as it had been dubbed by the U-boat commanders, had run its dreadful course. For the loss of twenty-two of their own submarines, they had sunk upwards of 400 merchant ships in which some 5,000 individuals – servicemen, merchant sailors and civilian passengers, women and children among them – had perished. By any reasonable measure, this was an avoidable tragedy.

Nor was it over yet. On 15 July Joseph Lubin, a senior official charged with collating the relevant figures, presented a memorandum to the president, informing him that, in the week ending 12 July, 'something in excess of half a million tons of shipping' had been lost. 'This is the highest loss for any week on record,' Lubin noted. Ominously, though, not all of these vessels had been sunk off the coast of America. 'Twenty-two of the ships lost during the week,' Lubin added, 'were on the Murmansk–Archangel run.'[65] So far from being over, the focus of the Battle of the Atlantic was merely shifting to other locations. The challenge to the Allies was more daunting than ever.

## 13.   Overstretched Everywhere

Churchill now found himself under intense political and diplomatic pressure. The experience – like the cause – was no less disagreeable for being familiar: the Royal Navy was once again being required to do too much with too little. Already overstretched by its commitments in the Indian Ocean, the Atlantic, the Mediterranean and the Arctic, the Admiralty was confronted by a crunch of simultaneous demands as London, Washington and Moscow vied for the resources needed to sustain a coherent strategy against the Third Reich. A reckoning was inevitable.

The prime minister had spent the last two weeks of June 1942 in Washington seeking to dissuade the Americans from opening a Second Front against Germany with a cross-Channel invasion of France later in the year, warning: 'No responsible British military authority has so far been able to make a plan for September 1942 which had any chance of success unless the Germans become utterly demoralized, of which there is no likelihood.'[1] As an alternative, he had advocated an Anglo-American landing (to be codenamed Gymnast) in Axis-occupied North Africa. This, he suggested, should become the launch pad for an invasion of Italy, which he was later to (mis)describe as 'the soft underbelly of the Axis'. Roosevelt's most senior advisors were deeply averse to the British proposal. When Marshall argued that 'the decisive theater is Western Europe. That is the only place where the concerted effort of our own and the British forces can be brought to bear on the Germans',[2] Churchill and his advisors, led by Brooke, held their ground. The choice between opening what Churchill would call, with breathtaking nerve, the 'true Second Front' in North Africa or the Second Front in Europe had become the most divisive issue facing the transatlantic alliance and the role of sea power was at the very heart of it.

This stand-off between the British and American negotiators was still unresolved when, on 21 June, reports reached the White House from the Middle East that the British garrison in Tobruk – a litmus test for Churchill of triumph or disaster in the struggle in the Western Desert – had fallen to Rommel's forces. Moreover, more than 30,000

British Commonwealth troops had lain down their arms virtually without a fight. The prime minister was in the Oval Office when he was given the news. According to those who were there, he blanched visibly. 'Defeat is one thing, disgrace is another,' he was to reflect many years later.[3] Nonetheless, he was comforted by Roosevelt's immediate response, which was to offer not merely sympathy but also material support. A few days later this was translated into a formal undertaking to deliver 300 new Sherman tanks for the desert front line. Crucial as this gesture turned out to be four months later, it was too late to arrest the next stage of Rommel's North African blitzkrieg, which by late June seemed to promise disaster of far greater import than the loss of an iconic outpost on the edge of the Mediterranean.[4]

Not pausing to savour Hitler's announcement that he was to be promoted to the rank of field marshal on account of his triumph at Tobruk, Rommel pressed on towards the Egyptian border, which he crossed on 23 June, whereupon he was authorized by the Führer to make an immediate thrust for the Nile Delta. Alexandria, Britain's naval headquarters in the eastern Mediterranean, was less than 300 miles away, Cairo only 120 miles further on, and Suez no more than eighty miles beyond that. If Rommel were to reach the Suez Canal – which, following the pell-mell retreat of the Eighth Army before his panzers, seemed quite possible – the entire Nile Delta would be in his hands. Not only would the Axis powers be masters of the Middle East but Churchill's imperial strategy would be in tatters.

To avoid this prospect, it had long been a British imperative to prevent Malta falling into Axis hands. For several months the island had been blockaded so effectively by the two Axis powers that between January and April not one British convoy had managed to reach Valletta with the supplies on which both the military and civil population relied. By the spring of 1942 the shortages had become so acute that civilian families had run out of kerosene for cooking and were driven to queue for hours at a time for a meagre ladle of thin stew. On 20 April the island's governor, General William Dobbie, had cabled London in despair to report that 'it is obvious that the very worst may happen if we cannot replenish our vital needs, especially flour and ammunition . . . it is a question of survival'.[5]

Despite the heroic efforts of a handful of RAF Spitfires, Malta was also subjected to a non-stop bombardment by wave upon wave of Axis aircraft. This onslaught rivalled in intensity the worst of the Blitz: in a six-week campaign during March and April, German and Italian planes dropped some 6,500 bombs on the island, almost half of which fell on the capital, killing many hundreds of civilians and destroying or damaging several thousand buildings. The Royal Navy was forced to flee the ruined port for the comparative safety of Alexandria while the RAF was reduced to a handful of serviceable aircraft.

As a result it had become virtually impossible to interdict, let alone to sever, the Axis supply lines between Italy and North Africa which fed, fuelled and armed Rommel's forces in the Western Desert. In February and March, more than 90 per cent of the goods and weapons despatched from Italy to North Africa reached their destination. In April not one Italian vessel was lost. By the early summer, Rommel's forces were so well provisioned that the Desert Fox was confident that his panzers would indeed seize Egypt, throttling Britain's direct connection with the rest of the Empire and thereby realizing Churchill's worst nightmares. To avert this, it would be essential to break the blockade and resupply Malta. To lose the British fortress would not merely be another humiliating setback, but, as Churchill reminded General Auchinleck, his Middle East commander-in-chief, its capture 'would give the enemy a clear and sure bridge to Africa, with all the consequences flowing from that'.[6] But every attempt to break the Axis blockade faltered or failed under the scale and ferocity of the enemy's assault on the British convoys running the gauntlet of the 1,000-mile maritime corridor from Gibraltar to the harbour at Valletta. With more than 450 aircraft based in the Mediterranean, the Axis prevailed time and again. By August, the British fortress was nearing the point of collapse. Churchill decided on drastic action.

On 9 August thirteen ships carrying a total of 30,000 tons of food and other supplies and – critically – a tanker, the *Ohio*, carrying enough petrol, kerosene and fuel oil to last ten weeks, steamed out of Gibraltar for the six-day voyage to replenish the British garrison. Escorted by two battleships, four aircraft carriers, three cruisers and twenty-six destroyers, the convoy steamed in four columns at a speed of fifteen knots. To no one's surprise, they very soon came under ferocious assault from the air and the sea. This attack signalled the start of a bombardment which was the heaviest and most concentrated against any convoy in the entire war – confirmation that the strangulation of Malta now mattered as much to the Axis as its survival did to the Allies.

Junkers 88s and Stukas attacked in waves of up to a hundred at a time, undaunted by the carrier-based fighters that hounded them from above for as long as they had the fuel to fly. On board the escort destroyer HMS *Ledbury* the captain, Lieutenant Commander Roger Hill, tuned his radio to hear British pilots as they yelled at their controllers in the aircraft carriers 'I've got no petrol' before landing with empty tanks. One or two pilots left it too late and burst into flames as they hit the deck. 'As the planes crashed,' Hill noted, 'they were just thrown over the side to keep the carriers clear.' No quarter was given on either side. When a parachute floated down and became snared on the edge of his ship, Hill presumed at first it was a British pilot whom he knew had just been shot down. 'I rushed over to pick him up. I hung over the side and said to my first lieutenant, "What is he, Jimmy?" and he said, "A fucking Hun, Sir. Three more parachutes coming down to starboard." "Let them go to hell," I replied.'[7]

On board the SS *Waimarama*, 'Freddy' Treves, a midshipman in the Royal Navy, found himself in the firing line when a German bomber scored a direct hit on his own ship. Treves was below at the time but rushed up on deck. 'There was black smoke everywhere, flames were burning aft of the bridge and the deck was slanting to starboard, so I thought, "Well, I'm a terrible coward, but I think I'd better go."' A poor swimmer, he nonetheless leapt into the water which had become a sea of debris and screaming people:

I saw my friend and mentor, Bowdrey. He was standing on a raft, his arms were outstretched and he was screaming for help, he couldn't swim. It was a picture I'll never be able to forget. He was drifting back into the flames on this raft. I started out towards him, but realized he was very near the flames and the raft would be too heavy to stop. So I turned and swam away. This has haunted me all my life. I was a coward.

John Jackson recalled the same incident but from a tellingly different perspective. The *Waimarama*'s junior radio officer was floundering in the water when Treves swam up to him and said, 'Jacko, lie on your back and don't move; I'm going to tow you away.' Jackson did as he was told:

I told myself, 'Don't struggle, Jackson, this guy's going to tow you away.' And so he did. He got me by the arms and pulled me, very slowly, away

from the flames . . . Then a whacking great spar of wood came alongside
and he said, 'Can you grab that spar?' and I did and I heaved myself onto
it . . . There was no question, he was a very brave lad.[8]

Jackson was fortunate: eighty of his shipmates were either drowned
or incinerated.

The most valuable target in the convoy – the *Ohio*, carrying 10,000
tons of fuel oil – was subjected to the most unrelenting bombardment of
all, some of which was suicidal. In the early hours of 13 August, two
Axis bombers crash-landed on her decks within minutes of each other.
Soon afterwards a bomb fell so close to the tanker's bows that two of her
forward tanks were split open, allowing water to gush into the fore-
peak. The next day another bomb carried away the tanker's rudder and
the engine room started to fill with water. It now seemed inevitable that
the ship, which was settling deeper and deeper by the stern, would soon
buckle under the strain. Yet her captain, Dudley Mason, remained calm
and, by a feat of practical seamanship for which there was no known
rulebook, the most important vessel in the convoy was finally shepherded into the Grand Harbour at Valletta on 15 August, still cradled
between the two British warships and co-steered by a huddle of local
tugs. The *Ledbury*'s captain had cause to rejoice: 'It was the most wonderful moment of my life. The battlements of Malta were black with
thousands of people, all cheering and shouting, and there were bands
playing everywhere. It was the most amazing sight to see all these
people who had suffered so much, cheering us.'[9]

Operation Pedestal, which Churchill had personally instigated, was a
triumph of resolve and ingenuity. The arrival of the *Ohio* not only
saved Malta but helped to secure the first significant British military
victory of the war. The Royal Navy, well supported by its own submarines as well as the surface fleet, and the RAF between them once again
seized the initiative in the Mediterranean with consequences that would
very soon alarm Rommel. By the end of August, only a third of supplies the Desert Fox required to sustain his offensive against Egypt
would reach their destination; by September, his Panzerarmee Afrika
would be low on ammunition and running out of fuel; and by October,
the British would have established such a stranglehold over the sea
routes from Italy to Tripoli and Benghazi that the Axis armies in the
Western Desert were doomed: the way would be clear for the British

Eighth Army to defeat Rommel at the final Battle of El Alamein in November 1942.*

However, the price exacted by the Luftwaffe for the liberation of Malta was substantial: of the fourteen merchant ships which had left Gibraltar only five reached their destination while the Royal Navy lost an aircraft carrier, two cruisers and a destroyer. Nor did Pedestal resolve the essential dilemma facing London and Washington: how could the two allies conduct a global maritime war without the means available to prevail on every front at once? Indeed, the promise of victory that now beckoned in North Africa served merely to bring this strategic challenge into even sharper focus.

In Washington, Churchill and the chairman of the chiefs of staff, Field Marshal Alan Brooke, had continued to argue for a joint Anglo-US invasion of North Africa without ruling out an early cross-Channel invasion of France. In the words of the prime minister's ever-astute aide, Colonel Ian Jacob, 'Our idea was to get them onto our side of the Atlantic so that they would be committed for the war against Germany [rather than Japan], and we hoped that if we had the forces in England we could persuade Roosevelt to use them in Africa.'[10] This manoeuvre required a degree of constructive ambiguity that Machiavelli would have admired. But, while it brought a temporary respite from one problem, it served merely to highlight another. As US Secretary for War, Harold Stimson, complained, it would not be possible to launch a cross-Channel invasion of France if American warships were 'tied up with an expedition to Gymnast'.[11] And this was to reckon without the Soviet Union.

In the summer of 1942 military analysts in both Washington and London were still seized of the nightmare thought that the Soviet Union might succumb to the Wehrmacht's onslaught and that Stalin would sue for peace to avoid the annihilation of the Motherland. Not only was Russia hungry for weapons but some parts of the country were also

---

* In August, Churchill sacked Auchinleck, who had served as commander-in-chief both of Middle East Command and, latterly, of the Eighth Army, and held the line at El Alamein. In his stead, the prime minister appointed General Sir Harold Alexander to oversee the Middle East; under him, Bernard Montgomery was placed in command of the Eighth Army.

desperately short of food. The Arctic port of Murmansk was under constant bombardment from Luftwaffe bomber squadrons based in Norway, which rained down destruction on a scale only otherwise endured by the citizens of Leningrad and Stalingrad. 'We had anti-aircraft guns but the Germans started to fly in very low and our guns could not target them without hitting our own people,' one Russian veteran recalled. 'So they just bombed and bombed. Nothing was left of Lenin Street except broken chimneys.' The city ran so short of food that the bread allowance was reduced to 200 grams for children and 300 grams for adults. 'It was not enough, of course, so parents would cheat – faking ration cards, doing anything to feed their children.' As the months went by, the rations had been further reduced: 'We ate berries and people boiled their boots and removed the bark from birch trees to eat the green sap beneath. Sometimes people took the needles from pine trees and screwed them into balls to chew.'[12] Leningrad, 800 miles to the south, had been under siege for nine months by the early summer of 1942, a German stranglehold which forced unspeakable torment on the city's inhabitants, some of whom were driven to cannibalism to avoid starvation.* On the face of it, therefore, the Soviet Union was indeed at bay.

Strategically, however, Stalin's predicament was not so grim as it might have appeared. Four hundred miles to the south of the old imperial capital, the panzer divisions which had threatened to take Moscow in October 1941 had not only been forced to lift the siege but had been driven back by a Soviet counteroffensive. By June 1942, to Hitler's growing concern, the Wehrmacht's offensive had been stalled for almost six months along a front line which ran for over 1,000 miles from Leningrad to Rostov-on-Don at the northern tip of the Black Sea. While Stalin awaited a renewed assault on Moscow, the Führer had decided on a thrust even further south. Anxious to secure a reliable supply of fuel and other materials, without which he feared Barbarossa would falter, if not crumble, he ordered the Wehrmacht to open a twin-pronged attack – to seize the oil wells around Baku on the edge of the Caspian Sea and, simultaneously, to march on Stalingrad, which occupied a pivotal strategic position on the Volga River, itself the principal artery

---

* The siege of Leningrad was not lifted until January 1944 by which time it had lasted for 872 days.

linking Moscow to the Caspian Sea. In due course, he imagined, 'European' Russia would thereby fall under the tutelage of the Third Reich: Germany would have more than enough Lebensraum to last at least 1,000 years. Operation Braunschweig, as this second phase of Barbarossa was called, had been ill conceived and poorly planned but initially it looked as though it might succeed.

If Stalin was hard pressed, the Führer was in a hurry. Following the safe arrival of the early convoys carrying Lend-Lease supplies from the United States (which Hopkins and Harriman had provisionally negotiated in Moscow the previous autumn), Hitler had become increasingly dismayed by the steady flow of weapons and supplies which had reached the Russian ports of Murmansk and Archangel. Aware of the threat posed by the rapidly growing military might of the United States, he was anxious to take Stalingrad as a prelude to renewing his offensive in the north. For this reason, his urge to arrest the flow of supplies reaching the Soviet Union through the Arctic was as pressing as Stalin's urge for it to be sustained and if possible increased.

While the U-boats rampaged up and down the Atlantic coast of the United States, Hitler's neuralgic mind was focused with characteristic obsession on another potential threat to his Eastern Front. In January 1942 he conjured up a strategic demon in the form of an imminent British invasion of Norway, which he regarded as a 'zone of destiny' for the Third Reich and therefore a 'vital' front line.[13] Accordingly, he ordered Raeder to despatch the entire German battle fleet to Trondheim to counter this threat, warning that, if the Kriegsmarine's commander-in-chief failed to follow his order, he would 'decommission' every battleship and transfer its guns and crews to meet the imagined threat in Scandinavia, insisting that 'every ship which is not stationed in Norway is in the wrong place'.[14]

Frustrated by the fact that a substantial proportion of the surface fleet had been blockaded in Brest for over a year, the Führer urged Raeder to order these capital ships to break out into the Channel and escape to their home ports in Germany, whence they could be despatched to Norway. At first, the Grossadmiral argued that such a move would expose the *Gneisenau* and *Scharnhorst* to the full might of the RAF and the Royal Navy and that it would be folly to take so great a risk with such a precious resource. But Hitler was adamant and Raeder backed down, though making it clear that it should be well understood the decision was not his, but the Führer's alone.

On 11 February Hitler's plan – Operation Cerberus – was put into action. Soon after 9 p.m. *Gneisenau* and *Scharnhorst*, flanked by the heavy cruiser *Prinz Eugen*, six destroyers and fourteen torpedo boats and shielded in the air by thirty-two bombers and more than 250 fighters, steamed out of Brest to begin their 'Channel dash'. It took a full twelve hours before the departure of the German squadron was detected, by which time they were well past Dieppe and only twenty miles from Boulogne. Radar on Coastal Command's reconnaissance aircraft had failed at crucial moments and, even more significantly, the Germans managed to jam almost every frequency on which the ground-based radar stations strung along the English coast operated. The Admiralty's predicament was aggravated by the absence of any heavy warships in the vicinity. By the time the Dover batteries opened up it was too late.

At noon on the 12th, five Royal Navy motor torpedo boats made visual contact with the enemy ships. But they were minnows facing sharks. From a distance of 4,000 yards they fired a salvo of torpedoes (all of which missed) before fleeing back to Dover to avoid what otherwise would have been certain annihilation. The first aircraft to target the two battleships were six Fleet Air Arm Swordfish biplanes loaded with torpedoes, but theirs was similarly a mission impossible. As they lumbered towards Calais at their maximum speed of 140 mph, they flew into a hailstorm of fire from a swarm of German fighters and the destroyers screening the two battleships. As they were escorted by only ten Spitfires, their fate was as inevitable as it was gallant. Although a couple of the Swordfish managed to release their torpedoes, all six planes were shot down; only five of the squadron's eighteen aircrew survived.* They too inflicted no damage on the Germans.

In the middle of the afternoon, five elderly destroyers left Harwich in an attempt to intercept the superior force which had now passed through the Straits of Dover into open water. Shielded by worsening weather which had reduced visibility sharply, they managed to get within 3,500 yards of the enemy before they came under heavy fire. After releasing a

---

* One of those to die was No. 825 Fleet Air Arm Squadron's commanding officer, Eugene Esmonde, who was awarded a posthumous Victoria Cross. He had already earned renown when he led the aerial attack on the *Bismarck* in May 1941.

salvo of torpedoes between them (all of which went astray), they had no sensible option other than to slink back into the security of the mist-shroud and return to base.

By this time Bomber Command had entered the fray, but to no better effect. A total of 242 bombers, supported by 398 fighters, attacked in three waves but they were thwarted by thick cloud and snow squalls. No more than forty pilots even set eyes on the German squadron; none hit their target.

Though the *Scharnhorst* was partially disabled after hitting two mines and the *Gneisenau* was slightly damaged by another, both battleships reached port safely, though it would be six months before *Scharnhorst* could go to sea again and the *Gneisenau* never returned to action. Hitler's 'Channel dash' was a propaganda triumph for the Third Reich which Goebbels exploited to the full. In Britain there was an outcry of wrath and despair in the press, with even *The Times* abandoning all restraint to thunder: 'Nothing more mortifying to the pride of sea-power has happened in home waters since the 17th Century.'[15]

As it happened, the Admiralty had been surprised by the timing but not by the audacity of the German operation. Ten days before the break-out from Brest, its staff had come to the conclusion that, although 'at first sight this passage [through the Channel] appears hazardous', it was nonetheless the likeliest route to be chosen by the enemy for any attempt to escape.[16] However, a combination of chance, accident, misfortune, poor weather and the Royal Navy's chronic shortage of suitable warships had been principally to blame. Nor, aside from the damage to reputation, was great harm done. Although 'the national wrath', as Churchill put it, was 'vehement', he and Roosevelt were determined to snatch victory from the jaws of defeat. 'When I speak on the radio next Monday evening,' the president cabled, 'I shall say a word about those people who treat the episode in the Channel as a defeat. I am more and more convinced that the location of all the German ships in Germany makes our joint North Atlantic problem more simple.' The prime minister replied, 'The naval position in home waters and the Atlantic has been definitely eased by the retreat of the German naval forces from Brest.'[17] It had hardly been a British triumph, but nor was it a national humiliation of the kind claimed by *The Times*.

Tellingly, the German naval staff agreed with the Allied leaders, summarizing the outcome as 'a tactical victory, but a strategic defeat'.[18]

Nonetheless, by the end of February 1942, although the *Scharnhorst* and *Gneisenau* were out of commission, the Kriegsmarine had assembled a formidable battle fleet in Norway: the *Tirpitz* was at anchor in Trondheim, where the great battleship was soon joined by *Prinz Eugen*, *Admiral Scheer* and another heavy cruiser, *Admiral Hipper* – a deployment, Churchill would write, which 'riveted our attention'.[19] The prime minister had long been awed by what he called 'the menace of the *Tirpitz*',[20] to the point where, earlier in the year, he had gone so far as to advise the commander-in-chief of the British Home Fleet, Admiral Tovey, that 'crippling this ship would alter the entire face of the naval war and that the loss of 100 machines [aircraft] and 500 airmen would be well compensated for'.[21] Tovey was no less mesmerized by the great German warship, claiming that to sink the *Tirpitz* would be 'of incomparably greater importance to the conduct of the war than the safety of any convoy'.[22]

In so far as it caught their attention at all, this perspective carried little weight with Roosevelt and none with Stalin. For so long as Russia's very survival appeared to be in question, the president was determined to satisfy the Soviet leader's persistent demands for more aid. Ever since Harriman had negotiated the terms of the billion-dollar package of Lend-Lease aid with the Soviet leader in September 1941, this had been an imperative that had to be obeyed. Aside from Bomber Command's assault on German cities, the supply of weapons, raw materials and food remained the only practical way of demonstrating the Anglo-American commitment to the imperilled communist state. For the time being, the only effective route for its delivery remained the Arctic Ocean. Following the safe arrival of PQ1 on 11 October 1941, eleven further 'PQ' convoys – the prefix derived from the initials of the Admiralty's director of operations, Commander P. Q. Edwards[23] – reached their Russian destinations without meeting any significant opposition; of the 158 freighters which made the crossing between September 1941 and March 1942, only one was sunk.[24] This was a relief to the Admiralty, whose warships had shepherded these convoys into port, but it offered no cause for rejoicing. As winter yielded to spring, so the days would lengthen and the ice floes would break up and drift south, forcing the convoys to steam within 200 miles of the Norwegian coast, bringing them within range of the Luftwaffe for longer periods of daylight. From Pound's perspective, the auguries were ominous.

Five days after leaving Iceland on 20 March, PQ13 – nineteen merchant ships escorted by two destroyers and three armed trawlers – steamed into precisely the kind of trouble the Admiralty had feared. The weather was atrocious as the wind rose and the temperature fell towards minus 40 °C. On board the SS *Eldena* John Haynes, an eighteen-year-old armed guard from Georgia, worked alongside other members of the crew in 'a constant battle to clear ice and snow off the deck and superstructure. Mast stays assumed gigantic proportions as ice encased them six to eight inches thick and they had to be attacked with sledge hammers to free them of ice. The ship itself was grinding through pack ice with a growling, cracking noise.'[25] On the fifth day, PQ13 was struck by a gale which roared down from the North Pole with such ferocity that

> the deeply laden ships pitched and rolled in the mountainous seas, and would sink into valleys of enormous waves with just their topmasts visible. Then the torturous climb to the next wave pinnacle revealed their salt-encrusted, scarified hulls with racing propellers before falling with a shuddering crash into the next trough. Thunderous seas poured over and down the decks, finding way into ventilators and cabins.[26]

As the gale howled through the rigging, one of Haynes's shipmates (whom he identified only as Mills) was overawed:

> [T]he air, laden with flying spume, froze as it struck the ship, turning it into a whiter, ghostly, spectra laboring through this hellish frozen world. Watch-keepers and gunners rapidly became ice-sculptured silhouettes, moving lethargically. The warm air they breathed out immediately froze into tiny icicles around the slits of their headgear. Eyelids were constantly brushed to stop them freezing together; hairs in the nose became icicles that pierced the nose when rubbed. Only later when thawing out, one felt the pain.[27]

As his ship drove into these seas, Haynes stared in wonderment as 'shuddering like a trapped animal' the *Eldena* struggled to rise through 'the colossal weight of water . . . At times I really thought we had been overwhelmed and were sinking.'[28]

The storm raged for four days. By the time it subsided on 27 March, the convoy was in disarray, scattered by the violence of the weather and separated by distances of up to 150 miles. The *Eldena* had been driven into a heavy ice floe which offered protection from any marauding U-boat but was close enough to the Norwegian coast to be dangerously in range of the Luftwaffe. On the following day, 28 March, the convoy partially regrouped only to be spotted by a German reconnaissance plane as the ships eased their way out of the ice field. In the afternoon, amid snow showers and fog, a swarm of enemy German bombers emerged through a break in the clouds to sink the *Empire Ranger* and the *Raceland*. The crew of the *Empire Ranger* were soon picked up by a German destroyer while the *Raceland*'s had time to lower four lifeboats, which they tied together with the intention of sailing for Murmansk, some 600 miles away. The next day, another storm drove them off course. Two of the boats sank and the other pair landed on the Norwegian coast with thirteen survivors who were immediately interned as POWs; thirty-two of their shipmates had perished, either in the bombardment itself or in the icy waters of the Arctic.

On the same day, the cruiser HMS *Trinidad* and two destroyers, under the command of Rear Admiral Stuart Bonham-Carter, made contact with the convoy. Operating as a 'close protection' force, in support of but independent from the convoy's escorts, the three warships attacked a trio of German destroyers. One of these was sunk by the *Trinidad*, which followed up by launching a torpedo at another in the middle of a heavy snowstorm. In a freak accident, possibly caused by the freezing temperature of the water, a faulty gyro inside the torpedo caused the missile to turn in a lethal arc. It struck its parent warship amidships, killing thirty-two of the crew, although the disabled *Trinidad* was able to limp into Murmansk. The cruiser was followed on 1 April by the last stragglers to reach the uncertain safety of the Russian port, where daily bombing raids had brought the city to its knees. Statistically, the losses incurred by PQ13 constituted a bearable rate of attrition: five merchant ships out of the nineteen which had left Iceland twelve days earlier. But with the hours of Arctic darkness diminishing by the day, the loss of one quarter of the ships which had sailed from Iceland ten days earlier was ominous – and both Pound and Tovey, who rarely saw eye to eye, were at one in their belief that continuing to operate the Arctic convoys over the summer months would be to court disaster.

On 8 April, a week after PQ13's battered arrival in Murmansk, the First Sea Lord on their behalf therefore submitted a formal note to the War Cabinet warning, in his blandly understated way, that 'geographical conditions are so greatly in favour of the Germans that losses . . . may become so great as to render the running of these convoys uneconomical'.[29] But his strictures were ignored, swept aside by the overriding imperatives which had made every Arctic convoy an essential component of American policy towards the Soviet Union.

Three weeks earlier, Roosevelt had written an effusive letter to Stalin, in which he undertook 'to bend every possible effort to move these supplies to your battlelines'.[30] But a logjam was starting to accumulate in Iceland caused largely by an acute shortage of British shipping. Though they never put the charge so crudely, the Americans clearly suspected that London – reluctant to deprive British forces in the Middle East and elsewhere to satisfy the Soviet leader – had started to operate a 'go-slow' on both the number and size of convoys to Murmansk and Archangel. Accordingly, on 24 April, Hopkins cabled Churchill, pressing him 'to explore this [accumulation of supplies in Iceland] at once . . . Hope I may have early answer because loadings are progressing.'[31]

Clearly irked by the high-handed tone of Hopkins's missive, Churchill replied brusquely two days later, indicating that the British government was doing its best to meet the challenge but that the arrangements which were currently in place were not open to review. The prime minister's evasive response provoked Roosevelt to intervene. In an unusually severe response on the same day, 26 April, he wrote:

> I am greatly disturbed by this because I fear not only the political repercussions in Russia but even more the fact that our supplies will not reach them promptly. We have made such a tremendous effort to get our supplies going that to have them blocked except for most compelling reasons seems to me a serious mistake . . . It seems to me that any word reaching Stalin at this time that our supplies were stopping for any reason would have a most unfortunate effect.[32]

Churchill opted for a tactical retreat. With the mildly reproachful reminder to the president that each convoy entailed a 'major fleet operation' and that 'with the best will in the world' it would not be possible to send more than three convoys every two months, he agreed to increase the number of ships in each Arctic convoy from twenty-five to thirty-five, insisting, however, that this was 'the absolute maximum number which it is safe to risk without further experience of the scale of enemy attack'.[33] This compromise averted an immediate stand-off between London and Washington but it was not the end of the dispute. Indeed, following his undertaking to increase the size of the Russian convoys, the pressure on Churchill grew steadily more intense.

Soon after his warning about the dangers of continuing with the convoys, Pound flew to Washington for a meeting with his American counterpart, Admiral King, who agreed that it would indeed be 'militarily impracticable' to sustain the convoys in the summer months.[34] However, he had less success with the president, whom he met on 27 April, the day after the latter's stern note to his prime minister. Goaded relentlessly by Stalin, Roosevelt overrode the concerns of not only the First Sea Lord but his own commander-in-chief as well.

Three days after dismissing Pound's fears, the president wrote again to Churchill about the 'urgent necessity of getting off one more convoy in May in order to break the logjam of ships already loaded or being loaded for Russia'. This time, Churchill did not yield. In the course of a long explanation of Britain's predicament, he stated bluntly that 'what you suggest is beyond our power to fulfil'.[35] Reminding the president that his own naval commander-in-chief, King, believed that the transatlantic convoys were already too thinly escorted, he warned that if Dönitz were to switch his U-boat fleet from US waters – where Operation Drumbeat was still wreaking havoc – to the North Atlantic, 'disastrous consequences might follow to our main life-line'. It was a simple point: the Royal Navy was already over extended and it did not have enough warships to protect the existing convoy routes, let alone to escort any more merchant ships to Russia. 'I beg you not to press us beyond our judgement in this operation,' he continued. 'I can assure you, Mr President, we are absolutely extended, and I could not press the Admiralty further.' In the face of this plea, Roosevelt reluctantly decided to draw back. On 3 May he replied, 'It is now essential for us to acquiesce in your views regarding Russian convoys.'[36] But this was still far from the end of the matter.

While these missives were flying back and forth across the Atlantic, two more Arctic convoys – PQ15 and QP11 (the prefix QP designating convoys returning from Russia to the West) – found themselves in the same kind of trouble as PQ13 had encountered. The thirteen merchant ships in QP11 were escorted by almost as many warships – six destroyers, four corvettes and an armed trawler, all of them under the command of Rear Admiral Bonham-Carter, who had transferred his flag from the damaged *Trinidad* to the cruiser HMS *Edinburgh*. The convoy was soon detected by German reconnaissance planes and U-boats. On the next day, 30 April, as she zigzagged at speed in front of her flock, the *Edinburgh* was hit by two torpedoes fired from U-446. One of these hit the flagship's forward boiler room, the other blew off most of her stern. Although severely damaged, the *Edinburgh* did not sink. Instructing the rest of the convoy to continue on its way, Bonham-Carter elected to take his stricken vessel back to Murmansk, accompanied by of the two destroyers. They were soon joined by four Royal Navy minesweepers which had sailed out from their base in the Kola Inlet to assist. In the hope of warding off any further U-boat attacks, the destroyers circled protectively round the *Edinburgh* as she steamed at four knots, a sitting target.

On 2 May four German destroyers appeared over the horizon in the hope of completing the task U-446 had begun. They opened fire at the sorry little flotilla from a distance of about four miles. Although the British escorts were heavily outgunned, they fought back. With suicidal courage, Commander Eric Hinton, who led the minesweeper flotilla from HMS *Harrier*, opted to charge directly at the German destroyers at the minesweeper's maximum speed of fourteen knots. From his position on the bridge alongside Hinton, the *Harrier*'s navigation officer, David Moore, watched mesmerized as the little ship bore down on the far more powerful German vessel, hoping to convince the enemy that it was the vanguard of a much larger force. 'The minesweepers were never intended to engage enemy surface ships,' Moore noted subsequently, 'but we all knew that our Captain would never entertain the thought of running away, even from a German battleship.'[37] Hinton's gamble paid off. Cautiously, the German destroyers kept their distance, laying down a smoke screen and dashing in and out of the cover provided by a succession of snow showers rather than closing in for what should have been an easy kill.

In a confused exchange, both British destroyers were hit and suffered severe damage. But the Germans did not escape unscathed either. The *Edinburgh* scored a direct hit on the *Hermann Schoemann*, whose crew was taken off by a sister destroyer before being scuttled. Soon afterwards, though, Moore watched as a torpedo slammed into the British flagship, all but cutting her in half. Bonham-Carter oversaw the tricky transfer of more than 800 men (including sick and wounded sailors, some of whom had been injured in other convoys) from the *Edinburgh* to two of the minesweepers, while the cruiser's last functioning gun turret continued to fire at the enemy until she was listing too steeply in the water for her weapons to be operated. Bonham-Carter decided she would have to be scuttled. Hinton duly fired twenty shells into her hull. Still the cruiser refused to sink. An attempt to finish her off with depth charges was equally ineffective. Finally, one of her destroyer escorts, HMS *Forester*, lined up carefully and fired her last torpedo at her from the effectively point-blank range of 1,500 metres. There was a pause that seemed to last far too long before 'the torpedo struck and exploded, and we witnessed the sad end of this fine cruiser as she rolled over and sank'.[38] Fifty-eight of her crew and a further fifteen men from her two accompanying destroyers had been killed, a remarkably low total which might have been far higher if the surviving German ships had not been hoodwinked.

Alerted to the experience of QP11 as the two convoys crossed paths, the men aboard the twenty-five merchant ships in PQ15 must have been grateful for the protection provided by the Royal Navy as they steamed towards Murmansk. Not only were two cruisers and two destroyers in immediate attendance but these were backed up by a 'distant covering force' of two battleships, an aircraft carrier, three cruisers and ten destroyers under the command of Admiral Tovey himself. Even so, on 3 May, a force of six torpedo-bombers flew in low over the convoy and sent three freighters to the bottom. Despite the fact that no more ships were sunk before PQ15 reached port on 5 May, the Germans had done quite enough damage to cause deepening dismay at the Admiralty. Although only four merchant ships had been lost from the thirty-eight which sailed in PQ15 and QP11, the damage to the escorts had been disproportionately heavy.

Following the loss of his two flagships, the *Edinburgh* and, soon afterwards, the *Trinidad* (which, after emergency repairs in Murmansk, was so badly damaged by a torpedo-bomber on her return journey that she too had to be scuttled), Rear Admiral Bonham-Carter gave formal warning of an unpalatable prospect. If the German airfields in Norway could not be put out of action, he argued, the Arctic convoys should be suspended until they could once again have cover of darkness:

If they must continue for political reasons, very serious and heavy losses must be expected. The force of German attacks will increase not diminish. We in the Navy are paid to do this sort of job, but it is beginning to ask too much of the men in the Merchant Navy. We may be able to avoid bombs and torpedoes with our speed; a six or eight knot ship has not this advantage.[39]

Both Tovey and Pound endorsed Bonham-Carter's bleak assessment, the latter writing to Admiral King on 18 May to comment that the Russian convoys 'are becoming a regular millstone round our necks . . . The whole thing is a most unsound operation with the dice loaded against us in every direction.'[40] Churchill, however, was hounded once again by *raisons d'état*. Stalin was now on the diplomatic offensive.

On 6 May, unwittingly echoing the White House, the Soviet leader wrote to the prime minister asking him 'to take all possible measures' in order to ensure the arrival by the end of May of some ninety ships which were 'loaded with important war materials' but were 'bottled up at present in Iceland or in the approaches from America to Iceland'.[41] Churchill's reply, three days later, was equally polite but firm:

We are resolved to fight our way through to you with the maximum amount of war materials. On account of *Tirpitz* and other enemy surface ships at Trondheim the passage of every convoy has become a serious fleet operation . . . We are throwing all our available resources into the solution of this problem, have dangerously weakened our Atlantic convoy escorts for this purpose, and, as you are no doubt aware, have suffered severely.[42]

Despite the resistance of the Admiralty, most forcefully articulated by the commander-in-chief of the Home Fleet, Admiral Tovey, the political pressure from the White House and the Kremlin did not abate.[43] By the middle of May, it was clear that Churchill would have to retreat under this twin-pronged attrition. In a note to the chiefs of staff on the 17th, he wrote:

Not only Premier Stalin but President Roosevelt will object very much to our desisting from running the convoys now. The Russians are in heavy action and will expect us to run the risk and pay the price entailed by our contribution. The United States ships are queuing up . . . Failure on our part to make the attempt would weaken our influence with both our major Allies. There are always the uncertainties of weather and luck, which may aid us. I share your misgivings, but I feel it is a matter of duty.

As if to emphasize the crucial nature of his decision, he told them: 'The operation is justified if a half gets through.'[44]

PQ16 left Reykjavik four days later with thirty-five merchant ships (the 'absolute maximum number' that Churchill had judged to be safe). The convoy was escorted by five destroyers, an anti-aircraft 'gunship', four corvettes, a minesweeper and four armed trawlers, which were both supported by a covering force of four cruisers and three destroyers and backed up by a distant covering force of two battleships, an aircraft carrier, two cruisers and thirteen destroyers. In mournful confirmation of the Admiralty's fears, even these forty warships were unable to prevent the loss of one quarter of the convoy they had been assigned to protect. For twenty-four hours a day, over six days, PQ16 was subjected to a relentless attack both from U-boats and from aircraft strafing, bombing and torpedoing in far greater numbers than before.

The torment began on 25 May. The statistics recorded that one US freighter, the *City of Joliet*, was attacked by eight torpedo planes and eighteen dive-bombers. Somehow the 6,000-ton vessel survived the initial onslaught and no ship was sunk that day. On the next, though, one of the Royal Navy's CAM ships – a freighter converted to launch RAF fighters – was fatally torpedoed by a U-boat. On 27 May – 'a day that no sailor who went through it will ever forget'[45] – the Luftwaffe returned with 108 aircraft to blitz the convoy with unprecedented ferocity. The bombardment started just after midnight and lasted for twenty-two hours. The bombers attacked in wave after wave from all directions, defying a wall of fire from the anti-aircraft guns of the destroyers and corvettes, which were supported by gunfire from those merchant ships which had been mounted with gun emplacements, operated by Armed Guards, trained for the purpose.* Once the enemy aircraft had released

---

* The US Navy Armed Guard was established in the Second World War to man the machine guns frequently mounted on merchant ships sailing both independently and in convoy. The Royal Navy had a similar unit manned by trained naval personnel and the Royal Artillery Maritime Regiment. The four cruisers in the original escort had been withdrawn because it was judged that the risk of losing such valuable ships to a land-based bomber attack on this scale was unjustifiable.

their bombs and torpedoes – often at point-blank range – they circled away to reload at airfields in Norway before returning for another run.

In that one day, the U-boats and bombers between them sank seven merchant ships. The 7,000-ton freighter *Ocean Voice*, the commodore's flagship, barely escaped becoming an eighth. 'I had little hope of her survival,' Commander Onslow reported, 'but this gallant ship maintained her station, fought her fire, and with God's help arrived at her destination.'[46] The bombardment from air and sea was unrelenting, and there were still three more days to go. Fortunately, PQ16 was saved from an even worse mauling by the arrival of three Soviet destroyers and, soon afterwards, six Royal Navy minesweepers, which steamed to the rescue from Murmansk.

Twenty-eight of the thirty-five freighters which had left Iceland on 21 May reached either Murmansk or Archangel to unload their cargoes. But the losses – 32,400 tons of weaponry, including 147 tanks, 77 aircraft and 770 other vehicles – brought into baleful focus the warning given by Pound that the Arctic convoys were in danger of becoming 'uneconomical'. And there was worse, far worse, to come.

## 14.   Disaster in the Arctic

The prime minister arrived back in London from his White House talks on 27 June, not to debate grand strategy but to confront a little local difficulty with Parliament. Following what he would himself describe as 'a long succession of misfortunes and defeats', the nation was resentful and recriminatory.[1] The diarist Nella Last expressed a popular sentiment when she wrote:

> Nearly three years of war. WHY don't we get going – what stops us? Surely, by now things could be organized better in some way . . . There is no flux to bind us – nothing. It's terrifying, not all this big talk of next year and the next will stop our lads dying *uselessly*. If only mothers could think that their poor ones had died usefully – with a purpose.[2]

The press echoed the public mood and Parliament was swift to respond. On 2 July a Conservative MP, Sir John Wardlaw-Milne, tabled a motion of no confidence 'in the Central Direction of the War'.[3]

One of the prime minister's critics was a Conservative MP, Sir Archibald Southby, a former naval officer. Noting that the German government had claimed to have sunk more than 3 million tons of shipping in the first five months of 1942 – a figure which he hoped was 'exaggerated'* – he waxed sonorous and prolix. Reminding the House that 'our hope of victory and the hope of salvation for all those who are now enslaved under the Axis' were at stake, he issued a clarion warning:

> If then by foolish strategy we suffer reverse after reverse which not only involve us in military defeat, but dissipate the sea power upon which the whole of our war effort is built, we render impossible the fulfilment of the task of guarding those merchant ships upon which we all depend.[4]

At the end of a long debate, Churchill rose to reply. Although he allowed himself a spasm of resentment against 'the nagging and snarling'

---

*It was. The correct figure was approximately 2.2 million tons (BritishNavalHistory.com).

of his critics, his summary – which acknowledged the succession of mishaps and misfortunes to which his adversaries had referred – was as assured as it was grandiloquent. Reminding his listeners that he had never promised less than 'blood, toil, tears and sweat', he urged that, when the House came to divide, those members 'who have assailed us [should be] reduced to contemptible proportions'. In this event, he perorated, 'a cheer will go up from every friend of Britain and every faithful servant of our cause, and the knell of disappointment will ring in the ears of the tyrants we are striving to overthrow'.[5] As he had predicted privately while he was still in Washington, his opponents were duly brushed aside. Of the 475 MPs who entered the lobbies, only twenty-five voted against him. The prime minister was unassailable. Had the debate taken place a few days later, Southby's foreboding might have had greater resonance among his colleagues.

As the prime minister spoke, convoy PQ17 was six days out from the Icelandic port of Hvalfjord, trundling towards Archangel, its thirty-three merchantmen (reduced from thirty-five when two damaged vessels had to drop out of the convoy soon after leaving Iceland) laden with 594 tanks, 297 aircraft, 4,246 trucks and gun-carriers and 156,000 tons of general cargo, which was 'enough to equip an army of 50,000 men'.[6] Escorted by six destroyers, four corvettes, three minesweepers, four armed trawlers and two submarines along with an oil tanker and three rescue ships, it was to enter the annals of naval history as a maritime disaster that Churchill would describe as 'one of the most melancholy naval episodes in the whole of the war'.[7] Given the ease with which Göring's Luftwaffe and Dönitz's U-boats picked off their victims one by one, the prime minister's lugubrious sentiment was an understatement of epic proportions: the wholesale slaughter of PQ17 – only eleven of the thirty-three ships in the convoy were to reach their destination – was an operational debacle of the greatest magnitude.

So far, to the surprise and relief of the Admiralty, the might of the German surface fleet based in Norway had seemed reluctant to engage with the Royal Navy. Instead of joining the U-boats and bombers to do battle against the convoys in April and May, *Tirpitz* and *Hipper* had remained at anchor at Trondheim while *Scheer* and her sister ship *Lützow* similarly remained on their moorings in Narvik. Unbeknown to the British, Hitler and Raeder had decided that the Kriegsmarine's capital ships should be held in reserve to protect against the threat of an Allied invasion of Norway unless they could be certain of success against the Allied convoys in the Arctic. Such circumstances might arise, Raeder suggested, 'when the enemy's exact position and strength were known and when sufficient air support was available'.[8] This cautious proposal found favour with the Führer, who authorized the establishment of a task force consisting of *Tirpitz*, *Scharnhorst*, two heavy cruisers and, as soon as she had been fitted out, the *Graf Zeppelin*, Germany's only prospective aircraft carrier.* Though he did not say where or when or in what way, Hitler proclaimed that this battle fleet would pose a 'serious threat' to the enemy.[9]

Yet the German battle fleet remained steadfastly at anchor, to the frustration of Admiral Otto Schniewind, who was in command of the Northern Front. Schniewind had been firmly instructed by Raeder that 'a naval reverse at this juncture would be particularly undesirable' and therefore to avoid any confrontation with British warships that might 'allow the enemy to score a success against the main body of the fleet'.[10] It may be presumed that Schniewind would have agreed with the mordant comment in the British Naval Staff History that 'Instructions more damping and cramping to the Commander of an Operation can scarcely be imagined.'[11]

In one of the great ironies of the naval conflict between the Kriegsmarine and the Royal Navy, the latter was scarcely less cautious than the former. By the spring of 1942, Admiral Sir John Tovey, commander-in-chief of the Home Fleet, who was responsible for the protection of the Arctic convoys, had grown increasingly concerned at their vulnerability. Enigma signals decrypted by Bletchley Park indicated that the *Tirpitz* was at large, waiting to savage any convoy that might cross its path. This, Admiral Tovey warned, was

> wholly favourable to the enemy. His heavy ships would be operating close to their own coast, with the support of powerful shore-based air reconnaissance and striking forces, and protected, if he so desired, by a

---

* Completed in 1938, the *Graf Zeppelin* was never operational. To prevent her falling into enemy hands, she was scuttled in March 1945 outside the port of Stettin (which was handed over to Poland four months later and renamed Szczecin). Raised by the Soviet Union a year later, the vessel was eventually sunk in a weapons test. A Polish survey ship discovered the wreck in 2006.

screen of U-boats in the channels between Spitzbergen and Norway. Our covering forces [battleships, cruisers, and aircraft carriers] would be without air support, one thousand miles from their base, with their destroyers too short of fuel to escort a damaged ship to harbour.[12]

Thus, in June 1942, so far from making preparations for an epic battle that would resonate down the years in the collective memory of all maritime powers, both the Kriegsmarine and the Royal Navy were resolved to avoid any risk of confrontation unless victory seemed assured. As a result – for the time being, at least – the stand-off between these two mighty fleets was a high-stakes non-event. Yet the failure of both navies to appreciate what was – and what was not – in the mind of the other, was a crucial element in what was very soon to become one of the great naval disasters of the twentieth century: the destruction of PQ17.

In addition to the twenty-three warships and support vessels that formed the convoy's escort, led by Captain John Broome, PQ17 had been given close cover by four cruisers and three destroyers, under the command of Rear Admiral Louis Hamilton. The Home Fleet, under Admiral Tovey, provided distant cover with two battleships, an aircraft carrier, two cruisers and fourteen destroyers. It was a formidable cavalcade of guardians that must have seemed all but impregnable to the merchant seamen whose lives depended on its ability and readiness to protect them.

The first attempt by the enemy to breach these defences occurred when the convoy was some seventy miles to the north-west of Bear Island. Just after 6.30 p.m. on 2 July, seven Heinkel torpedo-bombers appeared out of the mist from the starboard side of the convoy, skimming low over the water. Apparently indifferent to the barrage of anti-aircraft fire with which they were met, the bombers flew directly towards their intended victims until the fire became so intense that they were forced to drop their torpedoes wide of the convoy before making off again into the clouds.

A little earlier on the same day, Raeder had authorized the naval high command in Kiel to launch Operation Roesselsprung (Knight's Move), the largest operation of its kind yet essayed. Its formal purpose, which Hitler had authorized at a meeting with him at Berchtesgaden (the Führer's Alpine retreat in Austria) just over a fortnight earlier, was 'the annihilation of the PQ convoy in collaboration with U-boats and the

Airforce',[13] subject to the proviso that the battleships under Schniewind's command should not be put at risk. Quite how the admiral was supposed to reconcile these competing objectives was not explained to him. Nonetheless, that evening (a little after Churchill had defeated the no confidence motion in the Commons) a battle group, led by *Tirpitz* and *Hipper*, left Trondheim for their advanced base in Vestfjord; and, just after midnight on the 3rd, a second battle group, led by *Scheer* and *Lützow*, weighed anchor in Narvik bound for Altenfjord. The absence of clarity in their operational instructions did not augur well.

The operation started badly. Soon after her departure, *Lützow* ran aground in the notoriously treacherous waters of the Norwegian 'Leads', forcing the pocket battleship to return to port. A similar fate befell three of the *Tirpitz*'s destroyers, which hit a submerged rock as they entered Vestfjord. Schniewind was undeterred as he awaited the final authority from Berlin to sally forth against PQ17. In addition to the general constraints already imposed on his freedom of manoeuvre, Schniewind was mindful of a further specific decision which had been made jointly by Hitler and Raeder following the sinking of the *Bismarck*. This was to the effect that no convoy should be attacked until any accompanying aircraft carriers – 'which must be recognized as *the most dangerous opponents of heavy ships!*'[14] – had first been located and put out of action. Their fear was that an aircraft carrier could inflict enough damage on the *Tirpitz* for the Royal Navy's heavy ships to attack and sink what was left of the Kriegsmarine's surface fleet.

On 3 July, the low cloud which had covered the convoy's route for much of the previous six days yielded to a succession of fogbanks, which 'with sharp but invisible edges, would frequently snatch the convoy into cold cotton wool, returning it just as suddenly back into clear crystal sunshine'.[15] Though the Allied vessels were shadowed spasmodically both by reconnaissance aircraft and by U-boats, the weather gave them significant security from major attack. 'Fog' was 'any convoy's best friend' the escort commander, John Broome, aboard HMS *Keppel*, noted. 'In peacetime merchant skippers had dreaded fog at sea – specially with other ships around; now everyone in the convoy business welcomed it . . . we yawned as we raised our cocoa cups. "Long may it last".'[16] It did not.

In the late afternoon of the 4th, half a dozen torpedo bombers appeared over the horizon. They barely stayed long enough to launch their weapons before retreating under cover of cloud. The attack lasted for a few minutes only and caused no damage. It soon became clear, though, that this foray had merely been a 'softening-up' mission to test the escort's defences. Soon after 8 p.m. the bombers returned. This time twenty-five aircraft crept up on the convoy from astern, flying at low altitude. On this occasion, according to the official Navy Staff History, their leader 'showed great determination, hitting the *Navarino* in the middle of the convoy with two torpedoes, before he crashed in flames just ahead of the *Keppel*'.[17] As the *Navarino*'s crew jumped overboard, another freighter, the *Bellingham*, had to alter course sharply to avoid ramming the crippled vessel. The *Bellingham*'s second officer was moved to witness one of the shipwrecked seamen raise a fist from the water as he shouted, 'On to Moscow . . . see you in Russia.'[18] In quick succession two more merchant ships were hit. One of these, according to Broome, who invariably adopted a breezy tone in the midst of a crisis, was 'holed but happy'; the other two, including the *Navarino*, sank.[19] Most of the survivors from both ships were plucked swiftly from the water by the three rescue ships and pulled to safety.

As they scanned the emptying horizon from the insecurity of their raft, they tried to contain the nagging fear that no one had seen them. Imagining that they were presumed to have drowned, their spirits were lifted momentarily when a minesweeper steamed in their direction. But, evidently hastening to catch up with the convoy, it passed by, ignoring them. Appreciating the warship's priorities, the shipwrecked men stood up, self-mockingly, to 'thumb a lift'. According to one of them, the minesweeper's crew 'crowded the rails and cheered'. Reflecting ruefully that it had been 'an act of bravado on our part', he added, 'We would have liked it better had they stopped.' As it happened, they were eventually picked up by one of the convoy's rescue vessels.

From his perch on the bridge of the escort destroyer HMS *Ledbury*, Lieutenant Richard Walker found the five-hour battle

> wildly exhilarating, guns firing in every direction, planes flashing in the sun like swallows as they turned and twisted to attack, shells bursting just above the water, torpedoes dropping everywhere, tracer bullets, the Captain directing fire over the loud hailer: control, control, control, barrage, barrage, barrage, all the thrill of battle. I was staggered by the

beauty and excitement of it all. There was no time to be afraid. It was a matter of engaging aircraft all over the place. At times they came so close that we could see the expression on the pilot's face.[20]

When a British destroyer shot down a German bomber, the crew on one of the US cruisers reacted as though it was a game of baseball and 'cheered as if we were in New York, watching "dem bums" from Brooklyn'.[21] The crew of the *El Capitan* (loaded with warplanes destined for the Soviet air force) were similarly exuberant as they saw the downed aircraft's crew struggle in vain to escape from the burning cockpit. Perhaps forgivably, some of them shouted and jeered as they passed the wreck of the fuselage, 'hurling insults at the dying enemy'.[22] Broome estimated that, in all, four enemy bombers were shot down before the rest disappeared into the clouds. Elated by such good shooting and the overall discipline displayed by the convoy throughout the crisis, he felt a surge of pride and confidence: 'My impression on seeing the resolution displayed by the convoy and its escorts was that, provided the ammunition lasted, PQ17 could get anywhere.'[23]

At that moment, while the convoy was approximately 130 miles to the north-east of Bear Island and still some 800 miles from its destination, the First Sea Lord was in a crisis meeting. Twenty-four hours earlier, on the evening of the 3rd, Pound had left his office in the Admiralty to visit 'that vast monstrosity which weighs upon Horse Guards Parade', as Churchill described the bunker which housed the Operational Intelligence Centre (OIC). By this time, Enigma decrypts forwarded from Bletchley Park had intimated that the *Tirpitz* might be on the prowl in the vicinity of the convoy's projected route. After a briefing from Lieutenant Commander Denning, who, as head of the OIC, was charged to oversee the monitoring, collating and interpretation of every scrap of intelligence about these movements, the First Sea Lord apparently left without saying a word.

In the early hours of the next morning, Denning signalled Admiral Tovey (whose covering force was 250 miles to the south-west of the convoy) to inform him that a succession of enemy signals, which had yet to be deciphered, might 'indicate the commencement of a special operation by main units'.[24] Hamilton, whose cruiser squadron was to the north of PQ17, had been under orders from Tovey to break away from the convoy to take up duties elsewhere once it passed to the east of Bear

Island. However, at 7.30 p.m. on the 3rd, this order was countermanded by the Admiralty, who signalled 'Remain with convoy pending further instructions.'[25]

Pound's order must have come as momentary relief to Hamilton, who had been dismayed to be told that he was to leave the convoy at this point, knowing that it would then rely entirely on the protection of Broome's much weaker escorts and any Allied submarine that might be patrolling off the coast of Norway. Seven days earlier, on the eve of PQ17's departure from Hvalfjord, he had summoned the captains of the merchant ships to reassure them that, in addition to their escort ships, they would be heavily protected by the Royal Navy's covering forces throughout the journey. This assurance led one of the skippers present to log that 'it was stressed that PQ17 would have the strongest screen force yet employed in the protection of Arctic convoys'.[26] Hamilton's fresh instructions from the Admiralty offered him a glimmer of hope that he would not after all be required to breach the undertaking he had given at Hvalfjord. That glimmer was to be swiftly extinguished.

In London these were 'agonizing' hours, the agony exacerbated by the fact that between noon on the 3rd and 7 p.m. on the 4th the code-breakers at Bletchley Park were unable to decrypt the Enigma messages emanating from Germany.[27] As a result of this 'unreadability gap', neither the admirals at sea nor the OIC knew the whereabouts of the German ships or even if they had left port.[28] The only evidence available to them until this moment had been a sheaf of vaguely worded Ultra decrypts that invited speculation and conjecture. But at 7 p.m. on 4 July, new evidence arrived at the OIC, which appeared to indicate that, after all, the *Tirpitz* was not yet on the warpath.

This decrypt revealed that 'C-in-C Fleet [Admiral Schniewind] in TIRPITZ arrived Altenfjord 0900/4th July' and that 'Destroyers and torpedo boats' had been instructed by Raeder 'to complete with fuel at once'.[29] The same decrypt added that the heavy cruiser *Scheer* was also in the same port. Denning drew the obvious inference: the *Tirpitz* was at anchor, not at sea. He was in the throes of signalling this to Tovey when he was joined by Pound and two of his staff. After some discussion, Pound apparently reached the conclusion that the OIC's assessment was premature. Ordering Denning's interpretation of the evidence to be 'stripped out, leaving only the bald facts',[30] the First Sea Lord asked, 'Can you assure me that the *Tirpitz* is still in Altenfjord?' Denning replied that, 'although he could not give an absolute assurance, he was confident that she was, and expected that his opinion would be confirmed in the fairly near future', when he expected Bletchley Park to have decrypted more recent Enigma signals.[31] This was not good enough for Pound.

A little before PQ17's departure from Iceland, the commander-in-chief of the Home Fleet had had a telephone conversation with the First Sea Lord which had left him seriously perturbed. During it, Pound told Tovey that under 'certain circumstances the Admiralty contemplated ordering the convoy to scatter'.[32] Such an order meant precisely what it said: the escorts would be instructed to steam away from the convoy at speed and the merchant ships, thus deserted, were to scatter before finding their way independently to Murmansk. Tovey had openly opposed this approach, arguing that it was a 'vital necessity for ships to keep well up together for mutual support against the heavy attack that was certain', adding that 'he strongly deprecated such an order being given, except as a last resort in the actual presence of attack by overwhelming surface forces'.[33] In a private letter to the First Sea Lord, Tovey went further, insisting, with memorable passion, that an 'order to scatter' would be 'sheer bloody murder'.[34]

Very soon after his discussion with Denning, but in the absence of any further intelligence from Bletchley Park or from any other source, Pound summoned his staff to a meeting at 8.45 p.m. There would be no official record of what transpired in the course of the next thirty minutes but at least eight of those present argued against ordering the convoy to 'scatter'. The First Sea Lord found himself in a minority of two. According to Admiral Eccles, his director of operations:

> The way in which Admiral Pound reached his final decision was almost melodramatic: the First Sea Lord leaned back in his leather-backed chair and closed his eyes – an invariable attitude of deep meditation when making difficult decisions; his hands gripped the arm of the chair, and his features which had seemed almost ill and strained, became peaceful and composed. After a few moments the youthful Director of Plans, Admiral Lambe, whispered irreverently, 'Look, Father's fallen asleep.'*

---

* 'Father' was the nickname given Pound by his staff. He was prone to fall asleep in even the most important meetings. This habit greatly irritated the Chief of the

After thirty long seconds, Admiral Pound reached for a Naval pad Message and announced, 'The convoy is to be dispersed'. As he said this, he made a curious but eloquent gesture to the others, indicating that this was his decision, but he was taking it alone.[35]

The high drama of the moment was somewhat spoilt by the bathetic fact that Pound had failed to say precisely what he meant. As transmitted to Tovey, Hamilton, and Broome, just before 9.30 p.m., the message read: 'Immediate. Owing to the threat of surface ships convoy is to disperse and proceed to Russian ports.'[36] Reminded by one of his most senior staff officers, Admiral Moore, that the order to disperse would be interpreted to mean that the ships should remain bunched together – and therefore still make an easily detected and tempting target – Pound corrected himself, saying: 'I meant them to scatter'. Accordingly, a few minutes later a second signal ordered: 'Most immediate . . . Convoy is to scatter.'[37]

When the meeting broke up, one of its participants, the deputy director of the OIC, a retired rear admiral, Jack Clayton, told Denning what had transpired. The head of the OIC, who had just received a new Ultra intercept, which had confirmed his impression that the German squadron in Altenfjord had yet to weigh anchor, was evidently appalled. He persuaded Clayton to return to the First Sea Lord's office and explain that the OIC was more than ever convinced that *Tirpitz* was still in port and was likely to stay there. Pound refused to change his mind. 'We have decided to scatter the convoy, and that is how it must stay,' he insisted.[38]

When Broome received the order to scatter, he was aghast and incredulous. 'It seemed to explode in my hand,' he wrote later, adding:

> The order to SCATTER is the prerogative of the senior man on the spot when, and only when, an overwhelming force attacks his convoy, which would be more difficult to massacre if it remained concentrated. It is the last straw, the '*sauve qui peut*', and it is of course irrevocable . . . I was angry at being forced to break up, to disintegrate such a formation, and to tear up the defensive fence we had wrapped round it, to order

---

Imperial General Staff, General Alan Brooke, who was not aware that Pound was incapacitated by an as yet undiagnosed brain tumour which eventually proved fatal.

each of these splendid merchantmen to sail on by her naked, defenceless self.[39]

Nonetheless he passed Pound's message to PQ17's commodore, John Dowding, as he felt bound to do; the die had been cast.

Admiral Hamilton – who had already been instructed (by Pound himself), 'Most Immediate. Cruiser force withdraw to westward at high speed'[40] – was also appalled.[41] Like Broome, he presumed that the only explanation for such a drastic command was that the *Tirpitz* was about to appear over the horizon at the head of a posse of pocket battleships and cruisers that was poised to obliterate the convoy. 'Assuming, as we all did assume, that the scattering of the convoy heralded the imminent approach of the enemy surface forces,' Hamilton noted, 'we were – in the eyes of all who did not know the full story – running away and at high speed.'[42]

Mindful of the likely impact of such apparent pusillanimity on the morale of the officers and men serving in his squadron, he signalled all of them in terms which did not disguise his dismay at being instructed to leaving the convoy to find its own way to Murmansk. Making it clear that it was not his decision, he told them that a 'far superior force' was concentrating in the area, supported by shore-based aircraft. He did not add – but he did not need to – that to confront such a threat in open battle would have been an act of bravado. He concluded, 'I hope we shall all have a chance of settling this score with the Hun soon.'[43]

By this time, Captain Broome in *Keppel* had made a fateful decision: all five destroyers under his command were to follow him and join Hamilton's cruiser force. This left twelve small warships only – the corvettes and trawlers – to scatter with the now rapidly disintegrating convoy. Broome's decision, for which he was later to be severely censured, was, nonetheless, in strict compliance with Admiralty guidelines. It was also endorsed by Hamilton, who still presumed that an attack from 'an overwhelmingly superior force to the escort' was imminent.[44] In these circumstances, he explained later in his formal report, 'the addition of six destroyers to my force would have been invaluable, whereas the possibility of their being any protection to the scattering convoy was negligible in comparison'.[45] Like Hamilton, Broome expected that the chance would very soon come to 'settle the score' with the German fleet. It never did. As *Keppel* passed the commodore's flagship, Broome signalled Dowding, 'Sorry to leave you like this. Goodbye and good luck. It looks like a bloody business.' Dowding replied, 'Thank you. Goodbye and good hunting.'[46]

The merchant seamen under Dowding's command were appalled and bewildered by the news. Writing in his diary that night, Nathaniel Platt, an officer in one of the American freighters, summed up their feelings of abandonment: 'Received orders to disband convoy. It is unbelievable that we are being put on our own without protection – some ships with no guns at all. Everyone going every way on the horizon. Some ships sticking two or three together. We are going off alone.'[47] For a while Hamilton's warships still had sight of the vessels which they had been ordered to leave to their individual fates. Watching from the bridge of the USS *Wichita*, an officer noted bleakly, 'The ships are dotted around for miles. Some still burning and smoldering from [earlier] bomb hits, while others are just getting up steam. Their smoke makes it look like huge black ostrich feathers are growing out of tubs.'[48] They were, of course, sitting ducks.

At the fateful moment when the First Sea Lord issued his final order to PQ17, the *Tirpitz* – as the OIC had presumed – was indeed still at anchor in Altenfjord, 300 miles from the now scattering freighters. Apparently fearful that an Allied aircraft carrier was providing distant cover to the convoy, Hitler had yet to give his consent for the Kriegsmarine's capital ships to leave their Norwegian havens. That very morning, in a bitterly ironic appreciation, his headquarters re-emphasized that 'the presence of a heavy force with the convoy stood in the way of launching Knight's Move'. Unless the bombers or the U-boats that were now shadowing the convoy could put these enemy warships out of action, the *Tirpitz* and her accompanying armada of heavy warships was to remain well clear of PQ17.[49] Paradoxically, the fact that an aerial sweep by the Luftwaffe in the area of the last reported position of Tovey's fleet, which did include an aircraft carrier, had revealed 'no trace of this force' served only to reconfirm 'the impossibility of launching Knight's Move at the present time'.[50]

It was not until the early hours of 5 July, more than four hours after PQ17 had been ordered to scatter, that the German high command began to realize the bonanza Pound had gifted them. Just before midnight a U-boat reported that Hamilton's cruiser squadron had executed a sharp change of course to the south-west, and was steaming at speed away from the convoy. A little later, a reconnaissance aircraft radioed that the convoy itself was now spread over a twenty-five-mile swathe of the Arctic apparently heading in a variety of directions. Before long, the U-boats and the bombers began to close in on the virtually defenceless merchant ships which now had only the remnants of Broome's escort force – the corvettes and the armed trawlers – to provide them with any kind of shield. It was at this point, now knowing that his treasured battleship no longer had anything to fear from the British navy – that Hitler finally authorized the *Tirpitz* to weigh anchor to play her part in the 'annihilation' of PQ17.

By the time the great German battleship reached the open sea, the U-boats and bombers had already begun to pick off their victims. Between them, by the end of the day, they had accounted for no fewer than twelve Allied merchant ships, including Commodore Dowding's flagship, the *River Afton*. As if to add bathos to the hideous irony of this unfolding tragedy, their killing spree now led Raeder to instruct Schniewind to recall *Tirpitz* to the security of Norwegian waters. Fearful of Hitler's rage if any unforeseen accident were to befall the great battleship, the commander-in-chief gave the order in person, explaining Delphically that 'a defeat at sea would in the present situation . . . be very burdensome'.[51] Schniewind was bitterly disappointed, a frustration that seeped into a commentary on the fleet's inaction by the German naval staff: 'Every sortie attempted by our heavy surface units is burdened by the Führer's desire to avoid at all costs the risk of losses or defeats.'[52] Nonetheless, by 8 July the *Tirpitz* and her consorts were once again riding safely at anchor in Narvik. Though it did not form any part of Raeder's reasoning, the decision made operational sense: it was hardly worth the expenditure of manpower and fuel for a great battle fleet to hunt down a scatter of straggling freighters.

Out in the Arctic, as the U-boats and the bombers continued the massacre, the airwaves crackled with harrowing distress messages from the stricken vessels as they went down: 'On fire in the ice', 'Abandoning ship'. For the time being, the escort vessels left behind when Broome's destroyers steamed away to join Hamilton's cruiser squadron were impotent. Their escort commander had ordered them 'to proceed independently to Archangel'.[53] In light of this, the captains of the two anti-aircraft ships, HMS *Palomares* and HMS *Pozarica*, conferred.

Captain Edward Lawson, in command of *Pozarica*, argued that they should try to re-form the convoy, albeit with a vestigial escort, but he was overruled by Acting Captain Jauncey, who was his senior: Broome's order was unequivocal and had to be obeyed. Muttering, 'We can't leave these poor buggers,' and followed by three smaller escorts, Lawson elected to head for the nearest available refuge, Novaya Zemlya, a remote Russian archipelago 200 miles to the south, accompanied by three smaller escort vessels. His intention was to find temporary sanctuary there before weaving south-east through ill-charted waters to the port of Archangel, a further 600 miles away.

Soon after receiving Broome's order, believing that the German battle fleet was likely to appear over the horizon at any time, Lawson summoned his crew to a meeting. Were they to be attacked by a destroyer, he told them, they might survive; were it a battleship they would not. According to one of his men, he added: 'We will fight these ships to the last shell and if need be, go down fighting.'[54] Not surprisingly, this left his listeners 'rather despondent', a mood which was unlikely to have been lifted by his final thought for the day: 'Get as much sleep as you can and make peace with your maker.'[55]

The blitz began in earnest again the next morning. Helpless before this bombardment, a spirit of stoicism mingled with fatalism seemed to infect the abandoned freighters. As their ships shuddered, exploded, caught fire or splintered in pieces, threatening to toss them into the freezing waters (which at this latitude were only marginally south of the Arctic ice floes), the basic urge to survive inspired remarkable feats of endurance. While tanks, planes, trucks and ammunition disappeared to the bottom of the ocean, the survivors clambered aboard rafts and lifeboats or were fished out of the sea by other merchant ships which, even as the bombers and U-boats continued their onslaught, came to the rescue. An elderly American freighter, the *Olopana*, so slow that she fell behind the small group of merchant ships with which she had hoped to find comfort in numbers, caught up with three ships which were all at the point of sinking – the *Bolton Castle*, the *Washington* and the *Paulus Potter*. Laden with high explosives, the *Bolton Castle* burned 'like a giant Roman Candle'[56] before rearing into the sky as if to defy her persecutors and slipping beneath the waves. The *Washington* went down in the same manner while the *Paulus Potter* stayed afloat to be despatched later by a U-boat. Remarkably, their crews had survived and had taken to the lifeboats. Yet when the master of the *Olopana*, Captain Mervyn Stone, offered them refuge, all three crews declined, evidently preferring to risk the perils of the Arctic over the prospect of incineration. *Bolton Castle*'s crew decided to head for the Russian coast some 400 miles from where they had been shipwrecked; the other two crews opted for the nearer but bleaker protection of Novaya Zemlya. According to Stone, the crew of the *Paulus Potter*, who were crammed into four lifeboats (only one of which had an engine), merely asked for 'cigarettes, bread and lubricating oil' before setting off on their 200-mile voyage.[57]

Stone's own crew was not so stoical. Many of them, like those on many of the other vessels, came from a diverse range of nations which were not directly involved in the European war and their allegiance to the Allied cause was not so unequivocal that they felt bound to fight on to the bitter end. Stone, whose offer of help had so recently been rejected by three shipwrecked crews, found himself confronting a body of near-mutinous men. By 7 July many of them had not eaten a proper meal or slept for three days. In the near-permanent Arctic daylight, under constant threat of attack, they were cold, exhausted and frightened; apparently abandoned by the Royal Navy, they no longer had the stomach for further suffering. In *Olopana*'s engine room, which was partly manned by Hawaiians, this resentful despair was particularly acute. The fact that the *Olopana* was loaded with high explosives and petrol assuredly contributed to the growing apprehension. After consulting the ship's British gunners, who told him that their duty was 'to stand fast at the guns until the ship was put out of action',[58] Stone summoned the crew to his presence, where he 'suggested' to them that their lot was somewhat better than that of the men they had left in the ocean trying to reach a safe haven in open boats. Afterwards, Stone noted drily, 'I was assured they were feeling better about the situation.'[59] He spoke too soon.

As Stone sought to reassure *Olopana*'s fractious crew, Captain Stephenson, in command of the *Hartlebury*, watched helplessly as four torpedoes, fired in quick succession from a range of 800 yards, slammed into the side of his ship, slicing the British freighter into three pieces. In the ensuing chaos, some crew rushed for the lifeboats even before Stephenson had given the order to abandon ship. Lines were let loose prematurely. Boats were dropped in the water in a haphazard rush. Some were smashed, others were swamped. Stephenson waited until no one else was left on board the sinking ship before running up the sharpening incline of the deck to dive into the water as the *Hartlebury*'s stern reared up before she slid slowly backwards beneath the surface. He was hauled into a lifeboat, alive but with a severe head wound. Around him, men flailed in icy water or clung to wreckage before, as the cold seized them, losing their grip and the will to live, they too slipped silently away.

Arthur Carter, one of *Hartlebury*'s gunners, reached an undamaged raft which was already crammed with twelve men. He scrambled aboard shortly before a U-boat surfaced nearby. Two of the submarine's crew in the conning tower pointed machine guns at them. Carter thought he was about to die. Instead, he was about to become a photo opportunity for U-355's commander, Günter La Baume. Though La Baume had been scouring for quarry since the order to 'scatter', this was his first kill and he was not about to miss the chance to mark the occasion for posterity. As the cameras clicked, La Baume and his fellow officers shouted across, 'What ship are you? Where were you bound? What do want to go to Russia for? You are not Bolsheviks, are you?' Then, pointing in the direction of the nearest land, one of them apologized for not rescuing any of them but, as a gesture of humanity, passed across 'two bottles of Schnapps and seven loaves' to see them on their way.[60]

Others were less fortunate. When U-355 hailed the lifeboat which had rescued Stephenson, La Baume did no more than demand to know the name of the vessel to which they had belonged. Once he had established this, the U-boat commander departed, leaving the twenty men in the half-swamped boat to fend as best they might in the unrelenting misery of the Arctic. To the *Hartlebury*'s third officer, Needham Forth, who kept a detailed record of his experiences, La Baume's callousness 'seemed one of the cruellest things possible'.[61] The lifeboat was soon chilled by despair as, one by one, his shipmates surrendered to the elements.

The first to go was a fireman called Hutchinson, then a mess boy, who was followed by an able seaman, an electrician, a cabin boy, two more able seamen, the chief engineer, another fireman, two stewards, a cook, a gunner. As each man was added to the mournful tally, he was heaved overboard. There was no ceremony, only the need to remove as much weight as possible from the water-logged boat. With the exception of one of their number, Geoffrey Dixon, who went berserk as he tried to drown himself while his shipmates tried to restrain him, each one died quietly, falling in and out of consciousness, lost in an apparently painless delirium, until it was over.

Forth, who was himself up to his waist in water as he manned one of the lifeboat's oars, was clearly not given to expressions of undue sentiment, but he marked the moment of each individual death as though, by so doing, he gave dignity to the life and to the departure. After a while, he sensed that he might soon follow them. He noted later, 'I was slowly aware of the fact that I was going the same way as the others – the water having a stupefying effect on me.' He struggled forward to the bows, where he joined four other men – the only other survivors – to huddle together, 'frozen, feet absolutely stiff and white'.[62]

The cold was remorseless. Another of the *Hartlebury*'s rafts was already so crammed with survivors when it left the sinking freighter that the last four men who scrambled aboard were forced to stand among the sprawl of their exhausted shipmates sitting or lying on the bottom boards. As it turned out, this was their salvation. By stamping their feet, they warded off the frostbite and hypothermia that carried off every one of the other ten men aboard. The last to go was the ship's second engineer, Joseph Tighe, who, as his shipmates died about him, marked their passing by singing Psalm 23 – 'Yea though I walk through the valley of the shadow of death, I will fear no evil: for though art with me; thy rod and thy staff they comfort me.' Tighe's own death was observed by Richard Fearnside, the *Hartlebury*'s radio officer: 'He began to cry that he wished he was home in Glasgow. He was the last to die. He drifted off to sleep, and we tried to keep him awake, rubbing his feet, shaking him, talking to him, but it was no use.'[63]

Soon afterwards, Fearnside's little group came across another of the *Hartlebury*'s rafts. This contained one gunner wearing a duffel coat, who seemed lost in his own thoughts, and a dead seaman lying on the bottom boards. They tipped the corpse into the sea, transferred the gunner to their own raft and broke open a box of rations, which helped somewhat to fuel their resolve and almost certainly saved their lives. After drifting for another two days, they saw through a break in the sea mist which had surrounded them that they were just off the coast of what proved to be Novaya Zemlya. They were soon spotted by the crew of the *Winston Salem*, which had earlier gone aground on a sandbank, and a rowing boat was sent out to bring them to safety.

The survivors on Gunner Carter's raft were saved from the worst ravages of the Arctic by the bread and Schnapps provided by U-355. They were lost in the mist when a waterlogged lifeboat loomed into sight. It was Captain Stephenson with his three fellow survivors. Fortified by brandy, biscuits, condensed milk and tablets of Horlicks which they found on Stephenson's boat, the nine men bailed out his lifeboat before dividing into two groups, taking turns to row and rub one another's feet with whale oil to ward off frostbite. After several hours they sighted land, no more than three miles away. It did not take them long to reach a deserted bay, beach their lifeboat, and step ashore.

> The first thing we did on landing was to make a fire to dry ourselves out, the mate [the *Hartlebury*'s first officer, Stanley Gordon] split us into two groups, one to search for wood or anything burnable to keep the fire going, the other to look for anything eatable. Two birds were caught and a few bird's eggs found. The birds were obviously not afraid of us. They just sat there and let us take them . . . We made a stew, filling a biscuit tin with snow and putting bits of the birds in when it melted.[64]

Altogether only twenty of the *Hartlebury*'s crew of fifty-seven had survived. Most of the rest had been tested beyond endurance by 'fatigue, battle weariness and strain . . . their plight too desperate to sustain the slightest hope of relief'.[65]

At much the same time as La Baume's crew in U-355 was snapping the *Hartlebury*'s last moments for posterity, Kapitänleutnant Reinhart Reche in U-255 was enjoying an even better harvest. In quick succession on 7 July he sank two US freighters, the SS *John Witherspoon* and the SS *Alcoa Ranger*. He did not pause to celebrate. In the early hours of 8 July, as the *Olopana* lumbered south towards Russia, Reche manoeuvred U-255 into position and, at short range, fired a torpedo into her starboard bow. Among those killed by the blast were the half-mutinous Hawaiians in the engine room. With one lifeboat destroyed, the surviving crew members, led by their captain, Mervyn Stone, scrambled into the only remaining lifeboat and a couple of rafts to join the sorry scatter of shipwrecked seamen who were rowing, sailing or drifting through the icy seas in search of sanctuary. Before they set off, however, Stone's crew had a brief encounter with the U-boat which had sunk them. In a carbon copy of U-355's action, Reche surfaced to ask, 'Are you

Bolsheviks? No? Then why are you helping Russia?' At this U-255 slid below the surface once more, though not before Reche had delivered himself of a parting jibe: 'The ships of your convoy are all at the bottom of the sea,'[66] he told Stone. This was an exaggeration, but not so very far from the unfolding facts.

To their growing despair, Stone's men watched as, in his phrase, one corvette and then another, 'hunting around like bloodhounds',[67] loomed out of the gloom only to disappear without seeing their distress flares. But the *Olopana*'s captain would not allow his men to give up. Driving them to the point of exhaustion, he urged them to keep moving, both in the hope of reaching land and to stave off hypothermia. Two days later their efforts were rewarded. In the early hours of 10 July they set foot on the bleak shores of Novaya Zemlya where, up and down this coastline, a trickle of PQ17's shipwrecked sailors had similarly found sanctuary. Stone's crewmen were half-frozen, famished, and exhausted but they were at least alive. After a brief moment of respite, to allow 'everyone in his own way to meditate on his survival',[68] he organized them into small groups in an effort to turn a wasteland into a haven. Some built a barrier against the wind while others collected driftwood for a fire. Taking another officer with him, Stone set off in search of human habitation. They had identified a lighthouse from the sea and as they approached it now they saw a ship, evidently marooned, about three miles offshore. It was the grounded *Winston Salem*. Fearful that it would free itself and steam off without them, Stone climbed to the top of the lighthouse, tied a flag to the roof and lit a fire to attract their attention. After a while he saw a lifeboat put out from the freighter and head in their direction. The *Olopana*'s captain asked to be taken out to the ship, where he had a meeting both with her master and the injured captain of the *Hartlebury*, George Stephenson (who was to die a year later from his head wound). The three men decided that the *Winston Salem*'s supplies should be ferried ashore and that a base camp should be established on the beach in the hope that rescue would arrive in due course. By now there were encampments scattered along the coast, all facing the same predicament.

Berlin was cock-a-hoop. On the afternoon of 7 July the German high command broadcast a 'special announcement' from Hitler's headquarters, which, for once, did not need Goebbels to weave any significant fabrications to gild the facts. Its boast that PQ17 'had virtually been wiped out . . . [and that] the submarines and the air force have achieved what had been the intention of Operation Roesselsprung' was uncomfortably close to the truth.[69] Scores of thousands of tons of Allied supplies lay on the Arctic seabed while hundreds of merchant seamen, who had been reluctantly deserted by Hamilton and Captain Broome under instructions from Admiral Pound, were either dead, dying or striving to overcome the odds against survival. But PQ17's trauma was not yet over.

By the end of the first week of July, five freighters had stumbled to the protection of Novaya Zemlya, where they congregated in a narrow strip of water, sixty miles in length, that bisected the two islands which form the archipelago, marked on the charts as Matochkin Strait. Their crews were exhausted. Defying desperation, however, they summoned enough self-mocking resolve to rename their sanctuary 'Funk Cove'.[70] By this time most of the surviving escorts had already assembled there, under the wing of *Palomares* and *Pozarica*, which had taken up station at the entrance to the strait with their anti-aircraft guns poised to ward off any marauding bomber. The question which now haunted both the merchant skippers and the naval officers was whether to stay put in Matochkin Strait or run the inevitable gauntlet of bombers and U-boats to head south towards the White Sea and thence to their final destination, Archangel. Some of the merchant skippers wanted to stay put in the hope of receiving reinforcements from the Soviet navy and the British corvettes based in the region. Captains Lawson and Jauncey urged otherwise.

Considering themselves to have been released from Captain Broome's straitjacket, they decided to reform the remnants of PQ17, once again placing the merchant skippers under the command of John Dowding, who had been found a berth aboard one of the British warships following the sinking of the *River Afton*. They proposed to escort the five merchant vessels to Archangel at once. It would assuredly be a perilous voyage but it was preferable to staying put, waiting to be discovered by German reconnaissance aircraft which would at once call up the U-boats to blockade the entrances to 'Funk Cove'. The freighters and the escorts would be trapped with no means of escape.

The skippers saw the logic of this and soon after 7 p.m. on 7 July, Dowding's bedraggled little convoy weighed anchor and, escorted by a fragile phalanx of corvettes and trawlers, which had also made it to Matochkin Strait, nosed into the open sea. Their final destination was still some 700 miles away. It was a fine evening as they left Novaya Zemlya but they were very soon enveloped in a thick fog. This prompted one of the five merchant ships to turn tail and retreat into Matochkin Strait. The rest lost their bearings and any semblance of order collapsed. Before long, the vessels found themselves trapped by an ice floe which was denser and more widespread than they had been led to expect. No sooner had they 'gone astern' to escape from one semi-congealed mass of broken ice than they found themselves steering straight for another.

The only compensation for this new horror came when, by chance, the master of one of the freighters, *El Capitan*, peering into the fog, saw the vague outline of an open boat that was evidently imprisoned by ice. Forcing a passage through the thickening flow, *El Capitan* reached the lifeboat to find twelve men, shipwrecked when the *John Witherspoon* was torpedoed in the early hours of 6 July. After more than two days in an open boat, these survivors were suffering from severe exposure. To be taken aboard the freighter, their limbs massaged back to life, was to find hope where death had seemed a certainty.

It was not until the early hours of 9 July that the fog lifted, allowing the freighters to search for a way of escape from the encircling ice. To avoid the risk of further entrapment, they opted to make a long detour to the west before striking out again for the White Sea. In the process, they became so widely separated that it was impossible to regroup. Instead, they formed themselves into two mini-convoys, two freighters and six escorts in each, neither of which had any contact with the other. For a while all was quiet as both convoys skirted the ice barrier and, separately, began once more to head south for Archangel. They must have hoped that at last the worst was over.

As yet unaware of the existence of either of these two little groups, Admiral Schmundt, who was in command of the Arctic U-boats, had called off the hunt, believing that, between them, the Luftwaffe and his submarines had completed the destruction of PQ17. When this was reported to him, the commander of the Twentieth Army, based in Norway, signalled his 'heartiest congratulations' to the Kriegsmarine's command in Kiel: by destroying so many supplies destined for the enemy's front line, the general enthused, the navy had given decisive relief to the German Army fighting on the Russian Front.[71] Later that evening, however, Schmundt was alerted to a signal from Reche in U-255, who reported that he had sighted a small convoy, apparently heading towards the White Sea. Its location and its course would soon bring the ships within easy range of the German bomber squadrons based at the Banak peninsula on the north-western tip of Norway.

Just before midnight on 9 July, the escorts protecting the *El Capitan* (with the survivors from the *John Witherspoon*) and the *Hoosier* were alerted to the imminent approach of enemy aircraft. On board HMS *Lord Austin*, one of PQ17's escort trawlers, the crew watched as five specks on the horizon rapidly turned into dive-bombers accelerating down towards them and then separating as each selected a target. It was a terrifying experience. *Lord Austin*'s junior telegrapher, Johnny Rose, was transfixed:

> We saw the bomb get bigger and bigger, and I remember thinking that if I continued to look up in the air, my mouth would be dragged open and the bomb would fall right into it. It was surprising how smartly I snapped my jaws together . . . The coxswain behind me was straining his ears to hear the orders from the bridge. Already he had the wheel hard to port, and the old tub was answering painfully slowly. Johnny [one of the trawler's gunnery crew] was there on the Lewis, one eye on his Junkers target, the other on the whistling missile. Sweat poured down his face but he was still firing . . . The skipper [Lieutenant Leslie Wathen] was yelling 'Keep her hard to port!' and watching the bows shudder round . . . My knees felt like jelly . . . My head thudded and ached and I couldn't look upwards any longer . . .
>
> The scream of the bomb was earsplitting. Then, after what seemed like an eternity, it was down and smacking into the sea just off our bow, sending up a giant waterspout that doused the ship and all of us in its icy wave. Amazingly, it had not exploded.[72]

The *Hoosier* was less fortunate. Attacked by a swarm of enemy aircraft flying in a V-formation, she was helpless as three bombs tore into her hull, destroying most of the ship's engine room. As the bombs continued to rain about her, the crew were ordered to abandon ship; scrambling over the side into the lifeboats with as many of their possessions as they could gather up, they were picked up by one of the convoy escorts, HMS *Poppy*. Not far away the *Zamalek*, one of PQ17's rescue ships, already crowded with more than 200 survivors, was twisting and turning to avoid being hit herself when the crew of a Heinkel 115 parachuted into the water nearby, their plane brought down by another escort. The *Zamalek* was about to go to their assistance and had just started to signal her purpose when the rescue ship was engulfed by an eruption of water as two bombs exploded on either side of her hull. As she emerged from these water-spouts, her captain signalled again: 'I was about to say before being so rudely interrupted that if the Boche behave I will go back for them, but following this little package from the Fatherland, if they haven't frozen to death in this water they can either start swimming or bloody well tread water.'[73]

*El Capitan*, laden with 7,500 tons of munitions, eight tanks and four US bombers, was the next on the German hit list. Again and again, the Junkers 88s and the Heinkel 115s swooped down for the kill. Somehow, though, the freighter managed to survive seven hours of this onslaught before three bombs landed so close to her as to wreck the engine room. The vessel was finished but, miraculously, no one was killed. Her crew – among whom were American, Argentinian, Polish, British and Chinese seamen – was rescued by the *Lord Austin*, which then fired a volley of shells into her hull from 200 metres. According to one of the *Lord Austin*'s crew, *El Capitan*'s skipper 'stood on the bridge with tears in his eyes as the shells crashed into his ship'.[74] A while later, a lone German aircraft flew over to deliver the coup de grâce. The *El Capitan* was the twenty-fourth and final victim of the ill-fated convoy.

As these remnants of PQ17 straggled into the relative security of the White Sea towards Archangel, a lone Catalina flying boat, emblazoned with the Soviet Red Star on its fuselage, flew low over the remote spot where Captain Stone and his crew were setting up their camp on Novaya Zemlya. The pilot, Captain Mazuruk – who was renowned in Russia for his pioneering flights over the Arctic – had been despatched by the Soviet authorities in Murmansk to ferry medicines and supplies to the crews who had found themselves washed up on this inhospitable Russian archipelago and to airlift the wounded to hospital. On 13 July he landed in Matochkin Bay, where he made contact with another gaggle of ships which had just arrived, shepherded by an armed trawler, HMS *Ayrshire*, under the command of Lieutenant Leo Gradwell.

When he received Broome's order to proceed to Archangel, Gradwell had examined his charts and concluded that it would be suicidal to obey. Assuming that the Germans were bound to examine the same charts and move to cut off this line of retreat, he decided to ignore his commander's instruction and to head in the opposite direction. When a corvette signalled 'Where are you going?' Gradwell replied, 'To Hell. And the first one to come back, we hope.'[75] Flouting Broome's instructions yet again, he also picked up three merchant vessels en route as he headed towards the Arctic ice floe with only a sextant and a *Times World Atlas* to guide him. As the ice began to thicken around them, he took the extraordinarily bold decision to go deeper into it, judging this to be the surest way to avoid detection by any German reconnaissance plane. For an entire day, the *Ayrshire* navigated the little flotilla deeper into the thickening ice until they were twenty-five miles from open water and unable to go any further without ramming the icebergs which now loomed around them.

Gradwell ordered the three freighters to shut down their furnaces to avoid the black smoke from their funnels belching into a pale sky. He also instructed that the tanks mounted on their decks should be prepared for battle, their barrels aimed skywards. The enterprising master of the *Troubadour*, John Salveson, remembered that his ship carried a large stock of white paint, which Gradwell instructed should be used to camouflage all three freighters. It did not take long. 'The *Troubadour* was painted from stem to stern, from the waterline to her foretop in less than four hours,' one of her officers recalled. 'All of the deck cargo, deck-gear, hatches, superstructure, had been covered.'[76] Others went even further. The second mate on the *Silver Sword*, John Behnken, described how, in addition to painting their vessel, the crew 'spread white bed linen over the whole of our cargo deck and the hatches'.[77] The ruse worked: a low-flying enemy aircraft passed a mere twenty miles from them but failed to distinguish the ships from the ice in which they had concealed themselves.

After two days Gradwell decided to shepherd his little convoy along the ice-edge, gradually working southwards until, on 9 July, they made landfall at Novaya Zemlya, where they coasted south to Matochkin Strait without meeting any opposition. It was there *Ayrshire*'s captain discovered from the Russian pilot, Mazuruk, that there had been no set-piece battle between the Royal Navy and the German fleet following the First Sea Lord's order to 'scatter'. He was also told about the two mini-convoys which by this time had reached Archangel from Matochkin Strait. Gradwell now had to decide whether to follow their example, but he knew that the morale of the crews on the three merchant ships was crumbling and their captains were feeling the strain. Although he did not know it, other crews had all but mutinied, abandoning their vessels prematurely in the terror of a one-sided battle and potentially surrendering their precious cargoes to the enemy in the process. In any case, Gradwell took the precaution of scribbling a message for Mazuruk to take back with him for the naval authorities in Murmansk warning that, without assistance, the skippers would very probably refuse to leave the perilous security of 'Funk Cove': 'I much doubt if I could persuade them to make a dash for Archangel without considerably increased escort and a promise of fighter protection in the White Sea,' he advised; and, he went on, 'there has already been talk of scuttling ship . . . rather than go to what they, with their present escort, consider certain sinking'.[78] For this reason, he explained, he had decided to remain in Matochkin Strait until adequate protection was provided for the men who had placed their fate in his hands.

The authorities took this ultimatum as seriously as Gradwell had intended. Some days later, *Pozarica*, accompanied by three other British warships and two Soviet destroyers, steamed into Matochkin Strait to escort his three charges to Archangel. They arrived on 24 July – four weeks after leaving Iceland – without further alarums. There was no welcoming fanfare for their achievement but Gradwell's enterprise and initiative were to be recognized by both the Russians and the British: in disobeying orders he had single-handedly escorted his charges the entire way from Iceland to Archangel, an achievement for which the barrister-turned-RNVR officer was awarded the DSC.

Gradwell had won his medal for his outstanding leadership. It was a hard-won honour which no one who endured PQ17's travails begrudged him. However, for many merchant seamen, such awards seemed, parenthetically, to highlight the failure of the authorities to similarly recognize any of their comrades who had sacrificed themselves for a greater good on that dreadful voyage. Those who sailed in the Merchant Navy had long harboured resentment against their peers in the Senior Service, a latent animosity which, in the words of a judicious historian of the Merchant Navy's role in the Second World War, stemmed from 'bitterness resulting from social divisions, injustices, real and imagined, misunderstanding, mistrust and mutual ignorance'.[79] The tragedy of PQ17 aggravated this prejudice. The survivors were not slow to note that, by comparison with their suffering on this tragic enterprise, the officers and men who had deserted them at the moment of their greatest peril were relatively unscathed. In so judging, they of course overlooked the fact that the order to 'scatter' had been made by the Admiralty to the lasting dismay of the naval commanders charged to escort them to Archangel. They also forbore to recall that thousands of men serving in the Royal Navy had already been killed or mutilated on the high seas in defending the nation from their common enemy. It is cruelly invidious even to contemplate 'body counts' in this way, but that this occurred is nonetheless a measure of the 'ulcerous wound in the morale of the British Merchant Navy' which had been exposed by the horrors experienced by those who sailed in that Arctic convoy.[80]

Many survivors – a good number of whom had been rescued by the Catalina pilot, Mazuruk, who did not suspend his mercy mission to Novaya Zemlya until every seaman had been evacuated – were in a state of physical and nervous collapse, half-demented, their morale broken and, in some cases, their wounds severe. Frostbite was commonplace. Surgeon McBain, who was shipwrecked when another of PQ17's rescue ships, HMS *Zaafaran*, was sunk on 5 July, described his own experience with professional precision: 'I was fifteen minutes in the water . . . On boarding the raft, skin anaesthesia was complete to the neck. Joint sense was impaired and there was well-marked ischaemia [a lack of blood supply to internal and external organs like fingers and toes] . . . still showing traces after eight weeks.'[81] McBain was fortunate. Others required amputation of toes and feet; inevitably these men eventually left Russia with physical as well as mental scars that would remain with them for the rest of their lives.

The cost in lives was 153 Allied seamen of many different nationalities, a remarkably low figure given the travails endured by those who set sail from Iceland in PQ17 and a tribute, in part, to the resolution of the Royal Navy's rescue ships, themselves under attack as frequently as any other ship in the convoy. The material cost was far higher: 210 bombers, 430 tanks, 3,350 other vehicles and almost 100,000 tons of munitions – a total of 142,000 tons of military supplies which had been destined for the Russian Front – was now rusting in an Arctic graveyard. Of the thirty-five merchant ships which left for Archangel only eleven arrived; more than two-thirds of the convoy had been destroyed. Churchill's 'melancholy naval episode' was not only a military defeat – a wound that would fester for a long time – but it had grave diplomatic and political repercussions as well.

The immediate reaction of the British government was to shroud the disaster in secrecy. In the House of Commons on 29 July the Labour MP Emanuel 'Manny' Shinwell, who had evidently got wind of what had occurred, rose to ask the Financial Secretary to the Admiralty, George Hall: 'Is my right honourable friend aware that a recent convoy proceeding in a very important direction was denuded of protection almost at the last minute and that a large number of vessels were lost?'[1] Hall remained in his place, refusing to utter a word. When a chorus of MPs shouted 'Answer', Hall remained seated, staring silently at his papers. This bovine display of parliamentary arrogance served only to stimulate more conjecture and speculation. Nonetheless, it was the last mention of the incident in Parliament until after the end of the war.

The only inkling of what had really occurred was inadvertently provided by a hapless junior minister two months later when, on 28 September, the first contingent of PQ17 survivors arrived back in Glasgow in an American cruiser, the USS *Tuscaloosa*. They were ushered into St Andrew's Hall to be addressed by an under-secretary from the Ministry of War Transport, Philip Noel-Baker. 'We know what this convoy cost us,' he told the 1,500 weary seamen assembled before him, 'but I want to tell you, whatever the cost, it was well worth it.'[2] This sentiment did not go down well; whatever else Noel-Baker had to say was largely drowned out by the jeers of his audience.

The American authorities shared the British view that the consequences of the Admiralty's order to 'scatter' were too sensitive to be revealed. In both Washington and London, the mandarins were worried not so much about the human cost as about the diplomatic fallout. On 11 July, before the facts were fully known, a cable landed on Hopkins's desk in the White House from a senior US official which forecast – on what basis was unclear – that most of the ships yet to be accounted for would in due course arrive in Archangel; in which case, he averred, only a third of the convoy had been lost, a proportion 'deemed acceptable having in mind necessity of supporting Russia'.[3] This assessment was endorsed by Averell Harriman (who had helped negotiate the Lend-Lease deal with Stalin and had established close relations with Moscow in the process), subject to the proviso that future convoys were to prioritize the supply of tanks and planes over all other commodities.

Hitherto Churchill, bruised by the pressure from Roosevelt and Stalin, had been even more bullish, arguing that the convoys were justified 'if half of the ships in it were to reach their destination'.[4] Once it became clear, however, that neither a third, nor a half, but two-thirds of the ships in PQ17 had been sunk, he was thoroughly shaken. The losses were grim enough in themselves, but the damage done to Britain's reputation was even more disturbing. His first reaction was to demand an explanation for the decision to order Broome's destroyers 'to quit' the convoy. 'What did you think of this decision at the time? What do you think of it now?'[5] he demanded of the First Sea Lord, who had, of course, made the original decision that led to the fiasco. Pound's reaction, in the long tradition of senior officials, was to set up an internal inquiry. These proceedings lasted several months, at the end of which the Admiralty reached the predictable conclusion that, as no one had been directly responsible, no blame should be apportioned to anyone – a finding which prompted Churchill to comment drily, 'How could it do so in view of the signals made on the orders of the First Sea Lord?'[6]

Whether or not he held himself responsible, Pound was clearly bruised by the events his decision had precipitated. Mounting a rear-guard action against the very idea of using the Arctic to send supplies to the Soviet Union, he seized the moment to insist that no further convoys should be despatched to Russia until November. By this time, he argued, the night hours would no longer be illuminated by the sun; conversely, to send the next convoy, PQ18, through the enemy-infested Arctic before the onset of winter would expose the merchant ships and their escorts to a risk that could not be justified by any potential gain.

At first Churchill was doubtful. Mindful of the impact that such a long delay would have on Britain's standing in Washington and Moscow, especially now, when the Red Army was under growing pressure from the Wehrmacht, he urged the Admiralty to think again. Unable to restrain his urge to interfere in operational details beyond his competence, he suggested that PQ18 should be given an escort of two battleships, five aircraft carriers and at least twenty-five destroyers, all of which should be prepared to 'fight it out with the enemy'. With a fighter screen of at least a hundred aircraft, he claimed, 'we ought to be able to fight our way through'.[7] The Admiralty stood firm: it could not and it should not be done – or, as the prime minister put it with silky disdain, 'I could not however persuade my Admiralty friends to take this kind of line.'[8] To this extent only, PQ17 had inadvertently served Pound well.

The First Sea Lord's obduracy obliged Churchill to face the unpalatable task of informing Stalin that the next Arctic convoy was to be postponed. However, he took the precaution of seeking Roosevelt's approval before taking such a drastic step. Both men appreciated such a delay would breach the spirit, if not the letter, of the Lend-Lease understandings they had reached with the Soviet leader. In a carefully worded letter to the president, Churchill explained that the Admiralty was adamantly opposed to sending another convoy to Russia, on the grounds that it would be likely to suffer an even worse fate than its predecessor. Pointing out that further losses on the scale endured by PQ17 'cannot help anybody except the enemy', he asked Roosevelt to agree that 'the convoy should not be sent'.[9]

His message was accompanied by a draft of the cable he wished to send the Soviet leader. The following day the president replied: 'After consultation with [Admiral] King I must reluctantly agree to the position which the Admiralty has taken regarding the Russian convoy to the north and I think your message to Stalin is a good one. I assume you will send it at once.'[10] Pound's earlier correspondence with King had clearly not been wasted on the head of the US Navy.

Given the go-ahead, Churchill duly sent Stalin a long cable on 17 July. After informing the Soviet leader that his 'naval advisors' believed that the combined might of Germany's warships, submarines, and bombers 'would guarantee the complete destruction of any convoy to North Russia', he cut to the chase: 'It is therefore with the greatest regret that we have reached the conclusion that to attempt to run the next convoy, PQ18, would bring no benefit to you and would only involve dead loss to the common cause.'[11]

Stalin could barely restrain his fury. In a reply that Churchill described as 'rough and surly', he ridiculed the reasons put forward by the Admiralty as 'wholly unconvincing'.[12] His own 'naval experts' believed that 'with goodwill and readiness to fulfil the contracted obligations' these convoys could be 'regularly undertaken'. For good measure he added a sarcastic sideswipe at Pound, mocking 'the order given by the Admiralty that the escorting vessels of the PQ17 should return, whereas the cargo boats should disperse and try to reach the Soviet ports one by one without any protection at all' – his chosen terminology, incidentally, illustrating a similar confusion about the distinction between 'disperse' and 'scatter' that had previously afflicted the First Sea Lord. This decision, he had been advised, was 'difficult to understand and explain'.[13]

It was another phrase in Churchill's cable, however, that truly goaded the Soviet leader. In seeking to justify his decision to postpone PQ18, the prime minister had claimed that if one or two British battleships were 'lost or even seriously damaged' in the Arctic while escorting the Russian convoys, the Atlantic would be at the mercy of the *Tirpitz*. Not only would the food supplies – 'by which we [the British people] live' – be jeopardized but 'our war effort would be crippled'. In a passage which infuriated the Soviet leader even further, Churchill piled on the agony by warning that 'the great convoys of American troops across the ocean, rising presently to 80,000 in a month, would be prevented and the building up of a really strong Second Front in 1943 rendered impossible'.[14] His reference to the year 1943 was like a thunderbolt.

Until this moment, the carefully constructed ambiguities emanating from Washington and London had left Stalin with the impression that his Western Allies intended to launch a cross-Channel invasion no later than 1942. At the end of a visit to Washington by the Soviet Foreign Minister, Vyacheslav Molotov, in May, Roosevelt had virtually said as much, to the point of issuing a communiqué to the press which stated unambiguously that 'full understanding was reached with regard to the urgent task of creating a Second Front in Europe in 1942'.[15] In London, Churchill reiterated this commitment word for word in an Anglo-Russian communiqué issued on 11 June. Though he was also careful to warn Molotov that a shortage of landing craft meant that he could not 'promise' to launch the Second Front in August or September, the die appeared to have been cast. As not one political or military leader on either side of the Atlantic – with the possible exception of Roosevelt – thought that the Second Front in Europe could conceivably be launched before 1943 at the earliest, this undertaking by the two Western leaders was at best ill-judged if not disingenuous. Stalin's rage when he discovered that the 'commitment' had not been worth the paper it was written on was – for once – unfeigned. His response now was blunt: 'Taking fully into account the present position on the Soviet–German front, I must state in the most emphatic manner that the Soviet Government cannot acquiesce in the postponement of a Second Front until 1943.'[16] As he would very soon discover, however, this was to rage against a fait accompli: Roosevelt and Churchill had just agreed on a course of action that ruled out a Second Front in Europe until 1943 at the very earliest.

At the White House a month earlier, in talks which were overshadowed by the fall of Tobruk (see Chapter 13), the prime minister had failed to convince the Americans that a joint invasion of North Africa should precede any attempt to establish a Second Front in France. Impatient for a resolution of this impasse, Roosevelt had sent Marshall, King and Hopkins to London on 17 July, with secret instructions to reach 'immediate agreement' on 'definitive plans', insisting 'it was of the highest importance that US ground troops be brought into action against the enemy in 1942'.[17]

This had proved easier said than done. The competing perspectives of the American and British negotiators were acute; their efforts to maintain a civilized and rational dialogue complicated by mutual suspicion and ill-humour. In some cases this was aggravated by a degree of personal animosity – notably in the person of Admiral King, whom his colleague, an embarrassed Marshall, described as 'always sore' and 'perpetually mean'.[18] With the precision of a gifted mandarin, Alexander Cadogan, permanent under-secretary at the Foreign Office, encapsulated their predicament in his private diary:

> We have made up our minds against a Second Front this year. This I am afraid is right – sad though it might be. We want Americans to do *Gymnast* [the Allied landing in North Africa], President would probably be willing. But Marshall against. I fear that his idea is that, if *Sledgehammer* [the establishment of a bridgehead in France to prepare the ground for a full-scale invasion] is off, America must turn her attention to the Pacific. This is all rather disquieting.[19]

This was an understatement. After two days of fierce argument, the two sides had reached another impasse: the Americans were still determined to secure a commitment to Sledgehammer; the British were no less adamantly opposed. On 22 July, with time running out, Marshall and King decided to consult the president. He scribbled a reply, insisting that if the British still failed to give way, 'some other offensive be worked out for American ground forces in 1942'. As a postscript, he added the words, 'Tell our friends we must have speed in a decision.'[20] This settled the matter. When the British side refused point-black to participate in a cross-Channel invasion in 1942 on the grounds that it would result in a catastrophic defeat, the invasion of North Africa became the only realistic option on the table if Roosevelt were to achieve his objective of getting American boots on the ground in the battle against the Nazis. Overriding the objections of his military advisors, therefore, the president gave his blessing to Churchill's proposal. It was a seismic moment both for the relationship between the Western Allies and for the direction of the Second World War.

With the exception of King – whose hopes of shifting the focus of America's war from the Atlantic to the Pacific were thereby frustrated – the US negotiators accepted the outcome with a remarkable display of goodwill. Churchill was jubilant and cabled Roosevelt accordingly. Roosevelt replied, 'I cannot help feeling that the past few days represented a turning-point in the whole war and that we are now on our way shoulder to shoulder.'[21] Torch – the new code word for Gymnast – had been ignited.

It would take many weeks of transatlantic wrangling before the detailed plans for the North African landings were agreed. It would be a huge logistical enterprise, requiring more than 500 ships of all kinds to transport upwards of 100,000 troops across the Atlantic and subsequently to keep them supplied with the armaments, vehicles, fuel and all the other provisions needed to sustain a major offensive. As the Allies did not have enough ships simultaneously to run convoys to both North Africa and Russia, this had immediate implications for the Kremlin. The disaster of PQ17 thus became a convenient and misleading justification for a decision that was, in reality, based on the strategic aspirations of the Western Allies rather than the operational challenges of traversing the Arctic in high summer.

★

The question now for Roosevelt and Churchill was whether to take their cantankerous Soviet ally into their confidence and, if so, to what degree. So far he had been told only that Churchill had postponed the departure of PQ18, allegedly to avoid decimating the Royal Navy and thereby damaging the prospects for a Second Front in 1943. The revelation that the real reason for this decision was Operation Torch would assuredly fuel Stalin's suspicion that his duplicitous partners were once again preparing to dishonour their promissory notes to him. With his characteristic combination of political courage and self-belief, Churchill concluded that he should confront the Soviet leader in person with, at the very least, a simulacrum of the truth. With Roosevelt's approval, he therefore invited himself to Moscow for what promised to be a challenging encounter.

Innocent of the prime minister's purpose, Stalin responded with alacrity to what he described in his reply as an opportunity 'to consider jointly the urgent questions of the war against Hitler'.[22] Stopping off in Cairo to fire Auchinleck as Middle East commander-in-chief and to appoint General Bernard Montgomery to take command of the Eighth Army, he flew on to 'this sullen, sinister Bolshevik State' for what would become a famous tête-à-tête with the Soviet leader.[23] He arrived in the Russian capital on the evening of 12 August.

Although the 'totalitarian lavishness' of the Kremlin welcome cushioned Churchill's arrival, the talks began in an atmosphere which he described as 'bleak and sombre'.[24] With the diplomatic niceties accomplished, the prime minister opted for the direct approach, informing his host bluntly that he and Roosevelt had decided to postpone the Second Front in Europe until 1943. The conversation stalled. There was, Churchill wrote, 'an oppressive silence' until, with a showman's panache, he unveiled a map of the Mediterranean and sought to persuade Stalin that the Torch landings would constitute an alternative Second Front which would transform North Africa into the launch pad for an invasion of Sicily with the purpose of attacking the Axis powers from the south. Evidently intrigued by Churchill's adroitly argued proposition, Stalin broke the ice between them, exclaiming 'May God help this enterprise to succeed!'[25]

At their meeting on the following day, however, the mood darkened once again. Stalin produced an aide-memoire which he handed to Churchill and Roosevelt's envoy, Harriman (who, at Churchill's request, had joined the British party), in which he poured scorn on the Western Allies for breaching their undertaking to launch a Second Front in Europe during 1942; this breach, he fulminated, constituted 'a moral blow to the whole of Soviet public opinion'.[26] Thereafter the meeting went from bad to worse as his guests found themselves on the receiving end of what Harriman described as 'a very rough sledding'.[27] In this aggrieved mood, the Soviet leader had evidently also reflected overnight on the proposed North African venture and come to the conclusion that Torch was at best a sideshow and at worst an irrelevance: the Second Front, he fulminated, should not have been postponed for such a peripheral undertaking. Churchill tried a different tack, explaining the multiple perils involved in a premature cross-Channel invasion of France. At this, the Soviet leader went even further, implying that Britain's soldiers were frightened to take on the Germans with the same resolve as the Red Army had displayed. Churchill kept his cool, retorting, 'I pardon that remark only on account of the bravery of the Russian troops.'[28]

Despite these frosty exchanges, the Anglo-Soviet entente was somewhat restored following a banquet on the next evening at which Churchill did not hesitate to avail himself fully of a plentiful supply of food and wine. By the end of the next day – when a further meeting between the two leaders in Stalin's private apartment was once again lubricated by a marathon drinking session and another feast which ended only in the early hours of the following morning, the 16th – a casual observer might have concluded that this unlikely couple had become bosom friends. Having dismissed Torch only a few hours earlier, the mercurial Soviet leader now gave the North African operation his blessing once again. Much relieved, Churchill cabled Roosevelt to tell him that all was well, adding: 'Everything for us now turns on hastening Torch and defeating Rommel.' In similar terms, Harriman informed the president, 'The last meeting of the prime minister with Stalin when they met alone made a deep and favorable impression on the prime minister.'[29]

Churchill returned to London fired up by the need to assuage any lingering doubts that Stalin might still be harbouring about the good faith of his Western Allies. The most potent way of doing this, he thought, would be to reverse his own decision to postpone PQ18. With the Home Fleet back to strength following the return to Scapa Flow of a squadron of cruisers and destroyers which had been sent to the Mediterranean for Operation Pedestal, the Admiralty reluctantly agreed to the prime minister's volte-face: PQ18, Pound conceded, could go ahead after all. On 2 September Churchill duly cabled the Soviet leader to inform him the convoy had set out for Archangel. It was to be a mammoth naval operation. To ensure that 'we could fight a convoy through', Admiral Tovey set about assembling a task force of more than sixty warships to protect thirty-nine American, British and Soviet merchant vessels from what he forecast would be another mighty German onslaught.[30]

Hitler was not inclined to disappoint this expectation. Sharing Raeder's view that the flow of Allied supplies to Russia would 'remain decisive for the whole conduct of the war', he judged it imperative to wreak the same kind of havoc on PQ18 as on its predecessor.[31] On 10 September the bombers and the U-boat squadrons duly launched their double-pronged assault with renewed aggression. Yet this Arctic battle did not become a replay of the struggle that had been played out in the same waters two months earlier. Although thirteen freighters – one third of the convoy – were sent to the bottom of the Arctic in a grisly echo of PQ17, the other twenty-six reached their destination relatively unscathed. In the absence of any evidence that the *Tirpitz* would put to sea, and correspondingly no thought given to scattering the convoy, the escorts kept their stations throughout the voyage. Moreover, they counter-attacked with ferocity, shooting down forty German aircraft and sinking three U-boats. In these terms, the operation had been successful; more importantly, it appeared to have achieved its diplomatic purpose. However, the amity thus engendered between Stalin and Churchill proved to be short lived. Once again Torch was the problem.

In his discussions at the Kremlin, the prime minister had skirted round the degree to which the Torch landings would affect the Arctic convoys, contenting himself with generalities about the competing demands made on Allied shipping. In so saying, he did not so much conceal the truth as gloss over it. Yet he must have known at the time that something would have to give. A few days after Churchill's return from Moscow, a formal document – to which the prime minister would have been privy – landed in Hopkins's in-tray in the White House. Sent from London by the Admiralty, it stated explicitly that the 'escort commitments for Torch are so heavy' that it was 'out of the question to run a

PQ convoy simultaneously [with Torch] whatever risk is taken else-where in [the] Atlantic'. To ram the point home, the paper went on to insist that it was 'not possible to forecast the date at which [any] PQ convoy can be run after Torch'.[32]

Churchill loathed confronting any logistical challenge which threat-ened his strategic objectives. As his most senior military advisor, General Sir Alan Brooke, had noted earlier in the year, 'The situation as regards shipping is most disturbing and one that the PM will not face.'[33] Nor would he ever be disposed to do so. On this occasion, though, the Admiralty assessment was so unequivocal that even he could not ignore it. However, given the wrath that such news was likely to provoke in Moscow, Churchill forbore to broach the issue with Stalin until some days after PQ18's arrival in Archangel. Before he did so, he consulted the president once again. As the date for the Torch landings had by now been set for early November, he told Roosevelt that he intended to advise the Soviet leader that no convoy of any similar scale to PQ18 could possibly be sent until the end of the year.[34]

Roosevelt was dismayed. Only a month earlier, following the demise of PQ17, he had written an effusive letter to the Soviet leader, promis-ing to send more than a thousand tanks and aircraft to Russia by rail (through Persia) as well as by sea. He could hardly reject the Admiralty's advice out of hand but he was reluctant to renege so abruptly on such a very recent commitment. To resolve this predicament he favoured a sleight of hand, cabling Churchill to say that he felt 'very strongly' that 'this tough blow for the Russians' should be concealed from the Soviet leader until the very last moment. 'I can see nothing to be gained by notifying Stalin sooner than is necessary, and indeed much to be lost.'[35] Eight days later, on 5 October 1942, he reiterated, 'I feel most strongly that we should not tell Stalin that the convoy will not sail,' adding, vaguely, 'we simply must find a way to help them directly'.[36]

The president's verbal economy was no mere exercise in low cunning but reflected a genuine commitment to the Soviet Union. Notwith-standing his aversion to Bolshevism, he regarded the communist state as even more critical to the strategic interests of the United States than his anglophone ally across the Atlantic; his fear that the Wehrmacht might triumph over the Red Army or that Stalin might pre-empt that threat by suing for peace with the Third Reich remained a very real goad. To complicate Roosevelt's position further, Stalin had just cabled the two

Western leaders to warn them that the Germans were tightening their hold on Stalingrad. The Luftwaffe, he reported, had established air superiority over the city and, he added with an uncharacteristic hint of genuine despair, 'Even the bravest troops are helpless if they lack air protection.'[37] On 6 October he went openly on the diplomatic offensive by using the Communist Party's mouthpiece newspaper, *Pravda*, to give vent to his growing resentment. 'As compared with the aid which the Soviet Union is giving to the Allies by drawing upon itself the main forces of the German Fascist armies, the aid of the Allies to the Soviet Union has so far been little effective,' he grumbled in an open letter which was blazoned across the paper's front page. Not content with that sideswipe, he openly rebuked his allies for postponing the Second Front, calling on them 'to fulfil their obligations fully and on time'.[38]

There could be little doubting the seriousness of the Soviet predicament. Writing again to Roosevelt on the same day as the *Pravda* article appeared, Stalin conceded that the cargoes which the surviving PQ18 freighters were then unloading at Archangel were a 'great help' but made it clear that to hold the line at Stalingrad, let alone to reverse the German thrust, he would need much more assistance. Specifically, he sought a monthly delivery of '500 fighters, 8,000 to 10,000 trucks, 5,000 tons of aluminium, and 4,000 to 5,000 tons of explosives'; in addition he required 'two million tons of grain (wheat) and as much as we can have of fats, concentrated foods and canned meat' within the following twelve months.[39] Some of these supplies could be sent by train or truck along the 'corridor' which led from the Persian Gulf via Teheran to the Soviet cities of Baku and Beslan and some could be loaded into Soviet ships and transported to Vladivostok through the Pacific (where the Soviet Union's Non-Aggression Pact with Japan made them immune from attack),* but, in the autumn of 1942 the Arctic route remained by far the most important avenue for the delivery of heavy goods and weaponry.

For this reason Roosevelt decided to consult the head of the US Navy before approving the cancellation of PQ19. With Admiral King's help, he cobbled together an alternative, which he described as a 'different

---

*The 1941 Non-Aggression Pact was not abrogated by the Soviet Union, which finally entered the Pacific war just before Japan's surrender in August 1945.

technique in which the guiding factors are dispersion and evasion'. As he outlined the scheme to Churchill, the convoy would still sally forth but in small groups, two or three vessels at a time, sailing at intervals of between twenty-four and forty-eight hours. 'It is my belief', he wrote, 'that we would thus stand a good chance of getting through as high a proportion of the ships as we did with PQ18'.[40] Churchill was unimpressed and, two days later, replied, with unaccustomed vehemence: 'There is no possibility of letting PQ19 sail in successive groups with reduced escorts as you suggest. Neither can the fact that the convoy is not sailing be concealed from the Russians any longer.'[41] While he conceded that until this point it had been an 'advantage' to delay telling the Soviet leader that PQ19 would not sail – though why or in what way neither he nor Roosevelt was ever to vouchsafe – he now insisted that 'the blunt truth is best with Stalin . . . I feel strongly that he should be told now.'[42]

Roosevelt gave way. Two days later, Churchill despatched a long cable to Stalin. Reminding him of the timetable for Torch, he sought to sugar the pill by claiming that the Allied landings in North Africa would force Hitler to transfer planes and troops from the Russian Front either to shore up the Axis armies in Libya or to safeguard Italy and Sicily from the Anglo-American thrust across the Mediterranean which would assuredly follow victory in North Africa. In either case, Torch would serve to relieve the pressure in Russia. Stalin was not impressed. He was even less impressed to be told that, in the meantime, 'Naval protection [for any Arctic convoy] will be impossible' as so many warships would be required for the Torch landings. Nor was he mollified when, towards the end of October, he was informed that ten British merchant ships were to sail independently from Iceland with supplies for Russia.★ This, he judged – rightly – amounted to little more than 'gesture' politics by two Allies in whose good faith he could no longer place any trust. His response, four days later, dripped contempt: 'I received your message of 9 October. Thank you.'[43]

With the German and Russian troops at Stalingrad fighting hand to hand and street by street while the Luftwaffe systematically blitzed building after building until almost the entire city had been razed, it

---

★In the event thirteen ships set off for Archangel but only five reached their destination.

was hardly surprising that the Soviet leader was less than appreciative of the Western response to his nation's predicament. Nor was only Stalingrad at risk. The Red Army was also under such pressure along the thousand-mile length of the Eastern Front that a number of senior advisors in Washington, London and Moscow, including the British ambassador to the Soviet Union, Sir Archibald Clark Kerr, harboured the fear that the German onslaught might very well drive Moscow to the negotiating table with Berlin with a view to restoring their unholy alliance. Their respective leaders, however, were more sanguine, both of them confident that, in Roosevelt's phrase, the Russians would 'hold out this winter'[44] despite the suspension of the Arctic convoys.

Nonetheless, the president made another attempt to reassure their turbulent ally. On 15 October he sent Stalin a cable all but promising, in due course, to deliver the Soviet leader's entire shopping list: 'I have given orders that no effort be spared to keep our routes fully supplied with ships and cargo in conformity with your desires as to priorities on our commitments to you.'[45] This breezy but imprecise undertaking did little to soothe Stalin's sense of betrayal and he responded to this overture merely by demanding that the promised cargoes should be 'delivered to the USSR as scheduled by you'.[46] This curmudgeonly reaction irked Churchill, who commented that 'it would be a great mistake to run after the Russians in their present mood . . . the Bolsheviks have undermined so many powerful Governments by lying, machine-made propaganda, and they probably think they make some impression on us by these methods'.[47] However, when the two Western leaders compared notes about their Soviet ally's surly response, Roosevelt was insouciant. 'I am not unduly disturbed about our respective responses or lack of responses from Moscow. I have decided they do not use speech for the same purposes as we do,'[48] he observed with the laconic hauteur that was his diplomatic hallmark.

In conceding that the Arctic convoys should be postponed, the president had made a painful decision from which he had instinctively recoiled. But the great strategic plans to which he had committed himself gave him no alternative. He had agreed to prioritize the Western Front over the Pacific; he knew that victory in the Battle of the Atlantic was a precondition for defeating Germany; and he had been persuaded in favour of Torch over an early Second Front. Nonetheless, being acutely aware that only the Red Army could so weaken Hitler as to make eventual victory in Europe achievable, he was genuinely tormented by the decision to disappoint Stalin. For Churchill, conversely, the choice was stark and simple. Though he recognized that the Soviet Union was crucial to the defeat of Nazism, the order of his strategic priorities was shaped by Britain's imperial imperatives: the unyielding commitment to the Middle East, the control of the Mediterranean, the survival of Malta and their strategic corollary, the defeat of the Axis armies in North Africa. All these were trumped only by the Battle of the Atlantic, where the avoidance of defeat was both a sine qua non of eventual victory on all fronts and – from Britain's perspective – a matter of national survival. Belatedly, Roosevelt and Churchill had been forced to acknowledge that if none of their agreed commitments were to be abandoned, something else would have to give: for the time being that something would have to be the Arctic convoys.

The president was anxious to assuage their resentful ally while refusing to yield to the Soviet leader's charge that he and Churchill had violated an unequivocal commitment to him: 'I want us to be able to say to Mr Stalin that we have carried out our obligations one hundred percent,' he told Churchill at the end of October.[49] However, he gave no indication of how he thought this circle might be squared. Had the prime minister been prone to the use of such arcane phrases, he would have been inclined to reply, 'Fine words butter no parsnips.' Stalin would certainly have done so.

# 16.   Dönitz Seizes His Chance

The critical importance of the conflict at sea to the outcome of the Second World War was now in the sharpest possible strategic focus – or should have been. It was clearly impossible for the Allies to meet the accelerating demand for vessels of all kinds on all fronts at once: there were not enough ships simultaneously to support the military campaigns in the Mediterranean and North Africa, to sustain Britain's global supply lines, to defeat the Japanese in the Pacific and, most fundamentally of all, to fortify the Atlantic lifeline. The maritime resources available to the Anglo-American Alliance were already stretched to breaking point. Hostages to fortune abounded on every maritime front line.

In the Atlantic, the struggle had acquired a bitterness which had hitherto been notable for its absence. Mercy – the quality of which had been demonstrated by both sides in the early days of the conflict – had yielded to harsher rules of warfare in which chivalry on the high seas was replaced by a ruthless disdain for human life. On 17 September 1942 Admiral Dönitz issued a fateful order to every officer under his command:

> All attempts to rescue the crews of sunken ships will cease forthwith. This prohibition applies equally to the picking up of men in the water and putting them aboard a lifeboat, to the righting of capsized lifeboats and to the supply of food and water. Such activities are a contradiction of the primary object of war, namely the destruction of enemy ships and their crews.[1]

This injunction – the 'Laconia Order', as it became known – was provoked not by a sudden onrush of vindictiveness but by an incident which took place in the South Atlantic in September 1942, when five long-range (type IXC) U-boats were some 900 miles south of Freetown en route from the Bay of Biscay for operations off Cape Town. As dusk fell on Saturday the 12th, one of these submarines – U-156 commanded by Werner Hartenstein – sighted a large liner heading north. The *Laconia* was bound for Britain with more than 2,730 people on board – among them 1,800 Italian soldiers who had been taken prisoner in the Western Desert, some 290 Allied servicemen returning home on leave, 80 civilians and a crew of 463.

The twenty-one-year-old luxury liner had been requisitioned by the Admiralty on the outbreak of war and converted into a troopship, complete with mess halls in which soldiers could sling their hammocks. Her captain, Rudolph Sharp, who had been alerted to the presence of U-boats in the region, had been instructed to keep well away from the African coast, and he did so, knowing that it was unlikely that his ship would be detected in such a great expanse of ocean. Nonetheless, he took all necessary precautions. As the *Laconia* was a troopship, and armed with eight guns, she was a legitimate target under the rules of maritime warfare so, as darkness fell, every visible light was extinguished and the companionways to the upper decks were closed. It was a balmy tropical night and the atmosphere on board was untouched by anxiety as she steamed smoothly through a light sea.

A few minutes after 8 p.m. a violent explosion shuddered through the ship. It was the first of two torpedoes fired in quick succession by U-156. A young mother, Janet Walker, was putting her small daughter to bed when she heard a 'loud crash'. She opened the door of her cabin to find that 'water was pouring down the corridor and there were people running everywhere, crying hysterically'. With the little girl in her arms, she was transfixed in bewilderment. 'Everyone was pushing and it was hard to keep on our feet. One of the crew saw me standing there with Doreen in my arms – he grabbed me and told me to follow him.'[2]

With people 'screaming' all round her and 'numb with shock', Janet clung to her child as she made her way to a rope ladder. She was persuaded to climb down into a lifeboat while a member of the crew took Doreen in his arms, promising 'I'll hand her down to you.' Once she had clambered aboard, she looked up. Neither the sailor nor her baby was there. She tried to climb up the ladder again but an RAF officer said he would do so in her stead. He returned a few moments later saying that the little girl must have been taken to another lifeboat, adding, 'Don't worry – you'll see her in the morning.'[3] A missionary nurse, Doris Hawkins, was flung into the water when her overcrowded and half-flooded lifeboat capsized almost as soon as it had been launched. In the melee that ensued, she dropped the fourteen-month-old baby, Sally, who had been in her charge. 'I lost her,' she wrote later. 'I did not hear her cry . . . I am sure God took her immediately to Himself without suffering. I never saw her again.'[4]

One of the torpedoes had exploded in the holding pen in which the Italian prisoners had been entombed, killing many of them instantaneously. Frank Holding, who had survived the sinking of his ship, the *Beatus*, in the ill-fated convoy SC7, two years earlier, heard the surviving prisoners, who were 'nailed down below' under armed guard, 'panicking, crying – it's a terrible thing, men crying'.[5] Holding made his way to the port side and slid down a rope into a lifeboat, watching as some of the Italians leapt into the sea, crying out for help as they did so. Seeing that they might try to get into their lifeboat, one of the men crammed in beside Holding said, 'If any of them hang onto the side, call out and I'll give you a hatchet so you can chop their fingers off.'[6]

Fifteen minutes after the first torpedo struck, the great liner's stern rose high out of the water as the *Laconia* sank below the waves. As she went down, the surrounding sea 'shook and seethed, as if a volcano were suddenly going to erupt from the depths . . . Human beings, rafts, planks, hundreds of broken and bent pieces of wreckage, came to the surface again.'[7] Doris Hawkins had swum little more than a hundred yards as the *Laconia* slowly disappeared below the waves and, as she struggled to keep her head above water in the gurgling whirlpools created by the liner's slow immersion, the ship's boilers burst with an explosion so violent that she felt 'a sickening pain' in her back. Gasping for breath and inadvertently gulping down a foul mixture of oil and seawater, she was saved when a small raft drifted her way and she was hauled aboard. They meandered into the night through the detritus of the tragedy. 'We occasionally met other rafts, carrying men and women; we passed doors, orange-boxes, oars, pieces of wood . . . with men clinging on desperately and crying for help.'[8]

Seeing so many bodies in the water – alive and dead – and hearing the cries of the Italian prisoners, Hartenstein did what he could to pluck the living to safety. Soon after midnight, now fully aware of the scale of the disaster, he radioed Dönitz for further instructions. Under the prevailing rules of maritime warfare, the U-boat commander-in-chief would have been at liberty to instruct Hartenstein to leave the scene and proceed with his Cape mission. Instead – evidently influenced by the large number of Italians who were among the U-boat's victims – he ordered the other three U-boats which had been heading south with Hartenstein to join U-156's rescue operation. Hitler concurred with the proviso that he 'did not wish to see the Cape Town operations adversely affected, and that in any case the boats were to run no risks to themselves during the rescue work'.[9] Dönitz also instructed two more U-boats (U-506 and U-507), which were prowling off Freetown at the time, to head for the scene to join the rescue operation.

By the early hours of the 13th Hartenstein's crew had not only plucked more than 190 survivors from the water but U-156 also had four lifeboats in tow, filled with a further 200 men, women, and children. Overwhelmed by such numbers and mindful of the fact that scores more must be still in the water, he took it upon himself to summon assistance. At 4 a.m. – using the same waveband that the *Laconia*'s captain had used to send out a series of SOS messages as his vessel began to sink – Hartenstein radioed: 'If any ship will assist the shipwrecked *Laconia* crew, I will not attack her provided I am not attacked by ship or air forces.'[10] In effect he was offering to declare the surrounding seas a temporary 'no fire' zone so that the victims of his attack could be rescued by any vessel of any nationality.

The U-boat commander had taken this radical – even unprecedented – step without seeking higher authority. Though Dönitz was taken aback by Hartenstein's initiative, he did not seek to remonstrate. Instead, anxious that his U-boats would very soon be exposed to enemy attack, he ordered them to take on board only 'such numbers as will ensure that boats still remain fully operational when submerged'.[11] As he had hoped, Hartenstein's message was indeed picked up by the British authorities in Freetown but was initially discounted as a crude ruse by the enemy to lure unwary vessels into a trap. As a result, none of the very few Royal Navy vessels on patrol in that part of the South Atlantic were sent to the rescue. In the meantime, though, Hartenstein's call had been answered by the Vichy authorities, who ordered two French warships, the *Gloire* (from Dakar, the capital of Senegal) and the *Annamite* (from Conakry, the capital of neighbouring Guinea) to rendezvous with the submarines and take on board all their passengers. Mindful of this, and mindful of Hitler's instructions the evening before, Dönitz took the opportunity to order three of the Cape-bound U-boats to resume their voyage south.

In the long night following the sinking, the raft which had rescued

Nurse Hawkins was upended on more than one occasion by a rogue wave. It became harder each time to find the energy to clamber back on board. Some of the men, exhausted by the effort of keeping afloat for hour after hour, silently released their grip, fell back in the sea and disappeared from view. By dawn, Hawkins was not only soaked but chilled by a biting wind. As the equatorial sun rose towards its zenith, however, she and her shipwrecked companions felt the warmth return to their bodies only to discover that their arms, legs and faces had started to blister under the intensity of its rays. It was not until the evening of the 13th that they were seen by U-156 and lifted aboard, their legs so swollen and stiff from sunburn that they could hardly stand. Hartenstein and his crew treated them with 'great kindness and respect' and, as one of the four women among the 260 or more survivors who occupied almost every surface above and below decks, Hawkins was not only plied with nourishing food and refreshing drink but given eau de cologne and cold cream as balm to her blistered body. Hartenstein, she wrote, was 'particularly charming and helpful: he could scarcely have done more if he was entertaining us in peacetime. I did not hear "Heil Hitler" once; I saw no swastikas, and only one photograph of Hitler, in a small recess.'[12]

Holding (who had not found it necessary to chop off any fingers to repel Italian prisoners attempting to board his lifeboat) was given a similar welcome when Hartenstein came alongside. The (unidentified) British officer who had taken command of the little vessel had already set a course for the African coast, which he apparently estimated was some 900 miles away. According to Holding, the U-boat commander 'said we'd got no chance – it was too far, and we shouldn't move out of the area. We didn't believe him – you know, just a German telling lies.' Their attitude towards him changed when the U-boat commander invited anyone who had been wounded to come aboard for treatment. Holding, who had rubbed his hands raw sliding down a rope into the lifeboat, accepted gratefully. When his wounds had been dressed, he asked one of Hartenstein's crew for a cigarette and was astonished to be offered not one but a fistful. 'This German said, "Kamerad, give these to your mates." I thought, "This is a funny German. Not the way I've been brought up to think about them." They were brilliant.'[13]

On the morning of the 15th, the U-boats Dönitz had diverted from their Freetown operation – U-506 and U-507 – arrived at the epicentre of the disaster to join Hartenstein's U-156 in the rescue operation. U-507 – under the command of Harro Schacht – picked up Janet Walker, who was by now frantic with worry about her daughter. Schacht was sympathetic. With lifeboats and rafts now scattered widely across the horizon, he went out of his way to see if Doreen could be found, frequently summoning her mother to the conning tower and lending her his binoculars to see if she could pick out her daughter. She couldn't.

Schacht also came alongside the lifeboat to which Holding had returned with the fistful of cigarettes given him by Hartenstein's crew. Holding recalled that the U-boat commander passed over a supply of tinned bread, soup and a bottle of wine. Echoing Hartenstein's advice, he also told them to stay where they were and for the same reason. Holding noted, 'we had no choice but to take his word for it'.[14] It was a wise decision.

On the morning of the 16th, a four-engined bomber with distinct US markings on its fuselage flew overhead. At once, 'as proof of my peaceful intentions', Hartenstein ordered a 'a large Red Cross flag four yards square' to be displayed on the U-boat's bridge, facing the line of the aircraft's flight.[15] When it arrived overhead, Hartenstein signalled the pilot in Morse code apparently hoping to ask 'Are there any ships in sight?' Almost simultaneously the American plane challenged the U-boat to show its national flag. Neither appeared to understand what the other was trying to say before the plane – a long-range B-24D Liberator – flew off over the horizon.

On board the bomber, the pilot, Lieutenant James D. Harden, who – like his three-man crew – was on his first mission, radioed their base on Ascension Island seeking further instructions. A decision would have to be made rapidly as the aircraft was too far out to sea to remain airborne for more than another thirty minutes without running out of fuel. Captain Robert C. Richardson did not delay but ordered simply, 'Sink sub'.[16] Harden duly turned back to fly over U-156 at a height of 250 feet and dropped three bombs in quick succession, all of which fell wide. As he turned to fly in for a second attack, Hartenstein's crew made frantic efforts to cut themselves free from the lifeboats they had under tow so that the submarine could dive to safety without dragging the *Laconia*'s survivors down as well. This time the Liberator dropped another two bombs. One of these, Hartenstein noted, 'exploded, with a few seconds' delayed action, directly under the control room. Conning tower vanished in a tower of black water. Control room and bow compartment reported taking water.'[17]

Instructing the survivors crammed on U-156's deck to don lifejackets and jump into the sea, he put the submarine into a steep dive. Seeing this, the B-24's young and inexperienced pilot wheeled away to report, 'The sub rolled over and was last seen bottom up. Crew had abandoned sub and taken to surrounding lifeboats.'[18] Harden was either confused by the chaos he had caused or had allowed his imagination to run riot – or both. U-156 had in fact only sustained minor damage and escaped relatively unscathed.

By now Doris Hawkins, who had obeyed Hartenstein's order, was once again flailing in the Atlantic Ocean. She was a poor swimmer but an RAF officer, Squadron Leader H. R. K. Wells, saw her plight. Propping her up in his arms, he swam with her for fifty minutes through the swell until he caught sight of a lifeboat lifted on the crest of a wave. Hawkins was hauled aboard, where she found herself crammed into a thirty-foot open boat with sixty-six other survivors, all of whom, bar one, were men. The exception, she was relieved to see, was another young woman, Lady Grizel, Mary Wolfe Murray,* with whom she had formed a close friendship in the *Laconia*. As they drifted away from all other signs of human life, Wells – 'a very gallant gentleman', as Hawkins described him – was picked up by another lifeboat, all of whose occupants were to die from sickness and exposure within the next ten days.

When news of the B-24 attack on Hartenstein's submarine reached Dönitz later that evening, he was incensed. Signalling Hartenstein at once, he instructed: 'You are in no circumstances to risk the safety of your boat. All measures to ensure safety, including abandonment of rescue operations, to be ruthlessly taken. Do not rely on enemy showing slightest consideration.'[19] By this time Schacht, in U-507, had picked up ninety-one survivors, including fifteen women and children, and Erich Würdemann, the captain of U-506, advised that he had picked up a further 151, among whom were nine women and children. Armed with this information, Dönitz had second thoughts. After what he described as 'a very heated discussion' at his headquarters, in the course of which, he wrote, some of his most senior lieutenants argued strenuously that it

---

*Lady Grizel was the daughter of the Earl of Glasgow. She was returning from the Middle East after visiting her husband, a major serving in the Black Watch.

would be 'wholly unjustifiable' to put the U-boats at any further risk by continuing with the rescue, he nonetheless ordered the submarines to remain on station until the arrival of the Vichy warships. He also instructed them to offload all their passengers – with the exception of the Italian POWs – into the surrounding lifeboats: 'In view of the callous attitude, to say the least of it, adopted by the British authorities [in not sending any rescue ships to the scene] it seemed to me only logical that I, having accepted full responsibility for allowing the U-boats to continue their work of rescue, should now restrict their hazardous activities to the rescue of our allies, the Italians.'[20]

He soon felt vindicated. Just after midday on the 17th, U-506's lookout saw an aircraft approaching over the horizon. Schacht had just enough time to crash-dive and disappear below the surface before the B-24's bombs hit the water. Although the impact of the explosions was severe enough to send shock-waves through the vessel, the submarine was not damaged and Schacht made good his escape to join up again with U-507 for their prearranged rendezvous with the *Gloire* and *Annamite*. Like his first, Lieutenant Harden's second mission had failed.

That afternoon scores of British and Polish survivors were safely transferred to the two Vichy vessels which then set a course for Dakar and Casablanca. Among those thus brought to safety was Janet Walker, still desperate to find her daughter. Once on board, she darted this way and that through the throng of passengers, praying that she was about to be reunited with her little one, but there was no sign of her. The reality was unbearable. 'Even when I went back home I still didn't give up,' she recalled several years later. 'I thought maybe she'd been taken to some island. I used to spend money on fortune-tellers hoping they would give me some clue.'[21] A year later, though, she met a fellow survivor who told her she had seen a little girl who fitted Doreen's description being lifted into a lifeboat which overturned while it was being lowered into the water, hurling all its occupants into the sea. Hearing this, Janet Walker finally accepted that her daughter was dead. It was little comfort that she was herself among the thousand or more survivors, almost all of whom would have perished if Dönitz had not given his consent for the U-boats to pluck them to safety.

Not every survivor was picked up. Some either did not hear or did not heed Hartenstein's advice and opted to head for the African coast. Doris Hawkins, her friend Mary Wolfe Murray and their sixty-six male colleagues were 600 miles from land in a boat which had sprung a leak and required constant bailing; it had five oars but no sail and the rudder was missing. Between them, they had fifteen gallons of water, a quantity of ship's biscuits, Horlicks tablets, chocolate and some bars of pemmican.*[22] It was not enough to last so many people for more than a few days.

The lack of food was bearable but the water ration – two ounces a day – soon became hard to bear. 'When we received our precious drop, we took a sip, ran it round our teeth and gums, gargled with it and finally swallowed it . . . As we grew weaker, our mouths drier and drier, we only spoke when necessary.' Mary Wolfe Murray grew steadily weaker. On 25 September she seemed to fall asleep. 'Throughout that night I had my arms around her, in a last effort to keep her warm, but this night she didn't shiver, nothing disturbed her, and at six in the morning she just stopped breathing.' They held a short burial service but could not find the strength to sing 'Abide With Me' before lowering her body into the water.

She was but the first to die: 'Daily we saw our companions growing weaker, saw they had not long to live, and then sometimes found they were no longer with us. Some, despite all warnings, drank salt water and succumbed, and others became delirious. Their cries and rambling speech and often repeated pleas for water were terrible to hear.'[23]

Initially the lifeboat's rations had been allocated by the ship's surgeon, Dr Geoffrey Purslow, whose resolution in adversity had given encouragement to fainter hearts. He had been one of those who managed to fashion a makeshift mast with an oar and to rig a sail using the lifeboat's tarpaulin cover. In the process, he had managed to cut himself quite badly. In the absence of any medical supplies, the wound festered and the infection spread. Before long he was unable to stand for any length of time. Some nineteen days after the sinking of the *Laconia*, Hawkins saw that the doctor, apparently fearing that he would infect others, had come to a great decision:

> I stumbled over to where he was sitting and tried to speak to him, but no words came. He was quite conscious, and in a voice stronger than I had

---

*A nourishing compound of crushed dried meat, melted fat and other ingredients that was favoured by Arctic explorers.

heard for many days, he said: 'As I cannot be of any further help, and as I am now a source of danger to you all, it is better I should go.' As he heaved himself painfully up the side of the boat, I found my voice and said: 'Greater love hath no man than this that he lay down his life for his friends.' He said, 'Goodbye,' and with a long look took that final step backwards, The sea closed over him.[24]

In the following days, others perished at an accelerating rate.

It was not until Thursday 8 October, by which time they had been at sea for twenty-five days, that a naval rating saw the outlines of what looked like a convoy in the distance. Those who could do so roused themselves to watch the distant shapes with intense focus. After thirty minutes, when they realized that the ships must be riding at anchor, 'we knew that our prayers were answered and our dreams had been realized, that ahead of us was land'. Soon an RAF flying boat circled overhead. It dropped a lifebelt on which the crew had scribbled 'Help coming'. They were five miles off the coast of Liberia and sixty miles south of the capital, Monrovia. 'None of us had any idea where Monrovia was, but we knew what help was, and our hearts sang.' After a voyage of more than 600 miles in an open boat, Doris Hawkins stepped onto dry land. The nursing missionary was one of sixteen survivors from the lifeboat's original complement of sixty-eight souls.

At the time, the *Laconia* incident was hushed up by Washington and London. As in other incidents that were deemed likely to generate adverse headlines or 'give comfort' to the enemy, it was judged impolitic to draw public attention to a tragic episode in which more than 1,600 men, women and children had perished. It would be twenty years, courtesy of two diligent historians, Dr Maurer Maurer and Lawrence J. Paszek, before the truth finally emerged about the so-called 'mystery plane' that – in obedience to the order 'Sink sub' – had bombed those who were trying to rescue the shipwrecked survivors.

By his own account, Dönitz's Laconia Order – which was to form the kernel of the capital charge laid against him at Nuremberg in 1945 – sprang from a cold calculation of profit and loss.* 'I had realized', he

---

* At Nuremberg, the Allied prosecutors sought to prove that Dönitz's 'Laconia Order' had – in effect – authorized murder on the high seas and he was therefore guilty of war crimes which merited the death penalty. Their case was undermined when the commander-in-chief of the US Navy in the Pacific, Admiral Nimitz,

wrote after serving his ten-year sentence in Spandau jail, 'that in no circumstances must I ever again risk the loss of a boat and its crew in an enterprise of a similar nature.'[25]

His implacable edict (p. 327) concluded with an injunction that he chose to exclude from his memoirs: 'Be Hard. Think of the fact that the enemy in his bombing attacks on German towns and cities has no regard for women and children.'[26] The warning could not have been lost on his loyal U-boat commanders. In future, to save a fellow mariner from drowning would be to incur the wrath of an unforgiving commander-in-chief. Dönitz was not only a patriot but a zealot for whom the quality of mercy was a mark of weakness that no respectable Nazi should ever indulge.

From the Allied perspective, the statistics of the war at sea were starting to look very ominous indeed. Totting up the gains and losses, the War Cabinet in London saw a looming disaster in the Atlantic from which Britain could escape only with greater support of the United States. This was to prove a mountainous diplomatic challenge.

In August 1942 the total size of Dönitz's fleet had finally reached what was for him the magic number of 300 U-boats – the pre-war 'grand total' which, somewhat arbitrarily, he had advised Hitler was required to deliver a 'mortal blow' against Britain. Although repairs and servicing meant that sometimes little more than half this number were operational at any one time, the admiral had grounds for optimism. Between August and November, some 380 freighters were sunk in the Atlantic. In his War Diary, after sinking 119 ships in one month – a record number – he reported that 'successes in November . . . will probably amount to 900,000 tons. The time has come to regard these results in a true light.'[27] In fact, Allied shipping losses for that month totalled 720,000 tons; nonetheless, the autumn surge in Atlantic sinkings represented a 44 per cent increase from the 500,000 tons that had been sunk in August.

---

volunteered that ships under his command were authorized to wage 'unrestricted warfare' against the Japanese and were not expected to rescue survivors if there was any risk that this would jeopardize their mission. Although Dönitz was convicted of war crimes, he was spared the death penalty.

These figures prompted Churchill to send an unusually emotional cable to Roosevelt:

> The U-boat menace is our worst danger . . . the spectacle of all these splendid ships being built, sent to sea crammed with priceless food and munitions, and being sunk – three or four every day – torments me day and night. Not only does this attack cripple our war energies and threaten our life, but it arbitrarily limits the might of the United States coming into the struggle. The oceans, which were your shield, threaten to become your cage.

Urging the president to accelerate the building of new merchant ships and convoy escorts and to provide Britain with its 'fair share' of all shipping, he warned that already Britain's food stocks were 'running down with dangerous rapidity' and that 'in case of a renewed blitz on the Mersey and the Clyde or [an] exceptional concentration of U-boats on the Atlantic routes . . . I should be forced to reduce our general commitment to the overseas war effort.' Shorn of its grandiloquence, his special pleading – which contained an element of bluff – was essentially a simple shopping list at the top of which was the need 'to import 27,000,000 tons for our food and war effort in 1943'.[28]

The prime minister was not naive. Prone as he was to bandy mind-boggling statistics as though they posed answers rather questions, he knew that, to win his argument, he would need Roosevelt to override the competing demands of his own military and civilian advisors in and around the White House. To this end, he despatched to Washington a member of the War Cabinet, Oliver Lyttelton, the Minister of Production, to lobby Roosevelt on his behalf; Lyttelton, he told the president, 'is fully authorized to discuss all the above matters with you, and he is fully in possession of our views'.[29] The prime minister's envoy was a polished advocate but he soon realized that, to make headway, he would first have to negotiate the administration's Byzantine bureaucracy. As he explained soon after his arrival, 'I, therefore, determined at the outset of my mission to discuss all the subjects closely with the Services and only to ask the president to intervene where our vital needs were not being met.'[30]

His guide through Washington's administrative undergrowth was Arthur Salter, who, as head of the British Merchant Shipping Mission, had been labouring in that overgrown labyrinth since the spring of

30. (*top*) Arctic conditions on an Allied merchant ship. In this perilous region, weather conditions were routinely atrocious.

31. (*bottom*) One of at least 400 US merchant ships sunk by U-boats along the Atlantic coast of the United States in the first half of 1942 during Operation Drumbeat. This 'killing spree' alarmed Roosevelt and Churchill. Dönitz could hardly believe his good fortune.

32. (*top*) By 1943, the Atlantic convoys bringing supplies to Britain and Russia frequently numbered fifty vessels or more.

33. (*bottom*) U-boat POWs were few in number. Most crews perished.

34. Patriotic posters were distributed in British ports to remind workers that they had a critical role in feeding the nation.

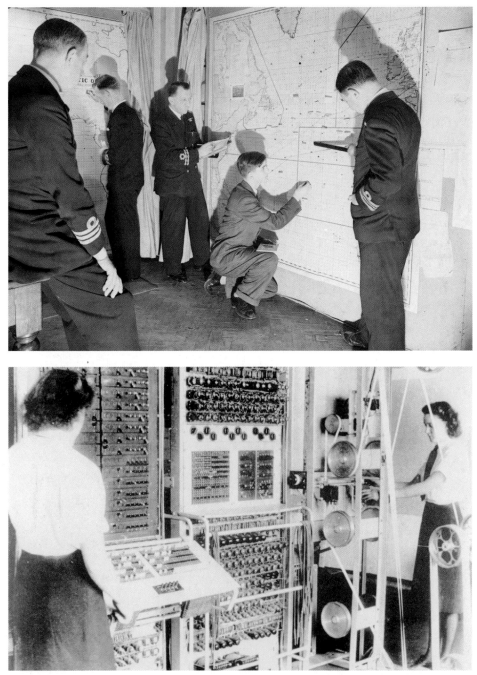

35. (*top*) Officers in the Plot Room at the Admiralty in December 1942, planning the routes of ships on large wall maps. By the spring of 1942 a handful of U-boats had destroyed 45 per cent of the shipping volume required to meet the demand for oil within the United States and Britain. These statistics alarmed the Allies.

36. (*bottom*) Bletchley Park, the secret headquarters of the Government Code & Cypher School (GC&CS), where they broke the Enigma code. This had less impact on the Battle of the Atlantic than is often claimed.

37. The Enigma machine, which the German high command used to encrypt secret military traffic. Inside the body of the machine were three parallel wheels, like aerofoils but with letters stamped along them. Each time a letter key was depressed, one or more wheels would rotate and a different letter would light up on a lampboard. By early 1940 a team of gifted mathematicians, scientists, engineers and analysts were on their way to breaking the Enigma code with the use of Alan Turing's 'bombe', which replicated the action of several Enigma machines wired together.

38. An emergency feeding centre in Liverpool. One of Churchill's greatest fears was that a serious food shortage would rock the morale of the British people.

39. A rating (P. S. Buckingham) inscribing another U-boat kill on the side of the wheelhouse on board HMS *Hesperus*. By the summer of 1943, the Allies had won the Battle of the Atlantic.

40. D-Day, 6 June 1944: British commandos storm ashore on Gold Beach. The invasion of Normandy – initially involving more than 156,000 Allied troops – was only possible because the Germans had already been defeated in the Battle of the Atlantic.

1941. In the intervening months Salter had become so entangled in the impenetrable thickets of bureaucratic intrigue that even his American allies in the relevant departments – who were very few in number – had proved unable or reluctant to liberate him. His task had not been made easier by the fact that from time to time British demands on American beneficence had been overstated by Whitehall officials anxious to ensure a comfortable surplus to guard against any unforeseen interruption of supplies. He was therefore accustomed to suspicious and adversarial scrutiny by his American counterparts. By late 1942 even the Anglophile Lewis Douglas – whose title of Deputy Director of the War Shipping Administration (WSA) belied his formidable influence – was unwilling to press his case in the absence of firm evidence that Britain really was in dire straits.

Douglas's reluctance to take Britain's case all the way to the White House was underpinned by his own predicament. With demand for shipping dramatically escalated by Operation Torch,* he was under growing pressure from his counterparts in the military. General Brehon B. Somervell, who bore overall responsibility for supplying the US Army's needs, had recently tried to browbeat him into ceding to his office control of the supplies designated for Britain as well as for America's own forces. Nor was Somervell above arguing that it would be 'desirable' for him to have the authority to 'cut off food exports'[31] to America's transatlantic ally. Douglas was also at loggerheads with Admiral William D. Leahy, who was formally the most senior military figure in the United States as the de facto chairman of the US joint chiefs of staff. When Leahy demanded that supplies to Britain be curtailed to meet the needs of the United States in the Pacific theatre, Douglas – who did not readily quail before officers in uniform, however senior they might be – lost his temper. Retorting that by exaggerating its demands the US military was endangering the overall conduct of the war, he asked icily, 'Did we want fighting and equipped allies, or did we prefer to fight alone?'[32]

In the absence of any strategic overview, decisions that would determine the outcome on the battlefield were being made in such an arbitrary

---

* The first wave of more than 100,000 Allied troops from the United States and Britain was due to land on the shores of Morocco and Algeria in the second week of November; they disembarked on the 8th.

and ad hoc manner, that an official United States government report was driven to conclude that not only were British interests being adversely affected but that 'problems directly affecting the [American] nation's survival are being met on a day-to-day basis without adequate information for proper decisions'.[33] Churchill's envoy had been fore-armed with a set of dire prognoses which – if he could secure a hearing for himself – would make a powerful case without need of exagger-ation. According to a leading historian of the increasingly bitter conflict over logistics which now bedevilled relations between Washington and London, 'Britain's shipping situation was becoming untenable by the autumn of 1942 and import programme forecasts indicated steady dete-rioration in the near future.'[34]

In April, British officials had estimated that the total of British imports for the whole of 1942 would be between 24 and 27 million tons; in fact the figure fell to 23 million tons, which, they advised, was likely to be even worse the following year. If their projections were accurate, only 9.5 million tons would reach Britain's ports in the first six months of 1943. An annual rate of, at most, 19 million tons would be a cata-strophic shortfall.

That was to reckon without the import of essential fuel oils, the life-blood of Britain's economy. By mid-December, Britain's reserves of commercial oil were projected to fall to 300,000 tons. With consumption running at 130,000 tons a month, the nation's industrial output – notably the production of steel and the manufacture of munitions – would soon be in jeopardy. The Royal Navy maintained a million tons of oil in reserve for an emergency, an essential contingency which, were it to be used for any other purpose, ran the risk of immobilizing the fleet.[35]

By the end of 1942, Allied shipping losses for the year would amount to no fewer than 1,664 vessels, 60 per cent of them sunk by Dönitz's U-boats. Although the United States and Britain were building mer-chant ships at the rate of 7 million tons a year, 8 million tons would be on the bottom of the ocean by the end of December. In every year since the start of the war the Allies had been losing more freighters than they had been able to build; it was little wonder that a senior member of the naval staff was to confirm, after more than three years of conflict, 'Our shipping situation has never been tighter.'[36] It was true that eighty-seven U-boats had been sunk or destroyed during the year, but Dönitz's fleet had still grown rapidly from a total of ninety-one operational boats in

January to a total of 250 by December. Thus, while the Allies were still losing merchant ships at a faster rate than they could produce them, the German U-Boat fleet was expanding at a faster rate than ever. It was as grim an imbalance as it was possible to imagine.

These projections formed the backdrop to Lyttelton's formidable objective of transforming Churchill's plea for Roosevelt's assistance into an American commitment to deliver. His first task was to persuade key officials like Emery Land, the Anglophobic administrator of the WSA, that Britain genuinely needed the 27 million tons of supplies for which Churchill had asked Roosevelt. By dint of charm and precision, Lyttelton accomplished this objective with less difficulty than might have been expected. His second task was to secure an undertaking from the US administration that this tonnage would be delivered in a timely fashion. This proved far harder; it was impossible to get any such commitment at any level of the civilian or military bureaucracy in the American capital. To untie the Gordian knot which threatened to ensnare him, he decided that the time had come to present his calling card at the White House. The only way of breaking the logistics logjam was a sign-off from the president.

On the face of it, Lyttelton's meeting with Roosevelt towards the end of November could hardly have been more productive. A few days afterwards, the president wrote to Churchill apparently committing the United States to filling Britain's shopping basket to the very brim.

> I am well aware of the concern with which your Government faces the serious net losses in the tonnage of your merchant fleet. It is a net loss which persists and I think we must face the fact that it may continue through all of next year. I, therefore, want to give you the assurance that from our expanding fleet you may depend on the tonnage necessary to meet your import program.

No commitment could have more unequivocal. However, there was a characteristic caveat, a presidential sting in the tail:

> You will, I am sure, agree that emergencies may develop which may require me to divert for our military purposes tonnage which it is now contemplated will be utilized for imports to Great Britain . . . [but] I wish to give you the definite assurance, subject to the qualifications I have indicated, that your requirements will be met.

In a single ambivalent paragraph, the president had given his officials all the wriggle room they would need to extricate themselves from an otherwise solemn pledge. However, this did not deter Roosevelt from adding, with the nonchalance of a brazen politician, 'I want you to feel that this letter, together with the agreements that Oliver is taking home with him, gives you the assurance that you need.'[37] Of course the implicit goodwill that underpinned his heavily qualified commitment made this letter of decidedly more worth than the paper it was written on. Yet it failed to offer respite.

It was not long before the WSA, which had the overall responsibility for implementing the presidential directive, seized on the qualifications in the president's letter, informing Salter that 'any figures of tonnage that may have been quoted . . . are taken as estimates only, and not as commitment to allocate a precise amount of shipping'.[38] This was precisely what the British representative most feared. With the U-boats holding the initiative in the Atlantic, Douglas's impeccably valid interpretation of the presidential intentions was bound to aggravate the already tense relations between US officials and their British counterparts as they wrestled over the challenge of delivering vital supplies to Britain without jeopardizing the national interest of the United States.

For a time, the potential impact of the shipping shortage on Britain gnawed at the personal relationship between Roosevelt and Churchill as they sought to resolve this worsening dilemma. In the middle of December, the prime minister warned that 'the acute shortage of shipping' forecast for early 1943 would lead to a cut in imports of all kinds including oil, the stocks of which, he advised, were already severely depleted.[39] Two weeks later, more anxious than ever, he warned that it had become a matter of 'mortal urgency' to provide more shipping for the Atlantic convoys than had been allocated so far. Asserting that imports were now projected to fall to an annual rate of 17 million tons (which was even lower than his officials had recently projected), he warned that such a shortfall would entail a severe cut in the consumption of food and raw materials. In terms which combined supplication and threat, the prime minister wrote: 'I must tell you frankly . . . unless our shipping resources are, in fact, as you so kindly propose I shall be forced immediately to reduce the British War Effort in overseas theatres even though this involves prolongation of the war and leaves you a greater portion of the burden we are eager to share.'[40]

His anxiety was unfeigned. By the end of 1942, Dönitz's fleet had not only grown to an overall total of 365 U-boats but upwards of 200 of these were operational at any one time, of which no fewer than 164 were now prowling the Atlantic Ocean. Recording the prevailing view of the Admiralty at the time, the navy's official historian observed: 'it was plain that the Battle of the Convoy Routes was still to be decided, that the enemy had greater strength than ever before, and that the crisis in the long-drawn struggle was near'.[41] He did not exaggerate.

# 17. Changes at the Top

By the end of the year, the Red Army was starting to turn the tide against the Wehrmacht in Russia while, following the Torch landings in November, the Axis powers were under pressure in North Africa as well. This made the role of the U-boat campaign even more critical to the Third Reich's hope of throttling the transatlantic lifeline. Dönitz not only saw this imperative more clearly than any of his peers but also, to his intense satisfaction, found himself thrust into a far stronger position to achieve that objective. The Führer had finally and irrevocably fallen out with the Kriegsmarine's commander-in-chief, Admiral Raeder, and Dönitz was now poised to inherit the naval crown.

The mutual antipathy between Raeder and Dönitz, which sprang from their conflicting views about the strategic purpose of naval warfare, had been aggravated by suspicion and rivalry as the senior officer's influence at the Führer's court began to evaporate. Frustrated by Raeder's failure to build up and equip the U-boat fleet at the rate needed to throttle the Allied supply lines, Dönitz went on the offensive. Without mentioning Raeder by name, he complained that it was 'irresponsible' and 'insufferable' that 'a painful decline in the sinking of enemy tonnage' was thereby inevitable.[1] Raeder was furious. It appeared to him as though Dönitz was deliberately seeking to undermine his authority. By constantly stressing the tonnage war he appeared oblivious to any other theatre of conflict; moreover, he seemed hell-bent on seizing powers to which he was not entitled, to the point where 'there was no aspect of the building, fitting out, repairing, experimental and development work on U-boats, or even the training of personnel which he was not trying to take over, reorganize and drive forward'.[2]

Raeder reacted by ordering his subordinate to confine his duties to the conduct of the U-boat campaign in the Atlantic. This proved counterproductive. According to Dönitz's propaganda officer, Wolfgang Frank, Dönitz's response was to ring Raeder's adjutant to say, 'Please inform the Grand Admiral that I cannot obey this order.' He then turned to his trusted staff officer, Eberhardt Godt, and said, 'If I were in

Raeder's place I would probably sack the BdU [Commander of the U-boats] for this; but we'll see what happens.'[3] Nothing did – except that Raeder apparently gave orders that Dönitz's name should be expunged from the caption of any photograph showing the two of them together.

Dönitz's arrogance was soon rewarded, though not in a way he could have foreseen. On 30 December 1942 a U-boat in the Arctic detected a convoy, JW51B.* Raeder told Hitler that he intended to intercept the merchant ships 'subject to confirmation . . . that no superior force [was] accompanying convoy'.[4] Hitler was increasingly anxious about the Wehrmacht's predicament on the Russian Front, where the Sixth Army, under General Paulus, had just been surrounded at Stalingrad. Raeder's scheme offered a realistic chance to starve the Russian enemy of crucial supplies at a critical time. The Führer gave the operation – Rainbow, as it was codenamed – his enthusiastic approval.

Unhappily for Raeder, poor weather and even worse intelligence intervened to turn Rainbow into a fading mirage. As soon as the convoy was sighted, the admiral in command of the operation, Oskar Kummitz, ordered the heavy cruisers *Hipper* and *Lützow* – which were leading two battle groups, each escorted by six destroyers for the purpose – to close on the convoy. Given to expect that he would meet little opposition, Kummitz was taken aback when two of the escort destroyers protecting JW51B suddenly emerged from the gloom to fend off the attackers. The German admiral, who had been instructed repeatedly that the Kriegsmarine's most precious surface vessels should not be exposed to any significant risk, was even more rattled when a British minesweeper, HMS *Bramble*, managed to collide accidentally with *Hipper* in the fog-tipped twilight. As the *Bramble* went down with all hands, Kummitz ordered his heavy cruiser (which had only been slightly damaged) to withdraw immediately. Wrongly presuming that an all-out British counter-attack with cruisers was imminent, he then instructed every vessel in both battle groups to follow suit.

Unfortunately, Kummitz's message to Berlin in which he reported this decision was misunderstood by both Raeder and Hitler. Allowing

* Following PQ18 in September, the Arctic convoys had been suspended until December when they were renewed but in smaller groupings and coded by the letters JW (outward) and RA (homeward), the series starting at JW51.

himself to believe that the admiral had withdrawn only because the Kriegsmarine had achieved its objective, the Führer boasted accordingly to his New Year guests. When the truth emerged, he was incandescent with rage. Ranting against the Kriegsmarine's failure to deliver a mortal blow against the enemy, he summoned Raeder to a meeting on 6 January at which he subjected the grand admiral to a ninety-minute tirade, inveighing against the inglorious history of the German navy and the pusillanimity of the present Kriegsmarine. Mocking the fact that the Raeder's beloved capital ships could apparently leave harbour only if surrounded by a cavalcade of smaller ships to protect them, he threatened to scrap all the big ships and to transfer their long-range guns to coastal defence. In a further insult, which Raeder interpreted as a direct attack on his own honour, he sneered:

> The number of one's forces in relationship to the enemy's has always played a great role with the navy as opposed to the army. As a soldier the Führer demands that once forces have been committed to action, the battle be fought to a decision. Due to the present critical situation, where all fighting power, all personnel, and all material must be brought into action, we cannot permit our large ships to ride idly at anchor for months.

Raeder bore what he later described as the Führer's 'vicious and impertinent' onslaught in silence, noting a few days later, 'I felt it beneath the dignity of the commanding officer of the navy to attempt to contradict in detail such utterly prejudiced statements.'[5]

When Hitler had finished his incoherent and self-contradictory rant (it had, after all, been at his insistence that the Kriegsmarine's most powerful warships had spent so many months at anchor), the grand admiral asked for a private meeting with the Führer at which he tendered his resignation, as Hitler clearly required. Advising that he should not step down formally until 30 January – which happened neatly to coincide with the tenth anniversary of the Third Reich – Raeder pointed out that this face-saving formula would allow his departure to be presented as no more than a timely moment to make way for a younger replacement. Raeder was a proud and obstinate man who would never concede that he had made some calamitous errors of strategic and operational judgement. But, at the age of sixty-seven, he was worn down by Dönitz's insubordination, his exclusion from the deliberations of the high command and the efforts of his peers to under-mine his standing with the Führer. In particular, the animosity he harboured for Göring had reached the point of no return. The stiff and dignified admiral had come to loathe the slippery and self-serving Reichsmarschall whom he held personally responsible for undermining his beloved Kriegsmarine with 'distorted and inaccurate' accounts of naval engagements in which the Luftwaffe had also been involved. His final words to Hitler as he took his leave were, 'Please protect the Navy and my successor against Göring.'

A more influential but far subtler adversary, however, was Albert Speer. An even smarter opportunist than Göring, Speer had been plucked by Hitler in the spring of 1942 from his relative obscurity as a commercial architect to become an influential member of his inner cir-cle. Given a plum job as Minister of Armaments over the head of the Reichsmarschall, who had coveted that powerful position for himself, he had swiftly insinuated himself into the Führer's favour to become an indispensable confidant.

In the months since his appointment, the new minister had estab-lished a strong rapport with the thrusting U-boat admiral. Quick to recognize the importance of the tonnage war, Speer endorsed the U-boat commander's urge to expand and modernize the U-boat fleet. It may be presumed that Dönitz's disdainful defiance of Raeder sprang in part from his knowledge that he was held in high esteem by Hitler's new favourite. Speer was certainly aware of the 'serious dissension' between Raeder and Dönitz and in early January 1943 he took advan-tage of an opening provided by Hitler to press the case for the U-boat commander-in-chief. Knowing that any 'direct attempt to influence [the Führer] was hopeless', the sinuous Speer, by his own account, 'merely hinted that all obstacles standing in the way of our U-boat plans could be eliminated were [Dönitz] given his head', adding, 'What I wanted to achieve was the replacement of Raeder.'[6]

If only to avoid any suspicion that he was being vindictive, or per-haps because he thought that Dönitz had the qualifications to be a contender, Raeder nominated his adversarial subordinate as one of his possible successors and he wrote to the Führer accordingly. Though he did not say so explicitly, his preferred candidate was without doubt Admiral Rolf Carls (who had earned a reputation for courage in com-bat). The choice of Dönitz, he wrote, 'would have the advantage of stressing especially the significance of the U-boat campaign as of war-decisive importance. The only disadvantage is the fact that Admiral Dönitz with his appointment as C-in-C would not be able to dedicate himself to the immediate conduct of the U-boat war to the same extent as formerly.'[7] It is hard to resist the conclusion that this caveat was intended to imply that Dönitz was not equipped for great strategic responsibilities and would be more productively confined to the operational role in which he had proved so effective. In any event, though Raeder's endorsement was less than whole-hearted, Dönitz had Speer as his principal cheerleader and his appointment was therefore a shoo-in. Promoted to the rank of Grossadmiral, he became commander-in-chief of the Kriegsmarine on the same day that Raeder 'retired' from the service which had been his life for thirty-nine years, an apparently seamless transfer of authority.

The very morning that he assumed office, Dönitz issued an Order of the Day to all those now under his command. It was an unambiguous assertion of the new commander-in-chief's priorities. Going out of his way to 'thank the submarine arm, for its death-defying readiness to fight, which is shown at all times, and its loyalty', he announced he would not only 'continue to command the U-boats' but in his new role would expect 'unconditional obedience, the highest courage, and devotion to the last. In that,' he went on, 'lies our honour. Gathered round our Führer, we shall not lay down our arms until victory and peace have been achieved.'[8]

As commander-in-chief, the new Grossadmiral enjoyed all the perquisites of high office. He and his family moved into a palatial residence in a suburb of Berlin which was filled with fine carpets, paintings and antiques. He travelled by limousine or private train or in the plane which was put at his disposal and he was escorted wherever he went by a squad of armed SS guards. By contrast with his colleague Göring, however, he was, by all accounts, 'upright and not out for personal gain'.[9] A better sense of what animated him is conveyed in a directive to his staff within days of taking up his new appointment: 'Our life belongs to the State. Our honour lies in our duty-fulfilment and readiness for action . . . with fanatical devotion and the most ruthless determination to win.'[10] Such a display of crude zeal might be thought to have been intended as an ingratiating echo of the Führer's own excesses, but Dönitz was every bit as fervent as Hitler; and, though he was canny enough to infiltrate himself into his leader's inner circle, he was not inclined to curry favour even with the man to whom he owed his present distinction.

Determined above all else to secure the resources he needed for the tonnage war, he made it his business to win over the Führer. To this end he paid 'frequent visits to Führer Headquarters', where he sometimes stayed 'for days at a time'.[11] The tactic paid off. When he came to the conclusion that Hitler's intemperate threat to scrap the capital ships would merely burden the Third Reich's exchequer without liberating new resources for the Kriegsmarine, he confronted the Führer openly. At first Hitler bridled at the prospect of countermanding his own very recent instruction but, according to Dönitz, he eventually 'very grudgingly agreed'. To this extent the Kriegsmarine's new commander-in-chief had stolen his predecessor's clothes: like Raeder, he had come to appreciate that to demobilize the surface fleet would do the Third Reich no favours at all. He was not to concede this change of heart, however, being content merely to report his relief that Hitler behaved towards him thereafter with 'exceptional civility'.[12]

Held in high regard by the Führer, he found himself at liberty to prosecute the war at sea according to his own precepts and he determined to make the most of it. From the start, he made it clear that he had no intention of being distracted from the tonnage war, on the outcome of which, he believed, victory or defeat in the Second World War would hinge.

It was not only in Berlin that this presentiment held sway. By the end of 1942 it was evident that a decisive struggle was in the offing, that the endgame could not be far away. In the words of the Royal Navy's official historian:

> It was plain to both sides that the U-boats and the convoy escorts would shortly be locked in a deadly, ruthless series of fights, in which no mercy would be expected and little shown. Nor would one battle, or one week's or a month's fighting, decide the issue. It would be decided by which side could endure the longer.[13]

On the face of it, the U-boats had the upper hand. Their killing spree, which had produced such spectacular results in the closing weeks of 1942, seemed set to continue in 1943. Indeed, the new year began with a spectacular incident which seemed to prove the point in a most alarming fashion.

The expansion of the U-boat fleet made it possible for Dönitz to threaten Allied shipping in several parts of the Atlantic at once. Although it remained his overriding purpose to sever the transatlantic artery between the United States and Britain, the network of capillaries in the Indian Ocean, the Cape route, the seas along the coast of South America, in the West Indies and the Caribbean provided easier pickings. A significantly higher proportion of the merchant ships that ploughed through these waters either went independently or in small convoys that were inadequately escorted and lacked air cover. Although finding them was often as much a matter of luck as judgement, on those occasions when they were detected the U-boats generally had little trouble in sending them to the bottom. The very first week of January 1943 provided one such opportunity.

On 3 January a lone U-boat prowling in the waters off Trinidad caught sight of a convoy of tankers heading northwards and signalled Berlin with its speed and direction. No prey was more enticing than a tanker and Dönitz was immediately on the alert. Presuming that the vessels were taking the shortest – Great Circle – route from the oil terminals in the Caribbean to the Mediterranean to resupply the US forces in North Africa, Dönitz decided to despatch a wolf pack – which was then a thousand miles away – to intercept the convoy. The commander-in-chief was well aware of the limitations of the operation in the absence of long-range reconnaissance aircraft. By his own admission, it was as though a military force had set off on bicycles 'from somewhere near Hamburg to intercept a force in the vicinity of Milan'.[14]

On this occasion, though, his gamble was favoured by fortune. On 7 January, the eight U-boats in Dolphin Group, as the wolf pack was codenamed, formed a patrol line in the waters some 500 miles to the west of the Canary Islands, directly in the path of the Mediterranean-bound ships. His 'intelligent guess' had proved correct. At dawn the following morning, the convoy of nine tankers, codenamed TM1, escorted by one destroyer and three corvettes, duly steamed into the very middle of Dönitz's trap.

There followed a series of infernos as, one by one, over the course of the next three days, seven of the vessels were torpedoed with fatal consequences. Crews were overcome by fumes, covered in oil or incinerated in the flames. Lifeboats were either destroyed or could not be lowered; when the *British Dominion*, carrying 9,000 tons of aviation fuel, exploded in flames, thirty-seven of the fifty-two crew died almost at once. When the *Empire Lytton* was hit by three torpedoes and caught fire, her captain, J. W. Andrews, ordered his crew to abandon ship, at which, according to his official report, almost all the men 'got into a panic, jumped into the port boat and lowered [it] into the water while the ship still had considerable way on her, causing the boat to break open and throw them into the sea [which was] heavily coated with fuel oil'. Andrews picked up eleven men in his own lifeboat, including his chief officer, who had been overcome by fumes and now 'unfortunately showed little sign of life. The boat was then too overloaded to take any more aboard, although I saw ten or twelve men still in the water.'[15] It was in such ways that – in ones and twos and tens – the unsung and almost unnoticed death toll of merchant seamen in the Second World War rose inexorably until it would eventually exceed 32,000.

The loss of these seven tankers was serious enough to reach the ears of the prime minister, though there is no evidence that he was ever told how the disaster had occurred: that it was in large measure due to a failure by the Admiralty to provide so important a convoy with adequate protection. The U-boats had been able to manoeuvre with impunity, darting in and out of the convoy, attacking en masse and severally as the escorts, overwhelmed by superior numbers, could do little to stop the carnage. By the time the four escorts were reinforced by three Royal Navy destroyers it was too late.

An official inquiry was inevitable. Revealingly, it was not asked to focus on the Admiralty's responsibility for providing such an important convoy with inadequate protection but on what had happened aboard the tankers. Specifically, the inquiry was charged to examine a variety of allegations and recriminations which surfaced about the conduct of the merchant ships in the convoy made by those who had survived the trauma. The *Empire Lytton*'s Captain Andrews was cross-examined about the indiscipline of the crew under his command and for his alleged failure of leadership, a charge which could have led to the withdrawal of his certificate of competency and the end of his career. Andrews fought back, claiming that 'he had never sailed with such a bad crew' and that their behaviour when the ship was torpedoed was 'disgusting'. However, he also insisted that the conduct of his officers had been 'splendid'.[16]

A far more serious allegation was levelled against the master of the *Vanja*, one of the two tankers which reached Gibraltar without damage. The inquiry heard that 'a certain amount of suspicion' had been aroused by the fact whenever another tanker was under attack the *Vanja*, a 6,000-ton Norwegian vessel, had managed to be well out of harm's way. Even more damagingly, two radio operators in other ships had apparently detected the *Vanja* sending out 'homing signals' on her radio. This, it was intimated, suggested that her captain was intentionally giving away the location of the Allied merchant ships to the enemy. In the absence of any evidence to support this conspiracy theory, it transpired that a more likely explanation was that her master had merely intended to alert the escorts to the fact that she had dropped out of her station in the convoy because her engineers were having trouble with her diesel engines, both of which had cracked cylinders.

After hearing all the evidence, the inquiry's chairman, Captain W. G. Parry, the commander of the battlecruiser *Renown*, concluded both that the *Empire Lytton*'s officers were blameless and that there was a perfectly innocent explanation for the *Vanja*'s poor station-keeping. Far more pertinently, he and his fellow adjudicators found that 'the fault lay with the weakness of the escort, which failure of the radar sets in *Pimpernel* and *Godetia* [two of TM1's three corvettes] had only made worse'.[17] This indictment served to highlight a disturbing side-effect of the military campaign in North Africa: the need for oil was paramount but the Allied navies were apparently unable to provide the warships in the numbers or with the equipment required to ensure its safe delivery. The omens were not encouraging.

## 18.  'The Battle of the Air'

The U-boat threat was top of the agenda at the Casablanca Conference which opened on 14 January 1943. Renowned in the history of the Second World War for Roosevelt's provocative declaration that the struggle would cease only with the 'unconditional surrender' of the Axis powers, the crucial business on the agenda at Casablanca was the means to that end. Roosevelt and Churchill had originally hoped that the conference would be a forum where the 'Big Three' would discuss their strategic vision for victory. In this they were thwarted when, despite their entreaties, Stalin bluntly refused to attend. The Soviet leader claimed that he could not absent himself from the Soviet Union 'even for a single day' on account of the unfolding drama at the front.[1] Since the Red Army had by now encircled the Germans at Stalingrad, the two Western leaders were both greatly irritated. But when, a few days later, the Soviet leader wrote again, pointedly reminding both Roosevelt and Churchill of their 'promise' to open a Second Front 'in 1942 or the spring of 1943 at the latest', the pair reflected that his absence would at least spare them yet another acrimonious debate about the decision to postpone the invasion of France sine die.[2] Notwithstanding Stalin's absence, the overarching purpose of the conference was to agree on a strategy for securing victory in the West.

Led respectively by Generals Marshall and Brooke, the joint chiefs of staff had a series of 'very heated' meetings which focused on strategy following the expected victory in North Africa.[3] Churchill insisted that, once this had been accomplished, their 'paramount task' should be a seaborne attack on 'the soft underbelly' of the Axis by landing an Allied army in Sicily.[4] The Americans were fearful, in Marshall's words, that the 'interminable' operations in the Mediterranean would leach resources from 'the main plot', namely the invasion of France. They pressed for an undertaking from their British counterparts that the British Mediterranean should at the very least form 'part of an integrated plan to win the war' and not just an opportunistic venture.[5] Again and again the Americans retreated, either directly or indirectly, to their default position that the liberation of France should be the Allied priority and that the Italian option was a distraction from this. The argument went round in circles, complicated by Admiral King's persistent attempt to hijack the debate by demanding that the Allies embark on an 'all-out fight to the finish against Japan and not merely a holding operation'.[6] After wrangling thus for five days, Brooke was exasperated. With characteristic disdain, he noted, 'Marshall has got practically no strategic vision.' For his part, King was 'a somewhat swollen headed individual' whose vision was 'mainly limited to the Pacific'.[7] Thanks as much to the fact that the Americans knew that their president tended to side with the prime minister whenever a showdown was in the making as to the fact that Brooke mounted the better argument, the British negotiators prevailed and on 23 January the Combined Chiefs presented a united front to their respective leaders: the 'soft underbelly' it would be.

Given its momentous implications, both Churchill and Roosevelt appeared remarkably relaxed throughout the conference as though their ten-day absence from their respective capitals offered a respite from the cares of high office. Only the absence of a brooding Stalin and, on the penultimate day of the talks, the boorish presence of General Charles de Gaulle, cast a shadow over the Moroccan balm. About Stalin little was to be done except to find a diplomatic way of telling him that he had once again lost the argument in favour of an early Second Front. De Gaulle, who had been coerced by the British Foreign Secretary, Anthony Eden, into dancing attendance upon his Anglo-Saxon benefactors in Casablanca, was at his most graceless and truculent. To facilitate the next phase of the war in North Africa, Roosevelt and Churchill required de Gaulle, as the leader of the Free French, to cooperate closely with General Henri Giraud, the leader of the Free French forces in North Africa. However, de Gaulle, who regarded himself as the sole representative of the Free French movement, refused to negotiate with Giraud, who, for his part, made it clear that he refused to serve under de Gaulle.

The impasse between the two *grands hommes* led Hopkins to advise the president to postpone a press conference which had been scheduled to coincide with de Gaulle's arrival in the Moroccan resort. Roosevelt reluctantly agreed and despatched Hopkins to the prime minister's villa to tell him. There, he found Churchill in bed in his customary pink robe, and having, of all things, a bottle of wine for breakfast. I asked him what he meant by that and he told me that he had a profound distaste on the one hand for the skimmed milk, and no deep-rooted prejudice about wine, and that he had reconciled the conflict in favour of the latter. He commended it to me and said he had lived to be sixty-eight years old and was in the best of health, and had found that the advice of doctors throughout his life, was usually wrong.[8]

Churchill found de Gaulle's hauteur ridiculous: 'He might be Stalin, with 200 divisions behind his words,' the prime minister observed after one meeting in his villa at which 'I made it quite plain that if he could not be more helpful we were done with him.'[9] Yet the general's skin was so thick that such barbed threats bounced off and he refused to relent. Roosevelt (who saw de Gaulle as a demagogue with dictatorial ambitions) was nonetheless determined to find a way out of this 'French quagmire'.[10] With a mixture of guile and thuggery, the president eventually prevailed upon de Gaulle to shake hands with Giraud in front of the cameras, as cold a display of public amity as it was possible to imagine. It was a relief, though, that the two Western leaders were able to hold a formal press conference at noon on the 24th to unveil the Casablanca communiqué. It was here that, apparently to the prime minister's surprise, Roosevelt announced to the world that only the 'unconditional surrender' of Nazi Germany would bring an end to the war.

The achievement of that political objective was severely circumscribed by one overriding factor: a lack of military resources of every kind. Throughout the ten days of competitive tendering for the alternative options facing the Allies, the negotiators were hobbled by the fact that they lacked the men and materiel required to deliver a fatal blow against the Axis powers on more than one front at once. It was not possible simultaneously to prosecute an offensive against the Axis powers in Sicily and the Pacific; to contemplate a cross-Channel landing in France as well as an invasion of Sicily; to sustain an attack on Sicily; and to maintain the Arctic convoys. The overriding constraint was shipping. A severe shortage of freighters and the escorts to protect them threatened to compromise any military offensive on any front, let alone two or more of these at the same time.

It is not surprising, therefore, that the Combined Chiefs' final report – 'The Conduct of the War in 1943' – highlighted one overarching priority: 'The defeat of the U-boat must remain a first charge on the resources of the United Nations.'[11] It could hardly have been put more starkly. The Battle of the Atlantic remained the most important struggle of the Second World War.

The implications of this conclusion had already been foreshadowed by a 'most secret' letter that was sent to the commander-in-chief of Bomber Command, Arthur Harris, on the opening day of the Casablanca Conference. The letter stated that:

> as a result of the recent serious increase in the menace of the enemy U-boat operations, the War Cabinet has given approval to a policy of area bombing against the U-boat operational bases on the west coast of France. A decision has accordingly been made to subject the following bases to a maximum scale of attack by your Command at night with the object of effectively devastating the whole area in which are located the submarines, their maintenance facilities and the services, power, water, light, communication, etc. and other resources upon which their operations depend. The order of priority of importance of the bases is as follows: – Lorient, St Nezzire [sic], Brest, La Pallice.

These Biscay ports were of critical importance. Were they to be isolated, the U-boats would lose the safe haven from which Dönitz had prosecuted the tonnage war against the Allied convoys. It was for this reason that, almost two years earlier, Hitler had authorized that the U-boat pens at all these bases should be rendered bomb-proof. It was against this background that Harris was instructed to start the bombing of Lorient 'immediately' and to continue until he was persuaded that the 'desired object has been achieved'. At this point he was to suspend operations to allow the results to be assessed from 'photographic reconnaissance and other sources of information as may be obtained'.[12]

Nine days later, reflecting the urgency implicit in the decision by the Combined Chiefs at Casablanca to make the U-boat threat a 'first charge' on their resources, the War Cabinet revised its instructions to Harris. On 23 January he was told that 'there should be no pause to assess [the] results of the attacks on Lorient before other U-boat bases in the Bay of Biscay are subjected to area bombing'.[13] He was to attack, attack, and attack again regardless of the consequences. Harris, who regarded any attempt to use his bombers to combat U-boats as a wasteful diversion from their important task of obliterating German cities, complied with extreme reluctance. Four days later he wrote a scathing report on Bomber Command's attempts to pulverize the U-boat bases: 'The desired result was unobtainable by the means indicated, the concrete shelters housing the submarines were impenetrable, and even the destruction of entire towns would only impede but not prevent their maintenance, while at the same time causing bitter resentment among the Bretons – some of Britain's best and stoutest friends.'[14]

Harris's scorn for a fruitless exercise was fully justified. Hitler's engineers and labourers had done a good job. For more than a year, the U-boat bays had been protected beneath a concrete canopy sixteen feet thick; not even the mightiest bomb could do more than dent the outer crust of such an edifice. This should have been recognized by everyone. The construction of these monumental shelters had been carefully monitored and recorded throughout by aerial reconnaissance. At least twice in the autumn of 1941, more than fifteen months earlier, Coastal Command's commander-in-chief, Philip Joubert de la Ferté, had written to the Air Ministry urging that 'these bases be bombed frequently' to frustrate their completion. He had been contemptuously rebuffed. 'Such attacks', he was told, 'would constitute a very considerable and unwarranted diversion' from Bomber Command's offensive against Germany.[15]

This was a disastrous decision which had enabled Germany to render the U-boat base at Lorient bomb-proof by January 1942. Not surprisingly, a belated attempt by US bombers to destroy the Biscay bases in ten raids mounted between 21 October 1942 and 3 January 1943 – which the Combined Chiefs at Casablanca appeared to have forgotten – yielded very little. In his report on these raids to the War Cabinet a few days later, the First Lord of the Admiralty was obliged to note that, apart from killing a number of French and German dock workers and putting one dry dock temporarily out of action, the U-boat pens had not been damaged at all.[16]

Quite why the War Cabinet should now think that Bomber Command would succeed where the Americans had failed is unclear, but the fact remains that Harris was right: the order to devastate the Biscay bases was demonstrably a futile gesture. After five weeks of sustained onslaught against the Biscay ports, Bomber Command had managed to destroy almost everything except the U-boat pens. This fact was not allowed to get in the way of policy, and by May ninety-eight aircraft had been lost in the course of more than 3,500 missions, while the U-boat shelters remained intact.[17] Bizarrely, since he was well acquainted with the facts, the First Sea Lord had not only supported the War Cabinet's decision to bomb them, but had gone out of his way to endorse what he described as the 'area bombing' of the Biscay bases.[18] In the absence of any other explanation, it might be concluded that he thought anything would be better than nothing. If so, he was wrong.

This fiasco had the most malign repercussions. For 'Bomber' Harris, the waste of effort, lives and aircraft forced on him by the War Cabinet was a political windfall which he used to reinforce his insistent claim that the Battle of the Atlantic was a 'defensive' sideshow in which Bomber Command should play no part. It also provided the Air Ministry with a powerful weapon in its struggle with the Admiralty, which, since Harris's appointment as commander-in-chief a little under a year earlier – had plumbed new depths of bone-headed animosity.

The long-smouldering tension between these two ministries had inadvertently been fanned into flames by the prime minister. His visceral belief – stated explicitly during the Blitz in the summer of 1940 – that the only way to 'overwhelm' Germany was 'an absolutely devastating, exterminating attack by very heavy bombers from this country upon the Nazi homeland',[19] gave a licence to Bomber Command which it would never relinquish. Neither a steady accumulation of evidence to the contrary nor the competing claims on a precious resource were allowed to permeate the carapace of conviction which led him to believe that the bomber was Britain's best available means of pulverizing the Nazi enemy. From time to time he wavered, but never for long enough to modify a strategic priority which had a profoundly damaging impact on the Battle of the Atlantic.

When an official analysis of some 650 photographs taken during a hundred bombing raids over Germany between June and July 1941 revealed that only 'one-fifth' of the 6,103 RAF bombers which took part even 'reached the target area', the Air Ministry had the gall to claim that this result served merely to confirm the need to build up 'an immense force [of bombers] to achieve decisive results by imprecise means'.[20] According to the Chief of the Air Staff, Sir Charles Portal, the

Butt Report had shown that 4,000 front-line bombers, assisted by improved navigational techniques, would be enough to destroy forty-three German towns, forcing some 15 million people to flee their homes. Advising this might take six months to achieve, he assured the prime minister that a force of this size could be counted upon to obtain 'decisive results against German morale'.[21]

In making this claim with such confidence, Portal was mindful of the fact that only a few weeks earlier the chiefs of staff, including the First Sea Lord, Admiral Pound, had formally advised the prime minister that there should be 'no limits to the size of the force required' and that 'a planned attack on civilian morale' if 'applied on a vast scale' might of itself 'be enough to make Germany sue for peace'.[22] Butt's report evidently gave Churchill cause to doubt. In his reply to Portal, the prime minister sounded a note of caution about the impact of mass bombing raids on German morale, commenting that 'all we have learnt since the war began shows that its effects, both physical and moral, are greatly exaggerated'.[23] But when Portal responded by reiterating that the bombers were 'a war-winning weapon' and by reminding him that this assessment had been at the heart of the strategy agreed by the chiefs of staff only a few weeks earlier, Churchill retreated. Though he warned against 'placing unbounded confidence in this means of attack', pointing out that even if 'all the towns of Germany were rendered largely uninhabitable', the Third Reich could very possibly still prosecute the war, he conceded that 'it may well be that German morale will crack and our bombing will play a very important part in bringing this about'.[24] More pertinently, he affirmed that he had 'no intention' of changing the bombing policy which had so recently been approved by the War Cabinet. Thereafter, when the occasion arose, Churchill nearly always sided with the Air Ministry against the Admiralty.

It was against this background that 'The Battle of the Air',[25] as Pound called it, now erupted between the two ministries, eliciting from the Second Sea Lord, Admiral W. J. Whitworth, his description of a conflict 'much more savage . . . than our war with the Huns, which is very unsatisfactory and such a waste of effort' (see p. 114).[26]

This futile inter-departmental struggle was exacerbated by the prime minister's stance. Though he persistently regarded 'the U-boat menace' as 'our worst danger', by continuing to take the Air Ministry's part against the Admiralty he very nearly ensured that it reached calamitous proportions.[27] Had Churchill permitted the long-range bombers, for which the Admiralty clamoured, to be diverted in significant numbers from Bomber Command to be modified for the war against the U-boats during 1942, there is little doubt that the tide in the Battle of the Atlantic – victory in which was a precondition for the cross-Channel invasion of France – could have been turned many months earlier. Moreover it would have avoided the horrendous loss of shipping which had occasioned Churchill's plea to Roosevelt in October 1942 (see p. 338)'.[28]

Of course, Churchill's paradoxical perspective was not shaped simply by raw prejudice. He was bombarded by conflicting advice by the principal combatants from both ministries. However, the 'Battle of the Air' was an unequal contest. The First Lord and the First Sea Lord were comprehensively outmatched and outsmarted by the air chief marshal and the commander-in-chief of Bomber Command. Portal and Harris formed a commanding double act: the former was clever and eloquent; the latter combative, obstinate and overly endowed with a gift for sub-Churchillian rhetoric. The 'one–two' combination of Portal and Harris was lethally effective against the lacklustre and malleable First Lord of the Admiralty, A. V. Alexander, and the visibly ailing and often somnolent Pound. Neither man seemed capable of offering a strategic alternative to area bombing with anything like the conviction and clarity required to prevail against the bombastic certainties of their adversaries. More fundamentally, the Admiralty duo never challenged the presumption – which Churchill shared with Portal and Harris – that it was essentially 'defensive' to bomb U-boats while it was unequivocally 'offensive' to bomb Germany. By conceding this conceptual high ground, they yielded the strategic battlefield to the point where their effort to secure the aircraft needed to thwart the U-boat offensive was lost even before they started to make the case.

Harris began his personal crusade in favour of Bomber Command almost immediately after his appointment as commander-in-chief in February 1942, a little before his fiftieth birthday. As a boy of modest intellect, he did not shine at his minor public school in Devon, although he did show resolve on the rugby field (but not so as to avert a severe drubbing (15–0) at the hands of the Royal Naval College in Dartmouth when he played for the first team in 1907). The teenager compensated for his lack of distinctive talent with a penchant for decisive action. At the age of seventeen, to the disappointment of his father, the embryo 'man of action' cut short his education to emigrate to Southern Rhodesia (now Zimbabwe), where he worked briefly as a gold miner before turning to farming, an experience that led him to nurture visions of owning a ranch himself. When the First World War broke out in 1914 Harris, who now regarded himself as a patriotic Rhodesian, joined the army, later flying to England, where he found a berth in the Royal Flying Corps. His aptitude as a pilot was soon recognized and, at the age of twenty-four, he took command of the United Kingdom's first bomber squadron (No. 38 Squadron, which in 1918 would be incorporated into the newly established Royal Air Force).

By this time he had established a reputation as a disciplinarian who favoured efficiency over camaraderie. Forceful by nature and intimidating in manner, he did not immediately endear himself to those under his command, though there were those who were entertained by his penchant for practical jokes. His habit of embarrassing junior officers invited to dine at his official residence by placing a whoopie cushion on one of their chairs apparently caused great mirth. But it was his achievements as a pilot (and his evident disregard for his own safety) which earned him their admiration. He also made his mark with his superiors, notably by speaking his mind without fear for the repercussions on his own career. His trenchant strictures on the inadequacies of the RAF, and his open disdain for the army and, even more, for the Royal Navy, may have ruffled some feathers, but such was his force of personality that they proved to be no impediment at all to his progress through the ranks. By 1937 he was an air commodore, by 1941 he had become Deputy Chief of the Air Staff, and by the time of his appointment as commander-in-chief, Bomber Command, he had been promoted to the rank of acting air marshal.

No individual was better equipped by temperament and attitude to implement the policy of area bombing, for which Portal had already secured the support of the War Cabinet. Sir Arthur Harris, as he had now become, was guided by a moral compass set on what he regarded as the only true course, from which he would not be diverted either by imaginative humanity or the quality of mercy. Nor did he conceal this from those about him: his biographer reports one of his squadron commanders as saying, 'We all love him; he's so bloody inhuman.'[29] His nerveless tenacity also blinded him to any evidence against his conviction that to kill German citizens of any gender or age was not only the best but also the only way to bring the enemy to its collective knees. To break a nation, he believed, you had to destroy its will to resist. Nor did he readily brook criticism or dissent.

Those who worked on his staff at Bomber Command's headquarters knew better than to challenge their remote and intemperate commander-in-chief. One of his team, Group Captain (later Air Commodore) Bufton, complained that Harris ruled his staff 'with a rod of iron which effectively deterred anyone from producing ideas that ran counter to his own'.[30] He was similarly dismissive of competing ideas when they came from above. When Air Chief Marshal Sir Wilfred Freeman, who had responsibility for exploring more effective ways of conducting the bombing campaign, urged Harris to extend an experiment with daylight bombing, he responded by bluntly informing his superior officer that what he had proposed was both costly and pointless. Infuriated, the air chief marshal wrote back to inform Harris that he had 'got accustomed to your truculent style, loose expression and flamboyant hyperbole, but I am not used to be[ing] told – as you imply – that I am deliberately proposing to risk human lives in order to test out an idea of my own which in your opinion is wrong. I should be glad if you would carry out the order given to you.'[31] Unabashed, Harris insisted that he would only proceed as ordered following 'an official directive to which I can register an official protest'.[32] Freeman backed down.

Harris was not alone in his convictions but surrounded by a phalanx of like-minded advocates. By far the most powerful of these was Churchill's trusted scientific advisor, Professor Frederick Lindemann. Raised to the peerage by the prime minister in 1941, Lord Cherwell (as Lindemann thereby became known) enjoyed the honorific title of Paymaster-General, which gave him a seat in the Cabinet. Cherwell was no less arrogant than Harris, though much cleverer. His special talent was to adduce statistics which appeared to offer scientific justification for the efficacy of area bombing, to which the German-born scientist was, in any case, viscerally and ideologically committed.

In March 1942 he provided Churchill with an apparently persuasive rationale for this approach. Extrapolating from the effects of the Luftwaffe's raids on British cities such as Birmingham and Hull, he argued that a force of 10,000 bombers – which he forecast should be available by the middle of 1943 – could drive 'the great majority' of the population of fifty-eight German towns to flee 'house and home'. The effect of bombing on this scale, he surmised, would so damage morale as to 'break the spirit of the German people'. Not surprisingly, Portal and Sir Archibald Sinclair, the Secretary of State for Air, seized on Cherwell's report, judging it to be 'simple, clear, and convincing'.[33] Adding the proviso that the government would need to deliver the means to achieve the proposed end, they advised not only would the bombers have to be produced at the rate forecast by Cherwell but also that it was imperative that they should not be diverted to any other task. Churchill agreed.

Cherwell was contemptuous of those who doubted his analysis. When an old scientific adversary, Sir Henry Tizard, the chairman of the Aeronautical Committee, had the temerity to question his figures, Cherwell swept him aside with the confidence of a man who – unlike Tizard – had the ear of the prime minister. On 15 April 1942 Tizard wrote, 'I am afraid that I think that the way you put the facts as they appear to you is extremely misleading and may lead to entirely wrong decisions being reached with consequent disastrous effect on the war. I think too, that you have got your facts wrong.'[34] In a withering reply, Cherwell retorted, 'I would be interested to hear what you think wrong with my simple calculation, which seemed to me fairly self-evident . . . My paper was intended to show that we really can do a lot of damage by bombing built-up areas with the sort of air force which should be available.'[35] This was not only arrogant but disingenuous. Cherwell's report had made a far greater claim for the efficacy of area bombing than was justified by the evidence.

The chief scientist had drawn heavily on an investigation by Professors John Bernal and Solly Zuckerman into the effects of the bombing raids on Birmingham and Hull, but had interpreted their findings to support conclusions which, as Zuckerman would later complain, were 'directly opposed' to those the two authors had reached. In their report (which did not appear until ten days after Cherwell's paper) Bernal and Zuckerman wrote:

> In neither town was there any evidence of panic resulting either from a series of raids or from a single raid . . . In both towns actual raids were, of course, associated with a degree of alarm and anxiety . . . which in no instance was sufficient to provoke mass anti-social behaviour. There was no measurable effect on the health of either town.[36]

Either Cherwell had misunderstood these findings or he had wilfully misconstrued them. In either case, the facts which were available at the time suggest that the decision to target civilian morale through the mass bombing campaign against Germany, which had been enshrined in a formal directive to Bomber Command on 14 April 1942, was, at the very least, based as much on wishful thinking as on valid evidence.

The impact of this misapprehension was of the greatest significance for the conduct of both the war in general and the Battle of the Atlantic in particular. The case for deploying long-range bombers to protect the North Atlantic convoys was not only compelling but had been clearly identified a year earlier. In the spring of 1941, the Battle of the Atlantic Committee (a sub-committee of the War Cabinet), over which Churchill usually presided in person, had urged that 'Coastal Command should be reinforced at the earliest possible date with long-range aircraft', noting especially that 'with adequate air co-operation a U-boat should find it impossible to shadow one of our convoys'.[37] Some months later, in December, the drama of HG76 (see pp. 237–8), when aircraft played a decisive role during a convoy battle which lasted for six days, had illustrated the point with compelling clarity; the German offensive was called off only because a lone bomber – the first of a handful of long-range bombers which Bomber Command had been instructed to hand over to Coastal Command – repeatedly forced the wolf pack to take avoiding action. Afterwards, the escort commander, Captain 'Johnny' Walker, had formally advised that aircraft were 'absolutely invaluable' to the protection of convoys. Despite evidence of this kind, however, the War Cabinet failed to act and the Admiralty continued to lose the argument. As one of Walker's equally renowned peers, Captain Donald Macintyre, was to point out, this failure 'to profit by the old lessons relearnt in the fight for HG76, [of which] the greatest was the necessity for continuous air cover if the attacks of U-boat packs were to be defeated', was unnecessarily to postpone the final reckoning in the Atlantic.[38]

The only aircraft capable of covering the entire convoy route across the North Atlantic was the American-built Liberator Mark 1, which had a range of up to 2,700 miles. The United States had begun delivering this version of the B-24 bomber to the RAF in the summer of 1941, but as a result of the 'Battle of the Air', Coastal Command was initially allocated only nine of these very-long-range (VLR) aircraft. Moreover, because they had to be modified to extend their range, these did not enter service until September of that year. They were quick to make their mark. Led by Flight Lieutenant Terry Bulloch (who was to become a legendary and highly decorated pilot), the resourceful crews of 120 Squadron pioneered ways of making the most of their flying time over the mid-Atlantic, attacking a U-boat for the first time in October.[39] But by the end of the year, though, many of their planes were grounded for lack of the replacement parts required after flying long hours over the Atlantic in often ferocious weather conditions. As a result, by early 1942, 120 Squadron was 'wasting away'.[40] With ill-concealed exaspera-tion the First Lord, Alexander, warned of the 'dangerous situation' that was likely to arise towards the end of the year if the rate at which mer-chant ships were currently being sunk was sustained; without the support of long-range bombers, he advised, the number of warships available to protect the convoys would be 'totally inadequate against the wolf-pack tactics we now expect'.[41] The following month, he sent a memo to the Battle of the Atlantic Committee, urging that the shortfall in long-range aircraft allocated to Coastal Command should have pri-ority over Bomber Command's demands for the same planes; and a few days later he followed this up by demanding that nine squadrons of American B-24 and B-17 aircraft be transferred from Bomber Com-mand to Coastal Command to close the Air Gap in the Atlantic.[42] He was soon followed by the First Sea Lord, who roused himself to open a session of the War Cabinet and state baldly: 'If we lose the war at sea we lose the war. We lose the war at sea when we can no longer maintain those communications which are essential to us.'[43] Warning that the loss of merchant shipping (carrying supplies) and tankers (carrying fuel) now threatened to paralyse Allied operations on the battlefield, he demanded that Coastal Command's allocation of land-based warplanes should be increased from just over 500 aircraft to a little under 2,000.[44] The Air Ministry was aghast. Portal retaliated five days later:

> Bomber Command could best contribute to the weakening of the U-boat offensive by offensive action against the principal industrial areas of Germany . . . To divert [the RAF's bombers] to an uneconom-ical defensive role would be unsound at any time. It would be doubly so now when we are about to launch a bombing offensive of which we have

high expectations and which will enable us to deliver a heavy and concentrated blow against Germany when German morale is low.[45]

On 19 March (following an inconclusive non-meeting of minds
between the competing ministries at the War Cabinet Defence Committee on the previous day) the Chief of the Imperial General Staff,
Alan Brooke, made a weary note in his diary: 'With the PM in his present mood, and with his desire to maintain air bombardment of Germany
it will not be possible to get adequate support for the Army or the
Navy.'[46] This was to prove the pattern for months ahead. Again and
again, the case mounted by the admirals was swept aside by an Air Ministry which knew that, in so doing, it invariably enjoyed the backing of
the prime minister. Coastal Command's urbane commander-in-chief,
Philip Joubert, was to reflect wryly on this bizarre predicament by noting that in the 'many battles' fought within the Atlantic Committee,
'The First Lord [Alexander], supported by his staff, with an occasional
friendly squawk from C.-C. Coastal Command [Joubert himself],
fought to increase the volume of air power devoted to the war at sea . . .
Bomber Command always won.'[47]

In early May 1942 Pound became so thoroughly alarmed that he once
again went on the offensive to demand 'with all urgency' an increase in
the number of aircraft 'necessary to guard our vital sea communications'. By this time he had enlisted his three most senior colleagues to
endorse his stance. Admirals Forbes, Cunningham and Tovey (the
Royal Navy's three most senior commanders-in-chief) formed a formidable trio who were by now incensed at the War Cabinet's persistent
failure to heed these warnings. They proposed drastic action – a showdown with ministers – arguing that 'the situation at sea is so grave that
the time has come for a stand to be made even if this led to their Lordships taking the extreme step of resignation'.[48] The moment passed.

Pound's failure to convince was partly a question of personality. Presuming, wrongly, that merely to make a valid case would be enough to
have it acknowledged, he was also drained of the intellectual and psychological energy needed to challenge the underlying assumptions and
dubious statistics deployed against him by the Air Ministry. Brooke's
diaries are peppered with cruelly dismissive comments about the First
Sea Lord's performance at key meetings of the chiefs of staff; in one of
many such observations, he noted that 'with an old dodderer like him it

is quite impossible for the COS to perform the function it should in the biggest Imperial War we are ever likely to be engaged in. He is asleep during 75% of the time he should be working.'[49] Had Brooke been aware at the time that the First Sea Lord was already afflicted by the brain tumour which would kill him the following year, he would undoubtedly have tempered his disdain with compassion. Nonetheless, his running commentary is a telling indication of why Pound kept losing the 'Battle of the Air'.

Noting that this struggle between the Admiralty and the Air Ministry was bedevilled by 'a welter of confusion and uncoordinated and wrong advice from the wrong people', Churchill's chief of military operations and Brooke's confidant, Major-General John Kennedy, proposed that the two ministries should be instructed to produce a joint paper laying out their competing views for the prime minister to decide between them. Clearly believing this would serve only to exacerbate the tensions between them, Brooke rejected the suggestion, which prompted Kennedy to note, 'The price we pay at sea and on land for our present bombing policy is high indeed.' Later he would reflect that 'Churchill's obsession for bombing Germany [which] resulted in the Navy being very short of long-range bombers at sea [was] the only well-founded ground for criticism of our central war direction'.[50] It was a well-aimed blow.

Churchill was mesmerized by Bomber Command. With a flair for self-promotion that would be rivalled only by General Bernard Montgomery, Harris had gone out of his way from the early days of his appointment to court public opinion. On the night of 30 May 1942, 1,000 bombers took off from various bases in Britain to attack Cologne. This was 'the greatest concentration of air power in the history of the world', but, as Sir Max Hastings has observed, there was 'no military magic about the figure of a thousand aircraft. It was the potential effect on popular imagination, on the politicians and on the Americans and the Russians that fascinated Whitehall.'[51] Harris made sure that his briefing to the aircrews taking part was subsequently released to the press. With such a mighty force, he told his men, Bomber Command had a unique opportunity to 'strike a blow at the enemy which will not only resound throughout Germany, but throughout the world . . . if you individually succeed, the most shattering and devastating blow will have been delivered against the very vitals of the enemy.

Let him have it – right on the chin.'[52] Montgomery could not have done better.

The propaganda impact reverberated just as Harris had hoped, but the material effect was somewhat less impressive. Although more than 12,000 homes were destroyed or damaged, rendering 45,000 homeless, subsequent photographic evidence revealed that 'the lasting damage to Cologne proved astonishingly slight in relation to the forces employed'.[53] However, Harris was exuberant, telling readers of the *Daily Express*, 'If I could send 1,000 bombers to Germany every night, it would end the war by the autumn. We are going to bomb Germany incessantly . . . the day is coming when the USA and ourselves will put over such a force that the Germans will scream for mercy.'[54] It was the kind of rhetoric that not only went down well with readers of the popular press but also with his own men. Though Harris kept his distance from the aircrews – he rarely left his office to visit one of his command's bases – he spoke their language to a degree that most of his peers were unable to emulate. His stock in Bomber Command could hardly have been higher.

Churchill was delighted. Congratulating Harris for Bomber Command's 'superlative' performance and the 'courage and skill' of the officers and men involved, he added menacingly, 'The proof of the growing power of the British Bomber Force is also the herald of what Germany will receive, city by city, from now on.'[55] Harris himself said, 'We are going to scourge the Third Reich from end to end.'[56] If only to the degree that the fire in their bellies was unquenchable, Churchill and Harris were kindred spirits. In the early months of Harris's reign at Bomber Command, he was accorded a welcome at Chequers, where, to the envy and irritation of his peers in the Royal Navy, he appears to have been given licence to rehearse his convictions over the dinner table. Though the two men were never to become close friends – Churchill felt there was 'a certain coarseness' about the air vice-marshal which clearly grated – the mutual admiration was evident to all.[57] Harris did not refrain from exploiting his access to the prime minister to make the case for Bomber Command against the Admiralty. In a breach of protocol, he sidestepped the formal chain of command by writing long papers for Churchill's private delectation in language which was often so intemperate that even those who shared his views were embarrassed by his excess of zeal.

In June 1942, soon after the 1,000-bomber raid on Cologne, he wrote a 'Secret and Personal' memorandum to the prime minister in which he declared: 'Victory, speedy and complete, awaits the side which first employs air power as it should be employed.' Boasting that his air campaign could 'knock Germany out of the war in a matter of months', and claiming – in defiance of the known facts – that Cologne had been 'virtually destroyed', he condemned, inter alia, the use of the RAF's bombers to

> bolster further the already over-swollen establishments of the purely defensive Coastal Command [which] achieves nothing essential, either to our survival or the defeat of the enemy . . . Coastal Command is therefore merely an obstacle to victory . . . Why nibble at the fringes of the enemy's submarine and sea power when we can obliterate with comparative ease the very sources of that power?[58]

It is inconceivable that Harris's egregious simplicities weighed quite as heavily with Churchill as the air vice-marshal might have hoped. Yet his bellicose declarations of intent not only reflected the prime minister's own proclivities, but may be presumed to have been music to the ears of a war leader who was otherwise surrounded by careful and cautious military and political advisors whose duty was to identify a complexity of challenges and to offer a range of alternative solutions before submitting their own recommendations for any particular course of action. Harris was impatient with such equivocation.

Sir Stafford Cripps, one of several cabinet ministers to visit Bomber Command's headquarters at High Wycombe, warned Harris that the abrasive excesses of his reports did not find favour with some members of the War Cabinet. Cripps advised, 'I think you would make your points better and achieve more if you were more careful about your form of expression.' Harris riposted, 'I am not a diplomat, God forbid – look where the diplomats have got us.'[59] Nonetheless, he decided to accept Cripps's offer to redraft one of his many strategy papers with the result that Churchill ordered it to be circulated to the War Cabinet, a distinct mark of prime-ministerial approbation.

For the most part, however, Harris's letters and papers were unrestrained in both style and content, regardless of any offence they might cause. On one occasion, after a particularly impolitic claim to the effect that RAF aircraft assigned to the Middle East should be returned to Bomber Command, he even managed to provoke the ire of his own boss. In a magisterial rebuke, the Chief of the Air Staff, Portal, wrote, 'I do not regard your letter as either a credit to your intelligence or a contribution to winning the war. It is wrong in both tone and substance.'[60] If Harris was to any degree abashed by this reprimand, he failed to show any contrition, doubtless mindful of the fact that the weight of opinion within the War Cabinet and beyond in favour of the bombing campaign gave him a latitude that few others could hope to indulge.

The Admiralty could not muster any advocate as potent as Harris, as eminent as Portal or as influential as Cherwell. Pound could never outbid this forceful trio, though in his dry and understated way he did his best. Soon after Harris's appointment, he scribbled a note in the margin of one of the routine documents which passed between them:

> Shall I hope to have a yarn with you and show you a paper we have just put in to the effect that unless we get at least as great an effort from the air over the sea as do our enemies then there will be a grave danger of our losing the war at sea and then amongst other things there will be no petrol for your bombers?[61]

Such genial barbs were lost on Harris, who did not even deign to pick up the gauntlet in retaliation.

On 25 July 1942 the commander-in-chief of Coastal Command, Joubert, wrote in despair to Pound, reminding him of what he knew already, that the Allies were losing tankers at a faster rate than they were being built and that the immense quantities of material and valuable lives thus lost meant that 'we are unable to conduct the offensives necessary for victory at the time, and on the scale, which are desirable'.[62] Their protestations were to little avail.

The chief beneficiary of this interminable Whitehall wrangle was Admiral Dönitz. It was an unexpected windfall. From early on, he had been only too aware of the threat that aircraft might pose to his U-boat fleet. By late 1941 the gradual build-up of Coastal Command's short- and medium-range bombers around the coast of Britain had forced him to make a tactical withdrawal into deeper waters. By the late spring of 1942, confirming the Admiralty's predictions, the wolf packs had started to congregate in the so-called Atlantic Gap, where – as a result of Bomber Command's obduracy – they could generally operate with impunity. Even so, on those rare occasions when a U-boat found itself on the surface within range of one of Coastal Command's aircraft, the consequences were invariably alarming, if not fatal. Dönitz was given a graphic illustration of this by one of his most successful aces, Reinhard 'Teddy' Suhren, who later described what happened when a British warplane appeared almost overhead, apparently from nowhere. In calm and clear weather, U-564 was on the track of a convoy and Suhren was hopeful of adding to his long tally of successes:

> I have already been on my feet for five hours. In an hour it will begin to grow dark. Ahead of us the horizon is as sharp as an etching. Twenty minutes later, on the starboard bow, mastheads show up. The convoy! . . . Scarcely has the radio-signal been sent than the look-out is already shouting 'Plane!' We are well aware that there are three other submarines in our patrol, and the old familiar song rings out again – 'Alarm!' 'Dive! Dive!' The plane must have seen us already. Tank 5 is beginning to hiss with escaping air as I jump down below. Being last, I close the hatch behind me. We glide down into the depths at a steep angle. At around 60 meters I give the order to level out. The depth-charges are sure to rain down on us now and it's always important to have the boat on an even keel when they go off . . . no sign of any depth-charges. So cautiously back up again . . . the boat is at periscope depth. A quick look-round; the plane has vanished. Surface! Look around with the naked eye. Nothing to see – but no sign of the convoy either, the tips of whose mastheads we had seen just now. The sea had swallowed them up again.[63]

Such missed opportunities were a source of intense frustration to the U-boat commander-in-chief. 'By systematically forcing the U-boats to submerge', he noted in September, 'it made them lose contact at evening twilight and thus spoiled all the [U-]boats' best chances of attack during the first four moonless hours of the night.'[64] As a result their prey usually escaped unmolested. Once forced to submerge, the submarines, which relied exclusively on battery power to propel them underwater, could travel at only seven knots – no faster, and often more slowly, than their quarry. At daylight, even when they had a good fix from B-Dienst, it would take them many hours, travelling at their full speed of seventeen knots on the surface, to catch up again; on those very infrequent occasions when a convoy was accompanied by an aircraft carrier, even this was virtually impossible without courting disaster in the form of an air-launched depth charge. But for most of the time this mattered little because there were so very few VLR bombers in the Atlantic.

By this time, the area of the Atlantic Gap killing ground had somewhat contracted. The gradual increase in numbers of medium-range bombers and long-range aircraft, notably the B-17 (better known as the 'Flying Fortress'), provided air cover to the convoys to a distance of up to 800 miles from their bases in Greenland, Iceland and Northern Ireland. But this still left an area of the ocean, roughly 300 by 300 miles, where the convoys were no less vulnerable and where, in Dönitz's words, 'we could be sure of finding them with no air cover at all'.[65] The Air Ministry's persistent refusal to make VLR Liberators available to Coastal Command in sufficient numbers to make an impact in these hazardous waters came as a surprise and a relief to Dönitz, who noted that he was 'gravely concerned' that they might soon be deployed to such effect to close the Gap.[66] Instead, by the last quarter of 1942, the U-boats seemed to be on course to win his tonnage war in the Atlantic.

Pound did his best to convey this fact to his peers and to the politicians. On 5 October he went so far as to warn that Britain's very survival was at stake, advising the Defence Committee that 'we have lost a large measure of control over our sea communications. This has already had and is having a far-reaching effect not only on the maintenance of the United Kingdom but on our ability to take the offensive.'[67] In his understated way, he could hardly have put the case more clearly. Once again, though, he was rebuffed. On 24 October Churchill, apparently soaring on Harris's flights of rhetoric, was implacable, instructing the War Cabinet, 'At present, in spite of the U-boat losses, the Bomber Offensive should have the first place in our air effort.'[68]

The First Sea Lord persevered. When Portal announced that, before long, Bomber Command would have up to 6,000 heavy aircraft with which to shatter Germany's infrastructure, Pound reiterated the point he had made so pithily against Harris four months earlier: that the RAF consumed a million tons of fuel a year as it was; to keep 6,000 bombers in service, Bomber Command would require five times as much oil, which could only reach Britain by convoys of tankers, and these would arrive safely only if they were protected from the wolf packs in the Atlantic Gap. This would prove impossible so long as the U-boats were virtually unchallenged from the skies. It was in these 90,000

'defence'. As a result they found it impossible to appreciate that the deployment of VLR Liberators in the numbers required to subvert the U-boat threat in the North Atlantic was every bit as 'offensive' as the bombing of Cologne. More to the point, this deployment was an essential precondition for securing victory against Nazi Germany. Had they recognized this fundamental truth when the Liberators became available in large numbers during 1942, the tide in the Battle of the Atlantic would have been turned many months earlier. As it was, Coastal Command had only one VLR squadron – twelve operational aircraft – by January 1943. This was nothing like enough to arrest a U-boat campaign which was about to reach an alarming climacteric.

# 19. A Very Narrow Escape

The storms at sea in the early weeks of 1943 were as severe and sustained as at any other time in the war as raging winds whipped the North Atlantic into a violence of tumbling waves that inspired awe and fear in warships, merchantmen and U-boats alike as they fought the weather as well as one another. It was an appropriately vicious environment for what was very soon to witness the bitterest convoy battle of the entire war.

For the men who crewed the U-boats in these conditions, life was somewhat akin to being tossed around inside an infernal washing machine: 'Giant waves sent icy torrents of seawater crashing over the top of the conning tower and down the hatches into the control room,' Hans Goebeler wrote. 'We control room mates were miserable, forced to sit for hours at a time being periodically soaked by the frigid brine. When we were wet the seawater burned our eyes with salt. When we were dry, the salt residue made us itch all over. We cursed the wretched winter weather.'[1]

In U-230, Leutnant Herbert Werner endured week after week of some of the worst weather ever recorded in the Atlantic:

> The sea boiled and foamed and leapt continually . . . U-230 struggled through gurgling whirlpools, up and down mountainous seas; she was pitched into the air by one towering wave and caught by another and buried under tons of water by still another. The cruel winds whipped across the wild surface at speeds up to 150 miles an hour . . . When we were on watch, the wind punished us with driving snow, sleet, hail, and frozen spray . . . Below inside the bobbing steel cockleshell, the boat's violent up-and-down motion drove us to the floor plates and hurled us straight up and threw us around like puppets.[2]

For those who sailed in the convoys there was but cold comfort in the fact that it was virtually impossible for U-boats to aim torpedoes accurately at the height of a storm, since heavily laden merchant ships were only too easily overwhelmed by the unabated ferocity of the elements.

On 23 January the *St Sunniva*, a Scottish ferry built to serve the route between Aberdeen and the Shetlands, but now operating as a rescue ship in support of the Atlantic convoys, became so heavily encrusted with ice in the worsening weather that she capsized and sank with the loss of sixty-four men. In hurricane-force winds on the following day, the *Ville de Tamatave* lost steerage when her rudder was smashed by a giant wave and the entire crew, including the convoy commodore, Admiral Sir Studholme Brownrigg, was drowned. Not surprisingly, the men who had to endure these oceanic horrors saw such weather as an enemy force every bit as terrifying as a wolf pack on the prowl. Writing of his own experiences, Captain Donald Macintyre noted, 'The enemy we knew we could cope with, but the vindictive savagery of the Atlantic gales and the mountainous waves they raised, which came snoring down the wind at us, towering high above our heads, many a time put the fear of God into me.'[3]

As it was, the malevolence of the Atlantic weather affected but did not determine the character of a war of attrition which had now lasted for almost three and a half years yet from which neither side yet showed any sign of recoil. On the contrary, the growing intensity of the struggle matched the ever clearer magnitude of its meaning: were the U-boats to prevail, the Western Allies would be unable to sustain the global strategy on which they had already embarked; conversely, if the Allies were to prevail, the Nazis were bound to face eventual annihilation.

At the start of this final phase of the Battle of the Atlantic, the balance of advantage seemed clearly to lie with the U-boats. In January, despite the appalling weather, they sank a total of thirty-eight merchantmen, fifteen of which were travelling in convoy. In February the numbers rose sharply. In a heavy gale on 2 February, the *Jeremiah Van Rensselaer*, one of fifty-seven ships in convoy HX 224, was torpedoed by U-456 and holed in two places. Without waiting to assess the damage (which, it transpired, was not beyond repair), some of the terrified crew lowered the lifeboats, two of which immediately capsized. Others leapt over-board and swam for the rafts. Of the ship's complement of seventy-one sailors and armed guards, forty-six lost their lives, including the captain, Lucius Webb. The following day U-632 sank a British tanker, the *Cordelia*, laden with 12,000 tons of oil, killing almost everyone on board; the only member of the forty-seven-man crew to survive was picked up by the U-boat.

In saving that life, U-632's commander secured a nugget of invaluable intelligence. Under interrogation, the hapless prisoner let slip that HX224 was being closely followed by another, slow-moving, convoy, SC118. The message was swiftly despatched to U-boat headquarters and within hours twenty U-boats were on their way to intercept the sixty-four merchant ships.\* On board U-230, Leutnant Herbert Werner was on watch as they closed on SC118 'through snow squalls, darkness, and a lashing sea'. Visibility, he noted, was 'close to zero' when he detected 'a string of shadows' which were screened by a zigzagging posse of destroyers. At one point he saw one of these listing so sharply as she drove into the 'towering breakers' that her guns 'touched the ocean's surface', a sight that caused him to reflect that he was 'safer aboard a submarine' and would not 'change to a surface vessel at any price'. Although U-230 fired several torpedoes at the convoy, none hit the target. But U-456 had greater success. Werner watched as 'three huge blasts sent fountains of fires and sparks into the sky. Then the flames collapsed and the three freighters burned quietly with their derricks grotesquely pointing into the night.'[4] In the course of the next three days, the wolf pack sank another five ships with the loss of 445 men, 272 of them aboard the troopship USS *Henry R. Mallory*, which sank within thirty minutes without apparently having time even to send out a distress signal. Despite an escort of twelve warships, twice the usual number for such a convoy, eight vessels were sunk in SC118, contributing to the total sixty-three ships lost in the Atlantic in February.

March was to prove even worse. On the 16th, an order was sent out from Dönitz's headquarters in Berlin: 'All U-boats proceed with maximum speed towards convoy grid square BD14. Over sixty ships course northeast nine knots.' It was the signal for the start of a sea battle between three wolf packs and two Allied convoys – SC122 and HX229 – that would create panic in the Admiralty.

Among the U-boats now hastening to the black hole of the Atlantic Gap was U-230. Despite 'the enormous strain of battling blizzards and

\* By this time, Professor Blackett had shown statistically – if paradoxically – that by increasing the number of escorts by a third a convoy of sixty vessels would enjoy the same level of protection as a convoy of thirty. This efficiency saving meant that Churchill's maximum of thirty-five ships per convoy (p. 279) ceased to apply.

enemy for seven weeks', Werner and the rest of the crew were in good spirits. A few days earlier they had successfully torpedoed two freighters in a slow convoy of sixty-nine merchant ships (SC121), twelve of which had been sunk by a fleet of twenty-three U-boats. Not only that, but U-230 had survived a retaliatory attack by three escort destroyers which, between them, 'in a hellish concert', dropped at least forty depth charges over and around them in the course of a nine-hour chase. Now, after 'cutting through a night of howling winds and brief snow squalls', they closed on SC122 as Werner imagined 'its officers and seamen constantly alert to the threat of being spotted, attacked, decimated, mutilated, killed'.

At 10.40 p.m. on the 16th, U-230's lookout shouted: 'Shadow on port, distance 6,500 [metres]. It's the whole herd.' Captain Paul Siegmann manoeuvred his submarine into range and prepared to launch an attack on one of the shadowy targets, which, according to Werner, seemed like 'dots the size of bugs, moving along the indistinct moonlit horizon'. When the U-boat was within 4,000 metres of the convoy, Siegmann veered away, intending to fire his torpedoes from its stern tube and then flee. Some thirty minutes later:

> the first destroyer of the inner cordon shot out of the obscurity. For a few minutes she cruised at high speed between us and the convoy and then changed course again . . . U-230 advanced far enough for Siegmann to swing into attack position. But as soon as we turned the boat began to rock hard, causing our treacherous white wake to spread wider and glisten in the moonlight like a thick torch.

The destroyer failed to notice this tell-tale evidence. Werner watched intently through his binoculars, waiting for Siegmann to give him the go-ahead to launch his torpedoes at the distant ships as they wallowed through the ocean, 'their masts stuck up along the horizon like a heavy picket fence'. As he prepared to open fire, Werner was nudged by U-230's oberleutnant, who murmured, 'Destroyers astern, closing in fast.' He glanced round at 'the white foam [that] leaped from their foredecks and bridges' as two escorts bore down on them. Suddenly, Siegmann yelled into the wind, 'Exec, select your targets!' 'Tubes, one to five, stand by!' Werner shouted down the hatch: 'Ready, ready,' came the reply. With the submarine in grave danger of coming under fire from the pursuing destroyers, he took aim at 'the fattest targets' in the convoy. Then

Siegmann yelled, 'Time is up, Exec shoot!' Werner pulled the firing mechanism five times as the U-boat veered sharply away to flee from its attackers. As they began their escape, the crew 'heard a terrific rumble of three hard explosions. Blinding flashes revealed innumerable cargo ships, destroyers and trawlers. Three of the vessels careered out of file, floating torches.' With no torpedoes left, U-230 managed to escape the convoy's escorts. As they began the voyage back to Brest, Siegmann – somewhat exaggeratedly – boasted to Dönitz's headquarters of their multiple triumphs in the course of the last few weeks. Werner himself recorded that he had been 'overjoyed with our spectacular victories. Everything seemed to be right with the world.'

U-230's successes were mirrored by others. In the early afternoon of 18 March, U-221 ran through the convoy, sinking the *Walter G. Gresham* with the loss of twenty-seven lives before her commander, Oberleutnant Hans-Hartwig Trojer, took aim at another easy target. On the bridge of the *Canadian Star*, Third Officer Keyworth watched as two torpedoes snaked unerringly in his direction. In a forlorn effort to outsmart the inevitable he put the ship's helm hard over. As he did so, one of the torpedoes smashed into the engine room, the other into a refrigerated hold. The *Canadian Star* at once began to sink by the stern. Her master, Robert Miller, gave the order to abandon ship. The twenty-four passengers – officers and their families who had been serving in the Far East and India – were mustered at the lifeboat stations. Four life rafts were launched without mishap, but two lifeboats were knocked over in the breaking seas. Keyworth was in one of these and watched impotently as water poured over the gunwales into his waterlogged lifeboat: 'It was useless to bale; the sea just swept through the boat from end to end. I could see the men, one by one, their eyes glazing and eventually losing their grip and being washed up and down the boat and eventually out of it altogether.'[5]

The ship's carpenter decided to stay with his ship. As her bows reared into the sky, he called out to an officer below, 'Good bye Sir, It was a good life while it lasted' before deliberately walking 'right into the path of a wave pounding across the after deck. It was like a minnow being swallowed by a whale.'[6] Of the eighty-four men who had boarded the *Canadian Star* a few days earlier, thirty-four had drowned or been frozen to death or, as in so many other cases, simply lost the will to live. As the battle raged, the Atlantic became indelibly pockmarked by a host of invisible tragedies as sailors and their ships disappeared for ever below the surface.

Three escorts were sent to hunt down the offending U-boat, following a line pinged back to them by ASDIC, which had located the vessel somewhere beneath the waves to the rear of the convoy. As they swept through the merchantmen, Surgeon-Lieutenant Humphrey Osmond on board HMS *Volunteer* saw two ships sinking, a beleaguered lifeboat and a lone man clinging to a spar:

> It was that appalling dilemma which a brave, decent and humane young captain had to face and decide on in about five minutes – the survivors or the submarine? We wallowed past them, the captain shouting through the loud-hailer: 'We'll be back' . . . I believe that decision hung around the captain's neck for the rest of his life. He could never be sure he had done the right thing because we didn't get the submarine.[7]

Unsurprisingly, not all the merchant crews, who had little experience of warfare and were drawn from many different nationalities, shared such an intense commitment to victory and, on occasion, they behaved with less spectacular courage than a romanticized version of the war at sea would allow. Aggravated by the shipowners' casual failure to provide their crews with the rudimentary equipment and training required to save lives, confusion and incompetence too often led to a greater loss of life than otherwise would have been the case. In this instance, the US Navy's official historian noted:

> There were numerous acts of heroism and self-sacrifice [but] it is sad to find instances of the same neglect, indiscipline and carelessness on board merchant ships that had been losing lives needlessly for four years. Lifeboats capsized and their painters parted, boats and rafts were cast off before the torpedoed ship stopped, tillers were missing, insufficient lifelines were rigged, rafts were not equipped with a heaving line to rescue men afloat, expensive lifesaving suits were abandoned, lifejackets lacked straps or handles to help a rescuer to pull an oiled-up survivor from the water.[8]

Yet, in these dreadful conditions, the will to survive generally triumphed. When the SS *Southern Princess* and the SS *Irénée Du Pont* were hit in quick succession, Captain Albert Hocken in *Tekoa* dropped out of line and went to pick up the survivors. 'Fellows were floating about, the red lights on their life-jackets like a carpet of fireflies in the water. Some men were whistling quite chirpily and others were shouting like mad.'[9] Over the next four hours, in an act of barely noticed heroism, the crew of the *Tekoa* risked all to rescue no fewer than 146 men from what would otherwise have been certain death. Elsewhere, the *Nariva* went to the help of one of the many rafts which had been sorely battered by the fierce gale. The freighter's second officer noted: 'As the raft got close, we could hear these poor, soaked U-boat victims shouting or crying for help until we could hear, borne down on us on the howling gale, the voices were lustily singing "She's a lassie from Lancashire, just a lassie from Lancashire". We didn't know whether to laugh or cry.'[10] By now, some forty U-boats were lined up in three patrols to attack both convoys. Together these comprised 110 heavily laden freighters escorted by thirteen warships. In the space of a few days, from 16 to 19 March, the two convoys were subjected to the most devastating U-boat onslaught of the entire war in the Atlantic, and it was on a scale that suggested Dönitz might be on the verge of achieving his ultimate objective.

In Berlin, they celebrated the latest killing spree. On 19 March, U-boat headquarters boasted, 'In all 32 vessels of 136,000 tons and one destroyer were sunk . . . This is the greatest success ever achieved in a single convoy battle and is all the more creditable in that nearly half the U-boats involved scored at least one hit.'[11] In fact 'only' 21 freighters out of the 110 in the two convoys had been sunk, but these vessels had been carrying between them 141,000 tons of supplies, a scale of loss which was even heavier than Dönitz had claimed. The destruction of HX 229 and SC 122 had brought to a terrible climax a U-boat slaughter in which more than half a million tons of shipping had been sent to the bottom of the ocean in twenty days.

In London and Washington, these losses provoked acute trepidation. Gripped by a very real fear that the convoy routes linking Britain to North America might be severed, the admirals pored over the statistics. These revealed that of the ninety-seven vessels lost by one means or another as they plied between Britain and the rest of the world in that month, two-thirds had been sailing in convoy – which was the only known means of limiting losses to what was regarded as an acceptable minimum. Haunted by the implications of this, the Lords of the Admiralty thrashed around for a means of escape. For a while they alighted on the most drastic option of all. On a visit to the headquarters of Western Approaches Command at Derby House in Liverpool, Lord Hall, the Admiralty's financial secretary, let slip that their lordships were 'secretly of the opinion that the convoy system should be abandoned and the merchant ships left to make their own way across the Western Ocean independently'.[12] Or, as it was put officially, 'It appeared possible that we should not be able to continue [to regard] convoy as an effective means of defence.'[13] To abandon the convoy system, the lynchpin of the Admiralty's maritime strategy, would have been a counsel of despair, explicable only by the fact that, at the time, the admirals must have felt that 'defeat stared them in the face'.[14] That it was even mooted was a measure of the degree to which the Admiralty had been gripped by dread, an intensity of feeling that was reflected in the Naval Staff Review at the end of the year, which formally recorded that 'the Germans never came so near to disrupting communications between the New World and the Old as in the first twenty days of March 1943'.[15] The shudder of remembered horror as they peered into that abyss is almost palpable.

Only one man seemed immune to this bout of collective panic. Admiral Sir Max Horton had succeeded Admiral Noble as commander-in-chief of the Western Approaches just before the end of November 1942. Noble had done much to sustain the morale of the men under his command, overseeing a new training regime, providing them with the latest technological devices, and joining them at sea to witness their predicament first hand. However, after eighteen months at the helm, he had been eased into a less exhausting but still demanding role as head of the British Naval Mission in Washington, a task for which his amiable nature and calm demeanour were well suited. By contrast, his successor was brusque, obsessive and blessed with boundless energy. Among his foibles, Horton favoured playing bridge until dawn and was given to commandeering junior officers to his whims. After one such long night in Derby House, he surprised his partner, Lieutenant Commander John Guest, by asking, 'Do you play golf?' When Guest conceded that he played regularly but explained that he did not have his clubs to hand, Horton was incredulous: 'What, a naval officer who doesn't carry his clubs with him?'[16] When Guest told him they were at his home in Woking, the admiral despatched a car to Surrey, where they were picked up and brought to Liverpool, petrol rationing notwithstanding.

Horton's domineering and sometimes brutal manner concealed a fine analytical mind; in the judgement of one of his peers, he was not only 'superb in his operational and administrative actions' but also 'had an intuition of what the Hun would do, which was quite uncanny'.[17] As a submarine commander in the 1914–18 war, he had distinguished himself by his unrivalled grasp of the immense complexities – human and technical – associated with the conduct of submarine warfare. In this, as in other qualities, he was a match for his principal adversary in the Battle of the Atlantic. 'With his knowledge and insight, his ruthless determination and his driving energy,' the navy's official historian wrote, 'he was without doubt the right man to pit against Dönitz.'[18]

As with Dönitz, so Horton's ruthless energy had been detected early in his career. In 1924, in terms remarkably similar to those which had been used about the young German officer, one of his commanding officers had reason to commend him: 'Discipline, Devotion to Duty and enthusiasm for your work which is so infectious that everyone near you feels it. All that you undertake is bound to prosper.'[19] In his new role, according to Captain Peter Gretton, Horton was intolerant of failure and 'had a quick way with incompetents'.[20] Those who failed to meet his exacting standards were removed from his staff at Derby House, or, if they were serving at sea, from the ships under his overall command. He was fanatical about training, thumping the table in meetings as he spat out the directive, 'Buy your experience in training and not when fighting the enemy.'[21] According to another of his subordinate officers, he 'drove, drove and drove' his officers and men with a 'personal interest' that was 'so intense that he almost defeated his own – absolutely correct – object'. One of his critical admirers noted that, as a result, 'Those responsible for training became so frightened of his insatiable inquiries that they were more interested in sending in satisfactory returns than in preparing ships to fight the enemy.'[22] Yet he was not so obdurate as to be deaf to sound advice; when a colleague summoned the nerve to point out that his overbearing manner could be counterproductive, he evidently eased off.

Like Dönitz, Horton was well aware that, while ill-trained men lose battles, well-trained men only win them if properly equipped to do so. Both the German and the Allied high commands also knew that the eventual outcome would not simply be a matter of ships, submarines and planes, or even highly trained crews – though all these were essential. To gain the upper hand, the adversaries had to win the technology battle as well. By late March, notwithstanding the grave losses of that month, Horton was quietly confident that, in this battle at least, the Allies would soon hold a commanding advantage.

At the core of this contest was the rapid development of more precise means of locating and destroying the intended victim, whether it be freighter or U-boat. The individual items in the navy's technological toolkit to achieve this had been painstakingly assembled over many months but were not yet fully operational. However, in the same moment that their lordships in the Admiralty contemplated the imminent catastrophe of a U-boat victory in the Atlantic, the diverse efforts of those teams of scientists, engineers, designers and technicians responsible for devising more effective means of warfare were about to shift the balance of power in the Atlantic.

By the spring of 1943 a high proportion of escort vessels had been fitted with a high-frequency direction finder (or HF/DF, known universally as Huff-Duff). This system could pick up even the briefest signal sent from one U-boat to another or the to-and-fro of messages between a wolf pack and U-boat headquarters, identifying it as a point of light on a fluorescent screen. Huff-Duff was not able to gauge the range of the boat which was transmitting the signal but merely indicated a bearing along which an escort could be despatched to hunt down the offending submarine in the expectation of forcing it to submerge before it could manoeuvre close enough to the convoy to release its torpedoes.

Of even greater significance were new radar devices that could be used in the Atlantic, either on warships or in the air. In effect, these were miniature versions of the land-based radar stations strung along the south coast of England which had given RAF Fighter Command early warning of an impending Luftwaffe attack during the Battle of Britain. Early in the war these had been at a primitive stage of development. Though they could be squeezed into the cockpit of a Coastal Command bomber, the early devices lacked the range and clarity to be of great use. When Dönitz countered in the autumn of 1942 by fitting the U-boat fleet with a radar detection device known as the Metox 600, they became virtually useless. The Metox was able to detect an intruding aircraft before it became visible to the naked eye. When this happened, an alarm would sound and the U-boat would crash-dive to safety.

By the spring of 1943, however, the Allies had developed a 10-centimetre-wavelength radar which was about to revolutionize the war at sea. As Dönitz would soon discover, this system not only had a range and clarity that had seemed inconceivable a few years earlier but was also a deadly weapon in the British armoury. With a maximum range of sixty miles, it could both identify the conning tower of a U-boat from twelve miles away and keep it in focus until the pilot was close enough to unleash his cache of bombs or depth charges with murderous accuracy. Since the Metox 600 was unable to detect the 10-centimetre radar, the new system was soon to become a source of great dread to U-boat crews who knew they had no answer to it.

As Horton was very well aware, however, no amount of discipline, training and technology would of themselves win the Battle of the Atlantic. On the very day that he took command of the Western Approaches, 19 November 1942, he wrote to the First Lord of the Admiralty and his colleagues to warn that 'unless a reasonable number of long-endurance destroyers and long-range aircraft come shortly a very serious situation will develop on the Atlantic lifeline'.[23]

The destroyers were to spearhead his new 'support groups', each of which was to form the equivalent of a cavalry unit, trained and equipped for the specific task of hunting down any U-boat patrol threatening the convoys. In this respect, Horton's aggressive instincts mirrored those of the prime minister, who as First Lord of the Admiralty had longed to create a somewhat similar force to comb the high seas. Horton's support groups, however, were to have a narrower and more clearly defined role. Instead of setting off on 'one wild goose-chase after another', his cavalry brigades were to operate in a planned and coordinated manner, not only with convoy escorts but also with the VLR bombers. Knowing that these aircraft should already have been deployed, Horton was insistent about this: 'I feel strongly that the solution of the German U-boat menace will be found only by the development of highly trained Support Groups working in cooperation with an adequate number of very long-range aircraft.'[24] The persistence with which he made the case for the support groups – which had already been advanced in less arresting language by his predecessor – was rewarded when the Admiralty agreed to establish five such groups in the North Atlantic. However, by March, none of these had completed the intensive training exercises upon which Horton insisted before unleashing them against the

U-boats; moreover, since the VLR bombers were still notable by their absence, Dönitz had every reason to suppose that the balance of power in the Battle of the Atlantic was still tipped heavily his way. It was – but not for much longer.

The fact that Horton did not have the authority to commandeer the VLR bombers from the Air Ministry did not deter him from pressing his cause with vehemence. In January 1943 he was rewarded by a visit from Sir Stafford Cripps (who had been appointed Minister of Aircraft Production a little before Horton's arrival at Derby House). According to Horton, Cripps declared that 'the VLR aircraft was the true solution to the U-boat menace' before going on to complain that

> the Admiralty had never made a clear and detailed case for VLR air-craft. They had simply asked for more aircraft for Coastal Command without giving detailed reasons and it was mainly owing to their not making out a clear and definite case that the Navy had not done better in the past in regard to its suitable aircraft. He reiterated . . . that the VLR had never been asked for before he suggested it.[25]

It is just possible that the sinuously ambitious minister genuinely believed what he was saying; if not, his assertion was an egregious dis-tortion. Horton, though, was wise enough not to look this ministerial gift horse in the mouth, even when the self-serving minister had the temerity to claim that it had only been when he had himself promoted the Admiralty's case in the newly established Anti-U-Boat Warfare Committee in November that this sub-committee of the War Cabinet provisionally agreed to allocate thirty-nine VLR Liberators to Coastal Command by the end of March 1943. Very little occurred to suggest that this commitment would be honoured until, at the Casablanca Con-ference in January, the Combined Chiefs had agreed that the threat of the U-boat menace should be a 'first charge on the resources of the United Nations'. At the same time, their planners confirmed that eighty VLR bombers would be required to cover the Atlantic Gap. In accept-ing this advice the Combined Chiefs decided to allocate these at a rate which would mean that half of them – suitably modified – would be delivered to Coastal Command by the beginning of April. In fact, a host of delays meant that Coastal Command had no more than twenty operational aircraft capable of operating in the Atlantic Gap by this promised date, too late to divert the disasters of that month.

It took the shock of the March sinkings finally to lift the scales from the eyes of those who had for so long refused to face the facts. A few days after the loss of SC122 and HX229, the First Sea Lord warned the Anti-U-Boat Warfare Committee that the Atlantic was now so 'saturated by U-boats' that it was no longer possible to evade them and therefore that 'we shall have to fight the convoys through them'.[26] This catastrophic prospect clearly made an impact on the air chief marshal, who finally conceded that the crisis in the Atlantic could no longer be sidestepped by his ministry. On 22 March, reacting to Pound's insistence that more VLR bombers were urgently required, Portal undertook to provide Coastal Command with no fewer than 150 Liberators by August at the latest. Two days later he not only confirmed this but also added a remarkable promise: the minutes of the meeting record him as saying that 'he was so convinced of the correctness of the policy of attacking U-boats around threatened convoys' that every one of the Liberators which had been earmarked for early delivery to Coastal Command would also be converted for VLR duties.[27]

Churchill's most trusted advisor, Lord Cherwell, was clearly put out by what must have appeared to him as a volte-face, if not a Damascene conversion, by Portal. In a direct riposte, he wrote to the prime minister the following day to observe sardonically that 'it is difficult to compare the damage done to any of the forty odd big German cities in a 1000 ton [sic] raid . . . with the advantage of sinking one U-boat out of 400 and saving 3 or 4 ships out of 5500'. With an adroit sense of what would carry weight with the prime minister, he added a velvety political aperçu: '[I]t will surely be held in Russia as well as here that the bomber offensive must have more immediate effect on the course of the war in 1943.'[28] As a confidant of the prime minister, who was trusted with state secrets and who was therefore privy to Stalin's resentment at the postponement of the Second Front, he was also familiar with Churchill's belief that, if it served no other purpose, the area bombing of German cities found favour in Moscow.

When 'Bomber' Harris heard about the air chief marshal's change of heart, he was driven to levels of hyperbole that were exceptional even by his own standards. Expostulating that it would be 'catastrophic' to divert the Liberators from the German offensive, he insisted that, in concert with the Russians, Bomber Command 'could knock Germany back behind her own frontiers, if not out of the war . . . in a matter of months'.[29] This time it was his turn to be ignored. Though both Cherwell and Harris would return to the fray, the chiefs of staff – thanks in significant measure to Portal's change of heart – had reached a decision that would very soon transform British fortunes in the Atlantic.

Though he shared the Admiralty's dismay at the losses in March, Churchill had other matters on his mind as well. To his great relief and satisfaction, the Torch landings six months earlier had been accomplished with hardly a mishap. To protect and supply the 100,000 Allied troops engaged in the operation with all their needs, not only had the Admiralty been forced to delay, reorganize and reroute shipping destined for Britain from Asia and Africa but, to the same purpose, Churchill and Roosevelt had provoked Stalin's wrath by suspending the Arctic convoys for almost three months until the end of December. Now in March they were about to do the same again – and Stalin would have to be told and given a credible explanation for their decision.

Although the November landings in Morocco and Algeria had been virtually trouble free, a combination of winter weather, the inexperience of the American GIs and grave tactical errors on the battlefield had slowed the Allied advance towards Tunis. In the meantime, the Axis armies in North Africa had been reinforced by 200,000 battle-hardened troops, most of whom had been airlifted from Germany in the weeks following Torch. Their resistance led to a severe delay in the Anglo-American timetable for victory and it was not until March that Rommel's forces were finally trapped by an Allied pincer movement. Throughout these weeks, the Allied navies, supported by Coastal Command, had been required to provide cover for the troopships and supply vessels which lumbered to and fro across the Atlantic to sustain the forces in North Africa.

Nevertheless, with the defeat of the Axis powers in North Africa now a foregone conclusion, Roosevelt and Churchill had their sights on the next phase of the war in the Mediterranean: the invasion and conquest of the Third Reich via Italy. The strain which the invasion of North Africa had imposed on Allied shipping, already aggravated by the heavy losses in the Atlantic, was about to be exacerbated yet further.

Operation Husky, as the invasion of Sicily was codenamed, was to be an amphibious assault by hundreds of thousands of Allied troops under the overall command of General Dwight D. Eisenhower, the commander-in-chief, North Africa. The operation would require ships and landing craft in similar numbers to those which had been deployed for Torch. With an urgent need for more warships in the Atlantic to counter the U-boat threat to Britain's transatlantic lifeline, it was obvious that something would have to give somewhere – and there was precious little debate about where that would be. Once again – and for the third time – Stalin had to be told that the Arctic convoys were to be suspended. This was not a prospect that either Roosevelt or Churchill relished.

Immediately after the Casablanca Conference in January, the two Western leaders had written a joint letter to apprise Stalin of their military plans for the following nine months. 'We believe', they wrote, 'that these operations, together with your powerful offensive, may well bring Germany to her knees in 1943.' After delivering themselves of this arresting but notably imprecise forecast, they proceeded to outline their intention to 'launch large-scale amphibious operations at the earliest moment' against Sicily; 'to concentrate in the United Kingdom a strong American land and air force' that would prepare the way for a cross-Channel invasion of occupied Europe 'as soon as practicable'; and, meanwhile, to intensify the bombing of Germany 'at a rapid rate'.[30] In a further message two weeks later, Churchill went so far as to hold out the prospect of a 'cross-Channel operation in August' or one 'with even stronger forces for September'. However, he added, the precise timing of this would 'be dependent upon the condition of German defensive possibilities across the Channel at this time'.[31]

So far from being seduced by this prospect, Stalin clearly detected the disingenuousness, if not perfidy, in the ambiguities and caveats with which Churchill's letter was sprinkled:

> It is evident from your message that the establishment of the Second Front, in particular in France, is envisaged only in August–September. It seems to me that the present situation demands the greatest possible speeding up of the action contemplated . . . [I]n order not to give the enemy any respite it is extremely important to deliver the blow from the West in the spring or early summer and not to postpone it until the second half of the year.[32]

The arrival of Stalin's cable coincided with Churchill taking to his bed with a high fever. An X-ray showed that he had a patch on his lung. Although his physician, Lord Moran, was not unduly perturbed, the prime minister, who had barely known illness in his sixty-nine years on earth, was somewhat alarmed to be diagnosed with pneumonia. Moran summoned a consultant, Dr Geoffrey Marshall. Prescribing a dose of tablets, Marshall urged him to rest until he had recovered, warning in jocular fashion that the pneumonia could otherwise get worse with the result that the prime minister could succumb to 'the old man's friend'. Churchill asked why. 'Because it takes them off so quietly,' Marshall replied. This clearly touched Churchill deeply. In Moran's account, the prime minister took 'a more serious view of his illness'[33] than his doctors; he certainly made sure that what he described as 'a very disagreeable experience' should not be underplayed, telling Harry Hopkins, among others, that he 'had had a bad time [which] might easily have been worse'.[34] Promising to relax by reading *Moll Flanders*, he undertook to receive only the most pressing of his official papers. Among these was his correspondence with Stalin.

On 24 February, while he was still bedridden, Churchill deemed it politic to send the Soviet leader a note explaining that, because his 'fever got so high', he had been unable to reply to his recent telegram but, within the next few days, he 'hoped to send you more information on the whole scene'.[35] In fact it was another fortnight before Stalin heard from him again. On this occasion Churchill more or less repeated his previous cable, reassuring the Soviet leader that the Second Front was still earmarked for August but warning that the supply of shipping required for such an operation was being outstripped by the growing needs elsewhere: to protect and provision thirty-eight British divisions strung out along a front that extended 6,300 miles from Gibraltar to Calcutta; to sustain the Allied campaigns in North Africa and against the Japanese in the Pacific; and to avoid further reducing the British imports which had already been 'cut to the bone'. All this, he concluded, meant that 'the shipping at our disposal and the means of escorting it' were simply not yet available on anything like the scale required to bring in the US troops needed for an earlier cross-Channel invasion.[36]

Not surprisingly, Stalin thought he was being strung along. In mid-March he wrote separately but in the same vein to both Churchill and Roosevelt:

I think I must give an emphatic warning, in the interest of our common cause, of the grave danger with which further delay in the opening of a second front is fraught . . . That is why the vagueness of both your reply and Mr Churchill's as to the opening of a second front in Europe causes me concern.[37]

From Stalin's perspective, there was worse to come. On 24 March, a few days after the mauling of SC122 and HX229, Churchill and Roosevelt finally confirmed that the Arctic convoys scheduled for the next few months would have to be cancelled yet again. Earlier in the year the prime minister had been greatly irritated by what he perceived as Russian ingratitude for the sacrifices which had already been forced on Britain to keep the Arctic lifeline open. When the Soviet ambassador, Ivan Maisky, accused the British of bad faith in January, for allegedly failing to allocate the promised number of merchant ships to the first convoy of 1943, Churchill had instructed Eden, Alexander and Pound that 'Maisky should be told I am getting to the end of my tether with these repeated Russian naggings, and there is not the slightest use trying to knock me about any more'. Whether or not his resentment lingered, he now seemed more than willing to be the bearer of bad news. Accordingly, on 30 March, with Roosevelt's approval he sent an unambiguous cable to the Soviet leader:

We feel it only right to let you know at once that it will not be possible to continue convoys by the Northern route after early May, since from that time onward every single escort vessel will be required to support our offensive operations in the Mediterranean leaving only a minimum to safeguard our lifeline in the Atlantic. In the latter we have had grievous and almost unprecedented losses during the last three weeks.[38]

Stalin's response was immediate:

I understand this unexpected action as a catastrophic diminution of supplies of arms and military raw materials to the USSR on the part of Britain and the United States of America. You realize of course that the circumstances cannot fail to affect the position of the Soviet troops.[39]

It might have been worse. Churchill must have been prepared for all manner of brickbats from allegations of perfidy to charges of treachery. Instead, when the prime minister responded to Stalin's reproach in conciliatory terms – albeit without yielding an inch of ground – Stalin favoured him with a surprisingly genial reply. Commenting on the Allied offensive in North Africa, he wrote: 'The speedy development of the Anglo-American advance in Tunis [sic] constitutes an important success in the war against Hitler and Mussolini. I wish you to kill the enemy and capture as many prisoners and trophies as possible. We are delighted that you are not giving respite to Hitler.'[40]

It may be that Stalin recognized the genuine predicament facing his Western Allies as they juggled their limited resources to overcome the double whammy of an acute shortage of warships and freighters on the one hand and, on the other, the alarming surge by the wolf packs in the Atlantic. But underlying Stalin's surprisingly agreeable tone was an important military development on the Eastern Front. The Soviet armies were at last on the offensive.

After one of the most gruelling and destructive battles in the history of warfare, the Germans were finally retreating from Stalingrad, leaving the way open for the Red Army to advance rapidly westwards to retake Kursk and Kharkov. Additionally, Hitler had ordered his forces to withdraw from the Caucasus. For the first time since the launch of Barbarossa almost two years earlier, the Wehrmacht was under pressure along the whole Russian Front. Although Leningrad was still under siege (and would not be relieved until 27 January 1944, by which time some 1.5 million soldiers and citizens would have died), German tanks no longer threatened Moscow. The panzers would fight bitterly in the months ahead to realize Hitler's insane vision, but they would seek in vain to sustain any counter-attack. The balance of advantage had shifted permanently from Hitler to Stalin.

## 20.  A Dramatic Turnabout

On 24 April 1943, fresh from their triumphs of the previous month, the crew of U-230 set off from Brest for the Atlantic Gap. On shore they had celebrated with abandon. While some of his friends took off to see their families, Leutnant Cremer remained on duty. It was an easy watch. He found time to walk in the French countryside, to indulge himself in the 9th Flotilla's country resort, Château Neuf, where he dined well, relaxed in a marble bathtub and explored the library. On one occasion he joined a group of fellow officers to sample one of the town's nightclubs. Skimpily dressed girls lined a dimly lit bar and plied their 'guests' with champagne. Werner danced with a girl who called herself Janine and later, after watching a blue movie, was enfolded in her arms for a customary denouement. But in the long hours of night, thoughts of Atlantic battles were rarely out of his mind. Assailed by memories of 'bellowing explosions of torpedoes, depth charges and bombs',[1] he thought of fellow officers who had not returned and was troubled by a sense that, notwithstanding the way in which SC 122 and HX 229 had been blitzed, the balance of advantage in the war at sea was changing, and not for the better.

As U-230 nosed out of her berth in the Bay of Biscay heading for the convoy routes, the mood among the crew was sombre. Only a month earlier, as their colleagues laid waste to those two convoys, Dönitz had urged them on with a bravura message: 'Bravo! Dranbleiben! Weiter so!' (Bravo! Keep at it! Carry on like that!).[2] This admonition no longer resonated. As the crew of U-230 knew from the tales told by returning colleagues, the Bay of Biscay had suddenly become a very hazardous 'bomb alley' from which there was very little chance of escape. Any U-boat leaving for the Atlantic Gap was now forced to play a life-and-death game of 'hide and seek', as Herbert Werner put it, until they had escaped the reach of Coastal Command's Wellingtons.[3]

The alarm had been sounded in the first week of March, when U-333, returning from an uneventful forty-eight-day voyage, was suddenly illuminated by a bright light from above. Caught in the glare of a powerful searchlight, the crew looked up in horror to see a low-flying twin-engined plane that had 'just jumped out of the darkness' making a bee-line towards them.[4] U-333's captain, Leutnant Walter Schwaff, was quick-witted enough to order his gun crew to fire at the aircraft as it came in for the attack. They scored a direct hit. The plane – a Wellington from Coastal Command – was at once engulfed in flames but, skimming low over U-333's conning tower, its crew managed to drop four bombs before crashing into the sea. Two of these hit their target, though one failed to detonate and the other inflicted only surface damage.

In other circumstances, Schwaff would have counted the downing of the Wellington as a signal victory, but on this occasion he felt far from celebratory. He and his crew had narrowly avoided death and the cause was an apparently inexplicable systems failure. Like almost every other U-boat, U-333 had been fitted with the Metox 600 the previous autumn. As this device could give early warning of an approaching aircraft that was fitted with radar from up to sixty miles away, Coastal Command's recent patrols over the Bay of Biscay had proved almost as fruitless as Bomber Command's simultaneous attacks on the U-boat pens. In the first two months of 1943 Coastal Command pilots occasionally sighted a U-boat on the surface but only one was sunk in this entire period. On this occasion, though, the Wellington had evidently managed to detect U-333 without itself being detected.

Thus, when Schwaff reported what had happened to U-333, there was consternation at U-boat headquarters in Berlin. It did not take long, though, for Dönitz to put two and two together and to conclude that the British bomber must have been operating on frequencies 'which lie outside the frequency of our (present) radio-locating receiver'[5] – a development to which Dönitz would later admit 'we had no answer'.[6] Dönitz could not know that U-333's attacker was equipped with the 10-centimetre radar system which, to Horton's delight, the Allies had just started to fit in Coastal Command's bombers and reconnaissance planes. Known as ASV III, the device was transformative. In combination with a powerful Leigh Light, fitted to the underside of the plane's wing to illuminate his unsuspecting target with precision and clarity, it was devastating. The delivery of these radar sets – which were still in short supply – was a tactical victory for Coastal Command. Portal had been reluctant to divert this new technology from Bomber Command's offensive against Germany, but Slessor, the new commander-in-chief, persuaded the air chief marshal that 'the desperate urgency' of arresting the U-boat onslaught should for once be given priority. Not only did Portal agree to release forty of the 10-centimetre sets but he was also persuaded to double the number of aircraft allocated to the Bay of Biscay. This raised to 150 the total number of planes available to patrol this 300-by-100-mile corridor, an increase in resources which, in Slessor's words, 'revolutionized the situation in the Bay'.[7] This was a dual benefit which, for the first time, tipped the balance of the struggle in those waters decisively in favour of the Allies.

Dönitz was consumed by gloom by these developments, noting that 'since February the effect of air surveillance has increased alarmingly when many boats are returning from big convoy battles'[8] and predicting 'there will be further losses'.[9] In an attempt to counter the new threat, he instructed his U-boat commanders who were within range of enemy aircraft to stay underwater at night and surface only during daylight hours to recharge their batteries. When this failed to diminish the danger, he performed something of a volte-face, ordering every U-boat to be armed with heavy anti-aircraft guns and instructing his crews 'to stay on the surface and fight it out'.[10] Initially, the appearance of these new weapons disconcerted fainter hearts in the Admiralty, but Slessor reassured his aircrews that 'the habit of fighting back may cost us a few more aircraft lost; but if persisted (which is at least open to doubt) will undoubtedly mean more U-boats killed'.[11] He was correct; the gallantry with which some crews obeyed Dönitz proved suicidal.

Against a darkening background of setbacks and threats elsewhere, which only the unhinged – like Hitler himself – could persistently ignore, the Atlantic had become the only theatre in which the Third Reich was still on the offensive. General Paulus had just surrendered at Stalingrad; Rommel was at bay in North Africa; the Allies had command of the Mediterranean, where they were throttling Axis supply lines and at the same time massing their own forces in preparation for the invasion of Italy; and the Luftwaffe was stretched to the limit by the need to counter Bomber Command's offensive. As a member of the Third Reich's high command, Dönitz was only too aware that the Battle of the Atlantic was now critical to Hitler's prospects of realizing his vision for the future of the world; in the words of his biographer: 'The only offensive force left to Germany was the U-boat arm, and it was natural that it should be used in a desperate throw to break out of the cycle of defeat.'[12] Despite his successes in March, Dönitz was far from confident that the struggle in the Atlantic would go his way: he needed more resources – both more U-boats and, no less vitally, more aircraft to support his wolf packs as they searched the Atlantic for vulnerable prey.

In February and March 1943 the Kriegsmarine's new commander-in-chief had four long meetings with the Führer. Though Dönitz went out of his way to display the loyalty and optimism which, at bleaker moments, sustained his leader's manifold self-delusions, he did not refrain from raising what he regarded as make-or-break issues. The first of these proved relatively straightforward. His precise shopping list was for a massive increase in production. He requred 800 new boats – better designed and with longer range – which would have to be built at a rate of almost one a day over the course of the next thirty months. To Dönitz's his relief, Hitler assured his favourite that the steel and other scarce metals required to meet this massive expansion of the fleet would be provided, as well as the 40,000 extra submariners that would be needed to crew the new U-boats.

Dönitz's other pressing need was for two types of aircraft: VLR aircraft to counter the impact of the Liberators, which were by now beginning to put in an appearance over the Atlantic, and several squadrons of multi-combat aircraft to challenge the growing number of enemy bombers now harrying the U-boats in the Bay of Biscay. In an uncanny echo of the 'Battle of the Air' which was simultaneously raging in Britain, Dönitz had been frustrated from the start of the war by the Luftwaffe's refusal to cooperate with the Kriegsmarine. According to Dönitz, Göring had behaved throughout his time in office as though 'everything that flies belongs to me',[13] a dog-in-the-manger attitude that had been aggravated by the personal animosity between him and Dönitz which had continued to simmer after their first confrontation in 1941 (see p. 136).

Rather as Portal refused to heed Pound, so Göring persistently stood in the way of Dönitz's attempts to secure the aircraft that any objective observer would have recognized as vital to the successful prosecution of the U-boat war. By the spring of 1943 the Kriegsmarine's new commander-in-chief – now the Reichsmarschall's military peer – had become so exasperated by this obstinacy that he began to confront Göring head-on. As a result, he reported, there were 'not a few collisions' between them, 'the most violent' of which took place in the presence of the Führer. 'I refuse to tolerate these criticisms of the Navy,' Dönitz had fumed. 'You would be better advised to look to your own Luftwaffe, where there is ample scope for your activities.' With some glee, the Kriegsmarine's commander-in-chief noted that the long silence which followed this outburst was broken when Hitler 'took leave of Göring with a shake of the hand and ostentatiously invited me to stay to breakfast with him'.[14] By this time, as this gesture pointedly confirmed, Dönitz's star was in the ascendant while Göring's was on the wane.

But Dönitz did not achieve all that he sought. Although Hitler undertook to deliver more JU-88 long-range fighters to ease the U-boats' predicament in the Bay of Biscay, he warned that no VLR aircraft were likely to be available on the timescale sought by Dönitz. There was nothing the Grossadmiral could do about this but their absence – 'one of the gravest handicaps under which we suffered' – continued to frustrate him; later in the same year he was to tell Hitler that 'future historians' would judge it to be 'wholly incomprehensible' that 'the German Navy, in this twentieth century, the century of aircraft, was called upon to fight without an air arm and without aerial reconnaissance of its own'.[15]

As U-230 ducked and dived her way through the Bay of Biscay into the apparent safety of the Atlantic, the crew felt a surge of optimism. As they sliced through calm seas under sunlit skies, 'the strain of the march through the Bay was soon erased by a series of beautiful days undisturbed by enemy planes',[16] Werner recalled. On 2 May they picked up a message from another U-boat reporting that it had sunk two freighters, which further raised their spirits and their hopes of yet more rich pickings. They had been given clear orders, they knew where they were heading and what to expect.

At U-boat headquarters the disposition of almost every convoy in the Atlantic was laid out for Dönitz and his senior staff. This was not so much because his U-boat crews weren't sharp-eyed (though they were), but because he had at his disposal detailed intelligence from B-Dienst, which, since the early days of the war, had been decrypting the great majority of operational orders sent by the Royal Navy to its ships at sea as well as almost every signal from the Admiralty detailing the latest known position of his U-boat fleet. For at least a year, since early 1942, according to Commander Tighe's excoriating post-war report for the Admiralty, B-Dienst had been developed to the point where German cryptanalysts could read 80 per cent of intercepted traffic within hours of its despatch. By the spring of 1943, he was even better informed: according to Tighe, 'the enemy . . . was reading most of the North Atlantic convoy traffic so quickly that he often had movements and diversion information ten to twenty hours in advance'. Crucially, there-fore, he 'was able to forecast alterations in convoy routes to avoid U-boats, and therefore to re-concentrate his wolf packs on our convoys. The patient and careful work of the submarine trackers was in fact being used against our own ships.' In particular, the destruction of convoys HX229 and SC122 could be 'directly traced to the information obtained by our signals'. In large measure this was because the Admir-alty had failed to take the precaution of investing the modest sums required to make its codes and ciphers as secure as they could and should have been. Even from the distance of many decades, it is not hard to detect the sense of horror and outrage with which Commander Tighe must have sifted the evidence before reaching his conclusion that 'this leakage of information through inadequate codes and ciphers . . . not only cost us dearly in men and ships but very nearly lost us the war'.[17]

It is not the least irony of the Second World War that OIC's 'compla-cency'[18] stood in the sharpest possible contrast to the care and energy which the same individuals had devoted to capturing and decrypting Enigma. After the war Harry Hinsley (the scion of Hut 4 at Bletchley Park who later became the official historian of the British intelligence services in the Second World War) would write that 'the regular receipt of naval Enigma decrypts from June 1941 . . . changed the course of the war by exerting a powerful influence on the outcome of most naval operations'.[19] The word 'most' is pertinent: Bletchley Park's contribu-tion to the Battle of the Atlantic – though far from negligible – was at best spasmodic and therefore significantly less critical to the outcome of the struggle than in other theatres. Though the genius of Alan Turing and his team in breaking the naval Enigma – which the Germans always presumed to be impenetrable – saved a significant number of convoys from steaming into the jaws of a waiting pack of U-boats (notably in the summer of 1941), Ultra was often of marginal use. In the early days this was because its decrypts were either incomplete or out of date by the time they reached the Submarine Tracking Unit. More pertinently, Ultra was effectively out of action at crucial periods.

The first six months of 1942 were a case in point. The spoke in Bletchley Park's wheel was the fourth 'rotor' which the Germans had added to the naval Enigma in the New Year. At a stroke it became impossible for Turing's team to break the German code, a blackout which was to last for ten months, in the course of which the U-boats enjoyed their longest 'happy time' of the war. Following the appalling damage inflicted by Operation Drumbeat on the eastern seaboard of the United States, the U-boat rampage in the Atlantic had continued long into the autumn, and to the Admiralty's despair and Churchill's alarm the graph of losses seemed to promise catastrophe. There was great relief, therefore, in the middle of December when Alan Turing's team was able to report they had finally cracked Shark – the menacing code-name coined by 'C' (Sir Stewart Menzies, the head of SIS) for the additional 'key' which had made such a murderous contribution to the U-boat campaign during those months. Once again, so it was hoped, the convoys would be able to take evasive action. But Bletchley Park's relief was short lived.

Less than three months later, on 10 March 1943, the OIC was once again in the dark. Two days earlier the Germans had replaced the code-book used to send back weather reports to U-boat headquarters and on which Bletchley Park was dependent for decrypting the remodelled Enigma. As a result the Submarine Tracking Unit was 'blinded' and would remain so until the Royal Navy could find a way of retrieving a copy of the new codebook. The First Sea Lord was dismayed. In a cable to the US vice-chief of staff in Washington, Admiral Henry Moore, he wrote gloomily that 'U-boat Special Intelligence has received a severe setback', which, he warned, might not be remedied for three months.[20] This blackout coincided precisely with the catastrophic days of March in the course of which HX229 and SC122 had been so horribly mauled by the wolf packs. It was therefore with relief that Menzies was able to advise Churchill on 19 March – by which time the remnants of those two convoys were through the worst – that, over the previous three days, Bletchley Park had broken back into Shark. This breakthrough gave the Admiralty little respite. Dönitz was now pouring U-boats into the North Atlantic in such numbers that it became almost impossible for the convoys to be diverted around one wolf pack without steaming into another. On the face of it, the intelligence gleaned by Dönitz from B-Dienst should have been of far greater use to him than the intelligence vouchsafed by Ultra to Admiral Horton: whereas B-Dienst could pinpoint the location of a convoy for Dönitz, Ultra was unable to provide Western Approaches Command with any means of escape from the wolf packs. Yet, for reasons which had little to do with intelligence, it did not prove to be so.

May was the pivotal month in the Battle of the Atlantic. By this time, finally and belatedly, the long-awaited VLR bombers – armed with 10-centimetre radar – had effectively closed the Atlantic Gap. In the words of Coastal Command's CO, Slessor, this had 'an instantaneous and dramatic effect' on the safety of the Allied convoys.[21] But it was not only the Liberators that were making a difference. Escort carriers, bristling with short-range bombers, had at last been released from the Mediterranean and the Far East to accompany most convoys through the most perilous parts of their voyage. Many destroyers, frigates and corvettes were now equipped with the latest Huff-Duff technology as well as the new 10-centimetre radar systems. They were also armed with the latest weapons like the bow-mounted Hedgehog, which could spray a volley of mortar rounds that were primed to explode on contact (rather than being timed or fused like a depth charge) at a retreating U-boat whether it was on the surface or under the waves.

Of no less importance, their crews were now rigorously trained and superbly led by battle-hardened commanders. Admiral Horton's support groups were also readily available to hunt down any U-boat bold enough to confront a protective umbrella which had at last become virtually unassailable. As events were about to prove, the Battle of the Atlantic was not to be won or lost by victory or defeat in the intelligence war but by men on both sides using all the resources at their command to fight one another with an unquenchable will to win.

As U-230 cruised towards its allotted hunting ground, Werner and his fellow crew members prepared themselves for the contest ahead. For several days they saw nothing. There was a lone merchant ship in mid-Atlantic, an easy target until they realized that it was a neutral (Swedish) vessel, which they allowed to continue unmolested. Occasionally the radio crackled but otherwise there was little to disturb an anticipatory mood in which enthusiasm and anxiety combined to keep them on full alert. This atmosphere changed dramatically when they heard a succession of radio messages from another wolf pack operating well to the north of them. As they absorbed the gist of these, shock-waves of dismay coursed through the vessel as one by one they heard the worst:

> 5 May: Destroyer. Attacked. Sinking. U-638.
> 5 May: Attacked by destroyers. Depth Charges. Leave boat. U-531.
> 6 May. Attacked by corvette. Sinking. U-438.
> 6 May. Aircraft. Bombs. Rammed by destroyer. Sinking. U-125.

The following day, when, despite repeated requests from U-boat headquarters, U-192 failed to report its position, Werner and his colleagues knew that at least five U-boats in the North Atlantic had been sent to the bottom in a little over twenty-four hours. All the signals had come from within the Atlantic Gap, the best killing ground in the entire ocean; something must have gone dreadfully wrong.

Two weeks earlier, on 23 April, a convoy of over forty freighters – ONS5 – escorted by seven warships, left from Liverpool for Halifax, Nova Scotia. For the first five days of the voyage they enjoyed a relatively uneventful passage. Only the buffeting they received from heavy seas and strong winds interrupted their steady progress. In HMS *Duncan* the escort commander, Captain Peter Gretton, chivvied his flock through the weather, chasing up laggards to ensure that none would be unnecessarily exposed to danger by falling out of the protective cocoon which his warships had woven around them. For Gretton, ONS5 was little different from the many he had already shepherded through these and other treacherous waters. On 28 April, as the convoy entered the Atlantic Gap, *Duncan*'s radio operator picked up a signal from a U-boat that was evidently dead ahead and keeping station with them. Gretton set off at speed to investigate. Although he found nothing, Gretton knew what was in store: 'it was clear that we were in for a heavy attack – again that horrible sinking feeling appeared'.[22] What he did not know was that, alerted by B-Dienst, Dönitz had lined up no fewer than thirty-nine U-boats in the ONS5's direct path.

Despite the worsening weather, which had the escorts rolling, pitching and wallowing through seas that poured down the decks, soaking the men responsible for loading and reloading the depth charges, they managed to fend off the first wave of attacks. The combination of radar and Huff-Duff in the hands of highly trained officers and men foiled the wolf pack's repeated efforts to pounce. On 1 May, though, the wind started to scream through the fleet at hurricane force, whipping up seas so monstrous that the convoy was brought to a standstill. 'Hove to' without steerage way, and thus effectively out of control, ONS5 was being slowly driven by the wind towards the ice packs which loomed off the coast of Greenland some thirty miles ahead.

At noon Gretton was pleased to see 'one of our old friends' – a Liberator from 120 Squadron – arriving overhead after flying more than 1,000 miles from its base in Iceland, 'a magnificent effort in shocking weather'.[23] The wolf pack had elected to ride out the storm in relative comfort far below the surface and therefore well protected from the Liberator – which was in any case soon forced to head back to its base for lack of fuel. By the following day, 2 May, the storm had scattered the convoy across a huge radius of ocean. Some of the vessels were thirty miles from the core of the convoy and thus dangerously exposed. Once again a VLR Liberator arrived, one of the thirty which were now operating over the Atlantic Gap. On this occasion the pilot played a key role in directing Gretton towards the location of numerous errant freighters; the speed with which the convoy was thereby reassembled allowed Gretton to steer a course to skirt the peril of the ice packs which were by now close enough to be visible off the starboard bow.

That afternoon the convoy was joined by five destroyers from the 3rd Support Group. Their arrival greatly strengthened the protective cordon which now embraced ONS5 and for a while all was quiet as the convoy resumed its passage to Halifax. As a result of the buffeting of the last few days, *Duncan* had been unable to refuel as it had been far too rough to pass a hose from the oil tanker accompanying the convoy. To make matters worse for Gretton, the destroyer had been so heavily battered by the storm that her fuel tanks had started to leak. With only just enough fuel left to reach Newfoundland, Gretton took the unpalatable decision to hand over his command to Lieutenant Commander Robert Sherwood in HMS *Tay* while *Duncan* limped away from the battleground. 'We were much depressed,' Gretton wrote, 'because we felt we left the group in the lurch and were thoroughly ashamed of ourselves, though there was really no one to blame except the staff who had decided in the 1920s the endurance of such destroyers.' It was the more galling because, as he would soon discover, 'the story of what happened after we left in the morning of 4 May is probably the most stirring of convoy history'.[24]

In the afternoon of that day, three of the five destroyers in the support group, which were also low on fuel, were forced to leave ONS5. Realizing that ONS5 was now dangerously exposed, Admiral Horton ordered the 1st Support Group (three frigates and two sloops), which was anchored at St John's in Newfoundland, to come to the rescue. It would take these reinforcements two days to reach the convoy, during which time it looked as though ONS5 might face a mauling to rival that endured by SC122 and HX229. Almost certainly picking up the to-and-fro of messages between the British vessels, Dönitz was aware that he had a window of opportunity that should be swiftly exploited. 'You are better placed than ever before,' he signalled the U-boats. 'Don't over-estimate your enemy, but strike him dead.'[25]

As the sky darkened and the fog closed on that evening, the wolf packs made their move, striking again and again at the flanks of the convoy while the remaining escorts raced back and forth, striving to protect their charges from this multidirectional onslaught. It was a long but unequal struggle in the course of which five freighters were sent to the bottom. Though some of their crews were rescued, others were lost entirely with their vessels or left to drown while their sister ships pressed on to avoid a similar fate. In the crude statistics by which victory and defeat were then measured, the score for the night was 5–0 to Germany.

By the following day, as the battle continued with undiminished intensity, Dönitz appeared to be on course for yet another triumph. That evening, with a bravado that bordered on the reckless, the U-boats pressed in to make their final attack, as though sheer numbers would ensure victory. U-266 hit three ships, among them an elderly liner, the *Gharinda*, which her chief officer had once described as 'the wreck of the British India Fleet'.[26] Her captain, R. R. Stone, and his half-frozen crew were rescued by HMS *Tay*. As his men shivered on the acting escort commander's deck, Stone asked to be taken back to his ship in the belief that she could still be salvaged. Sherwood told him that this was out of the question. He had good reason: with the help of her 10-centimetre radar and Huff-Duff, the *Tay* was tracking no fewer than seven U-boats in the immediate vicinity of the convoy, all of them manoeuvring for the kill. Against such a formidable array, the new technology could not possibly prevail. By the end of the day, although one submarine was destroyed, the tally of sunken freighters had grown from five to twelve, which was close to one-third of ONS5's original complement.

By the early hours of 6 May, a thick fog had descended which steadily reduced visibility to no more than a hundred yards. Nature's fortuitous intervention transformed the battle at once. With their radar sets clearly identifying any U-boat within range before they themselves could be seen by the enemy, Sherwood's escorts suddenly had a decisive edge. Reinforced by the arrival of the 1st Support Group, the British warships could now take the offensive. The ferocity with which they did so may be gauged by the fate of Kapitänleutnant Ulrich Folkers's U-125, which had unknowingly surfaced no more than a hundred yards from HMS *Oribi*. The destroyer charged directly at the U-boat slicing through the conning tower and causing serious damage before losing it in the fog.

Soon afterwards HMS *Snowflake* arrived to fire a sustained artillery barrage at the stricken sub. Unable to dive, Folkers evidently ordered his crew to scuttle the boat, which within minutes was shaken by a series of internal explosions which sent it to the bottom. When HMS *Sunflower* arrived on the scene to rescue Folkers and his crew, who were floundering in the water, the corvette's commanding officer, James Plommer, radioed Sherwood for instructions, and reportedly received the terse reply, 'Not approved to pick up survivors'.[27] *Sunflower* duly withdrew, leaving every one of U-125's fifty-four-man crew to drown.

Sherwood was operating within the rules of maritime warfare even though — with the exception of those U-boat commanders who stuck rigidly to Dönitz's Laconia Order (p. 327) — both sides in the war at sea still tended to observe the traditional convention by which shipwrecked sailors were treated with mercy and, where possible, saved from an otherwise certain death. But Sherwood was not alone. Although Captain Macintyre had never himself been forced to make a similarly 'agonizing decision . . . whether to ignore the call of humanity in order to keep the escorts to their primary task of preventing further sinkings by carrying the attack to the enemy', his own standing orders were unequivocal: 'survivors had to be ignored while an attack was in progress'.[28] In the heat of the struggle to protect his convoy, Sherwood shared that attitude.

The battle for ONS5 now began to turn decisively against the attackers. In quick succession the escorts sank three more U-boats, bringing the overall total to six. In the absence of any further convoy losses, the scorecard looked very different: in the space of thirty-six hours, Dönitz had lost one U-boat for every two freighters sunk. This ratio was unsustainable and he knew it. 'Notwithstanding the fact that twelve ships had been sunk I regarded this convoy battle as a defeat,' he wrote afterwards. At the time, his staff at U-Boat Command attributed this to two causes, to neither of which Dönitz had an answer. The first was 'the thick fog' which had 'ruined a golden opportunity'; and the second was the enemy's 'radar location' equipment which had left the U-boats in a 'hopeless position'.[29] Although the German shipyards were turning out more U-boats than ever before, the Grossadmiral now feared that the tide in the Atlantic was turning decisively against him.

At his headquarters in Derby House, Horton was of the same opinion and with even stronger reason. Even before this victory, the head of Western Approaches Command had been in buoyant spirits. It was not only that his escorts had sunk a great number of U-boats but also that Allied shipping losses for April had fallen by 50 per cent from the alarming total for March. The explanation for this had not been hard to find: in addition to the 10-centimetre radar and the advanced weaponry now fitted to a growing number of his escorts, the War Cabinet had been sufficiently shocked by the March calamities to provide enough ships and VLR aircraft to ensure that the Atlantic lifeline could not be severed – and even, in Horton's judgement, to eliminate the U-boat threat altogether. Between them, escorts from the Arctic, aircraft carriers from the Mediterranean and Liberators from Bomber Command had already made it harder by the week for the wolf packs to operate with any degree of security against the convoys. As Dönitz noted ruefully, all these factors had now combined to make his efforts to sever the Atlantic lifeline 'far more dangerous' than before.[30]

There was another devastating fact which, had Dönitz been aware of it, would have dampened his optimism even further. Despite his successes in March, he was more than ever anxious about the tonnage war, telling Hitler once again 'that the U-boat war will fail if we do not sink more ships than the enemy builds'.[31] But by April 1943 this had become an impossible ambition. Despite their losses, the Allies were at last building replacements at a faster rate than the U-boats could destroy them.

This was due to a revolution in shipbuilding that was now under way in the United States. Liberty ships – 9,000-ton all-purpose freighters – were entering service at the astonishing rate of 140 a month. The production lines for these vessels operated on the same underlying principles Henry Ford had devised to mass produce automobiles. Like the Model T Ford, the Liberty ship was to prove one of American capitalism's greatest triumphs, though exemplified in this case by an entrepreneur called Henry J. Kaiser. Born in 1882, the youngest son of a shoemaker who had emigrated from Germany, Kaiser had used his intelligence and determination to become a very rich man before his thirtieth birthday. By the time of Pearl Harbor, he was one of the nation's most powerful tycoons with an apparently limitless relish for new challenges. Among his many engineering projects he had pioneered the construction of large merchant ships that were built in sections held together by welds rather than rivets. This not only reduced the cost of production but increased the rate at which the vessels could flow off the production line. A role model for the American Dream, Kaiser was about to demonstrate that Roosevelt's 'great Arsenal of Democracy' could be filled to overflowing by the might of what President Eisenhower would later define as 'the military-industrial complex'.[32]

The keel of the first Liberty ship had been laid on 14 April 1941 to the specifications of the US government's Maritime Commission, which was to subsidize the cost of production. Five months later, on 27 September, the SS *Patrick Henry*, named after the Founding Father of that name, was launched by the president using words attributed to that champion of independence, 'Give me Liberty or give me Death'.* Designed to carry a wide range of goods from tanks and planes to iron ore and fresh food, the Liberty ships were 'bargain basement' vessels: 'There was no electricity or running water for the crew . . . the galley was lit with oil lamps, and there was no fire detection system . . . [The] ship was a sea-going boxcar.'[33] Required to run the U-boat gauntlet across the Atlantic, the lumbering Liberty ship was also presumed to have a very limited life expectancy.

Kaiser was as ruthless as he was effective. His son Edgar, who started to work for his father at the age of twelve, was instructed, 'You find

---

* Thought to have formed the climax of a speech Henry made on 23 March 1775, during which he advocated taking up arms against the British colonists.

your key men by piling work on them. They say, "I can't do any more," and you say, "Sure you can". So you pile it and they're doing more and more. Pretty soon you have men you can rely on absolutely.'[34] The proof was in the building. Kaiser had originally been commissioned to build 300 Liberty ships. In 1941 each took more than 200 working days to complete; by 1942 they were coming off the production line in half that time. Meanwhile, Kaiser's labour force expanded from 4,000 men and women in 1941 to more than 80,000 by the start of 1943. Many of these were evidently 'destitute laborers from the Dust Bowl States, like characters from the *Grapes of Wrath*',[35] willing to work long hours for low wages. Production lines were repeatedly streamlined, the workers apparently spurred to ever greater efforts by the competition which Kaiser engineered between the senior managers who between them ran eighteen shipyards, operating day and night to meet the demand. When one yard finished a vessel in twenty-three days, another managed ten. The record was set in November 1942, when the SS *Robert E. Peary* was assembled in under five days.* All this was good for publicity and morale but it was the average times which mattered; by the spring of 1943 it took no more than forty-five days from the moment at which the keel was laid to the point at which the vessel was eased down the slipway into the water.[36]

At this rate of production – which would eventually yield a grand total of 2,700 Liberty ships – Dönitz stood no chance whatsoever of winning the tonnage war. By May 1943 the graph of gains and losses revealed for the first time that a crucial cross-over point had been reached: not only was Allied shipbuilding growing almost exponentially but, despite the surge in production authorized by Hitler, the U-boat kill rate was also flatlining. Though Dönitz couldn't yet bring himself to admit it, this trend was irreversible. The dark clouds that were now gathering over his head were about to erupt in a perfect storm that would destroy every one of the operational, tactical and strategic plans upon which he had based his hopes of victory in both the tonnage war and, thereby, the Second World War itself.

With the devastating radio reports from the ONS5 front line still ringing in their ears, the crew of U-230 received orders from Dönitz's

---

* The *Robert E. Peary* survived the war, serving in the Atlantic and the Pacific. She was eventually sent to the breaker's yard in 1963.

headquarters to proceed to a new rendezvous to confront another convoy. Herbert Werner readied his bank of torpedoes. At 6.15 on 12 May, as the sun 'shot like a fireball over the ocean' he saw 'a smear on the horizon'. 'I called Siegmann to the bridge and said as he arrived, "I have a present for you, Sir." ' They watched as 'a mighty display of masts and funnels' hove into view. 'We were almost dead ahead of the parade . . . Within an hour, I calculated, we would have plenty of targets at our disposal.'[37] Werner and his team duly loaded the torpedo tubes and reported that U-230 was 'combat-ready'. As he did so, the submarine's radio operator reported that the convoy, which appeared to be protected by a cordon of twelve destroyers, was zigzagging away to the north-east. U-230 altered course accordingly to move into a better firing position.

At that moment a shout went up from the conning tower: '*Flugzeug!*' The *Flugzeug* in question was a biplane which appeared to be dropping out of the sun. As the alarm sounded, U-230 made an emergency dive. Within moments four explosions detonated immediately over their heads. The boat shook and fell sharply. 'Water splashed, steel shrieked, ribs moaned, valves blew, deck-plates jumped, and the boat was thrown into darkness.'[38] When the lights flickered on the crew looked at one another in astonishment. How was it possible for a small plane to be so far out in the Atlantic? There was only one possible explanation – and it was ominous: the attacker must have taken off from an aircraft carrier. For U-230, this was the start of a ten-day nightmare.

The ships that Werner had detected on the horizon belonged to convoy HX237, which had left New York bound for Liverpool on 1 May, escorted by Canadian warships under the command of Captain E. H. Chavasse. Hitherto, the Canadian escorts had enjoyed limited success and gained a poor reputation. Though the gallantry of their crews was not in doubt, they had been subjected to heavy criticism – much of it anecdotal – from their British counterparts who derided both the quality of their vessels and the inadequate training given to their crews. At the start of the war the Royal Canadian Navy (RCN) numbered 3,700 officers and men and possessed only seven destroyers and five minesweepers. This embryonic force had expanded at a rate which, according to the astute but acerbic critic Donald Macintyre, had been counterproductive. 'Discipline', he wrote, 'was weird and wonderful, equipment was ill-maintained and training in its use sadly lacking.' Though he regarded the zeal of the Canadian crews as 'magnificent', he could not refrain from observing that 'it would have been more valuable if quality rather than quantity had been the aim'.[39]

This disdain, which was expressed by others in cruder terms, may have owed something to the ineffable sense of superiority as well as devotion to discipline by which the Royal Navy was infected. But Macintyre's critique lacked that edge of neocolonial prejudice. For him it was 'a melancholy fact' that almost every convoy escorted by the Canadians in February and March 1943 'was a tale of disaster and sunken merchant ships' in which they frequently found themselves trapped 'in the confusion and melee of a massed wolf-pack attack' that results when 'a Captain is robbed of the atmosphere of careful search and undistracted investigation which is so vital to the detection of an enemy submarine'.[40]

Partly for this reason, the British had been surprised and dismayed in early March – at the worst of times in the North Atlantic – when Admiral King announced at a specially convened conference in Washington that he intended to withdraw the US Navy from all escort duties in this latitude to concentrate his resources on the convoy routes in the south to protect US troops on their way to North Africa. King's unilateral action put greater pressure on the Canadians, who now found themselves in sole control of the area to the south of Greenland on the western side of the 'chop line' at 47°W, where responsibility for the Halifax–Liverpool route was taken by the Royal Navy.

With this new disposition in place for barely a month, and with only five escorts to protect HX237's forty-seven freighters, all laden with military supplies, Captain Chavasse would have been forgiven for having indulged a frisson of relief at the news that the convoy was to be joined by Admiral Horton's 5th Support Group to help shepherd his convoy through the Atlantic Gap. In addition to four destroyers, this gave him the protection of HMS *Biter*, an escort carrier which had just undergone an overhaul after serving with the Royal Navy's covering force protecting Operation Torch.

Shaken by the wholly unexpected attack from the air on 12 May, the crew of U-230, in concert with another nineteen U-boats, continued to close on HX237, whose position, based on accurate reports from B-Dienst, was relayed to them from their Berlin headquarters. Fearing another murderous descent from the heavens, Werner continually scoured the sky as 'thickening white clouds scudded along at medium height under a stiff breeze from the west'. At just after 11 a.m. that morning, only two hours after the first attack, he detected 'a glint of metal between the clouds'. It was a small aircraft and it was diving towards U-230. Less than a minute later, four explosions sent shock-waves through the submarine's hull. The boat plunged to safety. When Captain Siegmann surfaced again 'in defiance of fear and sudden destruction', another aircraft appeared overhead almost at once. There was another shattering quartet of explosions around the submarine as she plunged back into the depths. Fearful that he would lose contact with the convoy, Siegmann came to the surface soon afterwards and was relieved to discover that the enemy was still in sight. A little after noon, his radio operator picked up a distress message: 'Attacked by Aircraft. Sinking. U-89.' One of *Biter*'s fifteen bombers had found its mark. Shortly afterwards, the coup de grâce was delivered by two of Chavasse's destroyers. Dietrich Lohmann and his entire crew of forty-eight were drowned. 'With a shudder,' Werner reflected, 'I pictured what would happen to us, once our own hull was cracked.'

There was no respite. Again and again, *Biter*'s aircraft returned to the attack, completely disrupting what had been intended as a coordinated U-boat offensive. At 1.15 p.m. U-230 was bombed for the fifth time. On this occasion, there was no time to dive. With the plane only 800 metres astern when it was detected, Siegmann ordered 'Right full rudder'. Werner rushed to the rear of the bridge with U-230's mate to man the U-boat's two anti-aircraft guns. 'The small aircraft grew enormous fast. It dived upon us, machine-gunning the open rear of the bridge . . . Neither the mate nor I were able to fire a single bullet; our guns were jammed.'[41] A moment later, the Swordfish dropped four depth charges, all of which erupted on the U-boat's starboard side. As the plane disappeared back towards the convoy, U-230's crew marvelled at their escape.

Twenty minutes later the radio operator picked up another message: 'Attacked by aircraft. Unable to dive. Sinking 45 North 25 West. Help.' This time the stricken boat was U-456, which, in tandem with U-403, had sunk a Liberty ship two days earlier. As the doomed U-boat was no more than twelve miles ahead, Siegmann decided to go to the rescue. As they closed on the stricken submarine, they could see U-456's bow was sticking out of the water. Some of her crew were clinging to the deck while others had hold of a steel cable that was strung between the bow and the bridge, the water up to their chests. An aircraft was circling overhead. With one of HX237's Canadian escorts advancing over the horizon in their direction, Siegmann had little choice but to abort his rescue mission to avoid a similar fate.

A short while later, U-230 came under attack yet again from the air. On this occasion, according to Werner, he and another gunner both took careful aim and fired a sustained barrage at their assailant:

> Our boat veered to starboard, spoiling the plane's bomb run. The pilot revved up his engine, circled, then roared towards us from dead ahead. As the plane dived very low, its engine sputtered, then stopped. Wing first, the plane crashed into the surging ocean, smashing its other wing on our superstructure as we raced by. The pilot, thrown out of his cockpit, lifted his arm and waved for help, but then I saw him disintegrate in the explosion of the four bombs which were meant to destroy us.[*42]

Their elation did not last. Later that afternoon, U-230's radio operator picked up yet another bleak signal. 'Depth charges by three destroyers. Sinking. U-186.' This was the eleventh report of this kind that Werner had noted since the start of U-230's voyage and by this time there was no doubt in his mind that 'a naval disaster seemed to be in the making'.[43]

U-186 had been sunk 200 miles to the south by Captain Macintyre's HMS *Hesperus*, one of the eight warships protecting SC129, comprising twenty-five vessels, which had left New York bound for Liverpool on 2 May. After nine months as an escort commander, Macintyre had yet to lose any merchant ship, a record he was determined to maintain. But with an unprecedented number of U-boats in the North Atlantic he expected trouble. Nonetheless, he was in good spirits, not least because the RAF was 'at long last allocating enough long-range aircraft to Coastal Command to enable them to close the gap of air cover in Mid-Atlantic'; and 'the new escort carriers would soon be at sea in sufficient numbers to accompany every convoy'.[44]

Moreover, *Hesperus* was fitted with 10-centimetre radar and Huff-Duff, a combination which, he was confident, would give him ample

---

[*]That the Swordfish was shot down is not in doubt. In the absence of any contrary evidence, there is little reason to doubt Werner's colourful account, especially as his narrative is consistent with the known facts.

warning of any encroaching U-boat. In addition, the code-breakers at Bletchley Park had broken back into Shark, which meant that Western Approaches Command once again had a clear picture of where the U-boats were likely to gather in wait. What he did not know, of course, was that the three wolf packs now operating in and around the Atlantic Gap were constantly being redirected towards the convoys on the basis of intelligence provided by B-Dienst. In effect, therefore, the moves and countermoves occasioned by the flow of intelligence to both sides more or less cancelled each other out.

For the first five days, Macintyre's convoy had been trouble-free. It was not until the afternoon of 11 May that *Hesperus*'s Huff-Duff picked up a radio signal suggesting the proximity of a disconcertingly large number of U-boats. Soon afterwards U-402 penetrated the convoy's escort screen and, in rapid succession, sank two merchant ships. To Macintyre's relief, the rescue ship, *Melrose Abbey*, moved in at speed to pick up the survivors – rescuing a total of eighty out of the eighty-three crew from both vessels. Once again the escort commander had cause to admire these little rescue vessels which 'performed a wonderful task at very great hazard, for by the nature of their job they were forced to lie stopped, sitting targets, for long periods at the very time when U-boats were known to be near'.[45] The fact that so many lives had thus been saved, though, was little comfort. By his own account, Macintyre was 'in a fury', not only at the loss of the two ships but also at losing his own 100 per cent safety record in the process: thus 'it was with rage in my heart that I awaited the attack that I knew must come with nightfall'.[46]

The mood aboard *Hesperus* that night was tense: 'The lookouts relieved each other with brief, whispered words instead of their usual cheerful witticisms. Out there in the blackness we all knew that a sinister menace lurked, and was sliding closer and closer to get in an attack. Our only doubt was the direction from which it would approach.'

No one slept. Then came a report from the radar room. 'Very small contact just come up, Sir. Bearing 230 degrees. Range five miles.' Macintyre swung *Hesperus* round to give chase, watching the while through the binoculars which he had confiscated from Otto Kretschmer over two years earlier (pp. 143–5). He soon saw the familiar white-wake of a U-boat, clearly on the retreat. As *Hesperus* approached, the submarine dived, leaving a phosphorescent whirlpool as the only physical evidence of its presence. The destroyer was over the spot to release a pattern of depth charges which caused a fountain of water that 'soared up to stand momentarily like pillars of light before tumbling back into the sea in a torrent of foam'. Knowing that the U-boat would have been severely shaken, Macintyre came in for a second run and unleashed another bombardment.

Beneath the surface in U-223, Leutnant Peter Gerlach and his crew waited in trepidation as the U-boat's hull was rocked by a shattering series of explosions. The lights fused and water flooded into the main compartment. With almost every instrument out of action and an electrical fire in the engine room, there seemed to be little hope. Recovering his poise, though, Gerlach sought to prevent the vessel plunging towards the bottom of the ocean. As it was, the U-boat fell to a dangerously low 700 feet below the surface before the crew managed to stabilize the vessel. Realizing that he had no means of escape, Gerlach blew the tanks and came to the surface just as the *Hesperus* began her third run. At this point, the two vessels were so close that U-223 was swept along the side of the destroyer. As it passed *Hesperus*'s stern, Macintyre ordered more depth charges to be unleashed at the now semi-wrecked U-boat.

*Hesperus*'s gunners joined in, pouring down a hail of gunfire at almost point-blank range, killing several of the submarine's crew and driving others to take shelter in the conning tower. To Macintyre's astonishment, U-223 still failed to sink. Within moments Gerlach's engineers managed to restart her engines. Now too close for the destroyer's guns to bear down directly on the target, Macintyre considered ramming the obstinate U-boat but, fearing that he might damage his own destroyer (as had happened once before to him), he thought better of it. Instead, he nosed slowly up to U-233's hull and tried to roll her over with a bump amidships. It almost worked. The U-boat began to turn turtle, only to right herself once more. Macintyre decided to withdraw far enough to allow his gunners to have another go. As he did so, U-233 managed to fire a torpedo at the retreating warship which only narrowly missed.

Several of U-223's crew had jumped into the sea, and Macintyre presumed the U-boat was at last in the throes of sinking. Mindful of the fact that he was now thirty miles behind his convoy, he opted to leave Gerlach and his crew to their uncertain fate. As it happened, Gerlach also thought his boat was doomed but he had done no more than order his crew to join him on deck. They now watched in astonished relief as the British destroyer disappeared into the night. Realizing that he had been offered a rare reprieve, Gerlach sent his crew back to their stations with orders to do all in their power to make the boat seaworthy again. It took them twelve hours but, after a herculean effort, they managed it and the battered craft set off on the slow journey back to the Bay of Biscay, limping into Saint-Nazaire just under a fortnight later.*

As he hurried to make contact again with the convoy, Macintyre studied a sheaf of Huff-Duff reports which showed the convoy was under threat from at least a dozen U-boats. By the morning of the 12th it became clear that these submarines were pulling steadily ahead of SC129, intending to lie in wait as the merchant ships steamed into their trap. A little after 11 a.m. Huff-Duff alerted him to the presence of a U-boat some nine miles distant. *Hesperus*'s ASDIC was activated and the sonar system very soon locked on. As the cry 'Contact!' came up from the ASDIC control room, Macintyre saw the tip of a periscope moving across their course. This time the depth charges were released at precisely the right moment. A sonar echo suggested that the U-boat was 'in desperate straits'. Moments later, the destroyer's crew felt the shudder of an underwater explosion. Macintyre was grimly gratified to see 'a spreading pool of oil with floating debris and smashed woodwork'. As evidence of *Hesperus*'s kill, he fished some of the wreckage out of the water, on one piece of which there was stuck 'a gruesome piece of flesh'.[47] The human remains came from U-186, news of whose demise had prompted Werner (still shadowing HX237 in U-230) not only to foresee an imminent naval disaster but also to insist 'we could not afford a moment of sorrow for all the men who died that one death that every submariner pictures a thousand times'.[48]

By this point, the slow convoy, trundling through the Atlantic Gap at seven knots, was being outpaced by its persecutors, travelling on the surface at more than twice that speed. In the absence of air cover, Macintyre was unable to mount a counteroffensive without leaving his charges exposed. 'It was', Macintyre wrote, 'maddening to be so close to so many enemies and be able to do nothing about it.' His only alternative was to order the escorts to zigzag at full speed to and fro around

---

* Following repairs to the damaged hull, U-223 was at sea again by September 1943. Seriously damaged on two further occasions, she was finally sunk in February 1944.

and between the merchant ships in the hope of preventing the U-boats mounting a coordinated attack against them.

Somewhat to Macintyre's surprise, the tactic worked. The wolf pack's offensive seemed to have lost momentum. It was as though the most recent intake of U-boat commanders – many of whom had very little experience of combat – lacked the will to commit themselves to the do-or-die efforts of their predecessors. Macintyre attributed this to 'the constant fear of being surprised on the surface by patrolling and escorting aircraft', which, he believed, 'was steadily wearing down the morale of the U-boat crews'.[49] The arrival of the aircraft carrier HMS *Biter* to join the convoy served only to confirm Macintyre's analysis. Released from providing aerial cover to HX237 – which by now was safely through the Atlantic Gap – *Biter*'s aircraft gave Macintyre instant respite. After thirty-six sleepless hours, the escort commander felt secure enough to retreat to his bunk, knowing that with 'her Swordfish patrolling round the horizon, I could rest with a quiet mind'. Thwarted not only by the new technologies, highly trained and well-marshalled warships but also by the threat from the air, the wolf pack gave up the hunt and stole silently away. It was a defining moment.

By 16 May, both HX237 and SC129 were out of danger. From Dönitz's perspective, it had been a disastrous few days. He had deployed more than forty U-boats to intercept the two convoys but, between them, they had managed to sink only five of the seventy-two heavily laden freighters which were now about to unload their cargoes in Liverpool without further impediment. The scorecard was even worse than it had been for ONS5: for every freighter sunk, a U-boat had also gone to the bottom. This 1:1 ratio was unsustainable. Assailed by these statistics, Dönitz could only conclude that 'the overwhelming superiority achieved by the enemy defence was finally proved beyond dispute'.[50]

Burdened by this prospect, the Kriegsmarine's commander-in-chief flew to Wolfschanze to see Hitler on 14 May. His mood was grim. 'The enemy's new location devices', he told the Führer, 'are, for the first time, making U-boat warfare impossible and causing heavy losses – fifteen to seventeen boats a month.' Hearing this, Hitler cut in to exclaim, 'These losses are too high. It can't go on.' In fact, Dönitz had understated the facts. As he well knew, his losses had started to run at twice that level; in the first two weeks of the month, he had already lost fifteen U-boats.[51]

Although he would never admit it, preferring to attribute any lack of daring or initiative to inexperience on the part of his commanders, Dönitz must have been aware that these losses were having an impact on morale. This was certainly the conclusion of the Anti-Submarine Tracking Room in London. Enigma messages decrypted by Bletchley Park made it clear that many U-boat crews had been intimidated by the savagery of the counter-attacks by which they were now so frequently assailed. 'The outstanding impression felt on reading recent U-boat traffic', the Admiralty reported, 'is that the spirit of the crews which are at present out on operations in the Atlantic is low and general morale is shaky. There is little doubt that [Dönitz] shares this impression.'[52]

As if to confirm this, the Kriegsmarine's commander-in-chief sent a message to all his U-boats on 15 May which was clearly intended to rally their crews. Acknowledging the enemy's radar equipment had robbed them of their 'most valuable characteristic, invisibility', he undertook 'to do everything in my power as C-in-C to take all possible steps to change the situation as soon as possible.' Meanwhile, he urged, 'I expect you to continue your determined struggle with the enemy by pitting your ingenuity, ability and hard will against his ruses and technical developments yet to finish him off.'[53] It was a hollow exhortation that did nothing to stave off the inevitable end.

By this time three further convoys were approaching the Atlantic Gap. The first of these, HX238 – forty-six vessels protected by five Canadian escorts – which had left Halifax on 9 May, was diverted from harm's way by a combination of Enigma decrypts and Huff-Duff. The convoy arrived in Liverpool eleven days later without even being detected. The second, HX239 – an especially valuable convoy with eleven oil tankers among its forty-two ships – left two days later. Heavily escorted by eight warships and accompanied by *Biter*'s sister escort carrier HMS *Archer*, the convoy was formidably protected. In his official report, the convoy's commodore, A. J. Davies, wrote, 'I cannot speak too highly of the handling of HMS *Archer* (Captain J. Robertson RN) . . . She kept continuously in the air for three days during daylight and never once got outside the escort screen.'[54] Helped additionally by the cover provided by Coastal Command's Liberators, HX239 also arrived in Liverpool without a single incident of note.

The third convoy was a little less fortunate but it was of the utmost significance as it demonstrated conclusively that Dönitz had lost the tonnage war. SC130 left Halifax for Liverpool on 11 May accompanied by Captain Peter Gretton's escort group, reinforced initially by five B-17 'Flying Fortress' bombers.* After what he regarded as his 'igno-minious retreat from ONS5', Gretton was 'rather looking forward to a battle now, and there was no longer that sinking feeling of anticipation for we were well on top of the enemy, we had a good escort and we were full of confidence'.[55]

By the evening of 18 May, twenty-five U-boats, guided by B-Dienst, were lying in wait on the edge of what was still called the Atlantic Gap, although by virtue of the VLR Liberators it had shrunk to the point where it hardly deserved that sobriquet. In the early hours of the fol-lowing morning, his 10-centimetre radar operated in tandem with Huff-Duff alerted Gretton to the enemy's patrol line. Veering off course to avoid them, he was gratified to hear the U-boats 'chattering away like magpies from a position on our original track, no doubt complain-ing bitterly at missing us'.[56] Later that night the convoy was reinforced by a sloop and three frigates from the 1st Support Group. Within hours, two of these had sunk U-954 with the loss of all lives, one of which was that of Dönitz's twenty-one-year-old son, Peter, who was serving as a watch officer on his first operation. Whatever grief Dönitz may have experienced on hearing this news, he concealed from those around him; nor was he to refer to it in his extensive memoirs written more than a decade after the end of the war.

Gretton was now on the offensive. Supported by VLF Liberators from 120 Squadron, he sent his destroyers to hunt down any U-boat as soon as it was identified. For the next twelve hours the escorts harried the wolf pack with venom. At one point Gretton found a chance to use HMS *Duncan*'s newly fitted Hedgehog mortar for the first time, when U-381 became one of the few submarines bold enough to nose into the middle of the convoy. The invader was detected by HMS *Snowflake* almost immediately. It crash-dived but failed to escape at least one of the destroyer's depth charges. At this point *Duncan* joined the hunt. When he neared the spot where the U-boat had last been seen, Gretton fired the Hedgehog, watching intently as a volley of twenty-four

* More than 12,000 B-17s were built. With a range of 2,000 miles, they were used extensively in the Pacific and later in the bombing campaign against Germany.

mini-bombs flew towards the target. They missed. On the second approach, however, they succeeded: 'It was most thrilling to stand, stop-watch in hand, waiting for the explosion – we saw oil rising and soon left the spot [to rejoin the convoy] . . . we came up through the columns at high speed, the signal "KILL" flying at both yardarms, and we got some cheery waves from the ships as we passed.'[57]

All forty-seven members of U-381's crew perished.

Later that evening, one of the Liberators made contact with three U-boats at the same time. In the course of a brief discussion with Gretton by radio-telephone about which of them to attack first, he joked, 'As Mae West said, one at a time, gentlemen please.' All three U-boats were forced to submerge. This was the pattern for the rest of the voyage. Though Gretton believed that the convoy was still being shadowed by up to thirty U-boats, not one of them appeared able or willing to get close enough to launch a torpedo; and, he noted with satisfaction, 'there seemed no reason why they ever should, if we continued to have an air escort in daylight'.[58] Spirits were so high and the mood so relaxed that on 19 May *Duncan*'s radio operator rigged a loudspeaker on the bridge so that the crew could hear the prime minister from Washington as he addressed both houses of Congress.

Churchill had arrived in Washington a week earlier, after crossing the Atlantic in the *Queen Mary*, accompanied by no fewer than a hundred officials and advisors.* With the Axis on the verge of defeat in North Africa, the purpose of Trident, as the conference was codenamed, was to discuss the priorities for the next stage of the war. It was a testing few days during which animosity frequently trumped amity as the Combined Chiefs took the chance to race their competing hobby horses. In his characteristic fashion, Brooke summarized their divergent views in his diary:

> King still remains determined to press Pacific at the expense of all other
> fronts. Marshall wishes to ensure cross Channel operation at expense of
> Mediterranean. Brooke still feels that Mediterranean offers far more

---

* Like her sister ship, the *Queen Elizabeth*, the *Queen Mary* was in constant use as a transatlantic troop carrier. Her maximum speed of thirty knots, which could be maintained except in the very worst weather, made her virtually immune from U-boat attack.

hope of adding to final success. Portal in his heart feels that if we left him a free hand bombing alone might well win the war. And dear old Dudley Pound when he wakes up wishes we would place submarine warfare above all other requirements. Out of the above compromise emerges and the war is prolonged, whilst we age and get more and more weary!![59]

Not surprisingly, Brooke claimed that compromise as his own, but, not for the first time, the prime minister had played a crucial role. By painting 'the big picture' and then arguing that the principal objective should be the defeat of Germany, he spiked King's guns. When it became clear that the Chief of the US Navy would be overruled, his acolyte, the aptly nicknamed General 'Vinegar Joe' Stilwell (who had been seconded by Roosevelt to become chief of staff to the Chinese leader, Chiang Kai-shek) was vitriolic: 'The inevitable conclusion was that Churchill has Roosevelt in his pocket. They are looking for an easy way, a short-cut for England, and no attention must be diverted from the Continent at any cost. The Limeys are not interested in the war in the Pacific, and with the President hypnotized, they are sitting pretty.'[60]

The sentiment was not only crass but it sidestepped the overwhelming argument in favour of annihilating the Third Reich before setting about the destruction of Japanese imperialism.

Once this fundamental commitment had been reaffirmed, the debate between the two sides focused on whether to follow the landings in Sicily with an invasion of Italy or, alternatively, to build up the Anglo-American forces already gathering in Britain for the earliest possible invasion of France. The Americans, led by Marshall, favoured the latter option but the British insisted on the former. Once again, Churchill's mellifluent diplomacy won the day. Stressing that 'the difficult beaches, with the great rise and fall of tide, the strength of the enemy's defences, the number of his reserves and the ease of his communications, all made the task [of a cross-Channel invasion] one which must not be underrated', the prime minister adroitly emphasized that he was unequivocally committed to 'a full scale invasion of the Continent as soon as a plan offering reasonable prospects of success could be made'.[61]

Once Roosevelt had been persuaded that it would be impossible to undertake a cross-Channel invasion before the spring of 1944, Churchill knew he had won. His ebullience was boundless. 'I have never seen him in better heart or form,' the British ambassador, Lord Halifax, wrote, 'an amazing contrast to the very tired and nerve-strained PM I saw last August in England.'[62] By the end of the week it was settled: the cross-Channel invasion should take place not later than 1 May 1944.*

As he listened to the prime minister's voice crackling through the ether, Gretton was exhilarated to hear one of his pithiest aphorisms as he told the assembled legislators, 'the proud German army has once again proved the truth of the saying "The Hun is always at your throat or at your feet" '.[63] Gretton felt much the same way about the Battle of the Atlantic but was more than ever confident that the U-boats were, metaphorically, at his feet. As he swung the convoy this way and that to avoid his adversaries, the escort commander noted that SC130 was man-oeuvring so 'beautifully' that 'the result would not have shamed a battle fleet'. Under constant threat from warships and Liberators, the U-boats hung back, clearly unwilling to commit suicide even in the name of the Führer. Five of their number had already been incapacitated, three of them by Coastal Command's bombers: if ever proof were needed that a combination of aircraft and escorts working in close harmony could make convoys virtually inviolable, SC130 was it. The pity was that it had taken so long for this to be appreciated. In this respect Bomber Command's bombast had a great deal to answer for.

On 21 May Gretton noticed that the wolf pack's chatter had ceased. Once again the U-boats had stolen away under cover of darkness. Like its immediate predecessors, HX238 and HX239, SC130 reached its destination unmolested. In this case, though, the U-boats had not been intimidated into flight but had been ordered to withdraw by their commander-in-chief. However, Dönitz had not quite given up. In a markedly defiant gesture, he sent them off immediately to attack another convoy with a most peculiar message that must have seemed to them as much like an ultimatum as an exhortation:

> If there is anyone who thinks that combating convoys is no longer pos-
> sible, he is a weakling and no true U-boat Captain. The battle of the
> Atlantic is getting harder but it is the determining element in the wag-
> ing of the war. Be aware of your high responsibility and be clear you

---

*D-Day was, of course, later to be postponed until 6 June 1944.

must answer for your actions. Do your best with this convoy. Be hard, draw ahead and attack. I believe in you.[64]

This was, though, the bluster of a commander-in-chief at bay, raging against the dark and consumed by chagrin. Almost at once he counter-manded his own order, instructing every U-boat in the North Atlantic to withdraw to the Azores on 24 May. This order was accompanied by a quixotic message which seemed to repudiate the very facts which had led him to this desperate measure:

At present you alone can take the offensive against the enemy and beat him. The U-boat arm by continuously sinking ships with war materials and supplies for the island [Britain] must subdue the enemy by a contin-ual bloodletting which must cause even the strongest body to bleed to death . . . I know that at the moment your battle out there is one of the sternest and most costly in losses because the enemy's new technical equipment is superior. Believe me, I have done and will continue to do everything to catch up with the enemy leap forward . . . We will not, therefore, allow ourselves to be forced on the defensive, nor rest, but where opportunity offers, strike and fight on with greater hardness and resolution . . . Then we shall be victorious . . . Heil dem Führer! Your C-in-C Dönitz.[65]

By suggesting that they had merely endured a temporary setback, Dönitz's hyperbole may have concealed the truth from his more gullible commanders but the facts were incontestable. With forty-one U-boats sunk in the month of May alone,[66] he had been forced to recognize that it was no longer possible to wage war against the convoys in the North Atlantic – 'the theatre in which air cover was strongest' – with any pros-pect of success.[67]

It was a most remarkable turnaround, a mirror image of the situation only two months earlier, in March, when the U-boats had been on the rampage, notching up record kills. The Admiralty had feared that the Atlantic lifeline was about to be severed; the War Cabinet had been alarmed; the prime minister had alerted the president; the crisis had been so acute that for a moment it appeared that Britain might no longer be able to prosecute the war. Now, two months later, the U-boat cam-paign in the North Atlantic was all but over.

By the time SC130 docked safely in Liverpool, the Allied navies had sunk or destroyed a grand total of thirty-three U-boats in just over a fortnight; by the end of the month this figure would rise to forty-one. Taken together, U-boat losses for April and May would total fifty-six, of which – notably – no fewer than twenty-eight were directly attributable to carrier-based and shore-based aircraft. Such losses, even if German shipyards could build the forty U-boats a month Hitler now promised, could not be sustained. Though Dönitz would fight on to the end, he knew the truth. By the end of May, as he would later concede, 'We had lost the Battle of the Atlantic.'[68] He had lost not only a record number of U-boats but the tonnage war as well.

There was no longer any risk that Britain's Atlantic lifeline would be severed. Not only that, but the build-up of American troops in England could be accelerated in preparation for the invasion of France. Thus the month of May 1943 marked a decisive turning point in the war. If the British victory at the Battle of El Alamein in November 1942 had marked 'the end of the beginning', then the German defeat in the Battle of the Atlantic in May 1943 was most certainly 'the beginning of the end' – and it was of decidedly greater significance.

# 21.   The Reckoning

For Nella Last, whose private diary shone a daily light on the life of a Barrow-in-Furness housewife, victory seemed a distant prospect. For week after week, year in, year out, she had struggled to maintain her energy, to help neighbours in trouble, to volunteer in the local WVS centre, where they made comforts for the men at the front, to make do and mend at home, and to turn her weekly allowance of rationed food into a nourishing diet for her stolid husband. Sometimes it all seemed too much; like so many others, who only knew what was happening at this or that distant front line from snippets of news that she read in the newspaper or heard on the BBC, she occasionally found herself close to despair:

> Am I growing old quickly – or is it the strain of ceaseless effort which tires me at times to my soul-case? It's a long time since I felt the keenness that always seemed a part of me. Is this what 'war weary' means? Will I ever feel gay and irresponsible again? Feel I could sing because the sun shines? Look forward to a holiday? I feel I am digging myself into a deep rut, and soon I'll not be able to see myself out of it – only along it.[1]

Her favourite son, Cliff, was serving in the Eighth Army in North Africa. Nella missed him with a raw intensity that she could express only in the privacy of her diary. She read and reread his letters, which now seemed all that she had left of the 'laughing lad' on whom she doted. On one occasion she went to his wardrobe, intending to take out his clothes to air them. She smelt the mixture of tobacco smoke and Harris tweed from a jacket which had been passed down to him from her brother. 'I stood with my face pressed against a jacket, and then pushed everything back and closed the door . . . sometimes a sadness beyond tears wraps me round.'[2]

Her husband had a job repairing houses that had been damaged in the air raids to which Barrow-in-Furness was still subjected. He appeared to take little notice of his wife but, as she was quick to note, even he was touched by the extent to which the ravages of war had affected their community. 'He comes in *horrified* – really shocked – to tell of people with no coal, no sugar till they went downtown for their rations, meat for only two days a week, bread and jam for tea, women *ill* with standing for hours in queues.'[3]

By contrast with the predicament now faced by millions of Germans, the shortages were not generally so acute as to cause real hunger. Those, like Nella, who knew how to eke out the weekly ration and who could cook well enough to create a nourishing meal out of scraps, did not suffer unduly. Nella Last's diary is a record of small culinary triumphs over minor adversities and the tyranny of the ration book. It was no comfort to her that the threat to Britain's lifeline had been nullified: Dönitz may have lost the Battle of the Atlantic but few people knew it. In contrast to the Eighth Army's victory at El Alamein in November 1942, when Churchill ordered church bells to be rung across the land, this naval triumph was not attended by celebrations of any kind; nor was it mentioned in public. Though the collapse of Dönitz's tonnage war was of far greater strategic significance than the Eighth Army's victory in the North African desert, only those at the heart of government or inside the military loop could possibly have been aware of it. No 'ordinary' citizen was aware that, at the nadir of British fortunes in the Atlantic, Churchill had been provoked to thunder 'British imports cannot be reduced by a single ship . . . the inroad on stocks is such that a halt must be called', or that British officialdom had warned that 'the wheels would cease to turn and rations would be jeopardized' unless the shipping crisis was rapidly alleviated.[4] For very good reasons of national security and morale, the public had been spared all knowledge of either this crisis or the bitter conflict between London and Washington which had helped to precipitate it. They were thereby in less than blissful ignorance of the fact that the battles fought in and around the Atlantic Gap during May 1943 had secured not only their own immediate future but had virtually guaranteed the victory they would finally celebrate two years later.

None of this meant that Dönitz had given up. At the end of May he went to see Hitler at his mountain retreat in Bavaria, the Berghof. It was an extraordinary encounter at which Dönitz might have been a conquering hero rather than the author of a terminal defeat. With a presence that none of his peers could emulate, he spoke with a conviction and zeal that fed the Führer's self-delusions and nurtured some of his own. He spoke of new technologies and advanced weapons systems that were in development and he urged Hitler to establish a naval air arm, and to expand the U-boat construction programme yet again. He failed, though, to press for submarines that could travel faster and for longer underwater, which offered the only real prospect of countering the superior technology developed by the British. Instead he merely urged the construction of a greater number of U-boats at a much faster rate. Hitler apparently consented to everything Dönitz proposed. 'I am of the opinion', the Kriegsmarine's commander-in-chief declared, 'that U-boat warfare must be carried on even if the goal of achieving greater successes is no longer possible, because the enemy forces tied up by U-boats are extraordinarily large.'[5]

Hitler apparently paced about the room while Dönitz spoke – though 'pacing' is perhaps not quite the term to describe the perambulations of a much diminished figure, with 'dulled eyes and pouchy skin' whose left leg 'tended to drag [while] his left hand trembled uncontrollably in his right behind his bent back'[6] – but now he interrupted Dönitz's monologue to reveal a belated strategic appreciation of the important role the U-boats could still perform as he insisted:

> Any let-up in the U-boat war is quite out of the question. The Atlantic is my first line of defence in the west and even if I have to fight a defensive battle there, that is better than defending myself on the coasts of Europe. The enemy forces tied up by the U-boats are so extraordinarily large that even if we no longer have great successes, I cannot permit their release.[7]

Any physical frailty by which Hitler was afflicted did not impair his ability to mesmerize his listeners; to this extent at least Dönitz was still as devoted an acolyte as any of his peers in the Führer's inner circle. Some days later, in one of his many entries in the U-boat War Diary, he gushed, 'The enormous strength which the Führer radiates, his unwavering confidence . . . have made it very clear in these days that we are all very insignificant in comparison with the Führer . . . Anyone who believes he can do better than the Führer is silly.'[8]

The die was thus cast: for the remainder of the war Dönitz would not seek victory in the Atlantic or in any other ocean. From now on his U-boat fleet was to harass the enemy in a war of attrition which at best could only delay the inevitable, though neither he nor Hitler could allow themselves to admit it.

Dönitz went out of his way to sustain the morale of the U-boat crews, visiting their bases to explain the new strategy and to exhort them to even higher sacrifice on the Führer's behalf. Oberleutnant Heinz Schaeffer, the commander of U-977, attended one of his pep talks.* His message was upbeat:

> If we stopped sending out U-boats, the enemy would stop escorting his convoys. As it is, we know that our U-boats are pinning down about two million enemy personnel in warships and in repair shops . . . So we must keep our U-boats at sea even if they never sink a ship. Their mere presence alone constitutes a success for us.'[9]

In the new order, to sink a merchant ship was a bonus rather than a purpose.

The human cost was to prove greater than the price exacted from any other theatre of the Second World War. That the men under his command rose to what was in effect a suicidal challenge was a mark of their devotion to duty and to the regard in which Dönitz was held by those who served under him. Schaeffer recalled the sangfroid with which he and his colleagues approached the prospect of yet another ocean patrol: 'Recently we had been compelled to make our wills before we went to sea,' he noted. 'So good for morale!' When their comrades departed for the hazardous crossing through the Bay of Biscay, now under siege from Coastal Command (which, in June and July, sank twenty-six U-boats and damaged seventeen more), they did not expect them to return: 'No more parties were given to celebrate the start of an operation now – we just drank a glass of champagne in silence and shook hands, trying not to look each other in the eyes. We had got pretty tough, but it shook us just the same. Operation suicide!'[10]

The atmosphere in every Biscay port was tellingly forlorn. The bands which had once greeted as heroes the crews returning from the Atlantic battlefront in the past were noticeable by their absence. There were no

---

* At news of Germany's surrender in May 1945 Schaeffer and his crew piloted U-977 to the coast of Argentina, an epic voyage of sixty-six days, for most of which time they remained submerged to avoid detection. In Argentina Schaeffer apparently found 'peace and quiet'.

crowds on the quayside. No aircraft on standby to fly them to Hitler's presence. No medals to bestow. When Herbert Werner returned to base on 28 May, he sat alone in his room among the familiar possessions which he had left a month earlier, feeling 'an overpowering sense of gratitude' that he had survived. He opened a parcel from home. 'Mother had sent me a birthday cake. It was already four weeks old, and had hardened and broken into many pieces. But I wished to honour my mother's belief in her son's longevity, so I ate a piece of cake anyway.'[11] It seemed to say it all. Yet, with a fortitude that defied the logic of their predicament, the U-boat crews rarely questioned the validity of the missions on which they were required to embark. 'Even in the times of the most terrible defeat they preserved their cohesion and discipline,' one of their most successful commanders, Peter Cremer, noted. 'They were always ready to fight on, even with the heaviest losses. To the end their spirit was unbroken.'[12]

In Brest, Leutnant Werner observed the eerie calm at the U-boat base where many of the mooring bays remained empty, as did the places in the mess halls where crews met for meals and to share their experiences at sea. The talk was heavy with gloom, though not with thoughts of defeat. The Allied raids on Brest (which preceded the Normandy landings) still made no impact on the U-boat pens themselves but inflicted severe damage on the surrounding area. When Werner hurried to the naval hospital following one of these raids, he noticed a 'Yankee' pilot being wheeled into the hospital precincts. Werner struck up a conversation with the downed airman, who did not refrain from expressing his contempt for the German officer's efforts to convince him that the Third Reich would eventually prevail. 'The war might be over for me,' the US pilot said, 'but it will be all over for all you Germans pretty soon ... We are going to pulverize your bases and your industry in a few months ... Whatever you Germans do, it will come too late. Time works for us – only for us.' Werner did not believe him but remained convinced that the American was 'a typical victim of Allied propaganda'.[13]

By the late autumn of 1943, on the heels of Italy's surrender, with the Wehrmacht on the retreat in Russia and the bombing blitz on Germany growing ever more intense, it was clear to the Kriegsmarine's senior staff that it was no longer possible to wage an offensive war at sea either: retrenchment or, in some cases, an orderly retreat were the only options. Yet Dönitz would hear none it. Overruling his advisors, he insisted that they should not yield 'until forced into involuntary retreat or surrender with huge and unnecessary losses of men and war materials'. In the words of his biographer, this was 'a negation of strategy'.[14] It was, though, a demonstration of Dönitz's unquestioning loyalty to the Führer and to their shared ideological conviction: his own lodestar – National Socialism – was as fixed in his as in Hitler's distorted firmament. Thus, in a speech on 8 December, he instructed his Flag Officers that every single individual in the Third Reich was required 'to put all his intellectual and spiritual powers and his willpower behind the fulfilment of his duty . . . In this struggle we can only hold our own if we follow it with holy ardour, and complete fanaticism.' It was inevitable, he told his senior staff, that the 'Anglo-Saxons' would attempt to invade Germany in 1944. The navy's task in preventing this would demand 'the most fanatical and complete commitment in which there is no yielding – not a metre'.[15] The only evidence that the strategic realities of the moment still impinged on him was the fact that by this time his command headquarters had already been transferred from the leafy suburbs of Berlin to a palisaded complex of timber barracks in the countryside some thirty kilometres from the capital to avoid destruction by Allied bombers.

This retrenchment coincided with statistics from the Atlantic which revealed an appalling catalogue of U-boat losses in 1943: a total for the year of 243, of which around 180 had occurred following the convoy battles of May which marked the turning point in the Battle of the Atlantic. Dönitz's response displayed such a surfeit of unreason as to suggest that he had momentarily succumbed to a Hitlerian bout of self-delusion. 'The day will come when I will offer Churchill a first-class U-boat war,' he told his men. 'The U-boat arm has not been broken by the reverses of the year 1943. On the contrary, it has become stronger.'[16] This was nonsense on stilts. By this time, the majority of those U-boats which put to sea did not return. In January, fifteen U-boats were lost; twenty in February; twenty-six in March; twenty-one in April; and twenty-four in May.[17] And so it would continue.

Even Dönitz could not avert his gaze from this rate of destruction. In March he had been forced to call off all U-boat operations against the Atlantic convoys, telling Hitler that these could be resumed only 'if we succeeded in radically increasing the fighting power of the U-boats'.[18]

His dream of once again menacing the convoys was embodied in the new type XXI U-boat, which was designed to travel at speeds of up to seventeen knots while still underwater. These submarines would travel faster than the fastest convoys but, fitted with a *Schnorchel* (snorkel), they could remain beneath the surface undetected by Allied radar for some thousands of miles.* The new boats were also to be fitted with a firing device that could unleash a volley of six acoustic torpedoes designed to home in on their target without need of precision guidance from within the U-boat. Had these visionary craft ever been used in anger and in enough numbers, they would most certainly have caused a very genuine threat. However, the prototypes were plagued by problems and, despite wildly surmising that they would soon come off the production line at the rate of six a day, Dönitz was only able to send two XXIs into action before the end of the war. Neither sank a single vessel.

As an interim solution, some of the existing U-boat fleet had been fitted with the new *Schnorchels*. They were not reliable. Herbert Werner described the moment in U-953 when the float at the top, designed to close the tube to prevent water flowing down it when the vessel was submerged, became jammed in the 'closed' position:

> With the air intake thus cut off, the port engine sucked most of the air out of the vessel before the diesels could be shut down. The men gasped for air, their eyes bulging . . . suffocation seemed imminent. The Chief gesticulated wildly, trying to tell his men to lay down the air mast, which might result in unlocking the float. With agonizing effort, the mechanics turned down the handles, lowered the mast by cable, then erected it again with the primitive winch. Painful minutes passed, but then the mast drained and the seawater gurgled down into the bilges. The float cleared with a snap and air was sucked into the boat in a long sigh. The sudden change in pressure burst many an eardrum. Some of the men covered their faces in pain and sagged to the deck plates. Others swallowed violently to equalize the pressure.

---

* The *Schnorchel* was a hinged air tube which could be raised above the surface when the U-boat was submerged. Thus air could be sucked into the main diesel engines and the exhaust gases expelled at the same time, allowing the U-boat to recharge batteries without the need to surface; in the absence of another effective counter to the 10-centimetre radar, this was the only way to avoid the risk of an unexpected aerial attack.

Some of the existing fleet had also been loaded with acoustic torpedoes. These had some successes against escort destroyers and corvettes which were no longer able to escape by zigzagging out of harm's way; in September 1943 three escorts were sunk in this way. However, the British countered by inventing a mechanical decoy which made far more noise than the warship itself. Towed behind as a decoy, it was called the Foxer and for the obvious reason: the torpedo was usually foxed.

The collapse of the U-boat offensive was easily measurable: from 629 merchant ships sunk worldwide in the last six months of 1942, to 314 in the first six months of 1943, 149 in the last six months of that year, and 67 in the first six months of 1944.[19] This was not only a catastrophic fall but conclusive evidence that Dönitz had comprehensively and irrevocably lost the tonnage war. As a result, nothing could now be done to prevent the Allied invasion of France from the launch-pad of the United Kingdom: the men and supplies required to sustain the greatest operation of its type ever essayed were finally free to cross the Atlantic with impunity. It was for this reason, above all others, that D-Day was not only imminent but virtually certain to lead on to victory.

In Liverpool, Admiral Horton could look at these statistics with some satisfaction. The commander of the Western Approaches was not given to triumphalism. Nonetheless, after the rout of the wolf packs in May 1943, he had felt able to send a victory signal to all the units under his command: 'In the last two months, the Battle of the Atlantic has undergone a decisive change in our favour . . . All the escort-groups, support groups, escort-carriers and their machines as well as the aircraft from the air-commands have contributed to this great success . . . The climax of the battle has been surmounted.'[20]

By May 1944 this had become unassailable fact. With the departure of the U-boats from the North Atlantic, the duties of an escort commander had become routine to the point of monotony. The escorts were still needed as a deterrent but precisely for that reason there was rarely a moment of drama or excitement. Donald Macintyre was relieved, therefore, to be given the task of leading a new support group (known confusingly as the 5th Escort Group) which comprised six frigates with a roving brief to hunt down any lone U-boat prowling for unwary or unescorted freighters. It took time, but on 6 May 1944, fifteen days after leaving Liverpool in his new American-built frigate, HMS *Bickerton*, Macintyre was guided towards a U-boat that was on weather patrol in the North Atlantic.

When U-765's captain, Oberleutnant Werner Wendt, was told that three enemy warships were approaching at speed, he ordered a crash-dive to a depth of more than 600 feet. Knowing that the U-boat could still manoeuvre out of harm's way at that depth, Macintyre adopted a tactic devised by Commander 'Johnny' Walker. With a stealth that had once been the hallmark of the German wolf packs, the warships crept up in a three-pronged movement from astern. Unable to detect the sound of the approaching warships above the noise from its own propeller, the U-boat's hydrophones lulled Wendt into a false sense of security. Once one of the frigates, HMS *Bligh*, had inched its way to a position where it was directly above the U-boat, it released a hail of twenty-six depth charges that plummeted silently towards the unwary target. As Macintyre gleefully recalled:

> A hundred fathoms deep, all was quiet in the U-boat and the crew had no inkling of the death that was sinking down through the water to them. With a shattering concussion the first charge went off alongside, plunging the boat in darkness. Another and another, creating utter confusion and cracking the stout pressure hull allowing the seas to pour in.

The U-boat crew could do nothing as tanks burst, water seeped into the control room and their vessel first plunged uncontrollably a further 200 feet towards the ocean bed before, as the tanks were blown, shooting cork-like towards the surface. Macintyre saw 'a cascade of foam and spray as the U-boat shot to the surface amongst the brown scummy patches left by the explosions'.[21] As U-765's twisted and broken conning tower broke surface, a Swordfish from the aircraft carrier HMS *Vindex* roared in to deliver the coup de grâce with two depth charges which dropped neatly on either side of the doomed vessel. The U-boat slid stern-first below the surface. A few moments later Macintyre heard a succession of muffled explosions as the hull imploded under the pressure of water as it sank to the bottom, taking with it thirty-seven of its forty-eight-man crew. Macintyre was 'enormously elated' by this kill, not least because, in his judgement, it had been 'a textbook operation' combining the technologies of Ultra, 10-centimetre radar, Huff-Duff and ASDIC as well that essential ingredient, the efficient coordination of warships and aircraft.

Eleven survivors from U-765 were pulled out of the water and brought aboard *Bickerton*. According to his own crew, Wendt had been the first to jump out of the conning tower as his vessel came to the surface. As he was also the first man over the side, 'abandoning ship without giving any further orders', they had been 'particularly disgusted'.[22] Macintyre took an immediate dislike to Wendt, who was, he wrote, 'an arrogant, strutting little braggart'. This impression was confirmed when *Bickerton* docked in Belfast and Wendt was handed over to an army escort. For a week he had lived in the warship's wardroom, where he had been treated as an equal by his fellow officers. Now, as he descended the gangway, one of them wished him farewell and expressed the hope that they might meet again once the war was over. Wendt replied, 'In the next war, I sink you!'[23] It was evidently not intended as a joke.

The end of the Battle of the Atlantic had finally liberated Churchill and Roosevelt from their residual fear that the U-boats could thwart their plans for victory. The elimination of the U-boat threat in the Atlantic was the precondition for establishing, provisioning and sustaining a multimillion-strong Allied force in Britain capable of liberating Europe from the Nazis.

This did not mean, however, that the strategic dilemmas that so often sowed discord between London and Washington were at an end. In the summer of 1943 this reached a crescendo in the Canadian city of Quebec.

The British party, led by Churchill, arrived aboard a freshly painted *Queen Mary* on 10 August for what promised to be a stormy gathering. The hottest topic on their agenda was Operation Overlord (the codename for the cross-Channel invasion of France). The pressure from those 'fools or knaves who had chalked "Second Front Now" on our walls for the last two years' had been a source of great irritation to the prime minister. Now, following months of detailed staff work by his senior military advisors, working closely with their American counterparts, he prepared to lay out before the president a 'majestic' and 'coherent' plan for the invasion of France.[24]

The Chief of the Imperial General Staff, Brooke, did not expect smooth sailing. Notwithstanding the formal agreements reached at a succession of earlier conferences, he felt sure that Admiral King was still viscerally reluctant to endorse any European operation that might distract from his Pacific priorities. He also feared that General Marshall, still bruised by losing the argument in favour of a cross-Channel invasion in 1942, might be obstructive when it came to negotiating such a mammoth undertaking as the invasion of France. He was additionally irked to discover that Churchill had agreed that an American – in the person of General Eisenhower – should be given command of Overlord although he had already promised it to him. 'It was a crushing blow,' Brooke recalled. 'Not for one moment did he realize what this meant to me. He offered no sympathy, no regrets at having to change his mind, and dealt with the matter as if it were one of minor importance.'[25] His disappointment did little for his relationship with Marshall, who had instigated the appointment of the American general.

At 'a most painful meeting' on 15 August, Marshall and Brooke duly argued about Overlord, the timing of which was complicated from the British perspective by the imminent surrender of the Italians following the successful occupation of Sicily. Marshall was insistent that Overlord should have absolute priority over the drive through Italy. Brooke was furious: Marshall had apparently not even read the detailed plans for Overlord, nor did he understand how it was linked to the southern thrust which was in part designed to siphon off enough German forces to weaken their hold elsewhere, and especially on the Western Front. Neither Marshall nor King had any enthusiasm for the occupation of Italy, the latter insisting that Italy was 'a liability whichever power controlled it, whether the Germans or the Allies'.[26] Nor did he refrain from reiterating that the war against Japan was every bit as crucial as the war against Germany and that significant resources should be redeployed from the European to the Pacific theatre (where the US Navy was, in fact, sinking far more Japanese shipping than he was willing to reveal). When the US chief of staff joined forces with the head of the US Navy by threatening to ditch the 'Germany First' strategy in favour of the Pacific unless the British surrendered the Italian option, Brooke, after one of their marathon sessions, noted, 'Another poisonous day.'[27]

The strategic conflict between the two sides was aggravated by ill-concealed personal animosities; at times their discussions became so heated that the principals ordered their staffs to leave them alone to settle their differences in private. The only light relief was provided inadvertently when, after one particularly fractious session, Admiral Mountbatten bounded into the conference room at the Frontenac Hotel intent on regaling the chiefs with his wheeze for establishing air cover for the Atlantic convoys. Habakkuk, as his scheme was codenamed, foresaw the construction of 'a self-propelled floating airfield' made from a mixture of ice and wood pulp called Pykrete.[28] To prove his point before a somewhat sceptical gathering, Mountbatten brought with him a block of 'pure' ice and another of Pykrete. Pulling a revolver from his pocket, he fired five shots into the 'pure' block, which duly splintered into smithereens, showering his audience with ice shards. Then he fired at the Pykrete block which demonstrated his case beyond argument: according to Brooke, the bullet 'rebounded off the block and buzzed round our legs like an angry bee'.[29] In King's account, the bullet came close enough to nick his trousers.[30]

Despite this graphic display of its potential, Habakkuk's day in the sun never arrived. Unwittingly, however, Mountbatten had been of more use than he might have imagined. The staff officers who were waiting in an adjoining room were startled to hear the sound of shots from behind the closed door and drew a ribald conclusion: according to Brooke, one of them shouted out, 'Good heavens, they've started shooting now!!'[31] Another kind of ice was broken, if only for a while.

In the end, after an exhausting and ill-humoured ten days, the two sides finally reached a reluctant accommodation. A while before the Quebec Conference, King had been asked by a journalist, 'What happens when the Combined Chiefs disagree?' King replied, 'The decision is up to the president and Churchill.' 'Who usually wins?' the journalist persisted. King evidently paused before replying with uncharacteristic delicacy, 'Mr Churchill is a *very* persuasive talker, you know.'[32] So it proved at Quebec. Subject to one or two minor caveats, the Allies reiterated that Overlord was their pre-eminent objective and that – as they had already agreed almost three months earlier – 1 May 1944 was still to be the target date for launching the cross-Channel invasion.

The Quebec Conference had exhausted all its participants. The ailing Pound seemed especially drained although, with his customary stoicism, he concealed the reason for this until the negotiations were over. But on the night of 28 August he told a close colleague that he had lost the use of his right leg some days earlier and that he had since lost the use of his right arm and that 'he felt it creeping up to the right side of his head – so the long and the short of it was that he couldn't go on'.[33] He returned by sea to London and went immediately to hospital, where he was diagnosed with 'a left-sided brain tumour of the most malignant form'.[34] No treatment was possible. He died on 21 October to be succeeded by Admiral Cunningham, the former commander-in-chief of the Mediterranean Fleet. Brooke, who had been scathing about Pound's lacklustre contributions at chiefs-of-staff meetings, was embarrassed when he became aware of the likely explanation for the fact that the First Sea Lord had latterly fallen asleep more frequently and more deeply; the admiral was, he noted subsequently, 'a very gallant man who literally went on working till he dropped'.[35] Pound had certainly lived long enough to see his memorable dictum 'If we lose the war at sea we lose the war' fully vindicated. Whether his successor, a man as clever as Portal and as forceful as Harris, would have been able to browbeat Churchill into realizing the implications of this fundamental early enough to have accelerated the victory in the Battle of the Atlantic can only be a matter of conjecture. That his abrasive and outspoken manner would have made a greater impact on his peers than Pound is hardly in doubt. Nor is the fact that the latter's honour and integrity were not enough to secure a hearing in the strategic roughhouse where Cunningham was equally at home as Portal and Harris.

Only one 'black spot', as he put it, marred Churchill's satisfaction at the outcome he had secured at Quebec: 'the increasing bearishness of Soviet Russia'.[36] Earlier in the year, Stalin had been furious when Churchill cabled to tell him that the Second Front was to be postponed in favour of Sicily. The prime minister had tried to mollify him by responding: 'It would be no help to Russia if we throw away a hundred thousand men in a disastrous cross-Channel attack such as would, in my opinion, certainly occur if we tried under present conditions and with forces too weak to exploit any success that might be gained at very heavy cost.'[37]

Recalling at length the numerous occasions on which the two Western leaders had apparently committed themselves to a large-scale invasion in 1943 at the latest, Stalin threw this sentiment back at Churchill: 'You say that you "quite understand" my disappointment. I must tell you that the point here is not just the disappointment of the Soviet Government, but the preservation of its confidence in its Allies, a confidence which is being subjected to severe stress.'[38]

On the eve of the Quebec Conference, the prime minister had been in touch with Moscow again. This time his message included a set of photographic slides depicting the devastation of Hamburg by Bomber Command and promised that, very soon, 'even greater destruction will be laid upon Berlin'. Informing Stalin as well that, over the last three months, the Allies had 'destroyed U-boats at the rate of almost one a day, while our losses have been far less than we planned for', he avowed that these successes 'will facilitate the establishment of the large-scale Anglo-American fronts against the Germans, which I agree with you are indispensable to the shortening of the war'.[39]

At the same time, the British came under renewed pressure from Moscow to renew the Arctic convoys which had been suspended in March. Churchill, who was anxious to mollify his mercurial ally, urged the Admiralty that, if this was 'humanly possible', he wished to accede to the Soviet demand.[40] At first the admirals resisted, citing a shortage of shipping, but the prime minister overrode their objections, insisting that at least five convoys could be despatched before the start of Overlord, and the first of these should leave in November.[41] Confirming this in a long cable to Stalin on 1 October, he wrote, 'I and all my colleagues are most anxious to help you and the valiant armies you lead to the utmost of our ability . . . we have always done our best in spite of our own heavy burdens to help you to defend your own country against the cruel invasion of the Hitlerite gang.'[42] So far so good. But there was a very sharp sting in the tail.

Before sending this cable, Churchill had made it clear to the Foreign Secretary Anthony Eden and the Admiralty that, in return for 're-opening the convoys we are entitled to make a very plain request to them for the better treatment of our personnel in North Russia'.[43] Now, for Stalin's benefit, he outlined a 'list of grievances' which had been drawn up by British officials in Murmansk, who had become increasingly frustrated by the pettifogging restrictions imposed by the Soviet authorities, which had not only frustrated the unloading and despatch of supplies but had aggravated the mutual suspicion by which relations with the Russians had long been bedevilled. Churchill cut to the chase. Pointing out that Stalin's officials had refused to issue enough visas to ensure the smooth flow of supplies, he demanded 'the immediate grant of visas for the additional personnel required and for your assurance that you will not in future withhold visas when we find it necessary to ask for them in connexion with the assistance that we are giving you'. He also demanded Stalin's help 'in remedying the conditions under which our Service personnel and seamen at present find themselves in North Russia': these grievances included a variety of restrictions on their freedom of movement and communication along with the censoring of 'private service mail'. Warning that 'the imposition of these restrictions makes an impression upon officers and men alike which is bad for Anglo-Soviet relations, and would be deeply injurious if Parliament got to hear of it', he urged the Soviet leader to 'have these difficulties smoothed out in a friendly spirit'.[44]

So far from being mollified, Stalin was aggrieved as never before. Churchill's failure to confirm that the prospective convoys were an 'obligation' as opposed to a promissory note riled him to the point of writing that it 'would be inadmissible to have the supplies of the Soviet armies depend on the arbitrary judgement of the British side. It is impossible to consider this posing of the question to be other than a refusal of the British Government to fulfil the obligations it undertook, and as a kind of threat addressed to the USSR.' For good measure, he not only refused to address any of the British grievances but added one of his own against them, referring to 'the inadmissible behaviours of individual British servicemen who attempted, in several cases, to recruit, by bribery, certain Soviet citizens for Intelligence purposes'.[45]

With Eden in Moscow, Churchill summoned the new Soviet ambassador, Feodor Gousev (who had replaced Ivan Maisky on the latter's recall to Moscow), to Downing Street. After observing the conventional courtesies he told Gousev that he could not bring himself to respond to the Soviet leader's cable as 'any reply which I could send would only make things worse'. For this reason, he would leave the matter in Eden's hands and would not accept the message himself. Whereupon he handed it back to the ambassador and escorted the crestfallen Gousev to the door.[46] Their meeting was over.

In retrospect, Churchill took some delight in recalling how he had faced down 'the Soviet machine' which, he had already advised the American president, was 'quite convinced it can get everything by bullying, and I am sure it is a matter of some importance to show that this is not necessarily true'.[47] In the event, with the diplomatic dexterity for which, in those days, he was renowned, Eden soon smoothed the contretemps away – though not before Stalin had told the Foreign Secretary that if only the British in North Russia 'had treated his people as equals none of these difficulties would have arisen'.[48] The Soviet Union's inferiority complex was never far below the surface, even in the person of its all-powerful leader, and there would be more such hiccups before the end of the war. However, these were usually resolved to the face-saving advantage of both protagonists. In this case, the Arctic convoys proceeded as Churchill had planned.

In May 1944, with the Soviet armies marching rapidly and mercilessly towards the German border, the prime minister was able to inform Stalin that, since the end of 1943, a total of 191 freighters had docked in Murmansk laden with 1,259,800 tons of military supplies to support this offensive. Despite 'heavy air attacks launched by a vigilant enemy', Churchill was happy to report that the Luftwaffe had managed to sink only five merchant ships and two destroyers, and had downed only one aircraft. 'All this has been very successful,' he wrote, adding with an effusiveness that reflected his unbounded confidence about the Allied advances on all fronts, that 'it rejoices my heart that these weapons should be reaching your gallant armies at a time when their great victories are occurring'.[49]

Estimates of the overall contribution of the aid provided by the Western Allies to Russia were to vary sharply from a Soviet low of 4 per cent to a Western high of 11 per cent. But such crude global statistics expressed merely in tonnage terms fail to highlight the pertinent facts: without Lend-Lease supplies of aviation fuel, aluminium and warplanes, the Soviet air force would have been significantly incapacitated; similarly, the 'shipments of specialized chemicals, metals, and industrial machinery', though modest in relation to the gross percentage of Allied aid, were crucial to the sustained production of weaponry from the Soviet Union's armaments factories. In addition, Lend-Lease provided the Russians with 500,000 miles of rail track, 2,000 locomotives and more than 11,000 railway wagons; more than 400,000 trucks and jeeps – which was almost enough to transport the entire Red Army of 11 million men.[50] Moreover, advanced communications systems developed by the US – radio transmission and receiving equipment, field telephones and improved cabling – gave Soviet commanders tighter control over their front-line troops, which is widely thought to have played an invaluable part in allowing the Soviet armies to match the manoeuvrability of the German forces. Much, though not all, of this assistance was delivered by the Arctic convoys: any disruption of those convoys deprived the Red Army accordingly.

Even Marshal Zhukov, the Red Army's commander-in-chief, a reluctant cheerleader for any Western initiative, would later concede that Lend-Lease supplies 'were of certain help', though he complained – with some justification – that this aid 'came in much smaller quantities than promised'.[51] Stalin was less equivocal. At the first 'Big Three' Teheran Conference at the end of November 1943, after the Arctic convoys had been relaunched and in the immediate aftermath of his spat with Churchill, he asserted that the assistance from the Western Allies, and especially from the United States, was 'an absolute necessity'.[52]

The degree to which the provision of munitions, weapons, petroleum products, machinery, raw materials and other supplies (calculated at the time to be worth more than $40 trillion) made a decisive contribution to the Soviet Union's eventual victory on the battlefield was inevitably to be a matter of future dispute. At the time, though, there is no doubt that it was regarded as crucial by all sides – and not least by Germany. For this reason – not to mention the political and diplomatic imperative – the convoys continued to sail (with a short break in the run-up to Overlord) until the very end of the war and even beyond. The final convoy to make the Arctic crossing was JW67, which left the Clyde on 12 May 1945, four days after the German surrender. The twenty-six freighters, escorted by an aircraft carrier, two destroyers and five corvettes, arrived at their destination on 20 May 1945 without incident and without fanfare. It was the last of seventy-eight convoys – some 1,400 merchant ships – which had steamed to and fro along this most gruelling and hazardous route escorted by scores of Allied warships (sixteen of which were sunk in the course of these duties). Between the despatch of the first convoy and the last, eighty-five freighters had been destroyed by a twin-pronged onslaught from the Luftwaffe and the U-boats.

These were epic struggles which had tested men to the limits of their endurance. Yet, in a shameful demonstration of prejudice and inertia, it would take successive British governments more than sixty years to give formal public recognition for their collective achievement to those civilians who sailed in the Arctic convoys. It was not until 2006 that the 'Arctic Emblem' was bestowed on those few veterans who were still alive, and posthumously awarded to the majority who were not. However, in another twist of bureaucratic cruelty, this was not a campaign

medal like the ones already given to those who had sailed in other theatres, including the Atlantic. It took another six years of sustained
pressure from the Merchant Navy Association before, in 2012, the award
was upgraded to the Arctic Star.

After the defeat of the U-boats in May 1943 the heat went out of the 'Battle of the Air'. The belated provision of a mere fifty VLR bombers from
Bomber Command to the Atlantic offensive against the U-boats had
proved the Admiralty's point beyond any doubt. Indeed the 235 VLR
aircraft which had earlier been promised for the protection of the convoy
routes by July 1943 were never delivered, largely because it became clear
they were not needed in such numbers: the combination of aircraft
and escorts, armed with appropriate weapons and technology, was quite
capable of seeing off any further U-boat challenge. And, as the Liberators
were coming off the US production lines at a rapidly growing rate (more
than 18,000 were to be produced before the end of the war), even 'Bomber'
Harris did not feel the need to oppose the provision of a small number to
Coastal Command. Nonetheless, he continued to claim that Germany
could be defeated by air power alone. On 13 October, in Brooke's sar-
donic account, he advised his superiors at chiefs of staff meetings that 'the
only reason why the Russian army had succeeded in advancing is due to
the results of [the] bomber offensive!! According to him . . . we are all
preventing him from winning the war. If Bomber Command were left
to itself it would make much shorter work of it all.'[53]

At least Harris had the courage of his convictions. Unlike the public
statements issuing from Sir Archibald Sinclair, the Secretary of State for
Air, to the effect that Bomber Command was principally attacking
enemy installations, Harris wanted the nation to know that Bomber
Command's role was 'to wreck enemy cities and turn them from assets
into liabilities'. The War Cabinet refused to release this information (or,
as one of Harris's sympathetic biographers was to note, 'the government, generally content to support Harris behind closed doors, was not
prepared to be honest to the world at large about what he was actually
trying to do'.[54]) The pretence may have been a political necessity to
minimize public disquiet at 'terror' bombing, but the strategy – which
could be realized only because monthly aircraft deliveries to Bomber
Command had risen to over a thousand by January 1944 – was rarely in
dispute.

Harris's objective made great demands on the airmen he sent on these missions. As Max Hastings has written:

> It is important to remember that losses had to fall below 4 per cent for a crew to have a favourable chance of completing a tour of operations. In January 1944, Harris was losing 6.1 per cent of aircraft dispatched to Berlin, 7.2 per cent of those which went to Stettin, Brunswick, and Magdeburg . . . on 30 March 1944, Bomber Command suffered its worst single disaster of the war, where ninety-six of the 795 aircraft dispatched to Nuremberg failed to return.[55]

Losses of this order placed demands of character and fortitude on the young men who flew in Bomber Command that were comparable to those displayed by their peers in Dönitz's U-boats, who continued to cross the Bay of Biscay on 'suicide' missions in the Atlantic. In the case of Bomber Command, however, the validity of a strategy which cost the lives of 55,000 British airmen (as well as 500,000 German civilians) was not only called into question at the time but with even greater bitterness after the facts became publicly known. The U-boat crews were never to endure such obloquy; though their mission was to prove impossible, its strategic validity was rarely challenged, except in detail, by any of those on either side who lived though those terrible years.

By March 1944 Harris had for two years been as dominant a force in Britain's war councils as in the public imagination but, in the approach to D-Day, which concentrated every military mind in Washington and London, his influence waned rapidly. Bomber Command no longer had a life of its own but was subjected to the greater endeavour for which the Supreme Allied Commanders had the power and responsibility. But, though the bombers now played a subsidiary role in the conduct of the war, Harris remained free to persist in 'terror bombing' German cities for another year. It was not until 28 March 1945 that, in a memorandum for the chiefs of staff and for the air staff (at whose insistence it was subsequently withdrawn to be substituted by a milder version), Churchill finally called this strategy into question:

> It seems to me that the moment has come when the question of bombing of German cities simply for the sake of increasing the terror, though under other pretexts, should be reviewed. Otherwise we shall come into control of an utterly ruined land . . . I feel the need for more precise

concentration on military objectives . . . rather than on mere acts of terror and wanton destruction, however impressive.[56]

Had the prime minister reached this conclusion in 1942, the VLR
bombers might have been made available for the Battle of the Atlantic
many months earlier and, in consequence, the 'U-boat peril', which
Churchill later claimed was 'the only thing that ever really frightened
me during the war',[57] would have been crushed long before May 1943.
Had the Admiralty been provided with the aircraft for which Pound had
pressed so ineffectually for so long against the clamour of Portal and
Harris, the prime minister would not have been driven to warn Roosevelt
in March 1943 that the Second Front would have to be postponed until
1944 on the grounds that Britain was 'crippled for lack of shipping'.[58]

It does not follow from this that D-Day should have been launched in
1943 rather than in the following year, or that it would have succeeded if
it had been so decreed. In 1943 the German defences in France were still
formidable; Hitler's armies were not so 'degraded' as they would become
after the hammering to which they were subjected by the Red Army's
counteroffensive; and the Luftwaffe – as the aircrews in Bomber Command knew to their great cost – was still a powerful adversary that could
inflict grave damage on any invading force. There can be no doubt,
though, that Churchill's clinching arguments in favour of attacking the
Third Reich's southern defences via Sicily in the spring of 1943 would
have been subjected to much closer scrutiny by Washington. Notwithstanding the inexperience of the American troops on the battlefield –
which had been alarmingly exposed during the campaign in North
Africa – Marshall would have been in a far stronger position to advocate
the earlier Second Front which he and his fellow chiefs of staff craved.
Churchill and the British chiefs might still have prevailed, but it would
have been a very much more difficult task.

If D-Day had been launched nine months sooner, it is conceivable
that the Western Allies would have reached Berlin earlier. If so, the
'carve-up' of Germany into three zones of occupation – which was ten-
tatively agreed at the Yalta Conference in February 1945 and brutally
confirmed at Potsdam five months later, when Poland was forcibly
co-opted into the Soviet bloc – might have been pre-empted by very
different 'facts on the ground'; Allied boots in occupation on a much
greater swathe of German territory might have provided their political

leaders with a far firmer base from which to argue their case. Had this
been so, the history of post-war Europe and its peoples would have been
very different.

Such speculation is tempting but it ignores a host of 'unknowns'
that make it perilous to contemplate. Yet, given the enormity of the
implications, such ventures are hard to resist, especially when it is
acknowledged – on the basis of facts readily available even at the time –
that the Battle of the Atlantic could and should have been won several
months earlier. Churchill was a great war leader: not only were his
powers of communication and persuasion unrivalled but also his strategic judgement was far sounder than is sometimes allowed. His vision
shaped the conduct of the Second World War in the West. Without his
rare energy and the overwhelming power of his personality, it is hard to
see how the Allies would have triumphed over the Third Reich as they
did. His aggressive instincts and clarity of purpose were crucial to steering them into a common purpose. Yet it is a paradox of his greatness
that it was precisely these characteristics which led to the single worst
error of his leadership.

Though he had doubts about both its efficacy and its morality, he saw
in the terror bombing of Germany a means of showing the world that
Britain's resolve was unshakeable. Its unrestrained aggression and its
unequivocal purpose – the destruction of the enemy's will to fight – not
only reflected his own nature but appeared to meet the essential criteria
for victory. However, not only did the bombing fail to have its intended
effect but, until the crisis of March 1943, it half-blinded him to the fact
that victory in what he mistakenly saw as the defensive Battle of the
Atlantic was a precondition for destroying Nazism and eliminating Hitler. He was never to understand that victory over the U-boats was every
bit as aggressive as the struggle against Nazism on any other front. The
magisterial judgement of the Royal Navy's official historian for this
failure of foresight therefore lingers in the mind. It was, he wrote:

> perhaps the most far-reaching and tragic strategic error, which can, at
> any rate, be laid at Churchill's door, since it was the shortage of shipping
> that delayed every offensive by the United Nations in every theatre up
> to mid-1944, and so prolonged the struggle at the cost of inestimable
> suffering to the peoples of the occupied countries.[59]

It is hard, if not impossible, to disagree.

# 22.   The Beginning of the End

In the early hours of 6 June 1944 the first wave of Allied troops – more than 150,000 men from the United States, Britain, and Canada – landed on the Normandy beaches under fire from the German guns on the cliffs above. An American reporter, accompanying the troops landing on Omaha, broadcast a first-hand account of the moment they disembarked:

> We came sliding and slewing in on some light breakers and grounded . . . All up and down the beach as far as I could see, men, jeeps, bulldozers, and other equipment were moving about like ants . . . I saw one small landing craft catch fire after taking a hit. Men came spilling out of it into the water waist deep . . . There were so many transports on the horizon that in the faint haze they looked like a shoreline. Destroyers were almost on the beach, occasionally jolting out a salvo that was like a punch on the chin.[1]

More than 4,000 landing craft, shielded by 1,200 warships and 11,500 aircraft – the greatest armada ever assembled – were subjected to a murderous barrage of shellfire from the cliffs. The water was choppy and the landings awkward. As the landing craft surfed in to grind to a halt on the beach, they came under a hail of fire from above. There were heavy casualties as the ramps were lowered and the troops stormed ashore. One member of the US 1st Division recalled:

> Some boats were coming back after unloading, others were partly awash, but still struggling. Some were stuck, bottomed out, racing their motors and getting nowhere, some were backing up short distances and trying again . . . I saw craft sideways being upturned, and dumping troops in the water. I saw craft heavily damaged by shellfire being tossed around by the waves. I saw craft empty of troops and partly filled with water abandoned, awash in the surf. Men were among them struggling for the pitiful protection they gave.[2]

According to another soldier, 'screams for help came from men hit and drowning under ponderous loads . . . There were dead men floating in the water and there were live men acting dead, letting the tide take them in.'[3]

The scale of the ambition and the critical importance of the Allied enterprise had made the Chief of the Imperial General Staff, Brooke, 'very uneasy about the whole operation' for fear that it might turn into the 'most ghastly disaster of the whole war'.[4] Though these were 'agonizing hours' for the British high command, they might have been far worse: another familiar source of death and destruction might have been waiting below the surface to intercept the troopships as they lumbered across the English Channel to land Allied armies on the Normandy beaches. However, not even one U-boat was there to colour the sea even redder with Allied blood. If these were indeed agonizing hours for Brooke, they were catastrophic for Dönitz.

A short while before D-Day, which Berlin knew to be imminent – though not when or where – the U-boat commander-in-chief's official diary offered a glimpse into the bleak prospect facing him: 'Now the chances of success have become meagre and the chances of not returning from operations have on the other hand greatly increased . . . Losses, which bear no relation to the success achieved, must be accepted, bitter though they are.'[5]

D-Day itself was a humiliating coda to Dönitz's defeat in the Battle of the Atlantic. As the first Allied troops disembarked on French soil, all forty-nine U-boats based in the Bay of Biscay were still in harbour. It was not until the afternoon of the 6th that their commanders were alerted to the landings and not until midnight that the first thirty-five crept out from their bases in Brest, Saint-Nazaire, La Pallice and Lorient to intercept the invaders. It was not only a belated start of a hopeless attempt to mount a counteroffensive but it also had no prospect of making even a marginal impact as they faced a virtually impenetrable barrier of Allied warships and aircraft. The waters between Land's End and the Brest peninsula were patrolled with such intensity by Coastal Command that no patch of sea was free from aerial scrutiny for more than thirty minutes at a time. Similarly, the Royal Navy, with ten support groups and three aircraft carriers, had effectively blocked the entrance to the Southwestern Approaches. No significant incursion towards the Normandy beaches was thus possible.[6]

Herbert Werner, now with his own command in U-415, was in little

doubt about this: his orders, as he described them, were to 'race unprotected towards the southern English coast at a time when the sky was
black with thousands of aircraft and the sea swarmed with hundreds of
destroyers and corvettes . . . madness'.[7] He did not exaggerate. Just
before midnight on the 6th, a patrol of Coastal Command aircraft
sighted a flotilla of eight U-boats leaving Brest. Within an hour they
came under attack as the bombers roared in at low level to blow them
out of the water. In the fierce battle which followed, the U-boats brought
down four aircraft but, in return, one of their number was sunk and five
more were so seriously damaged that they had to return to port. Among
these was Werner's U-415, which was attacked simultaneously by two
aircraft, one from dead ahead and one from starboard:

> This was the end . . . U-415 lay crippled, bleeding oil from a ruptured
> tank . . . a target to be finished off with ease . . . Suddenly, some men
> came struggling up the ladder, shaken, mauled, groggy, reaching for air,
> tossing inflatable rubber floats to the bridge . . . This, I thought grimly,
> was the way many of my friends had died – the silent way, leaving no
> word.[8]

U-415 managed to submerge and to creep slowly back towards
Brest. Werner had been wounded in the head but survived. By this time
he had come to the conclusion that 'the men who gave the orders had
lost their good judgement and even their common sense. But we were
trained to obey orders, sane or otherwise . . . We never voiced our
thoughts, never disturbed each other with any reference to our imminent senseless deaths.'[9]

The virtual absence of any U-boats in the Channel and the Luftwaffe
in the skies above made the Normandy landings in the early days of
June far less perilous than they would otherwise have been. One of the
BBC's war correspondents, flying low over the Channel, described the
scene below as the build-up of Allied forces on French soil accelerated:

> a sea crowded, infested with craft of every kind: little ships, fast and
> impatient, scurrying like water-beetles to-and-fro, and leaving a glis-
> tening wake behind them; bigger ships, in stately, slow procession with
> the [mine]sweepers in front and escort vessels on the flank . . . There in
> the distance was the Cherbourg Peninsula . . . and, there, right ahead
> now . . . Dozens, scores, hundreds of craft lying close inshore, pontoons

and jetties being lined up to make a new harbour, where six days ago, there was an empty shore.[10]

From the sea at least, nothing could be done to arrest the arrival of this armada. On 12 June, realizing the impossibility of their task, Dönitz recalled all the surviving U-boats to their Biscay bases, except those equipped with *Schnorchels*. These managed to penetrate further into the western fringes of the Channel but to nugatory effect: though they sank two frigates, only five of the thirty-five U-boats which Dönitz had ordered to counter the D-Day offensive – 'regardless of risk' – made it back to the Biscay ports. Almost 1,000 men had been shipwrecked at his behest, of whom only 238 were rescued.[11]

It was a comprehensive massacre. A little over a year earlier, in May 1943, by his own admission, Dönitz had lost the Battle of the Atlantic; now in the Channel, the Royal Navy and Coastal Command between them had delivered the coup de grâce. Not that you would have known this from an entry in his War Diary written a few days later, where he took denial to new heights of absurdity:

> After due consideration is given to the exceptional difficulties involved, the success achieved was satisfactory, and had been achieved at the expense of losses which were admittedly severe, but were not intolerable. Though these operations had no decisive effect upon the enemy's build-up, they had nevertheless hampered it to a considerable extent and by doing so lightened the burden of the [German] troops ashore.[12]

This was nonsense, and the fact that he never allowed himself to appreciate this – he was to reprint the entry in his memoirs – suggests that, for a while at least, his contact with reality had become almost as tenuous as that of the Führer himself.

Not long afterwards, Dönitz's humiliation was compounded when he was obliged to order every U-boat from the Biscay ports to evacuate France for the relative security of Norway to avoid being trapped by the Allied advance into Brittany that followed the landings. He was wise to do so. By September, after advancing against fierce resistance and losing 10,000 lives, the Americans surrounded and neutralized Saint-Nazaire and Lorient. This retreat severely inhibited his ability to mount the kind of threat in the Atlantic that had once 'gnawed' at Churchill.

Nonetheless, the U-boats could not be ignored. Even a small number, cleverly deployed at critical places in other waters, could still harass the convoys, especially once they were armed with technologies such as acoustic torpedoes and *Schnorchels*. To avoid unnecessary losses in the war of attrition that, from then on, was to characterize the maritime conflict, the Allies would still be obliged to deploy large numbers of warships and aircraft to protect the ocean arteries which fuelled, armed and fed their armies as they advanced across Europe. As Churchill was to note, 'The whole Anglo-American campaign in Europe depended on the movement of convoys across the Atlantic.'[13] Without those convoys it would have been impossible to maintain the flow of armaments, equipment and men required to sustain a campaign which was to last for nearly another year against a still-powerful enemy that fought with skill, tenacity and courage for every inch of occupied territory and, when forced back onto German soil, for the soul of the Fatherland as well.

Until the very end of the war Dönitz continued to send his U-boat crews on missions which both he and they knew to be suicidal. Yet his men went to their slaughter without complaint despite the loss of more than 200 boats in the ten months following the D-Day landings. They were able to do so only because – despite the best efforts of Bomber Command – replacement vessels continued to come off the production lines at such a rate that by the end of April 1945 Dönitz still had 166 operational U-boats (from a fleet total of 434), which was only twenty-two fewer than he had following D-Day. Yet in those eleven months they managed to sink only 121 merchant ships worldwide, of which – most importantly – only thirteen were lost on the North Atlantic convoy routes. It was a miserly tally that served to illustrate how comprehensively the U-boats had been defeated by the superiority of the Allied forces deployed against them.[14]

Dönitz may have been a skilled and charismatic naval commander, who thereby earned the grudging respect of his Allied counterparts, but his basic sentiments were no less squalid than any of his 'fanatical' peers. That his ideological commitment was as unequivocal as his military resolve may be presumed to explain in large measure why Hitler chose to designate him above his rivals to be his successor as Führer. Dönitz rarely refrained from an opportunity to parade his convictions. In an oration to the vast crowd gathered in Berlin for the 'Heroes Memorial

Day' parade three months before D-Day (when he was standing in for Hitler), he had delivered a lengthy address to the German people which was broadcast on national radio. In one particularly abhorrent passage, he asked rhetorically, 'What would our homeland be today if the Führer had not united us in National Socialism?' His answer lacked ambiguity: 'Divided in parties, permeated with the disintegrating poison of Jewry and vulnerable to it because we lacked the protection of our present uncompromising ideology . . . we would have succumbed long since to the burdens of this war and would have been delivered up to the pitiless destruction of our enemy.'[15]

On 1 May 1945, following Hitler's suicide, Dönitz duly inherited the Nazi crown – only to lay it down almost at once. Three days later, on 4 May, as Berlin fell to the Allies, he instructed his loyal U-boat crews to surrender, declaring, 'Undefeated and spotless you lay down your arms after a heroic battle without equal. We remember in deep respect our fallen comrades, who have sealed with death their loyalty to Führer and Fatherland.'[16]

With very few exceptions, the officers and men who took part in that 'heroic battle' had indeed fought for the cause with unquestioning resolve. For this reason they were held in honour not only by the German people but also by many of those against whom they had fought so dauntlessly; even Churchill could not refrain from paying tribute to the 'fortitude of the U-boat service'.[17]

Nor did capitulation break this spirit. In obedience to the undertakings he had been required to give to the victors, Dönitz made it clear in his 'surrender' order that all German warships were to be handed over and that none should be scuttled. According to Kapitänleutnant Peter 'Ali' Cremer, this 'touched us U-boat men to the quick, seeing we would have to hand over our boats to the Anglo-Americans without a fight'. As it happened, Cremer had just been assigned to join the new Führer's security unit. When his second-in-command rang from Kiel to ask whether he should obey these instructions, Cremer told him defiantly, 'Ali Cremer does not show a white flag and does not surrender his boat – so scuttle it.' Every other U-boat commander in Germany's home ports followed this lead and no fewer than 138 submarines were accordingly despatched in this way. By chance, Cremer was with Dönitz when word came through that the men under his command had – with unprecedented temerity – disobeyed the Führer's very clear order. 'The Grand

Admiral looked very surprised and at first disapproving, then a slight smile crossed his face. And we commanders also got away with it, for the Allied reprisals which we had expected did not occur.'[18]

Cremer was arrested a few days later but released soon afterwards by a sympathetic British naval officer. He became a free man in the ruins of Hamburg but they were bleak days with nothing to celebrate:

> All around me was emptiness. Most of my comrades were no longer alive, the years of my youth had gone. Like so many others I had given of my best in a war which very few of us had wanted and in which the faith and readiness for sacrifice of the German people . . . had been most terribly abused.[19]

Hamburg was in ruins. The BBC's Wynford Vaughan-Thomas bore witness to the devastation:

> Whole quarters have disintegrated under air attacks. There are miles upon miles of blackened walls and utterly burned out streets, and in the ruins there are still nearly a million people and 50,000 foreign workers living in the cellars and air-raid shelters . . . all that stirs in the streets is a British jeep or an armoured car . . . The docks are even more devastated than the town, the great shipyards of Bloem and Voss are a wilderness of tangled girders, and in the middle of this chaos fourteen unfinished U-boats still stand rusting on the slipways.[20]

There could hardly have been a better symbol of the last Führer's failure, the disintegration of the Third Reich. Between 1939 and 1945 he had presided over the loss of 781 U-boats as 30,000 young men out of the 38,000 who went to sea at his behest – four out of five – perished in the process; it was the highest rate of attrition for any branch of any armed service on either side of the Second World War. For the most part, they had lost their lives honourably for a criminal cause which was finally in ruins.

In his victory broadcast on 13 May 1945 the prime minister paid tribute to their victims – those who served in the Merchant Navy – for a 'devotion' to duty which was 'so rarely mentioned in the headlines'. By the end of the war, 32,248 of the 185,000 seamen who served in the Merchant Navy had lost their lives, often as they leapt from burning ships into waters where they could not swim or where rescue was not at hand.[21] Despite this attrition, the oversight to which Churchill had referred was to persist. They had delivered the means of victory, had spared Britain the prospect of defeat and made victory possible, yet their resolve would remain virtually unsung – the inevitable consequence of a prejudice in favour of derring-do exploits, the glamour of which more easily seized the popular imagination.

In the same broadcast, Churchill also paid tribute to the 'vast, inventive, adaptive, all-embracing, and, in the end, all-controlling power of the Royal Navy'. Of the approximately 800,000 officers and men serving in the Navy by the end of the war, 50,787 are recorded to have perished, a gallantry recorded rather more fully by posterity than that of those who served in the Merchant Navy (and who, proportionately, died in even greater numbers).

Towards the end of the broadcast, the prime minister delivered a valedictory warning:

> I wish I could tell you to-night that all our toils and troubles were over. Then indeed I could end my five years' service happily, and if you thought that you had had enough of me and that I ought to be put out to grass I would tell you I would take it with the best of grace. But, on the contrary, I must warn you, as I did when I began this five years' task – and no-one knew then that it would last so long – that there is still a lot to do.[22]

The following day, his private secretary noted, 'Victory has brought no respite. The P. M. looks tired and has to fight for the energy to deal with the problems confronting him.' These not only included the need to settle a date for the first general election for a decade (which took place on 5 July 1945, when the voters resolved that the great war leader should indeed 'be put out to grass') but also, which was of far greater historical moment, the future of Europe and 'the dark cloud of Russian imponderability'.[23] In a letter of commiseration to their go-between and trusted friend, Harry Hopkins, Churchill wrote, 'I understand how deep your feelings of grief must be . . . I feel a very painful personal loss, quite apart from the ties of public action which bound us so closely together.'[24] Nonetheless, as statesmen must, he soon established a bond of mutual respect with his successor, Harry Truman. Like Churchill, the new president realized that VE Day marked the beginning as much as the end of an era. On his behalf, therefore, Hopkins once again found himself in Moscow, where, for twelve days between 26 May and 6 June,

1945 he attempted to create a positive framework for the forthcoming conference with the Soviet leader. Despite his personal rapport with Stalin, he did not succeed.

At Potsdam, the fateful decisions were essentially in the hands of Truman and Stalin as the leaders of what were soon to be regarded as the world's two great superpowers. Britain (represented for the first ten days by Churchill, and from 26 July by the Labour leader and newly elected prime minister, Clement Attlee)* was relegated in substance, if not form, to the status of a junior partner. The negotiations were held in a collegiate atmosphere but the diplomatic language employed by both sides concealed the chasm of purpose and the clash of wills which were to shape the history of the rest of the century.

It was relatively easy for the Big Three to demand the 'unconditional surrender' of Japan, which, following America's decision to destroy Hiroshima and Nagasaki with atomic bombs, was duly accomplished on 15 August. The future of Europe was a different matter. Potsdam failed to bridge the ideological chasm which separated the Western Allies from the Soviet Union or to alter the distribution of authority granted to both sides by their relative positions on the battlefield. The United States (with Britain's support) was in control of what became Western Europe, much of which was later to be incorporated into NATO; the Soviet Union was in occupation of what became Eastern Europe, which was duly incorporated into the Warsaw Pact soon afterwards. The divided city of Berlin, isolated in the heart of East Germany, gave symbolic as well as substantial meaning to what became a global stand-off between the superpowers. If the seeds of the Cold War were planted at Yalta, they took root at Potsdam.

What mattered in 1945, however, was that Nazism had been defeated and a terrifying shadow had thereby been lifted from the world, something that would not have happened without that hard-won victory in the Battle of the Atlantic.

---

* Although the election took place on 5 July, the final count was not known until 26 July to allow for the return of ballot boxes containing the votes of British servicemen and women still based overseas.

# Epilogue: Fates Disentwined

So great was the death toll on both sides in the Battle of the Atlantic that there were to be few published memoirs from those who fought on that maritime front line. Among those who survived to tell their own stories, and who have therefore played a prominent part in this narrative, were three U-boat aces.

Peter 'Ali' Cremer, who spent altogether 381 days at sea, went on after the war to become general manager of a German electronics company. He died in Hamburg on 5 July 1992 at the age of eighty-one.

Reinhard 'Teddy' Suhren, the founder of the German Naval Association, who sank nineteen ships, spent almost a year in captivity at the end of the war. On his release he went into business, working for a petroleum company. He died from cancer in 1984 at the age of sixty-eight. His ashes were scattered off the coast of Spain, where twenty-eight of the crew under his leadership had drowned when U-564 was sunk by a Coastal Command bomber on 14 June 1943.

Herbert Werner served in four U-boats between 1941 and 1945, which sank six ships during his time aboard. After the surrender Werner was interned until July 1945, when, after a thorough interrogation by the British, he was apparently handed over to the French authorities. After a series of bizarre escapades which took him to Paris, and almost into the Foreign Legion, he eventually found his way back to his home city of Frankfurt. He later acquired US citizenship and became a successful entrepreneur in Florida where he died in 2013.

On the British side Peter Gretton, one of the Allies' most successful escort commanders, was promoted to become a vice-admiral, deputy chief of naval staff and Fifth Sea Lord. He was awarded a knighthood, a DSO with two bars, and a DSC. He retired in 1963 and two years later became the bursar of University College Oxford, where his writing on defence issues earned him distinction. He died on 11 November 1992 at the age of eighty.

Commander Donald Macintyre, who escorted twenty-eight convoys across the Atlantic, a total of 1,100 ships, of which only two were sunk, was awarded a DSO and DSC for his valour. At the end of the war, he left the navy to take up a successful career as a naval historian and became the author of eighteen books. He died on 23 May 1981, aged seventy-seven.

Of those who were at the heart of German strategy, Admiral Raeder was taken into custody by the Soviet authorities in Berlin at the end of the war and later taken to Moscow. Brought back to Nuremberg later in 1945, he was found guilty of war crimes and, in October 1946, sentenced to life imprisonment. He had assumed he was to be executed and, apparently wishing it had been so, he formally asked to face a firing squad – a request which was refused. He was released from custody in September 1955 on the grounds of ill health. He died on 6 November 1960 at the age of eighty-four

Admiral Dönitz was also charged with war crimes at Nuremberg but, in his case, prosecutors demanded the death penalty on the grounds, inter alia, that he had waged 'unrestricted submarine warfare'. When the US Admiral, Chester Nimitz, volunteered that he too had waged 'unrestricted submarine warfare' in the Pacific, Dönitz's attorney successfully argued that, as the Americans (and the British for that matter) had acted within the constraints of international law, so too had his client. Sentenced to ten years' imprisonment, he was held at Spandau, where he was once again in contact with Raeder. According to Albert Speer, a member of Hitler's inner circle who was imprisoned with them, the froideur between the two admirals persisted because Dönitz still blamed Raeder for his 'policy of bloated surface vessels' and his refusal to provide him with the U-boats he needed to triumph in the Atlantic.[1] On his release in 1956, Dönitz retired to a small village outside Hamburg, where, at the age of eighty-nine, he died on 24 December 1980, apparently reflecting that the war had been a mistake but still refusing to show remorse for his own part in it.

Of those who were at the heart of US strategy, Admiral Harold 'Betty' Stark became Commander of US Naval Forces in Europe after he was replaced as Chief of Naval Operations by Admiral King in March 1942. After supervising the US role in the Normandy landings, Stark faced a court of inquiry over his role in the events leading up to Pearl Harbor.

He was severely censured but avoided a court martial. He retired in April 1946 and died in Washington on 20 August 1972, aged ninety-one.

Admiral Ernest King, whose abrasive attitude towards his British counterparts did not soften following the success of the Normandy landings, was, by then, free to focus almost exclusively on the war in the Pacific. Three months after D-Day, at the Second Quebec Conference in September 1944, Churchill offered to help 'finish off' Japan by providing a British battle fleet to fight alongside the US Navy in the Pacific. Though Roosevelt accepted the offer in principle, the Chief of Naval Operations spurned it on the grounds that the Royal Navy would be a liability. According to the official record of an exceptionally acrimonious meeting of the Combined Chiefs of Staff (CCS), he said bluntly that he was 'not prepared to accept the British Fleet which he could not employ or support'. When every other member of the CCS dissociated themselves from what he had said, he was forced to relent – albeit, in the words of Pound's successor as First Sea Lord, Admiral Cunningham, 'with very bad grace'.[2]

In December 1945, four months after VJ Day – by which time it had become clear even to King that the British fleet had played a prominent and constructive part in the destruction of the Japanese Imperial Navy – he retired, admired but not missed by his peers in the United States as well as in Britain. In 1947 he was incapacitated by a severe stroke and spent much of the rest of his life in and out of hospital. He died of a heart attack on 25 June 1956 at the age of seventy-seven.

Harry Hopkins, who had presided over the Lend-Lease programme as well as facilitating the crucial transatlantic alliance between Roosevelt and Churchill, had intended to retire following Roosevelt's death. Truman persuaded him to postpone his departure for his final mission to Moscow in the weeks leading up to the Potsdam Conference. After his return from what had proved to be an arduous and unrewarding visit, Hopkins finally severed his relationship with the administration on 2 July 1945. Drained by illness and exhaustion, he retreated to New York, where he died seven months later, on 29 January 1946, at the age of fifty-five.

Of those at the heart of British strategy, Admiral Sir Percy Noble, after his departure from the Western Approaches Command to become Head of the British Naval Delegation in Washington, returned to London at the end of the war, retiring in the same year. He died at his home in London on 25 July 1955, at the age of seventy-five.

Admiral Sir Max Horton, Noble's successor as commander-in-chief, Western Approaches Command, took retirement from that role after the triumph of victory immediately after VJ Day, in August 1945. He died on 30 July 1951, aged sixty-seven.

Admiral Sir Charles Forbes, who served as commander-in-chief, Home Fleet from 1939 until May 1941, when he became commander-in-chief, Plymouth, retired in August 1943 to Wentworth in Surrey, where he lived until his death at the age of seventy-nine, on 28 August 1960.

His successor, Admiral Sir John Tovey, who orchestrated the sinking of the *Bismarck* and oversaw the Arctic convoys, served as commander-in-chief, Home Fleet until June 1943. He retired in 1946, and entered the House of Lords as Baron Tovey. He died in Madeira on 12 January 1971, aged eighty-five.

A. V. Alexander remained First Lord of the Admiralty throughout the war to become Minister of Defence in the post-war Labour government. As Earl Alexander of Hillsborough, he was Leader of the Labour Party in the House of Lords from 1955–64. He died on 11 January 1965, aged seventy-nine.

Sir Charles Portal remained as Chief of the Air Staff until the end of the war, when he retired. Raised to the peerage as Baron Portal, he became an industrialist and was appointed chairman of British Aluminium and then the British Aircraft Corporation in 1960. He died at his home near Chichester on 22 April 1971, aged seventy-seven.

Lord Cherwell, Churchill's close friend and principal scientific advisor, the most powerful civilian advocate of area bombing, remained at his post until 1945. After the election of the Labour government he returned to his post as a Professor of Physics at Oxford University. When Churchill became prime minister once more in 1951, the 'Prof' was recalled to the government to become Paymaster-General with a seat in the Cabinet, a post he held until 1953. He died on 3 July 1957, aged seventy-one.

Cherwell's wartime nemesis, Professor Patrick Blackett, was awarded a Nobel Prize in 1948 for his work as a geophysicist. For ten years between 1953 and 1963 he was head of the physics department at Imperial College London. An internationally renowned scientist, he campaigned for the British government to devote 1 per cent of Britain's GDP to development and was instrumental in the establishment of the Overseas Development Institute. He was elected President of the Royal Society in 1965, awarded the Order of Merit two years later and appointed a life peer in 1969, as Baron Blackett of Chelsea. He died on 13 July 1974 at the age of seventy-six.

Air Marshal Sir Arthur Harris remained as commander-in-chief of Bomber Command until the end of the war. In 1946 he was promoted to Marshal of the Royal Air Force and after his retirement in 1948 moved to South Africa, where he ran the South African Marine Corporation until 1953, when he returned to Britain. He died on 5 April 1984 at the age of ninety-one. A statue in his honour was controversially erected outside the Church of St Clement Danes in London in 1992; the inscription on it reads: 'The Nation owes them all an immense debt.'

Out of the total of 125,000 young men who flew as aircrew in Bomber Command during the Second World War, 55,573 were killed in action, a rate of attrition – 44 per cent – exceeded only by the young men who went to sea in German U-boats over the same period. Their gallantry was marked publicly and belatedly by the unveiling of the Bomber Command Memorial by Queen Elizabeth II in Green Park on 28 June 2012.

# Acknowledgements

When I embarked on this project my knowledge of the Battle of the Atlantic – like many people's, I suspect – was restricted to what I had read in some of the fine general histories of the Second World War. I was aware of one or two of Churchill's famous aphorisms about the importance of the struggle between the U-boats and the convoys, but little more. The gaps in my knowledge were thus oceanic in scale, and I have benefited enormously from the diligent research and often magisterial writings of others over the last seventy years. Among present-day authors, I am particularly grateful to Keith W. Bird, Lizzie Collingham, Robert Dallek, Michael Gannon, David Irving, Paul Kennedy, Marc Milner, Hugh Sebag-Montefiore, Kevin Smith, and Hubert P. van Tuyll for their illuminating insights.

Andrew Williams generously gave me access to interviews and research documents he compiled when producing the revelatory 2003 BBC series *The Battle of the Atlantic* and writing the book which accompanied it. James Crowden provided me with a number of documents and charts which had belonged to his grandfather, a navigation officer on convoy duty in an armed merchant cruiser. I am indebted to the Gadian family for allowing me to quote from letters written by Theodore Gadian, an RAMC officer serving in Iceland from 1941–2. Lord Norwich (John Julius Norwich) kindly gave me copies of the letters his mother, Lady Diana Cooper, wrote to him when as a ten-year-old boy he was evacuated to Canada. Three eminent naval historians – Peter Padfield, Professor Eric Grove and Professor Geoffrey Till – have given me the benefit of their expertise. The meticulous care with which they scrutinised the manuscript, their comments and their criticisms have been invaluable; I am grateful to them for sparing many blushes and for greatly improving my appreciation of the complexities of naval warfare. I am greatly indebted to Tony Cromer, the GCHQ Departmental Historian, who helped me to navigate through the intricacies of Enigma while steering me towards appreciating that Ultra made a far smaller contribution to the outcome of the Battle of the Atlantic than is widely supposed.

The novelist and TV producer Peter Grimsdale and the commissioner of many BBC TV history series, Martin Davidson, made time to read the manuscript; their comments were, likewise, constructive and stimulating. Although he was in the throes of writing his most recent military masterpiece, Antony Beevor found time to explore with me a speculative scenario about the potential implications for the D-Day landings had the Battle of the Atlantic been won six months earlier than it was.

I am grateful to Victoria Thompson, the Head of Friends at the Imperial War Museum; to the team at the National Archives in Kew; to Dawn Littler, the Curator of Archives at the National Museums Liverpool; to Margaret Jones, the Curator of the Western Approaches Museum at Derby House; and to the Churchill Archive Centre in Churchill College, Cambridge.

The staff in the Franklin D. Roosevelt Presidential Library at Hyde Park, New York State, guided me through the complexities of a huge archive in which, inter alia, the Harry Hopkins papers proved to be a treasure trove of illumination. David Rigby was my preliminary guide through the archival thickets of Washington and prepared some helpful research notes for me in that process.

I was fortunate that Dawn Berry, a history scholar with a sharp eye for a good story, agreed to be my researcher. Her ability to rifle through an archive at high speed but with great care, her academic rigour and her unbounded enthusiasm were not only infectious but, when my own diligence wavered, kept me afloat. Without her appreciation of my purpose and her readiness to help steer its focus, I might easily have lost my bearings.

The publishing team at Viking – notably Paul Martinovic, Poppy North, Jillian Taylor, Keith Taylor and Izzy Yates – have been enviably efficient and committed. My copy-editor, Trevor Horwood, has demonstrated yet again why authors scramble over one another to become the beneficiaries of his meticulous toothcomb. He has removed any number of egregious inconsistencies, errors and infelicities from my manuscript with diligence, patience, and good humour. I am greatly in his debt. I am grateful to Douglas Matthews for compiling a navigable index with great dexterity.

It was at the suggestion of my editor, Daniel Crewe, that – with some trepidation – I embarked on this project. He has been a fount of ideas and wisdom, helping to shape and focus the manuscript with suggestions and criticisms that invariably have been astute but always gently and, often amusingly, expressed. When I once wrote 'scampily' when I meant 'skimpily' or 'scantily', he commented in the margin 'I like the thought of that': the absurdity of the thought has stayed with me. He also wields his editorial scalpel with such masterly precision and delicacy that the patient barely feels the pain. Without his guidance and support, my own battle with the Battle of the Atlantic would assuredly have become a hundred years war.

My agent, Veronique Baxter at David Higham Associates, with the support of her colleague, Laura West, has been assiduous on my behalf and supportive; I am grateful for her continuing commitment.

My PA, Stella Keeley, who puts up with my manifold foibles but never draws them to my attention, has shaped order out of chaos with forbearance, patience and good humour. She also transcribed many hours of recorded notes, assembled them in a coherent order and catalogued them into files on which I became heavily dependent. She accomplished all this and a host of other tasks with speed and efficiency. When I raged at the computer, she even affected not to notice.

Family and friends, who must have noted my distraction, have been unfailingly encouraging. My greatest debt by far, though, is to my wife, Jessica. It is a challenge at the best of times simultaneously to have a demanding job at a primary school and bring up two small children. When the husband spends practically all his time, when he is not away, buried in his office, it is very much more testing. Jessica has been astonishingly tolerant of these errant ways. So far from complaining about my failure to fulfil my familial duties, she has been unfailingly generous. When I have felt close to the slough of despond and even despair, she has rescued me from that pit of self-pity. I cannot imagine how it would have been without her.

I should also mention my two youngest children, Daisy and Gwendolen, both of whom are at primary school. At the end of one of those long days when the thoughts had to be coaxed from the mind to the page, it was the greatest fillip to have two little girls rush into my office, leap on my lap and ask excitedly, 'Did you write a hundred words today?' – as though to have done so was the literary equivalent of climbing Everest. 'Yes, yes,' I could reply in honesty after barely achieving a fraught five hundred – and, my perspective thus restored, I felt very much better at once.

Jonathan Dimbleby
June 2015

# Select Bibliography

Alanbrooke, Field Marshal Lord, *War Diaries, 1939–1945*, ed. Alex Danchev and Daniel Todman (Phoenix Press, 2002)

Arthur, Max, *Forgotten Voices of the Second World War* (Ebury Press, 2005)

———, *Lost Voices of the Royal Navy* (Hodder and Stoughton, 2005)

Bailey, Roderick, *Forgotten Voices: Victoria Cross* (Ebury Press, 2011)

Bailey, Thomas A. and Paul B. Ryan, *Hitler vs. Roosevelt: The Undeclared Naval War* (Free Press, 1979)

Beevor, Antony, *D-Day: The Battle for Normandy* (Viking, 2009)

———, *The Second World War* (Weidenfeld and Nicolson, 2012)

Bird, Keith W., *Erich Raeder: Admiral of the Third Reich* (Naval Institute Press, 2006)

Blair, Clay, *Hitler's U-Boat War: The Hunters, 1939–1942* (Weidenfeld and Nicolson, 1997)

———, *Hitler's U-Boat War: The Hunted, 1942–1945* (Weidenfeld and Nicolson, 1999)

Broad, Richard and Suzie Fleming (eds.), *Nella Last's War: The Second World War Diaries of Housewife, 49* (Profile, 2006)

Brodhurst, Robin, *Churchill's Anchor: The Biography of Admiral of the Fleet Sir Dudley Pound OM, GCB, GCVO* (Leo Cooper, 2000)

Broome, Captain Jack, *Convoy is to Scatter* (William Kimber, 1972)

Brown, David K., *Atlantic Escorts* (Seaforth, 2009)

Buell, Thomas B., *Master of Sea Power: A Biography of Fleet Admiral Ernest J. King* (Naval Institute Press, 2012)

Calder, Angus, *The People's War: Britain 1939–1945* (Granada, 1969)

Caulfield, Max, *A Night of Terror: The Story of the Athenia Affair* (Frederick Muller, 1958)

Chalmers, Rear Admiral W. S., *Max Horton and the Western Approaches* (Hodder and Stoughton, 1954)

Churchill, Winston S., *Secret Session Speeches* (Cassell, 1946)

———, *The Second World War*, Vol. I: *The Gathering Storm* (Cassell, 1948)

———, *The Second World War*, Vol. II: *Their Finest Hour* (Cassell, 1949)

———, *The Second World War*, Vol. III: *The Grand Alliance* (Cassell, 1950)

————, *The Second World War*, Vol. IV: *The Hinge of Fate* (Cassell, 1951)

————, *The Second World War*, Vol. V: *Closing the Ring* (Cassell, 1952)

————, *The Second World War*, Vol. VI: *Triumph and Tragedy* (Cassell, 1954)

————, *Winston Churchill, His Wit and Wisdom: Selections from his Works and Speeches* (Hyperion, 1971)

Churchill, Winston S. (ed.), *Never Give In! The Best of Winston Churchill's Speeches, Selected and Edited by his Grandson* (Pimlico, 2007)

Collingham, Lizzie, *The Taste of War: World War Two and the Battle for Food* (Penguin, 2012)

Colville, John, *The Fringes of Power: Downing Street Diaries*, Vol. I: *1939 – October 1941* (Sceptre, 1986)

————, *The Fringes of Power: Downing Street Diaries, 1939–1955* (Weidenfeld and Nicolson, 2004)

Cooper, Artemis, *Cairo in the War, 1939–1945* (Penguin, 1989)

Creighton, Rear-Admiral Sir Kenelm, *Convoy Commodore* (Futura, 1976)

Cremer, Peter, *U-333: The Story of a U-Boat Ace* (Triad Grafton, 1986)

Crump, Simon, *They Call It 'U-Boat Hotel'* (Grizedale, 2001)

Cunningham of Hyndhope, Viscount, *A Sailor's Odyssey: The Autobiography of Admiral of the Fleet Viscount Cunningham of Hyndhope KT GCB OM DSO* (Hutchinson, 1951)

Dallek, Robert, *Franklin D. Roosevelt and American Foreign Policy, 1932–1945* (Oxford University Press, 1979)

Deane, John R., *The Strange Alliance: The Story of Our Efforts at Wartime Co-operation with Russia* (John Murray, 1947)

Dilks, David, 'The Twilight War and the Fall of France: Chamberlain and Churchill in 1940', *Transactions of the Royal Historical Society*, Fifth Series, 28 (1978): 61–86

Dilks, David (ed.), *The Diaries of Sir Alexander Cadogan, 1938–1945* (Cassell, 1971)

Divine, A. D., *The Merchant Navy Fights: Tramps Against U-Boats* (John Murray, 1940)

Doenecke, Justus D. (ed.), *In Danger Undaunted: The Anti-Interventionist Movement of 1940–1941 as Revealed in the Papers of the America First Committee* (Hoover Institution Press, 1990)

Doherty, Martin A., 'The Attack on the *Altmark*: A Case Study in Wartime Propaganda', *Journal of Contemporary History* 38(2) (April 2003): 187–200

Dönitz, Grand Admiral Karl, *Memoirs: Ten Years and Twenty Days*, trans. R. H. Stevens in collaboration with David Woodward (Frontline, 2012)

Easton, Alan, *50 North: An Atlantic Battleground* (PaperJacks, 1980)

Fergusson, Bernard (ed.), *The Business of War: The War Narrative of Major-General Sir John Kennedy* (Hutchinson, 1957)

Ferrell, Robert H. (ed.), *The Eisenhower Diaries* (W. W. Norton, 1981)

Fitzsimons, M. A., 'Roosevelt: America's Strategist', *Review of Politics* 7(3) (July 1945): 280–96

Freidel, Frank, 'FDR vs Hitler: American Foreign Policy, 1933–1941', *Proceedings of the Massachusetts Historical Society*, Third Series, 99 (1987): 25–43

Gannon, Michael, *Operation Drumbeat* (Naval Institute Press, 1990)

———, *Black May: The Epic Story of the Allies' Defeat of the German U-Boats in May 1943* (Naval Institute Press, 2010)

Gentile, Gary, *Track of the Gray Wolf: U-Boat Warfare on the US Eastern Seaboard, 1942–1945* (Avon, 1989)

Gilbert, Martin, *Winston S. Churchill*, Vol. III: *The Challenge of War: 1914–1916* (Heinemann, 1971)

———, *Winston S. Churchill*, Vol. VI: *Finest Hour, 1939–1941* (Heinemann, 1983)

———, *Winston S. Churchill*, Vol. VII: *Road to Victory, 1941–45* (Heinemann, 1986)

———, *The Churchill Documents*, Vol. XIV: *At the Admiralty, September 1939 – May 1940* (Hillsdale College Press, 2011)

———, *The Churchill Documents*, Vol. XVI: *The Ever-Widening War, 1941* (Hillsdale College Press, 2011)

Goebeler, Hans with John Vanzo, *Steel Boat, Iron Hearts: A U-Boat Crewman's Life Aboard U-505* (Savas Beatie, 2013)

Goette, Richard, 'Britain and the Delay in Closing the Mid-Atlantic "Air Gap" During the Battle of the Atlantic', *Northern Mariner* 15(4) (October 2005): 19–41

Gretton, Sir Peter, *Convoy Escort Commander* (Corgi, 1964)

Grove, Eric J., *The Price of Disobedience: The Battle of the River Plate Reconsidered* (Sutton, 2000)

Hastings, Max, *Bomber Command* (Pan, 2010)

Hawkins, Desmond and Donald Boyd (eds.), with Frank Gillard and Chester Wilmot, *War Report: A Record of Dispatches Broadcast by the BBC's War Correspondents with the Allied Expeditionary Force, 6 June 1944–5 May 1945* (Oxford University Press, 1946)

Haynes, John L., *Frozen Fury: The Murmansk Run of Convoy PQ-13* (America Star Books, 2010)

Heinrichs, Waldo, *Threshold of War: Franklin D. Roosevelt and American Entry into World War II* (Oxford University Press, 1989)

Heinrichs, Waldo, Marc Gallichio and Jonathan Utley (eds.), *Diplomacy and Force: America's Road to War, 1931–1941* (Imprint Publications, 1996)

Herman, Arthur, *Freedom's Forge: How American Business Produced Victory in World War II* (Random House, 2012)

Herwig, Holger H., 'Prelude to *Weltblitzkrieg*: Germany's Naval Policy toward the United States of America, 1939–1941', *Journal of Modern History* 43(4) (December 1971): 649–68

Hinsley, F. H. and Alan Stripp (eds.), *Code Breakers: The Inside Story of Bletchley Park* (Oxford University Press, 1993/2001)

Hinsley, F. H. with E. E. Thomas, C. F. G. Ransom and R. C. Knight, *British Intelligence in the Second World War*, 4 vols (HMSO, 1979–90)

Hirschfeld, Wolfgang and Geoffrey Brooks, *Hirschfeld: The Secret Diary of a U-Boat* (Frontline, 2011)

Holmes, Richard, *The World at War* (Ebury Press, 2007)

Howard Bailey, Chris, *The Royal Naval Museum Book of the Battle of the Atlantic: The Corvettes and Their Crews: An Oral History* (Wrens Park Publishing, 1994)

Howard, Michael, *The Mediterranean Strategy in the Second World War* (Greenhill, 1993)

Hughes, Robert, *Flagship to Murmansk* (Futura, 1975)

Huxley, Elspeth, *Atlantic Ordeal: The Story of Mary Cornish* (Chatto and Windus, 1941)

Iredale, Will, *The Kamikaze Hunters: Fighting for the Pacific, 1945* (Macmillan, 2015)

Irving, David, *The Destruction of Convoy PQ-17* (St Martin's Press, 1987)

Joubert de la Ferté, Sir Philip, *Birds and Fishes: The Story of Coastal Command* (Hutchinson, 1960)

Kaplan, Philip and Jack Currie, *Wolfpack: U-Boats at War, 1939–1945* (Aurum Press, 1997)

Kemp, Paul, *U-Boats Destroyed: German Submarine Losses in the World Wars* (Arms and Armour, 1999)

Kennedy, Michael, 'The Sinking of *Arandora Star*', *On-line Journal of Research on Irish Maritime History*, http://lugnad.ie/wp-content/uploads/war/The-sinking-of-Arandora-Star.pdf

Kennedy, Paul, *Engineers of Victory* (Random House, 2013)

King, Ernest J. and Walter Muir Whitehill, *Fleet Admiral King: A Naval Record* (W. W. Norton, 1952)

Kurzman, Dan, *No Greater Glory* (Random House, 2005)

Larson, Erik, *Dead Wake: The Last Crossing of the Lusitania* (Doubleday, 2015)

Loewenheim, Francis L., Harold D. Langley and Manfred Jonas (eds.), *Roosevelt and Churchill: Their Secret Wartime Correspondence* (Barrie and Jenkins, 1975)

Love, Robert W., Jr, *History of the US Navy*, Vol. I: *1775–1941*; Vol. II: *1942–1991* (Stackpole, 1992)

Lund, Paul and Harry Ludlam, *I Was There on PQ17, the Convoy to Hell* (Foulsham, 2010)

Lundeberg, Philip K., 'The German Naval Critique of the U-boat Campaign, 1915–1918', *Military Affairs* 27(3) (Autumn 1963): 105–18

Macintyre, Ben, *Agent Zigzag* (Bloomsbury, 2010)

Macintyre, Captain Donald, *U-Boat Killer: Fighting the U-Boats in the Battle of the Atlantic* (Rigel, 2004)

———, *The Battle of the Atlantic* (Pen and Sword, 2006)

MacLean, Alistair, *H.M.S. Ulysses* (Fontana, 1985)

Mallmann Showell, Jak P., *German Naval Code Breakers* (Ian Allan Publishing, 2003)

———, *Hitler's Navy* (Seaforth, 2009)

Marder, Arthur, 'The Influence of History on Sea Power: The Royal Navy and the Lessons of 1914–1918', *Pacific Historical Review* 41(4) (November 1972): 413–43

Maurer, M. and Lawrence J. Paszek, 'Origin of the Laconia Order', *Air University Review*, Maxwell Air Force Base, Alabama, USA, repr. *Journal of the Royal United Service Institute for Defence Studies* 109(636) (November 1964): 338–44

Messenger, Charles, *'Bomber' Harris and the Strategic Bombing Offensive, 1939–1945* (Arms and Armour, 1984)

Miall, Leonard (ed.), *Richard Dimbleby, Broadcaster* (BBC, 1966)

Middlebrook, Martin, *Convoy: The Battle for Convoys SC.122 and HX.229* (Penguin, 1978)

Miller, Lieutenant Commander Alan J. M., *Over the Horizon: 1939–1945* (Finavon Print and Design, 1999)

Milner, Marc, *Battle of the Atlantic* (Tempus, 2003)

Ministry of Foreign Affairs of the USSR (comp.), *Correspondence Between Stalin, Roosevelt, Truman, Churchill and Attlee During WWII* (University Press of the Pacific, 2001)

Monsarrat, Nicholas, *Three Corvettes* (Cassell, 1975)

———, *The Cruel Sea* (Penguin, 2009)

Moore, David, 'HMS *Edinburgh*', *Warship World* 3(8) (Autumn 1990); BBC archive, WW2 People's War, www.bbc.co.uk/history/ww2peopleswar/stories/18/a2076518.shtml

Moore, Robert J. and John A. Rodgaard, *A Hard Fought Ship: The Story of HMS Venomous* (Holywell House Publishing, 2010)

Moran, Lord, *Churchill at War, 1940–45* (Constable and Robinson, 2002)

Morison, Samuel Eliot, *The Battle of the Atlantic: 1939–1943* (McClelland and Stewart, 1993 [Little, Brown, 1947]), repr. as *The Battle of the Atlantic: September 1939 – May 1943* (Naval Institute Press, 2010)

———, *The Atlantic Battle Won: May 1943 – May 1945* (Naval Institute Press, 2011)

Mosley, Leonard, *Marshall: Hero for Our Times* (Hearst, 1982)

Mulligan, Timothy P., *Lone Wolf: The Life and Death of U-Boat Ace Werner Henke* (University of Oklahoma Press, 1995)

Munro, Captain A. D., *HMS Wellington Escorting Convoy SL 118 August 1942: Six Years on the North Atlantic 1939–45 and Operation Cycle* (Wellington Trust, 2013)

Nicolson, Nigel (ed.), *Harold Nicolson: Diaries and Letters*, Vol. I: *1930–39*; Vol. II: *1939–45* (Fontana, 1967/1970)

Offley, Ed, *Turning the Tide: How a Small Band of Allied Sailors Defeated the U-Boats and Won the Battle of the Atlantic* (Basic Books, 2011)

Padfield, Peter, *Dönitz: The Last Führer: Portrait of a Nazi War Leader* (Victor Gollancz, 1993)

Paterson, Lawrence, *Black Flag: The Surrender of Germany's U-Boat Forces* (Seaforth, 2009)

Pearce Jones, Guy, *Two Survived* (Lyons Press, 2001)

Peillard, Léonce, *U Boats to the Rescue: The Laconia Incident* (Cape, 1963)

———, *The Laconia Affair* (Bantam, 1983)

Pratt, Fletcher, 'The Battleship Comes Back', *North American Review* 248(1) (Autumn 1939): 127–39

Prien, Günther, *Fortunes of War – U-Boat Commander* (Tempus, 2000)

Probert, Henry, *Bomber Harris: His Life and Times* (Greenhill, 2006)

Prysor, Glyn, *Citizen Sailors: The Royal Navy in the Second World War* (Penguin, 2012)

Quinton, Marcelle and Anthony Quinton, *Before We Met* (Half Moon Press, 2008)

Richardson, General Sir Charles, *From Churchill's Secret Circle to the BBC* (Brassey's UK, 1991)

Roberts, Andrew, *Masters and Commanders* (Allen Lane, 2008)

Robertson, Terence, *Walker RN: Britain's Ace U-Boat Killer* (Pan Books, 1958)

———, *The Golden Horseshoe: The Wartime Career of Otto Kretschmer, U-boat Ace* (Frontline, 2011)

Rohwer, Jürgen, *Axis Submarine Successes of World War Two* (Greenhill, 1999)

Roosevelt, Elliott (ed.), *The Roosevelt Letters*, Vol. III: *1928–1945* (Harrap, 1952)

Roskill, Captain S. W., *The War at Sea, 1939–1945*, Vol. I: *The Defensive*; Vol. II: *The Period of Balance*; Vol. III: *The Offensive Part I: 1st June 1943 – 31st May 1944*; Vol. III: *The Offensive Part II: 1st June 1944 – 14th August 1945* (Naval and Military Press, 2004)

——, *Churchill and the Admirals* (Pen and Sword, 2004)

Runyan, Timothy J. and Jan M. Copes, (eds.), *To Die Gallantly: The Battle of the Atlantic* (Westview Press, 1994)

Schaeffer, Heinz, *U-Boat 977* (William Kimber, 1953)

Sclater, William, *Haida* (Oxford University Press, 1946; repr. PaperJacks 1980)

Scott, Peter, *The Eye of the Wind: An Autobiography* (Hodder and Stoughton, 1966)

Sebag-Montefiore, Hugh, *Enigma: The Battle for the Code* (Cassell, 2004)

Sherwood, Robert E., *The White House Papers of Harry L. Hopkins*, Vol. I: *September 1939 – January 1942*; Vol. II: *January 1942 – July 1945* (Eyre and Spottiswoode, 1948/1949)

Simpson, Michael, *A Life of Admiral of the Fleet Andrew Cunningham: A Twentieth-Century Naval Leader* (Frank Cass, 2006)

Slessor, Sir John, *The Central Blue: The Autobiography of Sir John Slessor, Marshal of the RAF* (Praeger, 1957)

Smith, Kevin, *Conflict Over Convoys: Anglo-American Logistics Diplomacy in the Second World War* (Cambridge University Press, 2002)

Soames, Mary (ed.), *Speaking for Themselves: The Personal Letters of Winston and Clementine Churchill* (Black Swan, 1999)

Speer, Albert, *Inside the Third Reich*, trans. Richard and Clara Winston (Macmillan, 1970)

Suhren, Teddy with Fritz Brustat-Naval, *Teddy Suhren Ace of Aces*, trans. Frank James (Chatham Publishing, 2011)

Syrett, David, *The Defeat of the German U-Boats: The Battle of the Atlantic* (University of South Carolina Press, 1994)

Terraine, John, *Business in Great Waters: The U-boat Wars, 1916–1945* (Wordsworth Editions, 1999)

——, *The Right of the Line: The Role of the RAF in World War Two* (Pen and Sword, 2010)

Trefousse, Hans L., 'Failure of German Intelligence in the United States, 1935–1945', *Mississippi Valley Historical Review* 42(1) (June 1955): 84–100

van der Vat, Dan, *The Atlantic Campaign: The Great Struggle at Sea, 1939–1945* (Birlinn, 2001) van Tuyll, Hubert P., *Feeding the Bear: American Aid to the Soviet Union, 1941–1945* (Greenwood Press, 1989)

Walling, Michael G., *Forgotten Sacrifice* (Osprey, 2012)

Werner, Herbert A., *Iron Coffins: A U-Boat Commander's War, 1939–1945* (Cassell, 1999)

Whittington-Egan, Richard, *The Great Liverpool Blitz* (Gallery Press, 1987)

Williams, Andrew, *The Battle of the Atlantic* (BBC Worldwide, 2002)

Wilson, Theodore A., *The First Summit: Roosevelt and Churchill at Placentia Bay, 1941* (Macdonald, 1969)

Winton, John (ed.), *Freedom's Battle*, Vol. I: *The War at Sea 1939–1945* (Book Club Associates, 1974)

Woodman, Richard, *Arctic Convoys, 1941–1945* (Pen and Sword, 2011)

———, *The Real Cruel Sea: The Merchant Navy in the Battle of the Atlantic, 1939–1943* (Pen and Sword, 2011)

# Notes

## *Preface: A Momentous Victory*

1 Peter Padfield, *Dönitz: The Last Führer* (Gollancz, 1993), p. 419.

2 Paul Kemp, *U-boats Destroyed: German Submarine Losses in the World Wars* (Arms and Armour, 1999), p. 8.

3 John Keegan, *The Second World War* (Arrow Books, 1990), p. 104.

4 Winston Churchill, *The Second World War*, Vol. V: *Closing the Ring* (Cassell, 1952), p. 6.

5 Fletcher Pratt, 'The Battleship Comes Back', *North American Review* 248(1) (Autumn 1939): 127–39.

6 Winston Churchill, *The Second World War*, Vol. II: *Their Finest Hour* (Cassell, 1949), p. 529.

7 Admiral Andrew Cunningham, letter dated 15 December 1942, quoted in Stephen Roskill, *Churchill and the Admirals* (Pen and Sword, 2004), p. 139.

8 Churchill, *Their Finest Hour*, p. 567.

9 Cited in Andrew Roberts, *Masters and Commanders* (Allen Lane, 2008), p. 52.

10 Roosevelt to Churchill, 4 May 1941, Elliott Roosevelt (ed.), *The Roosevelt Letters*, Vol. III: *1928–1945* (Harrap, 1952), p. 364.

11 Hubert P. van Tuyll, *Feeding the Bear: American Aid to the Soviet Union, 1941–45* (Greenwood Press, 1989), p. 72.

12 Padfield, *Dönitz*, p. 203.

13 Keith W. Bird, *Erich Raeder: Admiral of the Third Reich* (Naval Institute Press, 2006), p. 197.

## 1 *The Phoney War that Wasn't*

1 Richard Broad and Suzie Fleming (eds.), *Nella Last's War* (Profile, 2006). The diary was written for Mass Observation, an organization established in 1937 to monitor public opinion. Using volunteers to 'record the voice of the people', it has provided historians with an authentic archive, unmediated by pollsters and 'focus' groups by whom it was later was superseded.

2 Ibid.

3 Winston Churchill, *The Second World War*, Vol. I: *The Gathering Storm* (Cassell, 1948), p. 319.

4 Ibid., p. 320.

5 Max Caulfield, *A Night of Terror* (Frederick Muller, 1958), pp. 34–5.

6 Ibid., p. 87.

7 Ibid., p. 93.

8 Richard Woodman, *The Real Cruel Sea: The Merchant Navy in the Battle of the Atlantic, 1939–1943* (Pen and Sword, 2011), p. 15.

9 Caulfield, *Night of Terror*, pp. 144–5.

10 Sir Francis Bridgeman, cited in Roskill, *Churchill and the Admirals*, p. 20.

11 Richard Hough, *Louis and Victoria* (Hutchinson, 1974), p. 268; cited ibid., p. 22.

12 Churchill, *The Gathering Storm*, p. 320.

13 Ibid., p. 321.

14 Robin Brodhurst, *Churchill's Anchor: The Biography of Admiral of the Fleet Sir Dudley Pound* (Leo Cooper, 2000), p. 110.

15 Ibid., p. 11.

16 Ibid., p. 27.

17 John Colville, *The Fringes of Power: Downing Street Diaries, 1939–1955* (Weidenfeld and Nicolson, 2004), p. 709.

18 Brodhurst, *Churchill's Anchor*, p. 103.

19 Naval Staff History, *The Defeat of the Enemy Attack on Shipping, 1939–1945: A Study of Policy and Operations*, Vol. 1A: *Text and Appendices* (Admiralty Historical Section, 1957), p. 7.

20 Admiral Scheer, cited in Philip K. Lundeberg, 'The German Naval Critique of the U-boat Campaign, 1915–1918', *Military Affairs* 27(3) (Autumn 1963): 105–18.

21 Naval Staff History, Vol. 1A, p. 7.

22 Richard Dean Burns, 'Regulating Submarine Warfare, 1921–1941: A Case Study in Arms Control and Limited War', *Military Affairs* 35(2) (April 1971): 56–63.

23 Winston Churchill, *While England Slept: A Survey of World Affairs, 1932–1938* (G. P. Putnam's Sons, 1938), pp. 217–18.

24 British naval staff memo, 'Anglo-German Naval Discussion', The National Archives (TNA) CAB 24/222, cited in Padfield, *Dönitz*, p. 149.

25 Arthur Marder, 'The Influence of History on Sea Power: The Royal Navy and the Lessons of 1914–1918', *Pacific Historical Review* 41(4) (November 1972): 413–43, p. 421.

26 Ibid., p. 423.

27 Padfield, *Dönitz*, p. 191.

28 Ibid., p. 193.

29 Ibid.

30 Caulfield, *Night of Terror*, p. 197.

31 Bird, *Erich Raeder*, p. 139.

32 Padfield, *Dönitz*, p. 193.

33 Karl Dönitz, *Memoirs: Ten Years and Twenty Days* (Frontline, 2012), p. 57.

34 Ibid., p. 58.

35 Cited in Padfield, *Dönitz*, p. 15.

36 Ibid., p. 23.

37 Dönitz, *Memoirs*, p. 5.

38 Padfield, *Dönitz*, p. 120.

39 Ibid., p. 125.

40 Ibid., p. 144.

41 Bird, *Erich Raeder*, p. 2.

42 Ibid., p. 24.

43 Ibid., p. 60.

44 Ibid., p. xviii.

45 Ibid., p. 114.

46 Padfield, *Dönitz*, p. 31.

47 Ibid.

48 Bird, *Erich Raeder*, p. 127.

49 Padfield, *Dönitz*, p. 188.

50 Bird, *Erich Raeder*, p. 137.

51 Padfield, *Dönitz*, p. 188.

52 Dönitz, *Memoirs*, pp. 43–4.

53 Ibid., p. 123.

## 2 Caught Hopping

1 Broad and Fleming, *Nella Last's War*, p. 18.

2 R. J. Hammond, *Food and Agriculture in Britain, 1939–45* (Stanford University Press, 1954), p. 20.

3 Ibid.

4 Broad and Fleming, *Nella Last's War*, pp. 25–6.

5 Ibid., pp. 39–40.

6 Günther Prien, *Fortunes of War – U-Boat Commander* (Tempus, 2000), p. 93.

7 www.forces-war-records.co.uk.

8 Prien, *Fortunes of War*, p. 97.

9 Churchill, *The Gathering Storm*, p. 355.

10 Ibid., p. 359.

11 Ibid., p. 343.

12 Dönitz, *Memoirs*, p. 68.

13 Prien, *Fortunes of War*, p. 114.

14 Ibid., p. 121.

15 Churchill, *The Gathering Storm*, p. 339.

16 Ibid.

17 Dönitz, *Memoirs*, p. 56.

18 Churchill, *The Gathering Storm*, p. 357.

19 Ibid., p. 341.

20 Prien, *Fortunes of War*, p. 122.

21 Ibid., p. 123.

22 Quoted in Max Arthur, *Lost Voices of the Royal Navy* (Hodder and Stoughton, 2005), p. 223.

23 Ibid., p. 225.

24 Ibid., p. 226.

25 Interview with Sandy Robertson, Andrew Williams, *The Battle of the Atlantic* (BBC Worldwide, 2002), p. 38.

26 Prien, *Fortunes of War*, p. 124.

27 Ibid., p. 126.

28 Martin Gilbert, *Winston S. Churchill*, Vol. VI: *Finest Hour, 1939–1941* (Heinemann, 1983), p. 62.

29 Churchill, *The Gathering Storm*, p. 385.

30 Donald Macintyre, *The Battle of the Atlantic* (Pen and Sword, 2006), p. 27.

31 Donald Macintyre, *U-Boat Killer* (Rigel, 2004), p. 17.

32 Williams, *Battle of the Atlantic*, p. 55.

33 Naval Staff Report, quoted in Macintyre, *Battle of the Atlantic*, p. 24.

34 Churchill, *The Gathering Storm*, p. 389.

35 Dönitz, *Memoirs*, p. 58.

36 Padfield, *Dönitz*, p. 197.

37 International Military Tribunal document, Nuremberg, cited ibid., p. 198.

38 Padfield, *Dönitz*, p. 206.

39 Standing Order No. 154, cited ibid., p. 206.

40 U-boat Command War Diary, 1 October 1939, in Dönitz, *Memoirs*, p. 61.

41 Ibid., p. 124.

42 Williams, *Battle of the Atlantic*, p. 71.

43 Ibid.

44 Terence Robertson, *The Golden Horseshoe: The Wartime Career of Otto Kretschmer, U-boat Ace* (Frontline, 2011), p. 200.

45 Williams, *Battle of the Atlantic*, p. 59.

46 TNA ADM 199/141.

47 Mansion House Speech, 20 January 1940, Selected Speeches of Winston Churchill, The Churchill Archive Centre, Churchill College, Cambridge, UK.

## 3 Rash Moves

1 *New York Times*, 18 February 1940.

2 Cited in S. W. Roskill, *The War At Sea, 1939–45*, Vol. I: *The Defensive* (Naval and Military Press, 2004), p. 112.

3 Arthur, *Lost Voices*, p. 227.

4 Ibid., p. 231.

5 Ibid., p. 232.

6 Ibid., p. 5.

7 Ibid., p. 238.

8 Churchill, *The Gathering Storm*, p. 414.

9 Bird, *Erich Raeder*, p. 143.

10 Ibid., p. 141.

11 Quoted in Churchill, *The Gathering Storm*, p. 414.

12 *New York Times*, 19 December 1939.

13 Churchill, *The Gathering Storm*, p. 410.

14 Martin Gilbert (ed.), *The Churchill Documents*, Vol. XIV: *At the Admiralty September 1939 – May 1940* (Hillsdale College Press, 2011), p. 535.

15 Roskill, *The Defensive*, p. 106.

16 *New York Times*, 19 January 1940.

17 NORWAY AND SWEDEN, Memorandum by the First Lord of the Admiralty, 29 September 1939, War Cabinet Papers, 1939 CAB 66/2/7.

18 Churchill, *The Gathering Storm*, p. 430.

19 Gilbert, *Finest Hour*, p. 34.

20 Norway – Iron Ore Traffic, Note by the First Lord of the Admiralty, 16 December 1939, War Cabinet Papers, CAB/66/4/12.

21 Bird, *Erich Raeder*, p. 145.

22 Ibid.

23 Churchill, *The Gathering Storm*, p. 430.

24 Bird, *Erich Raeder*, p. 146.

25 Churchill, *The Gathering Storm*, p. 444.

26 John Winton, *Freedom's Battle*, Vol. I: *The War at Sea 1939–1945: An Anthology of Personal Experience* (Book Club Associates, 1974), p. 25.

27 Ibid., p. 26.

28 Martin A. Doherty, 'The Attack on the *Altmark*: A Case Study in Wartime Propaganda', *Journal of Contemporary History* 38(2) (April 2003): 187–200, p. 191.

29 Ibid., p. 194.

30 Ibid.

31 Churchill, *The Gathering Storm*, p. 445.

32 *New York Times*, February 1940.

33 Doherty, 'The Attack on the *Altmark*', p. 193.

34 Bird, *Erich Raeder*, p. 146.

35 Churchill, *The Gathering Storm*, p. 458.

36 Ibid.

37 John Colville, *The Fringes of Power* (Hodder and Stoughton, 1985 edn), p. 112.

38 Ibid., p. 113.

39 Churchill, *The Gathering Storm*, p. 484.

40 Arthur Marder, cited in Brodhurst, *Churchill's Anchor*, p. 139.

41 Neville Chamberlain to Ida Chamberlain, 13 April 1940, cited in David Dilks, 'The Twilight War and the Fall of France: Chamberlain and Churchill in 1940', *Transactions of the Royal Historical Society*, Fifth Series, 28 (1978): 61–86, pp. 75–6.

42 Brodhurst, *Churchill's Anchor*, p. 122.

43 Neville Chamberlain to Hilda Chamberlain, 20 April 1940, in Dilks, 'The Twilight War and The Fall of France', p. 76.

44 Winton, *Freedom's Battle*, p. 31.

45 Ibid., pp. 32–3.

46 Letter to Pound, 10 April 1940, in Churchill, *The Gathering Storm*, p. 474.

47 Conclusions of a Meeting of the War Cabinet, Wednesday, 10 April 1940, CAB/65/6/32.

48 Churchill, *The Gathering Storm*, p. 474.

49 Ibid., p. 475.

50 Sir Peter Gretton, *Convoy Escort Commander* (Corgi, 1964), p. 37.

51 Winton, *Freedom's Battle*, p. 34.

52 Gretton, *Convoy Escort Commander*, p. 37.

53 Ibid., p. 38.

54 Churchill, *The Gathering Storm*, p. 483.

55 Ibid., p. 482.

56 Admiralty's Director of Operations (Home), Captain Ralph Edwards, quoted in Roskill, *Churchill and the Admirals*, p. 105.

57 Churchill, *The Gathering Storm*, p. 487.

58 Dönitz, *Memoirs*, pp. 84–9.

59 Padfield, *Dönitz*, p. 211.

60 Ibid.

61 Bird, *Erich Raeder*, p. 148.

62 Ibid.

63 Ibid., p. 149.

64 Churchill, *The Gathering Storm*, p. 493.

65 Ibid., p. 495.

66 Ibid., p. 510.

67 Ibid., p. 511.

68 Hansard, 13 May 1940.

69 Winton, *Freedom's Battle*, p. 41.

70 Ibid., p. 42.

71 Dönitz, *Memoirs*, p. 91.

## 4 *The End of the Beginning*

1 Frank Freidel, 'FDR vs Hitler: American Foreign Policy, 1933–1941', *Proceedings of the Massachusetts Historical Society*, Third Series, 99 (1987): 25–43, p. 28.

2 'Quarantine Speech', 5 October 1937, Miller Center, University of Virginia, http//millercenter.org.

3 FDR to William Allen White, 14 December 1939, *Roosevelt Letters*, Vol. III, pp. 293–4.

4 M. A. Fitzsimons, 'Roosevelt: America's Strategist', *Review of Politics* 7(3) (July 1945): 280–96, p. 292.

5 Roosevelt to Churchill, 11 September 1939, in Francis L. Loewenheim et al. (eds), *Roosevelt and Churchill: Their Secret Wartime Correspondence* (Barrie and Jenkins, 1975), p. 89.

6 Churchill ['Former Naval Person'] to Roosevelt, 15 May 1940, Churchill, *Their Finest Hour*, p. 23.

7 Roosevelt to Churchill, 16 May 1940, Loewenheim et al. (eds), *Roosevelt and Churchill*, p. 95.

8 Naval History and Heritage Command Archives, Washington Navy Yard, Washington DC.

9 Churchill, *Their Finest Hour*, p. 51.

10 Robert Dallek, *Franklin D. Roosevelt and American Foreign Policy, 1932–1945* (Oxford University Press, 1979), p. 225.

11 Leonard Mosley, *Marshall: Hero for Our Times* (Hearst, 1982), p. 138.

12 Waldo Heinrichs, *Threshold of War: Franklin D. Roosevelt and American Entry into World War II* (Oxford University Press, 1989), p. 10.

13 Churchill, *Their Finest Hour*, p. 162.

14 Churchill to Reynaud, 13 June 1940, ibid., p. 164.

15 Roosevelt to Churchill, 14 June 1940, Loewenheim et al. (eds), *Roosevelt and Churchill*, p. 102.

16 Churchill, *Their Finest Hour*, p. 166.

17 Ibid., pp. 162–3.

18 Loewenheim et al. (eds), *Roosevelt and Churchill*, p. 103.

19 Churchill, *Their Finest Hour*, p. 167.

20 Ibid.

21 Dallek, *Roosevelt and American Foreign Policy*, p. 243.

22 Ibid.

23 Roosevelt to Robert James Farley (US Postmaster-General), quoted ibid.

24 Robertson, *The Golden Horseshoe*, p. 49.

25 Ibid., p. 50.

26 Ibid., p. 52.

27 Ibid., pp. 51–2.

28 Michael Kennedy, 'The Sinking of *Arandora Star*', *On-line Journal of Research on Irish Maritime History*, http://lugnad.ie/wp-content/uploads/war/The-sinking-of-Arandora-Star.pdf.

29 Robertson, *The Golden Horseshoe*, pp. 111–12.

30 Dönitz, *Memoirs*, p. 110.

31 Padfield, *Dönitz*, p. 222.

32 Dönitz, *Memoirs*, p. 113.

33 Churchill, *Their Finest Hour*, p. 531.

34 Dönitz, *Memoirs*, p. 102.

35 Roskill, *The Defensive*, p. 259.

36 Churchill to Roosevelt, 31 July 1940, Churchill, *Their Finest Hour*, p. 356.

37 Founded in 1940, the group met at the Century Club in New York. After the fall of France in June 1940, they campaigned informally for the United States to respond militarily to German aggression.

38 Dallek, *Roosevelt and American Foreign Policy*, p. 244.

39 *Roosevelt Letters*, Vol. III, p. 329.

40 Churchill, *Their Finest Hour*, pp. 361–2.

41 Ibid., p. 367.

42 *Roosevelt Letters*, Vol. III, p. 329.

43 Churchill, *Their Finest Hour*, p. 358.

44 Viscount John Julius Norwich, conversation with author, November 2013.

45 Diana Cooper, *Darling Monster: The Letters of Lady Diana Cooper to Her Son, John Julius Norwich, 1939–1952*, ed. Viscount John Julius Norwich (Chatto and Windus, 2013), p. 23.

46 Viscount John Julius Norwich, conversation with author, November 2013.

47 Ibid.

48 Cooper, *Darling Monster*, pp. 70–75.

49 A Statement to the House of Commons, 17 September 1940, Charles Eade (comp.), *Secret Session Speeches, by the Right Hon. Winston S. Churchill* (Cassell, 1946), p. 17.

50 Angus Calder, *The People's War: Britain 1939–1945* (Granada, 1969), p. 148.

51 Elspeth Huxley, *Atlantic Ordeal: The Story of Mary Cornish* (Chatto and Windus, 1941), p. 21.

52 Woodman, *The Real Cruel Sea*, p. 178.

53 Huxley, *Atlantic Ordeal*, p. 34.

54 Woodman, *The Real Cruel Sea*, p. 181.

55 *The Times*, 26 September 1940, p. 3.

56 *The Times*, 23 November 1940, p. 5.

## 5 U-Boats on the Rampage

1 Bird, *Erich Raeder*, p. 157.

2 Churchill, *Their Finest Hour*, p. 268.

3 Ibid., p. 274.

4 Bird, *Erich Raeder*, p. 159.

5 Ibid.

6 Dönitz, *Memoirs*, p. 114.

7 Bird, *Erich Raeder*, p. 156.

8 Ibid.

9 Dönitz, *Memoirs*, pp. 115–16.

10 Churchill, *Their Finest Hour*, p. 532.

11 Williams, *Battle of the Atlantic*, p. 85.

12 Macintyre, *Battle of the Atlantic*, p. 39.

13 Williams, *Battle of the Atlantic*, p. 88.

14 Ibid., p. 94.

15 Robertson, *The Golden Horseshoe*, p. 82.

16 Williams, *Battle of the Atlantic*, p. 95.

17 Robertson, *The Golden Horseshoe*, p. 88.

18 Williams, *Battle of the Atlantic*, p. 98.

19 Ibid.

20 Woodman, *The Real Cruel Sea*, p. 207.

21 Cited in Williams, *Battle of the Atlantic*, p. 106.

22 Woodman, *The Real Cruel Sea*, p. 202.

23 Defence Committee minutes, 15 October 1940, TNA CAB 66/13/2kl.

24 Macintyre, *U-Boat Killer*, pp. 18–19.

25 Defence Committee minutes, 15 October 1940, TNA CAB 66/13/2kl.

26 Max Hastings, *Bomber Command* (Pan, 2010), p. 40.

27 Memorandum to Minister of Aircraft Production, 8 July 1940, in Churchill, *Their Finest Hour*, p. 567.

28 John Terraine, *The Right of the Line: The Role of the RAF in World War Two* (Pen and Sword, 2010), p. 261.

29 Terraine, *The Right of the Line*, p. 262.

30 Churchill, *Their Finest Hour*, pp. 405–6.

31 Hastings, *Bomber Command*, p. 133.

32 Churchill, *Their Finest Hour*, p. 406.

33 In a letter to Admiral Andrew Cunningham, then commander-in-chief of the Mediterranean Fleet, dated 15 December 1942, quoted in Roskill, *Churchill and the Admirals*, p. 139.

34 Report of Interrogation of Survivors of 'U-100', TNA ADM 199/205.

35 Naval Staff History, Vol. 1A, p. 171.

36 Cited in John Terraine, *Business in Great Waters: The U-Boat Wars, 1916–1945* (Wordsworth Editions, 1999), p. 355.

37 Quoted in Padfield, *Dönitz*, p. 221.

38 Dönitz, *Memoirs*, p. 116.

39 Ibid., p. 117.

40 Churchill, *Their Finest Hour*, p. 529.

41 Broad and Fleming, *Nella Last's War*, p. 79.

42 Ibid., pp. 83–4.

43 Churchill, *Their Finest Hour*, p. 493.

44 Ibid., pp. 494–501.

45 Dallek, *Roosevelt and American Foreign Policy*, p. 255.

46 Basil Rauch (ed.), *Franklin D. Roosevelt: Selected Speeches, Messages, Press Conferences, and Letters* (Eastern Press, 1957), p. 269.

47 Ibid., pp. 256–7.

48 Ibid.

## 6 Churchill Declares 'The Battle of the Atlantic'

1 Gretton, *Convoy Escort Commander*, p. 55.

2 Leading Seaman Geoffrey Drummond, Commission Warrant John Arthur, Sub Lieutenant (later Lieutenant Commander) Roy Dykes, DSC quoted in

Chris Howard Bailey, *The Royal Naval Museum Book of the Battle of the Atlantic. The Corvettes and Their Crews: An Oral History* (Wrens Park Publishing, 1994), pp. 17–21.

3 Ibid.

4 Ibid.

5 Ibid., p. 105.

6 Ibid., p. 63.

7 Nicholas Monsarrat, *Three Corvettes* (Cassell, 1975), pp. 26–7.

8 Peter Cremer, *U-333: The Story of a U-Boat Ace* (Triad Grafton, 1986), pp. 59–60.

9 Ibid., p. 62.

10 Elizabeth M. Collingham, *The Taste of War: World War Two and the Battle for Food* (Penguin, 2012), p. 106. Maggie Joy Blunt, like Nella Last, was an 'observer' for Mass Observation.

11 Broad and Fleming, *Nella Last's War*, p. 104.

12 Ibid., p. 111.

13 Ibid., p. 130.

14 Ibid., p. 137.

15 Martin Gilbert (ed.), *The Churchill Documents*, Vol. XVI: *The Ever-Widening War, 1941* (Hillsdale College Press, 2011), pp. 315–17.

16 Kevin Smith, *Conflict Over Convoys: Anglo-American Logistics Diplomacy in the Second World War* (Cambridge University Press, 1996), p. 21.

17 Ministry of Labour memorandum (LAB 8/460) cited ibid., p. 18.

18 Philip Noel-Baker Papers, Churchill College Archives (CCC/NBKR 3/213), cited ibid., p. 21.

19 Ibid., p. 22.

20 Monsarrat, *Three Corvettes*, p. 191.

21 Poster held by Merseyside Maritime Museum, Albert Dock, Liverpool.

22 Prime Minister to Minister of Information, 14 April 1941, Winston Churchill, *The Second World War*, Vol. III: *The Grand Alliance* (Cassell, 1950), p. 128.

23 Note by Churchill, CAB 66/17, WP (41) 69, 26 March 1941, cited in Smith, *Conflict Over Convoys*, p. 24.

24 First Sea Lord's Records, 4 March 1941, TNA ADM 199/1933.

25 Prime Minister's Personal Minute, 5 April 1941, ibid.

26 Alexander to Churchill, 9 April 1941, ibid.

27 Churchill to Alexander, 11 April 1941, ibid.

28 Pound to Alexander, 15 April 1941, ibid.

29 Alexander to Pound, 18 April 1941, ibid.

30 Loewenheim et al. (eds), *Roosevelt and Churchill*, p. 141.

31 Dallek, *Roosevelt and American Foreign Policy*, p. 260.

32 Roosevelt to Churchill, 11 April 1941, Loewenheim et al. (eds), *Roosevelt and Churchill*, p. 139.

33 Churchill, *The Grand Alliance*, p. 122.

34 Robert E. Sherwood, *The White House Papers of Harry L. Hopkins*, Vol. I: *September 1939 – January 1942* (Eyre and Spottiswoode, 1948), p. 271.

35 Churchill, *Their Finest Hour*, p. 211.

36 Sherwood, *Papers of Harry L. Hopkins*, Vol. I, p. 276.

37 Colville, *The Fringes of Power* (2004), p. 453.

38 Churchill, *The Grand Alliance*, p. 3.

39 Robertson, *The Golden Horseshoe*, p. 112.

40 Dönitz, *Memoirs*, p. 137.

41 Ibid.

42 Ibid., p. 175.

43 Robertson, *The Golden Horseshoe*, p. 115.

44 Ibid., p. 114.

45 Ibid., p. 133.

46 Ibid., p. 138.

47 Macintyre, *U-Boat Killer*, p. 32.

48 Ibid., p. 35.

49 Clay Blair, *Hitler's U-Boat War: The Hunters, 1939–1942* (Weidenfeld and Nicolson, 1997), p. 257.

50 Ibid.

51 Robertson, *The Golden Horseshoe*, p. 147.

52 Macintyre, *U-Boat Killer*, p. 38.

53 Robertson, *The Golden Horseshoe*, p. 149.

54 Ibid.

55 Macintyre, *U-Boat Killer*, p. 38.

56 Ibid.

57 Robertson, *The Golden Horseshoe*, p. 151.

58 Macintyre, *U-Boat Killer*, p. 39.

59 Ibid., p. 43.

60 'Very Secret' Report, S.R.N. 178, TNA WO 208/4141.

61 Macintyre, *U-Boat Killer*, p. 44.

62 'Very Secret' Report, S.R.N. 178, TNA WO 208/4141.

63 Ibid.

64 Dönitz, *Memoirs*, pp. 174–5.

65 Gilbert, *The Ever-Widening War*, p. 461.

66 Ibid., pp. 468–9.

# 7 Moving the Goalposts Again

1 President Roosevelt Speeches and Statements, Home, www.usmm.org/fdr/emergency.html.

2 Sherwood, *Papers of Harry L. Hopkins*, Vol. I, p. 298.

3 Ibid.

4 Gallup Polls memorandum, 19 June 1941, TNA FO 371/26/72.

5 *New York Times*, 13 June 1941.

6 Memorandum for The President, 14 June 1941, Box 308, Harry L. Hopkins Files, Book 4, Franklin D. Roosevelt Presidential Library and Museum, Hyde Park, NY.

7 Sherwood, *Papers of Harry L. Hopkins*, Vol. I, p. 5.

8 Quoted ibid., p. 246.

9 Ibid., p. 245.

10 Churchill, *The Grand Alliance*, p. 21.

11 Roosevelt, Message to Congress on the Sinking of the *Robin Moor*, 20 June 1941, www.usmm.org/fdr/robinmoor.html.

12 Bundesarchiv-Militärarchiv, Freiburg im Breisgau, PG 32185, Case GE 240. ISKL. Teil C VII, p. 103, cited in Holger H. Herwig, 'Prelude to *Weltblitzkrieg*: Germany's Naval Policy toward the United States of America, 1939–1941', *Journal of Modern History* 43(4) (December 1971): 649–68, p. 661.

13 Hans L. Trefousse, 'Failure of German Intelligence in the United States, 1935–1945', *Mississippi Valley Historical Review* 42(1) (June 1955): 84–100, p. 96.

14 Herwig, 'Prelude to *Weltblitzkrieg*', p. 633.

15 Ibid., p. 661 (original emphasis).

16 Dönitz, *Memoirs*, p. 152.

17 Ibid., pp. 152–3.

18 Ibid., p. 153.

19 Roskill, *The Defensive*, p. 467.

20 Ibid., p. 379.

21 Churchill, *The Grand Alliance*, p. 270.

22 Bird, *Erich Raeder*, p. 176.

23 Roskill, *The Defensive*, p. 399.

24 Ibid., p. 402.

25 Winton, *Freedom's Battle*, pp. 135–8.

26 Ibid., pp. 138–9.

27 Bird, *Erich Raeder*, p. 200.

28 Ibid., p. 221.

29 Tovey succeeded Admiral Forbes as C.-in-C. Home Fleet in May 1941.

30 Churchill, *The Grand Alliance*, p. 275.

31 Herbert Wohlfahrt's War Diary, quoted in Dönitz, *Memoirs*, p. 169.

32 Ibid.

33 Roskill, *Churchill and the Admirals*, p. 124.

34 Ibid., p. 125.

35 Roskill, *The Defensive*, p. 413.

36 Churchill, *The Grand Alliance*, p. 286.

37 Dönitz, *Memoirs*, p. 412.

38 Churchill, *The Grand Alliance*, p. 282.

39 Roskill, *The Defensive*, p. 415.

40 Churchill, *The Grand Alliance*, p. 283.

41 Ibid., p. 286.

42 Churchill to Roosevelt (Churchill Papers 20/36), Gilbert, *The Ever-Widening War*, p. 732.

43 Letter to Hopkins, 17 June 1941, President's Secretary's File, FDR Library, Hyde Park, NY.

44 Churchill, *The Grand Alliance*, p. 120.

45 Rear Admiral Sir Kenelm Creighton, *Convoy Commodore* (Futura, 1976), pp. 89–90.

46 Ibid., p. 90.

47 This and the foregoing from 'The Letters of Theodore Gadian, July 1940–July 1941' (private collection).

48 Prime Minister to Foreign Secretary, Admiralty, War Office, 29 April 1941, TNA ADM 199/1933.

49 John Kennedy, *The Business of War* (Hutchinson, 1957), p. 133.

50 Churchill, *The Grand Alliance*, p. 308.

51 Churchill to Roosevelt (Churchill Papers 20/39), in Gilbert, *The Ever-Widening War*, p. 739.

52 Letter from Stark to Hopkins, 17 June 1941, PSF Diplomatic Files – Diplomatic Correspondence Iceland (Box 39, Military Files Series 1: Nos 50–53, Series 2, No. 18), FDR Library, Hyde Park, NY.

53 Letter from Lincoln MacVeagh to Roosevelt, 22 November 1941, ibid.

54 'Message to be sent by the Prime Minister of Iceland to the President', ibid.

55 'IF TIME PERMITS', 23 July 1941, TNA FO 371/26/72.

56 Letter from Lincoln MacVeagh to Roosevelt, 22 November 1941, PSF Diplomatic Files – Diplomatic Correspondence Iceland (Box 39, Military Files Series 1: Nos 50–53, Series 2, No. 18), FDR Library, Hyde Park, NY.

57 Franklin D. Roosevelt, Fireside Chat, 11 September 1941, www.presidency.ucsb.edu/?pid=16012.

## 8 *America Goes for It*

1 Quoted in Bird, *Erich Raeder*, p. 183.
2 Ibid.
3 Dönitz, *Memoirs*, p. 170.
4 Ibid., p. 177.
5 Monsarrat, *Three Corvettes*, p. 277.
6 Ibid., p. 278.
7 Ibid., p. 279.
8 Ibid., p. 60.
9 Ibid., p. 274.
10 Ibid., p. 300.
11 Dönitz, *Memoirs*, p. 428.
12 Monsarrat, *Three Corvettes*, p. 300.
13 Churchill, *The Grand Alliance*, p. 378.
14 Sherwood, *Papers of Harry L. Hopkins*, Vol. I, p. 315.
15 Ibid., p. 314.
16 Colville, *The Fringes of Power* (1985), entry for 1 August 1941, p. 505.
17 Sherwood, *Papers of Harry L. Hopkins*, Vol. I, p. 312.
18 Ibid., p. 322.
19 Ibid., p. 321.
20 Ibid., pp. 344–5.
21 'Military Secrets to Russia – Access of Russian engineers to plans', note by Assistant Secretary Berle, 30 July 1941, Box 305, Harry L. Hopkins Files, Book 4, FDR Library, Hyde Park, NY.
22 Berle to Hopkins, 30 July 1941, ibid.
23 BBC News, 31 August 2011, 'WWII Artic Convoy Veterans Recall "Dangerous Journey"', www.bbc.co.uk/news/world/europe-14723483.
24 Sherwood, *Papers of Harry L. Hopkins*, Vol. I, p. 348.
25 Churchill, *The Grand Alliance*, p. 381.
26 Colville, *The Fringes of Power* (2004), p. 506.
27 Theodore A. Wilson, *The First Summit: Roosevelt and Churchill at Placentia Bay, 1941* (Macdonald, 1970), p. v.
28 Sherwood, *Papers of Harry L. Hopkins*, Vol. I, p. 364.
29 Cited in Wilson, *The First Summit*, p. 106.
30 Cited in Dallek, *Roosevelt and American Foreign Policy*, p. 285.
31 Ibid.
32 Heinrichs, *Threshold of War*, p. 156.

33 Churchill, *The Grand Alliance*, p. 364.

34 David Dilks (ed.), *The Diaries of Sir Alexander Cadogan, 1938–1945* (Cassell, 1971), entry for 16 August 1941, p. 402.

35 Winton, *Freedom's Battle*, p. 141.

36 Ibid.

37 Quoted in Wilson, *The First Summit*, p. 224.

38 Churchill broadcast, 24 August 1941, http://www.ibiblio.org/pha/policy/1941/410824a.html.

39 'Shoot on Sight', Harry L. Hopkins Files, Book 4, FDR Library, Hyde Park, NY.

40 Ibid.

41 Dallek, *Roosevelt and American Foreign Policy*, pp. 273–4.

42 Ibid., pp. 275–6.

43 Churchill, *The Grand Alliance*, p. 390.

44 'Shoot on Sight', Harry L. Hopkins Files, Book 4, FDR Library, Hyde Park, NY.

45 Robert W. Love, Jr, *History of the US Navy*, Vol. I: *1775–1941* (Stackpole Books, 1992), p. 646.

46 Roosevelt's Labor Day radio address, 1 September 1941, The American Presidency Project, www.presidency.ucsb.edu/ws/?pid=16166.

47 Love, *History of the US Navy*, Vol. I, p. 646.

48 Samuel Eliot Morison, *History of the United States Naval Operations in World War II*, Vol. I: *The Battle of the Atlantic, 1939–43* (Little, Brown, 1947), p. 79.

49 Franklin D. Roosevelt, Fireside Chat, 11 September 1941, www.presidency.ucsb.edu/?pid=16012.

50 Morison, *The Battle of the Atlantic*, p. 80.

51 Halifax to Churchill, 11 October 1941, Premier Files, Churchill Manuscripts, TNA cited in Dallek, *Roosevelt and American Foreign Policy*, p. 289.

## 9 Secret Weapons

1 Dönitz, *Memoirs*, p. 129.

2 Padfield, *Dönitz*, p. 227.

3 Conversation with Peter Padfield, quoted ibid.

4 Cited in Terraine, *Business in Great Waters*, p. 305.

5 Operational Intelligence Centres: Formation and History, TNA ADM 223/286.

6 Roskill, *The Defensive*, p. 306.

7 Dönitz, *Memoirs*, p. 142.

8 Padfield, *Dönitz*, p. 228.

9 Dönitz, *Memoirs*, p. 142.

10 Hugh Sebag-Montefiore, *Enigma: The Battle for the Code* (Cassell, 2004), p. 134.

11 Ibid., p. 110.

12 Knox to Commander Alastair Denniston (Head of GC&CS from its inception in 1919), TNA HW 14/8, cited ibid., p. 109.

13 F. H. Hinsley and Alan Stripp (eds.), *Code Breakers: The Inside Story of Bletchley Park* (Oxford University Press, 1993), p. 93.

14 Sebag-Montefiore, *Enigma*, p. 81.

15 Ibid., p. 138.

16 F. H. Hinsley et al., *British Intelligence in the Second World War*, Vol. I (HMSO, 1979), p. 337.

17 Sebag-Montefiore, *Enigma*, p. 144.

18 Ibid., pp. 145ff.

19 Ibid., p. 150.

20 Ibid., pp. 152–3.

21 Interview with Heinz Wilde in Williams, *Battle of the Atlantic*, p. 132.

22 Ibid., p. 133.

23 Ibid., p. 134.

24 Ibid., p. 135.

25 Sebag-Montefiore, *Enigma*, p. 157.

26 Williams, *Battle of the Atlantic*, p. 138.

27 Sebag-Montefiore, *Enigma*, p. 158.

28 Ibid.

29 Ibid., p. 159.

30 Ibid., p. 162.

31 Williams, *Battle of the Atlantic*, p. 140.

32 Hinsley to Birch, 23 October 1940, TNA HW 14/7, cited in Sebag-Montefiore, *Enigma*, p. 142.

33 Ibid., p. 192.

34 Hinsley and Stripp, *Code Breakers*, p. 78.

35 Ibid., p. 79.

36 Message from admiral commanding U-boats, 24 June 1941, TNA HW 1/7.

37 Response to PM's comment on lateness of receipt of 6896, 28 June 1941, TNA HW 1/9.

38 Message from admiral commanding U-boats, 24 June 1941, TNA HW 1/7.

39 Cited in Sebag-Montefiore, *Enigma*, p. 200.

40 Quoted ibid., p. 201.

41 U-boat War Diary, 16 November 1941, cited in Padfield, *Dönitz*, p. 229.

42 Ibid.

43 F. H. Hinsley et al., *British Intelligence in the Second World War*, Vol. II (HMSO, 1981), Appendix 3, pp. 655–7.

44 Ibid., p. 657.

45 'Compromise of Convoy Movements Near the British Coast', Naval Section Report ZIP/ZG/62, 20 August 1941, TNA ADM 223/2.

46 'German Success Against British Codes and Cyphers', TNA ADM 223/505.

47 Ibid.

48 'Some Examples of the German Operational Use of the Intelligence obtained by reading British Naval Communications', TNA ADM 1/300 81.

49 'German Success Against British Codes and Cyphers', TNA ADM 223/505.

## 10 Fingers in the Dyke

1 Broad and Fleming, *Nella Last's War*, p. 162.

2 Smith, *Conflict Over Convoys*, p. 41.

3 Memorandum of 6 February 1941 cited in Churchill, *The Grand Alliance*, p. 649.

4 Calder, *The People's War*, p. 266.

5 Collingham, *The Taste of War*, p. 108.

6 Churchill, *Their Finest Hour*, p. 495.

7 Ibid., p. 503.

8 Smith, *Conflict Over Convoys*, p. 36.

9 Churchill, *The Grand Alliance*, p. 111.

10 Smith, *Conflict Over Convoys*, p. 67.

11 Ibid., p. 68.

12 Collingham, *The Taste of War*, p. 109.

13 Calder, *The People's War*, p. 275.

14 Mass Observation Diary, cited ibid., pp. 292–3.

15 Ibid., p. 293.

16 Broad and Fleming, *Nella Last's War*, p. 193.

17 Monsarrat, *Three Corvettes*, p. 120.

18 Calder, *The People's War*, p. 319.

19 Ibid., p. 317.

20 Monsarrat, *Three Corvettes*, p. 121.

21 Churchill, *The Grand Alliance*, p. 723.

22 Ibid., p. 689.

23 Ibid., p. 755.

24 Sherwood, *Papers of Harry L. Hopkins*, Vol. I, p. 388.

25 Dallek, *Roosevelt and American Foreign Policy*, p. 293.

26 Churchill, *The Grand Alliance*, p. 405.

27 Ibid., pp. 405–7.

28 Cripps to Eden, 4 September 1941, TNA FO 954/24, in Gilbert, *The Ever-Widening War*, p. 1159.

29 Churchill to Cripps, 5 September 1941, TNA PREM 3/401/1, ibid., p. 1171.

30 Churchill to Roosevelt, 5 September 1941, Churchill, *The Grand Alliance*, p. 409.

31 Hopkins to Churchill, 29 September 1941, cited in Dallek, *Roosevelt and American Foreign Policy*, p. 296.

32 Churchill, *The Grand Alliance*, p. 402.

33 Churchill to Stalin, 21 September, ibid., p. 414.

34 Roosevelt to Churchill, 8 October 1941, cited in Dallek, *Roosevelt and American Foreign Policy*, p. 296.

35 Churchill, *The Grand Alliance*, p. 402.

36 Ibid., p. 418.

37 Code Radiogram received at the War Department, 11.06, 10 October 1941, Russia Attacked, 39(b), Harry L. Hopkins Files, Book 4, FDR Library, Hyde Park, N Y.

38 Hopkins to Stimson, 14 October 1941, ibid.

39 Dönitz, *Memoirs*, p. 143.

40 Roskill, *The Defensive*, pp. 528, 536.

41 Bird, *Erich Raeder*, p. 170.

42 War Cabinet Directive, 28 April 1941, TNA CAB 120/10, cited in Gilbert, *The Ever Widening War*, p. 556.

43 Cunningham to Pound, 15 March 1942, cited in Michael Simpson, *A Life of Admiral of the Fleet Andrew Cunningham: A Twentieth-Century Naval Leader* (Frank Cass, 2006), p. 125.

## 11 *Shifting Fortunes*

1 Cited in Martin Kitchen, *Rommel's Desert War* (Cambridge University Press, 2009), p. 136.

2 Dönitz, *Memoirs*, p. 159.

3 Ibid., p. 161.

4 Ibid., p. 160.

5 Roskill, *The Defensive*, p. 540.

6 Churchill, *The Grand Alliance*, p. 512.

7 Creighton, *Convoy Commodore*, p. 134.

8 Ibid., pp. 132–6.

9 Ibid., pp. 140–42.

10 Ibid., p. 144.

11 SL87: Report of proceedings on Convoy and Court of Inquiry re. loss of ships (D/Key/4–5), Merseyside Maritime Museum, Liverpool.

12 Ibid.

13 *Northern Whig*, 14 October 1941 (D/Key/4–5), Merseyside Maritime Museum, Liverpool.

14 Winston S. Churchill to A. V. Alexander and Admiral Pound (Churchill Papers, 20/36), Gilbert, *The Ever-Widening War*, p. 1410.

15 Terence Robertson, *Walker RN: Britain's Ace U-Boat Killer* (Pan Books, 1958), p. 23.

16 Ibid., p. 28.

17 Ibid., p. 31.

18 Ibid., p. 33.

19 Ibid., p. 38.

20 Williams, *Battle of the Atlantic*, p. 158.

21 Robertson, *Walker RN*, p. 46.

22 Williams, *Battle of the Atlantic*, p. 159.

23 Robertson, *Walker RN*, p. 59.

24 Walker's War Diary, cited ibid., p. 53.

25 Ibid., p. 56.

26 Cited in Roskill, *The Defensive*, p. 467.

27 Dönitz, *Memoirs*, pp. 181–2.

## 12 Beating the Drum

1 Heinrichs, *Threshold of War*, p. 177.

2 Dönitz, *Memoirs*, p. 193.

3 Padfield, *Dönitz*, p. 236.

4 Map Room Files, Box 36, Military Files Series 1, FDR Library, Hyde Park, NY.

5 Navy Training Manual, cited in Morison, *The Battle of the Atlantic*, p. 127.

6 Interview by Michael Gannon, cited in Michael Gannon, *Operation Drumbeat* (Naval Institute Press, 1990), p. 136.

7 Ibid., p. 216.

8 Ibid.

9 Gary Gentile, *Track of the Gray Wolf: U-Boat Warfare on the US Eastern Seaboard, 1942–1945* (Avon, 1989), p. 12.

10 Ibid., p. 23.

11 Ibid.

12 Ibid., p. 24.

13 Ibid.

14 Morison, *The Battle of the Atlantic*, p. 130.

15 Dönitz, *Memoirs*, p. 202.

16 Ibid., p. 203.

17 Ibid.

18 Gentile, *Track of the Gray Wolf*, p. 126.

19 Gannon, *Operation Drumbeat*, p. 275.

20 Memorandum for the Secretary of the Navy, 26 February 1942, Box 169, A-16/3, FDR Library, Hyde Park, NY.

21 Ibid.

22 Ibid.

23 Roosevelt to Rear Admiral Adolphus Andrews, 9 March 1942, Navy Folder 2–42, A-16/1, FDR Library, Hyde Park, NY.

24 Robert H. Ferrell (ed.), *The Eisenhower Diaries* (W. W. Norton, 1981), entry for 10 March 1942, p. 50.

25 Quoted in Thomas B. Buell, *Master of Sea Power: A Biography of Fleet Admiral Ernest J. King* (Naval Institute Press, 2012), p. 187.

26 Ernest J. King and Walter Muir Whitehill, *Fleet Admiral King: A Naval Record* (W. W. Norton, 1952), p. 238.

27 Ibid., p. 239.

28 Ibid.

29 Eastern Sea Frontier, March 1942, p. 254, cited in Gannon, *Operation Drumbeat*, p. 352.

30 Harriman to Hopkins, 7 March 1942, Box 308, Harry L. Hopkins Files, Book 5, FDR Library, Hyde Park, NY.

31 Churchill, *The Grand Alliance*, pp. 539–40.

32 Ibid., p. 571.

33 Dallek, *Roosevelt and American Foreign Policy*, p. 331.

34 Harry L. Hopkins Files, Book 5, FDR Library, Hyde Park, NY.

35 Ibid.

36 Smith, *Conflict Over Convoys*, p. 73.

37 Comments by S. McKee quoted ibid., p. 85.

38  Winston Churchill, *The Second World War*, Vol. IV: *The Hinge of Fate* (Cassell, 1950), p. 103.

39  Ibid., p. 102.

40  Churchill to Hopkins, 12 March 1942, ibid., p. 104.

41  Roosevelt to Churchill, 20 March 1942, ibid., p. 105.

42  Churchill to Roosevelt, 29 March 1942, ibid.

43  Alexander to Churchill, 13 April 1942, TNA PREM 3/97/1.

44  Leathers to Hopkins, Box 308, Harry L. Hopkins Files, Book 5, FDR Library, Hyde Park, NY.

45  Memorandum on Shipping Losses from Mr Lubin [Joseph Lubin, Special Deputy Chief Investigator of the War Production Board], 17 April 1942, PSF Safe File, Lubin, Isador, Box 3, FDR Library, Hyde Park, NY.

46  Dönitz, War Diary, 15 April 1942, quoted in Dan van der Vat, *The Atlantic Campaign: The Great Struggle at Sea, 1939–1945* (Birlinn, 2001), p. 377.

47  Quoted in Gannon, *Operation Drumbeat*, p. 339.

48  Eastern Sea Frontier (ESF), Navy, November 1943, cited ibid., p. 344.

49  ESF, November 1943, cited ibid., p. 344.

50  Quoted in Gentile, *Track of the Gray Wolf*, p. 89.

51  ESF, November 1943, cited in Gannon, *Operation Drumbeat*, p. 345.

52  Morison, *The Battle of the Atlantic*, p. 130.

53  Gannon, *Operation Drumbeat*, p. 345.

54  Cremer, *U-333*, p. 98.

55  Personal letter from Roosevelt to Andrews, 24 June 1942, FDR Library, Hyde Park, NY.

56  King, *Fleet Admiral King*, p. 238.

57  King to Commanders, ESF and GSF [Gulf Sea Frontier], 17 June 1942, ESF, July 1942, chapter 10, pp. 1–10, cited in Gannon, *Operation Drumbeat*, p. 352.

58  Marshall to King, 19 June 1942, quoted in King, *Fleet Admiral King*, pp. 246–7.

59  King to Marshall, 21 June 1942, quoted ibid., pp. 247–8.

60  Roosevelt to King, 7 July 1942, Box 169, A-16/3, Warfare, November 1941 to October 1944, FDR Library, Hyde Park, NY.

61  King to Roosevelt, 9 July 1942, ibid.

62  King, *Fleet Admiral King*, p. 239.

63  See, for example, Blair, *Hitler's U-Boat War, passim*.

64  Morison, *The Battle of the Atlantic*, pp. 200–201.

65  Memorandum, Lubin to Roosevelt, 15 July 1942, PSF Safe File, Lubin, Isador, Box 3, FDR Library, Hyde Park, NY.

## 13 *Overstretched Everywhere*

1 Churchill, *The Hinge of Fate*, p. 342.

2 Roberts, *Masters and Commanders*, p. 206.

3 Churchill, *The Hinge of Fate*, pp. 343–4.

4 The Shermans were to make a crucial contribution to the Eighth Army's victory at El Alamein in November 1942.

5 Churchill, *The Hinge of Fate*, p. 272.

6 Ibid., pp. 275–6.

7 Arthur, *Lost Voices*, pp. 350–51.

8 Ibid., pp. 357–8 (Treves), 359–60 (Jackson).

9 Ibid., p. 371.

10 Roberts, *Masters and Commanders*, p. 111.

11 Quoted ibid., p. 190.

12 Conversation with author, cited in Jonathan Dimbleby, *Russia: A Journey to the Heart of a Land and Its People* (BBC Books, 2008), p. 19.

13 Bird, *Erich Raeder*, pp. 185–6.

14 S. W. Roskill, *The War At Sea, 1939–45*, Vol. II: *The Period of Balance* (Naval & Military Press, 2004), p. 116.

15 *The Times*, 14 February 1942.

16 Roskill, *Period of Balance*, p. 151.

17 Churchill, *The Hinge of Fate*, p. 100.

18 Roskill, *Period of Balance*, p. 158.

19 Churchill, *The Hinge of Fate*, p. 229.

20 Ibid., p. 200.

21 Churchill to Tovey, 22 January 1942, cited in Roskill, *Churchill and the Admirals*, p. 131.

22 Roskill, *Period of Balance*, p. 124.

23 David Irving, *The Destruction of Convoy PQ-17* (St Martin's Press, 1987), p. 3.

24 'Arctic Convoys, 1941–1945, Battle Summary No. 22' (1954), TNA ADM 234/369, p. 312.

25 John L. Haynes, *Frozen Fury: The Murmansk Run of Convoy PQ-13* (America Star Books, 2010), p. 28.

26 Ibid.

27 Ibid., p. 29.

28 Ibid.

29 Brodhurst, *Churchill's Anchor*, p. 237.

30 *Correspondence Between Stalin, Roosevelt, Truman, Churchill and Attlee During WWII*, comp. Ministry of Foreign Affairs of the USSR (University Press of the Pacific, 2001), p. 22.

31 'Urgent' telegram, Hopkins to Churchill, 24 April 1942, Box 308, Harry L. Hopkins Files, Book 5, FDR Library, Hyde Park, NY.

32 Roosevelt to Churchill, 26 April 1942, Loewenheim et al. (eds), *Roosevelt and Churchill*, p. 210.

33 Ibid., p. 211.

34 Brodhurst, *Churchill's Anchor*, p. 237.

35 Churchill, *The Hinge of Fate*, p. 231.

36 Ibid., pp. 231–2.

37 David Moore, 'HMS *Edinburgh*', *Warship World* 3(8) (Autumn 1990); BBC archive, WW2 People's War, www.bbc.co.uk/history/ww2peopleswar/stories/18/a2076518.shtml.

38 Ibid.

39 Roskill, *Period of Balance*, p. 130.

40 Brodhurst, *Churchill's Anchor*, p. 238.

41 Churchill, *The Hinge of Fate*, p. 232.

42 Ibid., p. 233.

43 Roskill, *Churchill and the Admirals*, p. 130.

44 Churchill, *The Hinge of Fate*, p. 234.

45 Morison, *The Battle of the Atlantic*, p. 173.

46 Roskill, *Period of Balance*, p. 131.

## 14 *Disaster in the Arctic*

1 Churchill, *The Hinge of Fate*, p. 392. Douglas Porch, *Hitler's Mediterranean Gamble: The North African and the Mediterranean Campaigns in World War II* (Cassell, 2004), p. 261.

2 Broad and Fleming, *Nella Last's War*, 25 June 1942, p. 209.

3 Hansard, House of Commons Debates, Vol. 381, 2 July 1942, cols 527–611.

4 Ibid., cols 224–476.

5 Ibid., cols 527–611.

6 Irving, *The Destruction of Convoy PQ-17*, p. 52.

7 Churchill, *The Hinge of Fate*, p. 237.

8 Bird, *Erich Raeder*, p. 187.

9 Ibid.

10 'Arctic Convoys, 1941–1945, Battle Summary No. 22', p. 54n.

11 Ibid.

12 Ibid.

13 Schniewind Operation Order, 14 June 1942, Fifth Air Force War Diary, quoted in Irving, *The Destruction of Convoy PQ-17*, p. 29.

14 Führer Naval Conference, 12 March 1942, File PG/32187, cited ibid., p. 10.

15 Captain Jack Broome, *Convoy is to Scatter* (William Kimber, 1972), p. 136.

16 Ibid., p. 137.

17 'Arctic Convoys, 1941–1945, Battle Summary No. 22', pp. 59–60.

18 Diary of *Bellingham*'s second officer, cited in Irving, *The Destruction of Convoy PQ-17*, p. 116.

19 Report of commanding officer, HMS *Keppel*, cited in 'Arctic Convoys, 1941–1945, Battle Summary No. 22', p. 60.

20 Walker, Department of Documents, Imperial War Museum, quoted in Glyn Prysor, *Citizen Sailors: The Royal Navy in the Second World War* (Penguin, 2012), p. 250.

21 From *The Sundial*, USS *Wichita*'s newspaper, 5 July 1942, cited in Irving, *The Destruction of Convoy PQ-17*, p. 116.

22 As reported ibid., p. 117, on the basis of an interview with *El Capitan*'s second officer, Captain Rupert Hall.

23 Broome, *Convoy is to Scatter*, p. 167.

24 Hinsley et al., *British Intelligence in the Second World War*, Vol. II, p. 216.

25 Ibid., p. 217.

26 Captain Mervyn Stone, *Olopana*'s voyage report, cited in Irving, *The Destruction of Convoy PQ-17*, p. 49.

27 Hinsley et al., *British Intelligence in the Second World War*, Vol. II, p. 216.

28 Ibid., p. 216.

29 Ibid., Appendix 11, p. 688.

30 Brodhurst, *Churchill's Anchor*, p. 243.

31 Hinsley et al., *British Intelligence in the Second World War*, Vol. II, p. 218.

32 'Arctic Convoys, 1941–1945, Battle Summary No. 22', p. 55.

33 Ibid.

34 Roskill, *Churchill and the Admirals*, p. 130.

35 Brodhurst, *Churchill's Anchor*, p. 246.

36 'Arctic Convoys, 1941–1945, Battle Summary No. 22', p. 62.

37 Brodhurst, *Churchill's Anchor*, p. 246.

38 Ibid., p. 247.

39 Broome, *Convoy is to Scatter*, pp. 182 and 187.

40 Roskill, *Period of Balance*, p. 139.

41 'Arctic Convoys, 1941–1945, Battle Summary No. 22', p. 62.

42 Ibid., p. 63.

43 Cited in Irving, *The Destruction of Convoy PQ-17*, p. 148.

44 Cited in Brodhurst, *Churchill's Anchor*, p. 24.

45 Cited in Broome, *Convoy is to Scatter*, p. 196.

46 Ibid., p. 192.

47 Diary of Nathaniel Platt, 4 July 1942, cited in Irving, *The Destruction of Convoy PQ-17*, p. 342.

48 Ibid., p. 136.

49 Ibid., p. 106.

50 Naval Group North's War Diary, 4 July 1942, quoted ibid., p. 107.

51 Raeder to Admiral Rolf Carls (Group Command North) cited in Bird, *Erich Raeder*, p. 188.

52 Cited in Irving, *The Destruction of Convoy PQ-17*, p. 183.

53 Broome, *Convoy is to Scatter*, p. 206.

54 Diary fragment by unnamed crewman, 'Life on HMS *Pozarica* in Convoy 17', Liverpool Maritime Archives and Library, Liverpool, ref. 0X1484.

55 Paul Lund and Harry Ludlam, *I Was There on PQ17, the Convoy to Hell* (Foulsham, 1968, repr. 2010), p. 101.

56 The *Bolton Castle*'s master, Captain Pascoe, quoted in Woodman, *The Real Cruel Sea*, p. 228.

57 Quoted in Irving, *The Destruction of Convoy PQ-17*, p. 195.

58 Lund and Ludlam, *I Was There*, p. 119.

59 *Olopana*'s ship's report, cited in Irving, *The Destruction of Convoy PQ-17*, p. 234.

60 Lund and Ludlam, *I Was There*, p. 114.

61 Richard Woodman, *Arctic Convoys, 1941–1945* (Pen and Sword, 2004), p. 239.

62 Needham Forth's Diary, 7 July 1942, quoted in Irving, *The Destruction of Convoy PQ-17*, p. 251.

63 Ibid., p. 253.

64 Lund and Ludlam, *I Was There*, p. 175.

65 Woodman, *Arctic Convoys 1941–1945*, p. 240.

66 Lund and Ludlam, *I Was There*, p. 120.

67 Irving, *The Destruction of Convoy PQ-17*, p. 296.

68 Ibid.

69 Woodman, *Arctic Convoys, 1941–1945*, p. 238.

70 Ibid., p. 235.

71 German Naval Staff War Diary, cited in Irving, *The Destruction of Convoy PQ-17*, p. 271.

72 Lund and Ludlam, *I Was There*, pp. 128–9.

73 Quoted ibid., p. 134.

74 Ibid., p. 136.

75 List of PQ17 signals maintained by Lieutenant Caradus in HMS *La Malouine*, cited in Irving, *The Destruction of Convoy PQ-17*, p. 145.

76 Narrative by Ensign Howard E. Carraway, 26 March 1945, quoted ibid., p. 146.

77 Quoted in Lund and Ludlam, *I Was There*, pp. 181–2.

78 Quoted in Irving, *The Destruction of Convoy PQ-17*, p. 299.

79 Woodman, *Arctic Convoys, 1941–1945*, p. 256.

80 Ibid.

81 Quoted ibid., p. 253.

## 15 *Goading the Bear*

1 Hansard, House of Commons Debates, Vol. 382, 29 July 1942, col. 489.

2 *The Times*, 29 September 1942, cited in Irving, *The Destruction of Convoy PQ-17*, p. 323.

3 Edwards/Drummond cable, 11 July 1942, 2021/2002, PSF Safe File, Hopkins, Harry, FDR Library, Hyde Park, NY.

4 Prime Minister to General Ismay for C.O.S. Committee, 17 May 1942, Churchill, *The Hinge of Fate*, p. 234.

5 Ibid., p. 238.

6 Ibid.

7 Ibid., pp. 238–9.

8 Ibid., p. 239.

9 Churchill to Roosevelt, 14 July 1942, Loewenheim et al. (eds), *Roosevelt and Churchill*, p. 223.

10 Roosevelt to Churchill, 15 July 1942, ibid., p. 224.

11 Churchill to Stalin, 17 July 1942, Churchill, *The Hinge of Fate*, p. 240.

12 Ibid., p. 241.

13 Stalin to Churchill, 23 July 1944, ibid., pp. 241–2.

14 Churchill to Stalin 17 July 1942, ibid., p. 240.

15 *Foreign Relations of the United States* (1942), cited in Roberts, *Masters and Commanders*, p. 176.

16 Stalin to Churchill, 23 July 1942, Churchill, *The Hinge of Fate*, p. 242.

17 Martin Gilbert, *Winston S. Churchill*, Vol. VII: *Road to Victory, 1941–45* (Heinemann, 1986), p. 149.

18  Roberts, *Masters and Commanders*, p. 251.

19  Dilks (ed.), *Diaries of Sir Alexander Cadogan*, entry for 15 July 1942, p. 462.

20  Roosevelt to Hopkins, Marshall and King, 23 July 1942, PSF Safe File, Hopkins, Harry, FDR Library, Hyde Park, NY.

21  Roosevelt to Churchill, 27 July 1942, Loewenheim et al. (eds), *Roosevelt and Churchill*, p. 227.

22  Stalin to Churchill, 31 July 1942, Churchill, *The Hinge of Fate*, p. 410.

23  Ibid., p. 428.

24  Ibid., p. 430.

25  Robert E. Sherwood, *The White House Papers of Harry L. Hopkins*, Vol. II: *January 1942 – July 1945* (Eyre and Spottiswoode, 1949), p. 618.

26  Ibid., p. 619.

27  Ibid., p. 620.

28  Ibid.

29  Loewenheim et al. (eds), *Roosevelt and Churchill*, p. 241.

30  Roskill, *Period of Balance*, p. 280.

31  Raeder statement at conference with Hitler, cited in Bird, *Erich Raeder*, p. 189.

32  Admiralty Memorandum, 19 August 1942, 23 July, PSF Safe File, Hopkins, Harry, FDR Library, Hyde Park, NY.

33  Field Marshal Lord Alanbrooke, *War Diaries, 1939–45*, ed. Alex Danchev and Daniel Todman (Phoenix Press, 2002), entry for 4 February 1942, p. 227.

34  Churchill to Roosevelt, 22 September 1942, Churchill, *The Hinge of Fate*, p. 513.

35  Roosevelt to Churchill, 27 September 1942, ibid.

36  Roosevelt to Churchill, 5 October 1942, quoted in Sherwood, *Papers of Harry L. Hopkins*, Vol. II, p. 636.

37  Telegram via the Russian ambassador, 5 October 1942, Churchill, *The Hinge of Fate*, p. 517.

38  Reply to question from Henry C. Cassidy, Associated Press, *St Petersburg Times*, Florida, 6 October 1942.

39  Stalin to Roosevelt, 7 October 1942, *Correspondence between Stalin, Roosevelt, Truman, Churchill and Attlee*, p. 35.

40  Roosevelt to Churchill, 5 October 1942, quoted in Sherwood, *Papers of Harry L. Hopkins*, Vol. II, p. 637.

41  Churchill to Roosevelt, 7 October 1942, Churchill, *The Hinge of Fate*, p. 518.

42  Ibid., p. 519.

43  Ibid., p. 520.

44  Roosevelt to Churchill, 27 October 1942, Loewenheim et al. (eds), *Roosevelt and Churchill*, p. 261.

45 Roosevelt to Stalin (received), 15 October 1942, *Correspondence between Stalin, Roosevelt, Truman, Churchill and Attlee*, p. 38.

46 Stalin to Roosevelt, 19 October 1942, ibid.

47 Note to Foreign Secretary, 27 October 1942, Churchill, *The Hinge of Fate*, p. 521.

48 Roosevelt to Churchill, 27 October 1942, Loewenheim et al. (eds), *Roosevelt and Churchill*, p. 261.

49 Ibid., p. 262.

## *16 Dönitz Seizes His Chance*

1 Dönitz, *Memoirs*, p. 263.

2 Williams, *Battle of the Atlantic*, p. 214.

3 Ibid.

4 Doris Hawkins, *Atlantic Torpedo* (1943), quoted in Léonce Peillard, *The Laconia Affair*, trans. Oliver Coburn (Bantam, 1983), p. 44.

5 Williams, *Battle of the Atlantic*, p. 215.

6 Peillard, *The Laconia Affair*, p. 63.

7 Ibid.

8 Quoted ibid., p. 72.

9 Dönitz, *Memoirs*, p. 256.

10 Ibid., p. 257.

11 Ibid.

12 Quoted in Peillard, *The Laconia Affair*, p. 118.

13 Williams, *Battle of the Atlantic*, p. 217.

14 Ibid., p. 218.

15 Hartenstein's War Diary, cited in Dönitz, *Memoirs*, p. 258.

16 M. Maurer and Lawrence J. Paszek, 'Origin of the Laconia Order', *Air University Review*, Maxwell Air Force Base, Alabama, USA, repr. *Journal of the Royal United Service Institute for Defence Studies* 109(636) (November 1964): 338–44, p. 342.

17 Ibid.

18 Ibid.

19 Dönitz, *Memoirs*, p. 259.

20 Ibid., p. 260.

21 Williams, *Battle of the Atlantic*, p. 219.

22 Peillard, *The Laconia Affair*, pp. 219–23.

23 Doris Hawkins, quoted ibid., p. 187.

24 Ibid., p. 189.

25  Dönitz, *Memoirs*, p. 261.

26  Padfield, *Dönitz*, p. 255.

27  U-boat War Diary, 30 November 1942, cited in Padfield, *Dönitz*, pp. 260–61.

28  Churchill to Roosevelt, 31 October 1942, Loewenheim et al. (eds), *Roosevelt and Churchill*, pp. 262–3.

29  Ibid., p. 264.

30  Smith, *Conflict Over Convoys*, p. 107.

31  Ibid., p. 83.

32  Ibid., p. 85.

33  Ibid., p. 82.

34  Ibid., p. 88.

35  Roskill, *Period of Balance*, p. 217.

36  Ibid.

37  Roosevelt to Churchill, 30 November 1942, Loewenheim et al. (eds), *Roosevelt and Churchill*, pp. 288–90.

38  Quoted in Smith, *Conflict Over Convoys*, p. 114.

39  Churchill to Roosevelt, 17 December 1942, Loewenheim et al. (eds), *Roosevelt and Churchill*, pp. 296–7.

40  Churchill to Roosevelt, 30 December 1942, cited in Smith, *Conflict Over Convoys*, p. 132.

41  Roskill, *Period of Balance*, p. 218.

## 17 *Changes at the Top*

1  U-boat War Diary, 14 December 1942, cited in Padfield, *Dönitz*, p. 261.

2  Ibid.

3  Cited in Bird, *Erich Raeder*, p. 201.

4  Ibid., p. 190.

5  Raeder's notes of 6 January meeting with Hitler (dated 11 January 1943), quoted in ibid., p. 203.

6  Albert Speer, *Inside the Third Reich* (Weidenfeld and Nicolson, 1970), p. 272.

7  Raeder to Hitler, 14 January 1943, cited in Padfield, *Dönitz*, p. 263.

8  Quoted in Terraine, *Business in Great Waters*, p. 522.

9  Padfield, *Dönitz*, p. 270.

10  Directive of 5 February 1943, cited ibid.

11  Dönitz, *Memoirs*, p. 310.

12  Ibid., p. 311.

13  Roskill, *Period of Balance*, p. 355.

14 Dönitz, *Memoirs*, pp. 318–19.

15 Woodman, *The Real Cruel Sea*, p. 580.

16 Ibid., p. 583.

17 Ibid., p. 584.

## 18 'The Battle of the Air'

1 Letter of 6 December 1942, *Correspondence between Stalin, Roosevelt, Truman, Churchill and Attlee*, p. 43.

2 Letter of 14 December 1942, ibid., p. 44.

3 Alanbrooke, *War Diaries*, entry for 18 January 1943, p. 361.

4 Sherwood, *Papers of Harry L. Hopkins*, Vol. II, p. 671.

5 Marshall, quoted in Dallek, *Roosevelt and American Foreign Policy*, p. 371.

6 Alanbrooke, *War Diaries*, entry for 14 January 1943, p. 359.

7 Ibid., entry for 20 January 1943, p. 364.

8 Note dictated on 22 January 1943, quoted in Sherwood, *Papers of Harry L. Hopkins*, Vol. II, p. 685.

9 Diary entry for 22 January 1943 in Lord Moran, *Churchill At War, 1940–45* (Constable and Robinson, 2002), p. 97.

10 Dallek, *Roosevelt and American Foreign Policy*, p. 377.

11 Churchill, *The Hinge of Fate*, p. 619.

12 Letter to Air Officer Commanding-in-Chief, Bomber Command, from Air Vice-Marshal Bottomley, Assistant Chief of the Air Staff (Operations), 14 January 1943, TNA AIR 8/424.

13 Letter to Air Officer Commanding-in-Chief, Bomber Command, from Air Vice-Marshal Bottomley, Assistant Chief of the Air Staff (Operations), 23 January 1943, ibid.

14 Note by Harris, 27 January 1943, ibid.

15 Air Historical Branch records 11/117/3(C) , pp. 30–31, cited in Terraine, *The Right of the Line*, p. 413.

16 Pound Memorandum, TNA CAB 86/3 1943/01/11.

17 Roskill, *Period of Balance*, p. 352.

18 Ibid.

19 Prime Minister to Minister of Aircraft Production, 8 July 1940, Churchill, *Their Finest Hour*, p. 567.

20 Report by D. M. B. Butt, for War Cabinet, cited in Terraine, *The Right of the Line*, p. 293.

21 Portal to Churchill, 25 September 1941, cited ibid., p. 295.

22 Pound to Churchill, 31 July 1941, AHB 11/117/1(C), cited ibid., pp. 290–91.

23 Churchill to Portal, 27 September 1941, cited ibid., p. 295.

24 Churchill to Portal 7 October 1941, Churchill, *The Grand Alliance*, p. 451.

25 Roskill, *Churchill and the Admirals*, p. 138.

26 Whitworth to Admiral Cunningham, 15 December 1942, cited in Brodhurst, *Churchill's Anchor*, p. 265.

27 Churchill to Roosevelt, 31 October 1942, in Loewenheim et al. (eds), *Roosevelt and Churchill*, p. 262.

28 Ibid.

29 Henry Probert, *Bomber Harris: His Life and Times* (Greenhill, 2006), p. 190.

30 Ibid., p. 155.

31 Ibid., p. 138.

32 Ibid.

33 Cited in Hastings, *Bomber Command*, p. 154.

34 Ibid., p. 157.

35 Ibid., p. 158.

36 Ibid., p. 159.

37 'Report of Committee on Winter Campaign of 1941–1942 in the Battle of the Atlantic dated 6th May 1941', Naval Staff History, Vol. 1A, Appendix 10, p. 345.

38 Macintyre, *Battle of the Atlantic*, p. 117.

39 Richard Goette, 'Britain and the Delay in Closing the Mid-Atlantic "Air Gap" During the Battle of the Atlantic', *Northern Mariner* 15(4) (October 2005): 19–41, p. 26.

40 Ibid.

41 Memorandum by the First Lord of the Admiralty, 11 January 1942, TNA CAB 86/3.

42 30th Meeting of the Battle of the Atlantic Committee, 10 February 1942, and A. V. Alexander, First Lord of the Admiralty, to the War Cabinet Defence Committee, 'Requirements of Long Range G/R Aircraft for Coastal Command and the Indian Ocean', 14 February 1942, TNA ADM 205/23 and PREM 3/97/1; cited in Goette, 'Britain and the Delay', p. 27.

43 Brodhurst, *Churchill's Anchor*, p. 263.

44 Air Requirements for the Successful Prosecution of the War at Sea, TNA AIR 19/9/243.

45 Air Staff paper, cited in Brodhurst, *Churchill's Anchor*, p. 266.

46 Alanbrooke, *War Diaries*, entry for 19 March 1942, p. 240.

47 Philip Joubert de la Ferté, *Birds and Fishes: The Story of Coastal Command* (Hutchinson, 1960), p. 150.

48 Cited in Brodhurst, *Churchill's Anchor*, p. 269.

49 Alanbrooke, *War Diaries*, entry for 17 February 1942, p. 230.

50 Kennedy, *The Business of War*, pp. 246–7.

51 Hastings, *Bomber Command*, p. 184.

52 Probert, *Bomber Harris*, p. 185.

53 Hastings, *Bomber Command*, p. 186.

54 Probert, *Bomber Harris*, p. 185.

55 Hastings, *Bomber Command*, p. 188.

56 Ibid.

57 As reported by Anthony Montague Browne, Churchill's last private secretary, cited in Hastings, *Bomber Command*, p. 166.

58 Harris to Churchill, June 1942, TNA AIR 14/3507.

59 Probert, *Bomber Harris*, p. 160.

60 Portal Papers, Christ Church Library, Oxford, Folder H81, E139, October 1942, Portal Folder 9, E63, cited ibid., p. 143.

61 Quoted ibid.

62 Cited in Brodhurst, *Churchill's Anchor*, p. 270.

63 Teddy Suhren with Fritz Brustat-Naval, *Teddy Suhren Ace of Aces*, trans. Frank James (Chatham Publishing, 2011), pp. 127–8.

64 U-boat War Diary, 3 September 1942, cited in Goette, 'Britain and the Delay', p. 24.

65 Dönitz, *Memoirs*, p. 242.

66 U-boat War Diary, 3 September 1942, cited in Goette, 'Britain and the Delay', p. 24.

67 Defence Committee minutes, 5 October 1942, TNA CAB 66/30 WP (42), p. 311, cited in Brodhurst, *Churchill's Anchor*, p. 300.

68 War Cabinet Memorandum by the Minister of Defence, 24 October 1942, Policy for the Conduct of the War, TNA CAB 66/30 1942.

69 Sir John Slessor, *The Central Blue: The Autobiography of Sir John Slessor, Marshal of the RAF* (Praeger, 1957), p. 498.

70 Ibid., p. 499.

71 Ibid., p. 505.

72 Professor Patrick Blackett, 'Recollections of Problems Studied, 1940–45', *Brassey's Annual* (1953), cited in Macintyre, *The Battle of the Atlantic*, p. 153.

73 Churchill to Roosevelt, 20 November 1942, Loewenheim et al. (eds), *Roosevelt and Churchill*, p. 282.

## *19 A Very Narrow Escape*

1 Hans Goebeler with John Vanzo, *Steel Boat, Iron Hearts: A U-Boat Crewman's Life Aboard U-505* (Savas Beatie, 2013), p. 104.

2 Herbert A. Werner, *Iron Coffins: A U-Boat Commander's War, 1939–1945* (Cassell, 1999), p. 90.

3 Macintyre, *U-Boat Killer* (Cassell, 1999 edn), p. 113.

4 Werner, *Iron Coffins*, pp. 92–3, for this and the following.

5 Martin Middlebrook, *Convoy: The Battle for Convoys SC.122 and HX.229* (Penguin, 1978), p. 247.

6 Second Officer W. A. Clarke-Hunt, quoted ibid., p. 250.

7 Quoted ibid., pp. 248–9.

8 Morison, *The Battle of the Atlantic*, p. 343.

9 Quoted in Woodman, *The Real Cruel Sea*, p. 620.

10 Second Officer G. D. Williams, quoted in Middlebrook, *Convoy*, p. 252.

11 Werner, *Iron Coffins*, pp. 99–102.

12 Woodman, *The Real Cruel Sea*, p. 538.

13 Roskill, *Period of Balance*, p. 367.

14 Ibid.

15 Ibid.

16 Wilson, *The First Summit*, p. 242.

17 Rear Admiral R. B. Darke, quoted in Rear Admiral W. S. Chalmers, *Max Horton and the Western Approaches* (Hodder and Stoughton, 1954), p. 77.

18 Roskill, *Period of Balance*, p. 217.

19 Letter from Admiral W. W. Fisher, Chief of Staff, Atlantic Fleet, 25 May 1924, quoted in Chalmers, *Max Horton*, p. 29.

20 Gretton, *Convoy Escort Commander*, p. 115.

21 Quoted in Chalmers, *Max Horton*, p. 207.

22 Unnamed officer quoted in Terraine, *Business in Great Waters*, p. 503.

23 Quoted in Chalmers, *Max Horton*, p. 160.

24 Ibid., p. 165.

25 Ibid., pp. 175–6.

26 Quoted from minutes of Anti-U-Boat Warfare Committee, 22 and 30 March 1943, cited in Hinsley et al., *British Intelligence in the Second World War*, Vol. II, p. 563.

27 Extract from A.U. (43), 12th Meeting, held on Wednesday, 24 March 1943 – Re-Equipment of Coastal Command Squadrons with Liberators, TNA AIR 8/1398.

28 Cherwell to Churchill, 25 March 1943 (copied to Alexander and Pound), cited in Roskill, *Churchill and the Admirals*, p. 228.

29 Memorandum by the Air Officer, Commanding-in-Chief, Bomber Command, 26 March 1943, TNA AIR 14/1454.

30 Roosevelt and Churchill to Stalin, 26 January 1943, Churchill, *The Hinge of Fate*, pp. 664–5.

31 Churchill to Stalin, 9 February 1943, ibid., p. 666.

32 Stalin to Churchill, 16 February 1943, ibid., p. 668.

33 Moran, *Churchill at War*, p. 106.

34 Cited in Prime Minister to General Alexander, 24 February 1943, Churchill, *The Hinge of Fate*, p. 660.

35 Prime Minister to Stalin, 24 February 1943, ibid., p. 668.

36 Prime Minister to Stalin, 11 March 1943, ibid., pp. 670–71.

37 Most Secret and Personal Message from Premier J. Stalin to President Roosevelt, 15 March 1943, *Correspondence between Stalin, Roosevelt, Truman, Churchill and Attlee*, p. 59.

38 Roosevelt to Churchill, 28 March 1943, Loewenheim et al. (eds), *Roosevelt and Churchill*, p. 323; Churchill to Stalin 30 March 1943, Churchill, *The Hinge of Fate*, p. 675.

39 Stalin to Churchill, 2 April 1943, ibid., p. 676.

40 Ibid.

## 20 *A Dramatic Turnabout*

1 Werner, *Iron Coffins*, p. 113.

2 Quoted in Padfield, *Dönitz*, p. 276.

3 Werner, *Iron Coffins*, pp. 111–13.

4 Cremer, *U-333*, p. 159.

5 U-boat War Diary, quoted in Cremer, *U-333*, p. 160.

6 Dönitz, *Memoirs*, p. 325.

7 Slessor, *The Central Blue*, p. 514.

8 Quoted in Cremer, *U-333*, p. 163.

9 Quoted in Roskill, *Period of Balance*, p. 369.

10 Ibid., p. 371.

11 Slessor, *The Central Blue*, p. 516.

12 Padfield, *Dönitz*, p. 267.

13 Dönitz, *Memoirs*, p. 132.

14 Ibid., p. 133.

15 Ibid., pp. 131–2.

16 Werner, *Iron Coffins*, p. 116.

17 German Success Against British Codes and Cyphers (by R. T. Barrett), drawn from the secret Admiralty report compiled by Commander Tighe in 1945, TNA ADM 223/505.

18 Ibid.

19 Hinsley and Stripp, *Code Breakers*, p. 80.

20 Sebag-Montefiore, *Enigma*, p. 271.

21 Slessor, *The Central Blue*, p. 499.

22 Gretton, *Convoy Escort Commander*, p. 139.

23 Ibid., p. 145.

24 Ibid., p. 147.

25 Quoted in Woodman, *The Real Cruel Sea*, p. 662.

26 Ibid., p. 664.

27 War and Military Records Online, compiled by Guðmundur Helgason, http://uboat.net/boats/u125.htm.

28 Macintyre, *U-Boat Killer*, p. 123.

29 Dönitz, *Memoirs*, p. 339.

30 Ibid., p. 243.

31 Quoted in Padfield, *Dönitz*, p. 280.

32 Farewell Address to the Nation, 17 January 1961, http://mcadams.posc.mu.edu/ike.htm.

33 Arthur Herman, *Freedom's Forge: How American Business Produced Victory in World War II* (Random House, 2012), p. 138.

34 Henry Kaiser Papers, Bancroft Library, University of California, Berkeley, cited ibid., p. 133.

35 Ibid., p. 180.

36 Morison, *The Battle of the Atlantic*, pp. 293–4.

37 Werner, *Iron Coffins*, p. 118.

38 Ibid., p. 120.

39 Macintyre, *U-Boat Killer*, p. 79.

40 Ibid., p. 81.

41 Werner, *Iron Coffins*, pp. 120–21.

42 Ibid., p. 122.

43 Ibid., pp. 122–3.

44 Macintyre, *U-Boat Killer*, p. 122.

45 Ibid., p. 123.

46 Ibid. for this and what follows.

47 Ibid., p. 131.

48 Werner, *Iron Coffins*, p. 122.

49 Macintyre, *U-Boat Killer*, p. 136.

50 Dönitz, *Memoirs*, p. 340.

51 Padfield, *Dönitz*, p. 296.

52 Admiralty Tracking Room Report, 19 April 1943, quoted ibid., p. 283.

53 U-boat War Diary, 14 May 1943, quoted ibid., p. 297.

54 www.warsailors.com/convoys/hx239.html.

55 Gretton, *Convoy Escort Commander*, p. 156.

56 Ibid., p. 157.

57 Ibid., p. 158.

58 Ibid., p. 159.

59 Alanbrooke, *War Diaries*, entry for 25 May 1943, p. 411.

60 Sherwood, *Papers of Harry L. Hopkins*, Vol. II, p. 726.

61 Gilbert, *Road to Victory*, p. 402.

62 Letter, May 1943, Lord Birkenhead, *Halifax: The Life of Lord Halifax* (Hamish Hamilton, 1965), p. 537, cited in Gilbert, *Road to Victory*, p. 411.

63 Churchill, address to both houses of Congress, 19 May 1943, Winston S. Churchill (ed.), *Never Give In! The Best of Winston Churchill's Speeches, Selected and Edited by his Grandson* (Pimlico, 2007), p. 350.

64 Quoted in Hinsley et al., *British Intelligence in the Second World War*, Vol. II, p. 571.

65 U-boat War Diary, 24 May 1943, cited in Padfield, *Dönitz*, p. 301.

66 Roskill, *Period of Balance*, p. 377.

67 Dönitz, *Memoirs*, p. 341.

68 Ibid.

## 21 The Reckoning

1 Broad and Fleming, *Nella Last's War*, 31 October 1943, p. 250.

2 Ibid., 10 March 1943, p. 235.

3 Ibid., 1 March 1943, p. 232.

4 Quoted in Smith, *Conflict Over Convoys*, p. 133.

5 Quoted in Padfield, *Dönitz*, p. 306.

6 Ibid.

7 Ibid.

8 Quoted in *Führer Conference on Naval Affairs, 1939–45* (Naval Institute Press, 1990), p. 360, cited in Timothy P. Mulligan, *Lone Wolf: The Life and Death of U-Boat Ace Werner Henke* (University of Oklahoma Press, 1995), p. 172.

9  Heinz Schaeffer, *U-Boat 977* (William Kimber, 1953), p. 127.

10  Ibid., p. 128.

11  Werner, *Iron Coffins*, p. 133.

12  Cremer, *U-333*, p. 183.

13  Werner, *Iron Coffins*, p. 174.

14  Padfield, *Dönitz*, p. 329.

15  Quoted ibid., p. 604.

16  Cremer, *U-333*, p. 222.

17  http://uboat.net/fates/losses/1944.htm.

18  Dönitz, *Memoirs*, p. 341.

19  Roskill, *Period of Balance*, Appendix O, p. 485; S. W. Roskill, *The War At Sea, 1939–45*, Vol. III, *The Offensive Part 1: 1st June 1943–31st May 1944* (Naval and Military Press, 2004), Appendix K, p. 389.

20  Quoted in van der Vat, *The Atlantic Campaign*, p. 471.

21  Macintyre, *U-Boat Killer*, p. 148.

22  'Report on Interrogation of Survivors from two 500-Ton U-Boats . . .', www.uboatarchive.net/U-473-765INT.htm.

23  Macintyre, *U-Boat Killer*, p. 151.

24  Churchill, *Closing the Ring*, p. 67.

25  Alanbrooke, *War Diaries*, commentary on entry for 15 August 1943, p. 442.

26  Buell, *Master of Sea Power*, p. 390.

27  Alanbrooke, *War Diaries*, entry for 19 August 1943, p. 444.

28  Roberts, *Masters and Commanders*, p. 405.

29  Alanbrooke, *War Diaries*, commentary on entry for 19 August 1943, pp. 445–6.

30  King, *Fleet Admiral King*, p. 278.

31  Alanbrooke, *War Diaries*, commentary on entry for 19 August 1943, p. 446.

32  Quoted in Buell, *Master of Sea Power*, p. 392.

33  Note from Admiral Noble to Admiral Cunningham, quoted in Brodhurst, *Churchill's Anchor*, p. 283.

34  Medical Report, cited ibid., p. 284.

35  Alanbrooke, *War Diaries*, commentary on entry for 28 August 1943, p. 450.

36  Churchill to Attlee, 25 August 1944, Churchill, *Closing the Ring*, p. 83.

37  Churchill to Roosevelt, 13 June 1943, Loewenheim et al. (eds), *Roosevelt and Churchill*, p. 342; and Personal and Secret Message from Premier J. V. Stalin to the Prime Minister, Mr W. Churchill, 24 June 1943, *Correspondence between Stalin, Roosevelt, Truman, Churchill and Attlee*, p. 74.

38  *Correspondence between Stalin, Roosevelt, Truman, Churchill and Attlee*, p. 76.

39  Churchill to Roosevelt, 12 August 1943, Loewenheim et al. (eds), *Roosevelt and Churchill*, p. 364.

40 Prime Minister's Personal Minute, 25 September 1943, TNA FO/954/3B.

41 This was greatly facilitated by the disabling of *Tirpitz*, which was followed in December by the sinking of *Scharnhorst*. This meant that the Kriegsmarine, despite a few alarums and excursions, thereafter ceased to pose a significant threat in the Arctic – or anywhere else for that matter.

42 Foreign Office to Moscow, 1 October 1943, TNA FO/954/3B.

43 Prime Minister's Personal Minute, 25 September 1943, ibid.

44 Churchill to Stalin, 1 October 1943, Churchill, *Closing the Ring*, pp. 234–7.

45 Stalin to Churchill, 13 October 1943, ibid., pp. 237–9.

46 Ibid., pp. 241–2.

47 Churchill to Roosevelt, 16 October 1943, ibid., p. 240.

48 Foreign Secretary to Prime Minister, 22 October 1943, ibid., p. 243.

49 Foreign Office to Moscow, 3 May 1944, TNA FO/954/3B.

50 Van Tuyll, *Feeding the Bear*, pp. 98–100.

51 Georgii K. Zhukov, *The Memoirs of Marshal Zhukov* (Delacourte Press, 1972), pp. 392, 466, cited in van Tuyll, *Feeding the Bear*, p. 73.

52 Quoted in Edgar L. Erickson, Foreword to Robert Huhn Jones, *The Roads to Russia: United States Lend-Lease to the Soviet Union* (University of Oklahoma Press, 1969), p. vii, cited in van Tuyll, *Feeding the Bear*, p. 73.

53 Alanbrooke, *War Diaries*, entry for 13 October 1943, p. 460.

54 Probert, *Bomber Harris*, p. 194.

55 Hastings, *Bomber Command*, p. 342.

56 Quoted ibid., p. 448.

57 Churchill, *Their Finest Hour*, p. 529.

58 Churchill to Roosevelt, 4 March 1943, Loewenheim et al. (eds), *Roosevelt and Churchill*, p. 319.

59 Roskill, *Churchill and the Admirals*, p. 230.

## 22 *The Beginning of the End*

1 Thomas Treanor, NBC, extract from Desmond Hawkins and Donald Boyd (eds.), with Frank Gillard and Chester Wilmot, *War Report: A Record of Dispatches Broadcast by the BBC's War Correspondents with the Allied Expeditionary Force 6 June 1944 – 5 May 1945* (Oxford University Press, 1946).

2 Quoted in Antony Beevor, *The Second World War* (Weidenfeld and Nicolson, 2012), p. 580.

3 Quoted in Antony Beevor, *D-Day: The Battle for Normandy* (Viking, 2009), p. 95.

4 Alanbrooke, *War Diaries*, entry for 6 June 1944, p. 554.

5 Dönitz, *Memoirs*, p. 420.

6 S. W. Roskill, *The War At Sea, 1939–45*, Vol. III, *The Offensive Part 2*: *1st June 1944–14th August 1945* (Naval and Military Press, 2004), p. 20.

7 Werner, *Iron Coffins*, p. 219.

8 Ibid., pp. 221–2.

9 Ibid., p. 228.

10 Richard Dimbleby, 11 June 1944, in Hawkins et al. (eds.), *War Report*.

11 Dönitz, *Memoirs*, pp. 422–3.

12 Ibid., p. 423.

13 Winston Churchill, *The Second World War*, Vol. VI, *Triumph and Tragedy* (Cassell, 1954), p. 472.

14 Roskill, *The Offensive Part 2*, Appendices X, Y, Y Y, and T, pp. 439–79.

15 Quoted in Padfield, *Dönitz*, p. 350.

16 Ibid., p. 419.

17 Churchill, *Triumph and Tragedy*, p. 474.

18 Cremer, *U-333*, pp. 277–8.

19 Ibid., p. 286.

20 Wynford Vaughan-Thomas, 4 May 1945, in Hawkins et al. (eds.), *War Report*.

21 Campaign Summaries of World War 2, September 1939 to August 1945, www.naval-history.net; BBC archive, W W2 People's War, bbc.co.uk/history/ww2peopleswar/categories/c1174/.

22 Prime Minister's Victory Broadcast, 13 May 1945, Churchill, *Triumph and Tragedy*, Appendix, p. 666.

23 Colville, *The Fringes of Power* (1985), 14 May 1945, p. 565.

24 Churchill, *The Hinge of Fate*, p. 413.

## Epilogue: Fates Disentwined

1 Cited in Bird, *Erich Raeder*, p. 221.

2 *Foreign Relations of the United States: The Conference at Quebec, 1944* (US Government Printing Office, 1971), pp. 330–35, cited in Buell, *Master of Sea Power*, Appendix VI, p. 539 (King) and p. 471 (Cunningham).

# Index